DAVID POLLOCK lives in Edinburgh and
shows in the city. He is an arts writer '
Scotsman, The List, The Guardian, The In
The Courier, The Stage and The Big Issue
Mixmag, Electronic Sound and Record C
Firsts and the annual Critics Awards for Theatre in Scotland

CW01401532

The Edinburgh Festival

A Biography

DAVID POLLOCK

Luath Press Limited

EDINBURGH

www.luath.co.uk

First published 2022

ISBN: 978-1-80425-012-9

The paper used in this book is recyclable. It is made
from low chlorine pulps produced in a low energy,
low emissions manner from renewable forests.

MIX
Paper from
responsible sources
FSC® C022174

Printed and bound by
Severnprint Ltd, Gloucester

Typeset in 11 point Sabon LT Pro by
Main Point Books, Edinburgh

For

Caroline, with love

Henry and Malcolm, who like going to see shows

Mum and Dad

*Everyone who has made the Edinburgh Festival what it is,
and tried to make it better*

Contents

What is the Edinburgh Festival?

MORE THAN ONCE during research for this book, after mentioning the title to people connected with the running of Edinburgh's August festivals, they said, 'you know there's no such thing as the Edinburgh Festival, don't you?'

It's true. The Edinburgh Festival isn't a single festival, it's a number of festivals happening within the city at the same time, overlapping with one another and occasionally working in tandem. But to the regular, casual visitor – whether they're arriving from York or New York, South Korea or South Lanarkshire – the distinction isn't immediately to the fore in their mind. Telling a story about the Fruitmarket's successful 2008 Festival exhibition of work by Janet Cardiff and George Bures Miller – technically part of Edinburgh Art Festival – the gallery's director Fiona Bradley sums this up:

> That show was in various reviews as 'the best thing you'll see on the Fringe', 'the best thing on the International Festival … People just don't make a distinction, and I like that. People are here for the Festival, they just say they're here 'for Edinburgh'. They're doing Edinburgh in August, you know?

That's why this book's title refers to the Festival, singular. The layperson sees it as all part of the same thing. To returning audiences and visitors, 'Festival' is handy shorthand for something they know is far larger and trickier to describe. To those who run and administrate the festivals, the distinction is, of course, an existential matter. The intention here is to at least begin from the simplest, least complicated starting point and unfold the explanation of each festival as we go. To break it down simply, though, a short glossary follows.

A note on the use of the word 'Festival'

It should be clear which individual festival is being discussed, generally by reference to its full name or acronym. However, often the word 'Festival' will be used on its own as a noun; before 1959 and the official arrival of the Festival Fringe Society, this likely refers to the International Festival, by some way the major element of what happened during Edinburgh's festival weeks up to this point. From '59 on, however, 'Festival' (or 'Edinburgh Festival') is shorthand for the combined total of everything that happens in Edinburgh during Festival time.

Edinburgh International Festival

Founded in 1947 as the Edinburgh International Festival of Music and Drama. A high-end selection of international-class orchestral music, opera, dance, drama and other activities, which was the bedrock foundation of the wider Edinburgh Festival. Terms: Edinburgh International Festival, the International Festival, EIF, the Festival (the latter only until the Fringe's official foundation in 1959).

Edinburgh Festival Fringe

Unofficially in existence since 1947, with the Fringe Society coming into operation in 1959. Originally a group of eight amateur theatre companies staging work at the same time as the first International Festival, the Fringe has grown to vastly outnumber the International Festival. In fact, it's the largest single arts festival in the world. Open access, in that anyone with a licensed stage to perform on can participate (a small participant's fee is required to appear in the official catalogue), it encompasses all art forms, but is largely known for theatre – from some of the world's finest companies to amateur dramatic and student theatre groups – and increasingly for stand-up comedy since the 1980s. Terms: Edinburgh Festival Fringe, the Fringe.

Edinburgh International Film Festival

Founded in 1947 as the Edinburgh Documentary Festival. At the forefront of the international film festival movement, it gained a huge industry reputation for key film premieres and star appearances during the latter part of the 20th century and is the world's oldest continually-running film festival. In 2008 it moved to a new slot in June. Following COVID disruption the 2022 edition is scheduled for August once more, although it's unknown if this adjustment will be permanent. Terms: Edinburgh International Film Festival, Edinburgh Documentary Festival, the Film Festival, EIFF.

Royal Edinburgh Military Tattoo

Founded in 1950. Although military-themed displays had been held alongside the Festival since it started in 1947, the first official Edinburgh Tattoo was held on the Castle Esplanade in 1950 and it has continued ever since. Featuring invited military bands and performers from around the world, it was televised internationally for many years and typically welcomes sell-out combined audiences of 220,000 over three weeks of performances.

A grand spectacle set against one of Edinburgh's most famous landmarks, it's synonymous with the Festival – is the Festival, in fact – to many people in other countries who only know Edinburgh from afar. Although a fully integrated part of the Edinburgh Festivals, however, its nature and origins set it apart from much of the other arts-based Festival activity. Terms: Royal Edinburgh Military Tattoo, the Tattoo.

Edinburgh Jazz & Blues Festival

Founded in 1978, officially named Edinburgh Jazz Festival the following year. Formerly running alongside the Edinburgh Festival, in recent years it has run immediately prior to it in July, serving as a musical appetiser for August's events. Terms: Edinburgh Jazz & Blues Festival, the Jazz & Blues Festival, the Jazz Festival, EJF, EJBF.

Edinburgh International Book Festiva

Founded in 1983 as the Edinburgh Book Festival. Star authors, discussions with key figures on current and historical affairs and children's events. On Charlotte Square every year until a move to the grounds of Edinburgh College of Art in 2021, with a further move to the new Edinburgh Futures Institute at Quartermile planned for 2023. Terms: Edinburgh International Book Festival, Edinburgh Book Festival, the Book Festival, EIBF.

Edinburgh Art Festival

Founded in 2004. Although classical and contemporary art has played some part in the Festival since the early days, it only came together in its own official festival in 2004, first as a printed guide collating details of all shows and soon after with an element of curation and commissioning under an artistic director. Terms: Edinburgh Art Festival, EAF.

Edinburgh International Television Festival

Founded in 1976. An industry event, generally held over the final weekend in August. No public tickets are available, but the Television Festival is notable for two reasons: one is the annual James MacTaggart Lecture, traditionally given by a leading figure in the industry and widely reported in the trade and popular press; two, the fact that delegates soak up the other festivals while in Edinburgh, which is a great deal of the reason why hit Fringe stand-ups, actors and playwrights can make a long-lasting television career happen by being talent-spotted during a successful Fringe run. Terms: Edinburgh International Television Festival, the Television Festival.

Other festivals in August:

The Edinburgh People's Festival (1951–1953) was an attempt to coordinate early Fringe activities under a socialist banner, put together by the poet Hamish Henderson and others in the Labour movement. It was short-lived, but it offered much – partly due to the involvement of Henderson and the American musicologist Alan Lomax – in terms of the beginnings of the Fringe spirit and the Scottish folk revival.

Edinburgh Mela (1995–present) is a community event founded by Edinburgh communities with roots across Asia. Although efforts were previously made to integrate it into the Festival as a programmed world dance and arts event, these have fallen away in recent years.

Fringe of Colour (2018–present) is an umbrella organisation which promotes shows by Fringe performers of colour and offers free Fringe tickets to young people of colour. During the COVID-19 pandemic it rebranded as an online film festival in 2020 and '21 and is taking a year out in 2022.

Since the late 1990s there have also been variously successful attempts to introduce a contemporary music strand to the Festival, under banners including Flux, Planet Pop, T on the Fringe, the Edge and Summer Sessions at the Ross Bandstand in West Princes Street Gardens. Only the latter still continues.

Other festivals outside August:

Edinburgh Science Festival (1989–present) is the largest science festival in the UK, taking place across the city in April.

Edinburgh International Children's Festival (1990–present) takes place across the city in May.

Edinburgh International Storytelling Festival (1989–present) is the only festival of its kind in the UK and it happens in October around the city. It's based out of the Scottish Storytelling Centre on the Royal Mile.

Edinburgh's Hogmanay (1993–present) is the only event in Edinburgh to equal the major August events in terms of international recognition. The centrepiece is a concert by a major artist at the Ross Bandstand around the 'Bells' – the chimes of midnight that signal New Year – with a huge firework display on the stroke of 12. Various official fringe events happen between 30 December and 1 January, and the city centre also hosts a German market, big wheel, skating rink and various other performances from late November.

Edinburgh International Magic Festival (2010–present) has taken place at various times of the year, but never in August.

Note on the Spotlights

BETWEEN THE CHRONOLOGICAL chapters, several key shows are profiled in their own 'Spotlight' sections – a drop in the ocean, in terms of the many thousands seen in August, but a key group of 21 events which have seen global careers made, the landscape of Edinburgh or its Festival permanently changed, or wider entangled stories about, for example, Scottish theatre or British comedy decisively developed on Edinburgh's stages.

INTRODUCTION

The Past

EDINBURGH IS A village. That's what people who live in the city say. The able-bodied visitor arriving by the high-speed East Coast Main Line from London can get from the platform at the central Waverley Station to the outer edges of the city centre quickly by foot. Seventeen minutes west along the park-lined central avenue, Princes Street, is the current home of new playwriting and sometime radical 1960s arts hub, the Traverse Theatre. Twenty-one minutes away across the Royal Mile – Edinburgh Castle at one end, Palace of Holyroodhouse at the other – and the Meadows is the arts complex and former Victorian veterinary school Summerhall, where the city bleeds into the suburban Southside.

Just ten minutes to the north on George Street are the 18th century Assembly Rooms, where Sir Walter Scott introduced King George IV at the Peers Ball of 1822, the first visit by a British monarch to Scotland in two centuries. Here, Scott himself was revealed as the author of the popular *Waverley* novels five years later. This is the city of the Scottish Enlightenment, the 17th and 18th century boom in humanist and rational thought which bled out into the world alongside the migrating Scottish people, taking with it the philosophies of David Hume; the economics of Adam Smith; the literature of James Boswell, Robert Fergusson and eventually Robert Burns; and world-leading developments in medicine, geology, mathematics and physics.

The land around Castle Rock and the other seven hills of Edinburgh[1] has been inhibited since at least the Bronze Age. The Romans had a camp at Cramond on the shores of the Firth of Forth, now a quiet suburb to the north-west of the city. Founded as a royal burgh by King David I in the 12th century, by the late 17th century the city had seen much political upheaval, including the 16th century Scottish Reformation, where the Presbyterian Church of Scotland broke with the Catholic Church in Rome; the Act of Union between Scotland and England in 1707; and occupation by both Oliver Cromwell's New Model Army and the Highland Jacobites in the decades which immediately followed.

In 1583 Tounis College was established, later the University of Edinburgh, the sixth-oldest university in the English-speaking world.[2] By the 18th century, the high-rise tenements within the city walls had created a primitively futuristic landscape in which 11-storey residential towers were occupied by progressively wealthier inhabitants as they rose, with poor workers housed near the ground and merchants on the upper floors. In this JG Ballard future city, which existed 200 years before the writer was born, overcrowding and squalor were rife. Slops and human waste were thrown from tenement windows at 10pm every night, their odour earning them the sarcastic nickname 'The Flowers of Edinburgh'. Drunks weaving their way home as the city's many bars closed had to have their wits about them. Despite its Presbyterian reputation, the city was notorious for a hard-drinking culture in which all classes mixed in the many taverns. Meanwhile, exclusive after-hours drinking clubs and societies flourished.

Daniel Defoe came to live in Edinburgh soon after the Act of Union of 1707 and Edinburgh's most powerful lords were split between those who stuck to their sense of Scottishness and those who embraced London's influence, as apparent in their continued use of the Scots dialect or their preference for a more supposedly cultured southern form of English. These questions of identity have remained to the fore in Scottish culture for more than 300 years. Meanwhile, the great figures of the Scottish Enlightenment – all male, of course – met and discussed at the Select Society, the Speculative Society and the Poker Club, held at the old Advocate's Library on Parliament Square, at John Row's nearby coffee house and in other central locations.

Another club was the Crochallan Fencibles, founded by the printer William Smellie, who later helped establish the *Encyclopaedia Britannica* in the city and published the Edinburgh editions of Robert Burns' work. Between the 18th and 19th century, the Scottish Enlightenment gave birth to a new Edinburgh, as printers, newspapers and the highly-regarded *Scottish Review* boomed amid the city's lively intellectual life. Architect James Craig's New Town sprawl of plush, one-family apartments extended to the north of the city, across the Nor' Loch in the gap between the Old Town and what's now Princes Street, which was drained in the 1800s and filled in by Waverley Station and Princes Street Gardens.

After the city's version of the Enlightenment was over, its impact lay within the changed structure and physical appearance of Edinburgh, all sandstone columns from nearby Lothian quarries to emphasise the Athenian ambitions of its great minds – these buildings and the city's seven central hills and nearby port of Leith are among the reasons Edinburgh is known as the 'Athens of the North', although the playwright Tom Stoppard once suggested its climate should make it more of a 'Reykjavik of the South'. The ideas of the Scottish Enlightenment travelled around the world thanks to the spread of the British Empire and the United States of America's founding.

The influence of post-Reformation Presbyterianism contributed to Edinburgh growing with no great history of music, opera or theatre, although the landscape wasn't barren. St Cecilia's Hall, the first bespoke concert hall in Scotland, was built on the Cowgate in 1763 and hosted regular concerts, until the Assembly Rooms on George Street opened in 1787 and took over as the city's premier music venue. The first Edinburgh Music Festival – no relation to the current Festival, but widely acknowledged as its first predecessor – was held in 1815 and consisted of three daytime concerts at Parliament House and three evening performances at the intimate Corri's Concert Hall on Broughton Street.[3]

The works of Haydn, Beethoven and Mozart were performed at this Edinburgh Music Festival and Handel, Beethoven and Mozart's music all featured at the second edition in 1819. This time it was held at the Theatre Royal at Shakespeare Square in the east end of Princes Street, a rough and disreputable neck of the woods in the early 19th century; the theatre once saw a riot when the audience refused to stand for the British national anthem at a concert which Walter Scott had been attending.[4] Later Edinburgh Music Festivals were held in 1824 and 1843.

Before the Theatre Royal and despite the strong disapproval of the church at the time, the Canongate Theatre had been founded in the city in 1747, which is where actor and theatre manager West Digges arranged for the production of *Douglas* in 1756, a new play by East Lothian minister of the Church of Scotland John Home. Although the verse tragedy was a big hit in Edinburgh and later in London, the Church forced Home to resign as a result and various prosecutions were threatened. Its public acclaim, however, contributed to the eventual official licensing of the Theatre Royal, the successor to the technically illegal Canongate.

Edinburgh's literary culture bubbled at a simmer until the early 20th century, with Scott himself, Robert Louis Stevenson, Arthur Conan Doyle and JM Barrie each claiming birth or residence in the city where Tobias Smollett and the author of *The Beggar's Opera* John Gay had also once lived. The great First World War poets Wilfred Owen and Siegfried Sassoon both recovered from shell-shock at Craiglockhart War Hospital in 1917. Nicknamed Dottyville by Sassoon, this was where Owen wrote his famous poems 'Dulce et Decorum Est' and 'Anthem for Doomed Youth'.

By the 1920s, a new wave of writing from the country was resurgent, primarily in the work of Dumfriesshire poet Christopher M Grieve, who used the alias Hugh MacDiarmid. This period was known as the Scottish Renaissance and it reacted against the sentimental love-of-country active in the previous century's Victorian-era Kailyard school of writing. Through MacDiarmid's 2,685-line narrative poem *A Drunk Man Looks at the Thistle* in 1926 and the work of contemporaries and followers of his including Edwin Muir, Sydney Goodsir Smith and Robert Garioch, the Renaissance writers tackled themes of Scots identity and cultural resurgence once more.

MacDiarmid formulated his own version of the Scots dialect named 'Lallans' and in 1927 co-founded the Scottish Centre of the organisation PEN in Edinburgh, alongside novelist Neil Gunn and Professor Herbert Grierson of the University of Edinburgh. PEN, which stood for 'Poets, Essayists, Novelists',[5] was founded in 1921 in London by a group headed by the writer Catherine Amy Dawson Scott, which included Joseph Conrad, George Bernard Shaw and HG Wells. Its purpose was to foster international co-operation between writers and to defend literature from the threats it might face around the world and in 1934 the 12th International PEN Congress came to Edinburgh, where the organisation formally pledged to defend free expression.

Both International and Scottish PEN continue to this day. So too, in a different fashion, does the other major organisation MacDiarmid co-founded, the National Party of Scotland, the first Scottish nationalist party, which emerged in 1928. In 1934 the left-wing National Party joined with the recently-formed Scottish Party to form the Scottish National Party, which has in the present, after a near-90-year journey, become the leading force in Scottish politics. By '34, however, MacDiarmid had already been expelled from the National Party for his Communist views, part of a tension between the two perspectives which also landed him in trouble with the Communist Party for his nationalist interests.

MacDiarmid only lived in Edinburgh for three years between 1908 and 1911, while he finished his studies at Broughton Junior Student Centre and worked briefly as a trainee journalist on the *Edinburgh Evening Dispatch* at the age of 18. Yet in his later years, he was often found holding court in the literary pubs of the central New Town, at places like Milne's, the Abbotsford and the Café Royal, which all still exist in their classic, wood-panelled, weathered glory today.

The beauty of MacDiarmid's writing and the defiance of his assertion of Scots identity made him one of the key figures – perhaps the most significant of all – in Scotland's cultural and political life of the 20th century, even as controversy followed him around his enduring support for the Communist Soviet Union and his often quite apparent Anglophobia. Edinburgh was his eventual place of death in 1978, aged 86, although until then he appears as both antagonist and protagonist in the story of the Edinburgh Festival.

In 1935, the Orkney-born, Hampstead-based poet, writer and contemporary of MacDiarmid's Edwin Muir began his *Scottish Journey* in Edinburgh, searching for the heart and soul of then-contemporary Scotland and finding a city in many ways unrecognisable from the present. He wrote of the Old Town that

> one feels that these house-shapes are outcroppings of the rocky ridge on which they are planted, methodical geological formations in

which, as an afterthought, people have taken to living... The smoke rising from innumerable chimneys produces the same ha f delightful, half nightmare sense of overcrowding that one finds in mountain villages in Southern Europe...[6]

In those days, the main shopping thoroughfare Princes Street represented the height of middle-class, Old Town opulence – its tea houses 'more strange than a dream', filled with stifling amounts of the 'floating sexual desire' Muir felt on the busy streets of the city. The Canongate, on what's now the tourist-trap Royal Mile, was a 'mouldering and obnoxious ruin' where unemployed young men waited and drank eternity away on the street and in doorways. The only place where most citizens let their hair down was in the pubs, where women were forbidden.[7]

Some things haven't changed, meanwhile. Muir imagined a dividing barrier between the east end of Princes Street and Leith Walk, the latter an avenue of a different class entirely, filled with 'ice-cream and fish and chip bars and pubs'. The Walk has gone up in the world somewhat, but you can still find all of the above in an area that continues to stand apart. In both worlds, Muir noted, drunkenness abounds, yet only on public display in the poorer parts of the city.

In Muir's eyes, Edinburgh was a soulless and past-obsessed place at heart. Born in Orkney in 1887 and subject to hard and poverty-stricken teenage years in Glasgow following the death of his parents, his relationship with Scotland was uneasy and he had been living in London for a decade and a half by the time of his journey through Scotland. A socialist and a nationalist by instinct, Muir was a key figure in Scottish PEN and argued successfully at the PEN Congress of 1932 in Budapest that the Scottish organisation should not be treated as a subset of English PEN.

At the PEN Congress of 1934 in Edinburgh, he presented a discussion at the Church of Scotland's Assembly Hall on the Mound and then travelled to Orkney to meet his wife and son, the latter recovering from a road accident which left him with permanent injuries. He had considered the capital city's character and described Edinburgh – despite all its recognised positive features – as an 'Anglicised and Americanised' city striking an uneasy balance between 'its legendary past and its tawdry present'.

Muir's chronicle of Edinburgh in the 1930s was among the very best accounts of the city's life immediately prior to the Second World War. The other wasn't published until 1961, the work of an author who was born in the city's well-off inner suburb Bruntsfield in 1918, educated at the old James Gillespie's School for Girls on Bruntsfield Links,[8] but living in a bedsit in Camberwell, south London, around the time her most famous book was written. The first draft, however, was completed in a four-week flurry in her parents' Edinburgh home over Christmas 1960.

Muriel Spark's *The Prime of Miss Jean Brodie* was based on the author's own schooldays in the early 1930s and its fictionalised title character borrowed elements of her own teachers, although Jean Brodie might well have been an allegorical satire of 20th century Edinburgh itself. Concerned with 'art and religion first, then philosophy; lastly science', she declared herself to be in her prime, yet teased and ultimately lost her admiring suitors, even as she sought to live vicariously on the youthful energy of the female students in her care. Her politics were conservative, to say the least.

Yet, in chronicling this pining for past glories, the writing of both Muir and Spark suggested potential waiting to flower, of stems pushing up through the gaps in the well-worn paving stones and cobbled setts of the city's streets. Muir related the experience of a ceilidh after a formal Edinburgh function:

> They are free without the affectation of Bohemianism. If one's sole acquaintance with Scotland were through them, one would be forced to believe that Scotsmen and Scotswomen were the most charming and light-hearted people in the world... at certain happy moments, in the first relief after a hardship passed, there are companies in Scotland which can strike this perfect balance between nature and art.[9]

The world was waiting to arrive in Edinburgh. Spark's protagonist and former student at the fictional Marcia Blaine School for Girls, Sandy Stranger, is asked many years after the novel's key events, in the first days of the 1960s, to remember her old tutor with the question, 'Who was Miss Brodie?' She responds: 'A teacher of mine, she was full of culture. She was an Edinburgh festival all on her own.'

* * *

When we consider the city of Edinburgh's last 500 years of history, significant eras present themselves. It's the city of the Reformation, the city of the Scottish Enlightenment and when future historians look back on this time, it will surely be remembered for generations to come as the city of the Edinburgh Festival too. While other cities had hosted festivals before 1947 and many more have taken up the mantle since, Edinburgh's international fame is founded on its originality, its enduringly monumental scale and its versatility across multiple art forms at once.

In many regards, the city did many things first – the concept of a fringe festival was unknown until 1947 – and it continues to do things bigger than anywhere else. In the pre-COVID year of 2019, the Fringe alone saw 3,012,490 tickets sold for 3,841 individual shows across 323 venues, most giving approximately one performance a day for three weeks. Among these shows, 154 nationalities were represented onstage and in audiences, with 1,661 international producers, programmers, talent agencies and festivals either presenting work or looking to find new talent to take to a worldwide audience. It's estimated this Fringe alone generated more than £1 billion for Scotland's economy. Such a sense of overwhelming volume, as we'll see, isn't always appreciated.

In some respects, the Edinburgh Festival has led the culture. In others, it's summarised and reflected what's happening around the world, within the heart of its village – actually a rapidly-growing conurbation and port city of a little over half a million people. The development of British comedy of the late 20th century, in particular, has its roots in Edinburgh, from the Satire Boom of *Beyond the Fringe* and the 1960s, to the explosion of stand-up comedy two decades later and its leading lights' subsequent takeover of UK television and beyond. Like the roots of two trees growing together, modern British theatre's main branch is in London, but its development and many of its seminal moments have happened in the superheated three-week laboratory atmosphere provided by the Edinburgh Festival.

Despite criticism that the Festival sits apart from Edinburgh as an act of artistic colonisation rather than a natural expression of the city's own year-round cultural life, its existence is firmly connected to, and influential upon, Scotland's culture and politics of the past 75 years. A biography of the Edinburgh Festival has to also be, in large part, a summary of Scotland's cultural and political life in the latter half of the 20th century and the beginning years of the 21st.

This book is an exercise in writing about place, about the development and shifting landscape of Scotland's capital city in the decades since the conclusion of the Second World War. As with any biography, it introduces a wide cast of individuals who have influenced its subject's life. Between the chronological chapters, several key shows are profiled – a drop in the ocean, in terms of the many thousands seen in August, but a key group of 21 events which have seen global careers made, the landscape of Edinburgh or its Festival permanently changed, or wider entangled stories about, for example, Scottish theatre or British comedy decisively developed on Edinburgh's stages.

As anyone – performer, audience member, one of thousands of staff, technicians, members of the media, or citizen of Edinburgh – who has experienced the Edinburgh Festival for three days, three weeks, or every year for three decades knows, it's a dizzying immersion in art and other perspectives. As the last of Scotland's mild weather and late, bright northerly nights bleed away with the summer, bespoke theatres, lively late-night bars, hot church halls and hotel meeting rooms all buzz until the early hours of the morning, filled with voices and views from across the globe.

It's a great thing, one of the finest creations of a country which hasn't been short of great inventions and new philosophies over the centuries. It's fair to say the Festival is also an imperfect thing at times, but reports of local dislike of it are greatly exaggerated, the statistics show. As the current director of the Edinburgh Fringe, Shona McCarthy, points out with reference to her previous career in arts administration in Northern Ireland, what Edinburgh has – its mix of festivals and the unique geography and official will to make them such a roaring success – is the jealous envy of cities across the world, many of which have tried and failed to replicate its success.

As the Edinburgh International Festival, Edinburgh Festival Fringe and Edinburgh International Film Festival all approach the 75th anniversaries of their founding in 2022, a post-pandemic hope that something approaching normality might be possible persists. In 2019, in my position as a freelancer reviewer for *The Scotsman* and others, I saw 139 separate events during August, a personal record in nearly two decades of attending professionally. The past two years of pandemic-induced cancellation and disruption have left a sense of loss on the city's streets, the feeling that something special and irreplaceable has been missing.

The Edinburgh witnessed by Edwin Muir was one steeped in its own institutions, but uncertain of its place in the world of the 20th century. A decade later, after war had passed, the Edinburgh Festival gave it global identity and purpose. For all the hopes that the Festival can be streamlined and improved as it rebuilds in 2022, the original International Festival spirit of 1947 is exactly what's required once more. After an international catastrophe its purpose was healing, understanding and togetherness, with the Fringe soon forcing its way into being to ensure democracy and diversity were also represented.

SPOTLIGHT

Bruno Walter and the Vienna Philharmonic Orchestra (1947)

ON THE EVENING of Monday 8 September 1947, as the famous Berlin-born conductor Bruno Walter lifted the baton to lead the 87 members of the Vienna Philharmonic Orchestra seated onstage at Edinburgh's Usher Hall, performing history formed around him.

For Edinburgh, this was its Festival's first true international blockbuster concert, as the debut year's programme delivered on its promise and set up many more major events to come. Walter was days away from his 71st birthday when he arrived in the city and an orchestral superstar. Born in Berlin's Alexanderplatz in 1876, the youthful musical prodigy first played piano with the Berlin Philharmonic at the age of 13. He became an apprentice to Gustav Mahler at the then Vienna Court Opera and when Mahler left the city under a cloud in 1907, chased out by rivals and antisemitic detractors, he wrote to the young Walter and told him he felt a special understanding with him.

Four years later in 1911, 34-year-old Walter was by Mahler's deathbed. Later that year in Munich, one of the crowning moments of Walter's personal and professional life arrived as he was selected to conduct the premiere of Mahler's unheard work *Das Lied von der Erde* ('The Song of the Earth'). The great composer had written it with his unhappy departure from Vienna, the death of his eldest daughter Maria in childhood and the discovery of the heart defect which would soon take his own life in mind.

By 1947, Walter had built a 40-year reputation as one of the world's finest conductors, from high-profile operatic directorships in Bavaria, Berlin and Leipzig to close orchestral associations with London and America, where he was now settled in California. So exciting was Walter's presence in Edinburgh, in fact, that his hotel had to detail a member of staff to guard the door of his room, to turn away resourceful fans and autograph hunters.

Yet, as the Edinburgh Festival's first director Rudolf Bing was well aware, the reunion of this particular conductor with the Vienna Philharmonic had far greater meaning beyond the simply musical. Both men were European Jews whose high standing within the operatic arts on the continent had been brought to an abrupt halt by the Nazis' rise to power. While each was living in Berlin in 1933, it was separately made clear upon Hitler's arrival that the paramilitary SA (the *Sturmabteilung*) would target their shows for disruption, so both left Germany and settled elsewhere. Walter had even been denounced personally in Hitler's speeches.

Bing went to work at 1934's inaugural Glyndebourne Opera Festival in England, while between 1933 and 1938, Walter's name became synonymous with Vienna, where he first came to prominence. Never a political artist, despite the Nazis' incorrect suspicion he was a Communist, Walter chose not to use his frequent conducting engagements across Europe and in America to denounce what was happening in his homeland, but rather to spread the sense of inspirational enlightenment and tolerance which he felt music fostered.

Appreciating the bulwark position taken against the Third Reich by Austria's government prior to the *Anschluss* of 1938, Walter took on Mahler's old role as director of what was now the Vienna State Opera in 1936 and shared conducting duties at the Vienna Philharmonic with his rival

Wilhelm Furtwängler. This was a golden period for the Philharmonic, during which Walter conducted a recording of Wagner's *Die Walküre* and the first ever recording of Mahler's *Symphony No.9*.

When Nazi Germany annexed Austria in May 1938, Walter was performing in Amsterdam and he knew it would be impossible to return home with his wife Elsa. In fact, his daughter Lotte was only able to join them two weeks later after being arrested and released, then crossing the Swiss border on the pretext of a non-existent singing gig. The next August, the Walters' other daughter Gretel was shot and murdered by her jealous husband while she slept in Zurich. Within three months the heartbroken family left Europe behind for good and set out by sea for America, where Elsa died in 1945.

The Vienna Philharmonic now entered the most contested period of its history, giving concerts at the behest of Joseph Goebbels and expelling Jewish members, seven of whom died during the war; five of them in concentration camps. Although Furtwängler's name was tarnished by continuing as the orchestra's main conductor, it's now known he defied Goebbels' wishes and attempted to shield Jewish players and their families on numerous occasions.

Bing was starting out with Hugo Heller's Viennese concert agency in the early 1920s when he first met Walter. Later he took the job of deputy intendant at the Städtische Oper[1] immediately after Walter left the post of musical director. Before Edinburgh had even been settled on as a venue for the International Festival of Music and Drama Bing was planning, the reunion of Walter and the Vienna Orchestra was the hot-ticket centrepiece he hoped to arrange for it. Walter's agreement to perform following an impassioned transatlantic letter from the hopeful Bing was the snowball that helped set the avalanche in motion. 'After that we were on the map,' Bing wrote in his memoir. 'Whenever anyone asked me what all this was about, I had merely to say that Bruno Walter was coming and no further questions were asked.'

Bing was aware, in fact, that many were deeply suspicious of the VPO and Austria itself immediately after the war and that Walter's presence would 'de-Nazify' the orchestra where one of its wartime conductors would virtually guarantee angry protest. Two previously expelled Jewish members had been invited to return to the VPO in 1946, but the violinist Arnold Rosé – Mahler's brother-in-law, whose daughter Alma had died in a concentration camp – angrily refused, before passing away later that year. The cellist Friedrich Buxbaum, who briefly played with the Glasgow Symphony Orchestra at the end of the 19th century, agreed to perform in Edinburgh, where he was presented with the orchestra's highest award, the Nicolae Medal, named after its founder.

The VPO arrived in Edinburgh on Thursday 4 September after a 48-hour journey by boat and road, bustling into the Carlyle Hostel in the southern suburb of Mayfield as the first ever Festival rain fell on Edinburgh after 11 days of sun. They were finally reunited with Walter – who had played a rare Schubert recital earlier in the week with singer Elisabeth Schumann – for the first time since before the war, ahead of their first rehearsal at the Usher Hall the next evening. 'Its members,' *The Scotsman* noted soberly, 'were looking forward to seeing him again after nine years' separation.'[2]

Bruno Walter and the Vienna Philharmonic Orchestra's first Edinburgh Festival performance paid tribute to Britain's compositional history with Ralph Vaughan Williams' *Fantasia on a Theme by Thomas Tallis* and closed with Beethoven's 'Pastoral' *Symphony No.6* and *Symphony No.7*. The second performance followed the same programme, and was attended by the Queen, Princess Margaret and the Duchess of Kent. *The Scotsman* recorded 'a concert probably unparalleled in the musical annals of the city', with thundering ovation after ovation from the packed hall greeting the performers at the end of the show. This was followed by a further series of cheers for the Royal party as they left the box.

It was a moment of great celebration, a pressure valve opening for a nation and a continent which had to stoically endure so much with little hint of light for the past decade. The key and most memorable moment of Walter's week-long stay in Edinburgh, however, came with his return to his old mentor Mahler's *Das Lied von der Erde*. The work was largely unknown in the UK, but it came alive through the voices of the tenor Peter Pears and the contralto Kathleen Ferrier. Both were recommended by Bing after appearing in Benjamin Britten's *The Rape of Lucretia* at Glyndebourne the year before, which had been written specially for Ferrier.

A village schoolmaster's daughter from rural Lancashire, Ferrier was a rising star of British opera at this point and Walter was immediately taken with her voice when Bing arranged introductions and auditions at the home of the publisher Hamish Hamilton. Walter said he believed her voice to be one of the greatest he had heard, even though she couldn't get through *Das Lied*'s sixth and final movement, 'Der Abschied' ('The Farewell'), due to the emotion of it.

Mysterious and otherworldly, the text in Mahler's work, written by the German poet Hans Bethge, speaks of weary men heading homeward to sleep, and then rediscover happiness and youth. These words envisaged the wars which would shatter the continent in the decades after Mahler died, but left with the hopeful image of the earth blossoming in spring and growing once more.

After the final performance on 14 September, the day's late-added second concert due to ticket demand, *The Scotsman*'s critic wrote:

One cannot perhaps maintain that the carefree warmth of sentiment runs naturally in the veins even of the Viennese nowadays, for we have all been chastened by bitter experience [but the performance contained] a wistful sighing for past loves and joys... that we can all understand and share.[3]

Together Walter, the Vienna Philharmonic, Ferrier and Pears had exorcised some of the hurt of recent times, pointed towards a brighter future and put Edinburgh's International Festival of Music and Drama on the world's map. Bruno Walter returned to life in California and his 1952 recording of *Das Lied von der Erde* is now recognised as one of the great operatic recordings. This record featured Kathleen Ferrier's voice once again, her career having springboarded from the Usher Hall to the great stages of America and Europe.

Ferrier became a regular performer in Edinburgh during August and with Walter returned to the Usher Hall, the scene of their history-making triumph, with the Paris Conservatoire Orchestra for Mahler's *Kindertotenlieder* in 1949. The greatest compliment she had ever received, was how Ferrier privately described that first request to sing with Walter, although her and the International Festival's life together was brief. Breast cancer cruelly ended her life and potential as one of Britain's operatic greats in October 1953 at the age of 41, the year after she performed *Das Lied von der Erde* in Edinburgh once more, this time with conductor Eduard van Beinum and the Concertgebouw Orchestra of Amsterdam.

Walter played in Edinburgh with the Vienna Philharmonic Orchestra again in 1953, but they didn't perform *Das Lied...* without Ferrier. 'She is one of the few irreplaceable artists,' remarked Walter at the time. He died from a heart attack at his home in Beverley Hills in 1962, at the age of 85, but in the intervening years he had returned to conduct masterfully on the once-forbidden stages of Berlin, Salzburg and Vienna.

'I felt that it was an invitation to be obeyed as a kind of command,' he told an Edinburgh press conference of his swift decision to appear in 1947.

The war was an interruption of very harmonious personal relationships, and when we met here after this interruption it was really a meeting of old friends who did not know if they were still friends. But they were.[4]

I

The Birth of the Edinburgh International Festival

ON BUSINESS AT a 1938 drama conference in Prague on behalf of his employer, the Glyndebourne Opera Festival in England, Rudolf Bing took time to visit family in his birth city, Vienna. By a stroke of extreme bad luck, he picked the days before 12 March 1938 to make the journey – the day of the *Anschluss*, Nazi Germany's sudden annexation of Austria. Turning around and fleeing his homeland on a train packed with desperate fellow Austrians, Bing watched fearfully as Czech guards made their way through the carriage at the border, roughly ejecting everyone holding an Austrian passport. Bing's wife, his career, his whole future remained in England. And he was a Jew carrying an Austrian passport.

Bing hid that passport deep in his belongings and as the guard arrived at his seat, he showed a document he was carrying instead. What is this? asked the guard in Bing's native German. Where's your passport? Pretending not to understand, Bing's fluent English and any tips he may have picked up from the actors he observed in his day job were desperately deployed. Can't you see who I am? Bing asked, pointing to the papers. They said he was the Liberal British MP Hugh Seely, travelling as an honoured guest of the Czech government.

As Bing was leaving England for the conference a few days earlier, a British Government official met him and told him Seely would also be attending. Here's a diplomatic pass for Seely, so he doesn't encounter any difficulties, said the official. Would Bing mind giving it to him when he saw him at the airport?' As it turned out, Seely had chosen not to take the trip, but Bing was still carrying his pass.

The border guard weighed up the situation and clearly decided it was more than his job was worth to cause trouble for a member of the British Parliament, so he waved Bing on. The hundreds of other desperate Austrian citizens on the train weren't so lucky. They were told to get off at the last stop before the border.

Bing sat alone and breathless in the empty carriage which carried him back to Prague. It was the last time he would see Vienna for nearly a decade.

* * *

'I find a particular fascination in wandering around a strange city, and imagining all the happiness and tragedy, hopes and disappointments, loves and hates that abide behind all these windows,' reflected Bing in 1972.[1] The impresario was looking back to his first arrival in London early in his career, when the 21-year-old's ambitions in publishing had been waylaid by his secondment to the Viennese bookseller Hugo Heller's operatic and theatrical agency, but his romanticism for the great cities of Europe was undimmed on his first proper visit to Edinburgh 17 years later.

In 1923, the year of that first London trip, the rakishly slim and dapper young Bing was awestruck by his surroundings as he assisted the tenor Alfred Piccaver while he played two concerts at London's Albert Hall. In Edinburgh in 1940, he was six years into his employment with the East Sussex-based Glyndebourne Festival Opera, where he'd served since 1936 as General Manager, resourcefully attempting to keep the show on the road as war approached.

Wartime restrictions prohibited the use of night lighting, so as not to allow enemy bombers an easy target and travel between cities and towns, let alone to and from Glyndebourne's countryside setting, was difficult enough for British citizens. Bing, however, was a potential 'enemy alien', an Austrian citizen who had to receive special dispensation and agree to check in at local police stations before he could tour with shows. Besides, Glyndebourne House had been repurposed as a home for child evacuees from London. For the first time since it staged an inaugural performance of Mozart's work in 1934, the by-now world-famous annual operatic season at Glyndebourne Opera House – conceived and built alongside the main house by landowner and organ builder John Christie and his wife Audrey Mildmay, the Canadian soprano – wouldn't be going ahead.

Instead, in 1940 the company's efforts were redirected into a nationally touring version of *The Beggar's Opera* starring Michael Redgrave and directed by John Gielgud. Bing and his wife Nina, a Russian former ballerina, had briefly seen Edinburgh at the end of a family holiday to England's Lake District some years before, but when the six-week *Beggar's Opera* tour arrived in Scotland's capital late during the first winter of the 1940s, he took in more of the city. This time Bing walked Princes Street and gazed up at Edinburgh Castle, seated on the lip of a sheer face of volcanic rock pitching away from Princes Street Gardens in the heart of the city. The view reminded him of Salzburg, and he remembered the summer music festival in his home country. Started in 1920 as an all-welcoming antidote to Prussian cultural inflexibility, the Salzburg Festival was now closed away on Nazi-occupied mainland Europe.

Bing's professional eye also liked the King's Theatre, where *The Beggar's Opera* played, and the grand Usher Hall. The hotels were not bad either. *The Beggar's Opera* transferred to London's Theatre Royal Haymarket and closed in May, a week before the evacuation of Dunkirk began. With the Phony War over and hostilities about to begin, the wartime prospects of even a highly-regarded opera manager were slim. Thanks to enthusiastic Glyndebourne patron Spedan Lewis, chairman of the department store chain the John Lewis Partnership, Bing spent most of the war years as a manager at the Sloane Square store Peter Jones, where he at least managed to return to his youthful professional interest and start a book section.

During the Blitz, Bing led overnight fire duty at the store, and from the roof of Peter Jones he could see fires strike up across the darkened city as the Luftwaffe's bombs landed. His store remained miraculously untouched, but one night a block of flats near the store was hit. He and his staff rushed to help, and Bing reached for the hand of a young woman rising from the rubble. The arm lifted away in his grasp, all that was left.

When he was on day shift, the commute from the Bings' home in Oxford and back made for a 12-hour working day, yet the time to think also sowed the seeds of a major idea Bing was developing to keep the name and reputation of Glyndebourne alive. Perhaps Salzburg was on his mind once more when he wondered to himself... what if a city, like Oxford perhaps, could be the site of a post-war festival of music and drama that would pay tribute to the sacrifice which the nation, the whole of Europe, had endured?

* * *

Rudolf 'Rudi' Bing was born in Vienna in 1902 and raised in a grand townhouse on Kaiser Josef Strasse in the city's predominantly Jewish Leopoldstadt district, with a view over Praterstern square. His parents were friends with Richard Strauss's family and Bing's middle-class upbringing gave him a youthful appreciation of opera, a taste for painting and singing and a good grasp of English; his family hired English governesses for the Bing children, a worldly decision which helped their son escape from Europe decades later. A difficult school student who grudgingly planned to continue studying only so his mandatory military service would be reduced from three years to one, both the First World War and the Austro-Hungarian monarchy itself ended before he finished school, so he was never called to serve.

In 1927, having served his apprenticeship with Heller's agency, he left Vienna for a job with an operatic talent company in Berlin, then became assistant Intendant to the renowned actor Carl Ebert at the Hessian State Theatre in Darmstadt. Ebert was a matinee idol, a handsome young leading man, who was making a shift towards a career directing for the stage now he was in his 40s. With little knowledge of the business side of running a theatre, Ebert hired Bing to do it. Under Ebert, the shows staged in this small-town theatre were progressive in spirit and often attracted local controversy.

Next, Bing arrived at Berlin's Städtische Oper, the 'Charlottenburg', following a brief, post-Darmstadt flirtation with the film industry. He was soon reunited with Ebert, when his old boss moved to the same organisation and Ebert once more handled the art while Bing handled the business. Bing's time at the Charlottenburg was in the latter days of the Weimar Republic era, the halcyon, bohemian artistic interregnum between the wars and before the fall of the fascist boot. This period was one of the most satisfying of his life, perhaps the biggest triumph of which was the production of Verdi's *Macbeth*, based on Shakespeare's 'Scottish play'.

In 1933 he and Ebert – a Jew and a social democrat, respectively – were summarily dismissed from their roles by the 'brown pest', the Nazi SA paramilitaries. Bing made his way home to Vienna, but in 1934 Ebert got in touch once more, this time with an unusual opportunity to assist with talent booking at a new opera festival Ebert was setting up with the conductor Fritz Busch at a rural stately home in England. The opportunity was a good one and Bing took it.

An unlikely but much-loved success story by the end of the 1930s, Glyndebourne was still Bing's main priority as the war came to an end. The international festival he was thinking of, in fact, was mainly meant to promote Glyndebourne's name and reputation until it could begin again. Through 1944, while he was still at Peter Jones, Bing was in discussion with Glyndebourne's founder John Christie and administrator HE Edwards about plans to bring it back to life, even though professional disagreements had forced Ebert and Busch apart. Bing left his brief career in retail and set up a new Glyndebourne office in London in late 1944. Under the company's name, he produced the Children's Theatre and a series of new plays at the Lyric in Hammersmith, both of which employed a young Alec Guinness.

Oxford seemed to Bing like the obvious city to stage his international festival, but talks with the University and city officials went nowhere. Glyndebourne also found the new Arts Council of Great Britain unsympathetic to any of their proposals – reputedly due to a dispute between Christie and its chairman, the economist John Maynard Keynes – but the British Council cultural organisation might be able to help. So in late 1944, with Christie and Edwards' blessing, Bing set up a lunch meeting in London's Hanover Square with the a few of the Council's people; among them, their representative in Scotland, Henry Harvey Wood.

What happened next isn't exactly clear, a *Rashomon* moment of differing perspectives telling conflicting stories of the same event. Bing's memoir says he already had the strikingly beautiful Scottish city he visited with *The Beggar's Opera* in mind as a location, remembering its resonance with

Salzburg. Yet in a 1947 piece for *The Scotsman* newspaper, Wood said he'd suggested Edinburgh as a location during that lunch meeting in London. Bing's specifications for a host city fitted perfectly: it should be able to accommodate 50,000 to 150,000 visitors in a month, but not be too big; reasonably well-served by concert halls and hotels; and it should be especially visually appealing. Either way, Wood was incredibly valuable to the birth of the Edinburgh International Festival and extremely enthusiastic about Bing's idea:

> [Bing convinced us] that such an enterprise, successfully conducted, might at this moment of European time, be of more than temporary significance and might establish in Britain a centre of world resort for lovers of music, drama, opera, ballet and the graphic arts... If, as now seems certain, the Festival succeeds, Edinburgh will not only have scored an artistic triumph but laid the foundations of what may well become a major industry, a new and exciting source of income.[2]

That the British Council was permitted to operate and grant funding in Scotland but not England was also a factor, apparently. Another was that the centre of Edinburgh had escaped the Luftwaffe mostly unscathed. Even Leith, Edinburgh's port area, suffered only minor damage compared to other industrial areas across the UK, despite the first air raid on Britain in the Second World War being the 'Battle of the River Forth' on 16 October 1939, as British Spitfires defended Rosyth Naval Base in Fife.

The two men were near-contemporaries, Bing the senior by only 20 months, yet Wood's apparent functionary position in a government organisation didn't tell the story of a life devoted to the arts. Known to all as 'Harry', he was an Edinburgh man himself, cultured, good-humoured and well-connected. He'd been educated at the grand, neoclassical Royal High School on the side of Edinburgh's Calton Hill, a school with a fine view of the city's Old Town.

Wood was talented enough as a student at Edinburgh College of Art that his work was shown in the Royal Scottish Academy and after also graduating in English Literature from the University of Edinburgh, he lectured at the university and wrote books on the poets Robert Henryson and John Marston. A close friend of the writer Edwin Muir, he was employed by the British Council to establish a Scottish office in 1940 and the following year also became a curator with an exhibition of *Inter-Allied Art* at the National Gallery of Scotland on the Mound. It featured artists from almost all the Allied countries, including the Norwegian Edvard Munch and the Polish war artist Felix Topolski.

Poland's World War II links with Scotland were strong and the more than 25,000 displaced Polish Army soldiers based near the city gave Edinburgh an unfamiliar cosmopolitan feel when they visited on weekend leave. Wood organised similar exhibitions, talks and lunchtime concerts in the National Gallery and its director Stanley Cursiter proposed him as a fellow of the Royal Society of Edinburgh in 1943. So Wood was naturally very well-inclined toward the kind of festival Bing was proposing and extremely well-placed to get him close to those who held power in the city.

Their job was to convince John Falconer, the then-Lord Provost and head of the Corporation that ran the city,[3] and Wood had a strategy to make the best impression possible. First, he set up a meeting with as many eminent city names as he could muster, so Bing could attempt to enlist their support. These included Eva Primrose, the Countess of Rosebery and Midlothian, a patron of the arts and friend of the Queen, who in 1943 had published an idiosyncratic but well-intentioned guide to the feminism of the time named *The Ambitious Girl*. As she passionately informed any young woman who might want to enter the theatre:

A play is not merely certain personages, words and deeds smoothly presented in a series of acts and scenes. It is a living thing, vibrant with the life and soul of the generation that produced it. The social, political, historical and religious topics of the day all have their part to play in it.[4]

Also in Wood's group were James Murray Watson, editor of *The Scotsman* newspaper and the physician Dr Osborne Henry Mavor, better known by his playwriting pen-name James Bridie, whose play *Tobias and the Angel* Bing had recently programmed at the Children's Theatre. Everyone agreed that Bing's plan was exactly what Edinburgh needed. What the continent would need, in fact, as the Allies took to the streets of Berlin and the torment of the past six years appeared to be nearly over.

A number of these people are often claimed as being somehow assistant founders of the Edinburgh Festival, but after Bing and Wood, John Falconer was the third person it truly couldn't have happened without – not that he was any great patron of the arts. More than two decades older than Bing and Wood, he was born in 1879 in Fortrose, a Highland town near Inverness on the Moray Firth and was a 'son of the manse'; meaning his father, Charles Falconer, was a Minister of the Church of Scotland. He went to school at the private George Watson's College in the smart suburb of Merchiston and studied law at the University of Edinburgh. He signed up for military service with the Royal Scots at the start of the First World War, served in Ireland and

France and was promoted to Major, returning to Edinburgh to practice law until he was elected to the local council in 1932.

Rising through the local political ranks, he unsuccessfully tried to become the right-of-centre Progressive Party's candidate for Lord Provost in 1938, but after serving as Edinburgh's chief air raid warden during the Second World War, he finally won the nomination and the post in 1944. Bing recalled of his first meeting with 'Sir John'[5] in February 1945 that he was 'an awfully nice little old man, a lawyer [who] had never heard of Glyndebourne... but he understood perfectly well my central argument'. That argument being, a festival like this was a potential money-spinner and prestige-builder for the city, especially while the great festivals of Europe were rebuilding.

Despite Bing's impression of him as unconcerned with artful things, Falconer welcomed this ambitious idea. Bing spent the summer of 1945 travelling to the city to deliver the same sales pitch to one Corporation functionary after another, a process he described as offering a crash course in local Scottish politics. He learned through trial and grievous error while making such faux pas, for example, that you don't refer to a resident of Edinburgh as 'English',[6] and nor does an Austrian Catholic offer to launch a Festival occurring in Presbyterian Scotland with a cathedral High Mass. Harvey Wood had to forcefully spell out the latter mistake to him.

The plan for a festival was first hinted at in the press in late 1945 and the plan was officially authorised by the town council in September of 1946 and launched with two simultaneous press conferences in the host city and in London the same month, the latter presented by Falconer. Representatives of all the groups which might have any kind of stake in the festival were then brought together for a meeting in November 1945, among them the Chamber of Commerce and representatives of the theatre, tourism and travel industries. At this meeting the Edinburgh Festival Society was created for coordination of the event, their job being to assist Bing and to approve decisions between a quorum committee of at least six members, at least two of whom had to be from the City Corporation. Wood was placed in charge of the first committee and this model carried on for two decades, acting as both help and hindrance to Bing's successors.

The new Scottish Tourist Board eagerly became involved, which wasn't surprising, as Lady Rosebery's husband Harry Primrose, the 6th Earl of Rosebery and briefly Secretary of State for Scotland, had been appointed its founding chairman in 1946. Funds were also provided from the racehorse Ocean Swell's unlikely win at the Derby run in Newmarket in 1944 – its owner was the Earl. Presumably while the couple were at home in their neo-gothic mansion Dalmeny House on the south bank of the Forth, which survives in the family to this day, they shared their enthusiasm for the thought of an Edinburgh Festival.

Thanks mainly to Falconer's nous and determination, this was the kind of fast-moving sequence of events we might not normally associate with local government. In fact, the Corporation were surprised when Bing told them the planning window for summer 1946 had already been missed and the first Festival would have to happen the following year. A large, excited article in *The Scotsman* on 24 November 1945 heralded 'probably... the first great post-war international art assembly in Europe', with the Lord Provost playing up to his role as salesman for the city by talking up Edinburgh as 'the most attractive venue in Britain [due to its] beauty, amenity and history'. Most of what we recognise in the contemporary Festival was established from the planning stages of what became the first Edinburgh International Festival of Music and Drama, with a promised event of three weeks to a month's duration, in summer or early autumn, presenting music, drama and ballet. Only the stated intention to feature British, Continental and American orchestras alongside Russian ballet feels less ambitious than the truly worldwide programme we see today. The benefit to tourism in Edinburgh and Scotland as a whole was baked into early coverage of the Festival, its commercial appeal sitting alongside the artistic potential.

As well as finding the money required to stage the Festival, thought had to be given to the volume of tourist accommodation required; a cruise liner berthed in Leith and an in-situ sleeper train were even mooted as options. Bing couldn't believe how well he managed to negotiate his own role and by extension that of Glyndebourne, where he still worked and whom he represented. In fact, as well as making arrangements in Edinburgh, he had organised *The Rape of Lucretia* by Benjamin Britten's English Opera Group as a one-off Glyndebourne performance in July 1946, with the festival there still on enforced hiatus.

In Edinburgh, he was employed to do the job of Festival Director as a representative of Glyndebourne, which would operate under the formal title of 'organising centre', but it was also written into the contract that any losses he or Glyndebourne made through organising the Festival or for any of the operatic shows they would stage themselves would be underwritten by the city. Despite the eventual success of the first Festival, Glyndebourne's losses were £37,000 at the end of it; Bing had anticipated them being roughly 50 per cent higher.

His duties, mind you, went above and beyond the normal, including making special arrangements with the war ministries in charge of fabric rationing to allow the hotels of Edinburgh to purchase new curtains to cover their previously blacked-out windows and brokering deals with American Express and the travel agent Thomas Cook to sell tickets overseas. The way Bing has it, there was also a general uphill struggle to early Festival organisation. Every major financial or programming decision involved boarding a sleeper train from London to Edinburgh to make his case to the committee, who had to rubber-stamp it.

Those in the wider cultural industry were equally intrigued by Bing's plans and perplexed by their location, an admittedly beautiful city with no great classical or operatic tradition of its own to speak of. Yet Edinburgh proved an easier sell than Glyndebourne itself, for back when Bing was brought in by Ebert and Busch to assist with the country house festival in 1934, he grew well-used to the blank stares and unsure correspondence of agents who had no idea what kind of audience or reception their clients might receive. This time, at least, Bing, Glyndebourne and Edinburgh itself were known quantities.

With Edinburgh, Bing also had a hidden card up his sleeve – one that he put in place early on and pulled out whenever he could sense the interest of a booking agent waning. That card was the name of one of the most famed orchestral conductors in the world: Bruno Walter.

* * *

Walter was top of Bing's list of preferred star guests, even ahead of such greats as the violinist Yehudi Menuhin and the pianist and composer Artur Schnabel, but some financial assistance from the city of Edinburgh was required to get the impoverished 87-piece orchestra and their instruments to Scotland. The city was willing to provide, for John Falconer recognised that only by refusing half-measures could the festival become a magnet for international audiences and for deep-pocketed tourist crowds.

Building upon the slow release of information unveiled over the previous few months, the press carried reports of the great orchestras which would be performing less than a year later, including the Vienna Philharmonic under Walter, as well as Paris' L'orchestré des Concerts Colonne, conducted by Paul Parey, the Liverpool Philharmonic under Sir Malcolm Sargent with soloist Artur Schnabel, and Manchester's Hallé Orchestra under John Barbirolli. While criticisms that Scottish drama could have been better-represented – as we'll see, leading to the arrival of theatre groups dubbed 'semi-official' and on the 'fringe' of the Festival – Scottish orchestras were well-represented.

The Scottish Orchestra was founded in 1891 in Glasgow and made its first Edinburgh Festival appearance on 7 September 1947 under principal conductor Walter Süsskind, another European evacuee from his home country of Czechoslovakia during the war. He led the orchestra from 1946 until 1952, rechristening it the Scottish National Orchestra in 1950, ahead of its Royal approval in 1977 and its present use of the name the Royal Scottish National Orchestra. They played with the pianist Arturo Benedetti Michelangeli in '47, while the other Scottish orchestra present that year – the BBC Scottish Orchestra, founded in 1935 by conductor Ian Whyte and presently named the BBC Scottish Symphony Orchestra – performed with the great violinist Yehudi Menuhin the following year, his first appearance of many in Edinburgh.

These concerts would all take place beneath the grand Beaux-Arts style dome of the Usher Hall, in the West End of the city, which had been completed in the same year the First World War broke out. Next door to the Usher Hall, the Royal Lyceum Theatre was created in the late-19th century by the great theatre designer Charles J Phipps, whose work also included London's Lyric, Garrick, Prince of Wales and original Shaftesbury Theatres, as well as the Gaiety in Dublin.

Remaining largely unaltered within even to this day, the Lyceum made a grand setting for the great French actor and director Louis Jouvet's company, as well as London's Old Vic Company, whom it was hoped would cement the Anglo-Scots feel of proceedings by staging a brand new, specially-written piece by James Bridie. This play didn't happen, but the two works they did bring included Shakespeare's *Richard II* in a version by director Ralph Richardson, with Alec Guinness in the title role.

Elsewhere, the King's Theatre – its foundation stone laid in 1906 by the Scots-American philanthropist Andrew Carnegie, who was born a few miles across the Firth of Forth in Dunfermline – would be the base for Glyndebourne Opera itself, which for three weeks was to present Mozart's *The Marriage of Figaro* and Verdi's *Macbeth* on alternate days, both directed by Ebert. The King's was the theatre which Bing so admired when he toured *The Beggar's Opera* in 1940 and there was much synchronicity in his returning with an opera which called to mind both his days in Berlin and his new links across the UK, a version of the 'Scottish play' by England's bard.

In fact, with the huge wheels of Edinburgh's Corporation behind the festival and Henry Harvey Wood and James Bridie increasingly involved in suggesting the artistic direction of the event, there were those who – behind closed doors – questioned the role of Bing and Glyndebourne in the organisation of it at all; who felt Bing's loyalty might be his primary place of work, with the Edinburgh location merely incidental. Yet Glyndebourne was taking no fee for its lead role in organising Edinburgh and the indefatigable and well-connected Bing had the confidence of both Wood and – very crucially – Falconer. Whether the death of Keynes in 1946 removed a barrier to Arts Council participation or not, thanks to the end of his supposed enmity with John Christie and by extension Bing, they also came on board with funding.

The Queen, Elizabeth Bowes-Lyon, consort of George VI and daughter of the Scottish Lord Glamis, had been announced as patron in October 1946 and for all of civic Edinburgh and those whose interest lay in a festival of the high arts, the excitement was left to build. As we'll find, that by no means meant everyone, yet the sense of expectation and tangible excitement would have been felt in the air throughout the city.

On 2 January 1947, a *Scotsman* columnist looked back to the archival glowing notices from the First Edinburgh Music Festival of 1815, and forward to a bill which 'should make 1947 an unprecedented year in the history of music in our midst.' Sadler's Wells Ballet were booked for the Empire Theatre, with the version of Tchaikovsky's *The Sleeping Beauty* in which the great ballerina Margot Fonteyn received some of her highest praise, as well as Usher Hall chamber concerts by premiere musicians Schnabel, Joseph Szigeti, William Primrose and Pierre Fournier, all together.

Another report had the University of Edinburgh's Professor Charles Saroléa, speaking in his position with the Edinburgh and Leith Consular Corps, calling for the creation of a municipal coffee house and restaurant, to liven up the dullness of Edinburgh at the weekend. No-one would mistake Edinburgh for Salzburg or Vienna, he said, without the kind of cosmopolitan 'coffee howff' like Edinburgh's very first, managed by John Row in a tenement near Parliament Square in 1673. Professor Saroléa would doubtless have been pleased by the coffee situation in 21st century Edinburgh.

* * *

By the time the Edinburgh International Festival of Music and Drama opened on Sunday 24 August 1947, the city was looking its finest in the late summer sunshine. Floral displays had been created in the public gardens and in baskets tied to the masts guiding the electrified trams through Princes Street, and a display of Scottish industries, arts and crafts had been arranged for shop windows. Through hotel derequisitioning and the help of citizens taking in lodgers following a massive public drive for support, several thousand visitors from across Europe and America were now discovering this previously modest Scottish capital.

Even now, our impression of mid-20th century Scotland and its relationship with the Church of Scotland – as much a de facto government for the time as the Scottish Office of the Westminster Parliament – might tell us that Edinburgh as a city valued sober worship and expressions of faith over the joy of art. While that may have been true up to a point, the Sunday afternoon opening ceremony in St Giles' Cathedral signified a reconciliation between the two fields, in a show of enlightened unity typical of the post-war years.

Before a congregation of 1,600, with several thousand more outside, having watched the formal procession from the City Chambers across the road, the Reverend Dr Charles Laing Warr, minister of St Giles', prayed in his sermon for:

> [A]ll writers, artists, dramatists and musicians, that their work may
> be done for Thine honour, and may increase the joy and beauty
> of our common life... Owing to causes located in the political and
> ecclesiastical controversies of a dead past, we have neglected the
> place of the heart and the emotions... It is the Church's duty, which
> it has not always remembered, to foster and promote aesthetic
> appreciation. Christianity... is, and must be, the friend of the Arts.[7]

That night, Paray conducted L'orchestré Colonne in works by Haydn, Schumann and Franck and for three weeks – until Saturday 13 September and a closing concert by Walter and the Vienna Philharmonic Orchestra, their originally-planned run of three shows growing to six to meet demand – the unusual but very welcome sense was that the artistic world's attention had settled upon Edinburgh, a feeling that the city found suited it. Reporting daily from the cultural frontline, *The Scotsman's* columnist wrote, tongue-in-cheek, of a new condition afflicting the normally introverted people of Edinburgh which they had christened 'Hysteria Festivalis'.

One surprise hit of the first Festival went on to establish a through-line for the next 75 years, a dependable constant for both International Festival and later its emerging Fringe. On George Street at the heart of James Craig's New Town, built in 1787 from public subscriptions in order to host the Caledonian Hunt Ball, the Assembly Rooms were purchased for public use by the Edinburgh Corporation in 1945. After a period of refurbishment they came into their own during the International Festival as a club bar and restaurant, which was accessible only to season ticket holders of what was named the Festival Club.

No doubt the allure of this building and its promise of all-day and after-dark socialising – often with the performers themselves – contributed to demand for tickets. One and a half thousand had been sold by the end of the Festival's first week, with the great demand causing many others to line up at the Assembly Rooms ticket office, lining up once for the privilege of joining another already-long queue to get into the Club. By the end of the festival, the number of tickets sold was 13,000.

It was in this hub the night before the official launch that John Falconer addressed a delegation including John Christie, Carl Ebert, Paul Paray, Lady Rosebery and Falconer's own wife Diana, declaring that 'this lovely city, so dear to Scottish hearts all over the world, awakens to a new future – to shine once more in the firmament of art'. Three weeks later, in the same spot, a party was held following the finale concert by Walter and the VPO, where artists and members of the public relaxed and drank and met together and the Lord Provost paid tribute to the border-crossing, cosmopolitan friendship of the Festival, which the spirit in this room best exemplified.

The Lady Provost was presented with flowers and the Provost himself accepted three grateful cheers from the crowd. The first Edinburgh International Festival of Music and Drama had been as perfect as humanly possible and agreement had already been reached that it was to return the following year. Even the one near-disaster, the possible suspension of the grand plan to illuminate Edinburgh Castle in the evening, had been overcome with personal appeals from dignitaries and serving MPs to Prime Minister Clement Attlee and the Minister of Fuel and Power Manny Shinwell. The request was to exempt the spectacle from strict post-war fuel conservation rules in place at the time, with members of the public even offering to donate their own coal ration and a compromise was reached in which four evenings of lighting was permitted.

Edinburgh residents flocked onto the streets to see their city anew beneath these lights, a beacon of artistic hope in Europe. On his first night in the city, Bruno Walter and his daughter Lottie admired the illuminations on the way to the Festival Club, a moment of tranquillity after the horrors their family had faced in the decade before. 'No-one, in a lifetime, would ever forget it,' said Carl Ebert, here representing Glyndebourne, but carrying with him something of the Weimar-era spirit in which the Festival's creator Rudolf Bing had also been forged.

* * *

As for Bing, his role as the main driving force behind the Festival's creation and delivery was perhaps not as celebrated at the time as it may have been. A pen portrait in *The Scotsman* in the Festival's closing days presents a modest man, at home with business and art, labouring away quietly in an attic room above the Festival Society office. In those days, it lay within the now-demolished Synod Hall on Castle Terrace, part of the block which still contains the Usher Hall and the Royal Lyceum, as well as the new Traverse Theatre. Fulfilling his Edinburgh vision of seven years before, the office afforded a perfect view of the Castle.

Bing's rule was that the management mustn't fraternise with the talent at the aftershow, so when his wife danced a reel with Lord Haig at a party in honour of Princess Margaret, he watched nervously from the sidelines. Who knows how he must have felt when he was dragged onstage by the Lord and Lady Provost at the Festival's closing party while Auld Lang Syne played?

When we speak of the creation of the Edinburgh Festival, we have to speak of Bing as first among the three equals – and the sizeable accompanying ensemble – who brought it to life. Wood suggested Edinburgh as a location and made the connections which allowed that to happen. Falconer brought a visionary willingness to drive the Festival through, in large part because he could see the financial rewards it would bring. But Bing was at once father and midwife to the whole thing.

The next two Edinburgh International Festivals happened under his stewardship, although after 1948 his role of Festival Director reported directly to the Edinburgh Festival Society. Yet he kept his post at Glyndebourne and worked tirelessly for its full-time return, which it did in 1950, the year after he left the UK, with the help of a grant from Bing's old department store boss Spedan Lewis. At 1948's Festival he programmed Rome's Santa Cecelia Academy Orchestra, conducted by Walter's old sparring partner Wilhelm Furtwängler and a theatrical *Medea* directed by John Gielgud. In 1949 came the Royal Philharmonic Orchestra, conducted by Sir Thomas Beecham and Gustav Gründgens' Dusseldorf Theater, amid controversy and protests about whether the director bore Nazi sympathies or not, despite Bing's extensive background checks on him.

Bing was lost to the Edinburgh and Glyndebourne Festivals for good in 1949, after a visit to New York earlier that year to try and secure some Glyndebourne shows in partnership with New Jersey's Princeton University. He also met representatives of the city's Metropolitan Opera, and they were impressed by the experienced administrator. Bing took the call offering him the New York Met job in May 1949, in the middle of lunch at the Ivy restaurant in London. After that year's third Festival, he and his wife Nina left for a holiday in the Swiss Alps. Their boat arrived in New York on 3 November 1949, and they moved into a 36th floor suite on Central Park South, with a view of Midtown Manhattan all the way to the harbour. He ruled at the Met – it's fair to say that's not an exaggeration, given the reputation he built – between 1950 and 1972, overseeing racial desegregation among leading roles in the 1950s and presiding over the demolition of the old Metropolitan Opera House and the building of a marquee new headquarters at Lincoln Centre. Such was his fame at the Met, he had to remind certain commentators of his proud role in creating the Edinburgh International Festival.

A naturalised British citizen from 1946, he became Sir Rudolf Bing in 1971. Two years later he was given a similar public award by Austria, the country he had fled exactly 35 years before.

Bing died in New York in 1997 at the age of 95, after suffering from

Alzheimer's Disease for some years. He outlived both Sir John Ireland Falconer, who was knighted in 1946 and stepped down from his role as Provost soon after the 1947 Edinburgh International Festival, dying in 1954 at the age of 74; and Harry Harvey Wood, who left Edinburgh in 1950 to work with the British Council in France and Italy, returning to Edinburgh University in 1965. He was 73 when he died of cancer at his home in London in 1977.

In *Banquo on Thursdays*, his idiosyncratic but entertainingly gossipy memoir of the Edinburgh International Festival's first five decades, future EIF publicist Iain Crawford – who was a cub reporter in Edinburgh in 1947 – credited Bing with a 'hard-headed practical sense', first and foremost. He also put forward the idea that the Edinburgh Festival's first principles were 'a strange amalgam of cultural banditry, civic enterprise and idealism', which sounds very much like the often-conflicting foundations upon which the following 75 years would be built.

SPOTLIGHT

A Satire of the Three Estates (1948–1996)

'THERE IS A PECULIAR irony in the fact that the Church of Scotland, which used to be known for its hostility to the theatre, to some extent owes its very existence to a play', wrote the playwright Robert Kemp in the Church's magazine *Life and Work* in June 1948, two months before his version of that play opened at the second Edinburgh International Festival. Sir David Lyndsay of the Mount's *A Satire of the Three Estates* was a seismic event in Scottish theatre when it first played in the mid-1500s and it became a transformational event in the early history of the Edinburgh Festival 400 years later.

Titled *Ane Pleasant Satyre of the Thrie Estaites* in Middle Scots (and with the subtitle *In Commendation of Vertew and Vituperation of Vyce* when it was published in 1602), we'll use the contemporary spelling here to avoid confusion between the various forms of the original subsequently used. Lyndsay, a courtier to King James V of Scotland and a member of the Parliament of Scotland representing his home area of Cupar in Fife, wrote *The Three Estates* as a provocation against the noble lords, the merchant bourgeoisie and the pre-Knox clergy – the three estates – of the mid-16th century's pre-Reformation Scottish realm. It saved its greatest anger for the latter, which Lyndsay credited with abuse of power and the corrupt taking of tithes from the poor.

These were heresies which could have had Lyndsay killed and the fact he survived suggests he must have had James v's permission to write such a work; in fact, the King may even have commissioned him. According to the only surviving report of a 1532 performance for the King, delivered by an attendee to the English court, James reacted viscerally to this early version, spurred to action about the clergy, although he died in 1542.

The Three Estates later had performances in Linlithgow in 1540, Cupar in 1552 and Edinburgh in 1554 – the latter on Calton playfield, where the Edinburgh Playhouse now stands and a short walk from the site of the Gateway Theatre, one of the founding venues of 1947's 'semi-official' festival. There's an argument the events of the Scottish Reformation of 1560 and therefore the primacy of the Church of Scotland for centuries to follow, were set in motion by the play's existence, but here the work falls foul of the irony noticed by Kemp. The Church of Scotland's deep, puritanical antipathy to theatre included this play and by the mid-20th century *The Three Estates* was a curio, known only to those with an interest in the histories of Scottish drama or the Church of Scotland.

Both groups counted Kemp and the Scottish playwright James Bridie among their number. The International Festival organising committee were sensitive to criticism about the lack of Scottish drama at 1947's Festival and Bridie was their expert of choice on the matter. They asked for a list of Scots plays for 1948 and Bridie sent them three, all with a clear link to pre- or post-reformation Scottish theatre. As his biographer Winnifred Bannister notes, Bridie himself was 'a product of the reaction against the dammed-up repression of a Knox-ridden people'.[1]

Not making the cut were the 1725 pastoral comedy *The Good Shepherd* by the Lanarkshire poet Allan Ramsay, persecuted by the Kirk for opening the first ever circulating library in the same year and the then-Reverend John Home's tragic but extremely popular *Douglas* (1756), which incurred the wrath of the presbytery, forcing Home to resign as a minister and move to London. Instead, the only complete surviving example of Scots drama from before the Reformation of the 16th century was chosen, the clergy-provoking, Reformation-inspiring *Satire of the Three Estates*. A perceptive *Scotsman* article back in July 1947 had suggested all three as contenders for a Scottish International Festival play.

A Church of Scotland minister's son who remained loyal to the Church throughout his life, Robert Kemp was born in Orkney in 1908 and educated in Aberdeen. He worked as a journalist with *The Manchester Guardian* (now *The Guardian*) and a broadcaster with the BBC in London during the '30s, reporting from France before the Nazi invasion of 1940. In Paris he interviewed the actor Louis Jouvet, whose company later staged the great

17th century playwright Molière's comedy *L'école des femmes* (The School for Wives) at the first Edinburgh International Festival.

That Kemp enjoyed and took influence from this play was just about his main contribution to 1947's Festival, although he was involved behind the scenes with the Reverend George Candlish and Sadie Aitken's Christian-focused but forward-thinking Gateway Theatre on Elm Row. The Molière play inspired Kemp to write an adaptation in Scots named *Let Wives Tak' Tent* (Let Wives Beware), a hit when it appeared at the Gateway in February 1948 – and later Glasgow Citizens and the London Embassy – with Duncan Macrae taking the lead.

On a shared post-theatre train journey from Glasgow to Edinburgh, Bridie suggested Kemp could work on a modern-day version of *The Three Estates* for the Festival of '48. Kemp agreed, abridging the work to two-and-a-half hours from the original length of somewhere between seven to nine hours. Tyrone Guthrie, no stranger to the Scottish theatre, would serve as director. Born in Tunbridge Wells in the English county of Kent in 1900, the tall (six foot four inches) and magnetically charismatic William Tyrone Guthrie was a relative novice during his last experience of Scottish theatre, when he spent two years as a producer (director, in today's terms) with the Scottish National Players between 1927 and 1928. Back then, he'd taken the company on a camping and performing tour of Aberdeenshire and Fife and directed Bridie's 1928 debut play *The Sunlight Sonata* at Glasgow's Lyric Theatre.

Starting out prior to the Players during the early days of radio drama at the BBC, Guthrie bore a powerful personal pedigree. His maternal grandfather was W Tyrone Power, Commissary General-in-Chief of the British Army and son of the 19th century Irish stage actor Tyrone Power, which made Guthrie a removed cousin of the American film stars Tyrone Power Sr and Jr. His paternal great-grandfather was the Scottish preacher and philanthropist Thomas Guthrie, whose statue stands on the edge of Princes Street Gardens, facing Castle Street.

Reflecting his founding of the 19th century 'ragged schools', which sought to help and educate children in desperate poverty, the statue's inscription describes the elder Guthrie as 'a friend of the poor and the oppressed'. This background gave the director a hereditary footing in the world of *The Three Estates* and he described himself as a 'mongrel Scot' who already knew from familial cousins in Edinburgh what impact the Festival had on the price of carrots in the city.

By 1948 Guthrie's reputation had grown enormously within British theatre – he directed the first London production of Bridie's The Anatomist in the early 1930s and was resident director at the Old Vic in London over two periods between 1933 and 1945, where his specialty was staging thrilling, contemporary Shakespeare productions. Guthrie's great triumphs of the period were 1937's *Hamlet*, starring Laurence Olivier, Vivien Leigh and Alec Guinness and the same year's version of *Henry V* – also starring Olivier and produced in honour of King George VI's coronation – which made a feature of an entirely bare stage. Even at this early stage, his interest was in challenging the formality of the traditional dressed set contained within a proscenium arch, in breaking down barriers between the space inhabited by the play and its audience. The raw proximity of a heaving football terrace was the kind of atmosphere he wanted to bring to the theatre.

Guthrie and Kemp were introduced; the director later remembered the writer walking in out of the Edinburgh drizzle in a thick tweed overcoat and cap, carrying a houseplant. The venue for *The Three Estates'* first contemporary production came in a flash of inspiration similar to the one which helped Rudolf Bing's creation of the Festival itself – the none-more-inspiring view of Edinburgh Castle from Princes Street. Bridie, Guthrie, Kemp and Festival assistant William Graham had spent a long, rainy day driving around the city in an old Daimler, scouring the stages of the city to find one suitable for their planned production and had come up empty. Everywhere was either booked for August or inadequate, including the swimming pool they were told could be emptied and the hall attached to a steam laundry. Fueled by the rum being poured by Bridie, the three men stood in different corners of the McEwan Hall clapping and shouting, testing the acoustics.

Kemp looked up at the view as the trio drove home along Princes Street and his gaze carried to the building alongside the Castle. Standing tall on the Mound, amid the north-facing wall of tenements which follow the course of the Royal Mile down towards Holyrood Palace, he saw the New College of the Church of Scotland, its H-shaped spires pointing towards heaven like the detail upon a crown. Containing the Church's General Assembly Hall, the New College was designed by the architect William Henry Playfair, who in the first half of the 19th century was more responsible than any individual for the visual profile of Edinburgh, with its grand, Grecian-style sandstone buildings.

The visitor to Edinburgh today is likely to marvel most at a building with Playfair's touch upon it. The New College, the adjoining Royal Scottish Academy and National Gallery of Scotland buildings on the Mound, the City Observatory on Calton Hill, the Royal College of Surgeons building at Surgeon's Hall and St Stephen's Church in Stockbridge are all city landmarks and defining Festival venues, while the grand Royal Circus and Regent, Carlton and Royal Terraces are some of the most beautiful residential streets in the country.

Accounts differ as to whether the Assembly Hall was first mentioned in conversation by Kemp or by Sadie Aitken – the passionate and resourceful manager of the Gateway Theatre, itself an example of the Church of Scotland's reforming post-war attitude towards theatre – but the idea had already been building in the other's mind. Bridie and Guthrie agreed it was a strong contender and with Aitken's help, agreement was reached with the Church to stage the play there. Guthrie's surname can't have harmed their chances either.

The shape and space of the Assembly Hall itself – completed in 1858 from designs by the architect David Bryce, who also planned Fettes College and the former Royal Infirmary by the Meadows – dictated the technical innovation which would be a major element of this performance and one of the signature revolutions of Guthrie's career. The rectangular, timber-lined hall was already laid out with a semi-circle of bench seating rising away from a lowered stage area on the floor, with further raised galleries behind this stage. With the Chair of the Moderator (the senior figure presiding over the Church's annual General Assembly) an inviolable feature of the lowered central area, Guthrie instead had an 'apron' or 'thrust' stage built over it.

Alongside this innovation, a flourish not seen in a production of this scale since the days of Shakespeare, Guthrie's plans were hugely ambitious. The cast included 60 performers, all Scottish and mostly drawn from the ranks of the Citizens Theatre in Glasgow. The entire auditorium would become their performance space, with processional entrances through the walkways and up the stairways on the thrust stage's sides, with banished players still visible in the gallery above. Molly MacEwen designed the scenery and the costumes, which were stitched together mostly by voluntary female helpers. Cedric Thorpe Davie composed a grandly sung score.

The initial response to news of *The Three Estates'* appearance at the International Festival fell somewhere between well-intentioned hope for this boldly Scottish production and uncertainty as to whether anyone would be interested. Ticket sales started slow, but picked up a little beforehand. Then, on 24 August 1948, came opening night, which was sparsely attended by students and enthusiasts – and impressed reviewers, whose reports stoked the kind of word-of-mouth that builds a blazing, hot-ticket success, the likes of which the International Festival hadn't experienced in its short life. Bridie's biographer Winifred Bannister wrote seven years later that:

> The effect of that first night was electric. There was majesty here,
> and enormous zest and sparkling comedy. The audacity of Lyndsay's
> attack, projected with such dynamic acting and such a glorious
> spread of pageantry, provided the theatrical experience of a lifetime.[2]

Lengthy queues began to form daily at the Festival's Synod Hall ticket office and many were turned away. By the end of the run, many thousands of people had seen *The Three Estates*. The Assembly Hall was returned as it had been given, the fake blood on the stage and all the melted candle wax in the aisles notwithstanding.

Calls for a repeat run in 1949 were acted on, this time counting the Queen among the audience; the first Royal performance of *The Three Estates* in 400 years. Pundits began to wonder whether the play might become an annually repeated standard during the Festival. This didn't happen – and would have become tiring before long – but *The Three Estates* returned to the Assembly Hall often over the next half-century. Guthrie's version reappeared in 1951 and 1959, after which his association with the festival ended due to a financial dispute. Between these productions, the great stage director and innovator perfected his thrust stage design at the Stratford Festival of Canada in 1952[3] and created a range of new productions for the Edinburgh Festival.

Guthrie's run of Edinburgh plays included Allan Ramsay's *The Good Shepherd*, finally staged in pre-midnight performances at the Royal High School during 1949's Festival, while he was also directing *The Three Estates*.[4] In 1950, with the Festival committee's confidence in contemporary Scottish drama clearly bolstered, he directed both Bridie's *The Queen's Comedy* and Eric Linklater's *The Atom Doctor* at the Lyceum, under the umbrella of Glasgow's Citizens Theatre company and in 1952 returned with the same company and the Old Vic for Kemp's adaptation of Joseph Mitchell's 1731 ballad-opera *The Highland Fair*.

Later, Guthrie took charge of high profile Edinburgh world premieres of new plays by the triple Pulitzer Prizewinner Thornton Wilder, *The Matchmaker* (1954, a complete rewrite of Wilder's 1938 play *The Merchant of Yonkers*) and *A Life in the Sun* (1955, renamed despite Wilder's objection from *The Alcestiad*) and there were performances of Sophocles' *Oedipus Rex* with the Stratford Ontario Festival Company (1956) and Ulster Group Theatre's hard-hitting Gerard McLarnon play about the sectarian divide in Northern Ireland, *The Bonefire* (1958).

Although drama came to be seen as a poor relation to music and dance in the early decades of the International Festival, its close 11-year association with Guthrie in the city of his father's upbringing helped give this strand international recognition. The 1973 revival of *The Three Estates* by the Royal Lyceum Theatre and their Scottish associate director Bill Bryden, before his move to the National Theatre in London, was part-tribute to Guthrie following his death at home in Ireland two years earlier. Both this version and 1959's featured the Edinburgh-born actor, director and broadcaster Tom Fleming, head of the Lyceum in the 1960s, who directed another International Festival revival of the play in 1984. It returned in August 1985 and again in 1991, the latter a stopgap caused by the loss of a

Bill Bryden-directed *Peter Pan* only one month before the festival.

This last *Three Estates* wasn't a great box office success and was, to date, the final International Festival appearance of Lyndsay's play in its 1948 version. What had once been a startlingly fresh new interpretation was no longer so, but it still had one last incarnation to go in the 1996 swansong of Glasgow's Wildcat Stage Productions. David MacLennan and Dave Anderson's spiritual and political successor to John McGrath's 7:84 company followed the latter in its taste for radical left-wing theatre aimed at working-class audiences and they reunited with McGrath as writer and director of the newly-titled *The Satire of the Four Estates*. Staged at the Edinburgh International Conference Centre as part of celebrations for the 50th International Festival, it featured rowdy and often deliberately low-rent mockery of a fourth target, the tabloid media's tone and political influence.

Where King James v had offered tentative promise of change when Lyndsay first wrote *The Three Estates*, the approaching Labour government fulfilled the same role in 1996, putting an end to a near-two-decade period of Conservative power which had continued almost as long as Wildcat's existence. Yet they lost their Scottish Arts Council funding the following year and soon folded, their creation of *The Four Estates* giving an oddly circular feel to the preceding half-century's revival of Scottish theatre via the Edinburgh Festival.

In 1948, Kemp, Bridie and Guthrie had looked back through centuries of the nation's stage history, but in the 1970s the founding 7:84 and Wildcat spirit had more in common with the anti-establishment, 'semi-official' plays which comprised the first Edinburgh Fringe in 1947. To look back on the various iterations of *The Three Estates* now is also to see much of the lineage of late-20th century Scottish acting talent laid out, including Duncan Macrae, Stanley Baxter and Fulton Mackay in the Guthrie versions; Rikki Fulton and Tony Roper in Bryden's; Gregor Fisher, Juliet Cadzow and David Rintoul in Fleming's; and Sylvester McCoy in The Four Estates. Yet the play's modern legacy in Edinburgh is about so much more than the individual qualities of each version.

Its 1948 revival, it was later suggested, defined the concept of a Scottish theatre as not just 'a question of national vanity, but... motivated by the existence of a distinctive theatrical voice.'[5] At the end of the first modern performance of the play, legend has it Bridie sighed in private prayer, 'now Lord, lettest thy servant depart in peace'. His life had been devoted to Scottish theatre – perhaps he sensed its future flourishing had begun here.

2

'On the Fringe of the Festival...'

WHEN WE SPEAK of the birth of the Edinburgh Festival, we celebrate the arrival of twins. One is barely older, more confident and self-assured, at ease with the role it's been handed alongside international peers at the very highest level. The other is younger, but essentially the same age; wildly creative, but often without its sibling's patience for creating a glossy finish. This twin rejects a sense of established order, but fights for attention however it can.

The birth of the Edinburgh Festival Fringe as we know it today – or the Festival Fringe Society, which attempted to bring some order to the chaos – didn't happen until 1959, long after Rudolf Bing's International Festival of Music and Drama launched with triumphant results in 1947. But the spirit of the Fringe was there from the very beginning – from before the beginning, in fact. Even as the new Edinburgh International Festival made a case for elite arts like opera and ballet being a reconciling force in post-war Europe, there were calls for work more representative of the people to be included.

The definition of this work, of art which is 'for' one group or another, is shaky, and this history won't pick a side, for surely art hopes to be open and accessible to all on some level? Yet, in the resettling period after World War II, as new social structures like the National Health Service and the Arts Council were being built from the ground up in the wake of the Labour Party's General Election win of 1945, the role of theatre was thrown into sharp focus. What part might it now play in reflecting the experience of ordinary people who had fought and suffered the deprivation of the war years?

Between the wars, the role of theatre in relation to class had become a hot subject for debate and worker's theatre groups had sprung up out of working-class and left-wing groups. In Scotland, most famously, a miner and poet from Cardenden in Fife named Joe Corrie had taken to playwriting around the General Strike of 1926 and his amateur Bowhill Players group toured the country as the Fife Miner Players, to communities where his play *In Time o' Strife* won huge support for its representation of working-class life during the Strike.

In North London in 1936, the Unity Theatre club was formed through explicit connection to the Left Book Club and the Communist Party of Great Britain. Like Corrie's group, it sought to represent the lives and concerns of working-class people, while taking in themes of agitprop and antifascism and it was extremely popular. As the name suggested, London Unity brought together disparate London theatre groups and clubs with similar aims under one umbrella and it inspired a network of up to 250 imitator groups to do the same thing around the country. The largest of these were in Liverpool and Glasgow, although Glasgow's group broadly rejected the Communist label in favour of a broader left-wing church.

On Thursday 30 January 1947, a line was drawn in the sand of *The Glasgow Herald*'s 'Letters to the Editor' column by actor Eveline Garratt, in her role as assistant director of Glasgow's Unity Theatre. Talks, she wrote, had already been held between Unity and Rudolf Bing about their – or any other Scottish theatre group's – participation in the upcoming first International Festival. Bing was asked whether any Scottish theatre groups had been invited to take part, or whether any groups planning to turn up anyway could be publicised along with the other entertainments. His answer, she wrote, was 'no' in both cases, compounded by his apparent insistence that 'no Scottish theatre is up to standard. '[1]

'Do the organisers,' she asked provocatively, 'think the rough, uncouth tones of the Scot will sound boorish beside the polished utterances of the Old Vic?' The response came two days later in the same column from the leading Scottish playwright and advisor to the International Festival's drama committee, James Bridie. Garratt's company was 'quite right to chance its arm' with its intended unofficial appearance in Edinburgh, he said, but she was suffering a 'lack of perspective' about Unity's ability to compete with the quality of some of the finest companies in the world.[2] The gloves had come off. For the next month, a war of words erupted through the Scottish arts establishment, via *The Herald*'s letters page.

Next up was the poet Hugh MacDiarmid – a complex figure in 20th century Scottish cultural history, whose political interests included communism and strident Scottish nationalism – and he unsurprisingly took the side of Garratt. 'Scotland... cannot develop culturally by taking in our neighbour's washing', he wrote, demanding the International Festival be condemned, 'since it can do nothing to stimulate the creative arts in Scotland'.[3] He believed only the commercial interests of the 'tourist racket' would be served and that the imposition of artists drawn from elsewhere would content bourgeoisie, moneyed audiences, with homegrown artists continuing to fulfil the role of second-rate 'pasticheurs'.

Another correspondent suggested assistance could be given to bring together Scotland's finest acting and creative talent under the banner of a temporary theatre company for the occasion, but this was dismissed as impractical. Meanwhile, others joined in who were less pessimistic than MacDiarmid. One suggested the poet was attempting to erect a 'granite curtain' between Scottish and other cultures, while Bridie himself responded to detractors in increasingly prickly fashion, accusing MacDiarmid of 'vulgar and unsupported abuse' of the festival organisers and suggesting his intervention might be ego-driven. Bridie declared that the Edinburgh Festival would be the best thing that could happen to the arts in Scotland and 'it would be pleasant to find a little comely gratitude on the part of persons interested in such matters'.[4]

Battle lines were drawn and many of these debates still resonate through the Edinburgh Festival's existence; Scottish localism versus a flood of visiting international work which might destabilise the nation's own artistic economy; the function of art as an elite and high-profile pursuit versus one that should be as open to the working classes as possible; and the very purpose of art itself, as spur for economic growth versus democratic instrument of betterment for all.

During the exchange, the great Scottish actor Duncan Macrae (writing as 'JDG Macrae') made a point that looked beyond the first Edinburgh International Festival. He believed Scottish theatre's long-term development didn't depend on what happened in Edinburgh that August, but whether structures could be put in place that would stop Scottish actors' professional choices being either a commitment to amateurism at home or a need to move to London to find prestigious work worthy of their abilities.

Following the Second World War, there were renewed calls for a London-based National Theatre for Great Britain and a National Theatre Act authorising funding was passed at Westminster in 1949, although the National Theatre building itself didn't open until 1963. Macrae caught the mood of these discussions by suggesting fundraising work by famous Scottish actors – among them Deborah Kerr and Alastair Sim – be put towards Scotland's own centre of excellence, alongside some of the proceeds of the International Festival itself.

Any profit from the Festival, Macrae wrote, would be best spent on 'a national school of dramatic art run in conjunction with a Scottish national theatre'.[5] One of these hopes arrived sooner than expected, but the other occupied discussion around Scottish theatre – and the Festival's place in it – for the next six decades. For now, though, the battle for the heart of the first Edinburgh Festival was on.

* * *

Glasgow's Unity Theatre might have been small fry in a sea of British performance where the Old Vic, Sadler's Wells and Glyndebourne Festival Opera were among the big draws, but they were hitting the crest of a decade-long wave of popularity in their home country when Garratt's letter was published. Throughout the 1940s, in fact, Unity rose from the amateur theatre groups of trade unions and Labour clubs in their home city to briefly take London's West End by storm, until its implosion at the turn of the 1950s consigned the company to Scottish theatre history – albeit a significant part of it, especially as inspiration for the radical theatre companies to follow.

Unity Theatre was an amalgam of five earlier amateur companies active in Glasgow, banded together at the end of 1940 when they were all depleted by call-ups to the war. These were the Workers Theatre Group, the Clarion Players, the Transport Players, the Jewish Institute Players and the Glasgow Players; the latterly formerly under the wing of the Scottish Labour College, which was founded by the hero of 'Red Clydeside' John Maclean in 1916. Beginning life with their version of *Awake and Sing*, Clifford Odets' treatise on working-class life in New York, Unity remained amateur for the first half of the decade, then split into amateur and professional ('part-time' and 'full-time') wings in 1945. The full-time group fell under the leadership of sometime electrician and trade union convener Robert Mitchell.

Determinedly proletarian, with strong links to the left, Unity in Glasgow combined the wider British Unity theatre movement's determination to make work for and about the working classes with an unashamedly Scottish voice. They called themselves a 'People's Theatre' and a 'Real Theatre' and took influence from the Irish nationalist playwright Sean O'Casey's work at the Abbey Theatre in Dublin, even producing new versions of his plays from the 1920s, including *Juno and the Paycock*, *Purple Dust* and *The Plough and the Stars*. Unity's belief was that 'a Scottish native theatre can only be built from the flesh and blood of Scottish authors, actors and producers'.

Future Scots stars including Russell Hunter, Duncan Macrae, Roddy McMillan and Ida Schuster were involved with the company as actors. They practiced what they preached, taking plays into hospitals and factories, staging theatre workshops and briefly publishing their own magazine, *Scots Theatre*, after the war. Unity's motto, borrowed from the Russian playwright Maxim Gorky and printed in their journal, was 'the theatre is the school of the people – it makes them think and it makes them feel'.

On 2 September 1946, four months before the exchange in the *Herald* began, the play which defined Glasgow Unity Theatre's professional wing received its first performance in their home city, on the stage of the Queen's Theatre, a sometime music hall serving popular entertainments to the working-class East End. *The Gorbals Story* was a huge popular hit, but it was also a call for solidarity and reform which resonated throughout post-war Glasgow.

The late Scottish theatre historian Bill Findlay wrote that the economic and social problems of Glasgow of the 1940s were 'partly redeemed by a resulting sense of community in adversity, and by a radical politics projecting utopian vision beyond present distress'.[6] The Unity playwright and sometime newspaper cartoonist Robert McLeish tapped into this spirit with *The Gorbals Story*, which rallied against the post-war housing crisis while offering the familiarity of community and plenty of Glasgow Scots humour.

When Unity demanded representation at the Festival, they were no strangers to rocking the Establishment's boat. At first they performed at the Athenaeum Theatre in the basement of Glasgow School of Music on St. George's Place, also home to the then-brand new Citizens Theatre.[7] Yet a disagreement behind the scenes meant they were forbidden from using this space for *The Gorbals Story* and had to relocate to the Queen's. On the opening night, with the Lord Provost of Glasgow and assorted city dignitaries in the stalls, a group of squatters were treated as guests of honour in the grand circle above. Their leader – one Peter Colin Blair McIntyre – made a pre-show address to this captive audience from the stage, taking aim at squalid tenement life and hotel evictions.

Did James Bridie have anything to do with Unity's enforced move from the Citizens building to the East End? His relationship with the young company wasn't exactly harmonious. By the early 1940s he was in his 50s and had lived a full life which seemed forged by a blend of privilege and personal over-achievement. Both Bride and Glasgow Unity were positive influences on the history of Scottish theatre, but it's not hard to believe they were also in some ways one another's nemeses.

* * *

Born Osborne Henry Mavor in Edinburgh in 1888, to engineer and industrialist Henry Mavor and his wife Janet, James Bridie was privately educated at Glasgow Academy, then graduated in medicine from the University of Glasgow in 1913. Straight away, he was commissioned as a Lieutenant and served during the First World War as a medic with the 42nd Field Ambulance, first at Ypres and the Somme in France, then on to Persia and the Caucasus, serving from Baghdad to Baku.

In his memoir of his father *Dr Mavor and Mr Bridie*, Bridie's son Ronald Mavor[8] recounts working with a friend of his father's from Glasgow who served with him during the war, who told him his father had been well-liked by his soldiers, organizing concerts and plays for them. At university Bridie wrote plays for his fellow students, and one inspiration for his love of theatre was Alfred Wareing's Glasgow Repertory Theatre. Active between 1909 and 1913 and one of Bridie's favourite diversions as a student, Wareing referred to this as a 'citizen's theatre'.

The younger Mavor's book title reflected his father's duality as a natural-bred social conservative, but also a theatrical egalitarian who was impressed by and often supportive of theatre makers from different backgrounds. In 1927 Bridie was part of the Scottish National Players' reading committee which turned down the Fife miner Joe Corrie's *In Time o' Strife*, staged the following year by Corrie and his Bowhill Players to great acclaim and ongoing influence, but in 1944 he overturned a similar decision by Glasgow's Citizens Theatre in favour of Corrie's *A Master of Men*.

After the war, Bridie became a General Practitioner in Glasgow's Langside, a doctor at the Victoria Infirmary and a Professor of Medicine at the Anderson College of Medicine, now part of the University of Glasgow. His pseudonym – adapted from his grandfather's name and grandmother's maiden name – was first used for the 1926 book which recounted his wartime experiences, *Some Talk of Alexander*. His debut play *The Sunlight Sonata* was staged at Glasgow's Lyric Theatre in 1928, using the pseudonym Mary Henderson and directed by a young Tyrone Guthrie, then the Bridie name arrived onstage with *The Switchback* in 1929.

Through the 1930s Bridie's plays appeared in Glasgow and London and when he retook his army commission in 1939 to serve as a medic during the early stages of the Second World War, he was recognised alongside JM Barrie as the key Scottish playwright of his time. Demobbed by 1943, he created his greatest legacy in Scottish theatre. The Citizens Theatre was established with its own acting company at the Athenaeum through the joint efforts of Bridie, Glasgow Art Galleries' director Tom Honeyman and George Singleton, local cinema magnate and founder of the Cosmo, now Glasgow Film Theatre.

It was Bridie's aggressive lobbying and fundraising which drove the project through. Installed as chairman, what he said went at the Citizens' first home in the Athenaeum and following its 1945 move to the Victorian Royal Princess's Theatre, south of the River Clyde amid the notorious slum tenements of the Gorbals. This building survives as the Citizens to this day, although it and the area are much altered.

At the very start, actors, crew and even plays were imported from London and Unity may have sensed the hand of the dominant and perfectionist Bridie in the decision not to grant the little-tested company space in the Athenaeum. Matters came to a head, though, when the Arts Council withdrew their funding to Unity Theatre on 11 August 1947. Bridie was involved with the Council's Scottish branch and it was just two weeks before Unity were to take to the stage in Edinburgh.

* * *

Bridie's biographer Winifred Bannister describes Glasgow Unity Theatre in those days as having 'the fervour of partisans shooting their way out of a cellar'[9] and there was certainly no holding back when Unity's James Barke, the novelist-biographer of Robert Burns and sometime Clyde shipyard worker, described the Citizens' version of JB Priestley's *Johnson Over Jordan* – its gala premiere at the renamed Princess's in 1945 – as being for 'the cognoscenti, the precious minority' in a letter to the *Glasgow Evening News*.

Whether any of this apparent personal bad blood fed into the Arts Council's decision not to fund Unity during the Festival can't be proven, although logical reasons were given at the time. The plays chosen, said Bridie's successor as Scottish chairman of the Arts Council James Welsh, hadn't been approved by the Council first and it believed they didn't stand a strong chance of commercial success. Bridie had already left the Council,[10] but was involved in telling Unity about the Edinburgh decision.

Privately he recognised their boldness, and the skill and good intentions of Mitchell and Unity's actors and designers, but found their administrative judgement lacking.

Glasgow Unity used this boldness to force their way into view in Edinburgh that summer. The original plan was to stage three plays, although the Arts Council decision meant they had to cancel one, *Starched Aprons*, a political hospital drama by Glaswegian minister's daughter and librarian Ena Lamont Stewart. It was inspired by her time as a secretary at the Royal Hospital for Sick Children in Glasgow during the 1930s.

Not to be deterred, Unity called a press conference in Edinburgh on 11 August 1947, making the press aware of the Arts Council's decision and issuing a bullish communiqué declaring their intention to perform during the Festival.

With international greats lining up on Edinburgh's biggest stages, *The Scotsman* reported in footballing terms that 'even if it only played the role of a netboy retrieving the ball behind the goal at the international, Unity was going to be there'.[11] In bringing two plays to the Little Theatre on the Pleasance, they were helped by two anonymous donations to the company totalling £900, received within a week of the press conference. One donor, in fact, found their work so important that they contributed despite having never attended a Unity show.

Unity's first Edinburgh play had premiered as part of the same Glasgow season as *The Gorbals Story* the year before. Robert McLellan's comedy *The Laird of Torwatletie* told of an 18th century landowner on the Solway Firth, where the river borders Scotland and England and his attempts to help a fleeing Jacobite soldier escape to France. Its performance at the Little Theatre on 25 August was preceded by an impassioned introduction from the firebrand Hugh MacDiarmid, who declared those involved in the decision to withdraw Unity's funding 'cultural Quislings'. No mean insult, with the occupations and collaborations of the Second World War so raw in the memory.

Unity's second play was their version of Maxim Gorky's *The Lower Depths*, the classic pre-revolutionary Russian social realist drama, which debuted in 1902 in Moscow under the direction of the great actor and director Konstantin Stanislavsky. Reflecting the hopeless lives and misplaced optimism of characters in a homeless shelter by the Volga River, based on the notorious Bugrov shelter in Gorky's home city Nizhny Novgorod, *The Lower Depths'* theme of extreme class disparity made it a popular choice among left-wing and Communist theatre makers of the early 20th century. The play's influence persisted. The French director Jean Renoir filmed an adaptation in 1936, which featured the actor Louis Jouvet, whose company appeared at the first Edinburgh International Festival. Eugene O'Neill's Broadway play *The Iceman Cometh*, first performed in 1946, also bore its influence.

The Unity version was still set in pre-revolutionary Russia, but was very deliberately performed in Scots. There might have been a nationalist edge here, but the use of language is more clearly understood in class-based social terms. Unity viewed the well-spoken, highest profile theatre being imported to Scotland at the Festival and elsewhere as a bar on working-class accessibility, with their voices and experience nowhere to be found on the big stages.

Unity's actors were former tradespeople with no dramatic training, let alone accent training. The raw Glaswegian tone was no barrier to *The Lower Depths'* success when it appeared at London Unity's Goldington Street Theatre in the summer of 1945, though, a run so triumphant that Colin Chambers' history of the Unity Theatre movement compared it the surprise General Election win of Clement Attlee's Labour Party that July. By the time their Little Theatre residency in Edinburgh was over, Unity's triumph upon territory marked out by the International Festival was that they held their own amid it all, drawing healthy audiences and good reviews.

Unity didn't arrive in Edinburgh and blow the competition away, as many simplified present-day accounts imply. Instead, they overcame the hurdles placed before them with dedication and ingenuity, when nobody had asked them to, in order to put on shows which they fervently believed in. In this respect, the spirit of the Edinburgh Festival Fringe as we know it now began with them.

* * *

Glasgow Unity weren't single-handedly responsible for the Fringe, though. In fact, they were just one of eight theatre companies staging unofficial work in '47, which *The Scotsman* referred to as 'semi-official' shows,[12] with the lumpen term 'Festival adjuncts' also used. Joining Unity at the Little Theatre was Edinburgh People's Theatre, founded in 1943 by the Edinburgh-born playwright Andrew P Wilson, sometime general manager of Dublin's Abbey Theatre and co-founder of the Scottish National Players in the early 1920s. With links to the Labour movement in Edinburgh, this group staged Robert Ardrey's *Thunder Rock*, about a man isolated on a remote lighthouse who communes with the ghosts of the past.

Its original, Elia Kazan-directed run on Broadway in 1939 had been short, but the play's bittersweet optimism for the future found favour in post-war Europe and particularly the UK. The People's Theatre's own records show the play was staged in late September, however, after the International Festival had ended; perhaps they were still surfing the wave of Festival enthusiasm tiding through the city.[13] Also at the Little Theatre was the Scottish Community Drama Association (Edinburgh District) with a version of Bridie's own *The Anatomist*, his key 1931 play about the bodysnatchers Burke and Harr and the physician they supplied. Edinburgh People's Theatre and Edinburgh SCDA both survive as amateur clubs to this day.

Only two unofficial companies were non-Scottish in '47. The first was puppet theatre revivalist Waldo Sullivan Lanchester, who staged short plays with his Stratford-Upon-Avon-based Marionettes in the bar of Clerk Street's New Victoria Cinema. The polished cream sandstone of architect George Washington Browne's 1915 YMCA building at 14 South St Andrew Street – just across Princes Street from Waverley Station and more recently a Chinese buffet restaurant – housed Edinburgh College of Art Theatre Group's version of August Strindberg's *Easter* alongside the amateur Christine Orr Players' take on Macbeth. Born in Edinburgh in 1899, Orr was a novelist, poet, playwright and broadcasting pioneer. Her 1936 appointment as 'organiser' of the BBC's Children's Hour in Scotland made her the highest-paid woman in the organisation outside of London and one of only three women in the BBC earning a salary of more than £500.

Orr taught drama classes at various colleges across Edinburgh and was the editor of the Church of Scotland's children's magazine *Greatheart*. While the influence of socialist theatre groups is often mentioned, the Church of Scotland also played a part in '47's unofficial aspect; in fact, the grandest of the year's non-International Festival plays wasn't happening in Edinburgh at all. Instigated by the Carnegie Trust and deemed worthy of the Arts Council's support, unlike Unity, the medieval Christian morality play *Everyman*, in an English translation of Austrian poet Hugo von Hofmannsthal's version, had its British premier during the Festival at Dunfermline Abbey, a ferry journey north across the Firth of Forth from Edinburgh.

Its title role was taken by Richard Ainley – son and half-brother, respectively, of the actors Henry and Anthony – who was returning to the stage after serious injuries sustained during the war cut short a promising film career. Following Everyman's journey through the world and into the afterlife and his realisation that only his own deeds count before God, John Hanau's impressive production was an unofficial accompaniment to the International Festival, but not so beyond the pale that the Princess Royal couldn't take in a performance on 4 September.

In keeping with the Christian theme, the final unofficial performances of 1947 were given at the Gateway Theatre by the Pilgrim Players, a touring company attached to the now non-existent Mercury Theatre of Ladbroke Road in London, which opened in 1933 as the home of Ballet Rambert.[14] The only major 'uninvited' group from outside Scotland appearing, the Pilgrims' plays were TS Eliot's *The Family Reunion* and *Murder in the Cathedral*, the latter about the assassination of Archbishop Thomas Beckett in 1170.

It was commissioned by the Bishop of Chichester for the 1935 Canterbury Festival through his diocese's 'director of religious drama' E Martin Browne and staged in the cathedral where the assassination took place. In 1939, Browne directed the first production of *The Family Reunion* at London's Westminster Theatre, with Michael Redgrave in the main role and founded the Pilgrim Players, who regularly staged the work of Eliot and James Bridie. Between 1945 and 1947, Browne was director of the Mercury, where he revived *The Family Reunion* and sent his Players to perform it in Edinburgh.

The Anglican Eliot's plays finding a home at the Gateway was little surprise. Sited within a tenement courtyard just off Elm Row at the western end of Leith Walk, where New Town Edinburgh bleeds into the working-class port of Leith, the building was opened in 1882 as a veterinary school and later used as a covered skating rink, a billiard hall, a cinema and a repertory theatre. Renamed briefly – and portentously – as the Festival Theatre in the early 1930s, then the Broadway Cinema in 1938, it fell into disrepair during the war, until owner AG Anderson gifted it to the Church of Scotland. He intended it to become a youth centre, with an emphasis on drama and film and the Church reopened it as the Gateway Theatre in October 1946.

In 1947, the union of Scotland's Church and theatre wasn't as unlikely as it seemed. Folk and religious plays flourished in medieval Scotland, prior to the Protestant Reformation of 1560, when the country's spiritual heart was remade in the image of the Presbyterianism preached by John Knox. Much art was forbidden as being disrespectful of God, theatres were burned, playwrights were persecuted and actors found other vocations. The great intellectual awakening of the 18th and 19th centuries' Scottish

Enlightenment softened attitudes, but the Calvinism of Knox still held much sway by the early 20th century. Even elements of the Church of Scotland felt drawn by the currents of post-war liberalisation, however.

The Gateway was put under the directorship of the Reverend George Candlish, a young minister who decided the theatre would show all manner of plays, not just the religious, for he believed the Church needed to relate to wider society upon its own terms. He was eventually assisted by manager Sadie Aitken and Robert Kemp.

* * *

As Glasgow Unity's successful incursion upon the first Edinburgh Festival was coming to a close, Robert Mitchell addressed the Unity summer school at the Pleasance:

> We should go and see West End plays and learn what we can from them. But we should not copy them... new standards [have] to be created, standards not of the West End, but specifically Scottish.[15]

James Bridie was already making moves to ensure Scottish theatrical representation at the 1948 International Festival, despite disappointment that the plan for the Old Vic company to premiere his play *John Knox* at 1947's Festival had come to nothing. Not enough Scottish actors were available for both Edinburgh and London runs, apparently, although there was also a suggestion the London theatre had found it 'too Scotch.' It debuted instead at the Citizens in Glasgow.

Bridie was undeterred. 'Edinburgh's dormant imagination has burst its chrysalis case and she has become a living city overnight', wrote Bridie to the actor John Laurie, outlining his determination to get an all-Scottish play together for 'The Sleeping Beauty' (his name for Edinburgh) the following year.[16]

Many histories record that Robert Kemp set the birth of the Edinburgh Fringe in stone, when an article he wrote for the *Edinburgh Evening News'* 14 August 1948 edition previewed the shows happening 'round the fringe of official Festival drama' that year. It's from this turn of phrase, many have said, that the adoption of the word's use in Edinburgh and the very concept of 'fringe theatre' as we know it today emerged. It's a tenuous connection, given that, for example, a 1947 *Scotsman* article previewing the first set of 'semi-official' shows described *Everyman* in Dunfermline as being 'on the fringe of the Festival'.[17] But Kemp was right when he identified unofficial activity building around the Festival.

The radical outsiders of Unity were being joined by others who had no need to be officially invited to Edinburgh.

In 1948, the Gateway hosted the Pilgrim Players once more, presenting the dramatist and screenwriter Christopher Fry's early-career liturgical play *The Firstborn*, and the Glyndebourne Children's Theatre doing George Bernard Shaw's *Androcles and the Lion*. Christine Orr returned to the YMCA with a play named *The Lady and the Pedlar*, while Robert McLellan's *Toom Byres* and Bridie's *It Depends What You Mean* were also staged by a group of Scottish companies which in 1948 totalled five.

The English theatre makers Joan Littlewood and Ewan MacColl's then-young touring company, the Theatre Workshop, arrived at the nascent Fringe in 1949. Their triple bill of plays at the Methodist Church's Epworth Hall on Nicolson Square comprised adaptations of the French *commedia dell'arte* playwright Moliere's 17th century piece *Le Médecin volant* (The Flying Doctor), Chekhov's short farce *The Proposal*, and Federico Garcia Lorca's *The Love of Don Perlimplin and Belisa in the Garden* (1928) about an elderly bachelor who falls in love with a young woman. Littlewood and MacColl's continuing presence in Edinburgh contributed to the short-lived but radical Edinburgh People's Festival in 1951.

In 1948, Glasgow Unity came up with an ambitious idea to stage McLellan's *The Flouers o' Edinburgh* – a period comedy set in the 18th century, about the Scottish upper classes' dithering between speaking English and Scots – for large audiences at the Ross Bandstand in Princes Street Gardens, but the plan fell through. Instead, they had to wait until the King's Theatre became available after the festival and the relative failure of the play in this new location after their hit festival in '47 illustrated the swift rise and fall of Glasgow Unity Theatre. *The Gorbals Story* had been a success in their home city and in 1948 it transferred to the Garrick Theatre in London's West End for six weeks, then to the Embassy Theatre. This was a huge achievement, but it cast Unity as part of the elite against which they had stood in their short life and divided their focus between Glasgow and London.

A 1950 film adaptation of *The Gorbals Story* was a critical and commercial failure and without the Arts Council's support they needed to keep touring their big hit. When Unity finally folded in 1951, they were a spent creative force, albeit an inspiration for others who later followed. Many of their actors found work with Bridie's Citizens Theatre, although by then it was sadly no longer Bridie's. Having worked on three films with Alfred Hitchcock and helped found the Glasgow College of Dramatic Art in 1950, James Bridie died unexpectedly of a stroke at the age of 63 in 1951.

Housed alongside the Royal Scottish Academy of Music at the Athenaeum building on Glasgow's St George's Place, the College of Dramatic Art was the centre of performing arts educational excellence which Duncan Macrae had hoped for in his letter to *The Herald* four years earlier. It evolved into the Royal Scottish Academy of Music and Drama and the present-day Royal Conservatoire of Scotland – had Bridie survived a little longer, maybe his fierce drive and ambition for the success of Scottish theatre would have cut short the further half-century wait for the National Theatre of Scotland's arrival.

* * *

The Fringe was to enjoy its own successes to match those of the International Festival over the following decades, but the spirit of '47 – whether officially requested, or uninvited but just plain determined – was the fuel that fed the Edinburgh Festival for decades to come. In January 1947, as letters to *The Herald* began to fly, Unity's lesser-known amateur company were debuting a play at the Athenaeum, which would ring down the decades as one of Scotland's greatest modern works. Her play *Starched Aprons* hadn't made the cut in Edinburgh and her work remained unstaged for decades while her name lapsed into obscurity, but Ena Lamont Stewart's *Men Should Weep* was a feminist play ahead of its time.

A troubling but darkly humorous look at the thankless role played by women in holding the family together amid the Great Depression, it was revived with great fanfare by John McGrath's radical 7:84 company as part of the Clydebuilt season in 1982. After this, *Men Should Weep*'s place in the canon has been assured. In 2010, it was given a starry production by the National Theatre in London, finally answering Eveline Garratt's question as to whether 'the rough, uncouth tones of the Scot... sound boorish beside the polished utterances of the Old Vic'.

Another example of the Fringe spirit's effect didn't play out until decades later. It involved another medical doctor who followed Bridie's path into the arts, Matthew Hall, who came from Surrey and trained in neurosurgery at the University of London, but discovered a new vocation after winning the Perrier Award for Best Newcomer in comedy at the 45th Edinburgh Festival Fringe in 1992.

As his bald-headed, big-shirted, absurdist comic creation Harry Hill, he went on to become one of British television's leading comedy and light entertainment stars for three decades and counting, an example of the Fringe's power in recent times to create national and international stars. His first full television series, simply titled *Harry Hill*, ran for three years between 1997 and 2000 on Channel 4 and featured among its colourful cast was Hill's supposed Nana, played by an actor already approaching 80 when the series began.

Born in Belfast in 1919, that actor had become a prolific recurring guest presence in many of the most popular British television series of the 20th century since her film debut in *The Gorbals Story* in 1950, and her final screen credit didn't come until 2009, six years before her death at the age of 95. Her name was Eveline Garratt and once, more than half a century before, she had written a fateful letter to a Scottish newspaper.

SPOTLIGHT

The Edinburgh People's Festival and Ceilidh (1951–53)

AS THE SHORES of New York disappeared over the horizon on 24 September 1950, 35-year-old Alan Lomax sat down on the deck of the liner RMS *Mauretania* and wrote in his notebook that he was 'a comrade of the world, longing to be everywhere.'[1] His destination was Brussels and he was embarking on one of the greatest musical missions of the 20th century – a quest to record and archive the forgotten folk songs of Europe, to be issued by Columbia Records on a selection of 30 long-playing discs. The label had provided him with a tape recorder, tapes and an assurance the project would be published, but otherwise he was on his own.

Born and raised in Texas, his father was John Lomax, also a musicologist, folklorist and oral historian. Lomax Jr helped his father record and collect American folk songs in the early 1930s and a decade later he was an archivist specialising in folk music at the Library of Congress and a radio presenter. In both roles, he helped popularise artists like Woody Guthrie, Lead Belly, Pete Seeger and Muddy Waters. What he told none of his friends or family, including his recently divorced wife and collaborator Elizabeth or young daughter Anne, was that there was an ulterior reason for his trip to Europe.

In the final days of 1949, Lomax was named in a newspaper article as a backer of a Civil Rights Congress dinner at a hotel on New York's Fifth Avenue in support of lawyers defending suspected communists, alongside *The New York Times*' music critic Olin Downes and the historian WEB Du Bois. The following summer, the infamous *Red Channels* pamphlet was published by anti-communist activists, which listed 151 suspected sympathisers in the US media. Lomax's name was on it, alongside Seeger, the playwright Arthur Miller, Dorothy Parker, Orson Welles and Leonard Bernstein.

Democrat senator Pat McCarran's self-titled act was close to becoming law, which would have exposed Lomax to registration and possible imprisonment as a suspected Communist, while effectively ending his broadcasting career, so the European trip was a useful way of evading the investigations of the US Government. At first, he planned to stay away until after Christmas of 1950; he didn't return to the United States until 1959.

From Brussels, Lomax made his way to Paris and finally to London, where he made contact with the BBC. Over the following months his song collecting took him to Ireland, Cornwall, Newcastle and Northumberland, where one of his guides was the singer and playwright Ewan MacColl, by now a participant with the Theatre Workshop in the unofficial Edinburgh Festival. MacColl had written to Lomax the previous year, upon publication of the American's book *Mister Jelly Roll: The Fortunes of Jelly Roll Morton, New Orleans Creole and 'Inventor of Jazz'*, to congratulate him on this work of Socialist Realism.

Together they researched workers' and railroad songs of England's northeast and MacColl wrote to a Scottish friend and colleague in February 1951 to suggest he record some songs for Lomax and introduce him to other Scots folk singers. His letter said:

> Just a brief note – there is a character wandering around this sceptered isle at the moment yclept Alan Lomax. He is Texan and none the worse for that... This is important, Hamish. It is vital that Scotland is well-represented in this collection.[2]

The Scottish friend's name was Hamish Henderson.

* * *

Born in Highland Perthshire on the first anniversary of the Great War's Armistice in 1919, Hamish Henderson was raised in London and well-schooled at Cambridge. He was a man of intriguing complexities; a pacifist, but so concerned about the Nazi threat that he ended up joining British Intelligence during the Second World War; involved in the North African campaign and the drafting of Italy's surrender document, but also an anti-war poet whose collected works *Ballads of World War II* and *Elegies for the Dead in Cyrenaica* meant he was rumoured to be banned from the BBC.

Much like his elder in the Scottish poetry community Hugh MacDiarmid, he was a communist and a Scottish Nationalist, which endeared him to the official wing of neither camp. On the Edinburgh Festival, his feelings were similarly difficult to predict. Speaking on a BBC radio programme in 1992, Henderson said he had expected the International Festival to bypass Scottish culture, but also that in his opinion, 'the greatest event in Scottish history, after the battle of El Alamein, was the Edinburgh International Festival'.[3]

In an essay published in 1998, Henderson recalled a Festival visit to the International House club on Princes Street, which catered to a cosmopolitan mix of Polish army officers and 'the arty sections of the Edinbourgeoisie', of which he was clearly one. Here he heard one of the International Festival's early guiding hands, the British Council's Henry Harvey Wood, excitedly telling an off-duty officer about plans for the nascent Festival and the (Henderson's words) 'celebrated foreign orchestras, opera companies, ballet light-footers and suchlike they might be able to attract to Auld Reekie'.[4]

Henderson rolled his eyes at the implied exclusion of Scottish artists from the line-up, but he disagreed with his comrade MacDiarmid's assessment that the event had to be resisted at all costs. 'The Communist Party had welcomed the festival [and] was greatly interested at the time in helping to develop a national cultural identity for Scotland,'[5] he wrote 50 years later. The Festival, Henderson considered, could be a route to this goal.

As a self-styled 'folk revolutionary', folklorist and song-collector himself, who believed that a powerful strand of Scottish radicalism lay in the dormant and undiscovered rural folk traditions, Henderson was well aware of Lomax's work. He took MacColl up on his suggestion, meeting Lomax in London in March. Lomax, not uncommonly for an international visitor, imagined Scotland was a kind of subdistrict of Britain, that its folk tradition might easily be encompassed as a small part of a wider conversation about England. Henderson corrected him. Lomax said:

The conversation was extremely important. Hamish feels that Scotland is the most interesting and important place on earth, with a real live people's culture, now on the march, and I must say he made me share his feeling.[6]

The meeting happened barely three months after the theft of the Stone of Destiny on Christmas Day 1950, when four University of Glasgow students and supporters of a devolved Scottish Assembly snuck into Westminster Abbey and took the Stone upon which British monarchs were traditionally crowned, bringing it back to Scotland. The Establishment saw this as a grave crime against the Crown, of course, but many Scots considered it the return of stolen property, after the Stone's removal from Scone Abbey near Perth by Edward I's invasion force in 1296. Scottish nationalism was an especially live subject in 1951.

On the first day of the year, the School for Scottish Studies at the University of Edinburgh was opened with the support of the University's Reid Professor of Music Sidney Newman and the behind-the-scenes encouragement of Henderson. Its first employee was the Scots Gaelic speaker and fellow folklorist Calum Maclean, who was raised on Raasay, a 14-mile-long Hebridean island in the straits between the Isle of Skye and the Applecross peninsula. Four years Henderson's senior, he studied Celtic traditions at

Edinburgh in the 1930s and had been sent by the Irish Folklore Commission to collect the songs and stories of his home island in the post-war years. By 1950 he had collected 11,000 pages of transcriptions and diaries.

Lomax's project was similar, but more time-limited. He arrived in Scotland on Wednesday 13 June for a summer tour with Henderson as his main guide, although first Henderson acquainted him with the School of Scottish Studies at its George Square townhouse, because their agreement was that Lomax's recordings would be copied and archived either there or with the BBC in Glasgow. Calum Maclean would be Lomax's guide to the Gaelic-speaking Hebrides and he conscripted his brothers Alasdair, a fellow academic and Sorley, the principal teacher of English at Edinburgh's Boroughmuir High School. Sorley wrote Gaelic poetry for which he'd received some recognition, especially in print from Henderson, and when they were finally translated into English in the 1970s he was acclaimed as the finest Hebridean poet of modern times and a significant Scottish literary figure.

Right away, Lomax recorded the talented 17-year-old bagpiper John Burgess on Edinburgh Castle Esplanade, then two Edinburgh-based singers from the Hebridean Isle of Barra, Calum Johnston and Flora MacNeil. On Monday 18 June he set out by car for the Isle of Skye and on to the Uists, where he met Alasdair Maclean. When he left a week later, it was with recordings of 250 Gaelic songs plus assorted verbal testimonies from their singers, then he drove to Glasgow, where he met an award-winning singer from the Isle of Lewis named Kitty MacLeod.

Henderson's own area of investigation with Lomax was going to be the Doric-speaking north-east and on Sunday 15 July the pair piled into Lomax's hired car and set off for the functional, stone-harled Commercial Hotel in the small North Aberdeenshire town of Turriff. Henderson was Lomax's guide, but also on a mission of discovery himself, using his dapper, tweedy, soft-voiced charm to ask around for local singers and voices who may be of interest. While Maclean made transcripts and Henderson learned the songs himself, Lomax was loaded for bear with a Magnecord Magnecorder PT6-A, a reel-to-reel tape deck which provided unparalleled recording quality. It came in two heavy parts, one carried by Lomax, the other by Henderson. Often it was easier to invite the singers they discovered into the hotel to sing.

One of these was Jimmie MacBeath, born to a Traveller family in the coastal town of Portsoy in the late 1800s. In the First World War he fought at Flanders with the Gordon Highlanders, then he served in the Anglo–Irish War at the turn of the 1920s, but the rest of his life was spent walking the roads of Scotland, England, the Channel Islands and even Nova Scotia. He laboured on farms and in kitchens, and sang for change in bars and on street corners. Henderson heard he was staying in nearby Elgin, but MacBeath was wary of Turriff, specifically the local police and he was only convinced to come and record with the promise of the finest room in the hotel.

MacBeath's specialty, like so many others in the north-east, was the 'bothy ballad', the songs sung by workers in the bothys – stone farm huts – where they slept after a hard day's work. Like the Gaelic waulking songs Lomax encountered in the Hebrides, sung by women as they beat freshly woven fabric, these were the communal songs of working people, of rich appeal to these travelling socialist ethnographers.

The pair also met and recorded John Strachan, a well-off farm owner from the countryside around Fyvie, born three-quarters of a century before, who had already been 'discovered' by the American Methodist song collector James Madison Carpenter in the 1930s. Others included the fishwife Jessie Murray, the Mearns family of Aberdeen and their children and the Lennox family, including the railwayman and activist Archie, whose granddaughter Annie – born three years after Lomax's visit – became internationally famous in the 1980s as the singer with Eurythmics.

Later that month, on 26 July, Lomax visited Dundee to record the great accordionist Jimmy Shand. His visit to Scotland was a whirlwind and rubbed some up the wrong way, especially the country's established collectors, to whom he paid short shrift. He wasn't done by the end of July, though. Exactly one month later, at the invitation of Henderson, he was in Edinburgh in the midst of the Festival for a special event to celebrate both the pair's work and the launch of a brand new event – the Edinburgh People's Festival.

* * *

By 1951, the same energy that had powered the beginning of the 'unofficial' festival remained. In many cases it manifested as simply amateur, independent theatre groups trying to drum up interest by choosing August to put on a show, but for others – including Glasgow's Unity Theatre, in the final throes of existence after bringing the future Fringe to life with such vigour in 1947 – it was about so much more than that.

Henderson wasn't the only one who believed the Festival platform could be used to spur more egalitarian ideas. Another was Martin Milligan, a Communist Party organiser in his late 20s from Glasgow and a recent graduate in Philosophy from Balliol College at the University of Oxford. He called a meeting in December 1950 at a club for Scottish miners on Rothesay Place in the West End of Edinburgh, to propose the formation of a committee which might plan a kind of complementary alternative to the International Festival. The committee grew to 40 individuals representing 17 trade union branches, five Labour Party organisations, the Musicians' Union and various other clubs and councils, whose intention was to embrace the local Scottish culture which they felt the International Festival ignored. The events would be affordably-priced, so whole families on working-class wages could attend.

Five years before the Soviet Union's bloody quelling of the Hungarian uprising and the split in support this caused across Europe, to be a left-winger and a trade unionist often went hand-in-hand with identifying as a Communist. Henderson did, for example, although he never joined the party. Serving in Italy, he was introduced to the Prison Notebooks of the Marxist philosopher Antonio Gramsci and – being multilingual – fell in love with their ideas while reading them in the original Italian.

One of the core concepts put forward by Gramsci during his imprisonment by the Fascists in the 1930s[7] was that of 'cultural hegemony' – that the ruling capitalist class reinforce their own superiority by spreading its message through cultural institutions. In which case, the only way the working class can break free is by establishing cultural institutions of their own. To Henderson, a People's Festival for Edinburgh seemed like a chance to enact this idea. 'Gramsci in action', he called it.

Others rallied to the People's Festival's cause, among them young folk song enthusiasts Norman and Janey Buchan, later active and well-known Labour politicians in the west of Scotland. Also involved were Ewan MacColl and Joan Littlewood, who had begun their Theatre Workshop in 1946 and built up a formidable reputation since. MacColl, in fact, had changed his name from Jimmie Miller as a partial result of the 'Lallans' movement adopted by Hugh MacDiarmid and others.[8] Lallans meant the promotion of the 'lowlands' Scots dialect from Scottish Central Belt, as so named in the work of both Robert Burns and Robert Louis Stevenson.

Although MacColl was born and raised in Salford, Lancashire, it was in a community of migrant Scots, including his own parents, who moved for work when his trade unionist father was blacklisted in Scotland. MacColl felt the pull of his parents' home country and its culture greatly and the Scottish Renaissance struck a chord within him. For a time, he even enjoyed keeping the fiction that he'd been born in Scotland alive. Littlewood, on the other hand, was an aspiring actor from a middle-class London family who had briefly attended the Royal Academy of Dramatic Art (RADA). Moving to Manchester soon after her 20th birthday in 1934, she joined MacColl's agit-prop theatre group the Red Megaphones (later Theatre of Action, then Theatre Union) and the pair were married.

At Theatre Workshop, Littlewood was in charge of the company and MacColl was the resident dramatist. They first visited the Edinburgh Festival in 1949, with a triple-bill of plays at the Methodist Church's Epworth Hall on Nicolson Square and Littlewood's memoir vividly recalls this visit:

A brawny chap in Highland dress drifted in [to the hall], followed by the caretaker who had six poodles yapping at his heels. The Scotsman read out one of his poems and asked what time we would be leaving.[9]

This was, apparently, their first meeting with Hamish Henderson. He took them drinking every night and once bundled them past the doormen at the exclusive Festival Club on George Street, where they sang songs about the radical Clydeside unionist John Maclean until they were thrown out. On the way out, they saw a group of young, shaven-headed men dressed in black – the entourage, apparently, of the controversial conductor Gustav Gründgens, whose alleged association with Nazism caused protests at the International Festival. Littlewood wrote in her autobiography:

All Scotland's wits, poets and gossips appeared in the local pub during the Festival. They didn't attend any of the concerts, operas or theatrical performances, yet they seemed to know exactly what was wrong with everything, and they had a fund of scandalous gossip about each other. Each one held court in his own particular corner at his own particular time and if frontiers were violated fighting could easily break out. Although none of them would admit it, they enjoyed watching these foreigners washed up on the high tide of culture. They needed a new audience for their diatribes and dithyrambs and if the payment was only a pint of the best, it was welcome.[10]

By 1951 Henderson, Lomax and the Theatre Workshop troupe were all close friends. The People's Festival was set for a whole week, the first of the International Festival, from 26 August to 1 September and the Workshop agreed to bring MacColl's play *Uranium 235*, a hit since it was first performed in 1946. It couldn't have been more current, written at the urging of scientist friends of MacColl's a year after atomic bombs were used on Japan. An expressionist documentary play, it used musical, dance and physical theatre elements, concluding that the people must take control of nuclear energy's monumental power. Hugh MacDiarmid compared it favourably to *A Satire of the Three Estates*.

The other big theatrical draw was the Fife miner Joe Corrie's *In Time o' Strife*, performed by Glasgow Unity Theatre in the fading festival pioneers' Edinburgh swansong. Like all of the first People's Festival, it was staged at the Oddfellows Hall on Forrest Road, discreetly hidden behind an ordinary tenement front. Also on the bill were Ena Lamont Stewart's *Starched Aprons*, a Unity play performed there by the Ferranti Drama Group, made up of workers at the major Edinburgh electronics and defence employer and choirs and drama groups from towns across the Scottish Central Belt including Barrhead, Tranent and Lesmahagow. There were talks by Henderson, MacDiarmid and MacColl, a festival club and a modest conference for 170 named 'Towards a People's Culture'.

The event with the most excitement around it and the widest repercussions, however, was the People's Festival Ceilidh, which began on the evening of Friday 31 August. Intended as a fundraiser, it was the event Henderson invited Lomax to record, a significant way-marker in both men's song-collecting careers and the modern history of Scottish folksong, where many of the singers they had discovered were invited to perform. For the audience, it was a revelation – an evening of song by performers who were raw but perfectly in command of their material, singing lyrics in Scots and Doric which didn't just engage musically, but which felt soaked of the stories and wisdom of times past and places far away from the city.

At this point in the 20th century, many of Scotland's Highland roads had been built for the purposes of decades before, for horsedrawn carts and farm traffic and it wasn't until the tourism boom of much later in the century that greater interconnection occurred; that anywhere north of Perthshire or Loch Lomond might be somewhere a Central Belter might naturally visit. These folk songs and the voices behind them were theoretical pleasures made flesh for many of the city folk in the audience at the first People's Festival Ceilidh.

Jimmy MacBeath sang with a raw traveller's buzz and Jessie Murray held a gorgeous tune on 'Barbara Allen', a well-known Scots Border ballad later covered by Joan Baez and claimed as an influence by Bob Dylan on 'The Girl from the North Country'. In tribute to what Henderson called 'the folk songs that have come out of the political struggles in the past', piper John Burgess played 'Blue Bonnets Over the Border', a tune that commemorates Bonnie Prince Charlie's march into England in 1795. At the age of 76, John Strachan proved to be a pure entertainer, full of jokes and bravura high notes in the choruses, but he was clearly exhausted by the end.

'I don't think we should sing onny mair, but yir the best audience ever ah sang tae,' wheezed Strachan near the end, but Henderson kept things going long past the projected 10pm finish time. He closed on his own 'John Maclean March' alongside a young woman known only as Mrs Budge, and then a spirited version of Burns' 'Scots Wha Hae' was taken up by everyone in the excited crowd. The loudest cheers, though, were for 22-year-old Flora MacNeil; although Calum Johnston also sang Gaelic songs, the tone of her voice was captivating, unearthly perfection.

When the Ceilidh was over, the audience walked under the last of the late-evening light to the other end of George IV Bridge, for a party in St Columba's

Church Hall, which went on into the morning on the slope of Castle Hill. The Ceilidh had been the week's great revelation and success and Henderson was asked to plan another for December, then another for the inevitable return of the People's Festival in 1952. This edition was the largest of the People's Festivals, with nearly 50 trade union organisations backing a full three-week festival of poetry readings, lectures, a People's Art Exhibition, local theatre performances, a People's Festival Ball at the Eldorado Ballroom in Leith and concerts of the music of Beethoven. A new film programme showed Vittorio De Sica's 1948 classic of Italian neorealism *Bicycle Thieves* alongside films from Russia and China.

The second People's Festival Ceilidh honoured the 60th birthday of the festival's new chair Hugh MacDiarmid, and although Lomax wasn't there to record it, Henderson later recounted what had been played:

> The veteran Barra singer Calum Johnston again sang splendid Gaelic songs and played the pipes; the famous Lewis sisters Kitty and Marietta MacLeod enthralled the audience with 'Cairistiona' and 'Agus Ho Mhorag'; an excellent bothy ballad singer from the North-East called Frank Steele sang 'Come All Ye Lonely Lovers'; the young Arthur Argo, great grandson of the famous Aberdeenshire folk song collector Gavin Greig, sang 'The Soutar's Feast' in a boyish treble; 18-year-old Blanche Wood sang songs she had learned from her aunt Jessie Murray; and Jimmy MacBeath gave of his best with 'Come All Ye Tramps and Hawkers' and 'The Moss o' Burreldale'.[11]

Theatre Workshop also returned, this time with the debut of MacColl's play *The Travellers*, the overtly pro-Communist content of which – coupled with Theatre Workshops performances in places like Moscow and Warsaw – caused consternation among Labour members of the People's Festival board, who transmitted their doubt to the Labour Party and the Scottish Trades Union Congress. Financial backing from both organisations was revoked, but Henderson and Norman Buchan ploughed on with a much-reduced event in 1953, whose single week was still notable for two more Theatre Workshop plays, their adaptations of Aristophanes' *Lysistrata* and Molière's *Le Malade Imaginaire* (The Hypochondriac). What proved to be the final People's Festival Ceilidh took on the third festival's theme of Celtic unity between Scotland and Ireland.

Alongside a performance by the Appalachian folk singer Jean Ritchie, Henderson introduced an unknown Aberdeen Traveller woman to this Ceilidh. He'd only met her the previous month, on a solo song-collecting trip to the north-east, but he remarked that her discovery was his biggest achievement and greatest pride. Jeannie Robertson was 45 when Henderson, acting on a tip, knocked on her door – she wouldn't let him in until he proved his authenticity by singing 'The Battle of Harlaw'. Song collectors had recorded her before, but it was Henderson's enthusiastic promotion at the 1953 Ceilidh and to friends including Lomax and MacColl that sealed her unexpected fame as one of the most significant figures of the traditional music revival.

She sang beautiful, tender ballads with a wistful timbre and sensitivity, but where there was meant to be humour in a line, she sold it well. Robertson's fame rocketed – by November an equally impressed Lomax was showcasing her voice alongside Jean Ritchie on *The Song Collector*, the broadcaster David Attenborough's BBC documentary on Lomax's work and a range of recordings and live performances until her death in 1975 inspired subsequent generations of folk singers.

Robertson's arrival was also the People's Festival's swansong, however. The egalitarian idealism of its founding had come unstuck amid political division and its three-year existence was half-parleyed into four, with a few associated events during 1954's Festival. Theatre Workshop were no longer involved – MacColl had performed some songs at 1953's People's Festival, his own swansong with the Workshop before he and Littlewood split. He briefly discussed a possible permanent Theatre Workshop base in the Scottish new town of East Kilbride with Henderson, but instead MacColl followed his own path as a folk singer. Littlewood and Gerry Raffles, her new partner and a Workshop member, renovated the Theatre Royal in Stratford and turned it into a powerhouse of independent British theatre which still continues following Littlewood's 1974 departure.

Lomax finally made it back to America in 1959, where he settled in a New York loft apartment as his recordings from Europe and continuing explorations of the American folk tradition became a Holy Grail to a new, young, hip generation of coffee shop folk singers. At one of the regular listening parties he held for aficionados in his apartment, one of them – a 20-year-old singer from Minnesota who had taken the name Bob Dylan – introduced himself and the pair became friends.

For Henderson the School of Scottish Studies became a vocation and he worked there from 1955 until 1987, collecting songs while writing his own poetry and music. His 'Freedom Come-All-Ye', written in 1960 as a song of internationalism and acceptance, is viewed as one of Scotland's many unofficial national anthems, while in 1958 he co-founded, with Stuart MacGregor, the Edinburgh University Folk Song Society, the first folk club in the city and one of the first in Britain. Henderson's regular 'office' was the Forrest Hill Bar on Forrest Road, opposite Oddfellows Hall[12] and a short walk from the School. The bar was nicknamed 'Sandy Bell's', in part tribute to the former owner Mrs Bell,[13] and this name was made official above the door at some point in the 1970s. To this day, it maintains a reputation for impromptu musical sessions by local folk players.

A certain revisionism tells us the Edinburgh People's Festival was essentially the official invention of the Edinburgh Festival Fringe, which is stretching the facts a long way. But it was the first formal gathering of some unofficial events under one banner and in its very first Ceilidh in particular, it lays strong claim to being the root of the Scottish – perhaps even British – folk revival, which would truly begin in earnest in the 1960s… once again, in Edinburgh during Festival time.

3

The Film Festival, the Military Tattoo and the 1950s

WHETHER THEY ORIGINATED in Vienna or Glasgow, many of the creative ideas that fed into the beginning of both the Edinburgh International Festival and its Fringe activity arrived from outside of Edinburgh. The third major festival whose roots were dug in the city in 1947, however, was founded on a medium that was already active in the city and which one Scot in particular helped to shape and create.

The birth of documentary film is synonymous with the birth of contemporary cinema as we know it. Across two centuries of technical development, film evolved from the crude magic lantern of the 17th century to the boom in projected moving images of the 1890s. Among the great early pioneers of the technology were the brothers Louis and Auguste Lumière of Lyon in France, whose invention of the Cinématograph system essentially forecast film cameras and projectors as they came to be known. In fact, their 1895 film *Workers Leaving the Lumière Factory* – widely recognised as the first motion picture – was a documentary, although the brothers referred to it as an *actualité* (news) film.

Over three decades until the 1920s, film evolved and the novelty of documentary mutated as filmmakers became cannier. At first, simple 'scenics' showed narrative-free moving images of places around the world, pushing a sense of exoticism at a time when most viewers in the transatlantic global north would have had little knowledge of cultures outside of their own. Soon filmmakers tried to weave stories within their work, to give more context on the people and cultures being shown and one of these was the pioneering American director Robert J Flaherty, who – despite a tendency to place his own interpretation on events and even direct his subject's actions – had a huge hit with 1922's *Nanook of the North*, which he had spent many years filming among the Inuit people of the Canadian Arctic.

Excited by Flaherty's success, Paramount Pictures sent him to Samoa to shoot a similar piece and the result was 1926's *Moana*, which in February of that year was reviewed by a pseudonymous critic for *The New York Sun* named simply 'The Moviegoer'. '*Moana*, being a visual account of events in the daily life of a Polynesian youth, has documentary value', wrote the critic. That use of the word 'documentary' was the first ever applied to a film, meaning The Moviegoer had invented a whole new cinematic genre.

The writer's real name was John Grierson, a Scot born in the Stirlingshire countryside in 1898, to schoolteachers who gave him a comfortable and intellectually rich upbringing rooted in socialist, humanist thought and Calvinist hard work; his mother Jane was an activist for the suffragettes and the Labour Party. By 1926 Grierson was a decorated First World War naval hero and an outstanding graduate in English and Moral Philosophy from the University of Glasgow, where he befriended James Bridie, an elder graduate of the university, who founded the *Glasgow University Magazine* which Grierson also wrote for.

In October 1924 Grierson sailed from the Clyde in Glasgow to Halifax, Nova Scotia to pursue the coveted Rockefeller Research Fellowship he had been given to study in the United States, first in Boston, then in Chicago and New York. He went out at night to hear the young Louis Armstrong play, began writing for newspapers and in Hollywood befriended actors including Charlie Chaplin, Harry Langdon and Raymond Griffith. In New York he was instrumental in preparing the English titles for the first release in the US of the Soviet filmmaker Sergei Eisenstein's enduring classic *Battleship Potemkin* (1925) and he came to know Flaherty too, amid the coffee houses of the city.

Grierson was a democrat, and he believed in civic education – of which he viewed documentary as an integral part – as an antidote to the unthinking top-down structure of a dictatorship. His interest was in the effect of propaganda as delivered through mass media, which led to his study of a particular type of film. In coining the word, Grierson assured his place in cinematic history and he's still referred to as the father of the documentary film. Twenty-one years after he wrote the review of *Moana*, he helped write another page in the history of contemporary film, when he became a founding inspiration for what's today known as the Edinburgh International Film Festival.

Grierson had returned to Britain in 1927 and taken a job with the Empire Marketing Board (EMB), an organisation which was idiosyncratic of its era even down to the name. Its purpose was to promote trade with the territories of the British Empire and through it Grierson wanted to set about creating his own version of what Flaherty had made in the US, a documentary film that filled its viewers' senses with a visual experience beyond their immediate environment.

Whereas Flaherty had travelled long distances to meet different cultures, however, Grierson wanted to take as his first subject the people of his own group of islands who weren't regularly seen or heard. His first film was *Drifters* (1929) and his and cinematographer Basil Emmott's subject was the fishermen of the North Sea, in keeping with Grierson's belief that documentary could be a potent tool to educate those living in democratic society about the world around them.

In years to come, his unique perspective on a new and developing medium, blended with his interest in the application of technique and political motive to that medium, placed him at the forefront of the Documentary Film Movement in cinema. The birth of this movement is widely recognised as being the screening at the London Film Society on 10 November 1929 of *Drifters* in a double bill with *Battleship Potemkin*, a film banned for its revolutionary aspect in the UK until 1954. Both Grierson and Eisenstein were in the audience for this British premiere of both films.

Early in 1930, Drifters was written about in the *Scotsman* by a barely 20-year-old reporter named Forsyth Hardy and Grierson contacted the paper asking to be put in touch with their insightful writer. The pair struck up a bond which lasted for the rest of their lives. Born in Bathgate, West Lothian, in 1910, Hardy was the *Scotsman*'s first ever film critic by 1932 and was deeply embedded in the nascent Scottish film industry by this point. He was there at the birth of the Edinburgh Film Guild in 1930, an organisation influenced by the pioneering London Film Society, which programmed that screening of *Drifters* and *Potemkin*.

In the 1920s the arrival of the 'talkie' exploded the creative potential of the medium, but it was still in its relative youth. There was no widespread film festival culture, no repertory cinema network and mainstream cinemas were concerned simply with commercial spectacle. For enthusiasts who wished to find obscure or artistic films, or fan the flames of the very beginning of a retrospective movement, film guilds and societies were the emerging forum of choice. Founded in London in 1925 by Ivor Montagu, 'zoologist, authority on table tennis and enthusiast for the cinema',[1] the celebrity members that the seminal London Film Society drew illustrated the kind of people who were excited by the cinema of the 1920s: the actor Dame Ellen Terry, the authors HG Wells and George Bernard Shaw and the economist and later Arts Council boss John Maynard Keynes.

Grierson also joined, as did Hardy later on, but first the *Scotsman* writer was one of those who created the Edinburgh Film Guild in the Film Society's image. The inaugural Guild meeting was in October 1930 at the Princes Cinema at 131 Princes Street, directly opposite the western end of Princes Street Gardens and the Castle,[2] where a constitution was drawn up and a board was appointed. The first President was James 'JH' Whyte, a former Cambridge University student, his vice-president was Hardy and they were joined by Norman Wilson, who worked in publishing, as honorary secretary. It was Wilson who first proposed the idea of a Film Guild, even though some dismissed the idea that Edinburgh needed another society and others sneered at a popular art like film's compatibility with the supposedly intellectual character of the city.

The fact meetings were held on Sunday aroused yet more suspicion, but Wilson responded simply that they intended to show films that were good quality, wherever they came from. The Guild was avowedly non-political, which cut a lot of slack with local authorities and hoped one day to begin making its own films, including a 'city symphony' – a visual documentary – of Edinburgh itself. Its official mission statement was 'to bring together those interested in the development of film art in Scotland and for the exhibition of films of artistic merit not generally shown in the ordinary commercial cinema'.

Based at the Caley Picture House on Lothian Road from 1931, with club rooms on North Bank Street in the shadow of the Assembly Hall, the Guild became a popular Edinburgh organisation during the next decade and a half. It compiled programmes of French, German, Russian and even Japanese films, attempted to create work aimed at the city's children and booked guest cinephile speakers including the author Compton Mackenzie, who in February 1931 made the rather bold theoretical statement that if Scotland gained its independence from the UK and he were appointed Minister of Arts, he would ban all films produced in American, despite his own suspicion of 'artistic' films.[3]

Other members and guests of the Guild included the University of Edinburgh's Fine Art professor David Talbot Rice, the BBC Orchestra's conductor Ian Whyte, the filmmaker Michael Powell – visiting in the immediate aftermath of completing *The Edge of the World* (1937) on the remote Scottish isle of Foula – and the British Council's ubiquitous man in Scotland, Henry Harvey Wood.

During this period the Scottish film industry formalised and Forsyth Hardy was at the centre of it. He became secretary of the newly-founded Federation of Scottish Film Societies, was involved in the foundation of the British Film Institute in 1933 and through his positions at *The Scotsman* and the Federation became a leading lobbyist for the creation of the Scottish Film Council, then a co-founder when it was created in '34. In 1932 the Edinburgh Film Guild also began publishing *Cinema Quarterly*, one of the earliest film journals, featuring contributions from Grierson, alongside figures like Graham Greene, Aldous Huxley and TS Eliot.[4]

Edinburgh Film Guild's position as the first and largest of the Scottish film guilds was thrown into national focus when the London Film Society and many other guilds across the UK closed down with the outbreak of war in 1939. The sourcing of films shown prior to the war had rarely been achieved through formal distribution arrangements, instead relying on tipoffs and suggestions from trusted contacts and this became an even trickier process when the supply of films from the continent dried up. Yet by finding occasional Polish, Dutch or Austrian works here or there and arranging an exhibition of 'film décor' at the National Gallery of Scotland on the Mound while its paintings were in wartime storage, the Guild bolstered its visibility and position.

When war was over in 1945 – the same year Norman Wilson published his enthusiastic 'film survey' of the country, *Presenting Scotland* – membership of the Guild ballooned to 2,500 as pent-up demand was released, making it the biggest guild in Britain. Audiences of 1,000 were coming to screenings and a forward-thinking series of educational talks from film practitioners began at the Gateway Theatre on Elm Row. In 1946, the Guild and local production company Campbell Harper Films went in together on a pair of smart, adjoining New Town offices buildings at six and seven Hill Street, a setted lane running parallel between Queen Street and George Street the Guild began showing films every day. The building was named Film House.

* * *

To Norman Wilson and Forsyth Hardy, the founders of the Edinburgh International Festival of Music and Drama's intention to create a world resort of all that is best in music, drama and the visual arts' represented a gross omission. They asked if they might be able to programme a film strand of the 1947 and were informed this wouldn't be possible. Yet Wilson in particular wouldn't be moved and he resolved to create an unofficial event running alongside the International Festival, in the same way eight unofficial theatre companies were planning to.

By this point, Hardy had left *The Scotsman* to become head of information at the Scottish Office, producing public information films like Budge Cooper's 1944 study of child delinquency in Dundee, *Children of the City*. His wider view of the industry told him Edinburgh had the perfect conditions for a celebration of film to run alongside the International Festival:

An informed community interest in the cinema resourcefully developed over some 15 years. The support of the film society movement. The encouragement and backing of the documentary film movement. A group of enthusiasts who were prepared to work hard day and night to give form to an idea.[5]

Yet what the Film Guild's planned project didn't have was the boost of public money. Although localised film events were hardly unheard of across Europe, the major precedents so far had arrived with major state backing. In 1932, the dictator Benito Mussolini had encouraged the founding of the

Venice Film Festival as a celebratory pageant of primarily Italian filmmaking, while in 1939 the Cannes Film Festival had been planned for France as a celebration of European and American filmmaking. War had delayed its start, meaning the 1946 first edition was to the film industry what Edinburgh in 1947 was to the performing arts.

To compete or even make an impression internationally, with no prospect of seeing any of the public investment being funnelled elsewhere in Edinburgh, would require radical thinking. From Hardy's perspective this meant simply concentrating on what the city was good at and in his friend Grierson the neighbourhood could at least lay claim to one of the most insightful visionaries of the modern filmmaking world at that point. By 1947, Grierson was in Paris working as the first head of information at another great post-war institution, the United Nations Educational, Scientific and Cultural Organisation (UNESCO), whose purpose was promoting international cooperation and peace through the fields of its title.

In 1933 the Empire Marketing Board had disbanded and Grierson had moved to the film unit at the General Post Office, with a remit which was little-altered. He directed only one film after *Drifters* – 1934's *Granton Trawler*, about a fisherboat leaving the Edinburgh port to work in the North Sea – but he became a prolific producer of key work by other documentarians, including Robert Flaherty's Irish-set *Man of Aran* (1934); Basil Wright's study of life and culture in what's now Sri Lanka, *Songs of Ceylon* (1934); the classic studies of British life and work *Housing Problems*, *Coal Face* (both 1935) and *Night Mail* (1936); and Alberto Cavalcanti and JB Priestley's tribute to internationalism, *We Live in Two Worlds* (1937).

In 1938, Grierson was invited to Canada to assess the country's film industry and the following year he set up the National Film Commission, later the National Film Board of Canada, which he ran during wartime, returning to Europe and the UNESCO job in Paris in 1946. Hardy made arrangements for him to attend the Edinburgh Playhouse – the scene of that Scottish premiere of *Drifters* which Hardy had reviewed 17 years before – to officially open the 1947 film event and with such a significant industry figure lending his name to it, another new Edinburgh festival was born. Modest in its wider ambition, it was internationally definitive within the area of its industry it represented.

The first Edinburgh International Festival of Documentary Films began with Grierson and Lord Provost John Falconer's addresses to the Playhouse on Sunday 31 August. *The Herald* reported on Grierson's opening address:

Mr Grierson said it was easy to see the reason in these difficult times to be sceptical about the place of the arts and culture, but he said that it was on a cultural level that the basis was to be found for the creation of a new world. All art was a study of harmony, and in that respect it had a great part to play today... The International Festival showed that Scotland was taking an interest in her culture, and UNESCO hoped that all countries would do likewise. In Paris... the press were taking notice of what Scotland was doing.[6]

The festival continued for eight days until the following Sunday. The first and final days (mirroring the potentially ungodly Sabbath scheduling of the Film Guild's screenings) were gala events at the Playhouse, with the days in between consisting of lower-key programming at Film House's modest theatre and a larger Friday evening show at the Methodist Central Hall at Tollcross. Seventy-five films were scheduled in total, most of them short enough to be bundled into package screenings and they had a truly international context, including entries from the USSR, Palestine and South Africa.

Films screened included the Swedish director Arne Sucksdorf's *Rhythm of a City*, a visual portrait of Stockholm and Mikhail Slutsky's Soviet *Festival of Youth*, which, despite the avowedly non-political stance of the festival, was considered a piece of Stalinist propaganda by *The Herald*'s critic. Francois Campaux's *Henri Matisse* told the great painter's story and showed him at work, Theodor Christensen's *Your Freedom is at Stake* was a story of wartime Danish resistance and Paul Rotha's *The World is Rich* – nominated for an Academy Award the following year – was a piece about post-war world food shortages which the director himself presented in Edinburgh.

Yet the centrepiece of the first Edinburgh Film Festival was the closing film, Roberto Rossellini's 1946 war epic *Paisà*,[7] which accentuated the concern many of the festival's selections had with the experience of the preceding decade in Europe.

The festival was a success, exciting audiences with films which 'opened windows on Europe and lands beyond long fogged by war',[8] and the decision was taken to expand the second festival of 1948 to the full three weeks of Festival time. This time the big premiere was Robert J Flaherty's *Louisiana Story*,[9] later Oscar-nominated, alongside Rossellini's unofficial sequel to *Paisà*, *Germany: Year Zero* and Nicole Védrès' study of the *fin de siècle* city *Paris 1900*. With a programme of talks and educational events from leading filmmakers, which mirrored the Film Guild's own programming, Edinburgh had become a place where, in contrast to the high-end showbiz of Cannes, a particularly worldly and artistic breed of filmmaker wanted their work to be seen.

The 1949 festival was opened jointly by Grierson, now resident in the UK again and the 65-year-old Robert J Flaherty, a revered figure to followers of the documentary form. The festival physically expanded within Edinburgh, into the Monseigneur News Theatre on Princes Street – the former Princes Cinema – and geographically around the world, welcoming films from Israel, Argentina and Australia, as well as Jacques Tati's clowning spectacle *Jour de Fête*.[10]

Already, the documentary remit which the festival had set itself was becoming stretched both by the availability of films and the demands of the Edinburgh audience. In 1950, its subtitle grew to encompass 'Realist, Documentary, Experimental' films and while the early years of the decade saw returning favourites like Rossellini,[11] Sucksdorf and Grierson, in his familiar capacity as semi-official voice of the festival, the 1951 event also premiered *Whisky Galore!* director Alexander Mackendrick's Alec Guinness-starring Ealing comedy *The Man in the White Suit*.

The festival of 1952 was officially opened by the Duke of Edinburgh and featured premieres for László Benedek's Stanley Kramer-produced adaptation of Arthur Miller's *Death of a Salesman* and Max Ophuls' *Le Plaisir*, while in 1953 it hosted the David O Selznick Golden Laurel Awards, presenting a trophy to the Hungarian director Alexander Korda and the year's Golden Laurel to Charles Frend's film *The Cruel Sea*, winning out over a shortlist that included Roberto Rossellini's *Europe '51*.

Although Edinburgh had chosen not to be an award-giving festival, the Golden Laurel's stated aim seemed perfectly in line with its own, to pay tribute to motion pictures produced anywhere in the world except the United States, or made by Americans abroad, which contribute to international understanding and goodwill. The awards were presented in the New Victoria cinema on Clerk Street – later the Odeon until its closure in 2003 – by the American ambassador to Britain.

There's no definitive point at which the renamed Edinburgh International Film Festival of the 1950s marked its evolution from being the premier documentary film festival in the world, to one of the leading film festivals, but with 70 years' hindsight the day when Orson Welles gave the festival's first celebrity lecture – holding court for two hours in the Cameo Cinema on Home Street on the subject of the film business – is an event which still sends shockwaves. Taking place in the latter stages of his acknowledged cinematic prime, two years after his *Othello* and four after his performance in *The Third Man*, reports illustrate a picture of a genial, charismatic visitor to the city, and an extremely enthusiastic advocate for the subject of cinema. He told his audience that the film industry should embrace the popular medium of television.

It was a prescient comment, both in terms of the evolution of independent cinema and Welles' own troubled career. The following year, the Cameo cinema – the 1914 King's Cinema, renamed when Jim Poole of Edinburgh's theatre-owning Poole family took it over in 1949 – was made a festival venue and the Hollywood director John Huston served as honorary president. He blagged a ticket for the International Festival's religious opening ceremony at St Giles' Cathedral and was entertained by the Film Guild at the North British Hotel, where his forthrightness was in contrast, said Hardy, to his taciturn demeanour at official engagements during a two-day visit from the set of *Moby Dick* in Ireland.

The Film Festivals of the mid-'50s brought Elia Kazan's *East of Eden*, Vincente Minnelli's *Lust for Life* and Kazan's *On the Waterfront*, starring James Dean, Kirk Douglas and Marlon Brando respectively. The New Victoria hosted gala events including the presentation of the Golden Laurel to Vittorio De Sica for *L'Oro di Napoli* (The Gold of Naples) by Douglas Fairbanks Jr in 1955 and the same prize to Laurence Olivier in '56, as well as a Royal Gala performance of Gene Kelly's *Invitation to the Dance* before The Queen, Prince Philip and Princess Margaret in the same year. Kelly attended the screening, as did the photographer Man Ray.

A '25 Years of Documentary' dinner at the George Hotel honoured Grierson and the premiere of *Drifters* and a *Sixty Years of Cinema* exhibition was held the year after. By this point several film festivals had sprung up around the world, including Berlin in 1951, the last of the present-day 'big three' alongside Venice and Cannes, but Edinburgh was certainly one of the biggest, with its own special link to film history and the added momentum that being swept along with the Edinburgh International Festival brought it. It continued to appeal to cineastes and to lovers of Hollywood cinema, and as the 1950s drew to a close it continued to outgrow its beginnings.

* * *

The founders of the Edinburgh International Festival of Music and Drama were all gone by the 1950s. James Bridie, the inspirational playwright and sometime drama coordinator, died suddenly at the beginning of 1951, the same year in which the unofficial Festival's co-instigators, Glasgow's Unity Theatre, folded under a weight of post-*Gorbals Story* expectation. Of the trio most influential in bringing the International Festival together, Sir John Falconer left his post as Lord Provost late in 1947, while Harry Harvey Wood's career with the British Council took him to live in France in 1950.

In Edinburgh, the job of Director of the International Festival passed on to Ian Hunter, a Scotsman Bing had known since Hunter was assistant conductor to Fritz Busch in the final pre-war year of Glyndebourne. The London-born son of a Scottish stockbroker, Hunter was raised in Spean Bridge in the Scottish Highlands and educated at the Edinburgh public school Fettes College, a pedigree that put him squarely within the elite group of society which founded the International Festival. He was an artistic soul, though. He learned the French horn and conducted the school orchestra and his youthful ambitions to conduct professionally brought him into Busch's orbit, following a time under the tuition of the University of Edinburgh music professor Donald Tovey.

For Hunter's generation, the Second World War came at the wrong time – he became a lieutenant colonel in the Royal Army Service Corps and when it was all over he knew the best years of his musical training had been missed.

Instead, he returned to Glyndebourne in 1946 under Bing's wing as a personal assistant, staying by his side until he left. The pair travelled to Edinburgh from London by overnight sleeper every week in the lead-up to the '47 Festival, their full-day meetings with the council preceded by a breakfast of kippers as the train rolled towards Waverley through the East Lothian dawn. Hunter had direct responsibility for the International Festival and Bing's other assistant, Moran Caplat, worked on Glyndebourne, although the pair co-wrote anonymous Festival gossip columns for the Edinburgh evening papers until Bing's departure.

Bing admired Hunter's sense of humour and his management skills. Although he was Bing's right-hand man – even starting the Bath Assembly Festival[12] on Glyndebourne's behalf in 1948 – Hunter was also well-liked by the Festival Society, including Falconer's replacement as Lord Provost, Sir Andrew Murray. The 30-year-old was seen as a skilled and promising young operator, who'd learned a lot about the workings of the Festival through his apprenticeship with Bing.

Yet Hunter wasn't trusted to take the reins straight away. Instead, while the Festival committee considered exploring other, more high-profile options for director, he was given the stopgap lesser title of 'artistic administrator' and appointed without fanfare. The first the press knew of it was when his name appeared alongside his new job in the International Festival's 1949 programme and it wasn't until 1951 that Hunter had earned a big enough foothold to officially become artistic director in his own right.

Hunter's greatest contribution to an Edinburgh August, in fact, had already happened before he got near the top job. In 1947, while the first Festival had been in its planning stages, he suggested to Rudolf Bing that a display of piping and dancing should accompany a Scottish festival. Then you had better do something about it, Bing told him.

By fortunate coincidence, Hunter's brother-in-law worked in Scottish Command at the British Army, so the young administrator asked if he might be able to help. Players from military pipe bands were drafted in, along with Scottish dancers and they gave informal displays on the Esplanade of Edinburgh Castle. The following year the regimental bands of the 1st Royal Scots and 1st Cameronians played at the Esplanade and the Ross Bandstand in West Princes Street Gardens. Beginning with around 2,500 standing audience members watching the earliest displays, these military events expanded until 1949, when *The Glasgow Herald* reported:

> The army presented their second festival show, *There's Something About a Soldier*, last night before 10,000[13] people at West Princes Street Gardens. Weather conditions were favourable. The Ross Bandstand, well illuminated below the floodlit Edinburgh Castle, was a suitable setting for the spectacle...The show is almost the monopoly of men of the Royal Scots. They provide pipes and drums, sword dances, automaton drill, a physical training display, and with the help of members of the Women's Royal Army Corps, a sixteensome reel. A band of the Highland Light Infantry accompanied the community singing.[14]

By this point, the military entertainment shown as part of the festival was already developing a formal structure, with *There's Something About a Soldier* and its sister show *The King's Men* devised for the occasion by Lieutenant Colonel George Malcolm, the 18th Laird of Poltalloch, who had experience of directing past military shows at Kelvin Hall in Glasgow and on Horse Guards Parade in London. The event was such a success that Lord Provost Andrew Murray and the General Officer Commanding the Army in Scotland, Sir Philip Christison, discussed how they could create a more formal event for 1950.

Their inspiration was the by-then traditional Military Tattoo, an ongoing feature of the British Army since the formation of the Aldershot Military Tattoo in 1894. The name took its inspiration from the 17th century Dutch phrase '*doe den tap toe*' ('turn off the taps'), which was what the drumbeat played in the evening at garrison towns meant to tavern owners. Adapted by the British Army, it came to mean the last activity of the day, and then a show put on in the evening for troops' entertainment. Between the First and Second World Wars, the Aldershot Tattoo was an extremely popular occasion with members of the public and Tattoos became a feature at other army centres, including Edinburgh's Dreghorn Barracks.

In part, the Edinburgh Tattoo of 1950 was a post-war revival of this recent tradition, but it became so much more. Co-produced by Lt Col Malcolm and Brigadier Alasdair Maclean, it ran for 20 performances between 21 August and 9 September, except Sundays. Grandstand seating was built on the north and south sides of the Esplanade, with a raised area for 1,600 spectators at the east end and a total of 500 military performers used, all of whom came together for the firework finale.

There was a sequence recreating the installation of the Castle's first Governor the Duke of Gordon in 1828, with a soldier on a striking white horse representing the Governor and a carriage on loan from the King. A well-managed 'Reveille' sequence featured, where the Castle appeared to awaken from silence and 64 dancers from the Highland Light Industry performed. Pipe Major George Stoddart played as the Lone Piper, one of the most famous aspects of the Tattoo through its history and it was a role he held until 1961. Sir Thomas Beecham conducted the bands and after a massed performance of 'Scotland the Brave', the performers left the arena playing 'Auld Lang Syne' as midnight approached.

The Tattoo was a roaring success and a complete sell-out and it was attended by the Queen of Belgium during the run and the Queen and Princess Margaret at the gala final performance. Around 100,000 spectators witnessed it, with many more tuning in on radio and television around the world. It was one of 200 BBC broadcasts from Edinburgh that summer, the Corporation's biggest-ever outside broadcast operation bar the Olympic Games. The American broadcaster CBS took highlights from the Festival, as well as 17 countries around Europe, but the future life of the Tattoo as a globally televised success, broadcasting to millions every year, was what made its blend of ceremony, music and fireworks the definitive image of Edinburgh in Festival time for many who've never been to the city.

* * *

Ian Hunter's tenure in charge of the International Festival – whether as administrator or director – lasted until 1955 and took advantage of the strong foundations he helped Rudolf Bing lay. In many ways his job was to take the rudder of a smooth-sailing ship and continue its journey, although this doesn't account for all the fresh work and negotiation required to bring the world's finest orchestras and performing companies together in the same place at the same time, year after year.

In 1950, Milan's La Scala orchestra came to the Festival for a series of seven concerts conducted by Guido Cantelli and Victor de Sabata, and the same year Hunter gave James Bridie's Citizens Theatre the Royal Lyceum for a trio of Scottish plays – John Home's 1756 tragedy *Douglas*, Eric Linklater's *The Atom Doctor* and Bridie's own *The Queen's Comedy* – which helped cement the nation's drama at the Festival. The Danish State Radio performed, conducted by Fritz Busch and Leonard Bernstein conducted France's *Orchestre National de la Radiodiffusion Française* at a concert which included William Schuman's *American Festival Overture*.

Hunter worked with Bing again on the long-planned visit of the New

York Philharmonic Orchestra in 1951, with conductors Bruno Walter and Dimitri Mitropoulos taking charge of a feast of 14 Usher Hall concerts which played the works of the great European composers. The same year, Sadler's Wells Ballet – with Margot Fonteyn and Moira Shearer in the company – presented a programme at the Empire Theatre headed by Tchaikovsky's *Swan Lake*. Other highlights of Hunter's time included John Gielgud taking the role of Leontes in Shakespeare's *The Winter's Tale* at the Lyceum and the Old Vic's 1953 version of *Hamlet* at the Assembly Hall with Richard Burton in the lead role, barely three weeks before the release of *The Robe*, which he received an Academy Award nomination for. Critics praised Burton's dignity and virility in the role.

In 1953, Hunter wanted to open up the festival to a wider audience, with ideas to put a big top or a live stage on the Grassmarket and stage international performances for the people of Edinburgh. In decades to come, long after he'd left, these ideas happened in one way or another thanks to the Fringe. A big departure during his term was the International Festival's relationship with Glyndebourne as its exclusive opera-producing arm. The cracks were showing in the lead-up to 1952's festival, when the Hamburg State Opera was invited to become the first international company to stage operatic events in Edinburgh in August, when it performed 18 concerts at the King's Theatre, conducted by Leopold Ludwig, Georg Solti and Joseph Keilberth.

The arrangement was meant to be a one-off, with Glyndebourne reinstated the following year and another big international name invited further down the line, but the Hamburg booking drove a wedge between Glyndebourne's John Christie and his former employee, Hunter. He soon tendered Glyndebourne's resignation and shortly after rescinded the Festival's use of the shared office space in London. Glyndebourne appeared with another Edinburgh operatic programme in 1960, but the end of their association was ultimately a good thing – now the Festival was free to contract the finest international operatic companies to appear every year.

Before Glyndebourne's departure was even hinted at, Hunter was known to be on his way. Contracted as artistic director until 1955, he was approached by the prestigious London-based classical music agency Harold Holt to take over, after the death of the man whose name the company bore in early September 1953. Founded by Alfred Shultz-Curtis in 1876, when it brought the music of Richard Wagner to Britain, the powerful agency had been run by Holt since 1924. Hunter asked to work with both organisations, but the Festival, already stung by Bing's split loyalties with Glyndebourne, was wary. In which case, it was generous that Hunter was allowed to take on the job with Holt in '53, but only if he gave the Festival the proper attention it required and informed the committee if the agency's clients were under consideration to appear.

The Festival had two years to find a replacement and they threw the job open to international applications. Among the 142 entrants were the Holland Festival's director Peter Diamand and George Lascelles, the 7th Earl of Harewood. The latter was a first cousin of the recently-crowned Queen Elizabeth II and had attended 1947's first International Festival with his mother Princess Mary, the Princess Royal, as personal guests of family friend Lady Rosebery. The Festival's founding advisor was still active behind the scenes and she actually lobbied for Diamand to be given the job, but the committee went the same route as led to Hunter's appointment – they looked within for his replacement.

* * *

By the turn of the mid-century, both the International Festival and the unofficial almost-Fringe had established themselves as annual events in Edinburgh and each was being taken seriously – the former, by the international opera, theatre and orchestral music communities at the highest level; the latter, by small British theatre companies like Joan Littlewood and Ewan MacColl's youthful Theatre Workshop.

The Fringe was being born mostly out of amateur enthusiasm, not theatrical radicalism. The first few years involved plays by amateur dramatic and increasingly student drama clubs, staged in church halls, meeting halls and social clubs, as all the official venues were tied up by the International Festival. The Little Theatre at the Pleasance, the Gateway Theatre and the YMCA on South St Andrew Street all continued to be well-used.

The Dunfermline Abbey experiment of 1947 continued for a time, funded by the Carnegie Trust, with Robert Kemp's *The Saxon Saint* (1949) telling the story of St Margaret in the abbey built in her honour and his *King of Scots* playing the same venue in '51. The Fringe was evolving into a home for new and obscure work. The Wilson Barrett Company, founded by the identically-named grandson of the famed Victorian actor, playwright and theatrical manager, began in London in 1938, but moved to Edinburgh after their premises were bombed during the Blitz. It used the Lyceum as a year-round base for popular repertory and toured to Glasgow and Aberdeen, until its closure in 1955. During 1949's Fringe it produced the great Norwegian realist Henrik Ibsen's 1891 play *Hedda Gabbler* at the Gateway Theatre.

The same year, future Fringe regulars the Edinburgh University Dramatic Society presented the Edinburgh debut of Ibsen's *Peer Gynt* at the Methodist Central Hall on Lothian Road, then in 1950 returned with Shakespeare's *King Lear* on an open stage at the Old College Quad. In 1951 Edinburgh University students took the first steps towards Fringe organisation, with the International Student Service providing food and accommodation for visiting companies at a hostel at 25 Haddington Place, opposite the Gateway Theatre. In 1955 Edinburgh students again tried to corral the city's Fringe activity with the opening of a communal ticket office which most of the student and amateur companies participated in,[15] and the same year EUDS inaugurated the university's new Adam House on the opposite side of Chambers Street with a new studio play named *The Daughter of the Dawn*. It became the society's home theatre.

Edinburgh's Moray House College Theatre soon presented work and students from the universities of Oxford, Durham, Aberdeen and Birmingham and the Edinburgh Academy school. The Newcastle People's Theatre did Chekhov's *The Seagull* at the Little Theatre in '51, the Dublin University Players arrived with a programme of Yeats in the Lauriston Hall in 1956 and London's recently-founded Rose Bruford Theatre School began a still-ongoing tradition of bringing work to Edinburgh. The Scottish Community Drama Association performed Robert Kemp's culture shock comedy *Festival Fever*, about a Russian musician arriving in Edinburgh, in the Little Theatre in '57, the same year the Edinburgh Shakespeare Players put on *Hamlet* and *Twelfth Night* at the Royal High School on the south slope of Calton Hill. Elspeth Douglas Reid was one of a number of actors returning every year with economical one-person shows, and the Players of Leyton produced *Hamlet* at Edinburgh Academy in 1957, with a young Derek Jacobi in the title role.

From 1952, the shape of the nascent Fringe changed with the arrival of the late-night revue show, among the first of which belonged to Fringe regulars the London Club Theatre Group. From 1950 they performed during August at St Mary's Hall on St Mary's Street, just off the Royal Mile, and their main presentation for 1952 was an adaptation of *The Ebb-Tide*, an adventure about the hijack of a cargo schooner loaded with champagne, written by the great Scottish author Robert Louis Stevenson and his stepson Samuel Lloyd Osbourne, and published in 1894. The play was adapted by a 32-year-old English actor named Donald Pleasence, whose stage career to this point had consisted of provincial repertory work and the hosting of entertainment at the infamous German prisoner-of-war camp *Stalag Luft I*, after his Lancaster bomber was shot down over France in 1944.

Before he became one of the most famed British stage and screen actors of his generation, both the play and Pleasance's performance were critical hits, and many satisfied critics hung around St Mary's Hall for London Club Theatre's revue *After the Show*. Written by Peter Myers and Alec Grahame, it ran from 10.30pm until midnight and its blend of risqué 'blue' comedy, song and burlesque included sharply topical jokes at the festival's expense, including a song about the tourist trade named 'Bureau de No Change'. This was the trick of the revues; student and amateur theatre faced stiff evening competition from the Festival's shows, but after hours they were the only choice available to night owls.

In 1953, the late-night revue really took off. As well as London Club Theatre's return, the actor Fenella Fielding starred in writer and composer Sandy Wilson's *See You Later* at the variety house the Palladium Theatre on East Fountainbridge,[16] while the Oxford Theatre Group made their first appearance at the Edinburgh Festival. In their first year they booked Riddle's Court, the 16th century merchant's townhouse just off the Lawnmarket formerly owned by David Hume and later went to Gillan's Close and then Edinburgh's former Parks and Burial Department headquarters at the Cranston Street Hall, further down the Royal Mile.

Oxford's programme followed the same format as London Club Theatre's, with a play followed by a revue. Specifically convened to marshal the efforts of both Oxford University Drama Society and its Experimental Theatre Club in Edinburgh, OTG first brought two attractive drama performances – August Strindberg's *Miss Julie* and Molière's *Tricks of Scapin* – alongside a new late-night revue called *Cakes and Ale*. The Molière piece was directed by a student named Frank Dunlop, much later the founder of the Young Vic in London and the director of the Edinburgh International Festival itself. In 1956, by which time there were four revues on the Fringe, students from Cambridge University first arrived in separate groups. The Cambridge University Players' revue was out of the way in the seaside suburb of Portobello's Town Hall, while the Cambridge University Actors presented Ben Jonson's 17th century comedy *The Alchemist* at the Masonic Hall on Forth Street.

Demonstrating some early Fringe topicality, Perth Theatre Company premiered the Scottish writer and novelist George Scott-Moncrieff's *Blood Upon the Rose* at Lauriston Hall in 1957, as a response to and reflection upon the previous year's Hungarian uprising. It was broadcast live by the BBC. Since the Gateway Theatre's reopening in 1946 it had become a key theatre in Edinburgh, staging works by Robert Kemp and other playwrights alongside films and community arts projects. Across Scotland, theatre was beginning to flourish; Perth Theatre, the tented Park Theatre in Pitlochry,[17] Dundee Rep and the Byre Theatre in St Andrews were all established or emerging and many brought Fringe shows to the Gateway.

Key to the Gateway's success was the irrepressible Sadie Aitken, who had recently turned 40 when she accepted a career change into managing the Gateway on behalf of the Church. She was an effective theatre administrator, she took care of much of the building maintenance herself and she had an easy, personable, community-building way, which involved teaming with the International Festival committee to arrange summer school visits by students from France, Canada and Wales. As Gateway manager, she was the first woman in Scotland to hold a theatre license and only the second to hold a cinema license.

In 1953, the Gateway formally launched its own resident theatre company, staffed by actors and administrators with experience of the old Scottish National Players, the Citizens Theatre, shows produced by the Gateway itself since 1946 and past International Festival productions of *A Satire of the Three Estates*, among them Tom Fleming, Lennox Milne and James Gibson. With Robert Kemp as chairman and a prolific source of new plays, the company members switched between acting and directing and the lynchpin of the company's season from 1954 until its closure in 1965 became their annual August production for the International Festival.[18]

The 11 Festival shows the company performed included four by Kemp, among them his Molière adaptation *Let Wives Tak' Tent* in '61, two by Bridie and Robert McLellan's Unity play from 1947, *The Flouers o' Edinburgh*. From its foundation in 1952 by playwright TM Watson and actor Duncan Macrae, the commercial touring company Scottishows also did good Fringe business at the Palladium Theatre on East Fountainbridge with revue shows and plays including Bridie's *Gog & Magog* in '54. Macrae, one of the letter-writers to *The Herald* in 1947, was born in Maryhill, Glasgow, in 1905, the son of a policeman. He started out with Glasgow's amateur Curtain Theatre in 1937, where he made a name for himself with the title role in Robert McLellan's *Jamie the Saxt*.

He moved on to Unity Theatre and then became a key player in Bridie's Citizens Theatre, tall and craggy and equally at home with comedy and drama. He was a familiar Scottish voice on the big screen through roles in the Ealing comedy *Whisky Galore!* (1949), Disney's RL Stevenson adaptation *Kidnapped* (1960) and *Greyfriars Bobby* (1961),and on pantomime stages with Stanley Baxter. He was also a continuing and vocal advocate of the National Theatre movement in the post-war period and of increased subsidy for Scottish theatre in general.

The Gateway's contributions to the International Festival – and occasional performances by the Citizens and later Perth and Dundee's theatres – were junior entries in a theatre programme still dominated by the Old Vic, but they were an important element of Scotland's still-developing, increasingly Arts Council-funded post-war theatre, especially in the face of television's growth. On Saturday the 31 August 1957, Scottish Television began broadcasting across the country from their new home at Glasgow's Theatre Royal and as television ownership increased though the 1950s, Gateway attendances began dropping. The Wilson Barrett company folded in 1955 and Scottishows stopped producing soon after.

A common theme during Edinburgh in August was the stuttering quest to unite the 'uninvited' yet increasingly talked-about Fringe events under one banner, often in the face of disinterest or direct opposition from the International Festival's committee and artistic directors, who felt these shows mainly meant unwelcome competition. As their number grew, the 'uninviteds' still mostly organised in complete isolation from each other. An early printed programme was put together by the newsagent firm John Menzies, and another list of 'Additional Entertainments' was gathered by the printing firm CJ Cousland in 1954, the same year the company's enterprising head Ian Cousland tried to create some organisation. During a meeting at the Moray Knox Arts Centre on the Canongate, the student and amateur groups were willing to establish 'a brain for the Fringe' to centralise booking and advertising, but Scottishows and London Club Theatre weren't involved; the latter was trying to gain recognition from the International Festival. The attempt to organise failed, but four years later they tried again.

This time the Oxford Theatre Group invited the 25 unofficial companies to a meeting at Cranston Street Hall on Friday 29 August 1958, led by 23-year-old Oxford student Michael Imison, later a BBC television director on *Doctor Who* and literary agent for Noel Coward and Terence Rattigan. The Festival Society was apparently too busy to attend, but this time arguments about collective representation, joint communication and marketing and shared responsibility for finding halls and hiring equipment cut through. Meetings continued and seven groups immediately expressed interest in paying five pounds each to get a society off the ground: Oxford Theatre Group, the Scottish Community Drama Association, Edinburgh University Drama Society, Edinburgh People's Theatre, the Players of Leyton, the Youth Theatre and Elspeth Douglas Reid. Nearly two weeks later and with other groups onboard, a new era began on Wednesday 10 September, as summed up by a simple report in *The Glasgow Herald* the next day:

> At a meeting last night of the committee representing 10 festival
> fringe groups a Festival Fringe Society was formed and a
> constitution was adopted. The following office-bearers were elected
> - President, Michael Imison, Oxford Theatre Group; secretary,
> Ian Cousland, 30 Queen Street, Edinburgh; treasurer, Neil Barber,
> Elspeth Douglas Reid's manager; publicity secretary, J. Gallagher,
> Edinburgh People's Theatre.[19]

In the summer of 1959, the new Society came into full operation. It was Cousland who suggested the companies should finalise an early programme and sell tickets months in advance, much like the International Festival and in 1959 he prepared 30,000 copies of a 22-page brochure, the predecessor of the stuffed packed programme we know today. The Fringe Society instated its own social hub at the YMCA where groups could meet up, the public could buy tickets and meals and hot drinks were sold.[20] 'Fringe' was no longer simply a handy term used by the press to describe a handful of disparate shows happening across the city and with the birth of the Festival Fringe Society the word passed into popular use. The gathering of shows it represented in August grew to dwarf every arts festival in the world before long.

* * *

Like Ian Hunter, the man he replaced, the International Festival's third artist director Robert Ponsonby was another youthful star of post-war arts admin in Britain – in fact, his appointment came at an even younger age than Hunter was when he inherited Rudolf Bing's job at 30. Born in 1926, the son of the organist at Oxford's Christ Church Cathedral, Ponsonby was 28 when he found out he'd got the job in early 1955 and 29 when his first self-programmed Festival, the tenth overall, arrived a year later.

The new director had travelled the same route as his predecessors, although his precocious age meant his first visit to Glyndebourne in 1938 had been at age of 12, to see Fritz Busch conduct Mozart's *Don Giovanni*. He was another product of the British Establishment and a keen organist while at school at Eton. At 18 he was called up for three years of military service as a 2nd Lieutenant in the Scots Guards regiment, most of which he saw out in England. During a brief posting to smashed and occupied Hamburg late in 1945, however, Ponsonby experienced German opera in the most unique and heartbreaking of circumstances.

The city had been flattened and burned by Allied firebombing raids, but in the immediate aftermath of the war, opera survived. One of the few remaining theatres was the Deutsches Schauspielhaus (simply, 'German Theatre'), which was taken over for Allied use and renamed the Garrison Theatre in the war's aftermath. The stage of the Hamburgische Staatsoper (Hamburg State Opera) also survived behind its fire curtain, despite the complete annihilation of the rest of the building. In this eerie open-air space audiences, including Ponsonby, congregated to hear some of the finest talent in German opera perform. His memoirs described the emotionally exhausting effect of hearing Wagner's *Tristan und Isolde* amid a Hamburg in ruins.

Demobbed in 1948, he went to Oxford as the university's Organ Scholar, singing with the University's Opera Club and hungrily attending performances. He visited Edinburgh International Festival in 1950, where he marvelled at Sera Jurinac's performance in Glyndebourne's *The Marriage of Figaro* and saw Thomas Beecham conduct the Royal Philharmonic Orchestra at the Usher

Hall. A year later, after a speculative personal enquiry, Ponsonby was installed as Glyndebourne's General Secretary in time to assist Bing's now-promoted former assistant Moran Caplat with the 1951 Festival of Britain revival.

After that, work had to be found for him and as Glyndebourne and the Edinburgh International Festival still shared their Baker Street offices in London, he began job-sharing as deputy to Ian Hunter. From the summer of '51, the two men regularly took the same monthly sleeper train north to Edinburgh that Hunter had shared with Rudolf Bing five years before. Appointed as Hunter's Edinburgh replacement three months before his predecessor's final International Festival in 1955 Ponsonby was recommended by the outgoing director as a safe pair of hands. Despite standing an attention-grabbing six and a half feet tall, he arrived in the days when the Festival's director wasn't a public-facing figurehead, but rather a capable behind-the-scenes administrator who might say a few words at a press conference when the year's big name arrived in the city.

Yet Ponsonby was taking on a huge responsibility – not just steering a major event in Scottish and British cultural life, but doing it in the tenth anniversary year, as the International Festival was coming into its own as the preeminent arts festival in the world. Across Europe, the great orchestral music festivals, which provided inspiration for Edinburgh – the Salzburg Festival in the city of Mozart's birth, the Wagnerian Bayreuth Festival in the bombed and rebuilt Bavarian town and Glyndebourne itself – had now been overtaken by the depth of multi-arts variety available in Edinburgh.

Despite his removal of the '...of Music and Drama' addition to the International Festival's name in 1956 – it was felt the remit had broadened since '47 – Ponsonby wasn't so much a reformer as a refresher. Mindful that the plan was to present another international opera in Glyndebourne's place in 1956, he went on a tour of Europe to find the best company he could, returning to his re-energised wartime haunt in Hamburg's Schauspielhaus, the Städtische Oper in Frankfurt and to Munich, a city now occupied with its own resurgent Opera Festival, founded in 1950 at the Bayerische Staatsoper.

He moved on to Zurich and then Prague, where he was asked by a friend in British Intelligence to look out for MIG fighters at the airport and check if his hotel was bugged. In Milan he experienced the new Piccolo Teatro, founded in 1947, the same year as Edinburgh's Festival and a production of Gorky's *The Lower Depths*, the same play Glasgow's Unity Theatre instigated the Fringe with. He went to Rome and Naples, where he heard Leonard Bernstein conduct the Israeli Philharmonic.

To International Festival watchers at the time, Ponsonby's 1956 edition was viewed as a high watermark. The Hamburg State Opera was his chosen visiting company and they delivered a full series of works by Mozart,

Stravinsky, Cornelius and Richard Strauss, while the Boston Symphony Orchestra also appeared at the Usher Hall. La Piccolo Teatro took up an invite to appear following Ponsonby's continental recce and appeared with two of their signature dramas, Carlo Goldoni's 18th century *Commedia dell'Arte, Arlecchino* (Servant of Two Masters) and the third part of Luigi Pirandello's 'theatre in the theatre' trilogy, 1930's *Questa sera si recita a soggetto* (Tonight We Improvise).

Sadler's Wells Ballet, now named the Royal Ballet, brought Swan Lake to the Empire Theatre, featuring their prima ballerina Margot Fonteyn at the height of her powers in her signature role. The Indian classical dancer Ram Gopal's hit show, *The Legend of the Taj Mahal* appeared at the same venue and Dylan Thomas' great Welsh play *Under Milk Wood* was read for the first of many times at the Edinburgh Festival, this time in the Lyceum three years after its author's death.[21] The great director Tyrone Guthrie also returned to Edinburgh with his Stratford Ontario Festival Company, who played on Guthrie's trademark thrust stage at the Assembly Hall, alongside the Michael Langham-directed *Henry V*, with a powerful lead performance from Christopher Plummer and a young William Shatner in the cast.

Of a privately but ambitiously proposed booking for the Audrey Hepburn version of Jean Giraudoux's *Ondine*, for which she won her Tony Award two years earlier, we can only imagine the attention it would have brought upon Edinburgh. The then-emerging film icon was too busy to do the show, so it didn't go ahead, but headlines were created in 1957 by another performer much coveted by the press for their image as much as their supreme talent.

The orchestra of Milan's famous 18th century Scala Theatre had already appeared in Edinburgh in 1950, but the modest King's Theatre just didn't have the size of stage required for La Scala's full operatic company. A solution came with the inauguration of Milan's La Piccola Scala in 1955, a 600-capacity theatre immediately adjacent to the original Scala. The smaller theatre's productions were more amenable to the size required at the King's and four of them were booked in for '57 – including a new performance of Vincenzo Bellini's 1831 opera *La Sonnambula* (The Sleepwalker), starring the great 20th century soprano Maria Callas.

'I am temperamental onstage while I sing,' said Callas during a press conference in Edinburgh. 'You would not want me otherwise'.[22] After a decade of her career at its height, the Greek-Italian soprano was already a well-known figure for her distinctive voice, her much remarked-upon beauty and her supposed 'diva' temperament. The description feels like an anachronism now, a put-down of female artists who accept no compromise or half-measures in their work. All contemporary reports say she was perfectly pleasant to deal with in Edinburgh and in her press conference, she also discussed the cold Scottish weather and the compact King's Theatre stage.

Unfortunately, a situation of others' making led to predictably overexcited press reports of Callas' behaviour in Edinburgh, which flashed around the world. She was contracted to play four performances of *La Sonnambula* between 19 and 29 August, but when Ponsonby asked La Scala for another show on 3 September, the company agreed. But nobody asked Callas' permission, or they would have known she planned to rest and holiday after Edinburgh and that she'd agreed to attend a party thrown by the American writer and high society gossip columnist Elsa Maxwell in Venice the same evening.

Callas had no intention of changing her plans for a booking she hadn't been consulted on and she left Edinburgh after the performance on 29 August. The immediate, indignant response in the press was to a performer who had gravely disrespected her audience by abandoning them to go to a party; the full story eventually came out, but the proverbial lie was around the world before the truth had its boots on. One person greatly benefited from the furore and that was 23-year-old Renata Scotto, Callas' covering singer in the role of Amina. She went onstage before a full house and gave an acclaimed performance, launching herself as one of the great Italian sopranos and later opera directors of her generation.

Robert Ponsonby later described Callas's time in Edinburgh in very positive terms. The famous singer's own words in her opening Edinburgh press conference, where she opened up about the lazy press treatment of her, proved prophetic: 'In New York the papers wrote a lot of nonsense and it hurt me very much. I don't go about showing my feelings, but that does not mean that I don't feel hurt'.[23]

Callas' appearance was still one of the resounding highlights of Ponsonby's time at the Festival, but there were other major talking points. One discussed for all the wrong reasons was Jonathan Griffin's brand new verse play at the Assembly Hall in 1957, *The Hidden King*, an expensive attempt to originate the new drama the Festival had been crying out for and a massive critical flop. Ponsonby still believed in it so much that he organised an event at the venue where the cast and creative team explained it before a receptive audience.

None of this did anything to dent the belief of national critics like Kenneth Tynan that drama was the weak link in the International Festival – a long trip to see shows which had either already been in London, were coming to London or weren't worth the effort in the first place. The idea persisted into the next decade, although 1958's drama offerings were strong, including the Ulster Theatre Group's Tyrone Guthrie-directed *The Bonfire* and New Watergate Theatre Club's British premiere of Eugene O'Neill's 1956 modern American classic *Long Day's Journey Into Night*, a Pulitzer Prizewinner the year before. Presented at the Lyceum before transferring to the Globe in London, this was directed by original Broadway director José Quintero and featured Anthony Quayle and future stars Alan Bates and Ian Bannen. Ponsonby also welcomed the Old Vic's 1959 presentation of William Congreve's 1693 comic play *The Double-Dealer*, a casting delight from the future, featuring Judi Dench and Maggie Smith, both 25 and Joss Ackland, 31, all professionals but unknown at the time.

One of the most unique International Festival shows of the era came during this period, when the concert trio of violinist Yehudi Menuhin, cellist Gaspar Cassado and pianist Louis Kentner played a late-morning show of Mendelssohn and Beethoven works on 11 September 1958 at the Embassy Cinema on Boswall Parkway, in the north Edinburgh housing scheme of Pilton. Following two shows at the Usher Hall earlier in the week, the idea was Menuhin's alone:

> We are so happy in Edinburgh, and like the city and the festival
> audiences so much that we want to show our appreciation [to]
> the people who really belong to Edinburgh and who have had no
> opportunity of attending festival concerts.[24]

With the artists playing for free and a small one shilling entry charge to cover costs, the show sold out all 1,500 tickets, with the venue reporting phone calls from as far as Aberdeen begging for tickets. The audience was a blend of festival regulars and Pilton locals, with a third of the tickets held for school parties and 1,000 disappointed customers left outside by the time the venue was full. An 11-year-old boy named Stephen Harvey managed to get in. When it was discovered the cinema lighting was too harsh, local doors were knocked on to ask for a standard lamp. Stephen told the venue staff they could borrow his mother's if he could have a free ticket; they obliged and he saw the show while his mother was left outside in the queue.

The chamber concert had been a huge popular success and the Embassy Cinema – now long since demolished – became a recurring festival venue. Menuhin, who performed in Edinburgh many times before his death in 1999, was given the Freedom of the City in 1965, placing him alongside such dignitaries as Walter Scott, Charles Dickens, Winston Churchill, Queen Elizabeth II, Sean Connery and Nelson Mandela.

Ponsonby also secured the Leningrad Symphony Orchestra under conductor Evgeny Mravinsky for the 1960 festival, but by this point the Festival's director had announced he would be leaving. Continually frustrated by the funding available from the city of Edinburgh and the creative timidity of those he had to deal with there, he later told Iain Crawford the city administrators possessed 'a generally philistine indifference towards artistic aspirations and policies'.[25]

This was beginning to have an effect on his programming and efforts to build bridges with Glyndebourne and tempt an angry Tyrone Guthrie back after 1959's *Three Estates* were stymied by finance. Peter Potter and not Guthrie directed Sydney Goodsir Smith's *The Wallace* for the Assembly Hall during 1960's Festival, a play about the Scots hero William Wallace which saw nationalists in the audience rise to loudly sing Robert Burns' *Scots Wha Hae* at its conclusion and royal visitor Prince Philip, the Duke of Edinburgh, left stymied by the play's Scots dialect.

Ponsonby, who died at the age of 92 in 2019, later said he viewed his time at the International Festival as an apprenticeship for a long career in the arts, which included periods as director of the Scottish National Orchestra and the BBC Proms, and controller of BBC Radio 3. Michael Imison, his very briefly-served opposite number at the new Festival Fringe Society, also left in 1960 for a job at the BBC. There's an irony to all of this, that the most resounding creative success of Ponsonby's tenure was the late-night 1960 revue *Beyond the Fringe*, a last-minute, shoestring-budgeted attempt to steal the Fringe's thunder.

SPOTLIGHT

Beyond the Fringe (1960)

AT 10.45PM ON Monday 22 August 1960, as a fresh International Festival audience took their seats in the smoky atmosphere of the Lyceum Theatre on Grindlay Street, its stage hurriedly stripped back from the three-hour Old Vic production of *The Seagull* which had not long finished one of the seismic moments of 20th century British cultural history happened.

Not that this was immediately apparent to the audience.

The six-night debut run of *Beyond the Fringe* was a hit at 1960's Edinburgh International Festival, but it didn't really catch fire until the following May, when the reworked show's transfer to the Fortune Theatre in London's West End made the wider world sit up and take notice. *The Observer*'s reviewer Kenneth Tynan declared with a certain tactlessness it was:

> [T]he funniest revue that London has seen since the Allies dropped the bomb on Hiroshima. Future historians may well thank me for providing them with a full account of the moment when English comedy took its first decisive step into the second half of the 20th century.[1]

This London run was the opened floodgate, the point where mainstream post-war British comedy stopped being about polite variety revues filled with nudge-nudge quips and jaunty musical numbers and instead insisted that deference to authority of the age – to the Royal Family, elected ministers of Her Majesty's Government, 'elders and betters', the very concept of the British Establishment – was no longer a given. Alan Bennett (26 when the show debuted in Edinburgh), Peter Cook (22), Jonathan Miller (26) and Dudley Moore (25) hardly invented satire, but these wayward products of the country's elite universities reinvigorated it for a country climbing out of a pit of drab post-war rationing and austerity, where the very Establishment Conservative Party had won three elections during nearly a decade in power, despite the national humiliation of the Suez Crisis in 1957.

A new youth movement was beginning to stir among those who were just children during the Second World War and what the Beatles were to the emergence of rock 'n' roll and ultimately pop music in the UK, *Beyond the Fringe* was to the satire boom and ultimately the stand-up comedy revival of the 1980s. The show's success in the West End and subsequent transfer to Broadway – where President John F Kennedy saw it – made household names of the four young men involved and in the short term directly influenced the magazine *Private Eye*, the London comedy and jazz club The Establishment and the BBC television show *That Was the Week That Was*. Peter Cook had a hand in all three, as respective co-funder, co-owner and scriptwriter.

Beyond the Fringe's influence unfolded yet further over the years, into the surreal adventures of Monty Python, into British punk rock – filtered through the self-consciously boundary-pushing obscenity of Cook and Moore's bootleg *Derek and Clive* double act of the 1970s – and into the very fabric of British comedy as we now know it. There are significant parts of the nation's psyche that imagine themselves contemptuous of bureaucracy, resistant to authority and armoured against the world by self-deprecating humour, the roots of which were at the very least nourished by *Beyond the Fringe*.

If the show's West End glory had a musical equivalent in the Beatles' 'She Loves You', the 1963 breakthrough that took the Western world by storm and became the biggest popular music hit of the decade, then its Edinburgh incarnation was the band's debut single 'Love Me Do', released the previous autumn to modest top 20 success; it was where it all began. More than that, the Edinburgh Festival was the very reason *Beyond the Fringe* – a title which none of the core quartet liked when it was handed to them by the International Festival's director Robert Ponsonby – existed in the first place.

With late-night university revue entertainment flourishing on the Fringe since 1951, Ponsonby had wondered whether the International Festival could create something really special after dark; that the quality of performer available to it could be beyond that of the Fringe. He made efforts in this direction in 1957, with Anna Russell's famed classical music and opera lampoon act, subtitled... *makes fun of the Festival* when it played at the Freemason's Hall and in 1959, when comic songwriters Michael Flanders and Donald Swann's 'after-dinner farrago' *At the Drop of a Hat* alternated with Russell over a dozen dates at the Lyceum.

Ponsonby's plan stepped up a gear in 1960, with three acts each doing a six-night run at the Lyceum over the festival's three weeks. Already booked were the French vocal quartet *Les Frères Jacques* and 66-year-old Beatrice Lillie, a Tony Award-winning, five-decade veteran of the stage. The planned guest for the opening week might have been one of the Edinburgh Festival's most thrilling bookings – the American jazz trumpeter Louis Armstrong, just four years after the 59-year-old had appeared alongside Bing Crosby and Grace Kelly in *High Society*.

Yet Armstrong's agent couldn't arrange enough UK bookings for his client to justify a transatlantic flight and Ponsonby needed a stop-gap replacement quickly. Talking to his assistant Johnny Bassett, he wondered if the Festival might consider playing the Fringe at its own game and putting on its own student revue.

Bassett had graduated from Oxford University in 1958 and he knew performers on the scene Ponsonby wanted to tap into. He thought of Dudley Moore, from working-class Dagenham in Essex, whose prodigious talents as a jazz pianist had won him a music scholarship to the elite Oxford. Bassett was a trumpet player himself, leader of his band 'The Bassett Hounds' and Moore had played with him in the clubs of Oxford and London. Nicknamed 'Cuddly Dudley', he was also good at acting and cabaret comedy, which helped counteract his self-consciousness as one of the few students at Oxford from a working-class background.

Moore graduated in 1957, studied for a postgraduate degree in music the following year, then moved to London to build a career as a jazz musician. He played with Bassett at the Dorchester and Savoy hotels, travelled to New York with Vic Lewis' band, took over as Johnny Dankworth's pianist and played the Royal Festival Hall with his own trio. For a time he was the in-house composer at the Royal Court Theatre, then he was offered the chance to make an album for Atlantic Records' awestruck founder Ahmet Ertegun in New York. His return flight to London, however, was booked for the next day, but he did cut a single named 'For the Birds' with future Beatles producer George Martin.

Moore had kept in touch with the student scene in Oxford, composing music for undergrad versions of Shakespeare's *Coriolanus* and Aristophanes' *The Birds*, the latter inspiring his single with Martin. He had a walk-on part as a pear-seller in *The Birds*, co-directed by the future film director Ken Loach, alongside student actors who later made their name in disparate areas; among them, *The Guardian*'s theatre critic Michael Billington, the three-decade artistic director of Glasgow's Citizens Theatre Giles Havergal and the news broadcaster Peter Snow. He also turned up in *Just Lately*, the Oxford Theatre Group's 1958 revue at Cranston Street Hall, and in 1959 accompanied the baritone Frederick Fuller with an eclectic late-night recital named *New Pills to Purge Old Melancholy* at the Gartshore Hall on George Street.

Like the rest of the Beyond the Fringe team, Moore was an ex-student feeling his way towards professionalism, but his roots were in the university revue scene Ponsonby wanted to evoke. Moore suggested another name to Bassett: Alan Bennett, a young medieval history don who also arrived at Oxford on a scholarship after his National Service. The Leeds-raised son of a jazz-playing butcher, Bennett was as working class as Moore, yet his learned, almost ecclesiastical manner couldn't have been more different. It was perfect, though, for his performing party piece, a satirical vicar's sermon, which was the toast of Oxford 'smokers'.[2]

Next, Bassett thought of a real star of the revue scene in the 1950s, this time one whose alma mater was Cambridge. Jonathan Miller's background was entirely different to Moore's and Bennet's and he seemed to be leaving performance behind. His father, Emanuel Miller, was a renowned psychiatrist and his mother, Betty, was a prolific novelist and biographer and young Jonathan was raised between London's Harley Street – where his father usually practiced – and wherever in England Emanuel was serving in military hospitals during the Second World War. Obsessed as a young man with the performer Danny Kaye, a Jewish American, as Miller himself was a Jewish Brit, a 13-year-old Miller sneaked into Kaye's London Palladium dressing room in 1948. I want to be a doctor, he told his hero. You'll never do it, shot back Kaye.

Miller performed mostly as a hobby on the side of his real vocation, medicine, but he was good enough to feature on a BBC radio programme for new talent named *Under Twenty Parade* before he'd even left school. After being persuaded to appear in the 1954 Cambridge Footlights revue *Out of the Blue*, he was the toast of its West End transfer to the Phoenix Theatre that summer, earning comparisons with Kaye and television appearances on ITV's *Sunday Night at the London Palladium* and the BBC's *Tonight*. Yet graduation from Cambridge in 1956 led to a deepening interest in neuro-psychology. He continued his studies and became house officer at London's University College Hospital.

It was a busy time of life for Miller, who in 1956 married Rachel Collet. She happened to be an old public schoolfriend of one Johnny Bassett, who approached Miller at the hospital and proposed a place in *Beyond the Fringe* to him. Miller agreed, simply for a fun summer respite from his demanding medical work. When Bassett asked if he knew anyone else who might want to get involved, he immediately recommended Peter Cook.

If Miller was by this point the most acclaimed revue performer in the group, then Cook was the most theatrically successful. Like Miller, he came from a successful establishment family; his grandfather Edward and father Alec both held high office in Britain's colonies in Kuala Lumpur, Nigeria and Gibraltar. Like Moore, Cook learned to play the clown to avoid bullying at school, albeit his school was of the prestigious boarding variety and when he went to study at Cambridge, he carried on being a relentless, everyday humorist. This made him difficult to know well, but it endeared him to a fashionable set of university friends which included later actors and television personalities like David Frost, Ian McKellen, Derek Jacobi, John Bird and Eleanor Bron.

Successful enough in Cambridge revues to have picked up an agent named Donald Langdon, Cook appeared in and wrote much of Bird's 1958 Cambridge Footlights show *The Last Laugh* and the response was so good that the producer Michael Codron hired him to write most of emerging *Carry On* film star Kenneth Williams' 1959 West End revue *Pieces of Eight*. An old-fashioned show of the sort *Beyond the Fringe* would edge towards the dustbin, Cook still loved the experience and the rewards of this gig. The same year he directed and mostly wrote the Footlights' revue *Pop Goes Mrs Jessop*, a tamer affair than his contingent of student fans had grown used to.

When *Pop Goes Mrs Jessop* appeared, Cook had already agreed to do *Beyond the Fringe* – a decision Langdon disagreed with, given that his client was a bona-fide West End success and the others were talented unknowns. Cook thought it seemed a fun project and decided to do it anyway, but Langdon at least negotiated his fee for the week up to £110, from the others' £100; infamously, his ten percent agent's cut meant Cook actually saw £99. As it turned out, Cook's second-class degree wasn't good enough to take him into the Foreign Service, as had been the plan, so the success of *Beyond the Fringe* was a handy safety net in place of the junior advertising copywriter's job in London he'd accepted as insurance.

The quartet's first meeting was in a restaurant near University College Hospital, for Miller's convenience – on Euston Road or Goodge Street or Warren Street, none of them could remember; they ate Indian or Italian, depending on whether Cook or Bennett is to be believed. They later agreed the mood was tense, a blend of nerves over who would crack the first joke and competitive spirit as to whether the others would find it funny. Moore corpsed while impersonating a violin which sounded like a baby, but redeemed himself by pretending to chaperone members of the female waiting staff to their customers, Groucho Marx-style. At five foot two, he felt uncomfortable with the sheer height of the others, all a foot taller than him, but although Cook had mocked the violin skit the loudest, Moore warmed to his charm the most.

Miller and the quiet Bennett were also nervous for their own reasons and Cook predictably filled the void. As Miller related, the sheer force of his personality seemed almost threatening to the others. A few days later, Bassett took them to visit Robert Ponsonby at the International Festival's London office on St James' Street – he liked what he saw and *Beyond the Fringe* was a go.

The plan was for each of the performers to bring their own solo material and write new sketches together. At parties and low-key revues at their old universities, they appeared as duos or trios in the months leading up to August, with Miller already having boldly told the press to expect an 'anti-establishment, anti-capital punishment, anti-colour bar and anti-1960' show. Eventually, one morning early in August, they set out at 6.30am to drive to Edinburgh from London, arriving 11 hours later after a most Bennettesque picnic in the Yorkshire Dales. The International Festival had put them up in a top-floor flat at 17 Cornwall Street, across the road from the Lyceum's stage door, around the corner from the Festival's Synod Hall office and with a view of Edinburgh Castle if you leaned out of the window.

With *The Seagull* taking up the prestige slot on the Lyceum stage, the Cornwall Street flat became *Beyond the Fringe*'s rehearsal room, although budgetary concerns meant they had no set or costumes anyway, beyond the smart suits and dark pullovers they'd bought themselves, the occasional prop hat and a bass player named Hugo Boyd. Cook later claimed 'a hundred chorus girls dancing around' would have been his preference. On being told by the actor's union Equity that he had to change his stage name to prevent confusion with the actor Peter Coke, he presented them with the suggestions 'Xavier Blancmange', 'Wardrobe Gruber' or 'Sting Thundercock'. He got to be himself, in the end.

Preparation was chaotic. Even the relaxed Cook was nervously re-rehearsing his parts and a run-through in the presence of a shocked Ponsonby saw the group screwing up their lines and collapsing into giggles. The night before they were still putting material together, which was when Moore wrote his comedic version of 'Colonel Bogey' in the style of Beethoven. He was wary in the presence of such perceived intellectual giants and his role in the show was to be 'Clown Prince'.

The text was two-thirds written by Cook, with the rest shared between Bennett and Miller. Later fleshed-out for the longer West End run by trial performances in Cambridge and Brighton, the hour-long Edinburgh original featured the Shakespeare parody *So That's the Way You Like It*, Bennett's signature sermon, riffs on nuclear war and the supposed nobility of combat and Cook's impersonation of then-Prime Minister Harold Macmillan as a very dusty and grey man, a defining turning point in British comedy's relationship with those in power. The playwright Michael Frayn, a contemporary of Cook and Miller at Cambridge, later wrote of the effect of the Macmillan sketch, 'TVPM', on the English middle classes during *Beyond the Fringe*'s West End run:

> The couple in front of me, a perfectly sound pair of young Tories, were right with us, neighing away like demented horses, until the middle of Peter Cook's lampoon on Macmillan, when the man turned to the girl and said in an appalled whisper, 'I say! This is supposed to be the Prime Minister,' after which they sat in silence for the rest of the evening. God knows what cherished family prejudices they had betrayed by then.[3]

Advance ticket sales were slow, adding to Ponsonby's nerves and on opening night the theatre was somewhere between one and two-thirds full, depending on reports. Then the outstanding reviews came in and the Lyceum was packed for the rest of the week, with return queues stretching along the block. When the short Edinburgh run was over, impresario Willie Donaldson signed them up to a West End run which made the quartet £75 a week each and the producers of the show half a million pounds, eventually.

It was a deal which the quartet came to regret. What the West End run brought each, however, was fame and recognition, which was parleyed, following the group's disbandment at the end of the Broadway run in 1964,[4] into enduring solo careers.

Bennett, almost ashamed of the youthful frivolity of *Beyond the Fringe*, became one of the key English playwrights of the late 20th century. Miller, the dictionary definition of the word 'polymath', became a leading medical researcher and writer, a world-class opera and theatre director, a prolific television presenter and guest and chair of the Edinburgh Festival Fringe board between 1983 and 1995.

Cook led the satire boom of the 1960s and changed the character of British comedy for good, continuing his working relationship with Moore in the cult comedy film *Bedazzled* (1967), the hit sketch series *Not Only... But Also* (1965 to 1970) and the deliberately extreme *Derek and Clive* (1976 to 1979). His dwindling success after this is often portrayed as a sad counterpoint to Moore's booming Hollywood career of the 1980s, for which he gathered an Academy Award nomination and two Golden Globe wins, yet those who knew Cook insisted he was happy with the life of a *bon viveur*, who valued entertaining friendships and good times over success. 'There never was a satire movement, only the Cook empire', Miller later dryly noted.

Other versions of the impact of *Beyond the Fringe*, seen from a distance, vary. Bennett's biographer Alexander Games noted that Jonathan Miller's work, in particular, shifted British comedy on from asking the question 'Wouldn't it be funny if…?' to 'Isn't it funny that…?', both personalising it and inventing the observational comedy genre. Bennett, the only surviving member at time of writing, noted that many people he knew were creating a similar kind of humour in private.

The last word on *Beyond the Fringe* goes to the late Peter Cook:

I may have done some other things as good, but I am sure none better. I haven't matured, progressed, grown, become deeper, wiser, or funnier. But then, I never thought I would.[5]

For everything he and his colleagues later achieved – together and apart – and inspired in many others who followed, it all began with those six nights in Edinburgh.

4

The Conferences and the Birth of the 1960s

A MIDDLE-CLASS SON of an American oil worker who was raised between Louisiana and Venezuela, who studied at a military academy in Atlanta, Georgia and who found himself stationed with the United States Air Force at Kirknewton – to the west of Edinburgh – was the most unlikely figure to go recatalysing the Edinburgh Festival for the turn of the countercultural 1960s. Yet Jim Haynes' difference was what made him perfect for the job.

Everyone who'd made a significant contribution to the festivals by this point – Rudolf Bing and other International Festival directors, the firebrand instigators of the Fringe and the People's Festival, even the fresh satirical voices of Beyond the Fringe in 1960 – were entrenched in one side or other of the British class divide. To Haynes, all of these things were a mystery.

As Haynes told it, he stumbled across the Atlantic and into a new life in Scotland in search of the easiest time possible. Living it up in New Orleans while he attended Louisiana State University, his compulsory draft into the US Armed Forces arrived in the early 1950s and he asked to go into the Air Force because it seemed to be less of a slog than the Marines. Thirteen weeks' gruelling physical training and a year learning Russian with the Security Services later, in 1957 he had a plan: to be transferred to a small airbase in Western Europe, but close to a major university.

The charming of one friendly posting officer later and Haynes found himself on a flight to Kirknewton within a month. In his memoir he wrote that despite the cold and dark, he fell in love with Edinburgh on his first aimless stroll around the city.

* * *

Thoughts of furthering his military career were far from Haynes' mind when he arrived at the stockaded fields on the edge of West Lothian. Instead, he planned to escape the military by attending one of the recognised great seats of learning in the world. With his base commander's blessing, he took on night duties listening to chatter from Soviet air traffic over the Baltic and the Black Sea for the CIA and studied by day at the University of Edinburgh.

He rented a smart room on Great King Street in the New Town and set about building a social life as fulfilling as his educational one. Able to mix a mean daquiri and with access to cheap drink from the Air Force bar, he went to late-night parties in Coates Gardens and Frederick Street. He made a second home of the Laigh Coffee House, one of the city's most bohemian hangouts of the day, which shared its name with Laigh Hall, meeting place of the Scottish Enlightenment's Select Society.

A series of interconnected basement rooms on Hanover Street near its northern junction with Queen Street,[1] the Laigh was owned by the actor Moultrie Kelsall and his wife, the musician Ruby Duncan. Kelsall performed with Tyrone Guthrie's Scottish National Players in the 1920s and in Guthrie's early International Festival iterations of *A Satire of the Three Estates.*[2] Named after the Scots word for low-lying land, the Laigh was a favourite with students, artists and Festival crowds. Officially opened by Sir Compton MacKenzie in 1956, it blended European café culture with a traditional Scottish sensibility long before this became common in Edinburgh's present-day tourist-trap cafes.

Beside the log fire which burned in winter, customers ate exotic hazelnut meringues and Haynes' favourite, the homemade shortbread, from morning until late at night, when bowls of creamy porridge came doused with a nip of whisky. One legend of debatable truth was that a Scottish housekeeper to President John F Kennedy ordered shortbread from the Laigh's kitchen to the White House in a diplomatic bag. If nothing else, it's a prime, pre-*Harry Potter* example of an Edinburgh café creating an instant, tourist-friendly mythology, but later visits to the Laigh by Sean Connery and Billy Connolly gave it less need of suspect Presidential approval.

The Laigh closed with the retirement of its long-serving manager Joan Spicer in 1999, more than four decades on from Haynes' discovery of it as one of Edinburgh's main cultural hubs while the city was still learning to be an international meeting point. Even as a young student, this handsome, smartly-dressed, laid-back and generous American was an Edinburgh curiosity in the 1950s. He befriended another of Edinburgh's most interesting characters.

Richard Demarco was born in 1930 on the west coast of Scotland and was raised in Edinburgh's beachfront suburb of Portobello. Between 1943 and 1949 he attended Holy Cross Academy in Leith, Edinburgh's first Catholic school, where he was a house captain and star rugby and cricket player with an intense fascination with art. His art teacher, Miss Clarke, sat him at the desk used by former celebrity pupil Eduardo Paolozzi. Fame with the Independent Group was still some years off, but Paolozzi had progressed from Edinburgh College of Art to Saint Martin's and the Slade in London. By the time Demarco left school in 1949, his predecessor had already produced his 1947 Pop Art collage *I Was a Rich Man's Plaything* amid Paris's post-war art scene.

Demarco followed in Paolozzi's footsteps, studying illustration and printmaking at Edinburgh College of Art. In his 20s he visited Paris and Rome, completed National Service with the army, commenced a decade-long career as an art teacher at the city's Duns Scotus Academy,[3] and met a certain Jim Haynes quite by chance on the corner of Blackfriars Street and the Royal Mile. Haynes was driving down the Mile in his signature black Volkswagen Beetle one busy Edinburgh Festival night in 1957, when he spotted Demarco and a group of stylish young friends and offered them a ride.

In her study of the Traverse Theatre's first 25 years, the theatre writer Joyce McMillan paints an absorbing picture of this era's scene, as young, vibrant, ambitious, art-adjacent people like Haynes and Demarco threw parties in a slowly loosening-up Edinburgh, to the sound of Sinatra's *Songs for Swinging Lovers*:

> Both are great socialisers, and keen and unapologetic woman-fanciers of the kind that flourished briefly in the window of opportunity between the decline of Victorian morality and the rise of feminism. The lace-curtained limitations on Edinburgh's cultural life – the men-only pubs that close at 9.30 or 10.00, the good restaurants that are few, stuffy, and expensive, the near-total absence of late-night eating and drinking places, the slightly creaky entertainment offered by the Lyceum and Gateway theatres – also cramp their social style. No-one has heard of the swinging '60s, but they are just around the corner.[4]

The pair's social and cultural thirst was more than whetted during the Festival's three weeks, but much like every other local regular – and Demarco is one of the vanishing few who's been every year since 1947 – the hangover-like sense of loss persisted for 49 weeks in business-as-usual Edinburgh. Haynes had a part-time job in the university bookshop and hungrily read novels at Kirknewton, waiting for the next burst of late-night Russian chatter. So, why not run his own bookshop?

Like the rest of the Haynes myth, it's as if he stumbled into his next move. With the decision to become a bookseller made, he sold his Volkswagen and arranged to leave the USAF, collecting a severance payment on the way. Then one day, walking along Charles Street on the Southside he noticed a tired-looking antique shop, stepped inside and offered the elderly woman who ran it £300 to take it off her hands. She accepted, Haynes gave away her remaining stock on the pavement and above the door he fitted an ornamental rhinoceros' head rescued from workmen throwing it away outside the New Club on Princes Street. He would often joke that Hemingway gave it to him, or that Ionesco's play *Rhinoceros* was named after this landmark fitting.

Bespoke new shelves were fitted by a Californian boatbuilder named Red Williams, who Haynes met on a bus and filled with cheap and accessible paperback books. Popularised first by US 'Armed Services Editions' during the Second World War, then as supposedly intellectually second-rate genre books picked up at markets and grocery stores, the paperback was beginning to boom when Haynes' Paperback Bookshop opened in the autumn of 1959. This boom began in the United States, but he was at its vanguard in Britain – apparently the owner of the nation's first dedicated paperback bookshop. He sought out exciting international publishers with challenging new fiction works and obscure textbooks for his bright young student clientele and his reputation spread.

Haynes' bookshop was also a coffee shop, an art gallery and a kind of meeting place and salon for the city's young and cultured people. John Calder, another key player in the Edinburgh Festival's early emergence into the countercultural 1960s, remembers the simple choice of drink as being a key factor in the cosmopolitanism of the Paperback Bookshop:

> There was no cash register, change was kept in a drawer, and Jim could easily be persuaded to lend books to those who could not buy them. They were seldom returned. He also – and this really shocked the local book trade – offered free coffee and tea, and had soft music playing. He was only a business man in so far as he had to take enough money to live and pay publishers: his motivation was enjoyment.[5]

Students, academics, doctors and actors used Haynes' bookshop and even the chairman of the Bank of Scotland was a regular customer. The basement was dug out so he could hold exhibitions of tapestry and pottery, and Demarco staged his first organised show there. In 1961 student Judith MacGregor, who married the future Liberal leader David Steel, had her graduation party at the Paperback.

There were Fringe shows too, beginning with the Scottish philosopher David Hume's 18th century *Dialogues Concerning Natural Religion* in August 1960, which debates the existence of God. The reviews were positive. Later Festival highlights included a 1962 exhibition by the Scots tapestry weaver and Pop Artist Archie Brennan and a well-reviewed if *Three Estates*-aping play about the Scottish Reformation entitled *Ane Tryall of Heretiks*, starring an actor named John Malcolm.

Six months after the Hume play, the Paperback's reputation as a home for the iniquitously alternative was sealed. In 1960, three decades after its completion and almost immediate banning for heavy-duty swearing and forthright descriptions of sex, DH Lawrence's *Lady Chatterley's Lover* was published by paperback imprint Penguin in the UK, an act virtually designed to force a stand-off with the new Obscene Publications Act of 1959.

On 2 November 1960, the jury in the high-profile trial at London's Old Bailey immediately and unanimously declared the book not obscene. It became legal to stock it and Haynes quickly and happily did. On Saturday 4 February 1961, a smart, conservatively-dressed lady named Agnes Cooper walked into the shop and asked if they had a copy. They did, so she bought it and asked Haynes to keep it until she returned. He knew something was up, so he rang a photographer friend, Alan Daiches and asked him to come quickly. Daiches arrived just as Ms Cooper returned with a fireproof oven dish, a pair of coal tongs and a jar of some kind of flammable liquid. She picked the book up with the tongs – in case its sinful touch might corrupt her – and took it outside, where the dish rested on a snow-covered wall. Standing in the winter slush, she lit the book on fire while giving a sermon about the evils of this 'iniquitous document'. Ms Cooper, a 62-year-old former religious missionary to the Belgian Congo who also lived on Charles Street, later said she hadn't read the book, but she knew it to be evil.

Daiches happily snapped away and one of his photographs became a key image of 1960s Edinburgh, as the city's old world met the new: Ms Cooper stands in smart Sunday shoes, coat and hat, while behind her Haynes and friends look nonplussed but amused. Haynes, particularly smart and laid-back in a V-neck sweater, tie and casual suit, half-smiles, but his eyebrows are arched in something like existential puzzlement. The rhinoceros isn't interested.

That week the story made national news across the UK and Allen Lane, the founder of Penguin, sent Haynes a letter of support. The pair later became good friends and beautiful, formerly stuffy Edinburgh was on the map as a city where you didn't just see high art and student revue shows in August, but where dangerous, challenging, sexual ideas and imagery might be found all year round.

* * *

Another high-flying publishing patron of Haynes' was Calder himself, son of a wealthy Scottish brewing heir father and a French-speaking Canadian mother whose family had links to the whisky trade. He was born in Montreal in 1927, on the anniversary of Robert Burns' birthday and raised between Canada, boarding school in North Yorkshire and the Calder family estate in the hills between Perth and Kinross.

In London at the turn of the 1950s, this son of the Establishment threw parties attended by Muriel Spark, went to pub poetry readings by Dylan

Thomas and befriended TS Eliot. While he worked in his family's timber business, he also invested some money in a friend's publishing venture, which grew through new iterations into a very respected operation under Calder. His list covered translations of works by Tolstoy, Chekhov and Dostoevsky, a number of sensitive books which discussed McCarthyism in America – setting him in early opposition to the censors – and from 1959 the early novels of Samuel Beckett, returned to print after the success of his play *Waiting for Godot*.

Calder also briefly owned a printing press, which published the film magazine *Sight & Sound* and the arts periodicals *Ballet* and *Opera*. George Lascelles, the 7th Earl of Harewood and director of the Royal Opera House until 1953, was involved with these titles and he and Calder became friends. As his 20s bled into his 30s, Calder was a high-living *bon viveur* who liked skiing, the company of women, parties populated by names that could be dropped and an enthusiastic soaking-up of international culture.

By 1960 he was publishing the plays of the French Absurdist playwright Eugène Ionesco, including the translation of the previous year's allegory for the rise of fascism *Rhinoceros*, as staged at London's Royal Court with Laurence Olivier and Joan Plowright under the direction of Orson Welles.[6] Another favourite was the French novelist and playwright Marguerite Duras, who was on the crest of a wave after her screenplay for Alain Resnais' classic of French New Wave cinema *Hiroshima, mon amour* received an Academy Awards nomination in 1960.[7]

In late 1960, Calder brought Duras to Britain alongside Nathalie Sarraute and Alain Robbe-Grillet for a package tour of talks by leading French writers. By the end of the two-week tour, Robbe-Grillet had returned to France but Duras and Sarraute made it to the small final session at the Paperback Bookshop. It wasn't the evening at the Paperback which stayed in Calder's mind after the tour, though – it was an earlier night in Coventry, where a packed, 800-strong audience of mostly teens and 20-somethings had hung on the authors' every word.

Even Calder was surprised literature could generate such excitement, as he told Lord Harewood when they dined a few weeks later at Overton's, an upmarket fish restaurant on St James Street in London. The Edinburgh International Festival's office in London was also on St James Street and Harewood was now the Festival's director following the departure of Robert Ponsonby – and Calder was here with a proposal. What if a world conference of writers could be held to tap into this enthusiasm for ideas and debate? And, what if it were to be held as part of the Edinburgh International Festival?

* * *

Of all the figures involved in the Edinburgh International Festival's early life, none was as close to the British Establishment as George Lascelles. He succeeded his father as Earl of Harewood in 1947, the year the Festival began, and was admitted to the House of Lords as Lord Harewood in 1956. The first grandchild of King George v through his mother Mary and Page of Honour at the 1937 coronation of his uncle King George vi, the Eton and Cambridge-schooled Harewood was firmly of the elite.[8] Yet he wasn't entirely detached, in his passions or his experience.

A captain in the Grenadier Guards during the Second World War, he was injured in battle and captured at Monte Corno in Italy in 1944, becoming one of the most valuable prisoners of war at the infamous Colditz camp. Only the actions of an ss general who realised that the war was lost and he shouldn't add to his crimes saved him from execution on Hitler's order. In 1961, the year he took over at the Festival, Harewood became president of his beloved Leeds United Football Club, while his love of opera came from a real enthusiast's perspective.

A regular Festivalgoer, Harewood was approached about the festival's directorship in the autumn of 1959 by Edinburgh's city treasurer Duncan Weatherstone and Lord Provost-elect Jack Dunbar, heir to his family's Leith-based soft drinks firm. Uncertain at first, with a comfortable role at the Leeds Festival, he thought the International Festival now lacked the sense of expectation he had felt in its earlier years.

Incredibly, Harewood actually had to travel to Edinburgh by sleeper train to interview for the post before the Executive Committee group, headed by outgoing Provost Ian Johnson-Gilbert, although there can't have been any doubt he was going to succeed. He travelled to Dalmeny and celebrated his appointment with a century-old magnum of family friend Lord Rosebery's wine, before heading south to start work at St James Street.

Harewood's focus during his tenure was on creating a sense of spectacle to snare critics' attention and build a new buzz around August in Edinburgh. One hope was that the city's operatic facilities would be upgraded from the chamber-adequate Kings Theatre to a hall big enough for the finest opera companies in the world. The 3,000-capacity, Art Deco-styled Playhouse on Greenside Place – built as a super-cinema in 1929, with the prolific Glaswegian cinema architect John Fairweather taking inspiration from the Roxy Theatre in New York – was the building he wanted, but the Council vetoed a potential bill of £50,000 for renovations.

Instead, Harewood's first festival in 1961 aimed to create an attention-grabbing classical programme. For the tenth anniversary of the great Austrian composer Arnold Schoenberg's death, his work was retrospectively celebrated, from the London Symphony Orchestra under Leopold Stokowski and the Scottish National Orchestra at the Usher Hall, to Amsterdam's Concertgebouw Wind Quintet at the Freemason's Hall. Harewood was excited that he could programme 25 of the composer's works into the Festival, but that its versatility meant anyone visiting could find plenty to amuse them without needing to take in one.

The Covent Garden Opera returned with a strong programme that included *Lucia Di Lammermoor* and *A Midsummer Night's Dream* – directed by Franco Zeffirelli and John Gielgud, respectively – and big strides were made in the other arts. Aware that theatre was seen as a poor relation to music at the International Festival, Harewood arranged funding for newly-commissioned plays including Nigel Dennis' *August for the People*, starring Rex Harrison and Rachel Roberts, at the Lyceum. The English Stage Company presented *Luther*, John Osborne's Albert Finney-starring study of the Protestant reformer, at the Empire Theatre on Nicholson Street.

Waverley Market, a covered Victorian structure between Princes Street and Waverley Station dating from the 1870s, with a beautiful roof garden and daily fruit and vegetable stalls which were regularly displaced by flower shows and funfairs, was pressed into use as a makeshift art gallery. An exhibition of 230 sculptures by Jacob Epstein, who'd died two years before, was a big popular hit, drawing 125,000 visitors in four weeks. The idiosyncratic male nude *Adam*, which Harewood purchased from the basement of Louis Tussaud's waxworks in Blackpool and later permanently displayed at his Yorkshire estate, was the centrepiece and the exhibition began a surge of posthumous recognition for Epstein. The poet and playwright Tom McGrath visited on a day trip from Glasgow, a formative experience in his own appreciation of art.

A weird footnote in Harewood's first programme, meanwhile, is mouthwatering to contemporary music fans now. A single night's showcase of electronic music at the Freemason's Hall was presented by the pioneering electronic musician Daphne Oram and featured 'Studie II' by the German composer Karlheinz Stockhausen, the first electronic music score ever published and an explicit rejection of Schoenberg's 12-tone composition technique. Harewood's debut Festival was so full, that he told Calder he could have until 1962 to prepare his conference.

Calder knew that Edinburgh's deep heritage was in literature, more than music or drama, and he believed that authors could provide as much onstage entertainment as other live forms.

Harewood allowed him to gather up to a hundred writers from across the globe on one condition – that the event not lose any of the Festival's money. Calder began contacting foreign embassies and consulates, asking them to sound out their finest national writers to attend.

Oddly, given the success of the tour that first inspired Calder, the French embassy reacted with a shrug, uncertain any of their writers would bother giving up their summer holiday for a work trip to Scotland, so the nation wasn't represented. The south of France was also of more interest to the great Scottish author Compton Mackenzie, nearing his 80th birthday, who chose to holiday there instead.

Yet Calder built a compelling programme. He enlisted Haynes and the extremely well-connected Sonia Orwell, widow of George, to assist and took *The Scotsman*'s arts editor Magnus Magnusson and BBC producer Finlay MacDonald for a wheel-greasing lunch at the Doric Tavern on Market Street, opposite Waverley Station. Along the road from the printers' entrance to the *Scotsman* building, the Doric in those days was a regular watering hole for journalists and intellectuals.

The University of Edinburgh's grand McEwan Hall was booked. A rotunda-like amphitheatre around the corner from the Paperback, it was built by the Alloa-born politician and brewer William McEwan, owner of the Fountain Brewery on Fountainbridge, and passed to the University in 1897. With seating for almost 2,500 and used mainly for graduation ceremonies, its dome's interior has an appropriate inscribed quotation from the Book of Proverbs in the Bible's Old Testament: 'Wisdom is the principal thing, therefore get wisdom, and with all thy getting, get understanding. Exalt her and she shall bring thee to honour'.

A programme for the conference came together around the loose theme of 'The Novel Today'. Across five afternoon sessions, groups of writers would assemble and debate a daily topic – 'Differences of Approach', 'Scottish Writing Today', 'Is Commitment Necessary?', 'Censorship Today' and 'The Future of the Novel'. Haynes enlisted a team of literary enthusiasts and bookshop customers, nicknamed the 'Charles Street Irregulars', to meet arriving authors and transfer them to accommodation in hotels and guesthouses across the city.

Meanwhile, the canny Calder found a novel way to drum up public interest. With the letters pages of newspapers typically groaning with views that attacked or defended the Festival, he sent fake letters in which whipped up both support for and opinion against novelists and their literature. 'The correspondence columns, which were much read in Edinburgh, were an excellent way of getting free advertising,'[9] he believed.

Excitement was building, although Calder suspected the International Festival saw his event as a quirky sideshow and many old-guard writers – Nigel Tranter, for one – believed there was little hope audiences would be interested in paying to hear writers who were usually quite happy to talk for free. The seating and miking-up of the stage was arranged so the authors could more easily debate, not simply address.

After a grand private house party in the New Town's Circus Place on Sunday night for all attending, then a buffet lunch with copious amounts of tongue-loosening wine on the Monday, Calder arrived at McEwan Hall to discover the lone box office member of staff was overwhelmed. A thousand people were queuing, with many more waiting to hire headphones for translation between the three official conference languages – English, French and German. The conference began half an hour late and soon its chair, the journalist and broadcaster Malcolm Muggeridge, was adjudicating between the great Indian writer Khushwant Singh, who authored the Partition novel *Train to Pakistan* and the gay, former Bletchley Park codebreaker Angus Wilson in a heated debate about whether love between men was a valid form of love at all.

In 1962, when gay sex was still a criminal act in the United Kingdom, such a discussion in public was scandalous. And there was more to come with the promise of Henry Miller's appearance, his sex and swearing-infused semi-autobiography *Tropic of Cancer* playing a similar, censorship-smashing role in America to *Lady Chatterley's Lover* in the UK. Welcomed with a tribute from Colin MacInnes, the chronicler of young 1950s London, Miller created controversy for unexpected reasons, as he declared he was here because he wanted to see Edinburgh and not discuss the novel.

Lines were drawn between those who argued for and against total artistic freedom versus censorship, and others who debated the effect of colonialism on literature. There was talk of the literary situation in Yugoslavia and behind the Iron Curtain, even though no writers from Russia, Poland or Hungary were permitted to attend by officials in their own countries. Their absence was a talking point, but the influential American critic Mary McCarthy paid tribute to Nabokov in his absence. Besides, there were 70 other writers to get behind – or not – in the following days.

The second day was designated for Scottish writers and busy with guests, including the rabble-rousing old communist and Scottish nationalist – and extraordinary poet – Hugh MacDiarmid, who had been a thorn in the side of the International Festival at its inception 15 years before. Also appearing were the novelist, poet and dramatist Sydney Goodsir Smith, whose play *The Wallace* was produced by the Festival in 1960, the once-censored feminist writer Naomi Mitchison and the poet and – four decades after this conference – first Scottish national Makar, Edwin Morgan.

Also appearing was the Glasgow-born *enfant terrible* Alexander Trocchi, who moved to Paris and then the United States a decade before, widening his literary circles even as many believed he'd eroded his own Scottish identity. As editor of the Parisian literary magazine *Merlin* and a writer of erotica for the hugely important 20th century French publisher Maurice Girodias' Olympia Press, Trocchi moved in the same international literary circles as Miller,[10] Jean-Paul Sartre and Terry Southern and was often billed as the first publisher of Ionesco, Beckett and Genet.

He was also adjacent to the Beat Generation and involved with the Situationist International and his most recent novel, 1960's *Cain's Book*, caused a furore by detailing his own heroin addiction in New York. Trocchi lived for 22 more years after the Writers' Conference and never wrote another novel, but on Tuesday 21 August 1962, his proximity to MacDiarmid provoked arguably the most infamous and controversial exchange in 20th century Scottish literature. Other writers were there – in fact, Norman Mailer chose the occasion to announce the birth of his daughter Kate three days before, with his third wife Lady Jeanne Campbell, daughter of the Duke of Argyll – yet history remembers the day for the dramatic headline that accompanied Magnus Magnusson's report in *The Scotsman*: 'Scottish Writers Stage Their Civil War'.

MacDiarmid, 70 years old, proudly Scottish in his kilt and unswerving in his stated belief that poetry was the superior written art form, was on home turf. The Glasgow University graduate Trocchi, on the other hand, had been away from Scotland for a decade. Although the intellectual tussle was painted as being MacDiarmid's firmly-rooted Scottish nationalism versus Trocchi's outward-looking internationalism, there might also have been personal antagonism between the pair.

MacDiarmid's natural habitat through the 1950s was Milne's Bar on the junction of Rose Street and Hanover Street, particularly the snug basement howff, around which the Scottish literary scene orbited. Nicknamed the 'Little Kremlin' for the political leanings of most of those involved, MacDiarmid often bent the ear of the likes of Sydney Goodsir Smith, Sorley MacLean and Norman MacCaig in there.

It was at Milne's in late 1961 that *The Guardian* journalist Alexander Neish introduced his then-interviewee Alexander Trocchi to MacDiarmid, a little over half of MacDiarmid's age, as the century's greatest Scottish novelist since Lewis Grassic Gibbon. Did MacDiarmid bristle at the young upstart? Neish recalled the meeting as cold – apparently MacDiarmid privately felt he had been barred from *Merlin* by its former editor.

In the McEwan Hall, the literary historian and writer David Daiches had replaced Muggeridge as chair, the jugs on the tables had been filled with whisky – which might help explain how things turned out – and MacDiarmid made a statement after niceties were out of the way. It railed against Scottish writers' perceived deference to the language of the English over their own, and took aim at the printed press, politicians, religious leaders and the

Scottish National Party. The latter had bounced MacDiarmid from their membership for his communism, but the Communist Party were equally unwilling to accept his Scottish nationalism. The Croat writer Petar Šegedin mentioned to Calder later that afternoon that he was surprised to find it wasn't just Yugoslavia which had nationalism.

Trocchi, who had taken heroin half an hour before proceedings began, took what bait was offered. The state of Scottish literature, he said, was:

[T]urgid, petty, provincial, stale, cold-porridge, bible-class nonsense. Of what is interesting in the last 20 years of Scottish writing, I've written it all. [MacDiarmid was] an old so-and-so, with a few rather old-fashioned quaintnesses that are not of my generation, [whose] hatred of the novel is just too crummy to be commented upon.

MacDiarmid made a not-very-veiled attack on Trocchi in turn, when he dismissed 'lesbianism, homosexuality and matters of that kind' as not fit for contemplation by serious writers.

'I'm only interested in lesbianism and sodomy!' snapped back Trocchi, before embarking on a defence of individualism over nationalism.

'I want no uniformity…' returned MacDiarmid.

'I want no uniformity either,' snapped back Trocchi, still digging, this time at his elder's dress. 'Not even a kilt'.

Edwin Morgan, Trocchi's tutor at Glasgow until his student overdosed on Benzedrine and dropped out, tried to move the conversation towards a gentler acceptance of internationalism; Muriel Spark teased MacDiarmid; Daiches attempted to calm the younger writer, although Trocchi told him if he wanted to get him out he'd have to throw him out. Sydney Goodsir Smith, drunk since lunch, nevertheless lucidly noted that the discussion appeared a somewhat stupid one.

Later, Trocchi said that MacDiarmid called him 'cosmopolitan scum' in private, an insult which has reverberated down the years.

Calder provided a post-mortem on the affair:

[MacDiarmid] was a natural enemy of Calvinist conformity and middle-class values, but underneath the rugged peasant exterior lurked an old-fashioned, often narrow-minded puritan.… Trocchi had lived in Paris, New York and California, advocated and belonged to the hippie lifestyle, and had experimented with every kind of drug.… They attacked each other with vehemence, although basically they were on the same side.[11]

Combining soap opera and politics, the day's events made national news across the country and established Trocchi as a new and uncompromising literary voice, although he couldn't capitalise on his fame. Rejected by MacDiarmid's Scottish followers, Trocchi didn't write another novel between *Cain's Book* in 1960 and his death in 1984. He carried the barest cult reputation in his home country until the 1990s, when his writing was reassessed after the emergence of the similarly inclined Irvine Welsh and its republication by the Rebel Inc imprint.

Trocchi's biographer Andrew Murray Scott wrote many years later that his subject was by no means opposed to Scottish Independence, nor the idea of a Scottish Parliament as an antidote to the British Establishment, but that he didn't think either would improve society much. He attempted rapprochement by letter with MacDiarmid, but his overtures were as failed as the cancelled 1964 Edinburgh Poetry Conference they were timed to coincide with.

The next day at the Writers' Conference of 1962, the subject was 'commitment' and MacDiarmid tried to claim he was the most politically committed writer on the stage. This time the chorus against, from writers who had travelled from Africa, the Caribbean and America, was more or less absolute.

* * *

The other major event of the Writers' Conference was Thursday's discussion on censorship, an already loaded issue in those days of societal change, rock 'n' roll and the post-McCarthy depths of the Cold War. What was otherwise an informative day's discussion, was notable as the moment a European audience began to take notice of a challenging and experimental new author named William Burroughs.

Although by this point Burroughs, the son of a well-off St Louis family, was nearly 50 and had published his key novel *Naked Lunch* three years before, he was still very much an unknown. During the 1950s he lived in Tangier and then Paris, where his literary experimentation matched his experimentation with hard drugs. Calder met Burroughs in Paris and when the author moved to London in 1960 they became even more friendly through Marion Lobbenberg, when she let her Kensington flat to him. With Calder & Boyars, Lobbenberg was soon to be Calder's business partner and Burroughs' publisher under her married name.

Calder invited Burroughs to the conference over a spring lunch in London and he accepted, fatefully sharing the same plane to Edinburgh as Trocchi, who he befriended during the journey. Burroughs had kicked heroin in

London, but Trocchi was still a user and they were lodged together at the home of a young Edinburgh doctor named Andrew Boddy, who wrote medicinal prescriptions for Trocchi. The writers became close and enduring friends, although Burroughs tried to keep his own heroin habit more low-key.

At the Conference, Burroughs also met his admirer Norman Mailer and made an even more impressed fan of Mary McCarthy. She spoke up early in the week for *Naked Lunch*, comparing Burroughs' words to the Action Painting of the late titan of American art Jackson Pollock. Amid the censorship debate, the reserved Miller offered some impassioned words against the business of the censor and Mailer put forward the view that the purpose of controlling what people consumed was to prevent their spirit going soft in case of war. Burroughs' ideas were even more evolved, explaining his belief that the entire, all-pervasive adverting industry is built upon the manipulation of unfulfilled sexual longing.

As the week drew to a close, Burroughs explained compositional techniques such as the cut-up and the fold-in. The former, borrowed from his painter friend Brion Gysin and recently used in Burroughs' *The Soft Machine*, involved literally cutting text up and reassembling it; the latter, folding two unconnected pages of existing text together to be read as a 'new' work.

The delegates were enthralled or disgusted by this non-traditional approach, and the final day's talk on 'The Future of the Novel' essentially became a trial over whether Burroughs really was the future of literature, or just a canny charlatan.

Mailer summed up the mood by appearing completely opposed to this style of writing, but thoroughly impressed by Burroughs' eloquence in defending it.

This strange new writer's words were reported around the world, his American publisher ordered more crates of *Naked Lunch* and his road to long-lasting notoriety was paved as a result of Edinburgh.

The first and only Edinburgh Writer's Conference ended the way it had begun, with another private party at the same plush New Town townhouse on Royal Circus, this time on the night of Friday 24 August 1962. The drunken revels rolled on until 4am, with much of the great and good of the literary world in attendance. Passes were made, discussions no doubt got heated and Burroughs later started a rumour that a gang of feral youths had beaten a helpless poet on the street before he found sanctuary in the house. In fact, recalled Calder, the 'poet' was the great translator of Russian literature Max Hayward, whose charming of Sonia Orwell apparently caused a drunk and belligerent Norman Mailer to remove him from the flat and throw him down the stairs. The poor, bloodied poet spotted by Orwell was Hayward making his dazed re-entry and trying to recover his drink.

Mary McCarthy wrote to her friend Hannah Arendt a month later:

I went to a Conference on the Novel in the middle of August – a fantastic affair, did you read anything about it? The most striking fact was the number of lunatics both on the platform and in the public. One young woman novelist was released temporarily from a mental hospital in order to attend the Conference, and she was one of the milder cases. I confess I enjoyed it enormously.[12]

Calder took an early flight to a family funeral in London the morning after the party. When he returned on Sunday, the literati had gone. He spent the next week soaking up the Festival in a daze, popping into the office to meet an elated Harewood. The Conference had been a huge success, generating fascinated column inches across the nation. What did Calder want to do next year?

A drama conference, wondered Calder? He was told to begin planning immediately.

*   *   *

Whenever one of the nightly parties was happening at the Writers' Conference, the Edinburgh socialite and fixer Haynes was never far away from its organisation. By this point he had bought into folk club the Howff at 369 High Street, right in the heart of the Old Town, with music promoter Roy Guest, who later went on to work for the Beatles' manager Brian Epstein and book Simon and Garfunkel's first London appearance. In the months after the Conference, Haynes was also among an ensemble of people desperate to give Edinburgh some kind of year-round artistic presence, who between them conspired, almost by accident, to craft one of the Edinburgh Festival's most significant and famous ongoing cultural legacies.

This story begins with the unlikely and not entirely artistic figure of Tom Mitchell, a Cumbrian farmer whose unspecified international work for the Ministry of Agriculture led him into meetings with Soviet premiere Nikita Khrushchev and a friendship with Pablo Picasso. He was one of British Rugby's most important figures – chairman of Workington Town, manager of the victorious British Lions tour to Australia in 1958 and briefly chairman of the Rugby League – and he also happened to spend a fair amount of time in Edinburgh, where he kept a flat overlooking the Meadows.

As he moved in fashionable circles, Mitchell inevitably came into contact with Richard Demarco's crowd, among them an Art College contemporary of Demarco's named Pete McGinn, whom Mitchell met in the Laigh and hired to caretake his flat while he was away. During the great British thirst of the 1960s for slum clearance and modernist post-war development, the tenements of the Old Town had become fair game for demolition and McGinn happened to show Mitchell one of these. It was a five-story, 400-year-old former flophouse and brothel named Kelly's Paradise – nicknamed Hell's Kitchen – in James Court, down an alley off the Royal Mile's Lawnmarket, in the shadow of Edinburgh Castle.

McGinn convinced Mitchell of a plan to turn the building into artists' studios, but once the businessman bought the place for a then-meagre £300, it stalled. Mitchell had the compact main room on the first floor cleared for use as the Sphinx Club during the festival of 1962 and Demarco heard some students from Cambridge University Theatre Company were looking for a venue. It was Cambridge's first official year in Edinburgh and they turned up mob-handed. Their 50-strong crew's main production was a Trevor Nunn-directed version of Ibsen's *Brand* at the Methodist Church's grand Central Hall just off Tollcross, but a pair of eager young students named John Cleese and Graham Chapman wanted to play comedy instead. They put on an early-evening coffee club cabaret at the Sphinx, and Henry Miller and Laurence Durrell both took time out of the Writer's Conference to attend.

Aware through Demarco and Haynes of what was happening at James Court, the great and good of Edinburgh's artistic landscape – John Calder among them – had taken an interest, not necessarily because of anything to do with theatre. 'Books and paintings and music and good food and company', were at least as important to [Demarco and Haynes]',[13] wrote Joyce McMillan. Instead it fell to John Malcolm, the actor who had just starred in *Ane Tryall of Heretiks* at the Paperback, to visit Mitchell as he recovered from typhoid in hospital and suggest a Fringe-style theatre could fill the space vacated by the Sphinx.

Costs would be saved by ripping seats out of the recently-closed New Palace Cinema, further down the Mile and opposite John Knox's House. A restaurant and bar upstairs could help pay the theatre's way. Entry should be by private membership rather than public admission charge, meaning the Lord Chamberlain's theatrical censorship wouldn't apply. The narrow, eight-foot high, 15-foot wide, 60-capacity room must have a non-traditional shape by necessity. Terry Lane, Malcolm's recently-recruited accomplice and old colleague from Pitlochry Festival Theatre, suggested naming the place after this shape; a transverse stage.

Except Lane got the terminology wrong and by the time he realised his error, the new theatre had already opened with a double-bill of Sartre's *Huis Clos* and Arrabal's *Orisons* on 2 January 1963, under the name the Traverse Theatre. Arguably no other venue has become more synonymous with the Edinburgh Festival in the following six decades. Before long Haynes took over its artistic directorship from Lane, but first he was to become involved with Calder's next conference. Calder was now a celebrity on the local arts scene, thanks to friends on *The Scotsman* including Magnus Magnusson and literary editor Bill Watson. He was invited to attend the Prix Formentor's earliest meetings – in Salzburg, not Mallorca, thanks to General Franco's illiberal displeasure with the whole thing – and speak to domestic Rotary Clubs on behalf of the Homosexual Law Reform Society.

At the turn of the 1960s, meanwhile, theatre was undergoing a renaissance internationally. In the UK this took the form of the Angry Young Men, led by John Osbourne and his 1956 Royal Court play *Look Back in Anger*, whose work was characterised by disillusionment with traditional British society. Calder thought a bit of this – allied with discussion of expressionism, surrealism, Brecht and the Theatre of the Absurd – would be perfect for drumming up more of the headline-grabbing controversy the Writers Conference had inspired. He reenlisted Haynes as his local fixer and a longlist of drama specialists was presented to Harewood. Although he wasn't Calder's first choice, *The Guardian's* outspoken and eminently recognisable critic Kenneth Tynan was immediately chosen.

Both co-organisers were allowed to indulge their own preferences and between them they knocked a very respectable line-up into shape, up to 130 from the previous year's 70 attendees. Calder invited Trocchi back and finally persuaded Robbe-Grillet and Duras over from France, while Tynan was fond of a small-time Hollywood cinema friend or two. There were big international playwrights including Edward Albee and Eugene Ionesco; an exciting array of Brits including Arnold Wesker, JB Priestley, Harold Pinter, Wolf Mankowitz, Joan Littlewood and John Mortimer; and great actors like Alec Guinness and the recently-married Laurence Olivier and Joan Plowright. Guinness and Plowright were appearing in Edinburgh that year, respectively in Ionesco's *Exit the King* at the Lyceum and George Bernard Shaw's *Saint Joan* at the Assembly Hall.

There were also Scottish Edinburgh Festival regulars, including Robert McLellan, Duncan Macrae and Moultrie Kelsall, as well as national personalities such as Peter Cook and David Frost. An ominous taste of things to come, however, arrived when Duncan Weatherstone, since 1962 Edinburgh's new Lord Provost, summoned Calder to his office and forbade him from bringing the controversial American comedian Lenny Bruce to Scotland. Calder recalled the preemptive dressing-down:

> I want no more talk about homosexuality and so on. If there is, I'll shut you down. And another thing. Don't go talking to the press about this. If you do, I'll cancel the conference.[14]

There was also discord between Calder and his co-organiser. Where the former wanted a public forum for debate about the issues of the day, allied with an educational sense of theatrical mystery unravelling, Tynan wanted the real heated debates to happen behind closed doors, an idea that almost came to pass. Calder wrote:

> The new upstarts from the red-brick universities were making waves, but the theatre-going traditional middle classes, who patronised Shaftesbury Avenue, didn't like them on both class and entertainment grounds. I wanted to educate, whereas Tynan wanted a forum for his chums, and an elitist prestige for himself. The better I knew him, the less I took him seriously.[15]

Under Haynes' management, the behind-the-scenes literary debauchery of the previous year was recreated with a welcoming party at a doctor's house in Murrayfield and more late-night, invite-only events at the flat on Circus Place. Haynes' flat on Great King Street became another hub – of drink and regrettable liaisons at night, according to Calder, who moved in to avoid the daily trip from his Perthshire estate by ferry or lengthy drive via Kincardine, in the days before a road bridge spanned the Forth. During the day was for hard work, though, very capably assisted by Sheila Colvin, who was one of the crew involved with the Traverse.

With the conference shifted to the International Festival's third week, from 2 to 7 September, the first day, chaired by Priestley, had little theme beyond a vague prompt about who bears most responsibility for a play – actor, director or playwright? It went badly. Pre-prepared statements were read and a bristling Tynan's angry opening remarks about Brecht's Berliner Ensemble being refused visas appeared to be the highlight.[16]

Calder cringed at the opening reviews but, with Harewood busy elsewhere and Tynan chastened, he began to rearrange things to recreate the adversarial nature of the year before. The next few days brought debates on the threat to theatre from other media, the value of state subsidy, Lord Chamberlain's censorship and – inevitably – nationalism, although the latter became a mild discussion more about translation than territory. Reports told of passionless discussions and a disinterested audience.

And then, on the final day, the Happening happened.

In attendance at the conference was the pioneering performance artist Alan Kaprow, who had devised the artistic 'Happening' in the late 1950s, taking influence from his tutor, the composer John Cage. An unstructured and unscripted sequence of events, which made a stage of the entire space and sometimes participants of the audience, a Happening was an experimental new form that blended art and theatre – precisely the kind of thing Calder wanted to present to an inquisitive Edinburgh audience. He scheduled one for the Saturday afternoon, as the conference's finale.

At first it was Joan Littlewood who put herself forward to stage it; 1963 had already been one of the most significant of her career, with the Theatre Workshop's controversial satire on conflict and Britain's role in it *Oh, What a Lovely War!* debuting at their Theatre Royal in Stratford in March. It transferred to the West End's Wyndham's Theatre in June, but only after Princess Margaret, a fan, intervened to stop the Lord Chamberlain's ban. Her ambitious plan involved workmen digging up the floor of the McEwan Hall during the event and something involving a nude model. She hired a 19-year-old woman named Anna Kesselaar for this job, the daughter of South African migrants who worked in the office of Basil Spence's architectural firm and did some photographic modelling at Edinburgh College of Art.

Yet, business in London called and when Littlewood had to pull out, other theatre makers – including Edward Albee – tried to devise something instead. Ultimately, the task fell to the American performance artist and 'Action Theatre' devotee Ken Dewey, then living in Paris. His piece was named *In Memory of Big Ed* by Scottish artist Mark Boyle, who was invited to help stage the work by Dewey after the American artist saw Boyle's work at the Traverse Theatre Gallery. It began with the critic and playwright Charles Marowitz giving a dry lecture on Beckett, when he was suddenly interrupted by a shouting, argumentative interloper in the audience; the playwright Charles Lewson, co-creator of the Happening.

Lewson invaded the stage and wrested the microphone from Marowitz, then a cacophony of bagpipes, discordant organ music and formless tape chatter created a disorientating soundtrack. An ornamental bust smashed to the floor, the American film actor Carroll Baker, star of *Baby Doll* and the controversial *Something Wild*, clambered through the audience in a silver catsuit and Mark Boyle's heavily-pregnant wife and collaborator Joan Hills wandered across the stage commenting on the events to her young sons.

Anna Kesselaar, already paid four pounds by Demarco on behalf of Littlewood, had been retained. The conference organisers later recounted her briefly being wheeled across the back of the stage on a trolley, naked from the waist up. At least one tabloid press report claimed – incorrectly – that she performed a striptease on the balcony, in full view of everyone, before being wrapped in a plastic raincoat and bundled away.

It was the first Happening ever to take place in the UK, but there was one more to come that day – while the audience had been sitting indoors, at last engrossed by some part of the week's proceedings, Kaprow had mounds of car tyres dumped at the door, which they had to climb over to exit as oil drums were hammered around them. Then the entire conference delegation was bussed to Calder's Ledlanet estate in Perthshire for a triumphant, alcohol-fueled party which went on all night.

By the next morning, he was the most notorious man in the country.

* * *

It's difficult to overstate the frankly apocalyptic levels of prudishness unleashed by the words 'naked from the waist up' in 1963, especially when there were newspaper photographers present who were all too willing to take snaps of Kesselaar backstage and show them to the Lord Provost. Calder and Harewood, both in attendance, thought the whole thing had been taken in amused, if baffled, spirit by the audience and that's certainly how they felt about it. At the time, Kesselaar described the whole thing as 'a giggle'.

Lord Provost Duncan Weatherstone, told about the events second-hand by reporters eager for a story, got his condemnation in early. He railed in the papers such irresponsibility and vulgarity. There was a vaguely conciliatory tone among the sternness as he suggested Edinburgh would continue to support the arts, but the freighted message was clear: the Festival had overstepped the mark and it was on notice.

In fact, the Provost wasn't alone in his dismay, although some other critics objected on purely theatrical terms. The Scottish actor Duncan Macrae called Dewey out for 'baloney' onstage immediately after the Happening, while Tynan's retrospective essay in the *Observer* a week later recalled how, sitting alongside Yugoslav theatre makers on the day, he felt embarrassment for the blow against social realist theatre which this spectacle represented. Although Littlewood and Trocchi were wildly supportive.

Elsewhere, a puritanical section of the Scottish public who considered moral guardianship their duty rose up to make complaints to the police and both Calder and Kesselaar – now nicknamed 'Lady MacChatterley' – were charged; the latter with acting in a 'shameless and indecent manner', and Calder with facilitating her. The trial began on 9 December 1963. Represented by the lawyer, socialite and later Tory MP Nicholas Fairbairn, the pair were helped by the testimony of Dewey, Duncan Macrae, the playwright Robert McLellan, BBC producer on the day David Jones and an unnamed housewife from Fife who attended the conference on the Saturday and approved of it.

Kesselaar was found not guilty, leaving Calder with no case to answer – yet, there were repercussions. Calder became *persona non grata* with the Lord Provost and any future conferences were vetoed, beginning with the proposed 1964 International Poetry Conference.[17] In the months after 1963's conference Calder founded his own Ledlanet Nights festival near Kinross instead, which ran for a decade, and he continued to be a significant figure in British publishing, instigating a trial in 1966 over Hubert Selby Jr's *Last Exit to Brooklyn* which represented a major victory against literary censorship. In years to come, his Drama Conference assistant Sheila Colvin became his third wife and associate director of the Edinburgh International Festival.

Harewood – between these events, murmuring criticism of his esoteric musical choices and the news he was expecting a child as the result of an affair – was gone before long, penning a resignation letter in 1964 which the Lord Provost was to accept in the event of his divorce. His final programmed festival was in 1965, but he went on to high-profile directorships with the Royal Opera House (again), the English National Opera and the Adelaide Festival. Calder believed Harewood's biggest mistake was letting the councillors call him George, rather than reminding them he was the Queen's cousin with the formal 'Lord Harewood'. The parting, as Harewood had it, was amicable.

In 2012, ahead of an event at the Festival to celebrate the 50th anniversary of the Writers' Conference, Anna Kesselaar finally spoke out about her experience to *The Scotsman*'s arts correspondent Tim Cornwell; about how Spence sacked her after the conference 'in a very nice way', how her boyfriend found out about it when he discovered her picture pinned up in a hut in Lapland on a Merchant Navy tour and how attempts were made by the authorities to take away her young son. She fled to London.

'I did it for art, and £4,' she said, noting that was a week's wages and she was a young single mother. In reference to the attitudes of certain sections of Edinburgh society at the time, she said, 'when you have a morality that dictates, you are in trouble'.[18] Her grandchildren still teased her about what she got up to half a century earlier.

The fiery debates of the Writers Conference and the boundary-challenging Happening of the Drama Conference were seismic events of their era, in the latter case front page news across the world. The 1960s didn't involve as many moral bets being off as those who build the decade's legend might suggest, but for all the social change that did occur before 1970, these weeks in Edinburgh provided plenty of grease for the wheels.

In the face of attempts to put a halt to Edinburgh being a stage for such change, the Festival as a whole found an ally in Bailie Tom McGregor, the judge who tried Kesselaar. He remarked upon the sensationalism and hypocrisy of certain sections of the press in building up the story, and speculated that they may have done the Festival lasting harm.

SPOTLIGHT

Rosencrantz and Guildenstern Are Dead (1966)

THE PLAY HAD no substance beyond its own terms, beyond its
apparent situation. It was about two courtiers in a Danish castle.
Two nonentities surrounded by intrigue, given very little information
and much of that false. It had nothing to do with the condition
of modern man or the decline of metaphysics... It was about two
blokes, right?[1]

Tom Stoppard was talking to *New York* magazine in 1977, about the work
that made his considerable name in theatre, *Rosencrantz and Guildenstern
Are Dead*.

The first appearance of his great extrapolation from the work of
Shakespeare was at the Cranston Street Hall church annexe, just off
Edinburgh's Royal Mile, the catalyst for the career of one of the 20th
century's great playwrights. Before long, it also helped to cement the Fringe's
greatest legend, which persists to this day – that you can appear in Edinburgh
as a complete unknown and leave the city an international star.

For many years, the '*Rosencrantz and Guildenstern* effect' was the widely
accepted term for the kind of bolt-from-the-blue, career-making fame that
every producer, playwright, director or actor bringing work to Edinburgh
dreamt of. When Stoppard's play arrived in Edinburgh in 1966, the
playwright wasn't exactly a complete unknown, yet the dream dynamic was
all there: student company brings promising new play to Edinburgh with
no fanfare whatsoever; one single good review catches the right attention;
success, fame and riches follow.

To add to the chance nature of the play's success, it wasn't even Stoppard's
main concern when it arrived in Edinburgh. Instead, the very same week saw
the release of his debut novel *Lord Malquist and Mr Moon*, which followed the
dandyish, out-of-time aristocrat Malquist on an adventure around Swinging
London of the 1960s, accompanied by his biographer Moon. Stoppard was
most excited for the book's publication, but in the meantime he headed to
Edinburgh to see how the Oxford Theatre Group's rehearsals were going.

Stoppard celebrated his 29th birthday the month before *Rosencrantz and
Guildenstern*'s Edinburgh debut, but to summarise even his pre-fame life is a
difficult task, given that his biographies stretch to many hundreds of pages.
It's fair to say his experience by this point was already rich in the incident
of the 20th century. Born in the Moravian city of Zlin in Czechoslovakia
in 1937 to Eugen and Martha Sträussler, young Tomáš Sträussler moved in

1939 with his family to Singapore, after his father's employers at the Bata shoe company decided to transfer all Jewish employees out of the country before the Nazi invasion. Two years later, his father – a volunteer doctor with the British Army – was killed when his boat was bombed by Japanese forces as it left Singapore.

Four-year-old Tomáš and his brother Petr were taken to Darjeeling in India by their mother, who Anglicised their names to Tom and Peter and after Martha remarried to British Army major Kenneth Stoppard, the family took his surname and moved to England in 1946. Privately educated in the north of England, Stoppard left school at the age of 17 in 1954 to work on local newspapers in Bristol. Here, he earned a reputation as a young bohemian-about-town and began to write drama criticism, striking up a close friendship with Peter O'Toole during the actor's formative years at Bristol Old Vic.

In 1960 Stoppard started writing his first play, less through a longstanding desire to become a playwright and more because people like Harold Pinter and especially John Osborne had made it the fashionable thing for any aspiring young writer to do. *A Walk on Water* – which was reworked, retitled *Enter a Free Man*, and staged in London in 1968 – found him an agent in Kenneth Ewing and his career took shape. He moved to London with his girlfriend, became theatre critic for a new magazine called *Scene* and wrote radio and television drama for the BBC and ITV. *A Walk on the Water* was filmed for the latter network, but it was a failed pitch for a television drama named *I Can't Give You Anything But Love, Baby* that set dominoes in motion.

Sharing a taxi back from the meeting, Stoppard and Ewing discussed the National Theatre's recent production of *Hamlet*, starring the now-famous O'Toole and the latter suggested the playwright could explore writing something with Shakespeare's characters Rosencrantz and Guildenstern. The characters are old friends of the Danish prince, sent to spy on him and then – possibly unwittingly – deliver him to the King of England to be executed. In the original, Hamlet wriggles free of the trap and Rosencrantz and Guildenstern meet his intended fate instead, although all we know of this is the line in the play's final scene; also the eventual title of Stoppard's play. But what exactly happened to them after they arrived in England? Stoppard was no great Shakespeare enthusiast, but the idea intrigued him.

After rereading *Hamlet* on holiday in Scotland in early 1964 – his first marriage happened the following year in Troon on the Ayrshire coast, by which point his parents lived in the Glasgow suburb of Milngavie – Stoppard participated in an outreach programme in Berlin involving young dramatists from both sides of the Iron Curtain, as organised by the Ford Foundation. Pretty much penniless, he was mostly interested in the grant money being awarded, but at the retreat's mansion accommodation in the city's south-western Lake Wannsee suburb, he wrote a one-act work-in-progress named *Rosencrantz and Guildenstern Meet King Lear*. This draft imagined Hamlet's roughly-drawn characters wandering into another of Shakespeare's plays in pastiche style.

Back in England, Stoppard rewrote the work and the new *Rosencrantz and Guildenstern* script found itself contracted to the Royal Shakespeare Company for a year before they decided not to stage it. While his work in television and radio picked up and he technically made his West End debut with credited revisions to a translation of Polish playwright Slawomir Mrozek's *Tango*, the National Theatre also considered *Rosencrantz and Guildenstern* and the Royal Court took a look.

In this context, Stoppard was hardly a complete unknown when his breakthrough play arrived in Edinburgh, but chances for it to find an audience were slipping away. Frank Hauser, director of the Oxford Playhouse, also turned it down, but he passed it on to a local student group named the Oxford Players, part of the Oxford Theatre Group. They liked what they read and wanted to take it to the Edinburgh Fringe.

* * *

When the Oxford Theatre Group's president walked into Kenneth Ewing's office in the weeks before 1966's Festival was due to begin, Stoppard's agent took some convincing to let him have *Rosencrantz and Guildenstern Are Dead*. Eventually he relented and the OTG added the play to their August programme alongside *Harry Love*, a film by future BBC staff director Colin Luke and the traditional Oxford revue show, this time titled *The Oxford Tattoo*. It was to be performed between Wednesday 24 August and Saturday 10 September.

Incredibly, the OTG also reportedly negotiated contractual clauses that meant ten percent of the play's earnings over the next five years would be payable to them – an extraordinarily good deal, as it turned out. Stoppard would also complete revisions to the text and in return be given a return journey to the city, free lodgings while he was there and permission to sit in on rehearsals. The play would star student actors David Marks and Clive Cable in the title roles and be in the safe hands of talented student director Andrew Snell, until he had to drop out at the 11th hour for personal reasons.[2] He was replaced by stage manager Brian Daubney, who was inexperienced even by student standards. Early preparation was reportedly chaotic.

Among the cast of 11 was Janet Watts as Ophelia, who in her post-university life became a long-serving staff writer on *The Observer*, including two significant profiles of Stoppard in 1973 and 1987 which pieced together some of the behind-the-scenes story of Rosencrantz and Guildenstern's first outing:

> The show was in shreds. The director and his leading lady/girlfriend had quarreled and dropped out, followed by their cronies. The stage managers had assumed the direction, much to the remaining actors' mutinous disgust. A few RADA students had been rounded up to fill the gaps in the cast. Everyone was baffled by the script, which seemed full of repetitions and non sequiturs. I played Ophelia, who had one scream and one line.[3]

When Stoppard breezed in for his authorised rehearsal visits, he set the play to almost-rights once more. The cast and crew were staying, not exactly in comfort, in the Roman Eagle Masonic Lodge on Johnston Terrace, ten minutes' walk toward the Lawnmarket end of the Royal Mile from Cranston Street Hall. Stoppard had showed up in the 'dungeon' where the students ate their breakfast one morning and immediately put them at ease.

Tall and exuding a calm confidence, he may not have been university-educated himself, but he was almost a decade older than all of them and strikingly poised and cool in his tweed suit. Stoppard's lanky frame suited the fact he liked to model his style on Mick Jagger, who later became a close friend. He read the script and noticed that parts of it made no sense because it had been mistyped, so he sorted this out, editing lines as he went and stayed up until the small hours with the main players, educating them in the precise rhythm of their lines.

Legend has it that one early performance of *Rosencrantz and Guildenstern* on the Cranston Street Hall's 'postage stamp-sized' stage only had one person in the audience, although that's a dubious distinction which several hundred Fringe shows can probably lay claim to by now. Many of these would still be envious of the amount of reviewer attention it received, even if much of it was unfriendly. 'As off-putting a piece of non-theatre as has been presented at the Festival for many a year', glowered *The Glasgow Herald*.

The words that mattered, though, came from the *Observer*'s Ronald Bryden, alongside a photograph of Stoppard looking foppishly mop-haired and puzzled:

> Behind the fantastic comedy, you feel allegoric purposes move:
> is this our relation to our century, to the idea of death, to war...?
> This is erudite comedy, punning, far-fetched, leaping from depth to dizziness. It's the most brilliant debut by a young playwright since John Arden's.[4]

In the 1950s and '60s the highly-politicised Arden was regarded in the same breath as the likes of Pinter and Osborne. In one of the loops of coincidence and synchronicity that surround the small world of the Edinburgh Festival's vast history, the Barnsley-born Arden studied architecture at Edinburgh College of Art at the turn of the 1950s and experiencing the International Festival's *Satire of the Three Estates* had greatly informed his view of theatre; he made its writer Sir David Lyndsay one of the key characters in his Scottish historical play *Armstrong's Last Goodnight*, which opened at the National Theatre in 1964.

Stoppard recognised the depth of the compliment eventually. He spotted the review on the train back to London and wondered whether Arden had written novels? It took him a moment to register that the review was of *Rosencrantz* and not *Malquist*. Meanwhile Kenneth Tynan, the *Observer*'s former theatre critic, was at the time working for Laurence Olivier as literary manager of the National Theatre. He read Bryden's piece, requested a script from Stoppard, and showed it to an admiring Olivier. The play opened at the Old Vic in April 1967 and was a success.

From there, history writes itself. *Rosencrantz and Guildenstern Are Dead* won its writer an *Evening Standard* Award and turned him into a theatrical rock star overnight. On Broadway in 1968 it was the New York Drama Critics' Circle play of the year and the winner of the first of five Tony Awards for Stoppard's plays. A long career on stage and screen followed, including one Academy Award and a film version of *Rosencrantz and Guildenstern* in 1990, which Stoppard directed himself.

The Oxford Theatre Group returned to Edinburgh in 1969 – this time to St Mary's Hall, just across the Royal Mile from Cranston Street – with the first stage versions of Stoppard's radio plays *Albert's Bridge* and *If You're Glad I'll Be Frank*. *Lord Malquist and Mr Moon* reportedly sold 688 copies in the UK. Cranston Street Hall, an established Fringe venue for many years, has now been converted into apartments.

5

The Howff, the Traverse and the Demarco Gallery

EVERYWHERE A PERSON of enlightenment and culture turned in Edinburgh at the beginning of the 1960s, there was Jim Haynes. With his Paperback Bookshop still building its reputation and long before either the conception of the Traverse Theatre or his assistance with John Calder's defining conferences, another investment of his caused wheels to turn which had cultural repercussions far outside Edinburgh. He put money in, although he got out again when it looked like he might lose it all.

The interest of young Edinburgh listeners in folk music had been smouldering throughout the 1950s, overtaking jazz as a hipster favourite ever since the Ceilidhs of the People's Festival gave way to the folky gatherings around the Edinburgh University Folk Song Society and Hamish Henderson's favoured pub the Forrest Hill Bar, aka Sandy Bell's. Taking up the challenge of progressing this scene was a man named Roy Guest, who had only arrived in the city in 1959 for a Fringe show as the guest of a nebulous bunch of Scottish nationalism-inclined student performers named the Sporranslitters.

Born in Turkey in 1934 to a Welsh railroad worker, Guest started out with an ambition to be an actor and studied at the Central School of Speech and Drama in London. After experiences travelling amid Paris's Left Bank crowd and in Montreal, he decided to take up folk singing. When he returned to London he busked and gigged enthusiastically. In the late '50s, Guest built a minor name for himself on the London scene.

The Sporranslitters liked him. They let Guest take on a part of their building up the stairs at 369 High Street, an old apartment block opposite St Giles" Cathedral on the Royal Mile, for regular folk sessions which continued beyond the Fringe of 1959. Since Henderson and Stuart MacGregor had founded the Folk Song Society at Sandy Bell's in 1958, revivalist folk culture was beginning to spread among a section of the city's youth. On the very first night the Society gathered, its founders met a 20-year-old singer named Dolina Maclennan, who'd recently moved from the Isle of Lewis.

She sang in Gaelic and Henderson and MacGregor immediately hailed her as the Society's first great discovery. At the request of landlord Ian Walker, who famously kept a portrait of the Queen and the Duke of Edinburgh proudly behind the bar for decades to come, Maclennan and singer and guitarist Robin Gray started performing regularly in the upstairs snug of the Waverley Bar on St Mary's Street, another outlet for folk music in Edinburgh and one of the first places most people in the city were able to hear live Gaelic song.

Guest named his weekend folk club using the same title with which the Sporranslitters had christened the building – the Howff, a word taken from the writing of Robert Burns which meant somewhere to meet and to rest. It quickly gained a reputation as a place where the emerging folk style met an emerging counterculture, a group of young and carefree people who were dropping out of mainstream life, or at least focusing their efforts on a career in music. This was a way of life largely unknown to urban working-class people even a few years older, who had lived through the war.

From Edinburgh, Maclennan, Gray and a talented local guitarist named Len Partridge got involved. Brother-and-sister duo Archie and Ray Fisher – who became enthused about this music while attending Norman Buchan's Glasgow Folk Club, the first folk club in Scotland open to the public – moved through, often visited by their old classmate, the lively eccentric Hamish Imlach. Also born in Glasgow, but raised on the post-war Edinburgh housing estate of West Pilton, was a quiet 17-year-old trainee gardener who was looking for a bit of direction and companionship in life.

Bert Jansch found what he was looking for at the Howff. Fisher and a friend of Guest's named Jill Doyle, who had also moved up from London, taught Jansch guitar, although his skills soon overtook almost everyone else's. The young Jansch was mesmerised by the players Guest brought to the club, including the Tennessee folk singer and guitarist Walter 'Brownie' McGhee and the harmonica player Sonny Terry, when they visited for an impromptu session after a concert at the Usher Hall in late 1960.

For the young musician, the Howff became a way of life. For several months he actually slept there, woken by the bells of St Giles' in the morning and Guest was happy to let the eager Jansch do all sorts of unpaid labour, from painting the walls to sweeping up. Ahead of one busy night, while soup was being prepared for the audience, Maclennan remembers the Howff's toilet breaking, so Jansch was sent on a mission to the nearby Mocambo Café on the pretext of buying a cup of tea, where he had to sneak into the toilet and steal the ballcock from the cistern.

In Guest's incarnation, the Howff existed from 1959 until 1962 and it caught the spirit of the precise moment where the rediscovery and reinterpretation of folk and traditional music – fuelled by the popular emergence of skiffle through artists like the Scot Lonnie Donegan – was a bright and exciting new sound for young folk devotees who spent their weekends drinking coffee by day and listening to raw and earthy music by candlelight far past midnight. There were parties afterwards at flats on St Leonard's Street, Rankeillor Street and Bristo Place and imitator clubs sprang up across Scotland, first in Dunfermline,[1] then Perth, St Andrews, Dundee and Kirkcaldy.

Yet the place brought young musicians and audiences together. Throughout 1961 the Howff's reputation soared, as it hosted historic Edinburgh concerts like the great American folk singer Pete Seeger and the rock 'n' roll originator Sister Rosetta Tharpe. Her fame in the 1940s for a blend of blues vocals and electric guitar influenced Little Richard, Elvis Presley and – following a 1964 tour with Muddy Waters – English guitarists like Keith Richards and Jeff Beck. Her concert in Edinburgh was so packed that Bert Jansch couldn't get in and had to wait on the Royal Mile outside.

Beyond the local community it built in Edinburgh, the big triumph of Guest and Haynes' partnership in the Howff was the Edinburgh Festival of 1961, when a series of bookings brought it to wider attention. For the folk aficionado, there were sets by the Irish political singer and songwriter Dominic Behan and the return to the festival of Hamish Henderson's source-singing People's Ceilidh discoveries Jeannie Robertson and Jimmie MacBeath.

The first Festival week's events were the big deal, though; a series of twice-nightly shows by the Austrian cabaret singer and former collaborator with Pete Seeger, Martha Schlamme, whose signature interpretations of Kurt Weill were accompanied by pianist Alasdair Graham.

Schlamme was a hit, well-reviewed by *The Guardian* and *The Herald*, and even the International Festival's director Lord Harewood intended to go along and hear her. It seemed the Howff was a major new arrival amid Edinburgh's cultural scenery – but by the festival of 1962, it was gone.

No-one knows quite why Roy Guest left Edinburgh, but among those who knew him – and even those who liked him a great deal, which was most people – there persisted an opinion he was essentially a likeable chancer and a bit of a rogue. Whatever condition the Howff's finances were in, which alarmed Haynes' lawyer so, there was nothing left when Guest vanished. The Edinburgh folk scene would go on to greater strengths, within and outwith the festival, but the Howff was over.

When Guest showed up a few months later, it was most unexpectedly in the pages of *Billboard* magazine, eagerly telling of his plans for the new folk club he was opening on St Mark's Place in New York's East Village with $1000 of MGM Records' money and special guest Martha Schlamme already installed. Its name – which demanded translation and explanation every time he mentioned it in the US press – was the Howff. Within a few years he was back in London, as one of the most powerful folk music bookers in the country.

* * *

After the Howff in Edinburgh folded and the 1962 Writers' Conference was behind him, Haynes turned his attention to the brand-new and ultimately longer-lasting venture a short walk up the Royal Mile. The Traverse Theatre had teething problems, from the departure of its originator, the actor John Malcolm, after a spat with his director friend and colleague Terry Lane in December 1962, to the accidental and near-fatal onstage stabbing of the actor Colette O'Neil on its second night with what was supposed to be a prop knife. She recovered quickly, but John Calder ordered his colleagues to milk the ensuing press for all it was worth. As Joyce McMillan wrote:

> The question of who, exactly, founded the Traverse remains an emotive one for everyone who was involved. The truth is that they all founded it, that the idea of this new, alternative kind of place – a theatre or an arts centre, a restaurant or just a meeting place – was alive, at different intensities, in all of these five principals [Haynes, Demarco, Malcolm, Lane and Mitchell] and in dozens of their friends, and it was because it was in all of them that it had such unstoppable force... [it was] more like a small force of history, and all the more remarkable for that.[2]

With Haynes out of the country taking his young family to see American relatives when the Traverse opened, Lane was de facto artistic director for that first year, although John Calder had significant input by way of offering plays by some of the exciting European writers he represented. These were blended with interesting versions of established works and by the time the Traverse's first Edinburgh Festival rolled around in 1963, the audience of subscribing local members had already seen Alfred Jarry's *Ubu Roi*, Henrik Ibsen's *A Doll's House* and Eugene Ionesco's *The Lesson*, alongside works by Genet, Coward, Brecht and George Bernard Shaw.

The Theatre's first festival brought visits from the likes of Kenneth Tynan and JB Priestley, both in town for Calder's Drama Conference, and featured a revival of Lane's production of *Ubu Roi* and a translation of the 18th century German dramatist Christian Dietrich Grabbe's *Comedy, Satire, Irony and Deeper Meaning*. There were also exhibitions in the upstairs gallery space, notably an Edinburgh Festival event in 1963 featuring the Glaswegian artist Mark Boyle who, together with his Edinburgh-born, then-uncredited wife Joan Hills, produced junk 'assemblages' of material found on building sites near their London home.

The pair had met in Harrogate and briefly lived in Paris. Their Dada-influenced works, like those of many contemporary American artists with an interest in assemblage, flew in the face of artistic convention. They evoked the urban decay and crumbling tenement squalor of undeveloped tracts of bombed-out post-war British cities like London and Glasgow.

When Hills popped into the Paperback Bookshop with some polaroids of their art while on a family visit to Edinburgh, Haynes was inclined to agree. Yet there was no space to get Boyle and Hills' large-scale works down the narrow stair to the basement, so Haynes suggested she ask at the Traverse Theatre instead. Here Hills met man-about-town Richard Demarco, who agreed with Haynes' assessment. The only trouble was, there was no dedicated gallery space at the Traverse, but Demarco wasn't deterred. He cleared some space in the upstairs café to house the work and the Traverse Gallery was born in August 1963.

The exhibition caused a stir. In *The Scotsman*, Sydney Goodsir Smith wrote that he disliked the religious-sounding titles. The visiting American artist Ken Dewey enjoyed the work and Boyle was invited to assist with the infamous Edinburgh Drama Conference 'happening' *In Memory of Big Ed*, alongside Dewey and the playwright Charles Lewson. The Edinburgh show was only Boyle and Hills' second exhibition, but his name[3] as an artistic *enfant terrible* was sealed.

Later in the decade, Boyle and Hills' work became synonymous with the counterculture scene in London through exhibitions at the ICA and the Indica Gallery, which was co-founded by William Burroughs' friend and biographer Barry Miles, Marianne Faithfull's husband John Dunbar and Peter Asher, the brother of Paul McCartney's girlfriend Jane. After falling in with the same management team as Jimi Hendrix and Soft Machine, Boyle and Hills also created liquid backdrops at the psychedelic rock club UFO in 1966, where Pink Floyd had a residency.

Despite being a protégé of the in-the-round theatre pioneer Stephen Joseph, Terry Lane was more conventional than the collection of theatrical radicals and eccentrics who clustered around the Traverse. By its second festival in 1964, Haynes had taken control as both chairman and artistic director, putting him in a prime position to exploit his international network of contacts. The first fruit of this came during the festival, with a range of plays by current European dramatists including the Pole Sławomir Mrożek and the Swiss writer Max Frisch, with a home theatre company which included the 22-year-old Scottish actor and later Tony Award winner and Academy Award nominee Tom Conti.

The big change that year was the sourcing of a new venue to stage a large and ambitious play for which there was no room in the Traverse itself. Directed by Michael Geliot, *The Happy End* was the first English translation of Kurt Weill, Elisabeth Hauptmann (as Dorothy Lane) and Bertolt Brecht's 1929 musical follow-up to *The Threepenny Opera*, run out of Berlin for alleged Communist sympathies at the time, but restaged in West Germany not long before the Traverse opened. This version was held at the Pollock

Hall on Marshall Street, a university building a couple of minutes' walk from the McEwan Hall and the Paperback Bookshop, which has since been bulldozed to make way for the Potterrow student union.

The play was recommended to Haynes at the Drama Conference of 1963 and he had such faith that he rustled up enough investment to spend £7,000 on a production with a cast of 20, a significant amount at the time.

The Guardian said it was exceptional, noting that by the look of the graffiti scratched into the wooden pew seating, Pollock Hall appeared to be a lecture theatre despite its church-like setting. This was the same production of *The Happy End* that transferred to the Royal Court in London the following year.

Haynes' vice-chair at the Traverse was Richard Demarco, and he pushed the venue's parallel reputation as a home of challenging new art. As well as Boyle and Hills, he presented his old Edinburgh College of Art friend – and subsequently one of Scotland's greatest 20th century painters – Elizabeth Blackadder, and Patrick Heron, a Cornish contemporary of Barbara Hepworth and Ben Nicholson. Boyle returned in 1965 for a large Traverse Gallery off-site show at the Bank of Scotland at 97–99 George Street, alongside artists from Barcelona, New York, Canada and Brussels.

The Traverse Theatre in the mid-1960s was a true cultural phenomenon and its inception was a transformative event both for Edinburgh and its Festival. It developed a reputation for new plays, both commissioned by the theatre and imported in, often debuts translation from Europe. Its reputation quickly spread – critics from London wanted to experience it and artists from all over became involved.

Some weeks after the 1964 festival, Liverpool revue group the Scaffold (the poet Roger McGough, Paul McCartney's brother Michael, and John Gorman, who later had a collective hit in 1968 with the song 'Lily the Pink') made their first Traverse appearance with *Birds, Deaths and Marriages* and over Christmas the great mime artist Lyndsay Kemp began his association with the theatre by presenting a physical adaptation of Dylan Thomas' *A Child's Christmas in Wales*. Haynes had been introduced to Kemp in Dublin by a mutual friend and theatre enthusiast named Jack Henry Moore, whom Haynes greatly admired, bringing him to work at the Traverse.

John Antrobus, already established as a television writer for Eric Sykes' show and *That Was the Week That Was*, premiered his play *You'll Come to Love Your Sperm Test* in 1964 and it transferred to London's Hampstead Theatre the following year. Work by Ionesco, Beckett, Mrożek, John Mortimer, Luigi Pirandello and CP Taylor was seen throughout the year and Harold Pinter's *The Dwarfs*, rewritten especially for the Traverse, and the premiere of Heathcote Williams' *The Local Stigmatic* – which quickly transferred to the Royal Court – appeared as a double bill in March '65. Kemp returned with his show *Bubbles* during the festival that year, this time alongside the counterculture musician, poet and Bonzo Dog Doo-Dah Band founder Vivian Stanshall in his cast.

A big-budget collaboration with the International Festival in 1965 brought the establishment and the exciting young pretender together, and although the Geliot-directed joint production of *Macbeth* at the Assembly Hall was widely viewed as unremarkable, the Traverse's legend remained untarnished by this fraternising with the mainstream. By this point it was a legend, a mythical place which fused the highest art and the most illicit thrills. A rumour went around that actors had sex on the stairs behind the stage doors to expel their tension before going on, compounding the idea that it was a place for horny young beatniks. Joyce McMillan wrote:

> Sex was all the rage at the Traverse, and sexual frankness a strong motif of many of the early productions, [but] sexual politics in the modern sense certainly wasn't the organisation's strong suit.[4]

Attractive young women filled most of the waiting and office roles and company secretary – later general manager – Sheila Colvin was a lone female voice on the all-male committee. Even within, there was dissent about this reputation.

There were also concerns about profligacy, with funds always an issue. The Traverse was overseen by a committee, but Haynes' skills certainly lay in befriending the great and interesting of the international theatre scene, not in office administration. The two areas were often at odds, such was the scale of Haynes' onstage ambition, and an increasing reliance on Arts Council funding applications came with conditions and oversight. This cut away at the freewheeling sense of endless possibility which had made the Traverse's name.

An internal struggle for power and a stormy AGM at Pollock Hall in early 1966 saw Haynes and Demarco left as the only original committee members, with Nicholas Fairbairn – the lawyer who defended John Calder from the fallout of the Drama Conference in 1964 – installed as Chairman. Yet pressure over finances and how the theatre was being run remained and there was disquiet about the fact Haynes' grand plan to open a second Traverse in London was drawing him away from the city.

This second Traverse happened briefly, when – with the counsel of the well-connected first Governmental Minister for the Arts Jennie Lee – Haynes took on the brand new Jeanetta Cochrane Theatre in Holborn in central London, then a partly-educational stage attached to the Central School of Art and Design.

Haynes' regular Traverse collaborators Moore, Geliot and Charles Marowitz joined him, but he was losing his grip in Scotland. Despite Fairbairn's stated intention to be a hands-off chair, he alienated Demarco by refusing him the Traverse's name for a new gallery he was planning on Melville Place, intended very much as an extension of the Traverse's work. Fairbairn ultimately accepted Haynes' resignation on 6 July 1966.

It's difficult to overstate just how much of a dial-shifting cultural phenomenon the Traverse was in its early years, under Lane and especially Haynes' management, but to give an indication of how much Haynes' was tuned into the cultural pulse of the day, his time afterwards in London put him at the heart of his era. On 29 September 1966, not even four months after he left Edinburgh, the London Traverse Theatre Company presented the London premiere of Joe Orton's seminal play *Loot*, directed by Marowitz, which transferred to the Criterion Theatre in the West End two months later. On 17 November the venue hosted a *Music of the Mind* concert by the Japanese-American Fluxus artist Yoko Ono, eight days after she first met John Lennon at the Indica Gallery.

From its opening issue of October 1966, both Haynes and Moore were on the editorial board of the cult, Tom McGrath-edited counterculture newspaper *International Times*, whose contributors included Writers' Conference alumni William Burroughs and Alexander Trocchi, Traverse veterans Heathcote Williams and Charles Marowitz and figures like John Peel and Germaine Greer.[5] The paper was launched by an all-night concert featuring Pink Floyd and the Soft Machine at Alexandra Palace and the offices were frequently raided by police.

Haynes left the Cochrane Theatre behind in 1967 to start the Arts Lab in a disused space on Drury Lane. Containing cinema, theatre and gallery space, it was a thoroughly alternative venue for those experimenting with hallucinogenic drugs and dropping out of the mainstream, including Lennon and Ono, who presented their exhibition *Build Around* there in 1968. Through the infamy of Haynes' invention, numerous smaller, independent Arts Labs sprang up around the country, like the one in Northampton that attracted the future comic writer Alan Moore, but the multi-platform creative model has mutated half a century later into the one used by any publicly-funded arts building.

Would any of this have happened in Edinburgh had Haynes stayed at the Traverse? Or would a Traverse in Edinburgh and one in London have meant those involved in Haynes' London activities would turn up at the Edinburgh Festival too? It's impossible to tell how a mainline into the heart of late-'60s counterculture could have impacted the Scottish city, although Lindsay Kemp did at least bring a bit of it to Scotland in 1970 when he staged his show *Pierrot in Turquoise or The Looking Glass Murders* at the Gateway Theatre on Elm Row, for recording by Scottish Television. The first version of the play that Kemp produced in 1967 featured a then-unknown David Bowie, whom Kemp taught mime and was briefly lovers with.

Despite the fact Bowie was now famous following the previous summer's hit 'Space Oddity', he agreed to perform in the show again for a rehearsal on 31 January and the recording on 1 February. The results lurk on the internet, an odd and eerily sexual piece with three little-known Bowie songs recorded for the occasion, 'Threepenny Pierrot', 'Columbine' and 'The Mirror', totalling five minutes of music. Bowie and his wife Angie stayed on a mattress on the floor of Kemp's basement flat on Drummond Street, and Bowie woke early to wander the empty Edinburgh streets and take in the architecture. Two months later he was recording *The Man Who Sold the World* in London.

It's extremely likely a continued Haynes reign at the Traverse would have been short-lived. His London Traverse lasted barely a few months, only until 1967, and by 1969 the Arts Lab was gone too. He moved to Paris, where he kept an *atelier* and an open house to friends across the world, until his death in 2021. In later years he remained an enthusiastic visitor to the Edinburgh Festival, where the legacy he left had been carried on in other ways. Richard Demarco established his own Demarco Gallery at 8 Melville Place, a Georgian former hairdresser's with a restaurant in the basement and a little space for performance. This was the venue for the Scaffold's return to Edinburgh over the festival of 1968, the same year a two-man, after-midnight revue featured the future broadcaster and moonlighting Cambridge Footlight Clive James.

Demarco's subsequent, decades-long work as a gallerist and curator in Edinburgh has been characterised by a near-obsessive exploration and presentation of Scottish and international artists, many of them for the first time. Offsite at the University of Edinburgh's David Hume Tower on George Square, The *Edinburgh Open 100* in 1967 was an exhibition of 100 emerging painters chosen from 1,500 entries from across the UK and Ireland, while in 1968 his festival exhibitions included group shows at Lord and Lady Rosebery's Hopetoun House and the North British Hotel on Princes Street.

Demarco also curated many nationally-themed group shows of artists, including 1973's *Eight Yugoslav Artists* at Melville College. It contained the first international performance by the then-unknown Marina Abramović, who presented *Rhythm 10*, in which she played the potentially dangerous knife-between-the-fingers game as an act of performance for the audience. Two years later Abramović returned to Edinburgh, again on Demarco's invitation, to perform at *Aspecta '75* at the Fruitmarket Gallery. His *Strategy: Get Arts* exhibition at Edinburgh College of Art during the 1970 festival is considered to be one of the most significant contemporary European art exhibitions of the late 20th century.

The Traverse, meanwhile, resisted widespread predictions of its post-Haynes demise. A Cambridge-born 25-year-old named Max Stafford-Clark had fallen in love with the theatre during his three visits to Edinburgh in 1965, first on tour with his rugby team from Trinity College, Dublin, then with a Traverse summer revue from the same institution and finally as director of and actor in the Fringe play *Oh, Gloria!* by Robert Shure. After this he stayed at the Traverse as assistant stage manager, but was suddenly thrust into getting a Fringe programme for '66 up and running when Haynes quit with two months to go.

The job of replacement artistic director, however, eventually went to Gordon McDougall, a hotshot, Cambridge-educated young theatre pro with trainee experience at the Royal Court. McDougall was also 25, and his partnership with associate director Stafford-Clark gave the Traverse exactly the youthful, countercultural buzz that Haynes was bringing to London.

Jim Haynes' time in Edinburgh lasted barely a decade, but during it he opened a nationally-renowned bookshop, had a hand in two cultural Conferences which gained international attention, helped lay some road for the British folk revival at the Howff and was instrumental in the creation of a key source of Britain's theatrical renaissance with the Traverse. A stew of combined energies brought that theatre into being, but Haynes was unequivocal in his sense of affection for and ownership of it.

SPOTLIGHT

Strategy: Get Arts (1970)

THERE WAS A time if ever you happened to be in Venice, Warsaw, New York, Bucharest or any other world capital, when you would hear Ricky Demarco had just been, or was just about to arrive, if you did not actually meet him in the street, stopping to talk, urgently, with infectious excitement about his latest project, his newest artistic discovery, before hurtling on like the White Rabbit, a bundle of papers under his arm, his camera tirelessly flashing. And if now he approaches 70 he has slowed down a little, it is only relative.[1]

THESE WORDS WERE written in March 2000 by the Scottish art critic and historian Duncan Macmillan and they help illustrate the long-term influence of Richard Demarco upon the recent history of art in Scotland and Edinburgh, in and out of Festival time. An obsessive enthusiast and collector of ephemera relating to his every activity, Demarco's Archive is an essential but undoubtedly overwhelming guide to the key European artists he's been at the forefront of popularising in the UK. At time of writing, the publicly accessible Demarco Digital Archive contains 10,000 distinct documents, among them photographs, programmes and correspondence.

Over three stories of his Georgian townhouse at 8 Melville Crescent, created with the support of Traverse Theatre Club members Andrew Elliot, John Martin and James Walker, his gallery made an immediate splash with an exhibition of 56 artists for the Festival of '66, followed by 126 more artists that Christmas. In March 1967 Demarco's enthusiasm for mass group exhibitions offering a snapshot of a country's contemporary art scene began in earnest, with – appropriately enough – *Contemporary Italian Art*, featuring 37 Italian and Italian-based artists of the Avant Garde, with debut or early shows in the UK for Jannis Kounellis, Giuseppe Capogrossi, Piero Manzoni, Lucio Fontana and Alberto Burri. These group shows continued through the decade, bringing artists from Poland, Brazil and Romania to Scotland.

Demarco's 1968 Fringe programme featured more than 150 artists at sites including Goldberg's department store and Hopetoun House, including 22 Canadian artists at Edinburgh College of Art. Young Scottish artists were also enthusiastically discovered and a little of the Traverse's performance thunder was stolen by a late-night Fringe revue from Cambridge Footlights Clive James, Tony Buffery and Pete Arkin in 1968 and '69, Geoff Moore's dance company Moving Being with the Incredible String Band in 1969 and Lindsay Kemp's *Crimson* and *White Pantomimes* in 1970 and '71. The Romanian programme of '69 and a solo show later that year introduced the Bucharest-born philosopher-sculptor Paul Neagu to the United Kingdom, where he settled and built a reputation.

Demarco estimated that between becoming a gallerist in the 1960s and the fall of the Berlin Wall in 1989, he crossed the Iron Curtain into Eastern Europe at least 100 times in search of new work. One of his very earliest journeys, however, was to *Rosc '67* in Dublin, the first in a two-decade series of international art exhibitions in the city, where works by Picasso, Matisse and Lichtenstein were on display. There he met and bonded with Günther Uecher, an artist from Dusseldorf who was part of Group Zero, a collective that created kinetic art focusing on light and motion, in response to the pictorial *Art Informel* style. Demarco was impressed that one of his heroes, the late Yves Klein, had been Uecker's brother-in-law and that both Uecker and Klein had a taste for Celtic culture.

In 1968 Demarco visited the Venice Biennale for the first time and, partly based on his connection with Uecker, the exhibition Documenta in Kassel, a city in central Germany near the East German border. Artist Arnold Bode founded Documenta in 1955 as a showcase of *Entartete Kunst*, the 'Degenerate Art' of Modernism, which was widely banned and destroyed by the Nazis, and it evolved into one of the leading modern art shows in Europe. Here Demarco had an epiphany about German art and one figure associated with it in particular. In retrospect, he wrote of his abiding Documenta memory:

> I see a large exhibition room full of long tables and strange objects which suggested the aftermath of a highly significant and complex science experiment. At a distance an extraordinary man unexpectedly imposed his presence upon the room and everything in it by examining and adjusting the objects with precise and dignified movements. He was dressed in a multi-pocketed grey fisherman's waistcoat, a white, open-necked shirt, and blue jeans. Sitting squarely on his head, half-obscuring his sallow-complexioned face, was a grey fedora hat, incongruously and splendidly formal. [2]

* * *

At this point Joseph Beuys was unknown internationally, although he'd built a degree of notoriety in Germany as a unique and uncompromising artist. By the time Documenta began in '68, he was already 47 years old and had lived an unconventional and controversial life. In 1936, at the age of 15, he was a member of the Hitler Youth and present at the Nuremberg rally of that year. During the Second World War he served in the Luftwaffe, was shot down on the Crimean Front and fought as a paratrooper on the Western Front. He was wounded in battle and captured by British troops following Germany's surrender, being released to go home three months later.[3] All through the war Beuys had drawn and made art and once it was over he enrolled on a course in Monumental Sculpture at the *Kunstakademie Düsseldorf*.

Fifteen years later, after various sculptural commissions, an extensive drawing project based upon James Joyce's *Ulysses*, a breakdown in 1956 and marriage in 1959, he became professor of the course he'd graduated from, where he eventually abolished entry requirements. By 1970 a class that was supposed to contain 20 students had 178. Beuys briefly flirted with the Fluxus movement, which took in figures including John Cage and Yoko Ono, and in 1964 he was physically attacked by right-wing students while taking part in a festival in Aachen on the anniversary of the assassination attempt on Hitler. This provocation seemed to please Beuys and it brought him to public notice. In November 1965, he drew attention entirely for his art with *How to Explain Pictures to a Dead Hare* at Galerie Schmela in Düsseldorf, for which he smeared his face with honey and paced a sealed-off room, observed through a window, as he cradled a dead hare in his arms and muttered to it about the pictures on the walls.

Beuys' interest was in nature, in its myths and 'invisible forces' and in their restorative powers. The consoling of the hare and the doubted but often-peddled story about being brought back to life after his plane crash in the warmth of Tatar nomads' animal furs and fat were in his mind, perhaps, a spiritual exorcism of the horrors of the war. Maybe he was even trying to dispel his own part in them. Beuys' art came to be about *Aktionen*, or 'Actions', a series of performance works which were close relatives of the Happening at the 1963 Drama Conference, but which he viewed as being closer to shamanic rituals. He emphasised the conceptual over all else. His great unfulfilled project was raising the Berlin Wall by three inches, and he thrived because of – or perhaps despite – the responses to such statements, whether they declared him a visionary or a charlatan.

Demarco was captivated by this mesmerising figure. At the beginning of 1970, he finally had an audience with Beuys in the house the artist shared with his wife Eva and two young children in the nice Oberkassel suburb of Düsseldorf, on the west bank of the Rhine. The city was just approaching the beginning of a period at the forefront of alternative German culture – the electronic group Kraftwerk had been formed there the previous year, splitting off into the equally influential Neu! in 1972 – and Beuys already had a following. Trying to draw the artist's attention away from the dozen friends crowded into the house, Demarco showed him postcards of idyllic Scottish landscapes.

Beuys told him they reminded him of *Macbeth*, and quoted Shakespeare. In May 1970 the artist touched down at Edinburgh's Turnhouse Airport in a thunderstorm. Within days, Demarco had shown him Arthur's Seat, the craggy hill in the heart of Edinburgh, the Forth Rail Bridge, and the haunting landscapes of Scotland's north; the desolate Rannoch Moor, striking Glencoe, and the castles on the banks of Loch Linnhe and the appropriately-named Loch Awe.

Demarco, still an artist at heart, came to define this route as 'the Road to Meikle Seggie'. Meikle Seggie itself is a farm sited midway between John Calder's Ledlanet estate and the village of Milnathort, on the boundary of Fife and Perth and Kinross, but in Demarco's definition it's a metaphor for the journey of artistic discovery taken in a life, through physical travel to find new experiences and the surprising diversions that might be thrown up along the way. At once it speaks of an affinity with and love for the Scottish landscape, but also a wider sense of internationalist curiosity, particularly on the European continent while the Second World War was still a fresh living memory for so many.

Impressed by his Canadian exhibition, the United States government invited Demarco to tour the country and research a projected large-scale exhibition for the Festival of 1970, which would assert the usA as the pre-eminent location for modern art in the world. Yet, Demarco's recent experience led him to believe instead that the Rhine-Ruhr valley region of Germany, encompassing Düsseldorf, Frankfurt and Bonn, held the title instead. The growing movement had a name, the *Wirtschaftswunder* ('Miracle on the Rhine') and many of its key figures were East Germans who had escaped in search of intellectual freedom before the wall went up.

In January 1970, Demarco was invited to tour West Germany by the country's Cultural Attaché in the UK Brigitte Lohmeyer and he enthusiastically accepted. Catching up with Uecker and soaking up the Düsseldorf gallery scene in ten days, what he saw convinced him German art had to be the Demarco Gallery's Festival subject that year.

With the blessing of the International Festival, despite Peter Diamand's scepticism that organising a multi-artist exhibition imported from continental Europe in the space of less than six months would be impossible, preparations began in earnest. From the bland working title *Dusseldorf in Edinburgh*, a variety of suggestions (*Happy Artsday*, *Paris on the Rhine*) eventually landed on the playful, palindromic *Strategy: Get Arts* in June '70.

Between 24 August and 12 September that year, the work of 35 artists was displayed in the halls and rooms of Demarco's alma mater Edinburgh College of Art. The work on display and available for experience bore a mischievous Dadaist 'anti-art' sensibility and often a disdain for accepted artistic norms, which gave the exhibition a rebellious tone. Klaus Rinke created a water installation over the entrance door, a jet at head height which issued sporadic blasts of water and had to be dodged on the way in. Stefan Wewerka arrived in Edinburgh, travelled to Burns Yard, a scrapyard to the east of the city and selected a group of wooden chairs that he then performed a participatory Action with – inviting everyone watching to help smash them to firewood on the main entrance stairs. The results were a tribute to Sergei Eisenstein's *Battleship Potemkin*.

Uecker covered both sides of a narrow corridor in knife blades pointing outwards for *Sharp Corridor*; a complaint and a visit from the police meant they had to be covered in a protective mesh barrier, creating the new work *Sharp Corridor Blunted by Police*. Blinky Palermo painted a mural named *Blue/Yellow/White/Red* high of the walls of the entrance hall, which the indignant and conservative College of Art authorities had painted over as soon as the show was over, much to the outrage of students. Gotthard Graubner's *Mist Room (Homage to Turner)* involved filling a room with stage smoke using a smoke machine borrowed from the Lyceum next door. It caught light and the fire brigade had to be called.

Dorothy Iannone's illustrated books contained images of nudity which the censor surprisingly passed without comment. Gerhard Richter, an early supporter of the possibility of the exhibition, created murky, austere paintings. Sigmar Polke, Dieter Roth and Hilla Becher all featured. And at the centre of it all, of course, was Beuys, the charismatic, inscrutable star of German modern art, making his debut amid the English-speaking art world in Edinburgh. He presented three works, including *Arena*, a photographic documentation of his past Actions in the very room where Demarco himself had been a student two decades before, and *The Pack*, Beuys' own beat-up Volkswagen camper van with a selection of husky sledges trailing behind it, mounted with rolls of felt, dishes of fat and battery-powered torches, a reference to the artist's own origin myth.

Beuys' third piece was the Action *Celtic (Kinloch Rannoch) Scottish Symphony*, which consisted of film of him shot at Rannoch Moor during a second visit earlier in August, this time by filmmaker Mark Littlewood and artist Rory McEwen,[4] accompanied by movement and activity from Beuys and music from the Danish composer Henning Christiansen.

Critics acclaimed *Strategy: Get Arts*. Some of them mocked it, in whole or in part. Others worked up a sense of righteous indignation at this shock of the new which had dared to set up camp in the heart of Edinburgh. It sealed many reputations, among them Richter's and Uecker's, and was the first stage in establishing Beuys as one of the major, most challenging and most controversial art stars of the 20th century. He represented Germany at the Venice Biennale in 1976 and 1980 and finally had an American career retrospective at the Guggenheim Museum in New York in 1979, whose programme notes referred to the major significance of *Strategy: Get Arts*.

In many ways, though, Beuys' presence in Edinburgh in 1970 was a sideshow. *Strategy: Get Arts* was the first major UK exhibition of contemporary German Art since *Twentieth Century German Art* at the New Burlington Galleries in London in 1938, a conscious, modernism-celebrating response to the Nazis' Entartete Kunst which personally displeased Hitler himself. Careers were made by *Strategy: Get Arts*, but a nation's artistic reputation was rehabilitated in the process.

* * *

The bond formed between Beuys and Demarco was strong and the artist returned to Edinburgh many times before his death in Düsseldorf in 1986 at the age of 64. By 1972, Demarco's vision for the Demarco Gallery had evolved into a series named *Edinburgh Arts*, a summer school intended to offer a longer working period to visiting artists and a more thorough immersion in the work for audiences. Workshops by Demarco, Paul Neagu, Tom Hudson and David Helder took place on Cramond Beach, Arthur's Seat,

Greyfriars Kirkyard and on Inchcolm Island in the Firth of Forth. This year also saw the first appearance of Polish theatre visionary Tadeusz Kantor's Cricot 2 Theatre company at the Edinburgh Fringe, on Demarco's invite.

In 1973 Demarco's Fringe operations largely moved to the old Melville College, a few doors from his gallery on Melville Crescent,[5] and Beuys performed an action there named *12 Hour Lecture: A Homage to Anacharsis Cloots*, in honour of the 'world federalist and international anarchist' Prussian nobleman of the French Revolution. The chalked blackboards with which he delivered the lecture were purchased by a gallery in America. In 1974, Demarco took Beuys to the remains of the Forrest Hill Poorhouse, a formerly grand, school-sized complex whose main building stood on the west side of Forrest Road, alongside Greyfriars Kirkyard, with other buildings on the east side, next to the New North Free Church – the building that later became the Other Traverse in the '70s and the Bedlam Theatre in the '80s.

By this point, the Poorhouse had largely been demolished for tenement housing, with the only remnants used as a plumber's yard at the end of Forrest Hill, the short lane alongside Sandy Bell's pub. Here Beuys performed the *Three Pots Action* in May '74, anointing the building's former use with drawings, cooking pots and ritual action. During the Festival he gave the three-hour *Black and White Oil Conference* lecture alongside the architect and futurist Buckminster Fuller, refuting the need for fossil fuel. Six years later Beuys co-founded the German Green Party, his artistic connection with nature perfectly feeding his prescient environmentalist views.

The Free International University for Creativity and Interdimensional Research (FUI) was founded in Düsseldorf in 1971 by Beuys, with German artists and philosophers including the Nobel Prizewinning writer Heinrich Böll, and assistance from the art critic Caroline Tisdall and a young Slade School of Art graduate named Robert McDowell. Its work was to explore the future of society through the holistic consideration of art, politics and economics. In 1976, Beuys and Tisdall visited the convicted murderer-turned-artist Jimmy Boyle in HM Prison Barlinnie in Glasgow and presented Boyle's sculpture *In Defence of the Innocent* during the Festival. Beuys continued the association with Boyle under the umbrella of the FUI at the Fringe of 1980, going on sympathetic hunger strike at Gladstone's Court on the Royal Mile.

A *cause célèbre* of the Scottish arts world at the time, including playwright Tom McGrath, who brought his story to the Traverse Theatre in *The Hard Man* in 1977, Boyle had been unsuccessfully defended at trial by Nicholas Fairbairn, the sometime chair of the Traverse who had defended John Calder in court after the Drama Conference of '63. From his youthful association with such liberal causes, Fairbairn infamously declared the industrial music group Throbbing Gristle 'wreckers of civilisation' in 1976,[6] and later became a member of Margaret Thatcher's government and a supporter of the proposed anti-gay Clause 28 legislation of 1988.

Boyle was released soon after Beuys' hunger strike, but Demarco believes this 1980 Action cost his gallery its Scottish Arts Council funding. Beuys' last visit to Edinburgh was in 1981 for the Festival exhibit of *Poorhouse Doors* – the crumbling doors of the Forrest Hill Poorhouse, removed before the room where he had exhibited was demolished – at the Scottish National Gallery of Modern Art in the Royal Botanic Gardens' Inverleith House. Made with the assistance of George Wylie, this piece was named *New Beginnings Are in the Offing*.

Demarco persevered, becoming instrumental in the creation of the Edinburgh Art Festival in the 2000s. In 2021, when Edinburgh College of Art lecturer Christian Weikop launched his thorough retrospective book on *Strategy: Get Arts*, it took place in Edinburgh International Book Festival's new home in the hall of ECA itself. Fifty-one years had passed and the exhibition's influence remained. In the front row of the audience, an ever-enthusiastic link to the memory of it all, sat 91-year-old Richard Demarco. Demarco said of Beuys in 2016:

Two weeks before he died, we spoke for the last time on the phone. He told me he was going to turn my gallery into a work of art so I could sell it and escape the art world. The last words he said were, 'Goodbye Richard, I love you'. And I said them back. Now, what curator would say that to an artist these days? But he wasn't an artist. He was my friend. [7]

6

Changing Landscapes in the 1970s

IN AN ERA when post-war rebuilding and regeneration projects were speeding up across Britain through sheer necessity, changes were wrought in Edinburgh which altered the landscape of the city and the Festival forever. Many more were attempted which would have left both unrecognisable today.

Amid prevailing political urges towards utopianism, improvement and legacy, many families in the city lived in crumbling tenement houses, especially around the Canongate and Holyrood areas, a situation which had only worsened since the war. Landlords left the country, failing to collect rent or carry out basic repairs and occupants were on decades-long lists to be rehoused. From the late 1950s, Labour councillor Pat Rogan set out on a one-person crusade to restore buildings, demolish others and rehouse families in new-build suburban housing estates and high-rises away from the city centre.

Patrick Abercrombie influence upon the shape of British urban development after the Second World War was immense. He was known for 1944's optimistically utopian Greater London Plan and for the Clyde Valley Plan of 1946, which saw nearly half of Glasgow's cramped and poverty-stricken population rehoused in high-rise suburbs and New Towns like Cumbernauld, East Kilbride and Glenrothes. In 1949 Abercrombie and his colleague Derek Plumstead also wrote a plan for Edinburgh.

This plan involved the complete razing of Princes Street to build a new multi-level road and rail route, the destruction of Leith, Gorgie and Dalry for conversion into industrial zones and large sections of the leafy city centre carved up to create dual-carriageway road access for growing numbers of car users; essentially a compact motorway, coring the heart of Edinburgh like an apple. With the Festival in mind, they also advocated the destruction of New Town designer James Craig's St James Square tenements on Leith Street to build a new theatre and concert hall.[1] The Abercrombie Plan was a bold and futuristic vision of an imagined city for the late 20th century – with the unfortunate by-product of smashing one of Europe's most beautiful cities, the home of the Scottish Enlightenment, into pieces under the wheels of progress.

Abercrombie died in 1957 and his plan was shelved for many years, but with slum clearance and modernist urban renewal picking up pace in the 1960s, it was partly revived. The two-tier road and rail system on Princes Street was abandoned, but the plan to tear down every building on the north side and build adjoining contemporary blocks with a linked, elevated walkway began. Only seven blocks were replaced in the end, but the New Club, designed by architect David Bryce, the Italianate-style Life Association and the North British and Mercantile Insurance Company were among the classic buildings to go. Princes Street remains an unusual, mismatched sight to this day.

Lord Provost Weatherstone was enthusiastic about these changes and on his watch Abercrombie's proposed Edinburgh Inner Ring Road began to progress in 1963. A dual-carriageway was to be built around the city centre, cutting its way through the Meadows and Inverleith Park, tunnelling under Calton Hill and thundering past quiet Stockbridge and the south edge of the Royal Botanic Garden. Led by the Edinburgh conservation group the Cockburn Association, which was founded by the judge Henry Cockburn in 1875, campaigners had this idea thrown out in 1965, although other aspects of Abercrombie's plan did come into effect. St James Square, a small grass park with run-down tenements on four sides, was eventually torn down in 1969, replaced not by a theatre, but by the functional St James Centre shopping mall and the St Andrew's House headquarters of the Scottish Office.

The planned opera house Lord Harewood had once wanted to see built had instead been earmarked for the site on Castle Terrace where the Synod Hall stood and the Edinburgh International Festival's original headquarters had been. Weatherstone – a bold enough man to ask the Beatles for a £100,000 donation to the Festival during a press photocall prior to their show at the city's ABC cinema in April 1964[2] – had already been instrumental in the removal of this admired theatre spaces to try and push the opera house through. Built in 1875 to Sir James Gowans' design, what became known as the Synod Hall was part of an ambitious plan to create a 19th century mega-theatre for Edinburgh, alongside a winter garden and an aquarium. The last two elements were scrapped before being built and the theatre was sold the year after its construction to the United Presbyterian Church for use as their Synod Hall.[3]

In 1882 the Royal Lyceum Theatre was built backing onto the Hall and when the adjoining Usher Hall opened in 1914, the Synod Hall had been in council ownership for general hire use since 1902. Edinburgh cinema magnates the Poole family took it on in 1928 and Poole's Synod Hall was still doing healthy business with daytime programmes and late-night horror screenings in 1965, when the council ordered the B-listed building's closure and demolition to make way for the new showpiece theatre and opera house project. With the Synod Hall went the Poole family's headquarters and the home office of the International Festival itself, which moved into the *Edinburgh Evening News'* old premises on Market Street, by Waverley Station, at a greatly increased rent.

Weatherstone and the Corporation, meanwhile, put their faith in the Edinburgh College of Art-schooled architect William Kininmonth, friend and former business partner of the great Basil Spence. His proposal was for a stark, modernist building made of smooth concrete, with a landmark tower, hotel, restaurant and two auditoriums – a 1,600-seat main hall and a smaller, in-the-round room for 800. Yet, the Corporation had misjudged how willing Prime Minister Harold Wilson's new Labour government was to underwrite big arts-related projects. Heels were dragged, funding was withheld, powerful figures expressed concern about Kininmonth's plan behind closed doors and bad press built around the project as it dragged on with no movement into the 1970s.

Eventually Kininmonth's firm was let go and the Edinburgh architect Robert Matthew was hired instead. A fan of modernist brutalism, his firm RMJM had made its mark on the city with 1963's David Hume Tower, part of the University of Edinburgh's controversial George Square redevelopment, and the Royal Commonwealth Pool, created for the city's hosting of the Commonwealth Games in 1970. Matthew's plan involved connecting the Lyceum, the Usher Hall and the new theatre, taking cues from the National Theatre and the Barbican in London.

It came to nothing. With funding still an issue, local government reorganisation meant the old Edinburgh Corporation gave way in 1975 to two bodies, the new Edinburgh District Council and Lothian Regional Council. The Festival Council itself was reorganised to give the Scottish Arts Council more representation. Ronald Mavor, son of James Bridie, became vice-chair of the Festival Council, but these reshuffles meant every council was a funding hurdle to be jumped annually.

The Conservative-led District Council comprised some amateur enthusiasts and others with an alarming degree of indifference to the International Festival, while the Labour-led Regional Council bore a pronounced antipathy to its perceived 'elitist' nature and significant opposition to the opera house, especially when the large and already-existing Playhouse needed refurbishment.

Soon after the reorganisation, the opera house project was cancelled altogether and the Festival itself became a political football to be kicked about by factions on the councils for years to come.

The site of Poole's Synod Hall, rashly torn down in anticipation of the new building in 1966, lay barren and overgrown with weeds until the early 1990s. Its replacement was a functional modern office block with a new home for a key Festival venue buried deep inside. The plan for Edinburgh to have a new, opera-worthy theatre also took two more decades to come to fruition, but in the meantime, what became known to locals as the Castle Terrace 'the Hole in the Ground' – the first of many in the city, amid a wave of stop-start late 20th century redevelopment – stood as a stark reminder of the fragile symbiotic balance that was now ingrained between Edinburgh and its Festivals.

* * *

Lord Harewood may not have left a new building in Edinburgh, but his programmes contained many International Festival highlights. In 1962 a wide range of Russian opera and music was presented, inspired by the previous visit of the Leningrad Symphony Orchestra in 1960, which Harewood researched with a visit to the country. He was an honoured visitor behind the Iron Curtain, which made sense to him because, as he put it, culture is 'the most genuine propaganda there is... it represents a people, perhaps untypically but... truthfully'.[4] His three-week trip 'revealed the warmth and the open-heartedness of the basic Russian character'.[5]

Harewood managed to secure the Belgrade Opera performing works by Prokofiev and Borodin, and the appearance of the composer Dimitri Shostakovich for a three-week visit to Edinburgh to hear many of the 25 of his works performed that year by the London Symphony Orchestra, the Polish Radio Symphony Orchestra and the Scottish orchestras. Harewood negotiated this visit during a private meeting with the composer (and interpreter) in his Leningrad apartment, during which he said Shostakovich earned his sympathy. The composer had recently broken his leg after a drunken fall and nervously struggled to light the cigarettes he smoked one after the other. After Shostakovich arrived in Edinburgh, they bonded further at the Sunday night parties Harewood threw when all the restaurants were shut, over the haggis smothered in whisky-infused gravy he liked to introduce as the 'house speciality' to artists from across the world.

The Russian theme of the programme was widely celebrated in Britain and in the Soviet Union, although the key Shostakovich works presented made an unusual pairing amid his output. On 7 September 1962, conductor Carlo Maria Giulini and the Philharmonia Orchestra gave the Western premiere of his *Symphony No 4 in C minor, Op 43*, which was written between 1935 and 1936, although its premiere later that year in Leningrad was scrapped by the composer following the Stalin-ordered 'Chaos Instead of Music' *Pravda* editorial of January 1936.

This article specifically criticised Shostakovich's opera *Lady Macbeth of Mtensk*,[6] a performance of which at the Bolshoi Theatre the leader had left early. The emerging formalism of the piece flew against all traditions of Soviet realism and such a denunciation would normally include a 'disappearance' and a death sentence. Yet Shostakovich survived and redeemed himself. Stalin died in 1953 and Shostakovich joined the Communist Party in 1960.[7]

In 1961, his *Symphony No 4* was finally performed in the Soviet Union.

Three days before this lost work was first heard by the West at Edinburgh's Usher Hall, the Philharmonia Orchestra premiered Shostakovich's *Symphony No 12 in D minor, Op 112* in the same venue, a work which he had composed in implied agreement that doing so would allow *Symphony No 4* to be heard again. As he'd apparently intended since the 1930s, *Symphony No 12* finally paid explicit tribute to the life of Vladimir Lenin and the Bolshevik Revolution – its subtitle was *The Year 1917*. Ambiguity about Shostakovich's commitment to Soviet ideals persisted long after his death.

Elsewhere, a series of ceilidhs, Scottish poetry readings and Gaelic concerts started at the Usher Hall and Leith Town Hall, the International Festival playing catchup with the folk tradition instituted at the People's Festival a decade before. In 1963 this led to the sometime refusenik and opponent of the International Festival Hugh MacDiarmid actually performing at it, reading his own work in Leith. Other notable moments of Harewood's tenure included recitals by Benjamin Britten and the tenor Peter Pears at Leith Town Hall in '61, Daniel Barenboim at the Usher Hall in '65, and operatic visits by Naples' Teatro San Carlo, the Hungarian State Opera and Ballet, Munich's Bavarian State Opera and Prague National Theatre in '64.

There were some retrospectively mouth-watering dramatic casts, including John Hurt, Richard Briers and Leonard Rossiter in *Hamp*, John Wilson's little-known play about desertion during the First World War, at the Lyceum in 1964. Alastair Sim, George Cole and James Bolam appeared in George Bernard Shaw's comedy *Too Good to Be True* at the same venue the following year. Haizlip-Stoiber Productions of New York arrived in 1965 with the great American writer James Baldwin's *The Amen Corner*, about the life of poor families attending a Harlem church. The company returned in '67, after Harewood had left Edinburgh, with a version of Eugene O'Neill's *The Emperor Jones*, about a black American man who sets himself up as emperor of a Caribbean island, and the dancer and choreographer Donald McKayle's *Black New World*. *The Emperor Jones* was directed by the off-Broadway director Gene Frankel and starred James Earl Jones.

The early 1960s also brought two major figures of 20th century popular culture to Edinburgh, at opposite ends of their career. With a commendable enthusiasm for non-European musical styles,[8] Harewood programmed an extensive range of Indian music in 1963. This opened with an introductory discussion between the Indian veena player and dance and music scholar VK Narayana Menon[9] and the violinist Yehudi Menuhin at the Freemason's Hall. Harewood had travelled in India before becoming Festival director and loved ragas for sitar and sarod since 1956, the year the sitar virtuoso Ravi Shankar first played small concerts in Europe, which Harwood had witnessed. By the time Shankar appeared at the 1963 Edinburgh Festival he was well-known in classical circles, but still four years ahead of discovery by the Byrds and the Beatles' George Harrison and the accompanying flush of countercultural fame which saw him play the Monterey and Woodstock music festivals.

Fifteen multi-genre performances of Indian music spanned the city in '63, including one at St Cuthbert's Church at the junction of Lothian Road and Princes Street involving Shankar, Menuhin and the great sarod player Ali Akbar Khan interpreting the works of Bach and Bartok. The great success of this strand was the *Bharatanatyam* dancer Tanjore Balasaraswati, already familiar to some Western audiences, but increasingly touring and performing outside India. Harewood saw her dance at a conference in Japan and when she arrived in Edinburgh her request for a hard floor rather than a sprung surface meant she danced in the hall of the then-Royal Scottish Museum on Chambers Street.

Indian music and dance continued during Harewood's tenure, but in Shankar he had brought a defining international music figure to Edinburgh while his fame was still emerging, and a friend to the Festival for years to come. Shankar's final performance in Edinburgh was at the Usher Hall during the 2011 International Festival, when he was 91 years old.

By 1964, on the other hand, Marlene Dietrich had already enjoyed decades of fame since becoming a star of German and then Hollywood cinema in the interwar years and had recently made her final film appearance of a prolific run stretching back to the early 1920s.[10] The 62-year-old was now making a lot of money as a star of big-budget touring cabaret shows and had been for a decade. Her week-long, late-night run at the Lyceum in '64 was greeted with fanfare.

Arriving onstage in her slim-fitting trademark 'nude' gown of peach or gold, depending on which report was most trusted, Dietrich performed a simple set which was all about the song and her own star power. Accompanied by pianist and musical director Burt Bacharach, a 36-year-old who made his own career while helping to revive hers, she evoked nostalgia for multi-generational childhoods among the audience. She sang songs in four languages, including Ray Henderson's 1929 song 'You're the Cream in My Coffee', which she had used to screen test for her breakthrough sound picture *The Blue Angel* and 'Falling in Love Again (Can't Help It)' from the film itself.

She performed 'My Blue Heaven', 'La Vie En Rose' and 'Lili Marlene', recalling Berlin's pre-war years. Dietrich returned for two encores and the crowd cheered for more, although an intended version of Peter, Paul and Mary's then-current hit 'Puff the Magic Dragon' remained unperformed, on the first night at least. She and Bacharach played the Festival again in 1965 and this time she was greeted by photographers on the runway at Turnhouse Airport, a conquering hero of a rich era for the Edinburgh International Festival.

* * *

If the back catalogue of Decca Records is anything to go by, the death of the Howff in 1963 was met with the arrival of a dedicated Edinburgh Folk Festival that year and the year after – or at least, *Edinburgh Folk Festival* was the name of two volumes of music recorded in the city and released across '63 and '64. There was nothing so formal as an actual festival, though. In 1961, 24-year-old English entrepreneur Nathan 'Nat' Joseph had founded his own label Transatlantic, with the aim of importing American folk and blues records and distributing them to the British market. In '63, he talked Decca into giving him money to travel to Edinburgh and record the best music he could find.

With the Howff gone, the people who gathered there were finding new places to perform. The Edinburgh folk scene was evolving, slipping into the cracks between the seam of traditionalism unearthed by Hamish Henderson at the People's Festivals and the oncoming wave of rock 'n' roll, and a young 'folknik' scene was emerging. These were serious folk heads, but ones influenced by Jack Kerouac, American jazz music and the availability of cheap Afghan hashish in the city, as much as the old music. Robin Williamson was one, an ex-pupil of George Watson's College, who dropped out to play jazz and then folk. He and Bert Jansch were flatmates, along with their friend Clive Palmer, a Londoner who'd come north to Edinburgh just as the Howff was closing down. They lived in ruined squats in some of the city centre tenements being eyed for destruction by councilor Pat Rogan, including one on the top floor of a West Nicholson Street tenement and another on the Grassmarket.

A third was in the deceptively glamorously named Society Buildings, across the road from Greyfriars Kirkyard and on the same Chambers Street block as the city's main museum. Mike Heron, another Edinburgh musician of the era, described a former Quaker meeting hall whose floor was covered in the tents and bedding of itinerant beatniks. Society Buildings didn't escape the attention of civic improvers and the wrecking ball soon came for it.

In the meantime Williamson and Palmer set up a folk night every Thursday at the Crown Bar on Lothian Street, by the McEwan Hall, as an addition to Archie Fisher's at the same venue every Tuesday. Jansch lit out for the road, hitching his way to France, Morocco and elsewhere. There were folk nights at the White Horse pub on the Royal Mile and at Hamish Henderson's haunt Sandy Bell's, where multi-generational folk players continued to congregate.

The place shut in the afternoon, typical of a Scottish pub in those days, so after lunchtime pints, everyone retired to a nearby flat on Forrest Road, to play more music until reopening time in the early evening.

For the Fringe of 1962 Martha Schlamme returned, this time to the much grander Palladium Theatre on Fountainbridge, although she lamented the loss of the Howff. During these three weeks, Archie Fisher hosted ceilidhs within the Outlook Tower at the base of the Castle Esplanade, formerly town planner Patrick Geddes' museum and later host to the Camera Obscura tourist attraction, as well as late-night parties at an old sweet factory on the Grassmarket. Hamish Imlach, never short of a florid recollection or two, said:

> It was a remarkable place. I recall seeing the conductor of the
> Berlin Philharmonic Orchestra, Cleo Laine and Geraint Evans all
> perched on the plastic cattle mats, and Albert Finney riding in on a
> motorcycle. The Police hated the place.[11]

The International Festival even got in on the act with this vibrant, youthful sound, engaging the Scots brothers Rory and Alex McEwen to host a concert at Haymarket Ice Rink in '62.[12] The McEwens were a strange pair amid the folk revival, a scene largely driven at that time by working-class musicians and the middle-class entrepreneurs bringing them together. The sons of a titled Conservative politician from the Scottish Borders, they were educated at the elite Eton College in England and at Cambridge University, where Rory performed with Cambridge Footlights. He became the art editor of *The Spectator* magazine and was the grandson-in-law of Hugo von Hoffsmanthal, founder of the Salzburg Festival.

Yet the brothers had a real love and enthusiasm for Scottish folk music, which Rory and Alex played during travels in 1956 across America, including to a national audience on Ed Sullivan's show. Rory became a broadcaster and folk expert for the BBC and the legend that he was the first person to play 12-string guitar on British television brought him a lot of fans. By the time the brothers hosted the International Festival's *Plain Song... and All That Jazz* event at Haymarket Ice Rink with performers including Dolina Maclennan and the jazz pianist George Melly, Rory was also renowned as the host of the short-lived folk and blues programme *Hullabaloo*.

The Haymarket show was a success and the following year the McEwens resolved to do something on their own, which fully indulged their personal tastes. They hired the Palladium Theatre for a late-night run of shows named *Straight to the Wood* and invited folk players from the city and elsewhere to get involved. It was into this milieu that Nat Joseph and his producer Bill

Leader bundled during August 1963, armed with Decca's tapes and money, looking to record any folk singers they could find. Much of this was done at Dolina Maclennan's flat above Napier's the Herbalist on Bristo Place, along the street from the Crown, where Dominic Behan was in festival residency with his show *Behan Being Behan*.

Issued on Joseph's Transatlantic Records imprint, later the key label of Britain's 1960s folk scene, the two *Edinburgh Folk Festival* volumes are now the key document of the sound of Edinburgh in those days and an important record of the nationwide folk revival's coming of age during the Edinburgh Festival. Between them, they contained recordings by old Howff regulars Archie and Ray Fisher, Dolina Maclennan, Owen Hand and regular visitor from Glasgow Hamish Imlach. There were also arrangements by Clive Palmer and Robin Williamson as a duo, the great English singer and close friend of Jansch's, Anne Briggs and by Birmingham's Ian Campbell Folk Group,[13] among them the future Fairport Convention violinist Dave Swarbrick.

These Festival nights were the final few gasps of the truly seminal folk era in Edinburgh, as musicians moved away to form formidable reputations elsewhere. Jansch left for London, where he became a founding member of the acid-folk supergroup Pentangle. Signed to Transatlantic, they set the standard in folk-styled acoustic guitar for decades to come.

Palmer and Williamson, meanwhile, started playing with their fellow local musician Mike Heron, who used to entertain Jim Haynes and other cocktail-sipping, burger-chowing US Air Force personnel at Kirknewton with rock 'n' roll covers. The three moved to Glasgow and evolved into the Incredible String Band, after which they were signed by Elektra Records, home of the Doors, Love and the Stooges. They had six hit UK albums by the end of the decade, influenced Paul McCartney and Led Zeppelin and played the Woodstock Festival in 1969. The same year they also provided music for Fringe performances by the multimedia theatre pioneer Geoff Moore's Moving Image dance company at the Richard Demarco Gallery.

The Edinburgh folk scene still played a part in the Festival. In 1962 a trio of former Edinburgh College of Art students played at Dolina Maclennan and Robin Gray's Waverley night as the Corrie Folk Trio, a packed summer evening's show in the upstairs snug which soon turned into a Festival residency. After some line-up changes, a profile-raising booking on the Scottish television folk show *Hoot'nanny* and a name change to the Corries, they became internationally-renowned exponents of the now-mainstream Scottish folk sound. In 1967 their member Roy Williamson composed the future unofficial Scottish sporting anthem 'Flower of Scotland'.

The Corries also hosted Festival showcase gigs at venues like the Goold Hall on St Andrew Square in 1963 and the much larger Caley Picture House on Lothian Road, freshly converted from a cinema, in 1968. On the bill at the latter show was a young singer from Dunfermline named Barbara Dickson, who arrived in the city in 1964 and often played and recorded with Archie Fisher. During the Fringe of 1967, Dickson befriended an unknown 21-year-old student, avid folk fan and part-time pub singer from Liverpool, the city of her mother's birth, who'd heard the legend of Sandy Bell's infamous folk sessions and was hearing one for himself when they met. His name was Willy Russell and he also wrote one-act plays for his student drama group while training to be a teacher at St Katherine's Training College.[14]

In 1971 this student group, collectively known as Cateysaints, performed Russell's piece *Keep Your Eyes Down* and in 1972 brought it and his plays *Playground* and *Sam O'Shanker*, an attempt to rewrite Robert Burns' *Tam O'Shanter* in English dialect, to the Fringe under the collective heading Blind Scouse. The playwright and founder of the 7:84 company John McGrath saw them and was impressed and he recommended Russell to Liverpool's Everyman Theatre, whose artistic director Alan Dossor commissioned him to write *When the Reds...* in 1973. It was Russell's professional playwriting debut and the next year the theatre presented his *John, Paul, George, Ringo... and Bert*. Going against the grain of expectation, the writer asked his Edinburgh folk friend Barbara Dickson to sing the Beatles' music for the play. It was a huge hit, playing to 15,000 people during an eight-week run and transferring to London's West End, where it ran for a year and gathered up *Evening Standard* and Critics' Circle awards.

Both Dickson and Russell's careers were further examples of the Edinburgh effect, where an August meeting in a noisy pub and the right person seeing a promising piece of amateur drama can make stars. Willy Russell became one of the UK's leading dramatists in the latter decades of the 20th century, with cinema-transferring stage hits including *Educating Rita* and *Shirley Valentine*, while Dickson achieved great fame as a pop star, a musical theatre singer and an actor. In 1983 they were reunited in Russell's eventually phenomenally successful musical *Blood Brothers*, which ran in London's West End for 24 years.

Other stars spent their early days in the Edinburgh folk scene too, like a young Glaswegian named Billy Connolly. Later in the decade he returned for gigs with his folk duo the Humblebums, who were inspired by the Incredible String Band, alongside Tam Harvey and later the future rock singer Gerry Rafferty. In 1969, an 18-year-old singer named Isla St Clair moved to Edinburgh from Aberdeenshire. Her mother was a singer named Zetta Sinclair, a close friend of Hamish Henderson's great source-singing discovery Jeannie Richardson, and St Clair (her stage name) sang folk since she was a child. Close friends with Barbara Dickson, St Clair made an unusual career change in 1978 when she became a household name as co-host of television quiz show *The Generation Game*.

In 1977 another document of the evolved Edinburgh folk scene emerged with *Sandy Bell's Ceilidh*, a record annotated by Henderson, which featured performances at the famous pub by a new generation of singers and players, among them the Leith songwriter Dick Gaughan, Edinburgh trio the McCalmans and nursing sisters Liz and Maggie Cruickshank, a harmony duo since the Howff. The famed accordionist Aly Bain also appeared, while his future musical partner Phil Cunningham was busy elsewhere in the city with he and his brother Johnny's folk band Silly Wizard.

Two years after this record an Edinburgh Folk Festival arrived, the real thing this time and its artistic director was an Englishman from South Shields in Tyneside named Ian Barrow. He'd already tried a smaller version of the same in 1968, just after graduating with a degree in physics from Edinburgh University, programming three weeks of concerts by musicians including Archie Fisher and Hamish Imlach that summer. Barrow went on to found Edinburgh Folk Club in 1973 and publish the *Sandy Bell's Broadsheet* folk newsletter, both with Ian Green and Kenny Thompson. In this festival's early years it hosted concerts by Silly Wizard, Richard Thompson and, as noted in Barrow's induction to the Scottish Traditional Music Hall of Fame:

[A] Planxty concert that coincided with a Scotland vs Ireland international at Murrayfield, a pub session series where staff couldn't pull pints fast enough, and a late-night club so popular it ran out of Guinness. [15]

The Folk Festival ran every year until 1999 and after its demise new, year-round traditional music strands like Ceilidh Culture and Tradfest have emerged in Edinburgh, although Barrow left the Festival's artistic directorship in 1982 to become a physics teacher at George Watson's College. He founded the Fringe venue the Acoustic Music Centre in the same year, programming folk and acoustic artists during the Festival ever since. The Centre was based on Chambers Street until 1995, then the University's Reid Hall on Bristo Square, the St Bride's Centre in Dalry and most recently the Edinburgh Ukrainian Club on Royal Terrace. From 2009, Barrow's Stoneyport promotions business has also staged folk and traditional concerts in and out of Festival time at the Queen's Hall.

On any weekend evening through the year, especially in the still-existing Sandy Bell's and the Royal Oak on Infirmary Street, impromptu folk jams among fellow patrons can still be heard, the democratic style of the movement unearthed during the People's Festival of 1951 continuing to ring through some of the city's last few unchanged barrooms.

* * *

By the late 1960s a new sense of radicalism was overtaking the world, its key point coming in the year 1968, with the Soviet suppression of the Prague Spring, the assassination of Martin Luther King and the Tet Offensive of the Vietnam War. Cities across the world rose up in protest and while street-rioting within the British Isles was largely confined to Northern Ireland, the events of this period were fuel for artists and students, inspired by sexual emancipation, growing civil rights movements, the loosening of Establishment cultural hegemony and a sense of experimentation assisted by the popularity of hallucinogenic drugs.

In Edinburgh, the spirit of '68 was most evident in the activities of radical Edinburgh University student activists. In 1966, playing on his reputation as a broadcaster with strong and uncensored views which often took aim at the Establishment, Malcolm Muggeridge had been elected as the University's student-elected rector. Well-known during the Edinburgh Festival as the chair of the 1962 Writers Conference, he had been intrigued by Communism as a young man and a strong critic of the Soviet Union following visits there, as well as an avowed anti-monarchist Republican and an early-adopting vegetarian. He was also an atheist, but in the immediate period following his election in Edinburgh, he undertook a conversion to Christianity which resulted in the publication of his 1969 book *Jesus Rediscovered*.

This personal moral journey coincided with articles in Edinburgh's university newspaper the *Student* about the potential benefits of consuming LSD and student campaigns to increase the availability of the female contraceptive pill on campus. These developments didn't sit well with Muggeridge and in January 1968 he invited the press to St Giles' Cathedral for the Rector's traditional term-opening speech; an event which turned out to be his very public and headline-grabbing resignation, in which he told students he could understand their sense of rebellion, but not the way it was expressed through drug use.

One of Edinburgh University's activists during this period was a teenaged history student named Gordon Brown, who had been fast-streamed to university from Kirkcaldy High School at the age of 16 in 1967. Staying on as a postgraduate, he became only the second student rector of the university following his 1972 election defeat of Sir Fred Catherwood, former Director-General of the National Economic Development Council.[16] This was an era when students were promoting anti-apartheid causes, protesting the 1970 Scotland v South Africa rugby international at Murrayfield and demanding the university divest its South African investments.

In 1973, the Edinburgh University Students Association (EUSA) was founded by the merger of the Students' Representative Council with the until-recently men-only Edinburgh University Union and the women-only Chambers Street Union. EUSA's role in the management and administration of Edinburgh University union buildings later gave it a significant role on the Fringe, while Brown, of course, became the United Kingdom's chancellor of the exchequer in 1997 and then Prime Minister in 2007.

At the Edinburgh Festival, the core embodiment of the radicalism of the 1960s remained the Traverse Theatre. Jim Haynes was long gone in 1966, but new artistic director Gordon McDougall and his general manager Max Stafford-Clark were well-attuned to the exciting, scandalous repertoire he'd built up. In his early days McDougall played it safe, with productions of John Osbourne's well-established *Inadmissible Evidence* and *Look Back in Anger* and topical documentary dramatisations of hearings into the Vietnam War and the Profumo Affair. Then in 1967, the pair established relations with the American playwright Paul Foster and the New York theatre he worked with, the Lower East Side's La MaMa Experimental Theatre Club.

A spiritual companion to the Traverse, La MaMa was opened in 1961 as Café La MaMa by Ellen Stewart, a former fashion designer for Saks Fifth Avenue and the 'Mama' of its name. She invited theatre makers to stage their work in her storefront boutique at 321 East Ninth Street, helping build the off-off-Broadway movement and among them was Foster, whose plays MacDougall staged at the Traverse in early 1967. Soon after, Foster visited Edinburgh and during that year's Fringe La MaMa's experimental and esoteric work provided an American spin on Traverse-style radicalism that was at least as headline-grabbing as anything Jim Haynes ever came up with. In the Traverse itself, Foster's anti-war piece *The Hessian Corporal* was performed,[17] along with *Balls*, which infamously featured only two ping-pong balls swinging back and forth as esoteric recorded monologues played. Elsewhere in the city at Barrie Halls, there was an array of Fringe works by then-unknown La MaMa playwrights including Leonard Melfi, future Pulitzer Prize for Drama winner Lanford Wilson, fellow future Pulitzer winner and Academy Award-nominated actor Sam Shepherd and Rochelle Owens.

The latter playwright's piece was *Futz!*, about an unconventional relationship between a farmer and his pig, which, in typical Traverse style, attracted fury from certain elements of the press. *The Daily Express*'s Brian Meek was one writer who went in strong on the play without having seen it, as he admitted during a public discussion at the Traverse which paired him with the show's director Tom O'Horgan. The play was grasped by many critics as a thoughtful and challenging satire on just the kind of herd-like moral furore which it inspired in Edinburgh, however. After seeing it in New York, James Rado and Gerome Ragi invited O'Horgan to make his Broadway debut as director of their musical *Hair* in 1968, which he followed with Andrew Lloyd Webber's *Jesus Christ Superstar* in 1971.

Elsewhere in La MaMa's Traverse's programme of '67, Foster's *Tom Paine*, about the 18th century American Revolutionary, premiered at the Church Hill Theatre in Morningside, while the Traverse itself produced Alfred Jarry's *Ubu in Chains* at the same venue, with live music by the psychedelic rock group and veterans of London Happenings the Soft Machine. With Robert Wyatt among their number, the group preceded the play's run in early September with their own show at Barrie Halls, subtitled *Lullabies for Catatonics*, featuring dancer Graziella Martinez and with visuals by artist Mark Boyle. For the *Ubu* show, illustrator Gerald Scarfe, who later provided the visuals for Pink Floyd's 1979 film *The Wall*, designed the Ubus as a pair of walking, talking male and female genitalia.

The play was poorly reviewed, but such notices did no harm to the Traverse's cult reputation. Joyce McMillan later wrote that this period was the zenith of the:

> [W]ildly exaggerated stories circulating about the drinking, dope-smoking, drug-dealing and lurid sexual practices that were supposed to take place there. At the time, the Traverse was a powerful focus for respectable Edinburgh's fantasies and fears about the new 'permissive' age.[18]

Later that year, Gordon McDougall left the Traverse and its punishing, non-stop work environment for Granada Television's Stables Theatre Company in Manchester and Stafford-Clark became sole artistic director. His first Festival in '68 welcomed the People Show, London's new and pioneering experimental theatre company – formed in 1966 around a Happening organised by Pink Floyd at the All Saints church in Notting Hill – for a series of midnight shows. The company returned to Edinburgh in years to come, often with the future film director Mike Figgis among their number as a musician and performer.

Then, as the festival of 1969 began, the Traverse as it was came to an end.

A combination of encroaching development and growing official concern about both the structural suitability and fire safety of the building at James Court saw the committee approve a rapid move to a new space in an old stone warehouse three times the size of old Traverse, which seated up to 100. In a courtyard behind the tenements at 112 West Bow, where the Grassmarket meets Victoria Street, the new Traverse was opened on 24 August by the UK arts minster Jennie Lee, just in time for Fringe presentations of the Traverse's version of *Dracula* alongside Traverse regular Stanley Eveling's play *Dear Janet Rosenberg, Dear Mr Kooning*. Soon after, the latter transferred to London's Royal Court.

Even more than McDougall, Stafford-Clark understood the emergent 1960s counter-cultural scene – and unlike Jim Haynes, he was a skillful creative producer in his own right. In late 1969, with the belief the Traverse now sat 'uneasily somewhere between an Arts Lab and a conventional repertory theatre', he abdicated his artistic directorship to set up the Traverse Workshop Company, a group of actors on a modest retainer who indulged his interest in pure theatrical experimentation. Using the old Traverse as rehearsal space, the TWC workshopped esoteric physical pieces intensively and to their own improvisational non-deadline, rather than the urgency of an opening night.

Here, Stafford-Clark pioneered an exploratory method of theatremaking which he took with him to his own Joint Stock Theatre Company in 1974, co-founded with the playwright David Hare and others. He became artistic director at the Royal Court in London from 1979 until 1993 – where he promoted playwrights including Hare, Caryl Churchill, Andrea Dunbar, Hanif Kureishi and Jim Cartright – and then head of his own Out of Joint company. For the Fringe of '76 he returned to the Traverse to direct Caryl Churchill's *Light Shining in Buckinghamshire*, part of a seemingly never-ending golden period of new playwriting for the Edinburgh institution, which by this point had managed to mature into a professional but still very adventurous new writing theatre.

Stafford-Clark's replacement in 1970 was Michael Rudman, an American with no previous Traverse experience and a resemblance to Jim Haynes only in looks and accent, such was his ability to present large amounts of great work while still balancing the books. Rudman was replaced on his departure in 1973 by Mike Ockrent, a former Edinburgh University student who'd become involved in the Haynes-era Traverse through student drama and been invited back by Rudman to direct after a period with John Knight's Perth Theatre.

Some key Traverse Fringe shows and actors during the early '70s included the 'seven-author play' *Lay By*, written by Hare, Howard Brenton, Brian Clark, Trevor Griffiths, Stephen Poliakoff, Hugh Stoddart and Snoo Wilson, Stanley Eveling's Ian Holm-featuring *Caravaggio Buddy*, the subsequent Hampstead Theatre transfer of Bertolt Brecht's *Drums in the Night* starring Petra Markham and Stephen Rea and Mike Leigh's *The Jaws of Death*, with Alison Steadman. There was also work by Steven Berkoff, Dominic Behan and more shows by Lindsay Kemp, the Scaffold and the People Show, while Simon Callow – who made his stage debut with a small role in the 1973

International Festival production of *A Satire of the Three Estates* at the Assembly Hall – became a key member of the theatre's ensemble.

Many more festival adventures lay ahead at the Traverse, but its foundation was in a spirit of emerging cultural adventure which was entirely of the 1960s.

The Traverse was no longer the *enfant terrible* of British theatre, but it's never become staid or uninteresting. Its Fringe programme announcement remains one of the highlights of the early-year Edinburgh Festival build-up to this day.

* * *

After the closure of Max Stafford-Clark's Traverse Workshop Company in 1974, the original Traverse was destined for eventual conversion into flats, just one of a series of changes to Edinburgh's landscape that impacted on the Festival and vice versa. While the devastating philistinism of the planned ring road around the city centre was headed off, there was destruction elsewhere – not just of the Synod Hall on Castle Terrace, but through a whole district on the Southside, near the university.

During the 1960s and '70s, the Potterrow area of the city – which adjoined the McEwan Hall, site of the '62 and '63 conferences and Hamish Henderson's School of Scottish Studies on George Square – was torn up for redevelopment by the University of Edinburgh. First to go were many of the terraced rows of Georgian houses around leafy George Square, an 18th century development set outside the old Edinburgh city walls, which formerly ran through Greyfriars' Kirkyard and along the back of what's now the National Museum of Scotland. Once home to Walter Scott, Arthur Conan Doyle and numerous Scottish politicians, including Henry Dundas, George Square was partly torn down on one and a half sides, despite opposition from architecture and urban planning pressure groups the Cockburn Association and the specifically-created Georgian Group of Edinburgh.[19]

These fine Georgian terraces, some of which can still be seen on the Square's east and west sides, were replaced by a utopian, utilitarian patchwork of Modernist concrete, including the multi-storey Appleton and David Hume Towers, the George Square Theatre lecture hall and Edinburgh University Library. Designed by Basil Spence's firm, this is now one of the largest academic libraries in the world, containing 1.8 million printed volumes, among them 400,000 rare books and 6 kilometres of archives and manuscripts.[20]

In the late 1960s and early '70s, Bristo Street, which used to cut diagonally across from Chapel Street to Bristo Place as a main artery into the city centre from the south, was entirely destroyed, alongside sometime Traverse Theatre offsite Fringe venues Pollock Memorial Hall and Barrie Memorial Theatre.

Parker's department store and public houses including the Woolpack Inn and the Argyll Arms went with them. Entire streets were removed, including Marshall Street, Park Place and Charles Street, the latter including the site of Jim Haynes' old Paperback Bookshop.

This area was slowly filled, first with the university's Potterrow student centre in 1973, an ugly grey construction with a greenhouse-like, domed social space in the centre and by the Bristo Square plaza outside the McEwan Hall a decade later, which soon became a meeting point and makeshift stunt park for Edinburgh's young skateboarders. The square on which the Paperback once stood was just a dirt car park for decades until the Informatics Forum opened in 2008, housing the University's artificial intelligence and computer science research departments.

On the spot where the Paperback Bookshop once stood, a small bronze rhinoceros head fixed to the Forum's wall and a bronze book on a plinth on the corner of Crichton Street now confuse visitors with little idea of Edinburgh's cultural history. Created by Edinburgh College of Art student William Darrell in 2011, the year the Art College merged with the University, they memorialise the fading echo of the wide-ranging cultural explosion which a group of people set off in Edinburgh in the 1960s amid these forgotten ghost-spaces.

For all that's come since, however, the new district created by the University of Edinburgh's expansionism has been anything but unfriendly to the Edinburgh Festival Fringe. From the end of the 1970s, the rapidly-growing Fringe has been harnessed by bands of arts producers and entrepreneurs who marshalled it into the form we know today and the new architecture of George Square and Potterrow has been an integral part of this evolution.

SPOTLIGHT

The Great Northern Welly Boot Show (1972)

AT THE TURN of the 1960s, a teenage apprentice Clydeside welder named Billy Connolly wandered Rose Street during festival time, crawling the pubs and marvelling at the long-haired folk singers and proto-beatniks bringing the city to life. Raised in Glasgow, in the demolished tenements of Anderston and then the post-war housing estate of Drumchapel, he completed his training and went to work on an oil platform in Nigeria for three months. When he returned, he bought a banjo at the Barras market in the East End of his home city and resolved to become a long-haired folk singer in his own right.

In the late 1960s Connolly made a name for himself in Scotland and further afield as part of the Humblebums, later famed for the band Stealer's Wheel[1] and his international 1978 solo hit 'Baker Street'. The Humblebums released three albums – the last two with covers by idiosyncratic Paisley painter John Byrne – and then split in 1971, as Connolly's fame for between-song comedy overtook his reputation as a banjo player. He played his first solo gig in late 1970 in Musselburgh, on the Forth coast just east of Edinburgh. His first comedy record, 1972's simply-titled *Live!*, appeared with a cover by Byrne on Nat Joseph's Transatlantic Records, also home to old Howff regulars Bert Jansch and Owen Hand.

The Great Northern Welly Boot Show had its roots partly in Connolly's interest in getting into theatre during the lull between the Humblebums fading away and his comedy career taking off – he and Tam Harvey had already provided music for a Glasgow Citizens Theatre play called *Clydeside* in 1966 – and partly in a play that appeared on the Traverse Theatre stage in February 1972. *Tell Charlie Thanks for the Truss* was a whimsical piece of proto-gig theatre, written by Glaswegian former schoolteacher turned poet Tom Buchan, a member of the same poetry enclave still congregating around the elderly Hugh MacDiarmid at Milne's Bar and the Abbotsford on Rose Street. An early entry in Buchan's playwriting career, his lyrics for *Tell Charlie* were set to music by pianist Tom McGrath, Jim Haynes' former appointee as editor of the countercultural *International Times*, now back in Glasgow to kick heroin, study English and develop his own poetry.

As a former shipworker in the yards of the River Clyde, Connolly played shows in 1971 to support former colleagues staging a 'work-in' in defiance of the collapse of Upper Clyde Shipbuilders, a high-profile campaign which attracted the attention of the Labour politician Tony Benn and the ex-Beatle John Lennon. Connolly wanted his first play to reflect this campaign while not actively being a documentary, so he took Buchan an idea about a work-in at a welly boot factory and asked him to co-write it. This first version of *Great Northern Welly Boot Show* played at the King's Theatre in Glasgow during the Clyde Fair International in spring 1972, an early iteration of a radical arts festival for the city and by all accounts it wasn't great – or rather, the songs and the humour stood out, but the drama didn't hang together properly, despite Buchan's best efforts.

At least, that was the verdict of three young actors from Glasgow named Bill Paterson, Alex Norton and John Bett, who saw and were enthused by the show at the King's. When it arrived in Edinburgh in August 1972, now with director Robin Lefevere attached, they were in the cast alongside producer Kenny Ireland[2] – later the artistic director of Edinburgh's Royal Lyceum for a decade until 2003 – and the 'token' English actor Patrick Malahide. The venue was the old, warehouse-proportioned Waverley Market next to the city's main railway station, where the co-operative cast and crew built the staging and seating themselves from scratch.

The show featured spectacles such as a woman stripping while standing between characters wearing masks of Conservative Prime Minister Ted Heath and his Labour opposite number Harold Wilson, and a range of bespoke comedy boots created by set designer and former Humblebums artist John Byrne. These included the Jack Buchanan Evening Welly, with a bowtie and silk lapels; the Dixie Flyer Cowboy Wellies; the Rustic Wishing Wellies; and the Reggae Wellies, a pair of enormous, half-peeled Fyffes bananas, which later became a famous part of Connolly's comedy image as the 1970s went on.

At the heart of it all, of course, was the co-writer himself, a fast-developing onstage talent who went out solo to tell his own jokes when curtain-up was delayed one night, sharp-witted and thoroughly Glaswegian, thriving before audiences of 700 when he'd previously been used to folk basements and attics. He'd told jokes onstage before, of course, but usually with a banjo to support him. Now he was instrumental in creating a new Scottish folk theatre.

* * *

Containing comedy, good songs and passionate if blunt political conviction, *The Great Northern Welly Boot Show* was the big hit of the 1972 Fringe, inspiring queues around the block for tickets. Thanks to Malahide's contacts in London it transferred to the Old Vic, where it was received warmly and no more. Connolly didn't look back, as his career in comedy raced away from this point, although he returned to the Fringe at the Traverse Theatre in the late 1970s for a little-acknowledged stint as a playwright.

An' Me Wi' a Bad Leg Tae (1976) was a well-reviewed slice of Glaswegian kitchen sink comedy, presented by new Ayrshire company Borderline Theatre and notable for the ever-dependable Bill Paterson's performance. The opening of *When Hair Was Long and Time Was Short* (1977), again with Borderline, was delayed due to a directorial disagreement. Porridge-like prison comedy *The Red Runner* (1979), a high-profile co-production between the Traverse and the International Festival, was widely-panned. After it, Connolly's stage career focused firmly on him telling the jokes.

It's fair to say Connolly's career as one of Britain's defining comedians has overshadowed the work of everyone else involved in *The Great Northern Welly Boot Show*, but an entire generation of Scottish artists' names were made with that run in Edinburgh. Norton, Paterson and Bett (and Malahide) had long and successful careers on stage and television, as did Ireland, before he took over at the Lyceum. In fact, members of this group returned for two Young Lyceum Company performances at the following International

Festivals. In 1973, Malahide was in Georg Büchner's *Woyzeck* at the Assembly Hall alongside an exceptional cast which included Simon Callow, David Rintoul, Tony Roper and future Doctor Who star Peter Davison and, in 1974, Sean McCarthy's adaptation of *The Fantastical Feats of Fin MacCool* at Haymarket Ice Rink reunited Paterson, Norton, Bett and Malahide, this time under the direction of Ireland, alongside Dolina Maclennan, Hamish Imlach and Muriel Romanes, with John Byrne once more designing the sets.

Patterson, Norton and Bett's involvement in the *Welly Boot Show* also led directly to their success with John McGrath's 7:84 company and during the Fringe of 1977 the trio played in John Byrne's debut as a playwright, *Writer's Cramp*, also directed by *Welly Boot Show*'s Robin Lefevre. Performed at the Calton Studios, a former television studio on Calton Road near Waverley Station, it was met with rave reviews. A year later, the first installment of Byrne's *The Slab Boys* stage opened at the Traverse in April 1978 with a young actor named Robbie Coltrane among the cast. The comedy about working-class young colour-mixers in a Glaswegian carpet factory later transferred to the Royal Court in London and alongside Byrne's television series *Tutti Frutti* a decade later, it established him as one of Scotland's leading dramatists. Perhaps most famously, Bill Paterson went on to play the father of Phoebe Waller-Bridge's character in *Fleabag*, the internationally successful television transfer of another Fringe hit staged 41 years after *The Great Northern Welly Boot Show*.

From the *International Times* and his work as composer for *Tell Charlie Thanks for the Truss* and *The Great Northern Welly Boot Show*, via his period between 1974 and 1977 as founder of the countercultural Third Eye Centre in Glasgow, in which city he booked Miles Davis and Duke Ellington for gigs, Tom McGrath became one of the most prolific and diverse cultural figures in Scotland. His own successful playwriting career of the late 1970s went in the opposite direction to Connolly's, although both were played out against the backdrop of the Fringe and particularly the Traverse Theatre's productions there under artistic director Chris Parr.

Parr was at the Traverse from 1975, for the first year as interim while Mike Ockrent took a sabbatical from which he didn't return. During his tenure various circumstances led the Traverse to swing towards commercial work and away from the experimental, partly at the instigation of the main funder, the Scottish Arts Council. An Oxford graduate from London who worked in theatre in Bradford and previously directed shows at the Traverse, Parr had an interest in making theatre accessible to audiences.

He wanted to take Traverse work beyond the theatre's own walls. For the Fringe of 1976 he established the 'Other Traverse' in the University of Edinburgh's Old Chaplaincy Centre at the apex of Forrest Road and George

IV Bridge, just across the road from Sandy Bell's bar and Greyfriars Kirkyard. Built in the 1840s to the designs of architect Thomas Hamilton, the imposing former New North Free Church stood alongside the site of Edinburgh's old poorhouse and had been used by the University since it was abandoned as a church in 1937. In August 1978, Byrne's *The Slab Boys* was revived at the Other Traverse, alongside two Tom McGrath plays, *The Android Circuit* – about an astronaut exploring sex with an android – and *The Hard Man*.

McGrath had already had a huge Traverse Fringe hit in 1976 with *Laurel and Hardy*, a popular, nostalgic show about the famed entertainers in the vein of *Welly Boot Show*; it starred Kenny Ireland and John Shedden in the title roles and later moved to the Mayfair Theatre in London. Substituting the physicality of comedy with the physicality of violence, *The Hard Man* was based on the life of Glasgow gangster and convicted murderer turned sculptor and author Jimmy Boyle, its co-writer. It premiered at the Traverse in the spring of 1977, the same year as Boyle's best-selling autobiography *A Sense of Freedom* emerged and when it made it to the Fringe after a run at the ICA in London and a UK tour, it was already a critical and commercial hit.

These collaborations between Parr's Traverse and various *Welly Boot Show* alumni were such a success that, in 1979, they were invited to premiere two shows at Moray House Gymnasium in association with the Edinburgh International Festival. One was Connolly's ill-starred *The Red Runner*. The other was Tom McGrath's acclaimed *Animal*, a remarkable, experimental piece, entirely at odds with the undeserved reputation for kitchen sink populism that *The Hard Man* had given its writer, in which a cast of 14 apes wordlessly observe the interactions of two human anthropologists.

Parr's Traverse commissions also included Michael Ondaatje's *The Collected Works of Billy the Kid* in 1976 and the 1979 Edinburgh International Festival hit *Rents* by Michael Wilcox, a queer comedy about two male Edinburgh sex workers which transferred to the Lyric Theatre Hammersmith. The comedian Mel Smith made an early-career stage appearance in the double act *Smith and Goody* during 1977's festival and in the times surrounding the 1979 Scottish Independence Referendum, Parr's support for new creative voices from Scotland – including actors like Robbie Coltrane, Maureen Beattie, Gregor Fisher and Tony Roper – helped set the shape and tone of the nation's culture for the rest of the century.

Before Parr stood down in early 1981, his final Traverse commission was McGrath's *1-2-3 Plays* trilogy and he also commissioned or produced plays by Tom Buchan, Bett and Norton. The latter pair and Bill Paterson were prolific as writers and performers with Scottish companies like Tom McGrath's Glasgow Theatre Club, established in 1978, which became the Tron Theatre two years later and Borderline Theatre, which for a time in the '80s made its Fringe base the Moray House Theatre on the Canongate as it created its own tradition of performing Scots translations of work by the great Italian playwright and activist Dario Fo.

One of Billy Connolly's memoirs told a story of his time at the Traverse which had him being banned from the bar for apparently dipping his own genitals in someone else's gin and tonic – a deliberate provocation to see how far he could push his behaviour before being told to quit. The purpose of his tale was to point out his own recklessness under the influence of alcohol, a drug he gave up in the mid-1980s, but it also illustrated what was undoubtedly a very masculine environment at the time.

With the opening up of the Traverse's festival stages to these working-class young Scottish men by Parr, a macho, competitive atmosphere was fostered for a time. But the transaction went both ways and the best Traverse writers of this era – rooted in the working-class Glaswegian origins of *The Great Northern Welly Boot Show* – wrote Festival plays which were able to excavate new emotional depths, to examine their own behaviour and find what lay at its root.

7

The Film Festival Meets the Movie Brats

'EVERYTHING WE DID, I have to say, was loathed by Forsyth Hardy,' says Lynda Myles, who was from 1973 until 1980 the director of Edinburgh International Film Festival. The first female director of a film festival anywhere in the world, in fact and as such the carrier of the torch which Hardy, Norman Wilson and others had lit back in 1947.

Myles is keen and correct to point out that much of what she achieved was a group effort, also deferring to Hardy and company's foresight and vision in starting the festival in the first place. She's quite probably the most significant single individual in Edinburgh International Film Festival's history – perhaps one of the most important figures in the development of the 20th century European film festival, in fact.

'It was so antithetical to everything they believed in,' she elaborates on the work she championed and the generational conflict it inspired; a conflict that began brewing in – appropriately enough, given the politics of the moment – 1968.

> Forsyth really tried to get me out on an annual basis. I mean, at one point he took the journalist Neil Ascherson aside and asked, didn't Neil think I was too radical? Unaware of the fact that Neil and I were actually sharing a flat, so it wasn't as damaging as it might have been. I respected what [Hardy and the rest of the Film Guild] did in the beginning, but they just wouldn't move, they were locked in the past.

Under the continued guidance of the Film Guild (although Norman Wilson left the chairmanship in 1960 to take up a new job in London) there had been many achievements in the late 1950s and through the '60s – notably the Guild's 1958 move from Film House to a four-storey townhouse at 3 Randolph Crescent with a cinema in the basement, which became a year-round centre of cinema in the mould of the National Film Theatre in London. The same period also saw the association of Ingmar Bergman's films with the festival, including *The Seventh Seal* and *Wild Strawberries*,[1] and the syncing of the programme in '62 and '63 to match the International Festival's Writers and Drama Conferences, showing films like Sidney Lumet's adaptation of Eugene O'Neill's *Long Day's Journey Into Night* and Clive Donner's adaptation of Harold Pinter's *The Caretaker*, starring Alan Bates,

Donald Pleasence and Robert Shaw. Yet 20 years on from its revolutionary inception, the near 60-year-old Hardy's version of the Film Festival didn't say enough to a younger generation.

In fairness, the letter that appeared in *The Scotsman* on 4 September 1967 might have reasonably fuelled Hardy's antipathy to the new generation. Declaring the Film Festival 'second to none in its dullness', it robustly went on the attack against the establishment Film Guild's running of the event. Its author was an undergraduate student of medicine at the University of Edinburgh named David Will, who ran the university's film society with his girlfriend Lynda Myles, then studying philosophy. The pair had met in fresher's week and begun dating and taken over the society, says Myles, through 'apathy on the part of everyone else'.

They were hungry film enthusiasts, inspired by the French New Wave of directors like Jean-Luc Godard, François Truffaut, Alain Resnais and Claude Chabrol and the determinedly left political film writings found in the French magazines *Cahiers du Cinéma* and *Positif*. Where the old film society had put a film on every week, Will and Myles screened daily, sometimes more than once a day, mostly for their own benefit. They programmed films they personally wanted to see and Myles wrote extensive programme notes for each. The pair were of a cineaste generation which firmly supported Truffaut, Godard and other filmmakers involved in the infamous cancellation of the May 1968 edition of the Cannes Film Festival, as political turmoil and student revolt overwhelmed France; a generation and a world apart from the sense of formal internationalism which had sparked Edinburgh's Documentary Festival. The couple holidayed together in Paris, watching films all day at the Cinémathèque Française and became friends with the archivists Henri Langlois and Mary Meerson.

'By the time of the letter Dave and I were going to a lot of music,' says Myles, who was born in Arbroath three months before the original Documentary Festival of '47, raised in Fife and inspired initially by theatre, as a regular teenage visitor to the Byre in St Andrews.

> Somehow we got into Boulez rehearsing *Rite of Spring*,[2] and it just seemed there was such a gap between the artistic level of the International Festival under Peter Diamand and the Film Festival. Dave's pet line was that the Film Festival's musical equivalent was Ivor Novello.[3] I mean, the Film Festival at that point was an absolute joke. I had great admiration for the founding fathers and the seriousness of what they did, but the Film Festival at that point had no status, no point of view. It had been dismissed by someone as the Shell Film Festival, because they were showing documentaries made by Shell.

The catalyst for Myles and Will's eventual seismic impact on the Film Festival came from – in Edinburgh Festival terms – a predictable source. 'Having written this letter to *The Scotsman*, a month or two later we were at an exhibition opening at Ricky Demarco's gallery,' says Myles (the exhibition was *16 Polish Artists*, which opened in October '67 at the Demarco Gallery). 'Ricky said to us, "would you like to meet the director of the Film Festival?" Oh boy, we thought – and that was when we met Murray Grigor for the first time'.

Far from the stand-up argument that the pair might have feared, they found Grigor to be thoughtful, friendly and engaging company. Born in Inverness in 1939 and educated as a biochemist at the University of St Andrews, Grigor was a film enthusiast who had become a young filmmaker himself while still an undergraduate, travelling to the Holy Land of Israel and Palestine with some friends to make a film which he sold to the BBC. Soon after, Grigor became a staff editor at the BBC in Glasgow, where he was when he applied for the Edinburgh Film Festival post.

In fact, it wasn't so much the Film Festival job that interested Grigor, but the position of assistant director of the Films of Scotland Committee which went with it, also based at Randolph Crescent. The Committee had been set up to promote the creation of films in the national interest in the 1930s and its first project was a series of seven documentary titles produced by John Grierson in 1938. Forsyth Hardy had been director of the Committee since 1955,[4] and Grigor saw the joint role afforded by the Film Festival directorship at least partly as a method of getting his dreamed-of documentary about the work of the Glasgow architect Charles Rennie Mackintosh made.

He had already tried and failed to make the film at the BBC and was astonished by the lack of knowledge at the Corporation's Glasgow base on Queen Margaret Drive, that part of the building had been designed by Mackintosh in 1895 when it was the women-only Queen Margaret College. With the assistance of the Committee Grigor managed to get *Mackintosh* made and it wasn't just the calling card for his later career as a filmmaker, but also the film which reinvigorated Mackintosh's reputation in the eyes of the Scottish nation.

In the meantime, he discovered that the directorship of the Film Festival – although it had been in place since the appointment of Callum Mill on a part-time basis in 1957 – was subordinate both to the needs of the Films of Scotland Committee role and to the collective programming decisions of the Edinburgh Film Guild's members. Although he only worked minimally on the 1967 festival, Grigor made a couple of key programming choices in Robert Aldrich's war classic *The Dirty Dozen*, which Hardy disliked intensely ('It posed but did not give a convincing answer to the question, "what is a festival film?"'[5]) and the Italian director Gillo Pontecorvo's startling *The*

Battle of Algiers, about Algerian rebels' conflict with the French government in the previous decade, which everyone loved whether they recognised the debt to Roberto Rossellini or not.

A relatively minor element of '67's programming was found amid the short films, yet it pointed to the future both for the Film Festival and for the entire movie industry. Written and directed by a University of Southern California film student named George Lucas, *Electronic Labyrinth: THX 1138 4EB* was a striking dystopian science fiction short which five months later went on to win first prize at the National Student Film Festival in New York, later re-emerging as Lucas's pre-*Star Wars* debut film *THX 1138* in 1971. Lucas was part of a new breed of filmmaker which was to transform the industry and – as Grigor recognised – Myles and Will were also part of this generation. He hired them as programme editors for the festival of '68, but until his departure in '72, they essentially drove the Edinburgh Film Festival's new and challenging identity as partners alongside him.

Early on, the trio decided to dispense with relying on the films offered to them by corporate sponsors and government-based national film bodies and to simply invite filmmakers they liked instead. In 1968, this meant the raw and defiantly commercial – and popular – American director and producer Roger Corman and screenings of his 1966 Peter Fonda-starring biker film *The Wild Angels*, his 1967 exploration of LSD counterculture *The Trip*, starring Jack Nicholson and the Corman-produced *Targets*, an early 1968 thriller by another of a new breed of filmmaker, Peter Bogdanovich. Crucially, these films were being seen for the first time in the United Kingdom, although Venice and Cannes had already had a taste of them.

Looking back 24 years later, Forsyth Hardy seemed guardedly impressed by the inclusion of Corman and pleased with Grigor's invitation to Grierson to both give the Celebrity Lecture and receive the festival's own bespoke Golden Thistle award for outstanding achievement in filmmaking, instituted in 1964 and first presented to the American filmmaker King Vidor. He was less impressed with the 'young turks' decision to reject his suggestion that Stanley Kubrick's *2001: A Space Odyssey* be shown, but he could see which way the generational wind was blowing. Grigor was a film enthusiast himself, but Myles and Will were the real radicals. Grigor had a weight of personality, though and an ability to sell the revolutionary to the Film Guild in terms of reference they could understand. Myles was less diplomatic.

'Murray's an incredibly generous soul,' she says. 'It wasn't his fault that he inherited a festival on its knees. Dave and I had the driving interest in work that was contextualising cinema and exploring new areas, and it's a great tribute to Murray that he let us run with it'. The festival had held retrospectives before, not least on the work of its regular contributor

Ingmar Bergman, but Myles and Will wanted to find some new heroes. Their choice for 1969 was the wayward former crime reporter and World War II infantryman Sam Fuller, who made low-budget genre films marked by their supposedly low-rent focus on fast-paced action and violence.

Aided by British Film Institute theorist Peter Wollen, Myles and Will programmed a range of Fuller's films, including the Westerns *I Shot Jesse James* and *Forty Guns* and the war films *Fixed Bayonets* and *Merrill's Marauders*. In recognition of Fuller's importance to the French New Wave, Jean-Luc Godard's 1965 film *Pierrot Le Fou* was also shown for the director's significant cameo appearance, while Will and Wollen edited a special publication with essays on Fuller's work, the first ever written.

Despite questions from some quarters as to whether Fuller was a worthy subject – Grigor was refused permission to award him the Golden Thistle – the seriousness with which the subject was treated found respect and admiration and the retrospective transferred to the National Film Theatre in London. The spotlight turned Fuller from a jobbing pulp director into an arthouse star in an environment away from the New Wave's spotlight, a serious director worthy of proper critical dissection.

Fuller later said of his Edinburgh experience that it boosted both his profile and his ego. He also spoke of his intention, through his or the interviewer's mishearing, to make a film in Edinburgh based on the real-life Jekyll and Hyde inspiration 'Dick and Brody' (Deacon William Brodie, 18th century city councillor and secret housebreaker):

> One day I would like to make this story in Edinburgh, the old
> Edinburgh down by Dean Bridge with its atmosphere – a certain
> type of cobble stone streets and gallows and everything else
> connected with execution and locksmiths.[6]

Fuller's larger-than-life transatlantic personality brought a buzz to Edinburgh and at a social event he met a 22-year-old Scottish filmmaker named Bill Forsyth, whose early, undistributed experimental work *Waterloo* had been screening at the festival. Fuller told him frankly that the film was 'an insult to your audience' and in that moment Forsyth rethought everything. A little over a decade later he was being touted as the Scots filmmaker of his generation, through 'well-made' narrative films like *Gregory's Girl*, *Local Hero* and *Comfort and Joy*. The 1969 Edinburgh Film Festival was a success for other reasons too, including the British premiere of Dennis Hopper's *Easy Rider* – Hell's Angel clubs from across Scotland lined up outside the Playhouse for it, with Peter Fonda appearing onstage – and an esoteric look at the film titles of Saul Bass.

A contemporary formula had been found and Grigor, Will and Myles decided to stick to it. In 1970, there were retrospectives of another pulp American director, Monte Hellman and the French New Wave auteur Claude Chabrol, while director Terence Fisher's Hammer *Dracula* films and more Corman productions also featured, alongside a new book on Corman's work by Will and theorist Paul Willeman.

'It's very hard to talk to anyone now about Sam Fuller or [later retrospective subjects] Douglas Sirk or Raoul Walsh as being forgotten, but at that point there had never been retrospectives', says Myles.

The only place that really paid attention was the *Cinémathèque* in Paris. If the National Film Archive in London had one print of a film, they'd just preserve it, whereas the *Cinémathèque* would show it until it fell apart. It's hard to understand what a fuss the Fuller retrospective caused. The guy who was head of arts at BBC Scotland radio said, 'he's no intellectual, so why are you doing it?' Then the next year, the tribute to Roger Corman caused hysteria. The rearguard of the festival and the Film Guild hated it. They wanted us to show traditional European art cinema, and we wanted to show everything – the avant garde, New York independents, new German cinema.

The furore about the bloody gangster flick *Bloody Mama*, which starred Shelley Winters and a young Robert De Niro, made the local papers. Yet behind the scenes another problem was brewing. The West German director Michael Verhoeven's film *OK* was scheduled to be shown, although the previous month the politics surrounding its content – the rape of a Vietnamese woman by American soldiers – had caused the cancellation of the 20th Berlin Film Festival. Now the Hollywood distributor of *Bloody Mama* threatened to pull the film if Edinburgh didn't cancel the 'anti-American' *OK*, which Grigor did.

The political fallout from the scheduling of both films was stark evidence of the new environment in which the Edinburgh International Film Festival operated. No longer simply used for entertainment, education or soft propaganda, as they had been at the time of the festival's beginning, films were now overtly political tools. The fallout from 1970 meant neither Will nor Myles were involved in 1971, but shifting landscape within the Film Festival meant Myles' influence upon it wasn't over by a long way.

* * *

At the beginning of the 1964 Festival, international business consultancy Urwick, Orr and Partners were hired by Edinburgh Corporation to look at its finances and one of their recommendations was that the artistic director become the Festival Director – charged with budgetary as well as creative responsibility, with more independence from the committee of the Festival Society.

The first incumbent in this new regime was Peter Diamand, a 62-year-old Berlin-born Austrian who became a naturalised Dutch citizen after spending most of the war in hiding there. Before the conflict, he was secretary to the pianist Artur Schnabel. After it, he worked with Netherlands Opera and the Concertgebouw Orchestra and had been long-term director of the Holland Festival.

His first Festival was 1966, coinciding with a major shift in homegrown theatre production in Edinburgh. Although the Corporation's grand plans for a new opera house and theatre languished in the Hole in the Ground for decades to come, they'd acted immediately to fund and establish, along with the Scottish Arts Council, a new Civic Theatre Company. Its home was to be the Royal Lyceum Theatre, which the Corporation had bought in 1965 from the Edinburgh speculator and philanthropist Meyer Oppenheim, who'd owned it for five years.

Thanks to television and the growth of publicly-subsidised theatres, the previously-booming, building-owning theatre empires of the Victorian era hit hard times, which created potentially catastrophic pressure upon the number of stages available to the International Festival. The first casualty was the Empire Theatre on Nicolson Street, which became a bingo hall in 1963,[7] seriously disrupting the International Festival's ability to continue hosting ballet and dance. The Empire hadn't been adequate for major international productions anyway, but now it was being hired back privately by the Corporation at extraordinary rates for esteemed guests like the New York City Ballet in 1967, while venues like Haymarket Ice Rink and the Church Hill Theatre filled in where possible.

The Howard & Wyndham organisation, Edinburgh-based but with theatres across the UK, was another victim. They sold the Lyceum to Oppenheim in 1960 and in 1969 the Edinburgh Corporation was essentially forced to buy the King's Theatre from them, to stop it being sold off to private developers. The Gateway Theatre also changed hands – in 1968 it was bought by Scottish Television as an east coast base to complement the Theatre Royal in Glasgow, but the Gateway Theatre Company had left already. In 1965 they moved to the Lyceum, were renamed the Royal Lyceum Theatre Company and took up the mantle of the city's first Civic Theatre Company. The Church of Scotland's involvement in Edinburgh theatre, meanwhile, moved to the new Netherbow Theatre alongside John Knox's House on the Royal Mile, which took the place of the demolished Moray-Knox Church and continues to be a Fringe venue today, following redevelopment as the Scottish Storytelling Centre in 2006.

In 1966 the Lyceum company took the place of the Gateway on the International Festival bill with Scots adaptation of a classical piece, Aristophanes' *The Birds*, renamed *The Burdies* in Douglas Young's adaptation for the Lyceum's founding artistic director Tom Fleming. Among the cast was an excellent array of Scots talent, including Fulton Mackay, Lennox Milne, 20-year-old future star Brian Cox and the great Duncan Macrae, who died seven months later. His death inadvertently signalled the end of an era – the temporary closure of his and others' dreams of a National Theatre for Scotland, in favour of publicly-funded, company-based models like those of the Lyceum, the Traverse and the soon-to-emerge radical theatres of the 1970s.

The early years of Peter Diamand's 13 International Festivals included two major anniversaries, the 21st edition in 1967 and the 25th in 1971. For the 21st he selected the works of Stravinsky and Bach to profile, with Scottish Opera making its first Edinburgh International Festival appearance five years after former Sadler's Wells musical director and Scottish National Orchestra principal conductor Alexander Gibson founded the company in 1962. For their debut they brought Stravinsky's *The Soldier's Tale* to the Assembly Hall and *The Rake's Progress* at the King's Theatre, conducted respectively by Gibson and regular Scottish Opera collaborator Peter Ebert, son of Glyndebourne founder Carl. The performances featured Una Stubbs and Gordon Jackson.

Also welcomed in 1967 were the Cleveland Orchestra under George Szell, the BBC Symphony Orchestra under Pierre Boulez and the Berlin Philharmonic under Herbert von Karajan, as well as a strong theatre programme. The famed mime Marcel Marceau appeared at the Gateway Theatre. For the 25th anniversary in 1971, a free concert was given at the Usher Hall the night before the Festival's opening for balloted members of the Edinburgh public. Yehudi Menuhin performed for no fee alongside the Festival Chorus, an ensemble of more than 100 local singers established as a permanent backing for Festival orchestras in 1965, as one of Harewood's final acts. The bill of '71 also included the *Deutsche Oper*, Scottish Opera and orchestral concerts by the Israel Philharmonic Orchestra, the Chicago Symphony Orchestra conducted by Carlo Maria Giulini, the major Scottish orchestras and the London Symphony Orchestra under Andre Previn and Claudio Abbado.

Diamand was known as a modest and unassuming Festival Director, not one of the biggest personalities to lead the Festival, but a canny operator who dealt as best he could with the usual push and pull of threatened and actual budget cuts, attempted creative interventions courtesy of the city's corporation and grisly politicking behind the opera house debacle and its fallout. Creatively he differed from his predecessor Harewood and his successor John Drummond in that he built good relationships with a select group of artists and invited them back over and over, where the others programmed fresh every year. Some said this led to a certain staleness after a while, but others believed it guaranteed quality.

In 1966 a brand new performance company named Pop Theatre had been founded especially for the International Festival by 39-year-old Yorkshireman Frank Dunlop, who'd already been resident director at Bristol Old Vic, artistic director at Nottingham Playhouse and director of the 1964 West End hit *Oblomov*, starring Spike Milligan. The company took over the Assembly Hall for successful versions of Shakespeare's *The Winter's Tale* and Euripides' *The Trojan Women*, with a company which included Jane Asher, Jim Dale and future *Doctor Who* Tom Baker. *The Trojan Women* earned rave reviews for its star, the jazz singer and actor Cleo Laine, who returned with Pop for *A Midsummer Night's Dream* and Ionesco's *The Lesson* at the Assembly Hall in '67.

Appointed associate director of London's Old Vic theatre that year, Dunlop founded its sister venue the Young Vic on the site of an old butcher's shop and a bombed-out baker's in 1970 and this company gave the International Festival one of its most retrospectively significant shows of the time. Dunlop brought the Young Vic to Edinburgh in 1971 for Shakespeare's *The Comedy of Errors*, starring Edward Fox and staged in-the-round in a marquee at Haymarket Ice Rink and the next year returned to the same venue with *Bible One: Two Looks at the Book of Genesis*. This new production contained two compact religious plays: the first, an adaptation of the *Wakefield Mystery Plays* version of the *Book of Genesis*; the second, a piece written by an Oxford drop-out rock 'n' roll obsessive and later Royal College of Music prodigy named Andrew Lloyd Webber and his writing partner since their teenage years, Tim Rice.

Although it was commissioned and performed as a school play by the private Colet School in 1968 and played by amateur companies in America from 1970 as a follow-up to the pair's hit *Jesus Christ Superstar*, the Young Vic's 45-minute Edinburgh quasi-performance of *Joseph and His Amazing Technicolour Dreamcoat* was the first professional production of what subsequently became one of the world's biggest musical theatre shows.

With Gary Bond in the title role, *Joseph* transferred to London's Roundhouse later that year and then to the West End's Albery Theatre in 1973, with the *Mystery Plays* element edited out.

Joseph was eventually extended into the full contemporary production which arrived at London's Haymarket Theatre in 1974. Among the Edinburgh cast had been an actor and Young Vic associate named Jeremy James Taylor, who in 1976 created a new student musical production featuring boys from the Belmont School in London named *The Ballad of Solomon Pavey*.[8] Co-written by Taylor and David Drew-Smythe and based on the life of the 17th century boy actor, it transferred to the lawn of St Mary's Cathedral in Edinburgh's West End that summer and won a Fringe First award.

Taylor continued to create productions for young casts on the Edinburgh Fringe, first at St Denis School on Ettrick Road in '78 and '79,[9] and then at George Square Theatre in 1980; the building had first been used as a venue by Edinburgh International Film Festival since its construction in 1970. In 1980 Taylor also officially founded his group as the charitable Children's Musical Theatre company and won two more Fringe Firsts for the original productions *Captain Stirrick*, about a gang of 19th century child pickpockets and *The Roman Invasion of Ramsbottom*, a *Monty Python*-esque comedy about Roman Britain. The latter was the first of a number of CMT's shows recorded and broadcast on ITV networks at Christmas over the next few years.

Children's Musical Theatre was renamed the National Youth Music Theatre in 1985 and became a fixture at the George Square Theatre until 1996, where its presentations of new and old work gathered acclaim and awards. The company was drawn into the official programme of the International Festival in 1984 with *The Tower of Babel* at St Mary's Cathedral, written by the company's David Nield and again in 1986 with Benjamin Britten's William Blake-influenced 1949 children's work *Let's Make an Opera!* in which the characters conceive a piece called *The Little Sweep* in the first half and then perform it in the second. The other NYMT show of that year at George Square Theatre emphasised the company's exceptional reputation for finding future talent.

Written by Nield and co-directed by Taylor, *The Ragged Child* was a piece about 19th century orphans which was so successful that it went to Sadler's Wells the following year, with original Edinburgh castmembers Jude Law and Jonny Lee Miller both still involved. Among other future stars appearing in Edinburgh with the CMT/NYMT were Toby Jones and Tom Hollander in the 1981 ensemble, then 15 and 14 respectively. The company appeared at the Fringe until 2002, latterly at the Assembly Rooms and Pleasance, although financial troubles, the departure of Taylor and a period of dormancy until 2005 mean it hasn't come back since. By 2003, however, the company had been involved in 59 productions during the Edinburgh Festival, winning seven Fringe Firsts, including one for 1994's *Pendragon*, which featured an 18-year-old Sally Hawkins.

In 1968 a strong year for theatre at the International Festival emerged, with Dublin's Abbey Theatre's *The Playboy of the Western World* by JM Synge, Glasgow Citizens' *The Resistible Rise of Arturo Ui* by Brecht, featuring Steven Berkoff and Leonard Rossiter and locals the Traverse Theatre with Eugene O'Neill's *Mourning Becomes Electra*. Also appearing was a young English company called Prospect Theatre, whose reputation for quality was taken to the next level the following year. They arrived at the Assembly Hall in 1969 with their versions of Shakespeare's *Richard II* and Christopher Marlowe's *Edward II* and the lead actor in both was a 30-year-old Cambridge graduate from Lancashire named Ian McKellen.

By this point McKellen was hardly an unknown, having appeared in the West End and been part of the Laurence Olivier's National Theatre Company at the Old Vic in 1965. Yet this summer in Edinburgh truly made him famous, as much for the controversy surrounding the work as the undoubted quality of it. The Theatres Act 1968 was passed on 26 July that year, which repealed a law dating back to 1737 which required plays produced in the UK to be passed to the Lord Chamberlain's Office for censorship and the type of boundary-pushing material previously found only at a private club like the Traverse was now no longer off-limits. At the first full Festival after the Act's repeal, *Edward II* featured a scene where McKellen's Edward and James Laurenson's Gaveston share a kiss and Edward dies by red-hot poker.

Despite the passing of the Theatres Act, many politicians and private individuals took it upon themselves to uphold morality on behalf of their fellow citizens' apparently delicate sensibilities. Among them was the independent Edinburgh Corporation councillor for Newington John D Kidd, an enthusiastic moral guardian. That other great censor Malcolm Muggeridge had opened the Festival of '69 with a sermon which railed against the erotic, but his return to London left Kidd to do the hard work of studiously recording and reporting all shows whose moral standards didn't come up to scratch.

Kidd had already made a name for himself in Edinburgh theatre circles by leading the backlash against the Traverse's *Mass in F* in February 1968, by the student Edinburgh Experimental Group, in which a woman, bare from the waist up, recounted her character's sexual history in monologue. The furore was such that the theatre's then-artistic director Gordon McDougall and its chair Nicholas Fairbairn presented their own response to the criticism a week later as a separate Traverse 'production' entitled *F in Mass*. After the Festival of 1969 Kidd planned to present his dossier to Home Secretary James Callaghan, but McKellen's kiss so outraged him that he went straight to the procurator fiscal to report a crime. The police were involved, but:

Ian Mackintosh, the company general manager, managed to persuade them not to call off the production by saying he himself did not object, and his father and grandfather were moderators of the Church of Scotland.[10]

Despite Kidd's protests, audiences voted with their feet and their open wallets. The plays were a huge success and McKellen's challenging but successful dual role was lauded. Returning to the Festival for performances including Marlowe's Doctor Faustus for the Royal Shakespeare Company in '75, the actor became one of British theatre's crown jewels, a Hollywood star and one of the most prominent LGBTQ+ activists of his time.

Although his 13 Festivals represent an exceptional innings, wrangling over finances caught up with Diamond in the end, following the cost-saving loss of the Gateway Theatre, the Church Hill Theatre and Haymarket Ice Rink as regular Festival venues during his tenure.[11] With only Thea Musgrave's operatic Mary Queen of Scots booked in for 1977, his long-held intention had been to produce a new version of Bizet's Carmen as the Festival's centrepiece that year. It went ahead and was a huge critical hit, with Claudio Abbado conducting, Teresa Berganza in the title role and Placido Domingo in the role of Don Jose after much negotiation from Diamond, but only after all involved had been asked to reduce their fee and requests for sponsorship brought in £35,000 from British Petroleum – the first but certainly not the last privately-sponsored International Festival show, in a landscape where it's now commonplace.

Domingo, of course, later became part of the Three Tenors group of operatic superstars, who launched the form to mass popular appeal when they performed to a global audience of 800 million from Rome the day before the same city hosted the 1990 football World Cup Final between West Germany and Argentina; their version of Puccini's 'Nessun dorma' has since become synonymous with the sport. All three singers had early-career experiences at the Edinburgh International Festival, the first being Luciano Pavarotti, 31 years old when he arrived at the King's Theatre in 1967 in the cast of Vincenzo Bellini's Capuleti e i Montecchi, a Holland Festival production conducted by Claudio Abbado.

Pavarotti returned to the International Festival just once more, singing Verdi's Requiem in 1974, as conducted by Carlo Maria Giulini, with Fiorenza Cossotto, Raffaele Ariè and Martina Arroyo singing alongside him (Arroyo was replaced by Rita Hunter on the second night due to illness). The third Tenor, José Carreras, also sang the Requiem for his only International Festival appearance in 1982, this time conducted by Claudio Abbado over two nights at the Usher Hall, which featured fellow soloists

Ruggero Raimondi, Jessye Norman and Margaret Price. Performed by the London Symphony Orchestra and the Edinburgh Festival Orchestra, this performance was so acclaimed that it was later broadcast by the BBC and made commercially available.

Diamand's last Festival was 1978's edition, the end of a run that had seen Daniel Barenboim make his first Edinburgh appearances and such singular events as Paco Peña performing late-night flamenco and Max Well playing the work of Buster Keaton. The outgoing director's tenure also included one of the most headline-grabbing events ever held at an Edinburgh Festival. Retiring from Hollywood after appearing in *High Society* in 1956 to become Princess Grace of Monaco, the Hollywood star Grace Kelly had performed extremely infrequently in the 20 years before she appeared at the Festival to celebrate the the United States Bicentennial. Giving four performances at St Cecilia's Hall on the junction of the Cowgate and Niddry Street and at the grand Signet Library on Parliament Square,[12] she and actors Richard Kiley and Richard Pascoe read poetry by Carl Sandburg, Ogden Nash, TS Eliot and Elinor Wylie.

For Diamand, it was just one good job seen through amongst many in Edinburgh. Aged 65 when he left the city, he settled into semi-retirement as artistic advisor to the *Orchestre de Paris* until his death in 1998. His replacement was John Drummond, a BBC executive who had been part of Cambridge Footlights in the 1950s during the same era as Peter Cook, Ian McKellen, Derek Jacobi and Michael Frayn. The son of a Scottish sea captain and an Australian singer, he had been a lover of the Edinburgh Festival since its earliest days, from family holidays in Scotland and Naval national service in the early '50s at Fife's Rosyth Dockyard. Drummond had cheekily made contact as a 23-year-old with Robert Ponsonby in 1958 and asked if a job as his assistant might be going. It was, but Drummond thought the pay was too low. Starting out on an 18-year BBC career by interpreting for Richard Dimbleby and David Attenborough in Moscow, he was finally offered the International Festival job in 1977, at the age of 43, but had to wait until after Diamand's final Festival in 1978 to begin programming.

One of the first things Drummond did at the Festival was to hire Sheila Colvin, formerly of the Traverse Theatre and the Conferences of the 1960s, as his assistant on the recommendation of Richard Demarco; by this point, apparently, she was working in London as the PA to the head of an American oil company. Colvin spent a decade at the Festival, staying in post after Drummond's tenure. His debut programme in 1979 made significant changes, the most tangible being the arrival of a new space for chamber concerts on the Festival.

Opened in 1822 as Hope Park Chapel, the grand church on Clerk Street in Newington was known as Newington and St Leonard's Church when it closed due to declining attendance in July 1976. A campaign was instigated by the Scottish Chamber Orchestra, Scottish Baroque Ensemble (now Scottish Ensemble) and Scottish Philharmonic Singers to convert it as their joint home, which reached fruition with its reopening by Queen Elizabeth as the Queen's Hall in July 1979, just in time for a programme of International Festival concerts the following month. Drummond thought the Freemasons Hall on George Street had bad acoustics and Leith Town Hall was gloomy and hard to get to, so he made the new venue a cornerstone for smaller concerts.

The Festival of 1979 also saw Jonathan Miller's return to Edinburgh in a very different context to *Beyond the Fringe,* as the director of Kent Opera's version of Verdi's *La Traviata* and the Edinburgh debut of Simon Rattle as conductor of a performance by the Philharmonia Orchestra. Noting the Festival opened on the 50th anniversary of the death of the Russian impresario and founder of the *Ballets Russes* Sergei Diaghilev – whose 25th anniversary had also been commemorated by Ian Hunter's Festival – an associated programme of two operas, three ballets, six concerts and the Citizens Theatre's production of Robert David MacDonald's *Chinchilla,* a play about Diaghilev's life, were all booked in.

After 13 years of Diamand's programming, Drummond promised a fresh look. Although, as is always the case with the International Festival, the view needs to be back towards tradition and forward to new opportunities at the same time.

* * *

For the Edinburgh International Film Festival, the only direction to move during the 1970s was forward. Following the furore of 1970 and the recovery year of '71, changes took place behind the scenes on EIFF's organising committee, with some elders unhappy with the way cinema in general was going, never mind the festival. Grigor, politically sharp as ever, brought in a new member of the committee, a fellow Scot named Colin Young, a significant figure in the history of both EIFF and the film industry in Britain and America.

Born in Glasgow in 1927, Young was another graduate of the University of St Andrews, who moved to the US to study film at the University of California, Los Angeles (UCLA). By 1965, he had become chairman of the university's film school and his tenure in charge saw many future star directors graduate, including Francis Ford Coppola, Paul Schrader, Barry Levinson, Lawrence Kasdan and John Milius. In 1971, Young returned to the UK to become the founding director of the National Film and Television School at Beaconsfield Studios in Buckinghamshire – then and now the leading film training facility in the country – and he also became an important voice on the EIFF committee.

In 1972, Myles and Will returned to the fold and although Myles says Young didn't much like what they were doing either, he firmly supported everything they – and later, she – did. That year the festival featured the British premiere of the Warhol Factory films *Heat*, *Trash* and *Blue Movie*, Jonathan Demme's debut film *The Hot Box*, which he wrote for director Joe Viola and the return of the retrospective, this time on the German-born Hollywood director Douglas Sirk. It showed 23 of his films from the early *Pillars of Society* to his final Hollywood film, 1959's *Imitation of Life*.

Sirk attended the festival and enjoyed it so much he came back the following year, while John Huston also returned following his honorary presidency back in 1954, this time with his film *Fat City* as the opening event. The festival has unsurprisingly dined out on the quote from the maker of *The Maltese Falcon* and *The African Queen* that 'the only [film festival] that's worth a damn is Edinburgh' ever since.

Film writers Laura Mulvey and Jon Halliday edited that year's publication on Sirk,[13] and Mulvey was also involved in 1972's other main event – not only the most important event of that year, but one of the Edinburgh International Film Festival's most significant contributions to film in its entirety, organised by Myles, Mulvey and fellow film theorist Claire Johnston. The Women's Event – also known as The Women's Film Festival – was an attempt to gather as many films made by women together for screening as possible.

The accompanying text illustrated that the independent production of the 1920s and of the present day had presented more opportunities for female directors than the big studio heyday, when women were less likely to be entrusted with the authority to control the economic and executive power involved in making a movie. The intention, it said, wasn't to pay homage to those who had survived in those circumstances, but to serve as inspiration for female directors who might follow. The selection of more than 30 films included Leni Riefenstahl's *The Blue Light* (1932), Leontine Sagan's *Mädchen in Uniform* (1933), Dorothy Arzner's *Dance, Girl, Dance* (1940), Nelly Kaplan's *A Very Curious Girl* (aka *La Fiancée du Pirate*, 1969), Barbara Loden's *Wanda* and Jane Arden's *The Other Side of the Underneath* (1972), as well as films by Ida Lupino, Judit Elek, Joyce Wieland, Barbara Loden and Vera Chitylova.

There was also a conference and a BBC Two documentary for a show named *Late Night Line-Up*, although sadly neither this or much other reportage or documentation exists. 'I'd started having women's group meetings in my flat in Marchmont,' says Myles. 'I was reading [the British psychoanalyst and feminist] Juliet Mitchell and all the American feminists, and had got to know Laura. We wanted to remind people of the great films there had been by women directors in the past, and also to draw attention to how few women directors there were at present, which has sadly not changed as much as one would like. I'd love to see [the *Late Night Line-Up* film] now, I remember there was one sequence where I was sitting with about 30 filmmakers on this very sunny day by St Bernard's Well [in Stockbridge]. We had invited as many of the directors as we could, a lot of it was about just meeting and talking with people'.

In 1975, Laura Mulvey published her hugely influential essay 'Visual Pleasure in Narrative Cinema' in the journal *Screen*, an important development in the emergence of Freudian psychoanalysis and especially feminism in film theory. In it, she elaborated on John Berger's idea of the 'male gaze', a convention in cinema where the active male looks upon the passive female and women seen onscreen are only understood through a man's interpretation of them:

> The magic of the Hollywood style at its best (and of all the cinema which fell within its sphere of influence) arose, not exclusively, but in one important aspect, from its skilled and satisfying manipulation of visual pleasure. Unchallenged, mainstream film coded the erotic into the language of the dominant patriarchal order.[14]

Organising the Women's Event was a major influence upon this work for Mulvey and in 1973 the Edinburgh International Film Festival pushed another boundary in terms of feminism in film. Myles had taken a predominant role in programming the 1972 festival, with Grigor otherwise engaged in filmmaking business and in '73 she was finally given the directorship full-time.

'The combination worked,' she says of her first half-decade as part of the Film Festival.

> During that time I was doing a philosophy degree, Dave was doing his medical degree and Murray was making films, so it was all slightly chaotic, and we had absolutely no money. Dave and I split up, which made life difficult, and he'd finished his medical degree and started psychiatric training. The nature of our split meant it was difficult to go on working together, but I make sure sufficient tribute is paid, because the fact is none of it would have happened without the three of us. Murray gave us the access, but the work wouldn't have happened without Dave's particular energy. The thing about being young is that you're fearless, and there was nothing to lose.

Myles's programmes continued to be successful and relentlessly diverse and intriguing, introducing films and filmmakers from around the world to British audiences. More retrospectives and publications emerged throughout her tenure, featuring Frank Tashlin, Irvin Kershner, Raoul Walsh, Jacques Tourneur, Paul Bartel and Joseph H Lewis, merging supposedly high and low culture, alongside expansive looks at Brecht and the Avant Garde movement through film. The film critic Barry Norman was so annoyed by the relentlessly highbrow nature of the Walsh book that he tore up a copy live on the BBC's *Film '74*.

'The book was kind of impenetrable...' smiles Myles of the publication, edited by Phil Hardy.

> I did overdo it, the Raoul Walsh year. I showed about 55 of his
> films, it was insane. Double bills at eight in the morning and double
> bills at night, and by the last day all the leading critics in Britain
> were asleep in the cinema. Nobody could cope with the pace, you
> just couldn't watch seven films a day.

These included the classics *High Sierra* and *White Heat*.

She brought new German films, 25 of them in 1973, including the work of Rainer Werner Fassbinder, Wim Wenders and Werner Herzog. Andrei Tarkovsky's triumphant *Andrei Rublev* appeared with work by George A Romero, Roman Polanski and Alexandro Jodorowsky. Perhaps most importantly to the era, the new generation of North American directors who were mirroring the New Wave style of the auteur were included, many of them Colin Young's former charges at UCLA. Francis Ford Coppola, George Lucas, David Cronenberg, Jonathan Demme, Brian De Palma and Victor Nunez all showed in Edinburgh at the very earliest stages of their careers, some also making the journey to Scotland and contributing to a unique social situation at the bar in Film House where filmgoers could turn up at the end of the evening and find De Palma or Sam Fuller, perhaps, holding court about movies.

This hubbub around the films mattered to Myles almost as much as the films themselves and having the directors in Edinburgh to add to the milieu was vitally important. Her budget was negligible, but she would stretch it to lay on treats for them. De Palma had a nice lunch at Prestonfield House, Hertzog visited the Western Isles (Myles: 'I thought the landscape would be up his street') and Wenders got a seat in the director's box at a Celtic game in Glasgow. Later, American screenwriter and pioneer of vegetarianism Anna Thomas returned to a Scottish castle in 1981 to direct her only film, *The Haunting of M*, with Fringe pioneer Evie Garratt in the cast.

Murray Grigor also returned with *Blast!* a study of the Vorticist painting movement in Britain, as narrated by *Great Northern Welly Boot Show* star John Bett and the Billy Connolly tour travelogue *Big Banana Feet*. In the event, Grigor's discovery of Myles and Will was his most significant contribution to the Edinburgh International Film Festival, but his legacy as a major actor within and chronicler of Scottish culture, particularly as a documentary maker, demands reassessment. His work includes 1982's *Sean Connery's Edinburgh*, a visual record of the city with his long-time friend – the pair were introduced by Richard Demarco, inevitably – and film profiles of the Scottish architects Robert Adam, Alexander 'Greek' Thomson and George Wyllie.

The 1983 Hogmanay television show *Scotch Myths*, directed by Grigor, was an extension of he and his wife Barbara's 1981 Edinburgh International Festival exhibition of the same name at the Little Lyceum, which poked fun and chipped away at the kitsch stereotypes surrounding Scottish cultural representations. Murray and Barbara Grigor were married in 1968 and she assisted with his stewardship of the Film Festival and was instrumental in the first major retrospective of Eduardo Paolozzi's work at the Royal Scottish Academy during the International Festival of 1983. Barbara Grigor died at the age of 50 in 1994; Grigor's American second wife Carol Grigor Colburn, who he married in 2011, helps run her family's philanthropic Dunard Fund, which has donated substantial amounts to the Edinburgh International Festival, the National Galleries of Scotland and the country's major orchestras.

In 1975 Lynda Myles' Film Festival demonstrated how firmly its finger was on the pulse with a short retrospective of a largely unknown 32-year-old director from New York named Martin Scorsese. At this point he only had three feature films in his catalogue,– *Who's That Knocking at My Door?* (1967), *Boxcar Bertha* (1972) and *Mean Streets* (1973) – but their explosive appreciation of pop culture and film history – the Scot and long-time friend of the Film Festival Michael Powell was Scorsese's great inspiration – had already been thoroughly noticed by the cognoscenti. He brought his new film *Alice Doesn't Live Here Any More* with him. The subsequent Academy Award for its star Ellen Burstyn's portrayal of a windowed mother traveling across the American Southwest was the biggest step yet on Scorsese's personal ladder to eventual godfatherhood of American cinema.

Scorsese's gift from the festival, apparently, was an extra night in Edinburgh's Caledonian Hotel, as he was enjoying the city and the immersion in film culture so much. His retrospective did much to legitimise and popularise his early work in the UK and he sat closer than most other directors to the Edinburgh International Film Festival of the 1970s' unique blend of cinema theory, commercial appeal and retrospective enthusiasm for the unrecognised greats of Hollywood and world cinema. As he was quoted on Sam Fuller in the EIFF programme:

I am crazy about Samuel Fuller! I have only met him once, but we
talked for a long time about emotional violence, which one mustn't
confuse with physical violence. Fuller's films taught me that, and
also that this emotional violence must not only be created by the
actor but above all by the director.[15]

Those who remember Scorsese at the time recall a shy but thoroughly
polite and enthusiastic man whose asthma seemed to not agree with the
Edinburgh weather, accompanied by his girlfriend and later second wife Julia
Cameron. He was no star yet, just a promising young filmmaker, and the
festival recognised his talent from afar. Soon, he returned with *Taxi Driver*
and then *The Last Waltz*.

Perhaps even more striking than Scorsese's presence in Edinburgh is the
story of how he and other Film Festival guests got around the city. One day
a 26-year-old aspiring actor, classic car enthusiast and Glasgow School of Art
graduate named Anthony McMillan turned up at the Film Festival's office and
asked if they needed anyone to drive film stars around. He pointed out into the
street, towards the gorgeous brown classic Dodge he'd turned up in and said
he'd happily put it to good use if the festival gave him some money for petrol
and insurance. The organisation had no funds for limousines, but Myles could
see this cheaper option was a better one. Scorsese reportedly loved the car and
its driver, who was already using the stage name Robbie Coltrane and whose
association with the Festival and the film industry wasn't done yet.

Also in 1976, the Film Festival paid tribute to the Scottish television
producer and director James MacTaggart, who'd died suddenly of a heart
attack in May 1974 at the age of 46. MacTaggart had made a name for
himself on key national drama strands *The Wednesday Play* and *Play for
Today*, commissioning much of the early work of director Ken Loach and
writer Dennis Potter and was friends with the creator of *Z-Cars*, Troy
Kennedy Martin and its sometime regular writer turned 7:84 founder,
John McGrath. Together with the BBC and Granada Television, Myles
programmed a retrospective of his work and a lecture in tribute, the latter
delivered on 25 August 1976 by McGrath.

The first James Taggart Memorial Lecture, delivered at the Royal College
of Physicians' building on Queen Street, was titled 'TV Drama: The Case
Against Naturalism' and, as anyone who knew McGrath's reputation might
have guessed, his warm sense of tribute was fused with a political purpose.
He questioned television drama's stagnation in the naturalist form, its lack
of ambition and most of all, the political changes that he believed had steered
the BBC away from its openness in the days when he, Martin and MacTaggart
had been working for it:

Anarchy is over. Centralised control, elaborate systems of command, supervision, check and review have been introduced. And on the personal level, the bully boys have moved in to stay.[16]

McGrath's words caused shockwaves, but people in the television industry were excited and keen to discuss the deeper meaning of their industry in a way it hadn't been before. The following March the Scottish editor of current affairs series *World in Action* and deputy director of the Edinburgh International Film Festival Gus Macdonald[17] met Jane Mills, a *World in Action* researcher, in London to ask whether she might be interested in organising another event like the previous year's.

She was, and with the support of William Brown, Macdonald's predecessor as STV MD, Alastair Hetherington of BBC Scotland and others – Lynda Myles says the original group comprised six people, herself included – they organised the first Edinburgh International Television Festival, a week-long event for 300 delegates in 1977. 'Britain had the best television in the world, but no television festival, what better venue than Edinburgh?' Macdonald later said.[18] He was also privately concerned that the Film Festival covered international work so well but appeared to have little room for British filmmakers, although Lynda Myles has a simple explanation for this:

In the mid-'70s, American money had disappeared from European cinema because the dollar was very low against European currency, so there was hardly any production at that point. Directors of the bigger European festivals would come to Edinburgh and say, 'what's Stephen Frears been doing?' or 'what's Ken Loach been doing?' Well, they were all doing *Play for Today* at the BBC, and the union made it impossible for us to show these films unless we set up a special event or a membership scheme or something.

The documentary maker Marcel Ophuls gave the 1977 MacTaggart lecture and both it and the Edinburgh International Television Festival itself have been annual events ever since. Beginning as a home for radical outsiders, EIFF has since become a thoroughly industry event, although it and particularly the MacTaggart Lecture are a major public forum where debates about the role of television broadcasting in Britain play out. Since '76, figures including John Schlesinger, Dennis Potter, Janet Street-Porter, Jeremy Paxman, Armando Iannucci, Michaela Coel, every Director General of the BBC and even Rupert Murdoch have used the MacTaggart to discuss censorship, privatisation, representation, new technologies and the future of public broadcasting and the BBC.

More than that, the concentrated presence of everyone who's powerful in British TV in the bars of the city, especially that of the George Hotel on George Street, has contributed to the Edinburgh Festival's reputation as a place where stars are made and discovered before they transfer to the screen.

Despite all of her successes, not everyone was happy with Lynda Myles' reign or the increasingly impenetrable programme notes. Yet the hits kept coming, first with Woody Allen's debut visit in 1977 with *Annie Hall* and his return with *Manhattan,* and then with a resurgence in Scottish filmmaking towards the end of the decade. The festival showed Bill Douglas's classic *Trilogy* of *My Childhood* (1972), *My Ain Folk* (1973) and *My Way Home* (1978), based on his own experience growing up in post-war poverty in the mining village of Newcraighall, near Edinburgh. In 1979, the gala opening at Calton Studios was the debut proper of Bill Forsyth – once chastised in Edinburgh by Sam Fuller for his experimental ways – *That Sinking Feeling.*

There were also retrospectives for the Scottish director John Mackenzie, including his television version of McGrath and 7:84's *The Cheviot, the Stag and the Black, Black Oil,* his screen version of Jimmy Boyle's *A Sense of Freedom* and the gangster classic *The Long Good Friday.* Bernard Tavernier's dystopian, Glasgow-filmed *Death Watch* appeared in Edinburgh and in 1978 a true lost curio of British cinema emerged directly from EIFF in *Long Shot.* Directed by sometime *Play for Today* director Maurice Hatton and starring Charles Gormley[19] and Neville Smith, it used the 1977 Edinburgh Festival as a backdrop for two fictional independent filmmakers trying to raise funds for their Aberdeen-set oil boom Western *Gulf and Western.* The cast list was a who's who of Edinburgh Festival and Film Festival cameos, including Wim Wenders, Stephen Frears, Bill Forsyth, Alan Bennett, Susannah York, Jim Haynes and a testy Richard Demarco, doorstepped for money in his gallery.

In 1980 Lynda Myles left the Edinburgh International Film Festival, handing over to her deputy Jim Hickey, who had worked with her and David Will since 1969 – the year before he also graduated from the University of Edinburgh with a Fine Art degree. She's astonished when she hears of film festivals now that have 200 or 300 staff, considering the small crew she got by with. Her team included head of publicity Rebecca O'Brian – more recently Ken Loach's regular producer – and Archie Tait, later cinema director at the ICA in London and a prolific producer and script consultant. Myles' next job was programmer of the Pacific Film Archive in Berkeley, California, which she calls 'one of the great programming jobs in the world'. Yet she didn't expect to return so quickly to something like her job in Edinburgh.

'I left [EIFF] partly because I'd run out of steam programming' she says.

We'd done so many of the things we wanted to do, and in fact
we did another women's event [near the end of her tenure] and I
thought it wasn't nearly as exciting. The women's movement had
become more fractious, so it was politically much more difficult to
deal with it all.

In 1978, she'd also programmed Kathryn Bigelow's first feature, *The Set-Up.*

It seemed that cinema was changing. There had been so much new
in the '70s, so much still to discover. Filmmakers still talk about
specific films they'd seen in Edinburgh in the early '70s that changed
their minds about what could be done, that from a humble base
and minimal resources you could still have an international reach of
some description.

Staying true to the Film Festival's roots, a *Documentary 50* event in 1979
once again paid tribute to Grierson and those who followed him, while a
major change for the festival happened in the same year. With the Randolph
Crescent townhouse now firmly outgrown by the Film Guild's activities, just
as Hill Street had been, a move was arranged into the former St Thomas's
Church at 88 Lothian Road, which had been designed in 1831 by architect
David Bryce.[20] Once the late former vicar of the parish, who had been
buried on the premises, was reinterred, the building opened in 1979 as the
Filmhouse. It continues to be the base of EIFF and the Edinburgh Film Guild
and it operates as one of the city's key arthouse cinemas along with the
Cameo on Home Street; the Festival and Guild are respectively the longest
continually-running film festival and the oldest film society in the world.

After two years in California, Myles has worked as a senior vice-president
at Columbia Pictures, commissioning editor for drama at the BBC and most
recently head of the fiction department at the National Film and Television
School. She wrote a book with journalist Michael Pye which defined *The Movie
Brats* generation of American filmmakers, inventing a phrase that Spielberg and
co. now refer to themselves by and produced *Sean Connery's Edinburgh* by
Murray Grigor in '82 and four adaptations of Roddy Doyle novels throughout
the 1990s, including Alan Parker's *The Commitments* in '91.

Her time at the Edinburgh International Film Festival broke boundaries,
promoted feminist filmmaking and introduced many of the key young
directors of the era, certainly in the UK. More than that, it simply presented
hundreds of great films while the eyes of the world were on Edinburgh. Even
her supposed detractors, for example Forsyth Hardy, had a great deal of
respect for her achievements, even if they didn't align with their own tastes:

What some critics found difficult to understand was how Lynda
Myles could equate her enthusiasm for the directors of American
B movies, made to meet the needs of a popular medium of mass
entertainment, with her support for those who looked at these films
as subjects for psychological analysis and windy theorising. Perhaps
the two attitudes could co-exist, but they tended to encourage
reservations about an elitist approach to a popular art.[21]

Yet Myles' festivals thrived on an informality that is entirely alien to any other
festival of a similar scale nowadays. Filmmakers and fans mingling in the same
bars was part of the point for her and, as a matter of course, she would only take
films because she wanted them. She blames Harvey Weinstein, she says, for the
current culture of VIP area access and horse-trading, where producers demand
festivals screen films they don't want to get the ones they do.

'We had no money to take people out for meals, so during the festival I
would invite 20 people round to my flat and somebody would cook for a
filmmaker,' she remembers.

It was hand to mouth, but with fewer bureaucratic restrictions that
one might have had. And the stories from the parties entered folkloric
dimensions. We had an opening night party and a closing night party,
and there was one big reception during the festival where you could
invite everyone who'd helped. The Commonwealth Pool had just
opened (in 1971), and somebody on our staff persuaded them to let
us use it for the party. The deal was that nobody could go in, and
idiotically the invitation said 'don't bring swimming costumes because
we can't go in the water.' So of course, come midnight, about 50
naked people jumped in. I remember standing with Colin Young and
wondering, which of us goes to jail for this? I remember Nick Nolte
was there. There was a lot of that going on back then.

SPOTLIGHT

Cambridge Footlights – The Cellar Tapes (1981)

WHILE THE OXFORD Theatre Group's late-night revues were inspiration for
Robert Ponsonby to create *Beyond the Fringe* in 1960, the success of that
show was a large part of what brought the Cambridge University Footlights
Dramatic Club to the Fringe afterwards. Students from Cambridge, Britain's
other leading university, had tried out Edinburgh shows here and there

during the late 1950s, but its leading student drama club didn't arrive in Edinburgh until after its alumni Peter Cook and Jonathan Miller had become stars.

Following the model established by the Oxford Theatre Group, the Cambridge University Theatre Company was specially established for the purpose of a three-week Edinburgh run, with works of serious drama accompanied by a late-night comedy revue. The Cambridge University Amateur Dramatic Club, founded in 1855, handled the drama and the comparatively youthful Footlights, around since only 1883, prepared the revue, although the University Theatre Company was a blend of both and actors tended to cross over. As with the Oxford group, the revue subsidised the drama to an extent, as all the International Festival's audiences and critics left the major evening shows in search of late-night revue fun.

Accompanying a version of Henrik Ibsen's *Brand* at the Methodist Central Hall on Lothian Road, directed by future Royal Shakespeare Company and National Theatre artistic director Trevor Nunn, the Cambridge Footlights' first Edinburgh revue in 1962 was a vintage one. *Double Take* featured performers John Cleese, Graham Chapman and Tim Brooke-Taylor and it made a firm attempt to escape the much-imitated dry satire of *Beyond the Fringe* by incorporating elements of the silliness and emphatic strangeness that later fed into the trio's respective comedy groups Monty Python and The Goodies. Some of Cleese's dialogue in one sketch, in fact, evoked the Pythons' later-famous 'Dead Parrot' sketch.

The future Edinburgh regular Miriam Margolyes and the actor Jo Kendall[1] were also part of this group, while 1963's revue return *A Clump of Plinths* swapped out the graduated Chapman for Brooke-Taylor's future fellow Goodie Bill Oddie. It also included Jonathan Lynn, later a film director in Hollywood and was a substantial breakthrough success after Edinburgh. Renamed *Cambridge Circus*, the show toured to New Zealand then transferred to Broadway, appearing on the *Ed Sullivan Show* in October '64 amid a post-*Beyond the Fringe* hunger for intelligent British comedy on American stages.

From *Cambridge Circus* on, Footlights had earned itself a reputation for revue comedy to match that of the Oxford Theatre Group's for theatre. Although a class to equal '62 or '63's didn't emerge for some time, the annual revues, which were prepared for the end of university term's May Week, honed in London then charged through the three weeks of the Edinburgh Fringe threw up a huge amount of talent. Cleese and Chapman's future Python Eric Idle joined in time for 1964's revue *Stuff What Dreams Are Made Of* alongside Goodie-in-waiting Graeme Garden.

Like *Beyond the Fringe*, the individual reach of those involved in *Cambridge Circus* extended far into the future of British comedy and entertainment. In

1964 the group devised the radio sketch comedy *I'm Sorry, I'll Read That Again* for the BBC Home Service and later BBC Radio 2, which ran until 1973. In 1972 Garden devised the improvisational panel show spin-off *I'm Sorry, I Haven't a Clue*, which continues to the present day on BBC Radio 4, with Brooke-Taylor as a regular until 2020. Cleese, Brooke-Taylor and Oddie co-created the ITV sketch programme *At Last the 1948 Show* in 1967, around the same time they began writing on *The Frost Report* for David Frost, a pre-Edinburgh Footlights alumnus of the same era as Peter Cook.

Former Footlights Cleese, Chapman and Idle worked together on Frost's show, which is where they met writers Michael Palin and Terry Jones, both former Oxford Theatre Group members and Idle's colleagues on the ITV children's show *Do Not Adjust Your Set*. Together with American animator Terry Gilliam, whom Cleese met during *Cambridge Circus*'s Broadway run and who was now living in the UK and working on *Do Not Adjust Your Set*, the quintet created the sketch show *Monty Python's Flying Circus*. This ran on the BBC between 1969 and 1974 and later developed into an acclaimed film series and various individually successful careers. Meanwhile Brooke-Taylor, Garden and Oddie's own absurdist sketch show *The Goodies* was a family hit on the BBC between 1970 and 1982.

The new term Footlights intake of October 1964 drew in the future broadcasters Clive James and Russell Davies and the first official female member of the club, the later writer and radical feminist Germaine Greer.[2] Others who experienced the intensity of a Footlights run in Edinburgh during their 1960s student days included Richard Eyre, associate director at Edinburgh's Royal Lyceum Theatre between 1967 and 1972, artistic director at the National Theatre in London from 1987 to 1997[3] and a prominent British film director; the author, screenwriter and *Downton Abbey* creator Julian Fellowes; and the singer and actor Julie Covington. Under the direction of Clive James, Footlights revues became more conventional, harking back to the pre-*Beyond the Fringe* style, although there was still an audience for them in Cambridge and Edinburgh.

The events of 1968 and a period of radical student sit-ins in the immediate aftermath demanded something more subversive to suit the times, however and Footlights wasn't delivering. *Gone with the Clappers*, the revue of 1971 whose title alone sounded like something from another era, was an Edinburgh flop and the club's financial problems meant that from 1974 it was reduced to begging for space at Oxford Theatre Group's St Mary's Hall for its Fringe shows.

For a time, the Footlights' lasting legacy wasn't the performers it produced but the broadcast executives who came through its ranks, including BBC Radio head David Hatch, BBC Radio producer and ITV television executive Humphrey

Barclay and Jonathan James-Moore, later the BBC Head of Light Entertainment who commissioned so many Fringe comedians of the 1990s into their own television series, including Steve Coogan, Harry Hill and Lee and Herring.

The revues of the 1970s didn't find the same unique blend of voices as the satirical *Beyond the Fringe* or the surreal Python-era Footlights, but plenty of future talents took some of their first steps onstage during Edinburgh Festival Fringes of the time, among them comedian and producer Griffith 'Griff' Rhys Jones, broadcaster Clive Anderson, comedians and co-founders of television production company Hat Trick Rory McGrath and Jimmy Mulville,[4] and the creator of *The Hitch-Hiker's Guide to the Galaxy* Douglas Adams, who directed and co-wrote 1976's revue *A Kick in the Stalls*.

* * *

By the very nature of three-year undergraduate degrees – plus optional postgraduate study, if the student chose to continue at Cambridge – a Footlights member's time in the company was naturally limited. The wheel turned again with a new student intake for 1979, which included the beginnings of a new classic line-up to match that of the early 1960s. One of the newcomers, Emma Thompson, a 19-year-old when she went up to Cambridge's Newnham College to study English in the autumn of '78, already had a family background in performance. Her mother is the Glaswegian actor Phyllida Law, daughter of a *Glasgow Herald* journalist and a fiercely Presbyterian mother; her father, who died in 1982, was Eric Thompson, the creator of the English version of children's television show *The Magic Roundabout*. From the start of her Footlights career she was known for being extraordinarily nice and extremely capable, especially as a comedian. Fellow Footlight Stephen Fry has said her nickname at the time was 'Emma Talented'.

Fry first saw Thompson perform a student production of Tom Stoppard's *Travesties* in 1979, co-directed by Brigid Larmour and Annabel Arden. 'The girl who played Gwendolen stood out like a good deed in a dirty world,' he later wrote. 'Her voice, her movement, her clarity, ease, poise, wit... well, you had to be there'.[5] Another of the 1978–79 year's Footlights students was two months older than Thompson and briefly her boyfriend in first year, the son of an Olympic rower who was heading for elite status in the same sport. John Laurie (who used and uses his middle name, Hugh) was on the Cambridge team that only just lost the 1980 boat race versus Oxford University, a strapping six-foot-two athlete who seemed fairly unremarkable beyond his physique and his background.

'He would be hanging about on the edge of a group of people, clutching a plastic bag',[6] was how one unnamed friend recalls Laurie's university social style. Although Fry wasn't in Footlights that year, it was a starry line-up in retrospect. Other members included McGrath and Mulville, in their final years; the future Comedy Store Player, author and broadcaster Sandi Toksvig; the later comedian and radio producer Jan Ravens; and Simon McBurney, co-founder (with Marcello Magni and Thompson's co-director in *Travesties* Annabel Arden) of Théâtre de Complicité, a company with its own subsequent Edinburgh impact. He was Thompson's partner for a time during university.

The 1979 Edinburgh revue was *Nightcap*, which got Thompson noticed by agent Richard Armitage of the Noel Gay Organisation. The following year Jan Ravens became Footlights' first-ever female president and she arranged the club's first all-female revue, *Woman's Hour*, for herself, Thompson, Toksvig and Hilary Duguid. The Footlights Edinburgh revue in 1980 was *Electric Voodoo*, which featured only Toksvig and Ravens from the previous year, although some material was written by Laurie, McBurney and Fry.

The London-born son of a physicist and inventor who spent time on remand in his teenage years for using stolen credit cards, but subsequently distinguished himself in his Cambridge entrance exams, Fry started his studies at the same time as Thompson and Laurie, but wasn't involved in *Nightcap*. That year, in 1979, he was appearing in Edinburgh at Adam House Theatre on Chambers Street with a science fiction-inspired production of *Oedipus Rex* by other Cambridge students and he didn't even see the revue until it arrived at the Fringe. As well as noting his friend Thompson was in it, he also noticed Laurie. That year Fry was also amazed by Rowan Atkinson's show at the Wireworks, after which he spoke to its designer, an old schoolteacher from Fry's days at Uppingham School named Christopher Richardson.

In 1980, Fry's Fringe was spent with Cambridge Mummers at Riddle's Court where one of the shows being staged was *Latin! or Tobacco and Boys*, a play he had written, as well as McBurney's *Notes of a Dirty Old Man* by Charles Bukowski and a version of Thomas Middleton and Thomas Dekker's 17th century play *The Roaring Girl*. One of the actors in this was Tony Slattery, a working-class Londoner who'd earned a scholarship to Cambridge and who also happened to be a youth judo champion. 'Handsome and amusing [with] the habits of an ill-trained but affectionate puppy,' was Fry's estimation of Slattery.[7] That year, Fry won a Fringe First for *Latin! or Tobacco and Boys*.

In the academic year 1980–1, Laurie and Thompson were both back at Footlights as president and vice-president, respectively and Laurie asked Thompson for an introduction to Fry, so impressed had he been by *Latin!* The two men began writing together and found they had an easy and natural rapport which sat nicely on the line between the era of posh Oxbridge revue comedy and the oncoming wave of Alternative Comedy. 'We're *students*, for fuck's sake', was their mantra, displaying a useful self-awareness that their experience came from a place of privilege. They rehearsed and performed throughout that year,[8] adding computing student Paul Shearer and Fry's old Cambridge Mummers friends Tony Slattery and Penny Dwyer to the group. The actor Tilda Swinton, not a Footlight but a contemporary at Cambridge, appeared in one of Fry and Laurie's sketches during term time and Jan Ravens was asked to direct that year's revue. Extra material was written by Toksvig and future Footlight and Edinburgh regular Neil Mullarkey.

The Cambridge Footlights show of 1981 was named *The Cellar Tapes*, a joint reference to the Footlights' basement club room, Bob Dylan's album *The Basement Tapes* and the inevitable pun on the word sellotape. Thompson's agent Richard Armitage – and Rowan Atkinson, also his client – had seen it in Oxford and was interested in representing those involved. At St Mary's Hall, shared as usual with the Oxford Theatre Group, it was a hit from the beginning. Even the poster, a photograph of discarded student ephemera, looked much better than Footlights' usual, like the album sleeve of an art school punk band's new record. The group were equally polished. They wrote sketches about the tuition of Shakespeare, posh revolutionaries, far-right politicians and Thompson's luvvie West End actor Juliana Talent and they did it all with a fresh assurance which suggested they were anything but novices.

Yes most of this Footlights team would have found fame anyway, but Edinburgh and the Fringe was an undoubted catalyst for them. The next step was a London run of *The Cellar Tapes* at the New End Theatre, a converted mortuary in Camden, as a late-night revue after the evening's performances of Steven Berkoff's *Decadence* had finished and a tour to Australia with the show teasingly renamed *Botham, the Musical*. A producer from Granada Television named Sandy Ross, who the group met in Edinburgh, paired them with hot young alternative comedian Ben Elton for a 1982 television pilot named *There's Nothing to Worry About!* although neither Dwyer nor Slattery took part.[9] This programme became the 1983 sketch series *Alfresco*, with Shearer replaced by Robbie Coltrane.

Next, Fry and Laurie cemented their reputation as a television double act through roles in *Blackadder* and the series' *A Bit of Fry and Laurie* and *Jeeves and Wooster* and have maintained a steady level of fame as, in Fry's case, a broadcaster and author and in Laurie's, a Golden Globe and Screen Actors Guild Award-winning television star of the series *House* and a successful musician on the side. Thompson returned to Edinburgh in 1983 with her solo show *Short Vehicle* and after successful stage and television gigs through the '80s, her 1989 film role in *The Tall Guy* – written by Richard Curtis and directed by Mel Smith, alumni of the Oxford Theatre Group at the Fringe – began a so far double Oscar-winning film career.

Paul Shearer continued to act and write, while Penny Dwyer moved out of the industry altogether and went to work for an engineering company which helped build the Channel Tunnel. After a period of illness, she died in 2003. Tony Slattery, meanwhile, was president of Footlights in 1982, for a revue featuring Neil Mullarkey, Richard Vranch and Steve Punt named *Promises, Promises...* whose costumes and sets were designed by future *Grand Designs* presenter Kevin McCloud. Then he went to work with Chris Tarrant and later became an extremely prolific comedy presence at the Fringe and on television, appearing in shows including *Whose Line is It Anyway?* and *Have I Got News for You.* In 2006 he and Fry discussed their shared experiences of bipolar disorder in the television show *The Secret Life of the Manic Depressive.*

Fry, Laurie, Thompson and Slattery were reunited in the cast of the 1992 film *Peter's Friends,* directed by and co-starring Thompson's then-husband Kenneth Branagh, which told the story of a fictional Cambridge University comedy group reuniting ten years on. The list of future stars to pass through Cambridge Footlights' revues in Edinburgh is long, but the class of '81 were more deserving of the mythology laid upon them than almost all of the rest.

* * *

At St Mary's Hall in 1981, on the very last day of *The Cellar Tapes'* performance at the Fringe, the deserved cheers that greeted the cast's curtain call stepped up in volume when a seventh figure took to the stage. The normally-shy Rowan Atkinson had an announcement to make and it involved a new comedy award instituted by Perrier; the 'bubbly water people':

> The organisers and judges of the award... were absolutely certain
> of one thing. That whoever won it shouldn't be the Cambridge
> bloody Footlights. However, with a mixture of reluctance and
> admiration, they unanimously decided that the winner had to be
> *The Cellar Tapes...*[10]

Now an Edinburgh institution and for a time (roughly between the turn of the 1990s and the change of sponsor in 2005) the single most important launchpad for new stand-up comedians in the UK, the Perrier Award was created in 1981 by executives from the British franchise of the French mineral water company Perrier. The names of the individuals who started the Perrier Award are lost in the fog now – Burns recalls an advertising executive who may have been named Daphne was involved – but it was a fully in-house venture for Perrier's marketing department at first and the connection with comedy just as its Alternative variety was beginning to flourish was extremely canny and forward-thinking.

'There were Fringe Firsts at the time, but there was no recognition of comedy,' says Burns.

> Perrier went to see the then-Fringe director [Alistair Moffat] and said we'd like to do this, and he helped them start it. It was a very different beast then, because there were only about 30 eligible shows and the judges didn't have to go back and see them again. The process today is much bigger, and the judges commit an immense amount of time to it.

The winners received a case of Perrier each.

Although the Perrier and its differently-sponsored successors became synonymous with stand-up, the shows the award championed were very different at first. Another early recipient was 1985's *More Bigger Snacks Now*, a punkish mime and physical theatre show by Théâtre de Complicité, the Jacques Lecoq Institute-trained company founded by Simon McBurney and Marcelo Magni and the show's movement director Annabel Arden.

Complicité, as the group simply came to be known, were yet another legacy of Footlights. Arden became a successful opera and drama director and McBurney, alongside a television and film acting career, returned to Edinburgh with Complicité in 2015. This time he was at the International Festival with the extraordinary *The Encounter*, a multimedia solo show at the Edinburgh International Conference Centre which told of Loren McIntyre's 1969 travels with the Amazon peoples of the remote Javari Valley.[11]

Cambridge Footlights and the Perrier weren't done with one another by a long way, although no dedicated Footlights troupe has won it again. in 1996, former Footlights comedy duo Alexander Armstrong and Ben Miller were nominated for the main award; alumni Matthew Holness, Richard Ayoade (as Dean Learner) and Alice Lowe were the stars of shortlisted supernatural spoof *Garth Marenghi's Fright Knight* in 2000 and the 2001 winner, *Garth Marenghi's Netherhead*. The trio moved into television with *Garth Marenghi's Darkplace* and *Man to Man with Dean Learner*, and Ayoade is now one of the UK's most ubiquitous comedy and entertainment broadcasters.

The year 1997 was a vintage one for Footlights, with Holness and Ayoade both appearing alongside future US late night television host John Oliver. Another emerged in 2001, when Footlights' own revue *Far Too Happy* was nominated for Perrier's Best Newcomer award. Tim Key, Mark Watson and Sophie Winkleman were in the cast and Watson and Key were both Newcomer-nominated individually in years to come; Key in 2003 alongside another ex-Footlight, Alex Horne, with Key winning the main award himself in 2009. Key, Tom Basden, Stefan Golaszewski and Lloyd Woolf (and originally Watson and Horne) also formed a hit Fringe sketch group named Cowards, and Basden won Best Newcomer in 2007. Other ex-Footlights Best Newcomer nominees were Natalie Haynes in 2002, Jonny Sweet in 2009 and Liam Williams in 2013, with Williams picking up a Perrier (now just the Edinburgh Comedy Award) nomination the year after.

Yet more famous Footlights to have performed in Edinburgh without getting near Perrier recognition include later *Peepshow* stars David Mitchell, Robert Webb and triple Oscar nominee (and winner) Olivia Colman; *Inbetweeners* stars Simon Bird and Joe Thomas; and comedians Phil Wang and Pierre Novellie. As recently as 2019, the club has continued to bring revues and Free Fringe shows to the Pleasance, C Venues and Just the Tonic spaces. It's unlikely they've finished gathering awards.

8

The Fringe Gets Serious

'STOP THE WORLD, Scotland wants to get on!' declared Winnie Ewing, a 38-year-old solicitor from Glasgow, outside the count of the 1967 British Parliamentary by-election in the Lanarkshire town of Hamilton. Achieved on 2 November, Ewing's win was a milestone moment – only the second time the Scottish National Party had won an electoral seat since their founding in 1934.[1]

Until Ewing's victory, the SNP's cause – to gain independence for Scotland from the rest of the United Kingdom via the ballot box, repeating what had happened in Ireland in the first half of the 20th century minus the civil war – had been a bubbling-under fringe concern, beloved mainly of radical thinkers like Hugh MacDiarmid and Hamish Henderson. Ewing's achievement changed everything overnight. Suddenly the SNP were a viable political force and over the next half-century, they gained dominance over the Scottish political landscape. It was tangible evidence of the spirit of '68 being felt in Scotland, a pushback against the established order and tied to a rising wave of Scottish 'cultural confidence': an awareness that the country could speak directly to itself about its own issues. Notably, the Anglo-Canadian journalist John Prebble's bestselling 1963 book *The Highland Clearances* had awakened many ordinary Scots to a historic injustice.

That spirit of '68 also helped light a spark for the resurgence of radical British theatre in the 1970s and the Scottish political developments of the decade put the nation at the forefront of this charge. One company led it in particular – 7:84, named after an article one of the company had read in *The Economist* which said seven percent of the UK's population owned 84 percent of its wealth. While its greatest successes happened across Scotland, the roots of 7:84 were intertwined firmly with the Edinburgh Festival. They didn't lie in the obvious places, though. In fact, they were in the same late-1950s Oxford Theatre Group shows at Cranston Street Hall that fostered the *Beyond the Fringe* group.

In the 1958 revue *Just Lately*, first of all, a young student from Glasgow named Elizabeth MacLennan appeared alongside Dudley Moore and the future film director Ken Loach. MacLennan, a member of Oxford's Experimental Theatre Group, had that summer just finished her second year at Oxford and at the beginning of her third she met a fellow student from Birkenhead named John McGrath, in a class on improvisation. Soon after, he directed her as Molly Bloom in a student adaptation of James Joyce's *Ulysses* at Oxford Playhouse and for 1959's return visit to Cranston Street Hall – as well as featuring in the revue once again, this time alongside Alan Bennett and the future director of Glasgow's Citizen's Theatre, Giles Havergal – she played a social worker in a new realist drama by McGrath named *Why the Chicken*.

MacLennan and McGrath were married in 1962 and spent much of that decade separately finding their way towards a shared destiny in 7:84. He spent time at the Royal Court after graduating and found it not as radical as he might have hoped. McGrath's belief was in socialist thought blended with popular appeal, so he went into television for a time, most notably as a writer and director on the gritty-for-its-time British police drama *Z-Cars*.

MacLennan's career as an actor, meanwhile, flourished. On stage, she appeared in a tour of *Why the Chicken* which was intended to transfer to the West End,[2] worked at Dundee Rep Theatre and appeared in productions on the West End and at the Royal Court. On television, she also appeared in *Z-Cars*, as well as the likes of *Dr Finlay's Casebook,* and was in a television play named *You in Your Small Corner* which featured one of British television's first interracial kisses.

McGrath found his way back into theatre with 1966's *Events While Guarding the Bofors Gun* at the Hampstead Theatre, directed by sometime Cambridge Footlight Richard Eyre, which looked back to the boredom of McGrath's own National Service in Germany in the mid-1950s. Then, in May 1968, he travelled to Paris, the epicentre of international student revolt, to visit and show support for those at the *Ecole des Beaux-Arts*. This spring journey was transformative for McGrath and he used it to inform his next play with Eyre, now the artistic director of Edinburgh's Royal Lyceum. Named *Random Happenings in the Hebrides*, it ran for four Lyceum performances during the 1970 Edinburgh International Festival, earning positive reviews for a piece about a Labour Party organiser (John Thaw) returning to the Hebrides of his youth and old flame Catriona (MacLennan), even as she's haunted by an incestuous incident with her brother (John Cairney) and the local fishing industry crumbles away. One trawlerman was played by a young Denis Lawson.

The broad consensus was that McGrath was a playwright full of ideas and although the incest angle was a cliché in stories of remote communities, the sense of political disillusionment in the wake of Labour Prime Minister Harold Wilson's unseating three months earlier was stark. He later wrote on the play's themes:

The furious banging on the bar counter for a drink that will
do no good when it comes is trying to say something about the

inadequacies of Labourism, the failure of the compromised hopes of the '60s.[3]

More than that, the play – subtitled 'The Social Democrat and the Stormy Sea' – began to expand on McGrath's ideas that the Highlands of Scotland were one of the ripest battlegrounds for political change in the whole of the United Kingdom. He

consolidated his disdain for 'the new bourgeoisie' who so unimpressed him at the Royal Court with declarations of admiration instead for the Workers' Theatre movements of the 1930s, the Unity Theatres of the 1940s – including the one from Glasgow which had 'gatecrashed' the Festival in 1947 – and for Joan Littlewood, Ewan MacColl and their Theatre Workshop. For all that had pushed hard against the norms of theatre during the Edinburgh Festival's lifespan, in other words:

As the Empire went, and the unions grumbled, and in 1956 the Suez adventure put paid to Britain's last fantasy that it could pillage the world at will by force of arms, so it became clear that the British middle class must change. We were the agents of that change.[4]

He was referring to those, like him, who benefitted from the 1944 Education Act, which opened up university education and a seat at the cultural table to a new generation of bright, young, working-class people.

McGrath outlined his belief in the potential of theatre yet further:

I do believe that there is a working-class audience for theatre in Britain which makes demands, and which has values, which are different from those enshrined in our middle class audience... middle class theatre is not by definition the only, or even necessarily the best, kind of theatre.[5]

These ideals were thoroughly shared by his wife, although MacLennan's background was significantly more privileged. Her parents were both successful doctors, her father becoming Sir Hector MacLennan in 1965 and the head of the Royal Society of Medicine in 1967. The only daughter among four siblings, Elizabeth, her brother David and his soon-to-be first wife Ferelith Lean were all in at the birth – with McGrath's next Edinburgh Festival show in 1971 – of the radical theatre powerhouse that was 7:84.

Trees in the Wind, that Edinburgh Fringe presentation, took McGrath and MacLennan back to the Cranston Street Hall, where a month was spent building three separate stages for the three bedrooms in the London flatshare where the play was set. In each lived a different woman: Gilly Hanna as a thoughtful social worker exploring sexual liberation; MacLennan as a razor-wielding radical feminist modelled on Valerie Solanas, writer of the SCUM ('Society for Cutting Up Men') manifesto and attempted murderer of Andy Warhol; and Deborah Norton as a devoted Maoist, in tune with a revived intrigue around and interest in Communist China.

The play's title, in fact, came from Chairman Mao's maxim that 'wind will not cease even if trees want rest', its implication being that politics will shape the lives of all, whether they engage with them or not.

Into this brew fell Victor Henry's lone man, there for sex and the announcement that he's giving up Maoism for capitalism. *The Scotsman* declared *Trees in the Wind* an unsung hit of that year, while Michael Billington demanded a London transfer in the pages of *The Times*. The following year 7:84 returned to the Fringe. This time the play was John Arden and Margaretta D'Arcy's *The Ballygombeen Bequest* at Old St Paul's Church Hall on Jeffrey Street, which distilled decades of troubled Irish history and politics into a tale of one peasant family's eviction.

Another seed that inspired a great Scottish theatrical legacy was sown during the Fringe of '72. As we've seen, *The Great Northern Welly Boot Show* at Waverley Market blended comedy, song and radical politics while kick-starting many Scottish stage careers, not least Billy Connolly's. It was playing barely a quarter of a mile from 7:84's venue and McGrath and MacLennan went to see it, where they recruited Alex Norton, Bill Paterson and John Bett for their next project. Inspired by the writings of John Prebble and his own journeys in the Highlands of Scotland, McGrath had been fomenting an idea for a show that explored the exploitation of the region by outsiders and the historic abuse of Gaelic culture.

His story ranged from the forced Highland Clearances of the 18th and 19th century, when landowners ran their tenants off the land and often deported them to the Americas in favour of more profitable sheep flocks, to the cordoning-off of swathes of the Highlands as hunting estates for the elite, to emerging fears in the 1970s that the approaching North Sea oil boom would have the same effect.

With 7:84 splitting into English and Scottish divisions in 1973, the latter producing the new play, McGrath and MacLennan were joined by Norton, Paterson, Bett and the Hebridean musician, Gaelic speaker and sometime Howff regular Dolina Maclennan (no relation to Elizabeth or David).

The result of their collective effort was the Scots classic of ceilidh-style gig theatre and entertaining political agitation *The Cheviot, the Stag and the Black, Black Oil*, which was first performed as a rehearsed reading in March 1973 at an Edinburgh conference organised by Bob Tait of *Scottish*

International magazine. A two-year Scottish and Irish rural tour followed, encompassing 'one hundred shows, over 30,000 people and 17,000 miles', [6] and the play's blend of music, comedy, drama and politics stirred wider Scottish audiences to the conversations that had won Winnie Ewing her seat six years earlier.

The discussion of Scottish theatre's wider voice amid the Edinburgh Festival had been a live one ever since its beginning in 1947, but with the birth of companies like 7:84 and Borderline and the making of several names in *The Great Northern Welly Boot Show* at the turn of the 1970s, it seemed it was finally speaking clearly and with some urgency.

* * *

Since its establishment by Michael Imison, Ian Cousland and the regular Fringe groups of the late 1950s, the Festival Fringe Society had carried on fulfilling its missions until the turn of the 1970s: to assist groups in finding venues, getting performing licences, navigating Lord Chamberlain's censorship and promoting their shows, especially through inclusion in the ever-expanding Fringe programme. There was a small subscription fee for Society services, but really, it was – and is – inclusion in the programme that's essential for visibility among every other Fringe group competing for audiences. The Society has never chosen shows to appear or forbidden shows from appearing on the Fringe and has no power to do so.

For its first 12 years the Fringe Society was entirely volunteer-run by people who had been involved in groups appearing at it. In 1978, then-Administrator Alistair Moffat wrote a history of the Fringe up to that point and his closer perspective led him to offer thanks to Edinburgh University Drama Society's Patrick Brooks, involved as Treasurer and then President between 1964 and 1972, as a driving force. Brooks was from Hereford but came to Edinburgh to study medicine in 1956 and later worked as a psychiatrist with the Scottish Office. He toured the UK with the Oxford Society, prizing a letter Harold Pinter sent him which complemented his performance in a student production of one of Pinter's plays and campaigned in the 1970s to help save the Edinburgh Playhouse.

Scottish Community Drama Association member Liz Willis and secretary and former Edinburgh Uni Drama Society member Janet Lewis were also key at the Fringe Society in the '60s. After she graduated, Lewis juggled this volunteer role with a full-time job importing Scandinavian furniture. In the early years of the Fringe a prize for the best student production was given, which in 1963 went to the future film director Stephen Frears for his Cambridge University Theatre Company production of *Waiting for Godot*.

If 1959 was a milestone year for the Fringe with the official inauguration of the Society, another came in 1968, with the abandonment of the Lord Chamberlain's veto on playscripts and an effective end to censorship in UK theatre. Content inevitably became edgier and more boundary-pushing, although this moment wasn't quite the watershed it might have been in other cities. The club nature of the Traverse meant it could already escape the Lord Chamberlain's editing pen and it had been well used to a moral panic or two, although that didn't stop Malcolm Muggeridge and Councillor Kidd keeping an agitated watch on moral standards during 1969's Fringe.

In the years before the passing of the 1968 Theatres Act, the Fringe was predominantly about the Traverse and the university groups, especially the high-quality theatrical output of Oxford Theatre Group and the noted comedy abilities of Cambridge Footlights. The Scottish student companies were doing so well, in fact, that a Scottish Students Drama Festival was held in Glasgow in the spring for a time, as of 1963. In 1961, students of the City Literary Institute in London brought a show named *Get Up and Gruts* to the Jacey Cinema on Princes Street, a building which was opened as the Princes Cinema in 1912 and later became known for screening 'continental' (ie sexually explicit) films until its closure in 1973.

A key player in *Get Up and Gruts'* writing and performance – who had briefly been featured on the BBC World Service by this point and also released his debut novel *Gruts* in '62 – was 29-year-old Glaswegian teacher Ivor Cutler, making his first Fringe appearance. The same year there was a 'poets cellar' in the city and in 1965 the great American harmonica player Larry Adler – who left his home country at the same time as Alan Lomax, also under accusations of Communism – performed an extremely popular revue at Morton House on Blackfriars Street, the historic 16th century home of James Douglas, the 4th Earl of Morton, which is now a backpackers hostel.

In 1965, one of Jim Haynes' final influences upon theatre in Edinburgh and on the Fringe itself was set in motion when he acted upon the good suggestion of a woman named Catherine Robins, an assistant stage manager at the Royal Court Theatre in London whom he'd recently met on a visit down south with John Calder. Visiting Edinburgh to read poetry at the Fringe in 1963, Robins completed her training as a drama teacher at the Central School of Speech and Drama in London in '64.

Soon after her meeting with Haynes, she posted her proposal for a pioneering community arts project to him. What she had in mind was a youth theatre group which would draw its members from the community and Calder, ever-open to fresh ideas, enthusiastically agreed. Robins moved to Edinburgh and, with local drama teacher Ros Clarke, set up her proposed group at the Traverse's rehearsal space on York Place. With a nod to the influence of Joan

Littlewood's group, it was called the Traverse Theatre Workshop.

This young company's first production was a Christmas show called *The Enchanted Square*, staged at the Traverse just before Christmas 1965, and regular productions followed at the Traverse and at St Mark's Unitarian Church on Castle Terrace, a few doors along from the Hole in the Ground, for the rest of the decade. These included the Workshop actors' involvement in the Traverse production of early 1968 named *Aberfan*, which pondered causal links between the Welsh mining disaster at Aberfan in 1966 and the Tay Bridge disaster of 1879. In 1970 the group gave its first Fringe production, a play named *Telephone* at St Giles' House on the Royal Mile and in the same year Margate-born Reg Bolton took over as director.

The Workshop was based at 66 Hanover Street and at Castle Hill School during Bolton's tenure up to 1974, with some performances given at the Traverse and elsewhere, but it wasn't the building-based work in and out of Festival time that drew the public's attention. Bolton's expertise was in physical street theatre and he had a hunger for community work, taking his puppetry, clowning shows and workshops – often in character as Dennis the Menace from the *Beano* – to children and community groups in the housing schemes of Pilton and Wester Hailes. During the Fringe of 1971, 25-year-old Bolton performed street mime at the foot of the Mound, outside the National Museum of Scotland building. This is widely viewed as a key event in the introduction of street theatre to the Fringe, as it now exists primarily on the Royal Mile.

The year after he left the Workshop, Bolton established his *Suitcase Circus* travelling workshop. In 1977 he ran a circus summer school in Edinburgh for three years, returning for Fringe shows at the Workshop before emigrating with his family to Perth, Australia in 1985. After this he became a highly-regarded circus theorist and academic, to add to his visionary creation of what he called 'social circus'. When Bolton left the Workshop in 1974 he was succeeded by his protégée Neil Cameron and the organisation finally found a long-term home at 34 Hamilton Place in Stockbridge, on the northern Fringe of Edinburgh's New Town and the banks of the Water of Leith. By this point ties with the Traverse had been cut and it was simply known as the Theatre Workshop, hosting year-round workshops and youth theatre groups, while making its 150-seat theatre and 50-seat studio available to external groups during the Fringe.

Theatre Workshop's future directors included Andy Arnold between 1980 and 1985,[7] who welcomed guest companies including Communicado, Impact and Rational Theatre, and Adrian Harris from 1985 until 1995, who increased the international dimension of visiting companies and made Theatre Workshop a frontrunner among disability access theatres with a complete refurbishment in 1990. The reopening party was a street parade along Hamilton Place by Pierrot Bidon's punk circus *Archaos*, known for chainsaw-juggling and motorcycle tricks, who set up in a tent on Leith Links for the Fringe around this time.[8] Harris was succeeded by Robert Rae, but in 2010 Theatre Workshop closed and the building was sold by Edinburgh Council for redevelopment following the financial crash of 2008.

The Fringe's own international identity increased in the late 1960s. In 1968 Georges Prudhomme, director of the *Institut Français Écosse* (French Institute for Scotland), started a programme of French arts on the Fringe, which continues to this day. Then based in a row of Randolph Crescent townhouses, the *Institut* was founded in 1946 by France's ambassador to the United Kingdom René Massigli as the Scottish outpost of the French Embassy. In 2018 it moved to grand premises at Parliament Square, just off the Royal Mile and continues to present Fringe work.

At some point in the early 1960s, a Kansas-born professor at the University of Southern California named John E Blankenchip arrived in Edinburgh during a sabbatical and took in some of the shows on offer in August and September. Wecan do better than this, he thought, after he'd seen what the Fringe had to offer. In 1966 he returned with some of his own students for shows at the Pollock Hall on Marshall Street. They were the first American company to perform on the Fringe and between this point and 2005 – Blankenchip died soon after at the age of 89 – the USC-USA company played 23 Fringes, presenting plays, musicals and new work by writers including Eugene O'Neill, Tennessee Williams, Neil Simon and Bob Fosse at venues including the Brunton Theatre in Musselburgh, the Southside Community Centre (formerly Nicolson Street Church, more recently known on the Fringe as Zoo Southside) and Drummond Community Theatre at Drummond High School in Bellevue.

USC won *Scotsman* Fringe First awards for two UK premieres, Stephen Sondheim's *Follies* in 1978 and Sam Shepard's *Buried Child* in 1979, and its Edinburgh student cohort at various times featured future film stars John Ritter, Ally Sheedy and Eric Stoltz. The Queen's sister princess Margaret went to see *Follies* in '78, as she'd done in 1971 for another acclaimed American student company which had followed USC's example and come to the Fringe. That year the College of Marin, also in California, brought a Wild West version of Shakespeare's *The Taming of the Shrew* to the Viewforth Centre at Viewforth Church on Gilmore Place, which featured 20-year-old drama student and future comedian and film star Robin Williams among its cast. It was Williams' first known stage role and reputedly the first visit by a member of the Royal Family to a Fringe show.

A small but historically significant symptom of the changes that occurred in the Fringe at the cusp of the 1970s came with the first appearance in 1970 of married theatre director couple Verity Bargate and Fred Proud's Soho Lunchtime Theatre Company in Edinburgh, with three plays at Cranston Street Hall including Spanish playwright Fernando Arrabal's controversial 1966 work *Solemn Communion*, which featured a scene of necrophilia.[9] Although the Soho company led a nomadic existence over the decades after it was established on London's Old Compton Street, it was the precursor of the current Soho Theatre on Dean Street, an important house for British new writing which has presented key plays at the Fringe in recent years.

Until the 1970s the main power as far as the Fringe Society was concerned was the student theatre companies and an argument in the pages of *The Guardian* in 1966 illustrated the problems that existed. Ahead of its annual general meeting at the end of that year's Festival, a representative of Oxford Theatre Group was quoted talking about a perceived lack of professionalism in the Fringe Society, including things like failure to list shows in the programme correctly and the inadequacy of the facilities at the YMCA. An independent reply on the letters page a few days later partially refuted the OTG's claims, saying they were as culpable as anyone for the apathy which existed among Society members regarding improvements.

Between 1961 and 1969 the number of shows at the Fringe had expanded from 30 to over 100 and in 1971 the pressure on its harangued part-time volunteers was at last eased with the fulfillment of an ongoing demand, the appointment of the Fringe Society's first paid member of staff, the part-time administrator John Milligan. This followed the formalising of the Fringe as a limited company with charitable status and a board of directors in 1969. An art teacher and sometime Scottish Arts Council worker and BBC researcher, Milligan worked three days a week at an office by the old Traverse in James Court. By 1972 he was full-time, the Fringe Club had moved from the YMCA to the Royal Mile Centre and he'd rapidly increased the number of companies attending. Edinburgh Corporation had given permission to use school halls and Milligan encouraged companies to increasingly share spaces, as happened at Cranston Street Hall and Heriot Watt University Students Union on Grindlay Street in 1970.[10]

After the Fringe of '72, however, Milligan had grown concerned about the poor box office for new writing on the Fringe – the Traverse excluded – compared to revue and repertory theatre. The solution he found to promote new work was a collaboration with *The Scotsman* newspaper's publicist Ian Thomson and arts editor Allen Wright, with the latter creating a new writing award named the Fringe First. A Fringe First is open to any new play or other rehearsed piece of theatre that is premiering on the Fringe (not the International Festival), with permission for up to six preview performances elsewhere beforehand. A member of *The Scotsman's* festival review team can nominate a play for its outstanding quality, which will then be seen by other reviewers and earn an award if there's broad consensus it's merited. Between 10 and 20 awards have been given annually ever since.

The very first Fringe First year in '73 was a vintage one and it justified their existence by singling out some of the very finest Fringe theatre makers of its era. Stanley Eveling was honoured for *Union Jack and Bonzo* at his regular home, the Traverse Theatre and Tadeusz Kantor was awarded for his second year at the Fringe, *Lovelies and Dowdies*. Presented by Richard Demarco at the decrepit, industrial Forrest Hill Poorhouse, this was a renamed version of pre-war Polish playwright Stanislaw Ignacy Witkiewicz's 1922 play *Dainty Shapes and Hairy Apes*, transformed by Kantor's Cricot 2 Theatre company into a dark, dehumanising but blackly amusing Holocaust allegory.

Kantor's first appearance at the Fringe was in '72 as part of Demarco's *Atelier 72* project, a sequel to his presentation of pioneering Polish artists in 1967 and a similar project to 1970's *Strategy: Get Arts*, although sadly Edinburgh College of Art was unavailable in '72 and it stood unused. Born in Austria-Hungary in 1915, prior to the reformation of the Second Polish Republic in 1918, Kantor ran the underground Independent Theatre in Kraków during the Nazi occupation and in 1955 he founded his Cricot 2 company. Th company was named after the previous Polish company Cricot, an emblem of the country's inspirational interwar Avant Garde scene.

Witkiewicz (known also as 'Witkacy') died by suicide shortly after the Soviet invasion of Poland in 1939. Although he was in relative obscurity at the time, he became a key influence on the post-war Theatre of the Absurd and the European Avant Garde, especially through Kantor's loose adaptations. Already 57 years old when he was 'discovered' by Demarco, Kantor's first play in Edinburgh adapted Witkacy's *The Water Hen*, mesmerising audiences with its physical intensity. It was 'conducted' by the director as he moved around the room mid-performance. Cordelia Oliver wrote in *The Guardian*:

> Everything done within the space – each gesture, human and spatial relationship, sound (for sound is integral, not only speech), change in temp, tone or pitch – strikes you as meaningful.[11]

Demarco's old friend Sean Connery took in a Cricot 2 performance in '73 and Kantor returned for another Fringe show, the Fringe First-winning *The Dead Class* in 1976, this time originated without referring to Witkacy.

There was also a communal Fringe First for the Pool Lunch-Hour Theatre at 76 Hanover Street, founded at the beginning of 1971 by Bradford Art College Theatre Group's Phillip Emanuel, who witnessed what the Soho

Lunch Theatre Company were doing at the Fringe in 1970. With a stage technician from Edinburgh named John Cumming and a writer named Lindsay Levy, Emanuel set up a theatre featuring small-cast plays of half an hour in length, serving open sandwiches, soup and coffee for lunch. The promise was that the audience could see a play and be back in time for work, and while lunch theatre clubs were fashionable in London, this was the first established elsewhere in the UK. The original plan had been to name it the Other Pool's (sic) Synod Hall after the previous occupant of the Hole in the Ground, but the potentially obscure in-joke was quickly done away with.

Opening on 1 February 1971 with Lindsay Kemp's *Turquoise Pantomime*, the Pool welcomed companies to the Fringe including Soho Lunchtime Theatre, Portable Theatre,[12] the Ken Campbell Road Show, Michael Almaz' Artaud Theatre and Edinburgh's own Theatre Workshop. A buzzing, central location which briefly rivalled the Traverse in Festival popularity, its Fringe First was awarded on the basis of a strong '73 drama programme which featured Hector MacMillan's play about Glasgow sectarianism, *The Sash,* and Alasdair Gray's early play *The Loss of the Golden Silence.* Financial issues and rising rent forced the Pool out for a fragmentary final Fringe around the halls of Edinburgh in '74. When Phil Emanuel resurfaced in the 1980s it was as the producer of Australian films including the Jeremy Irons-starring Ibsen adaptation *The Wild Duck* (1984) and *Rebel* with Matt Dillon (1985).

A friend of Emanuel's from Bradford who collaborated with him from the beginning of the Pool was playwright Richard Crane, who appeared with Cambridge Footlights in Edinburgh in the late '60s and won a Fringe First in '73 for *Thunder*. Another Bradford alumnus was later Traverse artistic director Chris Parr, for whom Crane and his wife Faynia Williams began creating Fringe shows throughout the 1970s, winning nine Fringe Firsts. In 1983 their Brighton Theatre became one of a number of Fringe companies to cross over to the International Festival when they premiered their acclaimed version of Dostoyevsky's *Brothers Karamazov* at the Freemasons' Hall, with Alan Rickman among the cast. In the years before this the International Festival also welcomed, as well as the Traverse, Fringe groups La MaMa for a trio of shows featuring Diane Lane at Moray House Gymnasium in 1976, and Cricot 2 with the premiere outside Poland of *Wielepole Wielepole*, a play about memory, religion and war, at Moray House in 1980.

There was often criticism that the International Festival did little to represent the wider population of Edinburgh, but a sense of political class-consciousness really began to enter the debate in the '70s. In part this was due to the election in 1972 of Councillor Jack Kane as Lord Provost, the first Labour politician to take on the role and a transformative political presence in Edinburgh. In 1974 he turned down a Knighthood, a slight that means the title is no longer automatically offered to Lords Provost, and after his term ended in 1975 he was a key agitator against the use of more public money on the 'elitist' opera house project. While in post, Kane worked closely with John Milligan, a Labour party activist, to promote Fringe events in the council estate suburbs of Pilton, Craigmillar, Sighthill, Portobello, Firhill and Gilmerton. While these weren't all a huge success, when Milligan left the Fringe in 1975 it was to take charge of the Craigmillar Festival.

Not part of the Edinburgh Festival itself and held in spring rather than August, the Craigmillar Festival was as much a landmark in UK community arts as the city's other festivals had been on the international stage. Its founder is recognised as Helen Crummy, a local mother of children at Peffermill Primary School, who in 1962 asked for violin lessons for her eldest son Philip and was told 'it takes us all our time to teach these children the 3Rs'.[13] With the support of fellow parents and her neighbour and councillor Kane, she started a small festival for local children in one of Edinburgh's most deprived areas to show their talents.[14] By 1970 it had become a fully-fledged festival in its own right, with local groups putting on new musical theatre productions and visiting artists getting involved.

By 1976 Craigmillar Festival Society was at its peak, with 600 people – including Milligan – involved in the organisation of it and 17,000 people attending. Around this time the Festival welcomed actors including Bill Paterson and Kenny Ireland for workshops and Richard Demarco assisted in commissioning the then still-imprisoned Jimmy Boyle to create the largest public sculpture in Europe for the area. Cast in concrete and inspired by Jonathan Swift's *Gulliver's Travels*, *The Gentle Giant That Shares and Cares* was an enormous, half-buried sleeping giant, so large that its arms and legs were tunnels which children could run through.

Billy Connolly unveiled the statue in '76 and four years later artist Pedro Silva created the similarly huge 'Mermaid Sculpture' on behalf of the Society, this time in physical protest against a planned new road which would have cut directly through the area. Part of the Scottish filmmaker Bill Douglas' *Trilogy* series was also based there and in August 1978 a *Rock Against Racism* concert featuring Aswad and local groups including the Scars took place in the shadow of Peffermill School.[15]

The environmental artist and thinker David Harding, who designed much of the art for the Fife new town of Glenrothes and later set up the highly-regarded Environmental Art degree at Glasgow School of Art, said of the Craigmillar Festival:

What is astonishing about the Craigmillar story is that, while incisive, creative thinkers like Augusto Boal, Paolo Friere and Ivan

Illich, among others, were publishing their ideas on approaches to the issues of the poor and excluded, intuitively the Festival Society was actually carrying them out. It had found its own route to the notions that given respect, opportunity and a platform for their own voices, the poor and excluded can achieve very special things.[16]

The Craigmillar Festival Society finally folded in 2002 and Boyle's 'Gulliver', now a vandalised blight, was torn down in 2011 in favour of redevelopment. Yet community activity still persists in new forms in Edinburgh's surrounding housing estates, including the recent archive project *Craigmillar Now*, which is dedicated to preserving the area's rich cultural history.

At the Fringe Society, Milligan was replaced by Alistair Moffat. He was 26 at the time of his first Festival in 1976, but already a veteran of local arts admin, having set up the Kelso Festival in his Borders hometown and the St Andrews Festival while he was a student at the university. He was also instrumental in the election of John Cleese as St Andrews' 'silly rector' in 1970,[17] as well as his friend Gordon Brown's election as student rector at the University of Edinburgh in '72, while Moffat was a postgraduate student there. In his five-year term with the Fringe, Moffat took what Milligan had done and ran with it, overseeing the move to the new and more accessible current ticket office on the High Street, a few doors from the Royal Mile Centre and proactively finding even more space for new companies to occupy.

New theatre company arrivals during Moffat's tenure included Paines Plough, founded in London in 1974 by writer David Pownall and director John Adams over a pint of Paines bitter in the Plough pub. Their 1976 Fringe debut *Music to Murder By* won a Fringe First, they were accepted by the Traverse with *Richard III Part II* in '77 and the company's Fringe association from there spanned decades. Founded in 1975 by Mike Alfreds, the Shared Experience company also appeared at the Fringe in '76 with a low-key school hall production of *Arabian Knights*. The playwright Stephen Jeffreys' first work *Like Dolls or Angels* was a hit for them in '77.

In 1979, six months after its premiere at the ICA in London and three months after his Science Fiction Theatre of Liverpool company put on the first stage version of Douglas Adams' *The Hitchhiker's Guide to the Galaxy* at the same venue, Ken Campbell staged five performances of his Guinness Book of World Records-entering 22-hour play cycle *The Warp* at Edinburgh's Regent Theatre during the Fringe. Written by poet, artist and Campbell's fellow spiritual adventurer Neil Oram, the play told the story of a man named Phil Masters through numerous reincarnated lives and was widely said to be 'lived through' by its audience, rather than simply seen. The London cast included Bill Nighy and Jim Broadbent, although it's uncertain whether they also appeared in Edinburgh.

Said Oram of the show's unique production after the disused cinema on the Royal Mile was found, preparation involved:

> ...squatting it... then draining it of a large six-feet deep lake at the bottom of the sloping ex-cinema... installing a water supply by digging up pavements... installing loos after looting un-occupied houses... digging up more pavements to get an electricity supply... mending the roof (the building had been empty for 20 years)... creating a café area... changing rooms... getting the building passed for public performance by the Edinburgh Building Department, which required proper architectural plans – which was achieved by Margo Sagov getting plans from the Edinburgh Archives, through bribing the Keeper with two packets of Capstan Extra Strong cigarettes – and then, she used these original plans to draw up new plans which she presented to the Building Department – who were astonished that she could produce these new plans. Margo calmly explained that she wasn't just a rock 'n roll guitar player, but a qualified architect. So the building was passed and the entertainment licence granted an hour before the show was due to begin'.[18]

Campbell's work in Edinburgh had grown from appearances at the Pool Lunch-Hour Theatre by his Roadshow company, which carried out small experimental works in unusual locations featuring young actors including Bob Hoskins and Sylvester McCoy. Thirty-nine years after The Warp and ten years after his death in 2008, his legacy on the Fringe took an unusual turn with a show at the Pleasance telling his story named simply *Ken*. It was part-produced by the team behind the popular Fringe hit *Showstopper! The Improvised Musical*, whose members Kate Alderton and Lucy Trodd had trained with Campbell. In fact, Alderton's parents, the actors Pauline Collins and John Alderton, had met while working on one of Campbell's productions, 'so he used to cackle with glee that he might be responsible for my very existence'.[19]

The Fringe started to evolve when John Milligan came on board, but Alistair Moffat turbo-charged the process with great enthusiasm. Edinburgh was changing too. Where once the only places to eat after 6.30pm were the Festival Club and possibly the restaurant of your hotel, now wine bars, restaurants serving continental food and pubs that dared stay open after 10pm were springing up to replace the formerly fashionable tearooms. By 1978, local institutions like Dario's had arrived, serving wine with Italian pizza and pasta until 4am on Lothian Road during the Festival, and Henderson's Salad Table on Hanover Street, Scotland's pioneer of vegetarian food.

The late 1970s saw a surge in protests against arts cuts during the Festival, in 1976 tied in with opposition to a planned hotel on the opera house site. These were led by, among others, Prospect Theatre Company and actor Prunella Scales, and in 1979 included a march from King's Stables Road to the Playhouse, co-organised by politician Janey Buchan. The Fringe, however, wasn't feeling the pinch. Where it had staged around 100 shows by 57 companies in 1969, in 1979 625 shows were staged by 324 companies.

* * *

Like the spirit of May '68, the arrival of punk rock in the late 1970s largely passed the Edinburgh Festival by.[20] In fact, the biggest manifestation of the punk spirit in the city at the time went mostly unnoticed, as a group from the University of Manchester followed the tried and tested 'early play and a late comedy' strategy in 1979. Their drama, a version of Eugene Ionesco's *The Bald Prima Donna* (aka *The Bald Soprano*) wasn't taken much notice of and the late-night comedy play *Death on the Toilet* only gathered some attention because of the quirky name.

The play's makers were a drama student comedy group named 20th Century Coyote, who'd formed as a five-piece in 1976 and staged a succession of eccentric, semi-improvised comedy plays named things like *My Lungs Don't Work*, *God's Testicles* and *How to Get a Man Out of a Bag*, in which one of their number would try to get out of a sealed bag for 20 minutes. That performer, Rik Mayall, was one of the only two members of the troupe left by '79, although sometimes their Manchester shows involved their flatmates Ben Elton and Lise Mayer. In Edinburgh, though, it was just Mayall appearing as Death and Adrian Edmondson as a man named Edwyn.

If doing the Festival played any part at all in the birth of Mayall and Edmondson's anarchic future television successes *The Young Ones* and *Bottom*, it's that it made them a little money, which showed the pair there was a future in the comedy game and encouraged them to move to London with Elton and Mayer. Once there, they met another duo named The Outer Limits – Nigel Planer and Pete Richardson – and between the six of them *The Young Ones* was born. Rick, Mayall's unbearably pretentious character in the show, was apparently also a result of the Edinburgh Fringe, where he'd stood up one night in the pub to mockingly imitate the poets performing and been received with warm applause when they thought he was serious.

The Fringe did become a key player in the eventual foundation of comedy as 'the new rock 'n' roll', a train that gathered pace through British popular culture from 1979 until the end of the century and beyond. Edinburgh's festivals had already helped set in motion the mutation of British comedy from early-century music hall humour towards something more contemporary and iconoclastic and tuned into the needs of broadcast media, through *Beyond the Fringe*, the Cambridge and Oxford revues of the 1960s and Billy Connolly's arrival. In the years since *Great Northern Welly Boot Show*, Nat Joseph of Transatlantic Records had surpassed his ambition to turn Connolly into a Hamish Imlach-style folk humorist, first with the surprise hit comedy record *Solo Concert* in 1974, then with Connolly's star-making, no-turning-back first appearance on Michael Parkinson's nationally-televised BBC chat show in 1975.

While Connolly was becoming internationally beloved for his uncensored flamboyance, another international star to get their start at the Fringe – and unwittingly set dominoes in motion which transformed the Fringe into a comedy powerhouse – was a quiet and reserved middle-class engineering student from County Durham in the north of England. At 24 years of age in 1979, his real breakthrough year in Edinburgh, Rowan Atkinson was already a Fringe veteran. His first appearance was in 1973 at the Lauriston Hall, close to Edinburgh College of Art, in a post-school production of Joseph Heller's 1968 anti-Vietnam War Broadway play *We Bombed in New Hampshire*.

It was an early dramatic role for Atkinson, who left St Bee's independent school in Cumbria the year before. He later told the Fringe's future director and biographer Michael Dale that what he remembered of Edinburgh was how long the traffic lights took to change, the 'primitive' lack of one-way systems and:

> [T]he Fringe reception, with people wandering around in white
> masks holding spoons in front of them trying to attract the media's
> attention... I thought, I hope I never have to do that.[21]

Studying for a degree in electrical and electronic engineering at Newcastle University, he returned in 1975 as Angelo in Shakespeare's *Measure for Measure* with Dundee University Theatre Group and in a two-handed, sparsely-attended lunchtime revue at the university's Roxburgh Reading Rooms on Roxburgh Place.

It wasn't until Atkinson arrived at Queen's College, Oxford, to study for his MSc in Electrical Engineering in 1975 that his performing persona and the links to help it develop emerged. His contemporaries included future comedians and actors Mel Smith, Angus Deayton, Helen Atkinson-Wood, Philip Pope and Tim McInnerny, who were all involved in drama societies, and future Prime Minister Tony Blair, Atkinson's near-contemporary at Chorister School in Durham as a child, who wasn't. The key friend he made, however, was a middle-class, independently-schooled English Literature student nearly two years younger than him named Richard Curtis.

The pair's differences somehow made them fit even more perfectly: Atkinson, an unassuming and ordinary-looking bloke from the north, with the air of a young university professor; Curtis, the handsome, charming, New Zealand-born son of a Czechoslovakian refugee-turned-marketing executive, who had lived in Sweden and the Philippines before he started in senior school. It was Curtis who got noticed offstage, but Atkinson's time in the Oxford Revue had a transformative effect. Assured and meticulously well-prepared, he figured out through long hours staring into the mirror that his unique face and the range of expressions it could conjure was his secret weapon. Both started out as performers at Oxford, but their fast-developing relationship saw Atkinson do more of the stagework and Curtis concentrate on writing.

At St Mary's Hall, by now the Oxford Theatre Group's Edinburgh base for well over a decade, they were involved with Oxford's Fringe revues of 1976 and 1977. In '76's show Atkinson was the stand-out performer and the sole agent of the many he invited to attend, Richard Armitage – heading his late father Noel Gay's organisation, which handled John Cleese and David Frost – immediately agreed to take him on. The next year the radio comedy producer John Lloyd was equally impressed, seeking Atkinson out after the show.

Atkinson's standing within the Oxford Revue was so high that he co-opted 1977's Fringe run as virtually a solo show, which he felt guilty but not sorry about. Reworking it as he went, cancelling performances if he felt the changes weren't quite ready, what resulted was *Beyond a Joke*, which transferred to the Hampstead Theatre in 1978, now with co-stars Elspeth Walker and Peter Wilson.[22] The humour was reportedly traditional and in some places even quite bland, but Atkinson's performance glowed. Delivering one line during the entire show in his own voice, he was compared to Jonathan Miller by Michael Billington in *The Guardian*. The rest of the performance involved silly voices, even sillier faces and the kind of mimed comedy that was a precursor to his and Curtis' huge global success with *Mr Bean* in the 1990s.

With a top agent, an up-and-coming producer and a reasonably-sized success in London already in his corner by '78 – an astonishing situation for a young man who had been doing student Shakespeare at the Fringe barely three years earlier – Atkinson's career was already on the way thanks to Edinburgh. He began to make inroads in broadcast, in both children's television and adult comedy and his Curtis co-written series of spoof biographies *The Atkinson People* appeared on BBC Radio 3 in April 1979. The same month a new topical ensemble sketch show, the John Lloyd-produced *Not the Nine O'Clock News*, was meant to begin with Atkinson in the cast, although BBC concerns about the political content with an election upcoming meant transmission was pushed back to October 1979.

With that show postponed for the moment, two key events for Atkinson came in the first summer after Margaret Thatcher's election. The first was *The Secret Policeman's Ball,* a series of all-star fundraising events for Amnesty International held at Her Majesty's Theatre in London between 27 and 30 June. Directed by John Cleese and featuring members of the Monty Python and *Beyond the Fringe* teams, as well as Billy Connolly, the Ball saw Atkinson sharing sketches with personal heroes like Cleese, Peter Cook, Michael Palin and Terry Jones.

The other key event was Atkinson doing something that was then unusual for a performer on the cusp of widespread comedy fame. He returned to the Edinburgh Fringe, the site of his discovery, for a show whose far-reaching effect was upon the Festival itself, more than Atkinson's already-secure career. Presented under his own name, it was made in Oxford for the most part. Once again his co-writer and co-star was Curtis, who was already picking up gigs writing for radio and television, including the forthcoming *Not the Nine O'Clock News*. They were joined by a third friend and collaborator, Howard Goodall, a musician, composer and first-class music graduate from Oxford.

Behind the scenes, the people arranging Atkinson's venue were also recent veterans of Oxford's theatre societies. The French-Lebanese stage director and banker's son Pierre Audi was involved in funding the show, and also involved were Oxford Theatre Group company manager Chris Naylor and theatre designer Will Bowen. The decision was not to try and hire one of the existing Fringe venues, but to create their own. The chosen space was a building dating back to 1840 on Old Assembly Close, just off the Royal Mile and close to the Fringe Society's new office on the High Street.

Built as a school for the George Heriot's Foundation,[23] this building had since been abandoned by the school and used as a printworks and then a wireworks under the ownership of Smith Fletcher & Co, whose names still appeared above the door when the Oxford group discovered it. Bursting with ambition, they set out to create an entirely new theatrical space in time for the 1979 Fringe, which meant the entire cast and crew would be shifting and assembling nearly 50 tons of scaffolding into banks of stall and gallery seating.

The group's chosen venue was so difficult to access via the narrow wynds of the Old Town, that just getting the material there was a huge effort. Actually building a working theatre was a major achievement. Speaking to Michael Dale, Atkinson remembered the all-night teching and stage-building sessions, a tradition established at the Oxford Theatre Group's shows, pulling tired 18-hour shifts to get it done. After all that, only the front row of the upper gallery could see the complete stage – but, had they built up the stage any higher, the first few rows of the stalls would have been looking at a sheer wooden wall.

One of the build team was a 40-year-old former soldier named Christopher Richardson, who worked as an art and design teacher at Uppingham School in the English town of Rutland, where he had taught the young Stephen Fry. Richardson was involved in the development of the school's 300-seat, professional-spec Uppingham Theatre, which regularly hosted Oxford Theatre Group for previews of their Edinburgh shows – this is how he became friends with Atkinson.

'I'd never been to Edinburgh before, but I went up because I'd offered to help Rowan build a staircase,' remembers Richardson now.

> It was this vast space which went all the way from the High Street
> right the way down to the Cowgate. You went in and there were no
> floors, but at the bottom there was a huge pile of scaffold. There was
> a hole in the roof, so water would pour in all day. There was a puddle
> on the stage at the bottom, and Rowan would try to work out how to
> do his sketch show on the puddle – the whole thing was completely
> mad. If you work out how expensive it was to buy all that scaffold,
> and you find it will only seat 90 people... financially it was an absolute
> disaster, but it was such an exciting time, I fell in love with it.

Word of mouth was fierce and the run soon sold out; others have said it didn't do too badly financially, despite the reduced seating capacity. Atkinson told Dale it was the most enjoyable experience of his Fringe career. The chaos of the venue aside, Atkinson won a Fringe First from *The Scotsman* that year, the first revue show to do so,[24] and the arrival of the Television Festival in '76 meant the perfect producers for his brand of visual physical comedy were now all in attendance.

All involved went on to success after the Wireworks show. Within months, Audi, Naylor and Bowen had co-founded the Almeida Theatre in Islington, north London, with a programme which included a range of eclectic international music and theatre. Audi was founding artistic director and later artistic director of the Dutch National Opera for three decades and concurrently the Holland Festival for a time. Naylor eventually became a local councillor in London and Bowen remains an in-demand theatre set designer, whose work included Atkinson, Curtis and Ben Elton's *The New Revue* at the Shaftesbury Theatre in 1986.[25] Richard Curtis became one of Britain's most famous film screenwriters, with popular light comedies including *Four Weddings and a Funeral* (1994), *Notting Hill* (1999) and *Love Actually* (2003), but not before writing extensively for Atkinson on *Not the Nine O'Clock News* (1979–82) and *Blackadder* (1983–89), and co-creating *Mr Bean* with him in 1990.

Not the Nine O'Clock News was finally broadcast two months after the Wireworks show and following a patchy first series it made Atkinson a star on British television, alongside Pamela Stephenson, his old Oxford Theatre Group acquaintance Mel Smith and young former Cambridge Footlight and producer of *The Atkinson People*, Griff Rhys Jones. Stephenson met her future husband Billy Connolly when he made a guest appearance on the show in '79 and made her own debut Fringe appearance at the Netherbow Theatre in 1980. She and Connolly moved to America a few years later when she became a series regular on *Saturday Night Live*, while Smith and Jones became famous as a television sketch show double act and powerful television producers through their company Talkback.

Despite his fame, Atkinson wasn't done with Edinburgh. He returned to the Fringe with his show in 1980, this time to the pristine, modernist George Square Theatre, which had been opened at the turn of the 1970s and was also the regular festival home of director and former *Bible One/Joseph and His Amazing Technicolour Dreamcoat* actor Jeremy James Taylor's Children's Music Theatre. Despite being a financial success, Atkinson wasn't happy with his 1980 set, a partially-reworked version of what he'd done at the Wireworks and. He was also stung by the press reaction, or at least the digs of the *Festival Times*'s over-eager student reviewers.

Atkinson's love for Edinburgh persisted, though. Invited by Alistair Moffat shortly before the Fringe's second administrator left in 1981, he joined the Fringe board and attended meetings until 1983, when too many other commitments forced him to stop. Atkinson later said he mainly accepted because it gave him an excuse to visit Edinburgh three or four times a year and he even considered buying a house in the city. He returned to the Festival once more in 1986, reunited with Curtis, Goodall and Deayton on *The New Revue*, a post-fame show so in demand that it went on after-hours at the Playhouse. The director was Robin Lefevre, who had previously been in charge of *The Great Northern Welly Boot Show* and John Byrne's *Writer's Cramp*.

In many ways, Atkinson's success in Edinburgh was a rerun of *Beyond the Fringe* nearly 20 years before. Although he was very much of the mainstream comedy establishment, his breakthrough success coincided with a defining point in a comedy evolution on the Fringe and in wider British culture. On the 19 May 1979 – 16 days after Margaret Thatcher's first election victory – the Comedy Store opened in London, creating a Year Zero moment for the young and establishment-baiting Alternative Comedy boom of the 1980s. Many of its graduates appeared in Edinburgh, the Fringe quickly rebranding itself as the centre of gravity for British comedy in the 1980s and beyond.

For the Fringe as an evolving idea, the real story wasn't about what Atkinson, Curtis and co. achieved in their few years in the city, although what they did was an inspiration. Instead, it was about the people on the periphery of their project – about Atkinson's friend, the teacher Christopher Richardson, for example, who returned to Edinburgh to help rig the show at the Children's Theatre venue in 1980. He had fallen for the Fringe and he wasn't finished with it by a long way.

In the audience at the Wireworks, meanwhile, was a manager with London's Cockpit Theatre named William Burdett-Coutts, who was born in Zimbabwe, schooled in the UK and not long out of university in South Africa. He'd already helped a group of friends from university arrange dates at the Old Vic in London that autumn for their premier production of South African playwright Pieter-Dirk Uys' play *Paradise is Closing Down*, about three women's lives set against the racially-charged backdrop of Cape Town in 1976 – he thought he might as well try and set up an Edinburgh run while he was at it.

Visiting the city and arranging a meeting with Fringe administrator Alistair Moffat for advice, Burdett-Coutts managed to secure the university's Old Chaplaincy Centre at the south end of George IV Bridge, the former church which the Traverse had taken over for the 1978 Fringe and now vacated in favour of Moray House Gymnasium. Like Richardson, Burdett-Coutts loved what he saw at the Wireworks. 'That was one of the first inspirations on me,' he says. 'They were very impressive, the way they took on a derelict building and turned it into a temporary theatre'.

As the 1970s became the 1980s and a wave of new comedy followed Atkinson, Curtis and their gang to Edinburgh, first Burdett-Coutts and then Richardson were at the forefront of reshaping the Fringe for a new generation of performers and audiences. Their own multi-site venues – Assembly and Pleasance, respectively – remain at the core of the Edinburgh Festival Fringe and the Festival itself, four decades later.

SPOTLIGHT

Mary Queen of Scots Got Her Head Chopped Off (1987)

IN TELLING THE story of the Edinburgh Festival as one huge, interlocking entity, some supporting characters feature more prominently than others. There are people like Jim Haynes, Richard Demarco and the venue owners of later years, who between them have taken a turn on the rudder or even helped build the boat that is the Festival. There are guest stars like Billy Connolly and the *Beyond the Fringe* crew, with their brief but eye-catching presence. And in the background is an ensemble of tens or maybe even hundreds of thousands of artists, idealists, entrepreneurs, amateurs and people who simply want to get involved.

No one person's contribution over the years summarises the Festival itself, but a couple of people come close. One is Richard Demarco, ubiquitous and always enthusiastic. Another is Liz Lochhead, who will helpfully remind of the synchronicity by pointing out she was born on Boxing Day 1947 in Craigneuk, a mining village in North Lanarkshire, barely four months after the Festival itself arrived. Then her breakthrough moment, the debut poetry collection *Memo for Spring*, was published in 1972, the year the Festival celebrated its 25th anniversary. She read from it at that year's Fringe alongside Norman MacCaig.

Lochhead was already a Fringe performer by this point. While she was still a student at Glasgow School of Art in the late 1960s, around '68 or '69, she and a group of poets who passed work around by post had their work read on the Fringe by a group of Scottish actors. During the Festival of 1971, the year Lochhead won the BBC Scotland Prize, the Scottish poet and playwright Joan Ure staged a couple of short plays named *Something in it for Ophelia* and *Something in it for Cordelia* in the Royal Society of Edinburgh building at 24 George Street, both critiques of Shakespeare in the form of scripted conversations between passengers at Waverley Station. Around these she arranged readings by some of Scotland's brightest young poets, including Lochhead, Tom Leonard, Alasdair Gray and Iain Crichton Smith.

Lochhead was a rare female voice in a male-dominated poetry world, although her dedication to working-class voices was in step with most of those writing around her.

Until 1978, she worked as an art teacher in Bristol, Glasgow and Cumbernauld, a job she didn't enjoy, even as writing and publishing poems gave her increasing satisfaction. In May 1978 she became a Traverse writer, of sorts, when she and her friend, the playwright Marcella Evaristi, put on a revue named *Sugar and Spite*. The same year she won the Scottish-Canadian Writers Fellowship, which was organised by the Scottish Arts Council and the Canadian Council and went to spend a year at York University in Toronto, then on to New York.[1]

In 1982, the 35th anniversary of the Festival's founding and her own birth, she became a playwright at last, with the Traverse Theatre's Fringe production of *Blood and Ice*.

Or rather, it was the first version of the first play that Lochhead, an infamous rewriter, was happy with. Telling of Mary Shelley's creation of the novel *Frankenstein* in a house on Lake Geneva in 1816, it was first seen as *Mary and the Monster* at Coventry's Belgrade Theatre in 1981. This version was directed by Michael Boyd, a former Edinburgh University Drama Society member and future director of Glasgow's Tron Theatre and the Royal Shakespeare Company, although it was completely torn apart and rewritten by Lochhead for the Traverse production.

By this point artistic director Chris Parr had left the Traverse after an uninspiring, budget-necessitated 1980 Fringe roster and his assistant Peter Lichtenfels had been made artistic director in his place. Following the move to other, bigger things enjoyed by key Traverse playwrights of the '70s like Tom McGrath and Billy Connolly, the very early '80s was a fallow time for new Scottish playwrights at the Traverse, with Lochhead's breakthrough standing as a shining light.

Not that Lichtenfels' more international outlook was doing badly by any means. The big hit of 1981's Fringe was the final version of Clare Luckham's *Trafford Tanzi*, an effervescent feminist piece about women wrestlers, which Liverpool's Everyman Theatre first staged in the city's pubs and clubs in 1978. In 1982, alongside *Blood and Ice*, Percy Mtwa, Mbongeni Ngema and Barney Simon's hit play *Woza Albert!*, about the second coming of Jesus Christ in apartheid-era South Africa, heralded a decade of increasing levels of anti-apartheid work on the Fringe. The Traverse's Festival offering for 1984 included Michael Tremblay's *Sandra/Manon*, Susannah York's adaptation of Jean Cocteau's *The Human Voice* and the Almeida Theatre Company's *Melancholy Jacques*, taken from the writings of Jean-Jacques Rousseau and starring Simon Callow.

Directed by Kenny Ireland, sometime castmember of *The Great Northern Well Boot Show*, *Blood and Ice* starred Gerda Stevenson and Ciaran Hinds and presented a view upon a story of horror and science which Lochhead perceived as a useful allegory in the nuclear age. Much like the critics, she thought her play was imperfect but had its moments. A change to tidy it up arrived with the Fringe of 1988, when second year Royal Scottish Academy of Music and Drama student David McVicar asked if he could stage a university production of it at that year's Fringe. Aided by her own script revisions, Lochhead loved this version, whose student cast included future professionals Daniela Nardini, John Kazek and Wendy Seager. McVicar is now Sir David McVicar, one of the UK's leading opera directors.

After the 1981 opening of Glasgow's Tron Theatre – which had its roots in the Tom McGrath co-founded Glasgow Theatre Club and was later under the artistic directorship of Michael Boyd for a decade from 1986 – Lochhead was asked to get involved in club revues at the venue. She'd met a Scottish student actor named Siobhan Redmond after seeing her in a play by Marcella Evaristi at St Andrews University, and Lochhead asked Redmond to be involved in the first of these revues, *True Confessions*. After this Redmond worked at the Bristol Old Vic and for Michael Boyd at Sheffield's Crucible, then in 1983 she got a gig on the new television sketch show, *Alfresco*, her first major screen part, alongside recent Perrier winners Emma Thompson, Stephen Fry and Hugh Laurie.[2]

Redmond still appeared in Lochhead's Tron revues in Glasgow, though. In April 1982, she and fellow actors John Cobb and Kevin McMonagle appeared in *Tickly Mince*, written by Lochhead, Tom Leonard and Alasdair Gray and in 1983 the same team plus writer James Kelman – under the name 'Merryhell Theatre Co' – brought *The Pie of Damocles* to Charlotte Square Gardens for the first Edinburgh Book Festival and a further Fringe week at Saint Columba's by the Castle. Lochhead continued to write plays, including the 1984 touring musical theatre show *Same Difference* for Wildcat Stage Productions, which featured a Glasgow University French and Philosophy graduate named Gerry Mulgrew. He'd played a talking dog called Toby Dug in the show.

A regular with Edinburgh's Theatre Workshop during the 1970s, Mulgrew was hugely influenced by the physical work of Tadeusz Kantor, which he'd experienced during the Fringe. In 1983 he and fellow actors Rob Pickavance and Alison Peebles, the latter an Edinburgh College of Art graduate who studied stage design at the Royal Scottish Academy of Music and Drama and fell into acting while working at Theatre Workshop, started Communicado Theatre Company. Their first production was *Robotnik*, in association with Theatre Workshop, a 'living newspaper' featuring 50 community volunteers and a seven-piece band, all in aid of the Polish solidarity movement.

Many years later, Mulgrew echoed the Czech dissident playwright and President Vaclav Havel's sentiment that theatre is about politics and the relationship of human beings to one another through power. Communicado told stories of international political movements in fresh and interesting style, including *Carmen* at Theatre Workshop during the Fringe of 1984, which updated Prosper Mérimée's original 1845 novel – rather than the opera which Georges Bizet adapted from it – to the setting of the Spanish Civil War in 1936. It won a Fringe First and later moved to the Tricycle Theatre in London, but not before a two-month tour of Scotland. When this tour arrived in Portree on the Isle of Skye, it was met by an old friend: Lochhead, in town to read poetry to pupils in the local high school.

This *Carmen* was in both Lochhead and Mulgrew's minds soon after, when he called and offered to take her for a Chinese meal in January 1985. The proposal he delivered was that 1987 would mark the 400th anniversary of the death of Mary, Queen of Scots, so did Lochhead want to write a Communicado show based on that story? That the commemoration was of her death – her execution on the orders of her cousin, Elizabeth I of England – and not her birth was a story in itself, he pointed out. 'I started reading up and doing research, and decided that I did want to do it very much, that it was a great story,' says Lochhead. She agreed and wheels were set in motion for what was to become Communicado's 'Mary Queen of Scots show'. Two and a half years later, with barely two months until opening, those wheels were skidding on ice.

It was 12 June, 1987. 'The day after the election, where Thatcher got in again,' says Lochhead, who was by this point ready to find an already-existing play about Mary for Communicado to use as their 'Mary Queen of Scots show' instead.

> I remember going over to Edinburgh to say to Gerry, there's just not a play to go into rehearsal with in six weeks. He was brilliant. He said, right, let's just tell it as a story, start with 'once upon a time'. That got me going, and it began to organically grow.

Inspired by his advice to imagine *King Lear* told in such a way, she wrote solidly for the next few weeks, and then after the first week of rehearsals, stayed up for three nights to completely reassemble the order of the scenes and the structure of the new play. Although workshopping of scenes and ideas had already taken place amid the free-flowing Communicado environment, it wasn't improvised by the company; Lochhead typed every word, in a race against time to get it ready.

Directed by Mulgrew at the Lyceum Studio, the now-demolished 'Little Lyceum', the play involved the story of Mary Stuart being told as a bustling, energetic cabaret to a group of characters after the fact while being shown to the audience in the present and the link between both elements was Myra McFadyen's narrator Corbie. This character had attitude and kept the audience informed all at once. Music was provided by fiddler Anne Wood and Frank McConnell's Riccio danced. Anne Lacey was Mary, Peebles was Elizabeth, Mulgrew was John Knox. The title *Mary Queen of Scots Got Her Head Chopped Off* came from the old Scots nursery rhyme and it was Mulgrew's work – apparently he forgot to make arrangements for poster printing, so when he arrived at the graphic designer's office in a panic one morning, he offered the final title on the spur of the moment. Lochhead loved it.

The political resonances spoke to Lochhead and to Communicado. The events in the play took place before the Act of Union of 1707, but they still spoke to the politics of the United Kingdom's two largest nations in the centuries since. 'It's a great Scotland and England play, a great [Scottish independence] referendum play,' says Lochhead.

> It's a story about women and power. I thought of Mary and Elizabeth as almost the other half of each other, and about how they ended up back-to-back and both trying to deal with the same

difficulty of being a woman in power, a female King. This was all happening at the time when we had Margaret Thatcher doing it the Elizabethan way, being an Iron Maiden. It was just a fabulous story.

Mulgrew's early hunch about the quatercentenary of Mary's death had been correct. As well as Communicado's show, the International Festival director Frank Dunlop staged Friedrich Schiller's classic *Mary Stuart* at the Assembly Hall with Hannah Gordon, while on the Fringe, Maureen Beattie starred in W Gordon Smith's *Marie of Scotland* at the Scottish National Portrait Gallery. Yet it's Lochhead and Communicado's acclaimed work which has persisted as one of the key pieces of Scottish theatre of recent times.

Neither was done with the Festival by a long way. Communicado's many Edinburgh productions featured Edwin Morgan's acclaimed translation of *Cyrano de Bergerac* in 1992, Georg Büchner's French Revolution-set *Danton's Death* at the St Bride's Centre for the International Festival in 1990 and a Fringe version of Robert Burns' *Tam O'Shanter* by Mulgrew, played at the Assembly Hall in 2012. The company has six Fringe Firsts, including one for *Mary Queen of Scots Got Her Head Chopped Off*, and Mulgrew continues to act and direct in and out of the company.

More than three decades after he wrote revues at the Tron Theatre with Lochhead, Alasdair Gray's supposedly untransferable classic novel *Lanark: A Life in Four Books* was beautifully staged at the Royal Lyceum by the reunited Suspect Culture team of Graham Eatough and David Greig, in a 2015 production mounted with the Edinburgh International Festival. Mulgrew was memorable in it, as he was in Frances Poet's *Still* at the Traverse Fringe of 2021.

Lochhead collaborated again with Communicado on the large-scale *Jock Tamson's Bairns* at Glasgow's Tramway for the city's European City of Culture year in 1990, and was about the only person who didn't see it as a magical experience; she just didn't feel the same magic had occurred as with *Mary Queen of Scots Got Her Head Chopped Off*. She returned to the Traverse 16 years after her debut there with *Perfect Days*, a play about a woman (Redmond) approaching middle age who wants to have a baby, and it was a hit on the Fringe in 1998 before a transfer in '99 to the Hampstead Theatre and the West End.

She directed her own Scots version of Molière's *Tartuffe* on the Fringe in 1994, nine years after writing it, and then funded a revival at the Assembly Rooms in 2019 as a belated 70th birthday present to herself. In 2000 Lochhead's Maureen Beattie-starring adaptation of Euripides' *Medea* for Theatre Babel was a huge success, first in Glasgow and then at the Fringes of 2000 and 2001. In 2022, after five years as Scotland's Makar – or

National Poet – between 2011 and 2016, she's finally scheduled to make her Edinburgh International Festival debut with a new version of *Medea* starring Adura Onashile as the immigrant in Greece. Michael Boyd will direct, his first time on one of Lochhead's plays since Coventry in '81, and the 75th anniversary of the Festival will also see her celebrate 50 years of *Memo for Spring* at the Book Festival.

The synchronicity continues, but her highlight in Edinburgh is clear. 'You've got to have a basic gut feeling, and I knew I should do *Mary Queen of Scots Got Her Head Chopped Off*,' says Lochhead.

Life in the theatre is up and down, some things work out and some things don't, but at that point the stars were aligning for us. It's such a great story, and I'm very proud and pleased I was able to be part of it. I think if I'm remembered for any play it will be that one.

9

'Supervenues' and the Arrival of the Big Three

IN THE ABSENCE of the majestic, much-promised new opera house at the Hole in the Ground, it's ironic that the patch of muddy ground backing onto the Lyceum Theatre – also flatteringly known as the 'Castle Street Crater' – was where the landscape of the Edinburgh Festival started to be altered for good. Ever since 1947 the shape of the city in August had been in a state of evolutionary flux, but the arrival of the supervenue turbocharged the change.

Since the Fringe's beginning, each company traditionally found their own venue and stuck to it, although increasing competition for available space in the 1970s meant companies began to share locations. Eight companies famously began the activity that later became the Fringe; by the formation of the Festival Fringe Society in 1959, that number had roughly trebled. By Alistair Moffat's final year as administrator in 1981, 485 separate groups were involved, staging 6,484 individual performances across three weeks.

In particular, Moffat's transformative impact on the Fringe is laid bare by comparing the figures for John Milligan's final year in charge in 1975, when just 143 companies staged a comparatively meagre 1,971 performances.[1] In six years, the Fringe had more than trebled in size. In 1981, Moffat launched Fringe Sunday, during which crowds thronged the Royal Mile to watch acts perform part of their shows. The official event later moved to Holyrood Park and then the Meadows, ending in 2009, but what occurred on the Mile that year has since become the norm on the Fringe, all day, every day.

Beginning in 1980, two individuals grasped the opportunity to take what the geography of Edinburgh was capable of hosting to the next level. One was William Burdett-Coutts, who had been so impressed with the Wireworks' DIY, multi-show approach the year before. The other was a man named John Rettalack, who in 1977 became the founding artistic director of a small London theatre troupe named Actors Theatre Group (then and now shortened to ATG Theatre). His group had already come to Edinburgh and won a Fringe First with their version of *Don Juan* in 1978 – in 1980 they returned with their own venue, the first step in an ambitious, transformative four-year cycle which burned briefly but incredibly brightly.

In 1980 and '81, ATG were based at St Columba's Church Hall on Upper Gray Street, a leafy residential side road on the fringe of Newington, where the city centre bleeds into the well-off residential suburbs of Mayfield and the Grange. The venue had been suggested to them by Alistair Moffat, in fact, after his wife had attended National Childbirth Trust classes there while she was pregnant. Proudly boasting a food and wine bar, a garden marquee and a deceptively convenient '13 minutes' walk from Fringe Office', as it was advertised, ATG programmed 77 Fringe performances from a total of 10 shows by six theatre and dance groups. Among them were Hull Truck Theatre Company, the Ensemble Theatre of Sydney and ATC themselves, with their own well-received adaptation of *The Life and Death of Don Quixote*.

In 1982, the ambitions of Rettalack and ATG – and particularly the company's administrator Eric Starck, a key figure – vaulted. Following talks with and visits by planning officials stretching back to January of that year, they were given permission to erect a 500-capacity tent within the Hole in the Ground, which would – as with St Columba's – be hired out to various other companies. The venture was named the Circuit and it worked very well, with the 20-foot depth of the muddy site providing surprisingly good acoustics. Seven daily shows ran from 10 in the morning until the early hours of the next day. Two rooms at the Heriot-Watt University Students Association building on Grindlay Street and the Little Lyceum theatre, which backed onto the Hole in the Ground, were also commandeered, nearly doubling its capacity.

For 1983, the Circuit's ambition increased, this time with three tents and a capacity nearing 1,000 between them. A total of 36 shows were booked in, including theatre, comedy, music and even opera, meaning the site of the ill-fated opera house was finally hosting the medium, after a fashion. Highlights included ATC's own return to *Don Juan*, Footlights star Emma Thompson with her solo show *Short Vehicle*, American playwright and performer Eric Bogosian with his off-Broadway hit of grotesque, all-American vignettes *Funhouse* and Berlin's Freie Theateranstalt with *Ubu oo*. Again, much enjoyment was had all round, although the Circuit collapsed under the weight of its own technical and financial burden when that year's Festival was done. A particular issue had been noise bleed between the tents during performances, an issue that gave rise to one of the most eccentric anecdotes in the Fringe's history.

Also appearing at the Circuit in '83 was the infamous compere, comedian and prankster Malcolm Hardee, who took a dislike to Bogosian even before he realised the part of the American's set that blared out AC/DC came during a quiet sequence of his own show. No compromise could be reached, so Hardee decided to co-opt the section of his set where he attempted to leap a row of cars in a ride-on tractor borrowed from a local garden centre to pay a visit to Bogosian's show – by taking the tractor on a tour through the adjoining tent flap and leading his audience across Bogosian's stage, through the tent and back into his own.

By his own account, Hardee was naked when he did this, not an unusual situation for a comedian whose set *The Greatest Show on Legs* ended with him completely unclothed, aside from a couple of strategically-placed balloons. It was only the first chapter in the legendary Fringe career of Malcolm Hardee, who managed to discover the means by which reviews were filed to *The Scotsman* newspaper in 1989. An early pioneer of playing alphabetical tricks to ensure his show appeared at the front of the Fringe programme and annoyed at not being covered, he asked fellow comic and early Fringe adopter Arthur Smith for a convincing write-up of Hardee's Pleasance revue *Aaaaaaaaaargh The Tunnel Club Comes to Edinburgh!* which he could send to the paper under the name of regular *Scotsman* writer William Cook.

Smith's review declared it the funniest show in Edinburgh that year, although perhaps to throw the subeditors off the scent, he also made uncomplimentary remarks about Hardee's badly-fitting suit and his suspicion that the comedian lived in a bus station. Hardee delivered it to the production door of *The Scotsman*'s North Bridge office at 9am and it was published the next day. The pair were the toast of that year's Fringe comedy circuit and shortly after Hardee's death at the age of 55 in 2005, his friend John Fleming inaugurated the Fringe's Malcolm Hardee Awards, which were taken over by the British Comedy Guide website in 2019.

The Hardees offer awards for Comic Originality (for performers themselves, rather than – and sometimes despite – the quality of their shows), for the Act Most Likely to Make a Million Quid and for a self-promoting Cunning Stunt in the vein of Hardee and Smith's review trick. Here a willingness to aggravate people, ideally those with some degree of importance, was at least as crucial as raising a laugh.

As for Bogosian, a Fringe regular in the 1980s, he recovered enough to write the play *Talk Radio*, which was Pulitzer Prize-nominated and then turned into a film starring its author by Oliver Stone in 1988.

The Circuit was over as quickly as it had begun, but it helped set precedents which became normal at the Fringe over decades to come, including the idea of a multi-show venue under sole control of one operator and ad-hoc tented venues taking the place of already-scarce theatres and civic halls. John Rettalack wasn't done with the Fringe, returning with his later young audience Company of Angels and winning Herald Angel awards for his own *Hannah and Hanna* in 2001 and his adaptation of Richard Milward's novel *Apples* in 2010. While Circuit had been happening, meanwhile, William Burdett-Coutts was doing exactly the same thing with a venue that had been familiar to the Festival since the very beginning.

* * *

Once upon a time, the Festival Club on George Street had been the height of post-war elegance on the Edinburgh International Festival – a bright, spacious, continental-style dining room where people enjoyed the hubbub of European accents and foods in a classily-lit Georgian hall filled with attractive and cultured people from around the world.

More than three decades later, the Festival Club had lost all trace of its postwar glamour, and had instead become a kind of self-service restaurant where tea and shortbread was taken by Festival tourists. It was a liability for both Edinburgh Council, the owners of the building and for the Edinburgh International Festival, which had long-since seen interest in the Club as the social hub of the Festival migrate to the Fringe's younger and more exciting spaces.

Over the years Fringe social activity had spread out from the YMCA on South St Andrew Street to sites on Chambers Street and at the Royal Mile Centre and ultimately all the way to the university union building at Teviot Row House. Opened in 1889 alongside the McEwan Hall and the later site of the Paperback Bookshop, Teviot was designed by architect Sydney Mitchell – also known for the Ramsay Garden housing development by the Castle Esplanade – and is the oldest purpose-built student union in the world. The Fringe Club became a huge success as a social and performance space from 1981, staging samples of many shows performing on the Fringe until late in the evening, with audiences able to wander in and out of the warren of rooms, which created an early Fringe rite of passage for comedians hoping not to be barracked or walked out on.

In 1979, meanwhile, the old Festival Club finally came to an end and the Assembly Rooms were mothballed. 'My memory [of the Assembly Rooms] when I walked past was of people in uniform outside the door, like one of those buildings you couldn't get into,' says William Burdett-Coutts. 'It felt rather exclusive, I was somewhat intimidated by it. But it was run-down, so it had a faded grandeur which was quite fascinating.' Burdett-Coutts' relationship with the Assembly Rooms building was to change substantially just two years after his first festival in 1979, when he arrived with some old university friends from South Africa and staged playwright Pieter-Dirk Uys' *Paradise is Closing Down* at the Chaplaincy Centre on Forrest Road.

The son of English parents, whose mother and farmer-turned-stockbroker father had moved to Zimbabwe – Rhodesia as was – after the Second World War then had him in 1955, Burdett-Coutts' had returned to the UK after university to avoid being conscripted to the Rhodesian army. An anti-apartheid piece about the Cape Town riots of 1976, *Paradise is Closing Down* reflected Uys' concerns over the state censorship of theatre in South Africa. Death threats had been sent to the company, but Uys told *The Herald* that he knew being a white playwright gave him a privileged position to speak about this. The play was a small taste of the uncomfortable reality of the wider world that the Fringe increasingly came to present in years to come.

By 1980 Burdett-Coutts was studying for a Master's degree in drama at the University of Essex and directing his own plays and he decided to bring his version of East German playwright Ulrich Plenzdorf's piece *The New Sorrows of Young W* to Edinburgh that summer. This time the Old Chaplaincy Centre was out of bounds, as it had become the exclusive year-round home of the Edinburgh University Theatre Company. Since Richard Crane and Faynia Williams of the University of Bradford Drama Group first took over the Chaplaincy Centre as a Fringe Theatre in 1977, both the Traverse and Burdett-Coutts' group had shown the potential of the place for performance. Given the attention-grabbing name, the Bedlam Theatre – inspired by its proximity to the former site of the city's asylum – it remains in use by the EUTC today.

Instead, with the help of Alistair Moffat once more, Burdett-Coutts sourced the Harry Younger Hall as 1980's venue and this time his ambition was enhanced by what he'd seen at the Wireworks in '79. 'I got some money out of my student union, as many people do, and arranged to rig and run the venue for the period of the Festival to help pay for it all,' he recalls. 'We built our venue, sublet it to other companies, and I put two or three plays on that year – I was in one, I directed another and I ran the venue.' Opened in 1969, the unassuming Harry Younger Hall, tucked away down a lane near the foot of the Royal Mile, had in fact been designed by the architect Basil Spence, sharing a lineage with Coventry Cathedral, New Zealand's parliament building the Beehive and the Edinburgh University Library on George Square.

Owned by the nearby Canongate Kirk and named after a son of the local brewing firm who died in the Second World War, the hall was opened as a sports centre for local boys. Its architectural pedigree didn't make any impression on Burdett-Coutts. 'It was like a scout hall,' he says.

> We didn't really know what we were doing and we had to invent it as we went along. I hadn't heard about licensing before we started. I lost the keys for the venue, and I had to sleep there overnight so we didn't get broken into. It's one of those classic Fringe stories – sleep in the venue, act in a play, direct a play, sell the tickets, clean the toilets. Perfect Fringe training.

It was successful too and the legacy of this modest venture continues today – as recently as 2019 the Harry Younger Hall was still in operation as a Fringe venue, the simply-named Venue 13. In 1981, however, Burdett-Coutts was on the lookout for a new space. Moffat, ever the resourceful fixer when it came to finding performance nooks in the city, showed him more university buildings. He also presented him with the Assembly Rooms, where Burdett-Coutts took one look at the modest Wildman Room on the ground floor and realised it was perfect. He wrote to the Council asking for use of it during the Fringe. They got in touch and asked if he'd like to use the whole building. 'Being somewhat adventurous I said, why not?'

Soon after he heard this news, Burdett-Coutts was in London with another play he was touring. 'I sat in a dressing room at the back of the Old Vic and basically arranged a programme for the Assembly Rooms. Without a penny to my name, but ordering up kit and all the rest of it. And it just worked. We set up about 50 shows in the first year, and it did remarkably well'. He and the technical team from the previous year at the William Younger Hall planned every single room in the A-Listed building, including the 500-capacity Music Hall and other spaces with capacities of between 80 and 350, moving scaffold up the grand staircases on either side of the wide foyer. Their seating banks had to neither harm the interior walls of the building, nor be too heavy and plunge through the floors.

The first year the place was run on a shoestring – with only a dozen staff doing everything, just as they had at the Younger Hall – but it was a roaring success. At one point during the festival of 1981, the three biggest-selling shows of the Fringe were all taking place at the Assembly Rooms: the Griff Rhys Jones-starring revue *An Evening Without*, featuring fellow former Cambridge Footlights Clive Anderson and Rory McGrath; the revue version of BBC Radio 4 show *RadioActive*, featuring Oxford contemporaries of Rowan Atkinson including Angus Deayton; and the Jacques Lecoq-trained trio *The Moving Picture Mime Show*. *NewsRevue* first appeared at the Fringe here, after starting out at the Gate Theatre in London in 1979 under the direction of former Cambridge University students Mike Hodd and Jack Thorington. It's continued ever since, later moving to C Venues and the Pleasance Courtyard, entering the Guinness Book of World Records as the world's longest-running live comedy show in 2004 and welcoming a roster of A-list comedians over the years.

Also at the Assembly Rooms, the great Scottish absurdist and songwriter Ivor Cutler's *Life in a Scottish Sitting Room Vol 2* took place with his partner, the poet Phyllis King. As well as running the venue, Burdett-Coutts directed his own play once more, this time a version of Kantor muse Stanislaw Ignacy Witkiewicz's 1923 Dadaist work *The Madman and the Nun* – at this point, theatre director was still his first choice of career. Despite sharing a name with an ancestor who founded the Coutts banking empire, his side of the family had nothing to do with it. The funds for the Assembly Rooms were raised by the sale of his car and the remortgaging of both his parents' house and that of jazz promoter Roger Spence, who came in on the venue to programme late-night live jazz for its first year.

The success of Festival jazz in 1981 – both Spence's shows and the Edinburgh Jazz Festival, more of which later – was underlined not just by the Assembly Rooms' involvement, but by the Mardi Gras-style Jazz Festival parade of international music marching along Princes Street on Sunday 23 August, followed by a concert in the Grassmarket to celebrate the opening weekend. The great jazz pianist Oscar Peterson also appeared at the King's Theatre. For Alistair Moffat's closing year at the Fringe, there was the beginning of what was to grow into a Festival landmark – the closure of the Royal Mile at the High Street, just outside the Fringe Office, to enable six stages presenting half-hour extracts from ten shows to entertain passers-by.

Crowds thronged and street performers turned up to juggle, ride unicycles and play music. The event only lasted for five hours, but in years to come the same scene would greet visitors and tourists – and frustrate locals taking a short-cut across town – every day of the Festival. Elsewhere on 1981's breakthrough Fringe, Cambridge Footlights' *The Cellar Tapes* at St Mary's Hall placed its undiscovered undergrad stars together onstage and Nabil Shaban and Richard Tomlinson's pioneering disability arts theatre company Graeae made its first Edinburgh appearance at the Theatre Workshop in Stockbridge.

While Circuit's emergence the following year looked to give Burdett-Coutts some competition, its swift departure helped seal the Assembly Rooms' status as the original, one of the best and definitely the longest-running of the Fringe 'supervenues'. Despite the moral objections to these new venues by Festival veteran Richard Demarco, who saw them primarily as money-making rather than artistic ventures, large multi-space venues with a single management team soon came to dominate Edinburgh.

'The energy that came out of turning the Assembly Rooms into a Fringe venue was just fantastic,' says Burdett-Coutts now. 'When it was fully running, when you had five spaces and a social area operating in there, I always felt it hummed, it was like being on a boat'. Recapturing some of the glory days of the Festival Club, it had a restaurant, two bars, a temporary bookshop run by Tom McGrath's Third Eye Centre in Glasgow and, more importantly, the sense it was now the most exciting show in town, that the Traverse Theatre was finally not the only cool place to hang out. Cutler, Rhys Jones' *Not the Nine O'Clock News* accomplice Mel Smith and Scaffold member turned Assembly Rooms performer Roger McGough had appeared at the Traverse in previous years, but now there was a venue that accommodated each type of artist, amid music, theatre, revues and emerging stand-ups.

Burdett-Coutts never did take up that directing career, although as well as founding the Assembly Rooms – which employed nearly 800 staff by August 2019 – he was hired in the late '80s to oversee Glasgow's Mayfest celebration, the city's short-lived equivalent of the Edinburgh Festival and later worked as head of arts at Granada Television in Manchester, founding director of the Brighton Comedy Festival and artistic director of Riverside Studios in London. All the time, he's remained head of the Assembly Rooms, which later evolved into the multi-venue Fringe organisation named simply Assembly. It's one of the most reliably interesting but undoubtedly powerful institutions on the modern Edinburgh Festival Fringe, but other contenders have risen up to challenge that claim.

The Fringe as it was had been changed for good in 1981, between the culmination of Alistair Moffat's tenure of promotion and expansion and the arrival of Assembly Rooms and the brief flourish of Circuit, both venues which pointed toward the future. Elsewhere, *The Cellar Tapes* won the inaugural Perrier Award for comedy, presented to them by Fringe veteran Rowan Atkinson. The next major space to arrive also had its roots in his defining 1979 venture at the Wireworks.

* * *

Just like Burdett-Coutts, Rowan Atkinson's old friend and staircase-building accomplice at the Wireworks Christopher Richardson arrived cold in Edinburgh in 1979 and immediately fell for what went on in the city in late summer. Born in Haywards Heath, West Sussex, shortly after the outbreak of the Second World War, he had been raised in Sussex and Berkshire. After compulsory National Service during the 1950s, he hung around to make the military his career, yet he secretly held artistic ambitions. In the 1960s he left the army, dismaying elder members of his family and enrolled at the Royal College of Art to study interior design. His contemporaries included David Hockney and members of the Bonzo Dog Doo Dah Band, including Vivian Stanshall.

At the age of 26 in 1966 – the same age William Burdett-Coutts would later be when he founded the Assembly Rooms – Richardson graduated and took a job as a teacher at the nearly 400-year-old Uppingham School in the English county of Rutland, near Leicester. Its alumni included the town planner Patrick Abercrombie, the actor Boris Karloff, the film director John Schlesinger and, of course, Stephen Fry. Richardson was hired as an art and design teacher, establishing the A-level Design curriculum, but when it was announced Uppingham Theatre was to be built to serve the school's drama students, he enthusiastically volunteered to help.

The interior of theatrical spaces had been a particular interest at college and Uppingham Theatre was based in part upon the Leipzig *Gewandhaus*. Once it was finished, Richardson spent 12 years running the theatre and designing shows there, which is how he met visiting Oxford students – including Atkinson – and spent his summer helping out with the Wireworks build in '79. Although that venue was only in operation for one Fringe,[2] Richardson returned in summers to come, first assisting with Atkinson's 1980 show at the Children's Music Theatre at George Square Theatre, then with CMT's other productions in following years. He also produced a Fringe show himself, for a group of visiting American summer school students.

'[Children's Music Theatre at George Square] was another lovely little theatre which sort of ran itself,' says Richardson, 'but I also thought I knew how it could work better.' His talent as an organiser was noticed in Edinburgh. Somebody – he can't remember who, but probably a representative of Edinburgh University Students Association – asked if he might like to get involved in running a theatre.

> I said no, I've spent my time in Uppingham running one and that
> was difficult enough. But they asked me to come and have a look,
> and I did. I walked into the Pleasance Courtyard and looked around,
> and it was one of those days in Edinburgh when the heat comes out
> of the cobbles and you've got steam everywhere. I thought, God, this
> is terribly exciting, there's something cold and mystifying about it.
> Of course, it *was* bloody cold. I told them I'd love to do it.

Like the Assembly Rooms itself, what was then known as the Pleasance Little Theatre was one of the key buildings used in the very first year of the Festival. While the Festival Club at the Assembly Rooms was the social hub of the International Festival itself, the main theatre at the Pleasance was where the unofficial incursion by Glasgow's Unity Theatre took place, when they presented Maxim Gorky's *The Lower Depths* to much enthusiasm. If anywhere deserved to stake a claim as the birthplace of the Fringe, it's this strange collection of buildings, like a small cobbled hamlet wedged between the east end of the Cowgate and Holyrood Park.

The Pleasance – named after the street on which it stands – had been a base for the University of Edinburgh's societies and sports clubs since the late 1930s, before which it filled the same role for the people of the area under the banner of the charitable Pleasance Trust. Going back to the 19th century, it began life as a complex housing two breweries, a Quaker Meeting House and a gymnasium, before passing into the hands of the Church of Scotland's New College in 1875 as a missionary centre for minister training named the New College Settlement.

In recent Fringe times, the theatre space was unused until the Scottish company Wildcat Stage Productions brought it back to life in 1980, naming it the Wildcat Theatre Complex for their own programme of shows. Wildcat was a spinoff of John McGrath and Elizabeth MacLennan's activist 7:84 Scotland company, formed in 1978 by MacLennan's brother David and Glaswegian actor Dave Anderson to stage popular, socially-conscious theatre, but with a rock 'n' roll flavour.

The first year of what Richardson renamed simply the Pleasance Theatre was modest, especially by comparison with what later emerged; at the time, he had only the 100-capacity cabaret bar downstairs on the courtyard and the main theatre upstairs, which he managed to get 300 people into. In the courtyard there was food, a creche and a small art gallery. The flyer advised patrons were able to 'drink all day'. The highlight of that first Pleasance programme of 1985, with hindsight, was the final Fringe show by Scottish comedy group the Bodgers. Founded in 1980 as a nine-piece troupe by Sixth Form pupils of George Watson's College, when they put on a modestly successful Fringe show in the hall of Infirmary Street Primary School, they'd since cut their number to four and picked up a Perrier Award nomination for their 1984 show *Arfington Arfington*.

Their Pleasance swansong, *Mr Hargreaves Did It*, earned another Perrier nomination, by which time two of the Bodgers, Jack Docherty and Moray Hunter, had begun writing scripts for BBC Radio 4 series including *RadioActive* and television comedy shows like *Spitting Image*, *Alas Smith and Jones* and *The Lenny Henry Show*. In 1985 the Bodgers quartet – Docherty, Hunter, Gordon Kennedy and Pete Baikie – were given their own Radio 4 series *In Other Words... The Bodgers*, which became for its second season *Bodgers, Banks and Sparkes*, with the addition of ex-Cambridge Footlight Morwenna Banks and stand-up comic John Sparkes. The sextet later created the eccentric and much-loved television sketch show *Absolutely* for Channel 4, running from 1989 until 1993.

Despite the loss of their entire stock of tickets shortly before opening in 1985, which led to a hurried reprint to foil touts and the near-immediate crash of their automated ticketing system in 1986, the Pleasance was a success, at least as far as audiences were concerned. Richardson is fond of telling the story that his venue turned a small profit in his first year of a little under 200 pounds, then it was another decade before he made any money from the Pleasance again. He managed to quit his job as a schoolteacher, though and started a theatre design consultancy to pay the bills. His project in Edinburgh appears to have been a labour of love in those early days.

'Well... not pure love,' says Richardson now.

I mean, I thought it could work. You're very optimistic when you're involved in theatre. You've got to have a great deal of faith, not only in yourself but in the whole system, even if you're let down or it doesn't work.

In 1986, outside investment allowed him to convert the Quaker Meeting House on the site into a new theatre – It became Pleasance 2, alongside the rebranded Pleasance 1 in the main hall – and the Pleasance grew incrementally from there into one of the most irresistible forces on the Fringe.

* * *

William Burdett-Coutts was an inspiration to the Pleasance, in being first to solve what Christopher Richardson calls the 'patching wars' of the Fringe. With greater sharing of venues during the 1970s, separate companies might have barely an hour to hand over between shows, leading to sometimes chaotic, disorganised and fractious scenes as the incoming company tried to hustle their predecessors out of the building and set up their own scenery and lighting plots.

By operating as the overall proprietor of the venue, with their own tech crew, organisations like the Assembly Rooms and the Pleasance were able to smooth and professionalise this process, bringing the discipline of a proper theatre to the chaotic, high-turnover jumble of three weeks' worth of shows arriving in spaces which often hadn't been designed as any kind of performance space. With a system which allowed this intensity to be maintained and built upon, others used this blueprint to create umbrella Fringe organisations around the city in years to come and the very next to arrive was the final part of a trio which unofficially became known as the 'Big Three' of the Fringe.

By 1985, Alternative Comedy had long since arrived in the UK. The election of Margaret Thatcher in 1979 coincided with the opening of the Comedy Store in London and a new set of establishment targets. *Beyond the Fringe* had mocked Conservative governments before, but after the satire boom of the 1960s the emerging Oxbridge comedy strata had busied itself more with the surreal sketches of Monty Python or the classic physical comedy of Rowan Atkinson. The big stand-up draws prior to the Comedy Store were matey and illiberal, stars of working men's clubs like Bernard Manning and the just-emerging Jim Davidson.

The Comedy Store very quickly became a pushback against all of that, particularly under its first compere (or 'master of ceremonies') Alexei Sayle, the aggressively outspoken son of Liverpool Communists, who helped institute what was intended to be a non-sexist, non-racist brand of performance at the club. The early days of the Comedy Store and its spin-off revue *The Comic Strip* – whose television series became a hit for the opening night of the Channel 4 network in 1982, launching the careers of Rik Mayall, Adrian Edmondson, Dawn French, Jennifer Saunders, Nigel Planer and more – was a London story, but all involved performed in Edinburgh soon enough, helping to make the Fringe the eventual centre of gravity for the British comedy industry.

Wild-eyed, pugnacious and all at once a celebration and parody of the kind of bristling, combative picket line firebrand who terrified the Establishment, Sayle was a trailblazer in many ways – in Alternative Comedy and in the introduction of truly working-class voices to the intelligent end of a genre previously reserved for the middle class in Britain. He was also a first in Edinburgh. In 1980, he and the comedian and playwright Tony Allen, his accomplice in the Comedy Store's Alternative Cabaret, were the first of the alternative stand-up wave to play the Fringe, when they were invited to put on a show at Heriot-Watt's student union on Grindlay Street, under the banner of a group of university students from Bristol.

The pair weren't, however, the first stand-ups to play the Fringe. Birmingham's stand-up pioneer and later Factory Records recording artist John Dowie first appeared as a 21-year-old in 1971, when even he wouldn't have described what he did as 'stand-up'. In 1975, 22-year-old recent University of Birmingham graduate and contestant on TV talent show *New Faces* Victoria Wood appeared as part of Roger McGough's *Wordplay* revue and the following year she shared a Fringe bill with comedic Birmingham folk musician Jasper Carrott. At the time she was more of a writer and sketch comedian, but when she made the full transition to stand-up with her first solo show *Lucky Bag*, it was premiered at the Fringe in 1983 and recorded for later album release.

'Though we were still in the United Kingdom, it was surprising how foreign Edinburgh felt,' Sayle later wrote of his arrival at Waverley Station.

All the craggy grey-stone buildings set about with towers and tiny windows appeared designed to repel some nameless, invading horde; even the libraries, schools and the family-planning clinics looked like they could be defended against a determined enemy.[3]

They might be set in defence, he speculated, against the mimes taking over every other street corner.

The difference to London must have been palpable. In 1980, the wholesale urban refurbishment of cities into similarly-planned spaces for retail and restaurant chains was a long way off and Edinburgh was in the final throes of the days when its wider reputation for being stony and dour contained an element of truth and wasn't just the outdated and undeserved stereotype it is now. Sayle marvelled at the lack of diverse Asian groceries of the kind he might find in London and Scotland's peculiarly-named leading chain store of the day, *What Every Woman Wants*. He stayed in a caravan near the Pentland Hills and walked to the nearby dry ski slope hoping to see people fall over for a morning's entertainment. The 1980s' Fringe boom in supervenues and alternative comedians, of whom he was in the advance guard, were key factors in the city's cultural modernisation.

The third of the supervenues to open in Edinburgh in the 1980s had its own indirect link to the Comedy Store, through two comics who started out there not long after Sayle. Stephen Frost and Mark Arden were collectively known as the Oblivion Boys and they wanted to put their own show on in Edinburgh, but were dismayed by the ongoing scarcity of venues. By late 1984, before the Pleasance arrived the following year, there was the Assembly Rooms, there were various small church halls and adapted spaces and that was it.

Frost and Hunt happened to mention their frustration to a friend, a woman named Karen Koren, who they knew was from Edinburgh. Born and raised in the city, Koren's family history lay in the strong historic shipping links between Norway and the Forth shipping port of Leith. In 1851 Christian Salvesen, the son of a Norwegian shipping magnate, moved to Queen Charlotte Street in Leith and with his brothers set up what became one of the world's leading shipping companies, branching out over the next century and a half into whaling and road freight logistics. In 1921, the year after Leith was officially incorporated into the city of Edinburgh, Koren's own grandfather, a Norwegian ship's captain, moved to Leith and settled down with his family and a new ship chandlery business.

In the few shorts years she was away from the city, Koren became involved in the 1960s pop scene in Glasgow, dancing with a band alongside another woman at the Locarno Ballroom and following the band to London; the man she briefly married was in the group. After she returned home to Edinburgh she took whatever jobs she could to survive, including secretarial work at the Norwegian Consulate in the city, where being fluent in the language was an advantage, but she didn't lose touch with London. Another of her jobs was showing houses to possible tenants for an Edinburgh estate agent, which is how dominoes were set in motion that led to a dramatic change in career.

One of the landlords who used the company she worked for was an Edinburgh businessman named Brian McNally and he told her about his plan to open an upmarket bar and restaurant with a casino above it in the West End of the city. With her knowledge of the Comedy Store and her awareness of what the Oblivion Boys and their friends thought Edinburgh was lacking,

Koren suggested that instead of a casino, why didn't he consider using the space for something that couldn't be found anywhere else in Edinburgh? He was interested and asked her to make a comedy club happen.

In February 1985, with the bar and restaurant downstairs, McNally's comedy club opened on the first floor of the townhouse at 6 Palmerston Place in the West End of Edinburgh, just around the corner from Haymarket Station. With a year-round weekly schedule to fill, the enthusiasm with which she'd source new comedians throughout her career and the knowledge there was plenty of talent in the pubs and clubs of Scotland which deserved wider recognition, Koren began booking names from across the country.

In its short life, McNally's saw a number of outstanding bookings by then-unknowns, including a 23-year-old, New Jersey-born Glaswegian magician and stunningly frank comedian named Jerry Sadowitz (then going by Gerry Sadowitz), who'd been doing gigs at future comedian Janey Godley's Weavers Inn pub in Glasgow since 1983 and who was already commuting to London to play the Comedy Store. Koren also booked a pair of recently-graduated students from the Royal Scottish Academy of Music and Drama in Glasgow named Alan Cumming and Forbes Masson, actors who'd adopted the comedy personas of Victor and Barry, a smoking-jacketed, ridiculously pretentious duo from the eternally-gentrified neighbourhood of Kelvinside in Glasgow's West End. At 1984's Fringe, Cumming and Masson had appeared at the Harry Younger Hall alongside other RSAMD students, adopting the familiar, keen young Fringe performer tactic of wandering the Royal Mile in character as Victor and Barry, dishing out flyers to tourists.

After a poor review from a junior reporter at *The Scotsman* named Andrew Marr, Cumming and Masson incorporated an unflattering song about him into their set. Marr went on to become one of the BBC's main political correspondents. In 1985 Cumming was back at the Fringe in Borderline Theatre's version of Dario Fo's play *Trumpets and Raspberries*, alongside Elaine C Smith and Andy Gray, but Victor and Barry turned up in late-night revue at McNally's. To many Scots, Cumming and Masson's names and faces – or Victor and Barry's, more precisely – became synonymous with Edinburgh Fringe performance, cementing the 'luvvie' image they were sending up.

McNally's first and only Fringe in 1985 also welcomed Billy Connolly and Pamela Stephenson in the audience and three young performers from the Comedy Store, Dave Cohen, Kit Hollerbach and Paul Martin (later Paul Merton), with a show named *Three Weeks to Live*. In the changeover between shows, the trio got to know a double act named Mullarkey and Myers, comprising Neil Mullarkey, a former member of Cambridge Footlights and Mike Myers, a 22-year-old Canadian spending a couple of years in the UK.

Within two months, the quintet had founded the improvisational group the Comedy Store Players, which still exists with Merton among its number today. Three years after returning to Canada in 1986, Myers joined the cast of *Saturday Night Live* and became internationally famous through film roles in *Wayne's World* and *Austin Powers: International Man of Mystery*.

Koren also booked London sketch trio The Jockeys of Norfolk, featuring Chris Lang, Andy Taylor and the pre-fame actor Hugh Grant, an alumnus of Oxford Theatre Group's recent excursions in Edinburgh. Their enjoyable stage show was showcased on a Fringe television special presented by Russell Harty, but the humour didn't come across and the group eventually went their separate ways.[4] Despite these successes and the fact Koren had clearly tapped into a vein of entertainment that the Fringe and Edinburgh itself was crying out for, she says Brian McNally was never entirely convinced by the idea of a comedy club over the casino he'd originally wanted to run in the snug, 80-seat upstairs space.

In 1986, she was approached by a former Edinburgh College of Art student named Andrew Brown who, after graduating in 1977, started running exhibitions around the city, first at Gladstone's Land's Saltire Gallery on the Royal Mile, then at a studio at 369 High Street; formerly the Howff. He called it the 369 Gallery and it became one of the most exciting contemporary art spaces in Edinburgh. The 'Glasgow Boys' Peter Howson, Stephen Campbell and Adrian Wiszniewski all showed there, as well as other leading Scottish artists like Joyce Cairns and Pat Douthwaite and the Malaysian artist and Glasgow School of Art graduate Hock-Aun Teh.

In 1984, Brown was successful in raising funds from the Scottish Arts Council to take over a derelict three-storey warehouse on the Cowgate, opposite the foot of Blair Street, in a corner of the Old Town which was grimy and obscured from the sun. The building above the warehouse was part of Edinburgh's 'multi-storey city', the former J & R Allan's department store on South Bridge and the warehouse that had served the store lay empty since its closure, reaching all the way down below the Bridge to Cowgate level. Brown got permission to convert the building into the new 369 Gallery, with education and studio space, a restaurant and an 150-seat auditorium upstairs.

The closed restaurant alongside it for some reason bore the unusual name of 'the Gilded Balloon'. What it meant is only speculation, although it may have had something to do with the intrepid 18th century Italian aeronaut Vincenzo Lunardi, who in October 1785 flew a hydrogen-filled air balloon 46 indirect miles over the Firth of Forth, from the grounds of George Heriot's School in Edinburgh to Ceres in Fife. Lunardi's adventures in Scotland made him a celebrity and commemorative novelties were created such as the balloon-shaped and impractical hat named the 'Lunardi bonnet', which was referenced in Robert Burns' poem *To a Louse* the year after the flight.

The restaurant's name might have referred to a milliner on South Bridge that kept an antique version of the hat in stock, possibly even James Spittal, who commissioned the building's construction in 1823 and was the previous occupant of the department store before J & R Allan. Or it might not. Either way, the quirky name 'Gilded Balloon' soon took on a new meaning when Andrew Brown asked Koren to leave McNally's and put together a programme of Fringe entertainment in the 369 Gallery's arched upstairs performance space in 1986. Shifting the entire operation she'd built at McNally's to the new space, together with the lengthy list of contacts she'd already built up in Scotland and London, she called it the Gilded Balloon.

The first Gilded Balloon programme of 1986 featured the 50-year-old Glaswegian comedian Arthur Brown, who'd only recently given up his career as an accountant after becoming a hit at the Comedy Store, the redoubtable Scots playwright and poet Liz Lochhead and Fringe First-winning former Cambridge students the Balloonatics. Other early beneficiaries of the new venue were Koren's old friends the Oblivion Boys, desperate to play in Edinburgh, who devised an anarchic late-night show named *The Boys Have a Night of Raw Sex with Fluffy Girlies*, featuring a live band led by comedian Rowland Rivron.

This title was a lumpen reference to the fact the band were named Raw Sex and the roster of six resident comedians were gender-balanced, three male and three female. The gig ran from midnight until 1.45am, a comparative all-nighter in a city where shows were done by midnight or 1am at a push, even during the Festival. The flyer for it bore the discreet motto in small print, 'As Seen on TV, Late and Live'. The moment those last three words appeared in August 1986 signalled the birth of one of the most infamously lawless and anarchic shows of the Festival Fringe and the moment comedy truly got a grip on Edinburgh.

* * *

While the Assembly Rooms made an instant impression upon the Fringe, the Pleasance and the Gilded Balloon took longer to grow and build their spaces and reputations. Despite the persistent public impression that Fringe venue managers make money hand over fist, there's been an imbalance between the three organisations since the beginning. The Assembly Rooms has always run its own bars and done nicely from them, but the Pleasance and the Gilded Balloon live on premises managed by Edinburgh University Students Association (EUSA), which operates its own bars and gives them both a cut of the income.

It's a recurring theme, which has only increased in importance over the decades since – as the University of Edinburgh has grown, it's become increasingly integral to the Fringe, with lecture theatres, student union halls and bars and even university-managed student accommodation becoming key to the Fringe's wider existence. Hand-in-hand, letting these spaces to Fringe operators, performers and audiences over summer gives the university an enormous economic boost which isn't available to most other academic institutions.

In the early days of venue expansion, a space that looked like it may have once become a major player attempted a revival in 1986. A collaboration by Cornish promoters Elephant Fayre and Brighton-based cabaret the Zap Club, the Elephant Tent was another attempt to make use of the Hole in the Ground alongside the Lyceum, following the Circuit's departure. Among the highlights were the *Time Out Chat Show*, hosted by Muriel Gray and Arthur Smith and a music programme which featured Factory Records' A Certain Ratio.

The Elephant Tent returned in 1987, hosting scrap sculptors, performance artists and Glastonbury Festival regulars Mutoid Waste Company, although that year the Zap Club weren't involved, making the entirety of Rose Street their venue instead by taking over multiple pubs and pedestrian areas. In 1986 the International Festival also experimented with canvas, putting circus on in a tent named the Dome, programmed by former Theatre Workshop director Andy Arnold. Based at Pilrig Park, just off Leith Walk, it attempted to broaden the geographical boundaries of the Festival into previously-ignored areas of the city, a response to claims it was too elite and exclusive. Attracting noise complaints from locals, it wasn't a success and didn't return.

By 1987, the Pleasance was being referred to as a 'mega-venue' in the same breath as the Assembly Rooms and both found their originally theatre-heavy programmes incorporating more stand-up in the second half of the decade. These years saw the Pleasance take on shows by Paul Martin (aka Merton), Mark Steel, the Bodgers' Jock Docherty and Moray Hunter – appearing with the couch from their Edinburgh flat – and the double act Black and Baddiel as hosts of the late-night cabaret, featuring former Cambridge Footlight and future superstar of '90s comedy David Baddiel. The year before he had been with Cambridge Footlights when they first played the Assembly Rooms, where they were ostracised by the regular comics. Although not as badly as the Oxford Theatre Group – featuring later comedian, playwright and stage director Patrick Marber – who turned up for a gig at the Gilded Balloon's *Late 'n' Live* to find every comic in town was there to torment them with heckles.

At the Assembly Rooms, meanwhile, things were beginning to happen. The bill in 1982 included a cappella vocal group the Flying Pickets, who had developed their style touring the country for a year as actors in 7:84's production of John Burrows' *One Big Blow*, a musical drama about a militant colliery brass band. In the van between shows they sang along, barbershop quartet-style, to pop songs, which received an unexpectedly overwhelming response when they were repeated in the pub. They put the group together for the Fringe of '82 and by 1983 their cover of Yazoo's 'Only You' was the Christmas number one hit in the UK. Apparently the song was Margaret Thatcher's favourite of the year, an irony considering the band's name referred to striking miners.

In 1983, the uninspiringly named *Stand-Up Comedy* show arrived at the venue, with sometime 20th Century Coyote Rik Mayall, his old flatmate Ben Elton and Comedy Store regular Andy de la Tour on the bill. In fact, de la Tour was the only bona fide stand-up comic performing. Elton was a writer who got in front of a mic mainly to get his own work heard and Mayall was a comic actor and the only one of the trio who was well-known, both for Rick in *The Young Ones* and his character Kevin Turvey on BBC Scotland's *A Kick Up the Eighties*. This Fringe run was where Elton and Mayall both got bitten by the stand-up bug, though and live comedy was a major part of their careers from then on. The same year, however, comics Gareth Hale and Norman Pace didn't like the hothouse Fringe atmosphere at the Assembly Rooms and didn't return. Their 1982 debut Edinburgh show was in the bar above the Playhouse and it was seen by hardly anyone – except the producers who made them stars on television. They had no need to return.

In '83, Eric Bogosian escaped from Malcolm Hardee by playing the Assembly Rooms and the following year his fellow American Rita Rudner was there amid a package group of comics from the country. In '84, the Perrier-winning success of Los Trios Ringbarkus also inspired more Australian artists to make the long trip to Edinburgh. John Sessions made an early career appearance at this venue, as did French and Saunders and Patrick Barlow's comic abridged theatre company The National Theatre of Brent, then a two-hander with Jim Broadbent.

Fringe comedians were making the jump from television, rather than the other way around. Former *Tizwas* presenter Lenny Henry was a widely known figure when he appeared as a stand-up at the Assembly Rooms in '85, as were Edinburgh-born impressionist Rory Bremner in '86, Harry Enfield – a zeitgeist-capturing 1980s figure, with characters like Loadsamoney and Stavros – and young Liverpudlian Craig Charles, the latter pair having appeared on Channel 4's briefly starmaking stand-up show *Saturday Live*. Old friend of the venue Ivor Cutler returned and he and Phyliss would paint Edinburgh Castle or collect shells at Portobello beach when their show wasn't on.

The Assembly Rooms also hosted Simon Fanshawe, pianist and *The Tube* presenter Jools Holland and Dillie Keane's comedy song trio Fascinating Aida. This latter group started out at the Circuit in 1983, where theatre impresario Ian Albery told them they needed a director. That night Keane bumped into actor and director Nica Burns when she was getting out of a taxi and Burns agreed to do the job. The following year Aida were nominated for a Perrier and they went on to be a West End hit and a Fringe success at the Playhouse in 1987. Keane wasn't the only one to find the comedy scene of the time very competitive and boorishly masculine, but her first solo show was also nominated for a Perrier in 1990, just as comedy on the Fringe was beginning to really boom.

In 1987, the Gilded Balloon's single room grew to include the Wilkie House theatre alongside and Scottish comedians – including those Karen Koren had first brought to Edinburgh at McNally's – were becoming stars. One was a 22-year-old punk drummer from the new town of Cumbernauld named Craig Ferguson, who'd once played for former Velvet Underground singer Nico on a Scottish tour and taken up stand-up comedy on the advice of his equally unknown bandmate in the Glasgow group the Dreamboys, a young actor named Peter Capaldi. In 1986, Ferguson had taken his character Bing Hitler – a ranting, shouty sociopath entirely at odds with Ferguson's later years as the smooth host of the CBS talk show *The Late, Late Show* – to the room above the grand Café Royal lounge just off Princes Street for a 1am show. The character was a safety net for Ferguson, because he knew audiences were judging it and not his own persona.

Ferguson did each gig, then at 2.30am ate a bad cheeseburger at an all-night kiosk in Waverley Station and slept in a photo booth until the first Glasgow train at 6.15am. His first shows had 12 people in a 150-capacity room, then *The Scotsman* and the *Edinburgh Evening News* gave him glowing reviews. He appeared on Scottish Television's Fringe arts show *Acropolis Now*, interviewed by Muriel Gray and people had to be turned away at the door by the end of his three weeks in the city. This debut Fringe found him sell-out audiences, an agent and television offers. In 1987 'Bing' shared a show with Harry Enfield at the Assembly Rooms and later he sold out the 2,000-capacity Pavilion Theatre in Glasgow. Soon enough Ferguson tired of the persona and moved into straight theatre alongside stand-up under his own name. His show at the 1989 festival was at the enormous Playhouse, a venue he returned to on the Fringe in 2019, after finding sobriety and huge late-night cult success in America.

Victor and Barry, meanwhile, continued on a while longer in their affected am-dram personae, playing a one-nighter at the Gilded Balloon in 1986 and making semi-regular returns at the Assembly Room until 1991.[5] Regulars on televised Fringe round-ups and Scottish television Hogmanay programmes, the characters were decisively killed off onstage at the London Palladium in 1992 and Alan Cumming later impressed with a wide-ranging and diverse theatre and film career, winning Oliver and Tony Awards for his work on the stage. In 2007 he returned to Edinburgh as Dionysus in playwright David Greig's soul musical adaptation of Euripides' Greek tragedy *The Bacchae* for the Edinburgh International Festival, directed by John Tiffany, which transferred to the Rose Theatre in New York.

In recent times, Cumming has performed Edinburgh shows of music and storytelling in *...Sings Sappy Songs* (2016) and *...Is Not Acting His Age* (2021) and he hosted the fiercely entertaining late-night Festival cabaret *Club Cumming* at Leith Theatre. Like Ferguson, he's reached the status of elder statesperson at a Festival whose life in comedy was being born at the same time as their own. While they both went on to greater careers in years to come, comedy at the Fringe was also set to boom even further in the 1990s and before long the Big Three of the Assembly Rooms, the Pleasance and the Gilded Balloon stopped being the exception and instead became the model to aspire to.

SPOTLIGHT

I Am Curious, Orange (1988)

'THE ADVANTAGE OF presenting Michael Clark's *I Am Curious, Orange* at the beginning of the Edinburgh Festival was that it defined the rock bottom, the level below which no later production could fall without actually sinking a bore hole into the lower layers of visual witlessness and acoustic ugliness'. These words were *The Guardian* critic Gerald Larner, writing ten days after the final performance of Clark's dance piece at the King's Theatre for the Edinburgh International Festival.

The bitter taste of the show clearly still lingered with Larner. In the absence of a five-star rave from an Edinburgh Festival critic, these kinds of reviews can be the next most attention-grabbing for a prospective audience – the ones which suggests a singular experience can be found in Edinburgh that is at least cataclysmically, historically bad. *I Am Curious, Orange* certainly wasn't historically bad. But it was very much a punk contemporary dance performance, defying the opinion of anyone who wasn't in tune with its own wilfully playful, obscure and confrontationally eccentric aesthetic.

It didn't care what its critics thought, in other words, an attitude that shaped the work of its principal creators throughout their careers, including 26-year-old dancer and choreographer Michael Clark, who grew up the youngest of five children on a farm in rural Aberdeenshire. His conventional working-class Scottish upbringing featured atypical Scottish country dancing lessons with his sister from the age of four and an admiration for the music and convention-challenging gender fluidity of David Bowie. As a gay man discovering his sexuality as he grew, 1970s Scotland wasn't the kind of place where Clark could freely express himself.

In 1975, as punk was about to break, he joined the Royal Ballet School in London, where – contrary to rumour – he wasn't expelled for sniffing glue. He was caught, but as the lead in the school production there was no way he was going to be expelled. On graduation he turned down the Royal Ballet itself, joining the Ballet Rambert under Richard Alston and then the New York-based company of 'punk ballerina' and protégé of Merce Cunningham, Karole Armitage. In November 1982, he appeared onstage at the Traverse Theatre as part of a showcase of new dance with his early piece *Of a Feather, Flock* and he performed on the Edinburgh Fringe.

Clark's first wider exposure – literally – to the British public came during a 1983 performance on the British music show *The Old Grey Whistle Test*, for which he choreographed a spiky but graceful ballet for himself and three other dancers, wearing Bowiesque leotards, sequins and military flat caps. Memorably, two of the costumes had porthole-like apertures cut around the dancers' bottoms. The performance they were accompanying was the song 'Lay of the Land' by the Manchester post-punk group The Fall, of which Clark was a fan. The couple at the core of The Fall, their founder Mark E Smith and his wife Brix, an American musician and former drama student, had first seen him dance on Channel 4's youth culture television show *The Tube*. He caught their attention and soon afterwards, by coincidence, his manager got in touch to say he'd love to work with them.

Clark and The Fall bonded over debauched nights out in Manchester and London. In 1984, at the age of 22, he started his own dance company. One of the pieces he produced around this time was *New Puritans* (1984), soundtracked by The Fall. A performance of it was filmed by video artist Charles Atlas – also a frequent Merce Cunningham collaborator – for the esoteric, experimental film *Hail the New Puritan*, in which Clark and the Smiths read Burroughsian cut-up gibberish in the manner of late-night television hosts shrouded in clouds of cigarette smoke.

Working on his own pieces, Clark built a team of friends and regular collaborators around him, including The Fall, Atlas and Royal College of Art graduate and sometime Derek Jarman assistant Cerith Wyn Evans. Later an internationally-celebrated sculptor and installation artist, at this point Evans was creating video clips as backdrops for Clark's pieces. Other regular accomplices were the New Romantic-era fashion label BodyMap, whose designs were worn by Boy George and Marilyn and the polysexual performance artist, designer and club promoter of the infamous nightclub Taboo, Leigh Bowery.

Clark made a conscious decision to work with designers outside of the stage tradition, keen to find people who would try and impose their own personality on his work rather than meekly accommodate his. In 1984 he was enough of a known quantity within the mainstream world of contemporary dance that he performed *New Puritans* at the Assembly Rooms, while in 1986 he gave a late-night premiere of his tribute to Marc Bolan *our caca phony H* at the Lyceum as part of the International Festival.

For 1988's Holland Festival, Clark agreed to create his first ever commissioned piece of work – a commemoration of the tercentenary of the ascension of the Dutch William of Orange to the English throne in 1688, as husband of Queen Mary II. Styled as William III when he took the throne, the monarch became a figure of fascination to Clark, not least because of the hold he retains in Scotland. As a bastion of Protestantism, the name of 'King Billy' still means a great deal to one side of the sectarian divide in the west of Scotland, which is particularly manifest with many fans of Rangers Football Club; the Scots Protestant community from which it was founded has traditionally been viewed as the binary opposition to Glasgow's other big football club, the Irish Catholic Celtic.

During development work, Clark was fascinated by a visit to Glasgow's Barras market, where he found T-shirts, tea towels and other memorabilia bearing the image of William. This informed the eventual title of the show, *I Am Curious, Orange*, a dual reference to William's title Prince of Orange and the erotic Swedish dramas of the late 1960s, *I Am Curious (Blue)* and *I Am Curious (Yellow)*. He was also intrigued by the historical rumour that William had been gay.

Playfulness with the meaning of the costumes aside, this element took the piece beyond its original historical subject and brief. Homosexuality had been a facet of Fringe shows for many years, especially since the Traverse Theatre's opening and the legalisation of sex between men in 1967, but *I Am Curious, Orange* brought it to the fore with audiences of the official Edinburgh International Festival, particularly with its adoption of the New Romantic and Blitz Kid aesthetic and the presence of Clark and Bowery, two of the queer icons of their generation.

Co-created with Mark E Smith, as lyricist of the songs and Brix Smith and The Fall as musical composers, *I Am Curious, Orange* premiered at the Holland Festival in July 1988. Its first British run was at Edinburgh's King's Theatre between 15 and 20 August, before a visit to Sadler's Wells in London the following month. Clark also ran a club night at Leith Assembly Rooms to celebrate the conclusion of Edinburgh performances, which became an all-night crawl towards Edinburgh's seminal gay club Fire Island on Princes Street, a fine send-off for the venue after a decade in existence hosting artists like the Village People, Eartha Kitt and Jimmy Ruffin. The following month it closed and the building is now the Princes Street branch of Waterstone's the bookseller.

The show was playful and outrageous, featuring dancers dressed in Celtic and Rangers strips scoring a goal with a bomb, a spray of giant fast-food fries over a backdrop depicting the Houses of Parliament and Brix Smith being wheeled around the stage sat atop a giant hamburger – her nickname throughout the production was 'Burger Queen'. Clark's dancers performed with the raw, overt sexuality of his past shows. In his innovative merging of classical and contemporary styles and the music accompanying them, Clark pushed a precise if sweatily youthful physicality to the fore.

At the back of the deep stage, Mark E Smith barked along with his band, the primal rhythms of the music countering and enhancing the delicacy of the movement. The title and lyrics of 'Big New Prinz', one of the group's key songs, were written in direct reference to William. Studio versions of the music written for the show were released on The Fall's album *I Am Kurious Oranj* two months after the Edinburgh performances and a live recording from the 1988 Edinburgh shows named *I Am Pure as Oranj* was issued in 2000.

Smith's lyric from his 1980 song 'C'n'C-S Mithering', which alludes to the conventional and the experimental exchanging places, has been directly used in reference to Clark's work in the past. Critics have suggested *I Am Curious, Orange* was neither his nor The Fall's best work, but it was a watershed for the Edinburgh International Festival and the wider range of performance it represented. Writing in the *NME*, Stuart Maconie noted:

> [A] gorgeous authoritarian noise trashing everything in its path. In
> the aisle in front of me sit two mature blue-rinsed lady patrons of
> the arts. Their eyes have glazed over, their fingers are jammed in
> their ears. This is the weird and frightening world of modern ballet.[1]

On a big stage, the show foregrounded both a playful, lighthearted sense of queerness in contemporary dance and the indefinable indie cool of the nebulous Fall. *I Am Curious, Orange* remains spoken of fondly by those who were there to this day.

* * *

Michael Clark developed a heroin addiction and in the wake of Leigh Bowery's death in 1994, he retreated to his old bedroom at his mother's house in Fraserburgh, near Aberdeen, for four years, prompting rumours he had died of an overdose or of AIDS. Reemerging in 1998, he became artistic associate at the Barbican in London and in 2009 the International Festival's director Jonathan Mills commissioned a sight-unseen and very well-received suite of new work from him for the Playhouse, soundtracked by the music of

David Bowie, Iggy Pop and Lou Reed.

Soon after the performances of *I Am Curious, Orange* were over, Mark and Brix Smith separated in January 1989 and were divorced later that year. Before he arrived in Edinburgh, all Smith knew of the city was the footballer Arthur Mann, who played for the Edinburgh-based club Heart of Midlothian FC and became the record signing for his own beloved Manchester City in 1968.[2] In the late 1980s he was sick of the emerging ecstasy and acid house culture in his home city of 'Madchester', as it had become known. 'I'd rather drink whisky, thank you very much', he said. 'I'd rather read a good book.'[3] Associated throughout his career with his hometown of Prestwich in Greater Manchester, Smith moved to Edinburgh on his own and lived there for a year from 1989, first in a flat in Leith and then in the New Town, enjoying relative anonymity in the pubs of the city.

'I was accepted straight away,' Smith said of what he described as his exile in what he named 'the poor man's San Francisco', because of all the hills. 'Leith's good, it's a bit more the real Edinburgh'.[4] He made himself at home in the Scotch Malt Whisky Society building down by Leith's Shore, across from the forbidding housing block Cable's Wynd House – known as the 'Banana Flats' for its curved shape – and walked the streets of the city. Arts writer Neil Cooper wrote of Smith nursing 'his seemingly unquenchable drinking habits in Black Bo's, the Meadow Bar and Millionaires nightclub'.[5] After he'd moved back down south, Smith said of Edinburgh:

I loved it. The thing is, I liked it too much. I couldn't get any work done. But it was a lot cheaper in those days. We're talking about 1990 here. Then it was 25 quid a week, now it's 200 quid a week. Same in Manchester.[6]

By this point in 2012, he'd grown to prefer Glasgow. The Fall's final gig was at Glasgow's Queen Margaret Union in 2017, two months before Smith's death.

On the band's 1991 album *Shift-Work*, The Fall released one of the most tender and emotional songs of Smith's 31-album career in 'Edinburgh Man', a reflection on his time in Scottish exile, whose lyrics spoke of walking home from pubs and parties across the bridges of the city centre in the early springtime dawn. He expressed a desire to stay away from the Festival, to enjoy a quarter-gill of whisky in a pub instead. Despite the lifelong admiration for Smith from one of the Fringe's definitive comedians, the singer always preferred Bernard Manning to Stewart Lee.[7]

10

The Birth of the Jazz and Book Festivals

THE IDEA EDINBURGH existed as a cultural desert whose drought was ended by the International Festival in 1947 ignores an art form widely disregarded by the festivals in their early years. From the end of the Second World War the city was a hotbed of modern jazz, with talented young players springing up to fill an ever-growing range of clubs, of which the city fathers and authorities were no fans.

The unlikely birthplace of this jazz scene in Edinburgh was the Royal High School, a smart neoclassical building on the north side of Calton Hill, designed by the great Edinburgh architect Thomas Hamilton in the 1820s and declared one of the two finest buildings in the country by the architectural theorist Alexander 'Greek' Thomson in 1866.[1] One thing the school had going for it in the 1930s and '40s was an exceptional music department and the list of pupils it turned out as skilful young musicians and future jazz stars was exemplary.

They were collectively known as the 'Royal High School Gang' and they included the clarinettist Alexander 'Sandy' Brown, born in 1929 in Uttar Pradesh, India, where his father was a railway engineer and trumpeter Alastair 'Al' Fairweather, born in 1927 in Edinburgh. The pair went to Edinburgh College of Art together after school – they were contemporaries of Richard Demarco – and made their names in the band of local players that supported Big Bill Broonzy at his seminal Usher Hall gig in February 1952, a show attended by many of the later Howff gang.

Soon after this, the pair left for London, where in 1957 they recorded the first in their *McJazz* series of records, named by *Melody Maker* two years later as one of the top 12 finest jazz records to date. With a particular interest in African styles, Brown later went into business in acoustic architecture, first with clients including the BBC, although he still played with musicians including Kenny Wheeler, Humphrey Lyttleton, Pee Wee Russell and members of Count Basie's band. He died tragically young in 1975, at the age of just 46. Meanwhile, Fairweather went on to play with Acker Bilk and Cy Laurie, then returned to Edinburgh later in life.

Brown and Fairweather's old schoolmates included clarinettist Archie Semple, born in 1928, who played with Mick Mulligan and Freddy Randall, before his alcoholism killed him the year before Brown. Among the most celebrated of this group was the pianist, drummer and son of a Joppa piano tuner Stan Greig, who in 1956 played on the first jazz hit in the UK, Lyttleton's Joe Meek-engineered 'Bad Penny Blues' and later appeared in Dick Lester's 1962 film *It's Trad, Dad!* with Acker Bilk's band. Particularly revered as a jazz and blues pianist, Greig and Fairweather founded the celebrated London Jazz Big Band in 1975. Alex Welsh was also a fellow Edinburgh boy and a fine cornet player who recorded his music for Decca, although not a Royal High alumnus.

Before their careers took them away from Edinburgh, however, the Royal High Gang made noise in the jazz clubs of city as the 1940s bled into the '50s. These included the Edinburgh Jazz Club, on Riego Street near Tollcross, which began life as the Edinburgh Rhythm Club at city centre music shop Methven Simpson's Limited. Another club was held on the top floor of the striking India Buildings on Victoria Street, a 19th century office complex comprised of tiered, circular balconies under a domed rotunda, which gives it an air of ornate, Venetian mystery.[2] Sandy Brown created the Stud Club on Lothian Street (it was short for 'student'), although this kept moving venues as each new one was closed by the police. In postwar Scotland, jazz clubs were seen as a corrupting source of illicit substances and activities.

There was also the West End Café in a Shandwick Place townhouse, with a grand entranceway, a restaurant in the front and a 20-foot-high performance space through the back where hot, strong coffee was the only drink on offer. It was owned by Pete Chilver, one of the first British musicians to play electric guitar, who quit the London jazz scene to manage a hotel in North Berwick and residencies were played there by musicians including Johnny Dankworth and George Melly. The latter wrote:

> Even the name of the café, in appearance a conventional Scottish tea-room, was the same as a venue in Chicago where [Louis] Armstrong had played in the early 20s. Another advantage was that we could play jazz all evening with no waltzes or sambas.[3]

There were jazz events at the Palais de Dance on Fountainbridge, a grand venue bearing a sprung dancefloor and a levered revolving stage and one of a number of pre-war big band ballrooms inspired by London's Hammersmith Palais. Jazz Band Balls took place at Oddfellows Hall on Forrest Road, the same venue where Hamish Henderson inaugurated the People's Festival around the same time. Both venues were distinguished in that their shared bouncer was a sturdy Edinburgh bodybuilder from Fountainbridge known as 'Big Tam', a jazz fan who had been a member of the Edinburgh Rhythm Club.

Among other odd jobs, Big Tam worked as a milkman, a coffin polisher and, in 1952, a life model at Edinburgh College of Art, where he was painted by both the art student trumpeter Al Fairweather and Richard Demarco. The future art impresario remembered him straight, shy and with Adonis-like good looks, which clearly served Big Tam Connery well when he started using his middle name Sean and became the 20th century's most famous Scot, by way of James Bond and a sterling film career.

Another of the Royal High School Gang of jazz musicians, a younger member who was born in 1934, was Mike Hart, who started out as a teenage drummer and felt all his dreams had come true when Sandy Brown invited him to sit in with his band one night at the West End Café. He played with Brown at the Royal Albert Hall in London in 1952 and following his return from National Service with the RAF in 1954 he hooked up with Edinburgh trumpeter Charlie McNair and later co-founded the Climax Jazz Band. Hart never stopped playing, although he didn't achieve the same fame as many of his contemporaries. Through to the 1970s he took jobs in agriculture, antiques and as tour manager of Andy Stewart and Jimmy Shand's *White Heather Club* variety show. He got married, had kids, got divorced and variously took up sailing, flying and deep-sea fishing.

Then in 1978, by now in his early 40s, Hart took a holiday that resulted in a powerful legacy for him and for Edinburgh – the destination was the Old Sacramento Dixieland Jazz Jubilee in California.[4] While he was there he wondered if something similar might work in a festival city like Edinburgh? Hart decided to give it a try and an unheralded three-day event took place at Stewart's Ballroom at Abbeymount in the summer of 1978 – also known as gig venue the Astoria, long since demolished, with student accommodation now occupying the site. It wasn't billed as such, but this low-key local event was the first edition of what became known in 1979 as the Edinburgh Jazz Festival and in 1980 as the Edinburgh International Jazz Festival, taking off rapidly as more people came to know about it.

In particular, the 1980s hit a sweet spot for this new strand of the Edinburgh Festival, as it grew bigger while mostly managing to remain within the bounds of informality. From early on, as the Jazz Festival expanded from five days in 1979 to eight days, the format included an eye-catching Mardi Gras parade on the opening Sunday, with floats filled with 300 performers moving along Princes Street towards a celebratory party on the Grassmarket. Throughout the city centre, meanwhile, pubs threw open their doors to jazz musicians, with daily free sessions held the length of Rose Street and around.

Sponsored first by local breweries Dryburgh's and then by Scottish Brewers' McEwan's brand, offering free access to each set of brewery-run pubs for audiences, this 'Jazz Crawl' was the lifeblood of the Jazz Festival until the early '90s, providing open access to local jazz sounds for anyone, alongside an increasing number of official venues. As the music became more contemporary and broader definitions of jazz became more interesting to Hart and his programming team – Van Morrison first appeared in the mid-1980s and the Sun Ra Arkestra performed in 1990 – so the Jazz Festival grew and grew.

The first official event in 1979 featured 18 bands, which by 1986 had grown to 37 bands. The 1987 bill included Acker Bilk, Humphrey Lyttleton, Dave Shepherd and Stan Tracy. There was a concert at the Usher Hall and the birth of 'Gold Star' venues which required a paid-for pass, including the 'Jazz Amphitheatre' on Lothian Road, the 'Cotton Club' at the Potterrow Edinburgh University Student Centre on Bristo Square, the 'Jazz Headquarters' at the Royal Overseas League Club on Princes Street, with a striking view out across to Princes Street Gardens and Edinburgh Castle and the 'Jazz Big Top' on the Meadows.

Gigs also happened at the Caledonian Hotel, in the courtyard of the bustling and student-friendly Southside pub the Pear Tree House and in the Spiegeltent on Charlotte Square, a style of 'magical mirrored marquee' which first arrived in the city in 1985 and was soon to become emblematic of the Fringe. The Edinburgh International Jazz Festival hit just the right tone for the fast-growing Fringe of the 1980s, between the spectacle of the opening parade and the sense that music might be found behind any pub door a visitor opened.

Demand for jazz was so great, in fact, that the Platform Jazz network, which had been programming year-round jazz concerts across Scotland since 1973, backed Edinburgh promoter Roger Spence's *Round Midnight* programme at the Queen's Hall during the festivals of the 1980s. [5] What appeared to be a competitor event was more of a collaboration in many ways and following the collapse of Platform, Spence rebranded as Assembly Music and went into partnership with Hart on the Jazz Festival in 1996.

The Jazz Festival formalised in the 1990s, doing away with the entertainingly informal Jazz Crawl as its brewery sponsorship left, before evolving into its current version at the end of the decade. The Jazz Festival Club moved to the George Hotel on George Street, the Cotton Club to the Cavendish nightclub at West Tollcross and then the University Staff Club on Chambers Street and St Giles' Cathedral was used for special events. *Jazz on a Summer's Day*, an opening weekend concert at the Ross Bandstand in Princes Street Gardens, was touted by Mike Hart as the largest jazz event in the country.

Hart had created such a pillar of the Edinburgh Festival by 1995 that he was awarded an MBE and the Jazz Festival's modest two-day blues focus evolved to the point that the whole event was rebranded the Edinburgh International Jazz & Blues Festival in 1997, now expanded to ten days and scheduled for the week immediately prior to the opening of the International Festival and Fringe. Tommy Smith's National Jazz Orchestra of Scotland also made their debut in 1996, while in 1997 Hart and Spence finally went into official partnership on the festival, inviting headline-grabbing names like BB King, Gil Scott-Heron, Diana Krall and Dr John before the end of the decade.

After a quarter of a century in charge of what remains one of the key tentpoles of the Edinburgh Festival season, Mike Hart retired from his creation just before his 70th birthday in 2003 and enjoyed another 15 years of family life before his death in 2018.

Before Hart finished work, he saw the jazz style that was so important to Edinburgh's nightlife in the late 1940s come full circle half a century later, with the rise of Latin jazz in the bars and clubs of the city, a sound that Edinburgh enthusiastically adopted. For a brief but wonderful time, Mansfield Place Church at the foot of Broughton Road became the heaving club venue Cafe Graffiti, where nights like Lizard Lounge and Big Beat pushed revivalist funk, soul and Latin sounds to a young audience and artists like the Salsa Celtica orchestra – later Jazz Festival regulars – and the hugely talented Leith DJ and producer Joseph Malik thrived.

After decades of dilapidation and misuse, Mansfield Place Church had reopened during the Festival in the early 1990s for a display of the striking murals of artist Phoebe Anna Traquair covering its interior and grew through a few years of Fringe cabaret into use as an impressive nightclub space. Its brief boom ended with the millennium and the sale of Mansfield Place Church for development, although the restoration of Traquair's murals was a positive result. Now known as Mansfield Traquair, it's a wedding and corporate event venue – an oddly more exciting fate than the gentrifying wave of conversion into apartments or student flats, which has taken out many old Fringe venues in the 21st century. Testament to the durability of Mike Hart's vision, the Edinburgh Jazz and Blues Festival continues to roll along.

* * *

Jenny Brown can't quite remember the first Edinburgh Festival she attended as a non-civilian, but she remembers the effect it had on her. It was some point in the late 1970s and the Edinburgh-raised Brown was studying English at university in Aberdeen. Between her first and second year she took a summer job back in her home city, helping out at the Fringe Society ticket office.

'I used to shepherd the queue', she remembers.

There was some telephone booking, but most people had to queue up right down to the Wireworks, so I would have to go down the

queue and say, 'anyone queuing for Cambridge Footlights?' I had
to tell them, sorry, it's sold out for tonight. We all worked really
hard, then went to two or three shows a night. That's what started
the rhythm of the year for me, which everyone who works in the
Festival knows so well. Everything builds up to the summer, then
September comes and it's back to 'plainclothes and porridge' again.
But it's wonderful once that's in your system. I still have that –
everything leads up to August.

Brown's graduation coincided with Alistair Moffat looking for another
full-time member of staff to assist him and she got the job. She was there
for two or three years, then another alongside Moffat's replacement Michael
Dale, before her own big opportunity came up. She remembers the buzz of
this period around 1980 as the tipping point for the Fringe – the moment
when professional shows began to outweigh the amateurs.

When William Burdett-Coutts came up to stage his first Fringe play in
'79, Moffat arranged for him to stay with Brown and her flatmate and Fringe
colleague Shona Munro in Gloucester Lane.

'Bill would be using the telephone, phoning theatre companies in South
Africa and all the rest of it, with us getting nervous about the phone bill,'
remembers Brown.

We were barely out of university, we had no money whatsoever, but
it was an exciting time. Even though we were so young, we felt right
in the centre of things. There was a theatre company called ACME,
they would do a show in your house, and Scottish Television decided
they wanted [to film] a midnight show of *A Streetcar Named Desire*
in our flat. The actors came up the stair and absolutely didn't engage
with us, we followed them round from room to room. They went
into the bathroom and even used my toothpaste, it was great.

In 1982 a new job opportunity came up. A one-off festival was planned
for the following year under the umbrella of the Scottish Arts Council and
the Scottish wing of the National Book League (now the Scottish Book
Trust), to reintroduce a literary element to the Edinburgh Festival. Following
John Calder's ambitious 1962 Writers' Conference and the definitive demise
of such events after the infamous Drama Conference of '63, authors hadn't
had much representation at the Festival. This made sense, of course – writing
for print isn't exactly a performative medium. Yet little effort had been made
to find the right format for literature.

With the near-combative element of the old Conference a no-go, the

International Festival had made an annual series of small poetry and prose recitals part of their programme since 1969, with an occasional classic thrown up. Moira Shearer and Ludovic Kennedy had read together at St Cecilia's Hall in the 1970s, for example, while Judi Dench took part in a programme of macabre supernatural stories in 1975 and Ian McKellen read a selection of his own choice and some Shakespeare in '76 and '77. Also involved later in the decade were Diana Rigg, Robert Powell, Joan Bakewell, the Scots Norman MacCaig, Sorley MacLean, Iain Crichton-Smith and Dolina MacLennan and Dench again, this time alongside her husband Michael Williams.

The most ambitious literary happening in Edinburgh since 1962 came in 1980, with International Festival director John Drummond's attempt to finally resurrect the Writers' Conference, this time with five events themed around the subject of 'Whose Language is it Anyway?' at the temporarily reopened Assembly Rooms. Some A-list names appeared on the panels – Gore Vidal, Anthony Burgess, Seamus Heaney, Kingsley Amis, Jonathan Miller, John McGrath, Margaret Drabble – and the event was well-received, but controversy and therefore wider excitement levels were low. The finest literary debate on the Festival was to be found at the 'Meet the Author' events at the George and then Roxburghe Hotels since the early 1970s, small-scale affairs where writers including Edna O'Brien, Piers Paul Read, Lavinia Derwent and Nigel Tranter faced an audience.

Following in the spirit of 'Meet the Author', the Scottish Arts Council and the National Book League wanted to try something different. They appointed a man based in London named Tony Gould Davies as the founding director of the Edinburgh Book Festival and Jenny Brown was appointed assistant director. In a letter to *The Bookseller*'s edition of 15 January 1983, Gould Davies outlined the intention:

> The objective of the festival is to have a major, consumer-orientated book event, associated with the Edinburgh Festival, supported by relevant events and celebrities from all media, to increase the awareness of the range and depth of books available, and to sell as many books as possible.

The origin of the Edinburgh Book Festival seems at least as much a commercial imperative as it was rooted in ideas – or certainly, the intention was to get audiences buying books where they might otherwise not have. At the time, Brown says, there had recently been a survey saying a majority of members of the public would feel too intimidated to enter a bookshop and it was this attitude the Book Festival intended to counter.

In February of 1983 Gould Davies had to leave his post unexpectedly before the Book Festival began and Brown was promoted from assistant director into his position. She had six months to plan a festival happening from 21 August until 3 September, whose venue had already been set as Charlotte Square Gardens, just off the West End of Princes Street. The intention was to hold the festival somewhere central and accessible, which would absorb the carnival atmosphere of the entire Edinburgh Festival itself and Princes Street Gardens was initially chosen – until an old bylaw apparently aimed at discouraging 19th century peddlers was discovered.

Incredibly, it was illegal to sell books within Princes Street Gardens. By the time the law was changed by the council much later, the Book Festival had already agreed the Charlotte Square move – a far better site on reflection, says Brown. After taking charge, she and her team set up in an office on George Street donated by principal sponsors the Bank of Scotland and began planning. They were in uncharted territory. The only other similar event that existed in the UK at this point was the Cheltenham Literary Festival, founded in 1949 and despite its own literary history and wealth of booksellers, Edinburgh was a city devoid of the late-night bookselling culture we know now. The leading Edinburgh Bookshop on George Street closed its doors at 1pm on Saturday and didn't open again until Monday morning.

'I didn't sleep,' says Brown of the first year. 'But our board had a lot of people who were very well-known in the book world, like Ainslie Thin, the director of leading Edinburgh academic booksellers James Thin,[6] and that inspired confidence'. At a meeting in London André Deutsch, the publisher, said to Brown he wouldn't give her any money, but he'd bring her John Updike.

And he did. So the very first Book Festival happened, we had one theatre which seated 250, one huge book sales tent and a very good programme. John Updike, Anita Desai came from India, Doris Lessing... it was starry, because there was no competition. It felt pioneering.

All of the elements fell into place. A consortium of Edinburgh booksellers including WH Smith, John Menzies, Bauermeister's and the Stockbridge Book Shop all came together to supply huge quantities of books, catering was laid on and the already-familiar 'Meet the Author' strand from the Roxburghe Hotel was incorporated to provoke some discussion with and between authors. Crucially, says Brown, one of the key elements of the Book Festival from the start was the fact that around a third of the events were aimed at children, again to encourage new readers, as programmed by her colleague Val Bierman.

'There's a great moment that I like to think sums up the spirit of the first

Book Festival,' says Brown. 'John Updike was walking to a packed theatre, and he was stopped by a little boy saying, excuse me, are you the man selling the balloons?' The first children's event began at 10.15am and the last event was scheduled for 6.30pm, because there was a general impression among the organisers that no-one was going to choose a ticket to hear a writer speak over a night at the theatre or opera.

Finances meant the number of international authors was limited, but homegrown Scottish publishing was entering a thriving period in 1983. The first Book Festival also featured William McIlvanney, Edwin Morgan, Liz Lochhead and Alasdair Gray, who had just published the modern classic *Lanark* and Edinburgh publishers including Canongate and Mainstream were developing strong lists. All of the approximately 60 authors were paid the same fee, an egalitarian touch which has become the accepted standard at Scottish book festivals and the fact the festival charged admission – all but unheard of to hear authors talk in those days – didn't dampen enthusiasm.

In 1983, the Edinburgh Book Festival was never intended to be anything more than one-off event, a way to celebrate books and writing at the world's biggest arts festival. The building of marquees on Charlotte Square cost a lot of money and there was no way it could become an annual event. It was, however, a great success and all concerned decided that a biannual event might be possible instead. The second Edinburgh Book Festival took place in 1985 on the same site. Brown and her all-female team moved to a 'garret' at 25a South West Thistle Street Lane and began typing, mailing and faxing prospective guests and their agents. 'Publishers are always interested if they're going to sell books, aren't they?' she says. 'By 1985 we had a much more ambitious programme, our success rate [of authors agreeing to attend] was maybe one in three to begin with, now it was up to one in two'.

That year the Book Festival invited James Baldwin, although he didn't have a book out and even his publishers thought he was unlikely to come.

He came! People were crawling under the tent flaps to get in to see him, it was such an event. The word got out by 1985 that this was a festival worth supporting, and a lot of London publishers came up to see what was happening. It was a rarity, and we found that authors wanted to take part, because perhaps their friends were at the festival or they wanted to go to the festival themselves.

In Brown's opinion, the Book Festival can only work in its original position of late August, so it's complimentary to the other Edinburgh Festival activity around it, while also straddling the return of local children to school. That way they can be brought to events as school parties, rather than individually by interested parents, which is a good way of letting young readers be exposed to something different.

In 1983, Jenny Brown and her team started a new festival – in 1985 she unwittingly inaugurated a brand-new Edinburgh Festival tradition. With a square full of functional but uninspiring white marquee tents to rebuild, she was told by her friend William Burdett-Coutts about a new innovation he had discovered. In Britain for the first time for a festival at Camden Lock in London, Dutch entrepreneur Jelle van der Zee was touting around a grand new circular tent made of fabric, wood and mirrors, rich in character and atmosphere. He'd named it the 'Mirror Tent', which translates to the far more glamorous-sounding 'Spiegeltent' in Dutch.

Van der Zee didn't actually invent the Spiegeltent, instead he'd found one in a barn in Belgium in 1979 and bought it from its owner, renovating it for special occasion hire. Nineteen metres in diameter, the tent is a 'dance salon' built in Herentals in the Flemish region of Belgium in 1920, which would usually be fitted with its own organ – unfortunately, the one with van der Zee's tent had been lost. It is, says its current owner David Bates, the largest of only six remaining antique Spiegeltents in the world and it toured Belgium, Holland and France throughout the 20th century. Marlene Dietrich reputedly performed on this very Spiegeltent's stage in the 1930s.

Born in the village of Bilthoven in the province of Utrecht, van der Zee first played trumpet as a young man in Dutch jazz bands at the turn of the 1960s, but music wasn't his main gig. He was a talented young hockey player, a player with the Dutch national team in his youth and a European Cup winner as coach of the Dutch junior team. He was also a public relations man by trade, helping to broker the sponsorship deal between Dutch soccer idol Johan Cruyff and football boot manufacturer Puma. It was this latter skill that helped him sell the undeniably attractive Spiegeltent around Europe.

When Brown saw it in 1985 she wanted it for the Book Festival so much that she booked it while funding still wasn't signed off for that year's event. With beer sponsorship in place, the Beck's *Spiegeltent* was an instant hit and soon the Jazz Festival were subletting it for performances. Before long, other sharp entrepreneurs on the continent were discovering their own dance salons in barns and soon the number in circulation – and at the Edinburgh Festival – had multiplied. To try and set his own tent apart, van der Zee branded his the 'Famous Spiegeltent'.

Brown remained in charge of the Edinburgh Book Festival until 1993, overseeing five-and-a-bit festivals in total, welcoming her old flatmate and joint payer of those phone bills to South Africa Shona Munro as her assistant director in 1987, who then took over in 1993. 'I'd done it for five festivals, which is really long enough,' says Brown. 'It was much healthier for the Book

Festival that they had a change of director, a change of emphasis.'

Munro remained in post until 1996, when she was succeeded by the late expert in Latin American music and culture Jan Fairley, who had experienced being smuggled out of Chile during the coup of 1973 and in turn by the Book Festival's press officer Faith Liddell in 1997, who rebranded the event as the Edinburgh International Book Festival in 1999. Brown's career blossomed further away from the Book Festival, from broadcasting with Scottish Television and writing for *The Scotsman*, to heading a reading initiative named 'Readiscovery' and six years as literature director of the Scottish Arts Council. She's now Scotland's leading literary agent.

She remembers the intermittent problems with on-site power plunging the main tent into darkness and Maya Angelou reading on regardless, Gore Vidal packing out the theatre with every visit, Jimmy Boyle discussing *A Sense of Freedom*, Magnus Linklater chairing a discussion between the Ottoman expert and *A History of the Crusades* author Steven Runciman and Fitzroy Maclean, writer of *Eastern Approaches*, about their memories of travel in the first half of the 20th century. She and her audience heard of Christabel Bielenberg's experience of escaping Nazi Germany and Jung Chang's tale of leaving China, both at the same event. Hunter S Thompson was booked and didn't get on the plane, so Ralph Steadman appeared on his own.

'All the authors used to go to the Roxburghe Hotel before their events,' remembers Brown, of the days before onsite yurts.

> There was a moment in 1983 where Anthony Burgess spotted John Updike in the breakfast room, and said to him the immortal words, 'Updike? Burgess. We have corresponded.' Then there was this wonderful photo somewhere of Ben Okri shaking hands with Amos Oz. There was a sense that Charlotte Square could be this international meeting place for authors – and remember, they weren't meeting anywhere else back then.

When she was growing up in the city, says Brown, the sense that Edinburgh was a literary city was all around. She saw the Walter Scott Monument, the largest in the world to a writer and Waverley Station, named after one of Scott's novels. On Anchor Close, off the Royal Mile, had once been based the printworks where William Smellie had published the first edition of the *Encyclopedia Britannica* in the 18th century and Chambers Street is named after former Lord Provost of Edinburgh William Chambers, who with his brother Robert first published the *Chambers Dictionary* in the city in 1872.

At the turn of the 19th century the major publishing, printing and bookbinding firm Oliver & Boyd set up operations in Tweeddale Court, another narrow courtyard off the Royal Mile and remained there until the 1970s. The building was taken over by publisher Robin Hodge, who began producing the listings and culture magazine *The List* in 1985, one of the key publications of Edinburgh Festival and Scottish cultural life ever since. From 1911, John Bartholomew and Son begin printing their now world-famous brand of maps in Duncan Street, near sometime Fringe venue St Columba's Hall on the edge of the southern suburb of Mayfield.

Jenny Brown sensed the presence of all this history in her youth. 'They were mapping the world from Edinburgh,' she says.

> That's all gone, of course, but if you looked for them there were all the signs that this was a city built on books. What was missing was the sense of vibrancy in the contemporary literature, it was like the tail end of something that had been glorious, and it needed to be built up again. The Book Festival has helped – literature's now apparent and celebrated in the city, in a way it wasn't before.

* * *

The Film Festival was resurgent and the birth of the Jazz Festival and the Book Festival increased audience competition for the original and still reputationally predominant International Festival. John Drummond's final year as Festival Director was 1983 and his replacement was Frank Dunlop, who had, since establishing Pop Theatre at the International Festival in the 1960s and premiering *Joseph and the Amazing Technicolour Dreamcoat* at Haymarket Ice Rink in '72, made an international name for himself as a theatre director.

After founding the Young Vic, he worked with the Royal Shakespeare Company and set up a theatre company at the Brooklyn Academy of Music (BAM), enjoying a number of hits in London and New York. These included a revival of William Gillette's 1899 stage version of *Sherlock Holmes* (1973), which ran on Broadway for two years,[7] Dunlop and actor Jim Dale's *Scapin* (1974), their Tony Award-nominated adaptation of Molière's *Les Fourberies de Scapin* ('The Trickery of Scapin') and the 1980 Broadway revival of the 1960 hit *Camelot*, once again starring Richard Burton as the king of English legend.

There was a level of controversy around Dunlop's appointment in Edinburgh, because he was absolutely a 'theatre man', while the Festival's focus had always been on music and opera. He was also known to be outspoken – his time in Edinburgh certainly didn't alter this reputation – and on his appointment Michael Billington used the words 'a born populariser and showman with an appetite for novelty' to describe him.[8] Dunlop was 56 when he accepted the job.

Drummond's five-year tenure had enjoyed many highlights although, like every other director of his era, he'd struggled with a lack of adequate venues and a general sense of intransigence when dealing with the council. '[W]hat was seen in London as one of the great glories of the Scottish year was for many in Edinburgh a tiresome, expensive irrelevance', he wrote.[9] One elderly councillor became furious with him when he'd pointed out that all the benefits of the International Festival came for roughly the same cost as was spent on the maintenance of Edinburgh's graveyards, as though he was suggesting people not be buried, while a period of high inflation meant wealthy tourists from Europe and America were staying away and Fringe-friendly young backpackers were becoming the wider festival season's tourist staple.

With Sheila Colvin's help and experience of the original Conferences, though, he welcomed writers for that revived Writers' Conference at the Assembly Rooms in 1980 and moved the International Festival's once-great but now-failing Festival Club to the University of Edinburgh's Basil Spence redesigned Staff Club at 9–15 Chambers Street. Drummond's finest year for opera, he has said, was in 1980, when the Cologne Opera conducted by John Pritchard and directed by Michael Hampe were a last-minute replacement for L'Opéra du Rhin of Strasbourg, who had to pull out. Cologne's versions of Mozart's Cosi Fan Tutte and Domenico Cimarosa's Il Matrimonio Segreto ('The Secret Marriage') at the King's Theatre were very well-received, as were Scottish Opera's The Cunning Little Vixen by Leoš Janáček and Wozzeck by Alban Berg, the latter under the Opera's principal conductor Sir Alexander Gibson.

This year also saw the premiere of the great Orkney-based composer Peter Maxwell Davies' most famous work The Lighthouse at Moray House, an atmospheric piece about a lighthouse crew who infamously all went missing on the Scottish Flannan Isles in 1900. The work has been widely performed since, although Drummond's tenure didn't repeat such operatic heights. The Lighthouse was also the first and most successful recipient of the short-lived Tennant Caledonian Award for new work, which ended with Drummond's tenure.

Although he failed in some attempts to bring major theatre works from China and Poland to Edinburgh, Drummond did convince Tadeusz Kantor to make the International Festival switch with Wielepole Wielepole at Moray House in 1980 and the following year attracted the National Theatre of Romania for a version of Terence's Roman comedy The Woman from Andros, directed by the actor Grigore Gonta. In 1980, the National Theatre staged the Wakefield Mystery Plays at the Assembly Hall, directed by Bill Bryden, with Brian Glover and Brenda Blethyn among the cast and in '81 the same company premiered Tom Stoppard's On the Razzle at the Lyceum, although its seven performances were rather impudently billed as just previews. In 1982, Drummond's EIF produced a version of Nikolai Gogol's *The Marriage*, directed by and starring Peter Ustinov.

As well as the opening of the Queen's Hall and a hit 1979 exhibition of Degas' art from a century before, Drummond's greatest legacy as International Festival director was in the consistent quality of music he brought to Edinburgh. Conductors including Riccardo Muti, Claudio Abbado, Simon Rattle, Jerzy Maksymiuk, Georg Solti and Dmitri Shostakovich's son Maxim all appeared during his tenure and soloists including Claudio Arrau, Yo-Yo Ma and Yehudi Menuhin appeared, the latter in the twilight of his performing career in 1981. In 1980 the former Prime Minister Edward Heath, a keen conductor, led the European Community Youth Orchestra at the Usher Hall alongside Abbado.[10]

Although it was a big success, the 1,200-capacity venue on the Meadows known simply as the Tent had been expensive to put on and difficult to gain planning permission for. Its sole appearance as a dedicated dance space came during the Festival of 1979, when the Royal Ballet of Sadler's Wells presented the world premieres of Kenneth MacMillan's *Playground* and David Bintley's *Punch and the Street Party* and the National Ballet of Cuba hosted work including *Giselle*, choreographed by Alicia Alonso.

The fact the Tent didn't continue was no reflection on Drummond's instinct for the popular. Behind the scenes he made efforts for an event which would have been incredibly memorable, but sadly agreement couldn't be reached to persuade Paul McCartney and Wings to play on the Castle Esplanade during the Festival of 1979. In a strange act of synchronicity, though, young Edinburgh promoters Pete Irvine and Barry Wright staged what was billed as 'the largest rock festival ever staged in Scotland' at the Royal Highland Showground at Ingliston that year, under the banner of their new company Regular Music.

Decades later, under different ownership, Regular would finally bring big summer concerts to the Esplanade, putting on shows in July using the seating arena built for the Tattoo in August. The Edinburgh Rock Festival of '79 was hugely ambitious, with headliner Van Morrison supported by Talking Heads, Squeeze, the Undertones, Steel Pulse and local folk artist Dick Gaughan and while only 13,000 of its expected capacity 30,000 attended, it was both a critical success and the first example of the modern rock festival to be held in Scotland.[11] 'Wright expressed pride to the press about the fact that real ale and toilets were among the event's attractions and conveniences, a taste of major music festivals to come.

While Drummond's attempts to found a tented venue on the Meadows and a home for rock music on the Esplanade were the right ideas at the wrong time, however, one new development stuck. At 10.30pm on the evening of Sunday 2 September, with the sponsorship of Glenlivet whisky, the Scottish Chamber Orchestra under conductor Trevor Pinnock staged a free performance of works by Haydn and Handel at the Ross Bandstand in Princes Street Gardens. At the conclusion of Handel's *Music for the Royal Fireworks*, written in 1749 for George II and the end of war in Austria, fireworks were let off above Edinburgh Castle, a spectacle that had crowds thronging the Gardens and Princes Street itself. The annual Edinburgh International Festival Fireworks Concert has become arguably the single most popular event in the International Festival's calendar to the present day.

Having turned down an extension to his contract, Drummond's final Festival of 1983 successfully revolved around a consolidating theme. The year before he had seen the Hamburg State Opera give performances of the late Austrian composer Alexander von Zemlinsky's works *Eine Florentinische Tragodie* ('A Florentine Tragedy') and *Der Geburtstag der Infantin* aka *Der Zwerg* ('The Birthday of the Infanta' aka 'The Dwarf') – both adapted from the work of Oscar Wilde – and immediately wanted to bring them to Edinburgh. Sheila Colvin asked him who Zemlinsky was and why he was relatively unknown. These were good questions and the *Vienna 1900* theme of that International Festival was an attempt to answer them, to represent the *fin de siècle* milieu in which Zemlinsky's work had been created and to put forward Drummond's own theory that Vienna during this period was a 'furnace' which had bred many of the big ideas of the 20th century.

With help from the art historian Peter Vergo, a programme was conceived which the Hamburg State Opera headed, while Scottish Opera performed Benjamin Britten's *Death in Venice*. The Municipal Theatre of Haifa staged Yoshua Sobol's play *The Soul of a Jew*, about the conflicted Viennese philosopher Otto Weininger. Glasgow's Citizens Theatre performed two relevant plays, both translated by Robert David MacDonald, in a four-hour adaptation of Karl Kraus' *The Last Days of Mankind* and a dramatisation of Hugo von Hofmannsthal's libretto to Richard Strauss's *Der Rosenkavalier* ('The Knight of the Rose') and the casts for both included Ciaran Hinds and 25-year-old Gary Oldman, a regular with the Citizens' company in the early '80s.

There were performances of Schoenberg, Debussy and Johan Strauss's music, talks at the Church Hill theatre and a *Vienna 1900* exhibition at the National Museum on Chambers Street. The International Festival of '83 also hosted Joan Plowright in Chekov's *The Cherry Orchard*, directed by the filmmaker Lindsay Anderson, the 7:84 Theatre Company with John McGrath's adaptation of Aristophanes' *Women in Power* (along with *The Soul of a Jew*, this marked a brief return to the Assembly Rooms' Music Hall for EIF), an extensive series of pieces from Ballet Rambert, choreographed by Merce Cunningham, Robert North and others and Sandra Kotze and

Elsa Joubert's theatre version of Joubert's apartheid-era South African novel *Poppie Nongena*.

It was a popular and well-programmed swansong year for Drummond, although as the buzz died down the old problems returned. He could see that Labour were going to take over the city council in the next year's elections and he disagreed with what he called the party's 'little Scotland' attitude. That not enough was spent on culture in and around the city during the other 11 months of the year was something he did agree with, but not that this was the Festival's fault or that it should suffer for the council's lack of commitment.

More than this, he was disheartened by the fact he couldn't squeeze any more financial pips from the District Council, yet £13 million could fairly easily be conjured when the 1986 Commonwealth Games were announced for Edinburgh. Meanwhile, the theatres looked ever more decrepit and unsuited to contemporary standards. The city had, Drummond suggested, an ambition it wasn't willing to back up.

Drummond returned to the BBC as controller of Radio 3 with special responsibility for the Proms, keeping on the latter part of the job until his retirement in 1995. Before he left, he later wrote, the then-Lord Provost Thomas Morgan asked if figures like Jonathan Miller or Melvyn Bragg might be interested in succeeding him. Drummond had to point out that the salary for his job was a fraction of theirs. Attracting a candidate was difficult, but Drummond, who died at the age of 71 in 2006, was surprised when Frank Dunlop got the job. 'Surely some knowledge of music was essential,' he thought, adding that the form 'was not well-served by Dunlop's eight years as director.'[11]

The Edinburgh Festival was the job Drummond said he'd wanted all his life, but after half a decade of it he'd come up against a problem familiar to its past directors. In a valedictory interview he bemoaned the way the set-up of the Festival's funding, hierarchy and many answerable parties meant innovation was all but impossible: 'You get sick of apologising in this job.'[12]

* * *

Where Drummond had come in with grand and unfulfilled plans to put rock music and foreign cookery somewhere on the International Festival's bill, Frank Dunlop arrived saying that an exhibition football match could conceivably be a Festival event. Of all the definitions of 'festival' he'd seen, 'not one of them mentions culture... They all talk about joy and celebration and revelry and merrymaking.'[13]

What did please Drummond about the effervescent Dunlop's tenure, viewed from after the fact, was the way his successor finally managed to get things moving in the city, with great strides towards modernisation of its stages and theatre buildings, all badly needed since 1947. Dunlop knocked a great deal of the stuffiness out of the International Festival's image, said Drummond and he was right to modestly add that some of the roots of this modernisation started with him.

In the event, it was Drummond's abrupt departure which caused the appointment of Dunlop, as much as anything. Although the outgoing Director was merely fulfilling his five-year contract, the offer of a five-year extension had seen him tentatively agreed to two. Nothing had been signed, but when he decided the stress of doing the EIF job – of negotiating with new funders as well as artists[15] – he decided against signing the contract after all. Dunlop was doing well directing on Broadway, but as an International Festival regular he took it upon himself to ring the Council and give them some ideas on how it should be run so as not to alienate the wider public. Soon after he made contact, he found himself being offered the job. Not long after accepting it he quickly changed EIF's dates to a week earlier for 1984, in order to catch more summer tourists, as the clash with the big European opera festivals of 37 years before was no longer a material issue.

With Dunlop's appointment, an old relationship was restored. Alistair Moffat left his role at the Fringe in 1981 to become the head of arts at Scottish Television, after instigating boom times during his period as director and he was replaced by 31-year-old Michael Dale, who had previous with both Moffat and Dunlop. Born in Perth, Scotland, to a Scottish mother and English military father, Dale was brought up in Cairo until Brits were expelled following the Suez Crisis, then went to school in Cheltenham. He attended the University of St Andrews, where he discovered many of his classmates had failed to get into Oxford, just like him.

St Andrews was where Dale met Moffat, a fellow history student and rugby player and he helped him move some pianos around during Moffat's St Andrews Festival in 1971. Five years later Moffat, still only 26, was appointed director of the Fringe and Dale took holidays in Edinburgh to catch up with him and attend shows every summer after that. Ironically, it was Dale who had the background in 'proper' theatre before taking over the Fringe. While Moffat self-started the St Andrews and Kelso Festivals on the side while studying to be an art historian, Dale moved to London after graduation and started out as a cleaner at Shaftesbury Theatre, then moved up to tearing tickets at performances of *Hair*. A friend from university told him there was an assistant manager job going at the Young Vic and he applied and got it, which meant Frank Dunlop was now his boss.[16]

'When Frank took over (at the International Festival) he came marching through the door of the Fringe office and said, 'here we are again, boy, you and me",' remembers Dale.

John Drummond and I got on well, partly because of our backgrounds. Alistair had been prone to make statements like, 'the Fringe is now more important than the Festival', which I don't think John appreciated at all. I mean, John wasn't the easiest person in the world, but he had proper flair and a huge, wide-ranging knowledge. He was very charismatic, and he knew absolutely bloody everybody – seriously famous people.

Their reunion in Edinburgh was brief. Dale left the Fringe in 1986 to work for the planned Glasgow Garden Festival of 1988, the third in a series of five biannual British regeneration festivals, held on the banks of the River Clyde where major ship docks used to stand.[17] His replacement as director was Mhairi Mackenzie-Robinson, who had been an assistant at the Fringe Society since Alistair Moffat's tenure. The Fringe grew during Dale's tenure, but at a much more modest rate than during the '70s. In 1986 there were 494 Fringe groups, next to 1981's comparable 485, but the number of shows they performed had ballooned to 959 from 740 (or 8,592 individual performances in 1986, compared to 6,484 in 1981).

Meanwhile, Dunlop fell straight into a political furore in his first year in charge, with the Labour group having taken over Edinburgh District Council for the first time at the local elections in May 1984. On 18 August a forum was held on the Festival, chaired by the new head of the Council's Recreation Committee Mark Lazarowicz, which involved representatives of the Scottish Arts Council and Greater London Council in attempting to put forward ideas 'to make the arts more accessible and more relevant to the man in the street'. In the background, though, there was concern that the Labour group was now claiming all political seats on the Festival Council – previously they had been held by representatives of all parties – and that a purge driven by a kind of reverse snobbery was going to be enacted upon the International Festival.

With withering sarcasm *The Herald*'s Raymond Gardner commented that the *Komische Oper Ballet* 'hail from that part of Berlin round which the local district council built a wall to stop the local citizenry being corrupted by the elitism and free enterprise of the West.'[18] While certain council members were loud and angry in their dismissal of the Festival, however, the same paper's arts editor John Fowler reported of the forum that it was chaired by 'neither cultural Luddites nor wild Philistine bogeymen', but rather intelligent people who believed 'that culture is a good thing'.[19]

Despite an ongoing controversy stoked by the press in Dunlop's early days, those on the council relaxed when they got to know him and realised he had a taste for the popular and that he could bring a Festival in below budget, as he did in 1984. In 1986 the Festival Council's chair James Dunbar-Naismith also succeeded in having the number of political seats on the 12-strong Council reduced by the 200 members of the Fringe Society who voted it in, so as to remove their majority. For the first Festival of Dunlop's in '84, that most supposedly elitist of arts, opera, was poorly served due to a combination of Dunlop's lack of expertise and the increasing difficulty of convincing international companies to put up with the city's substandard facilities. Yet the Playhouse hosted the Komische Oper to wide acclaim, while the 46-year-old Rudolf Nureyev made his first Festival appearance, dancing Swan Lake at the Playhouse with the Paris Opera Ballet, of which he was director at the time.

There was also a mini-series of Samuel Beckett's performances and talks, part-programmed by John Calder; there was classical dance and music from Thailand at the King's Theatre, the Arifuku Kagura masked dance troupe in Princes Street Gardens; and an especially good year for visual art. The American psychiatrist and philanthropist Arthur Sackler funded a display of his art collection from the Smithsonian Institution in Washington, DC at the Royal Scottish Museum on Chambers Street, with a focus on Chinese painting at the University of Edinburgh's Old College.

There was also work by Jean Michel Basquiat and John Cage at the Fruitmarket Gallery, Henry Matisse at the City Art Centre, Edinburgh's own Eduardo Paolozzi at the Royal Scottish Academy and an exhibition named *Creation: Modern Art and Nature* at the Scottish National Gallery of Modern Art on Belford Road. This new landmark was set in a leafy estate just beyond the West End, with the Water of Leith running through the valley behind it.

Since 1960 the SNGMA had been based at Inverleith House in the Royal Botanic Gardens, but now it took over this much larger space, which had until 1975 been John Watson's Institution, a school for fatherless children. Founded in 1762, it was built in its current form in 1825 by William Burn, son of the architect Robert, who also designed the Nelson Monument on Calton Hill. William's own work included the Church of St John the Evangelist at the West End of Princes Street, the Melville Monument on St Andrew Square and – echoing the grand mood of Watson's Institution – Cliveden House in Buckinghamshire and a number of other English stately homes.

Dunlop was in charge of the Edinburgh International Festival until 1991's edition and certain hallmarks kept returning to any commentary concerning his time there – chief among them, the fractious relationship with the District Council and funding matters and also the perceived substandard nature of opera and music during his tenure. While many commentators believed he ignored these in favour of his first love, theatre, Dunlop was quick to point out that the musical forms still took up the majority of the Festival budget.

In light of both talking points, there was also a certain irony that one of his earliest successes in Edinburgh was the acclaimed arrival of the

Opéra de Lyon under John Eliot Gardiner in 1985, whose performances of Emmanuel Chabrier's *L'Etoile* ('The Stars') and Claude Debussy's *Pelléas et Mélisande* showed off the King's Theatre's new 100-capacity orchestra pit, a much-needed improvement. That year's International Festival also saw an inventive method of fulfilling the Festival's 'international' mission while increasing the level of much-demanded local content by taking as its theme the 'Auld Alliance' of Scotland and France. Gardiner also conducted the *Opéra de Lyon* Orchestra in a programme of Mozart at the Usher Hall, where Daniel Barenboim took charge of two performances by the *Orchestre de Paris* and the *Orchestre National de France* were conducted by Charles Dutoit and Thomas Fulton.

There was dance from Scottish Ballet and the French companies *Ris et Danceries* and *Groupe de Recherche Chorégraphique de l'Opéra de Paris*, exhibitions including a Matisse-themed show at the Royal Scottish Academy and *L'Ecole de Paris 1900–1960* at the Scottish National Gallery of Modern Art and talks and readings on Scottish, Scots Gaelic and French subjects. In association with Perth Theatre, Rikki Fulton and Denise Coffey adapted Molière's *Le bourgeois gentilhomme* as the Scots comedy *A Wee Touch of Class*, directed by Joan Knight at the Church Hill Theatre and Tom Fleming's *The Three Estates* from the year before returned at the Assembly Hall alongside the same director's revival of Sydney Goodsir Smith's *The Wallace*.

Elsewhere, 1985's International Festival programme revealed the scope of Dunlop's taste for quirky variety, which audiences appreciated and many critical purists – perhaps betraying a sense of the elitism that many Labour council members railed against – turned their noses up at. Michael Clark made his first EIF appearance with *our caca phony H* at the Lyceum, future Fringe favourites the Moscow State Circus played the Playhouse, the Ross Bandstand and Leith Theatre and the extremely popular American acrobats the Flying Karamazov Brothers played a few dates at the Lyceum and the Assembly Rooms. A collaborative Jazz Festival All-Stars concert was also inaugurated at the Usher Hall, with players including Humphrey Lyttleton and Buddy Tate.

The undoubted stars of '85, though, were the Toho Company of Japan, directed by the great Yukio Ninagawa, whose version of Macbeth at the Lyceum took the breath of all who saw it. Toho Company returned to much acclaim as part of Dunlop's first World Theatre Season in '86, with a stunning outdoor version of Euripides' *Medea* in the quad of the University's Old College and Ninagawa returned with his own company to perform *The Tempest* in '88, Yukio Mishima's *Sotoba Komachi* in '90 and Kunio Shimizu's *Tango at the End of Winter* in '91. The latter was an English-language play, with Alan Rickman and Robert Glenister in the cast. Rickman's first professional acting job after graduating from the Royal

Academy of Dramatic Art had been at the Festival, in Birmingham Rep's 1976 adaptation of Ben Jonson's *The Devil is an Ass*.

Dunlop's World Theatre programmes proved to be one of the most successful aspects of his programming in Edinburgh and between its first appearance in 1986 and 1991, he welcomed companies from Germany, Sweden, South Africa,[20] Spain, France, Japan, Poland, Israel, Italy, Canada, Korea, India, New Zealand, Australia, New Guinea, Denmark, Romania, Czechoslovakia, Yugoslavia, the USA and various regions of the USSR, as well as Scotland, England and Ireland. Among the many interesting plays that Dunlop booked during this time were *Greek Tragedy*, devised and directed by the English film director Mike Leigh with Sydney's Belvoir Street Theatre company in 1989; a 1990 double bill of *King Lear* and *A Midsummer Night's Dream* from director Kenneth Branagh's Renaissance Theatre Company, featuring Branagh, Emma Thompson, Siobhan Redmond and Richard Briars among their casts; and a return for Tadeusz Kantor's Cricot 2 with *Today is My Birthday* in 1991. In 1987 alone, the Berliner Ensemble, the Gorky Theatre of Leningrad and Dublin's Gate Theatre all appeared.

As much as some critics enjoyed prodding Dunlop's selections for their supposedly lowbrow qualities, he picked several winners in his time. The company of Sweden's Folkoperan Theatre performed at Leith Theatre – the former Leith Town Hall, reactivated as an EIF venue in the 1980s – and became a popular centrepiece of the venue's reinvention as a decentralised hub for small-scale opera. In 1990, the Cleveland San Jose Ballet played *Coppelia* at the Playhouse with 52-year-old Rudolf Nureyev appearing among the dancers three years before he died. A slew of big-name classical soloists and recitalists included the extravagant pop violinist Nigel Kennedy, Montserrat Caballé, Evelyn Glennie, Ravi Shankar, Stephane Grappelli, Yo-Yo Ma and Yehudi Menuhin.

Jimmy Logan performed the work of the late Scottish entertainer Sir Harry Lauder at Portobello Town Hall in 1986 and there were readings of Edward Lear at the Royal Museum of Scotland in 1990 by broadcaster Nicholas Parsons, who had visited the first Edinburgh international Festival as a 23-year-old in 1947. He became an Edinburgh institution in his elder years, beginning his chat and cabaret show *The Happy Hour with Nicholas Parsons* at the age of 77 in 2001. Parsons returned to the Pleasance Cabaret Bar to host it every year until 2018, when he was 94; he's believed to be the oldest person to appear in a Fringe show.[21]

Dunlop celebrated 40 years of the Edinburgh International Festival with an Usher Hall Gala Concert in 1986, which was part-hosted by Sean Connery and in the same year Ingmar Bergan directed Strindberg's *Miss Julie* for Stockholm's Royal Dramatic Theatre at the King's Theatre. That year also featured one of the oddest but retrospectively most interesting turns of his EIF career. Presented at the Church Hill Theatre, *The Road to Immortality (Part 2) aka LSD (...Just the High Points...)* was a difficult to penetrate, partially verbatim piece which explored the written works of Burroughs, Kerouac, Ginsberg, Huxley and others, scenes from Arthur Miller's The Crucible and excerpts of the 1982 debate tour between cultural opponents Timothy Leary and G Gordon Liddy. It was the first appearance in Edinburgh by the New York experimental company The Wooster Group, with Willem Dafoe and Steve Buscemi among its cast.

The 1980s were a period of great change for the Festival as a whole. While the Fringe boomed and seemed to find a kind of purpose in that growth, the International Festival appeared to be struggling to justify its very existence. Extraordinarily hard-working, unafraid to do all the work he didn't want delegated, often brusque with colleagues, politicians and the press and reportedly quite a shy man who never owned a house in the UK during his entire Festival tenure, just an apartment in Manhattan and a succession of hotel rooms, even the indefatigable Dunlop found the constant round of funding and political squabbles wearing.

He had intended to quit after his fifth Festival in 1988 and a failed attempt to get an Italian-themed programme off the ground, but a fundraising programme by *The Scotsman* to help raise the £60,000 necessary to bring Houston Grand Opera's production of *Nixon in China* by John Adams to the city raised £90,000 from 2,000 members of the public. In the face of such gratifying support, Dunlop ploughed on for three more years and while the same old problems didn't turn his own fortunes with the Festival around, what was happening through in Glasgow inadvertently gave the International Festival the reinvigorated standing it had been seeking for years.

SPOTLIGHT

A One Night Stand with Sean Hughes (1990) Frank Skinner (1991) Steve Coogan in Character with John Thomson (1992)

IN 1982, A former drama student from London named Nica Burns fulfilled an ambition and took a show to the Edinburgh Fringe. Based on HE Bates' 1953 short story *Dulcima*, in which a Gloucestershire farmer's daughter seduces a wealthy old landowner, the then 28-year-old says she invested all of her savings to start a tiny theatre company so she could make it happen.

'I adapted it with a guy I was at university with who directed me in drama society plays,' says Burns.

I was the leading lady, it was a two-hander at the Celtic Lodge on the Royal Mile[1] at 8 o'clock. Three days in *The Scotsman* gave us an excellent review, and then we sold out for the rest of the run. It cost £600 to stage – if we couldn't afford a bit of set we mimed it, and everything had to get into my battered Ford Escort or it didn't go to Edinburgh. We made a total profit of £48, which I split with the director. I didn't expect that. I expected nothing.

For all the considerable production skills she's shown throughout her life, Burns says she learned them all in those early days in Edinburgh. Born in 1954 in British Malaya, now Malaysia, her parents were a doctor and a nurse, there to help vaccinate people in rural villages. Raised in London, she studied to be an actor at the city's Webber Douglas School, but the Fringe was a crash course in new skills; in writing and producing, especially.

'You've got two things on your passport,' she says, referring to the main attributes she believes a performer possesses to influence their own success.

One is talent and the other is the determination to make it happen. The people who do it have to have ambition, they have to have determination, and they have to learn about the business side. Somehow they scrape the money together. You can do all of those things, but it's no good if you're no good, and it's no good being brilliant if nobody else recognises it. If you can't get through the traditional doors, the Fringe gives you an opportunity to smash those doors open.

Burns certainly used the Edinburgh Fringe to open doors. She returned in 1983 with three productions in different venues, among them the Cowgate warehouse which would later become the Gilded Balloon and the Market Street nightclub alongside Waverley station named Buster Brown's. Getting out of a taxi to visit a restaurant on Leith Walk one evening, she also recognised the woman getting in after her. It was Dillie Keane of the musical group Fascinating Aida, then in their first year at the Fringe, who had just had it bluntly suggested to them that hiring a director would improve the show. Keane asked Burns to do it on the spot, Burns agreed and the following year Fascinating Aida won the Perrier Award for their show at the Assembly Rooms.

Burns went on to direct the show for 17 years and although Keane and co. didn't achieve the same crossover success as future Perrier winners, they were extremely popular at the Sydney Festival, with BBC Radio 4 listeners and in the West End, nominated three times for the Olivier Award in the Best Entertainment category in 1995, 2000 and 2005. Their songs have been covered by Bette Midler, Amanda Palmer and future Fringe star Camille O'Sullivan, while Keane's own solo career during a split in the group from 1989 until 1994 began with a Perrier nomination for her show *Single Again* in 1990. She returned in '91 with *Citizen Keane.*

Burns' breakthrough year in '83, meanwhile, finished with her taking over the artistic directorship of the Donmar Warehouse in Covent Garden, a 19th century brewery which had been used since 1961 as a private rehearsal studio under the ownership of theatre producer Donald Albery and then his son Ian.[2] Since 1977, the space had been owned by the Royal Shakespeare Company as their rehearsal space and occasional studio theatre, hosting hits including the premiere of their 1976 production of *Macbeth*, which bore a strong Edinburgh connection, given that it starred Ian McKellen and Judy Dench and was directed by Trevor Nunn, all veterans of the city at some point in their career. In 1980 the venue also hosted the premiere of Willy Russell's *Educating Rita*, directed by former Traverse artistic director Mike Ockrent.

After rapidly building a name for herself in Edinburgh, Burns stayed at the Donmar until 1989. The roots of her other major project of this era – the production of the Perrier Award itself – also came in '83. That year's Perrier was won by the Melbourne duo *Los Trios Ringbarkus*, whose success opened the door to a flood of Australian cabaret and comedy acts on the Fringe from the next year on. They weren't the act that caught Burns' attention, though. Another group that had been tipped for the award came from Brighton, a street music and theatre ensemble named Pookiesnackenburger, created by two 20-something friends named Luke Cresswell and Steve McNicholas.

The pair came together in their home city for a punk show named *Romance is Not Dead*, which 'commemorated' – after a fashion – the wedding of Prince Charles and Lady Diana Spencer in July 1981. The following month they were making their first appearance on the Edinburgh Fringe as Pookiesnackenburger, a raw and noisily inventive ensemble of street musicians. For five years they appeared at the Fringe, sometimes alongside their sister theatre company Cliffhanger, performing shows at locations including the Wireworks Playground, a tenement courtyard just off the Royal Mile behind the Fringe office.[3] 'When money got a bit low because we'd drunk it all, we'd go out and busk,' said former Pookiesnackenburger member John Helmer of the Edinburgh experience. In one afternoon's busking, he said, they 'earned all the air fares there and back.'[4]

Pookiesnackenburger performed at every Edinburgh Fringe until 1985, earning enough popularity that they made a number of television appearances and briefly had their own Channel 4 show. On their way to this brief flush of success and later, greater triumphs, Nica Burns saw them in Edinburgh and booked their show *Eureka! Bongo!* for the Warehouse in late 1983, where

The Guardian predicted they would copy the Flying Pickets' success. That prediction didn't come true for Pookiesnackenburger, but Cresswell and McNicholas were bound for much greater global success via the Fringe.

After devising a 1986 advert for Heineken beer which involved bins being rattled in tune, adapted from a part of their live show, Pookiesnackenburger faded away in the mid-1990s, re-emerging as jazz-funk group The Yes/No People, who briefly flirted with pop music success. Meanwhile, Cresswell founded the Urban Warriors, a duo who played percussion on bits of scrap metal, including their own homemade armoured suits. The Warriors enjoyed some cult success, appearing on Channel 4 music show *The Tube* and creating large-scale 'junk percussion' shows around the country, until in 1991, Cresswell and McNicholas combined the aesthetic of the Heineken commercial and the Urban Warriors for a new Fringe show.

Featuring an ensemble of seven players, *Stomp* had been developed from a series of Yes/No People sketches on the previous year's environmental television show for teens, *A Beetle Called Derek*, presented by the later film director Andrea Arnold. Tucked away in a late-night Assembly Rooms slot which began just before midnight, the format suddenly clicked in a big way with audiences and critics. It toured internationally for the next three years, winning an Olivier Award and transferring to the off-Broadway Orpheum Theatre in 1994, then playing the Academy Awards at Quincy Jones' invitation in 1996 and recording an HBO special the following year. The recast Stomp remains a present-day touring hit, thanks to Edinburgh. Cresswell's younger brother Addison also made progress in the city in the 1980s, becoming one of the country's key comedy agents with his company Off the Kerb.

It was during Pookiesnackenburger's run at the Warehouse that a representative of Perrier came to see the show, took a look around the theatre and liked what they saw. Burns was asked to take over the production of the Perrier Award from the following year. 'I said no, not as they are now,' she recalls. 'It's too small, I'd like a bigger idea. The prize money had to go up and the winner would come down to the Donmar for a three-week season. In those days nobody was bringing shows from Edinburgh back to London, it wasn't the thing'.

Burns' plan was for each Perrier winner to be the centrepiece of week-long, multi-show mini-seasons which recreated a small slice of the Fringe in London, with theatre companies including Gerry Mulgrew's Communicado and the newly established Cheek by Jowl transferring successful plays from Edinburgh. Founded in 1981 by Declan Donnellan and Nick Ormerod, Cheek by Jowl's very first show was a two-week run of William Wycherley's 17th century play *The Country Wife* at St Columba's by the Castle during that year's Fringe and they returned with William Makepeace Thackeray's

Vanity Fair – which won them a Fringe First – and Shakespeare's *Pericles*, both at the Bedlam Theatre in '83. The latter pair were packaged up with Jean Racine's *Andromache* at the Donmar in January 1985, earning Cheek by Jowl an Oliver Award for Best Newcomer that year and a nomination for Donnellan, their first of seven Olivier wins and eight nominations during a career which has been closely linked with the Donmar.

'As we developed the Perrier, we realised the comedy industry was developing,' says Burns.

> New stand-ups were learning to do a 50-minute show, which is a serious amount of material for a comedian. Suddenly there were people who were starting to be very experienced, they'd been doing it for five, six, seven years. By 1991 we had this absolutely extraordinary Perrier show, with just a massive amount of talent.

* * *

Contrary to the perception of the Edinburgh Comedy Award for the last three decades, the earliest years of the Award were very light on stand-ups. The big winners were revues like the famed Cambridge Footlights group of '81, or quirky, high-concept performance comedy like *Los Trios Ringbarkus* in '83 or Theatre de Complicité's *More Bigger Snacks Now* in '85. Fascinating Aida being among the nominees in 1984, Burns' first year as producer, caused the show's director some discomfort, although she had no involvement in the judges' decision. Despite the fact more conventional, straight and character stand-ups like Ben Elton, Rik Mayall, Lenny Henry and French & Saunders played Edinburgh during the '80s, however, this form of comedy was little-represented among the Perrier's nominees and winners.

In 1985 stand-up pioneer John Dowie, who had first come to Edinburgh in the early '70s and was viewed as a guru by younger comics like Alexei Sayle, Tony Allen and Mark Steel, was shortlisted but lost out to Complicité. The first stand-up comic to win the Perrier was Arnold Brown in 1987, although his show *Brown Blues* at the Gilded Balloon was novel in that it was partly a musical set, featuring Barb Jungr and Michael Parker. That year's shortlist was a taste of things to come, though; the first one to feature all stand-ups, with Nick Revell and John Sparkes joining the following two years' winners Jeremy Hardy and Simon Fanshawe.

While Sparkes' geeky Welsh poet character Siadwel and his television appearances on *Naked Video* and *Absolutely* helped him into a career as a writer and actor and Hardy and Fanshawe were both highly-regarded stand-ups who enjoyed lengthy careers on stage, radio and television, no genuine stand-up stars emerged at this time.[5] Other nominees around this time included Robert Llewellyn for his show *Mammon, Robot Born of Woman* in 1988, whose lewd robotic title character was what got Llewellyn noticed and cast by the producers of the sci-fi comedy *Red Dwarf* as the robot Kryten and John Peel-approved performance poet, comedian and later Edinburgh regular John Hegley with *Can I Come Down Now, Dad?* in 1989. The first genuine stand-up star to appear on a Perrier shortlist, however – and actually win the thing – was Sean Hughes in 1990.

Born in London in 1965, Hughes was raised in Dublin from the age of six, but after starting out in stand-up in his home city, he returned to London in the late '80s and began playing the circuit there. He was a regular visitor to the Fringe, often inviting the audiences at his ultra-low-key shows to the bar afterwards. In 1989, he and Stephen Frost took the conceptual stand-up piece *One Man and His Show* to the Gilded Balloon, a precursor to the following year's *A One Night Stand with Sean Hughes* at the same venue. This was less a straight stand-up show, more an exercise in storytelling, autobiography and surreal humour in the mould of The Goons, with Hughes exploring his past relationships with women and with his father.

Hughes – a Smiths and Morrissey obsessive – pitched the darkness and self-deprecating gloom perfectly for his young audience. When he won the Perrier that year, he was its youngest recipient yet at the age of 24. 'Sean was the only possible winner if the Perrier was to retain any credibility', wrote *The List*'s correspondent Philip Parr after the winner was announced at a ceremony at the 369 Gallery, beneath the Gilded Balloon, adding he believed the comedian was 'stretching the barriers of comedy.' [6]

Playing a version of himself in the show, a hungover, down-at-heel bedsit dweller with an overactive imagination who quotes Samuel Beckett and Morrissey, Hughes struck a chord with his audience. His Perrier win, the arrival of Vic Reeves and Bob Mortimer's *Vic Reeves' Big Night Out* on Channel 4 in the same year and the influence of American comedians like Bill Hicks and Denis Leary heralded a new, post-Thatcher era of British comedy, one that was less political, less indebted to the influence of either the Comedy Store or the history of Cambridge Footlights, but which found room to playfully pay tribute to what had gone before in its pursuit of the postmodern.

Before *The Mary Whitehouse Experience* arrived on television in 1991 and two of its stars David Baddiel and Robert Newman (both experienced student performers in Edinburgh) defined the 'comedy is the new rock 'n' roll' era by playing to 12,500 people at Wembley Arena in December 1993, Sean Hughes was the British Isles' first comic rock star of the 1990s. He was 'NME famous', moving into acting in Alan Parker's film *The Commitments* (1991) and television with his own surreal hit *Sean's Show* (1992). Such fame proved at odds with his personality, though, and he soon tired of playing arenas full of teenage fans.

Paying the bills as a team captain on panel show *Never Mind the Buzzcocks* and with acting gigs like *Coronation Street*, Hughes wrote novels and occasionally plays. His post-Perrier return to Edinburgh in 1991 was with the stand-up show *I Shouldn't Be Telling You This, But...* at the Gilded Balloon, but he and fellow Irish comic Owen O'Neill also brought the two-handed comedy play *Patrick's Day*, about two Irish barmen in London on the national holiday, which made fun of British interpretations of Irish culture. In 1999 the pair reunited at the Assembly Rooms for two short plays named *Dehydrated* and *Travellin' Light*, which again examined aspects of Irish culture and this time won them a Fringe First.

Before his early death in 2017 at the age of 51, Hughes had been back in stand-up for a decade, taking more autobiographical shows to the Fringe – for example, *Life Becomes Noises* at the Pleasance in 2012, which again discussed his father two years after his death. The writer Bruce Dessau, in his obituary of Hughes, described him as:

[O]ne of the most important figures in the evolution of modern long-form stand-up comedy. Until [he] won the Perrier award for best show, most alternative comedy shows at the Fringe were little more than extended comedy club sets, gags shamelessly stitched together. Hughes did something different, weaving a narrative into his performance.[7]

A new wave of young Irish comics also followed him to the Fringe, many of them veterans of Dublin's Comedy Cellar. Soon after his Perrier win came O'Neill and Jimeoin, then from 1994 the Gilded Balloon hosted an annual package show named *Young, Gifted and Green*, whose early stars included Ardal O'Hanlon, Andrew Maxwell and Ed Byrne. Raised in suburban Dublin, Byrne studied horticulture at the University of Strathclyde in Glasgow, where he tried out stand-up at the student union and started a club, also called the Comedy Cellar, at the 13th Note bar. Acts he booked there included Fringe regulars – as he was to become with great success – Phil Kay, Ford Kiernan and Greg Hemphill, as well as Armando Iannucci's brother David.

The idea that Sean Hughes was a fresh voice and an obvious winner amid the Perrier's 1990 shortlist was the reverse of the following year's award. This time, only one artist couldn't be counted as part of a new generation who would come to define British comedy and broadcasting in the next decade; the irony being that this performer – the American clown, magician and vaudevillian Avner 'the Eccentric' Eisenberg – was the only nominee who was at the time genuinely famous. He'd played his own show and in straight theatre on Broadway and in 1985 was the titular holy man of the hit film *The Jewel of the Nile*, playing alongside Michael Douglas and Kathleen Turner. As many international artists were coming to realise, he saw a successful Fringe run as his way into the British and European market.

Yet that defining Comedy Award shortlist of 1991, which Burns picked out as one of the finest, was very much about the breakthrough British artists it contained. From London came printer's son and Comedy Store newcomer Jack Dee, who had appeared in a two-handed stand-up show with Jenny Lecoat at the Assembly Rooms the previous year and who was now back with his own show. *The List* – somewhat prematurely, given the competition – declared the hangdog observational comedian probably the best stand-up of that year. The writer also got in what may have been a veiled dig at Hughes and the lure of playwrighting for stand-ups that year, or perhaps it was a reference to Arthur Smith's hit *An Evening with Gary Lineker* at the Assembly Rooms, in which five men gathered in a hotel room to watch the previous year's World Cup semi-final in Italy.

The third nominee was Eddie Izzard, a former drama student who was born in Yemen and raised in Northern Ireland and Wales. She had been performing a street escapology act across Europe – including on the Royal Mile during August – throughout the 1980s, until she became a Comedy Store comic in 1987.[8] In '89 and '90 she performed Fringe shows at Greyfriars Kirk House, serving her audience in the bar before the show. In 1991 her nominated show *Just the Words* at the Counting House pub on West Nicolson Street showed off her well-honed, esoteric observational delivery just two months after her appearance at the *Hysteria 3* benefit for the Terence Higgins Trust AIDS charity at London's Palladium made her name in comedy.

Lily Savage, meanwhile, was a veteran of the Fringe, of live performance and of the comedy circuit, although the latter had only come more recently. The drag queen alter-ego of former social work and care worker Paul O'Grady, who was born in 1955 and raised in Tranmere, Lily was a self-styled 'radical Marxist sex kitten', a sharp and lewd heckler's nightmare whose persona had been built over more than a decade in drag performance. Since 1978, O'Grady had played the gay pubs of London, appeared in fellow drag artist David Dale's show *If They'd Asked for a Lion Tamer* at Nica Burns' Donmar Warehouse and was part of drag groups including the Playgirls, the Glamazons and the Disapointer Sisters. He and Dale were also part of a trio named LSD (Lily, Sandra and Doris) which played the Edinburgh Fringe in 1983. From 1984 he began compering at pubs and clubs, which honed his act as Lily into full stand-up.

'By all accounts there was quite a lot of shagging going on in Edinburgh during those three weeks,' reminisced O'Grady of his and Lily's '91 visit to the city, making an observation of all the straight stand-ups around him. 'It didn't matter if you had all the appeal of a whelk with dysentery, if you were a male stand-up'.[9] He stayed in a flat off Broughton Street and performed *The Live Experience* at the Assembly Rooms' compact Wildman Room at midnight every night, by day taking on endless gimmicky photo opportunities. On the *Edinburgh Nights* television roundup show, he told host Tony Wilson that Lily and the celebrity madam Cynthia Payne – also promoting her own show – were operating a brothel somewhere in Leith.

'The Edinburgh Festival changed my life', wrote O'Grady later. 'The experience opened doors for me that would otherwise have been firmly closed'.[10] Even without winning the Perrier, Lily Savage returned for a sell-out run at the Assembly Rooms' Ballroom the year after and three sold-out shows at the Usher Hall in 1993. The winner of the award in '91, meanwhile, had only become a stand-up comedian in the first place because of the Fringe. Frank Skinner's first experience in Edinburgh during August was in a Halesowen College student production of Ron Hutchinson's play *Rat in the Skull* in 1987, in which he played a corrupt Met police officer.

Appearing under his birth name, Chris Collins, the 30-year-old from West Bromwich was an English lecturer with the college at the time and he took the part for a bit of fun. The play was a failure, averaging an audience of five people, but Collins soaked up the Fringe atmosphere otherwise. He later wrote that one of the most transformative experiences of his life and career was going to Ivor Dembina's late-night *12.12 Cabaret* at the Pleasance that year, which was his first-ever experience of alternative comedy. The main attraction that night was the post-Footlights double act Black and Baddiel, who made a huge impression on him, although he didn't talk to them. The next night he went to see Julian Clary as The Joan Collins Fanclub and revelled in being picked for a bit of onstage audience participation.

By the time he returned to Birmingham, Collins had already decided he was going to become a stand-up and soon afterwards he contacted the Coventry-based company Tic Toc to book a slot at the following year's Fringe. Unaware that beginner comedians usually start with 15 or 20-minute slots on group bills, then possibly a shared one-hour show with another comic, he booked a full hour at Calton Studios and spent a year learning stand-up. In the end, his show did worse than the previous year's play – its daily average attendance was only four people – but a couple of positive reviews and a good experience in the bearpit environment of the Fringe Club convinced him he'd found his calling.

Soon afterwards, while applying for Equity membership, he realised there was a northern English club singer named Chris Collins, so he became Frank Skinner, in honour a member of his dad's old pub dominoes team. His next run at the Fringe came in 1990, when he was asked to support a *Spitting Image* scriptwriter and budding stand-up named Steve Coogan at one of the Pleasance's upstairs rooms. The next year, in 1991, Skinner was back with his own full show at the Pleasance Cabaret Bar, the very same room where he'd witnessed Ivor Dembina's late-night show four years before and decided on his future career.

This show took to the stage in Edinburgh a few days after Skinner's first major television project aired, a short-lived Channel 4 sitcom with Jenny Eclair and Henry Normal named *Packet of Three* and for two weeks he lived with Denis Leary in what Skinner called 'the filthiest flat in Edinburgh', littered with the pair's pizza boxes and chip shop wrappers. For the final week Leary was replaced in the flat by David Baddiel, from that show of Dembina's in '87, who had been the American's support act. Here, he and Skinner cemented a friendship which led to the hit collaborative television shows *Fantasy Football League* and *Baddiel and Skinner Unplanned* between 1994 and 2005 and the enormously successful unofficial English footballing anthem 'Three Lions' in 1996, released with The Lightning Seeds to commemorate England hosting the Euro '96 tournament.

On the final Saturday night of the Fringe, Skinner's show ended with the Perrier team taking to the Pleasance stage and surprising him with the award. In a vintage year, he later recounted, what swung it for him was that his Fringe had been going so well that he jettisoned all his old jokes and dug out new ones from his vast bank of material. When the judges came back to all the shortlisted shows again to re-evaluate the nominees, what they got from Skinner was a whole new set that was just as good as the first.

* * *

During its first decade in existence, the Perrier had built a formidable reputation, but by 1991 it was now the single most important, career-shaping event in British comedy. For Steve Coogan, the comic who had invited Skinner to support him in 1990, his friend's win was also 'probably the most depressing point in my life'.[11] A fiercely competitive environment at the best of times, the effect of the Perrier nominations, especially in those days, was to guarantee full houses and media interest for all involved and to suck the momentum out of every other comedy show on the Fringe.

Despite being the nominal headliner the year before, reviewers had been lukewarm at best about Coogan in '90, while eagerly praising Skinner. Even Skinner agreed in his autobiography:

To be honest – and Steve is very open about this – I blew him off the stage most nights, which, in the end, I think was the best thing that ever happened to him.[12]

Noting that Coogan was 'a naturally funny bloke who would have me rolling around', Skinner suggested he was stuck in a rut picking up well-paid voiceover jobs and not focusing on his act.

Coogan didn't disagree, worrying he had become a bargain version of the incredibly popular and blandly mainstream impressionist Bobby Davro. Prior to his show with Skinner, he'd been to the Fringe in 1988 with a London Weekend Television showcase, then in '89 with Mike Hayley for a double-act show at the Playhouse Studio named *Seaside Special*, which received modest reviews. In *The List*'s review of that 1990 show with Skinner, though, Philip Parr noted that his character Duncan Thickett was an unfunny, nervous comic who forgets his lines – not too far from his estimation of Coogan. Skinner hid his copy under the sofa in their shared flat to spare Coogan's blushes, but he'd already seen it, picking up a copy one sunny blue morning in a newsagent by the Castle.

Professionally, Coogan knew something had to change. One day he had lunch with another young comic who was appearing at the Gilded Balloon, Patrick Marber, who he vaguely knew from television. Marber encouraged Coogan, telling him there was no great gulf between his work and Skinner's. The only difference was what Coogan already knew, that Skinner had worked harder. As the pair talked, they came to a similar realisation to the one reached by Rowan Atkinson and Richard Curtis more than a decade before; that Coogan wanted to be a performer, but Marber really wanted to be a writer. Bonding over 'a mutual discontent' was how Coogan piut it. The pair agreed to come back together with a great show in 1991.

As it turned out, Coogan's next show wasn't ready in time for the next Fringe. He watched Hughes win the Perrier with his first Edinburgh show, giving comedy on the Fringe a youthful, rock star aura, then his friend Skinner in '91, definitively leapfrogging him in terms of fame. That summer Coogan wasn't in Edinburgh, he was making money doing poolside gigs to holidaymakers on the island of Rhodes. He was pleased for Skinner, of course, but distraught for his own career. By the time the Fringe of '92 came around, things had improved. Keen to get out of the reductive box of being 'just' a good impressionist, an admittedly lucrative creative dead-end for others before him, Coogan had joined the cast of spoof Radio 4 news show *On the Hour*, led by Glaswegian BBC producer Armando Iannucci, with Marber also on the team.

The first episode aired during the Fringe of '91 and it ran for two series until May the following year. A favourite character on the show was Coogan's bullish but not very bright 'sports reporter' who, by the time of '92's Fringe, had just been recorded in a pilot episode for his own radio series to air before Christmas. A chat show featuring guests from the world of theatre, politics and 'emotional tragedy', *Knowing Me, Knowing You with Alan Partridge* was instigated by co-writer Marber and produced by Iannucci. The character eventually proved extraordinarily successful for them, especially Coogan, transferring to television with *On the Hour* spin-off *The Day Today* in 1994 and then *Knowing Me, Knowing You* later that year, the first of a series of onscreen outings for Partridge which continue to the present.

It's clear all concerned would have been successful anyway, but the Fringe of 1992 was a kind of symbolic fulcrum point in the British comedy story of that decade. Coogan had been raised in Lancashire in a comfortable working-class family, studying drama at Manchester Polytechnic and playing early stand-up gigs in support of his brother Martin's band the Mock Turtles, who had minor chart success in 1991 with the 'Madchester'-era hit 'Can You Dig It?'. Marber – who directed the show – was a firmly middle-class Londoner who studied at Oxford, and his perceived assurance and maturity in Coogan's eyes led him to become almost a mentee of Marber's.[13]

The third member of the group involved in their late-night show at the Gilded Balloon was John Thomson, a Lancastrian just like Coogan and a classmate of his at Manchester Polytechnic. As the title suggested, *In Character* was all about character comedy. Thomson compered as Bernard Righton, his politically correct version of Bernard Manning, who arrived onstage gravel-voiced with a cigarette in one hand, a pint of bitter in the other, subverting the style of old-fashioned gags with racist or misogynist punchlines by expressing his support for racial equality and women's rights.

Coogan, meanwhile, went with his dreadful stand-up from Fringes past, Duncan Thickett; fastidious handyman Ernest Moss; Alan Partridge, in his first appearance before a live audience; and Paul Calf, a drunken, thuggish Northern lad with a 1980s feathered haircut, who was to briefly become at least as big a star as Partridge in the beer-guzzling era of Britpop and *Loaded* magazine. It was an era that Coogan personally presaged during Edinburgh that year; he's written in the past about drinking heavily that August and first trying cocaine there, which led to hospitalisation with panic attacks. Incredibly, he still managed to do two runs of different shows in 1992, *In Character* and *The Dum Show* in the afternoon at the Pleasance. Despite a retrospectively dream line-up of Coogan, Marber, Stewart Lee, Richard Herring and Simon Munnery, the latter wasn't a hit.[14]

In Character was, though, and within a week Coogan and Thomson went from audiences of six or seven to full houses. When they won the Perrier, he felt vindicated after the previous years' setbacks:

I thought, 'They can say what the hell they like now. I don't care. I'm a Perrier winner'. It remains the most exciting award I've ever won in my life. More than any of the BAFTAs, although the Oscar nominations come close. You can go from zero to hero in four weeks in Edinburgh. it's like having a career in microcosm.[15]

* * *

There are many dozens of other stories that can be written about the winners and nominees of the Perrier Award in the first 20 years of its existence – even about 1992's shortlist itself, which featured hot favourite Jo Brand, Scottish comedian Bruce Morton, reliably enthusiastic political agitator Mark Thomas and character comic and inspiration to Coogan and Thomson Graham Fellows, in his alter-ego as nerdish folkie John Shuttleworth. The three years between 1990 and '92 changed the face of the Perrier and helped define the British comedy landscape for decades to come.

Hughes gave comedy a young, esoteric, largely apolitical appeal; Skinner used old-school technique to bring the alternative into the heart of the mainstream; Coogan married both extremes, his characters – especially Partridge – becoming subversive student favourites and edgy light entertainment staples all at once. In the mid-'90s John Thomson was arguably even more successful in this field, as one of the cast members of acclaimed sketch series *The Fast Show* between 1994 and '97, alongside comedy actors including Paul Whitehouse, Arabella Weir and the late Caroline Aherne.

Patrick Marber, meanwhile, moved quickly away from comedy and further into writing, as he'd always wanted to. His debut play *Dealer's Choice* appeared at the National Theatre in London in early 1995, winning Evening Standard and Writer's Guild awards for its depiction of gambling addiction, then touring to the Fringe Club during the Festival of 1996. In years since, he's won an Olivier Award for his 1997 play *Closer*, was nominated for an Academy Award for his screenplay to the 2006 film *Notes on a Scandal* and has directed plays by Tom Stoppard, Harold Pinter, Dennis Potter and David Mamet. He's attributed his foray into stand-up, most likely tongue-in-cheek, to 'bad luck'.

Throughout the rest of the 1990s other big stars including Lee Evans and Bill Bailey were a part of the Perrier, while another vintage year to match 1991 came in '97. That year Graham Norton, Johnny Vegas, 'pub landlord' Al Murray and Milton Jones were all shortlisted, although the winners were The League of Gentlemen with their second show in two years at the Pleasance, a character comedy which made Coogan and Thomson's work look almost rudimentary.

Featuring inbred shopkeepers and other weird denizens of the imaginary rural English town of Royston Vasey, Mark Gatiss, Steve Pemberton and Reece Shearsmith (and co-writer Jeremy Dyson) created a detailed, in-depth world for their characters, which transferred to television on BBC 2 between 1999 and 2002 and then a feature film in 2005.[16]

The trend for character comedy started by Coogan and Thomson and developed by The League was taken further by 1999 nominees *The Arctic Boosh*, who had won the Perrier Best Newcomer award the previous year for their debut show *The Mighty Boosh*. Founded by comedians Noel Fielding and Julian Barratt, who met at a comedy club in High Wycombe, Buckinghamshire, the Boosh had previously appeared on the Fringe in Stewart Lee's 1997 solo show at the Pleasance *King Dong vs Moby Dick*. Partially about Lee apparently being forbidden by the Fringe Society from putting an erect penis on his flyer, Fielding and Barratt played the titular penis and whale, respectively.

Introducing the pair's eccentric zookeepers Howard Moon and Vince Noir, with Rich Fulcher as their boss Bob Fossil, 1998's *The Mighty Boosh* was directed by Cal McCrystal, who previously performed with French master clown Phillipe Gaulier in his show *The End of the Tunnel* at the Assembly Rooms in 1991 and directed the physical theatre company Peepolykus' breakthrough hit *Let the Donkey Go* in 1996 at the Pleasance. In '98 at the same venue, he directed both the *Boosh* and Cambridge Footlights' *Between a Rock and a Hard Place*, starring Richard Ayoade, Matthew Holness and John Oliver. In 1999, Stewart Lee directed *Arctic Boosh*, featuring the cast as postmen on the frozen tundra.

In 2000, the final part of the trilogy, the motor-themed *AutoBoosh*, arrived in Edinburgh, and from there Fielding and Barratt won a commission for a 2001 BBC radio show, which led to the hit BBC Three television version of *The Mighty Boosh* in 2004. The same year, Fielding was Perrier-nominated for his solo show *Voodoo Hedgehog*. Meanwhile, Holness and Ayoade had taken up the character comedy baton at the Fringe with their horror author Garth Marenghi and his assistant Dean Learner, Perrier-nominated for *Fright Knight* at the Pleasance in 2000 and winners with *Netherhead* in 2001. This show also transferred to television and two decades on Ayoade, like Fielding, is one of Britain's most successful mainstream television personalities.

Other veterans of the Perrier's golden years include 1995 winner Jenny Eclair for her show *Prozac and Tantrums*, a bawdy examination of sex and unfulfilled ambition from the perspective of a 30-something mother. A former Manchester Polytechnic student who graduated several years before Coogan and Thomson, this was Eclair's 12th year at the Fringe. Her career had already evolved to the big stages after making a name for herself on the

London cabaret circuit, but it hadn't gone unnoticed at the time how male-dominated the British comedy industry was. Eclair was the first solo female winner of the Perrier.

In 1996, the winner was Irishman Dylan Moran, who started out at the Comedy Cellar in Dublin in 1992 and won the Gilded Balloon's *So You Think You're Funny?* in 1993. He skipped '94's Fringe and returned with the well-received *Selected Drivel* at the Pleasance in '95, cementing his reputation as a blend of Oscar Wilde and the great comedian Dave Allen, following in the footsteps of Sean Hughes with the Perrier-winning *Dylan Moran is Indisposed* at the same venue in '96.[17] In the late 1990s he and his Scottish wife settled permanently in Edinburgh's leafy Bruntsfield area, at the West End of the Meadows, and he's been a regular at the Fringe ever since, most recently with *Dr Cosmos* at the Stand in 2018, with which he discussed becoming teetotal.

Executive-produced by Assembly's William Burdett-Coutts, who paired Moran with co-creator and fellow Irishman Graham Linehan, Moran's Channel 4 sitcom *Black Books* co-starred Fringe veteran Bill Bailey and gained a cult following during a run which lasted from 2000 until 2004. Although the story of Moran's misanthropic independent bookseller Bernard Black was set in London, it's believed to have been inspired by the bookshops of Edinburgh, primarily the maze-like antiquarian stores of West Port and the idiosyncratic Deadhead Comics, formerly on Candlemaker Row.

In 1992 the first Perrier Best Newcomer Award was surprise-announced moments after Coogan won the main award and it went to Harry Hill, who had been at the Fringe Club the year before in a joint show alongside impressionist Alistair McGowan named *When Harry Met Ally*. This time he had a typically eccentric solo show at the same venue named *Flies!*. Hill's sparse crowds had been boosted by a *Guardian* review from William Cook which hailed him as the future of comedy, and the win led to his breakthrough BBC Radio 4 show *Harry Hill's Fruit Corner* in '93.

Hill wasn't a fan of the competitive Fringe atmosphere though, especially around the buzzing Gilded Balloon bar on the Cowgate:

> It wasn't a particularly nice place to be unless you were plastered. There was a lot of anger in that bar; a lot of comics up against it with mixed reviews of their shows, poor audience numbers, money worries and, as if to compound it, everyone knew how everyone else was doing.[18]

This was in the days, he says, before Fringe reviews had been 'dumbed down' by star ratings, so everyone read every cutting comment made at the expense of their fellow comics.

As well as his own show in 1992, Hill was also appearing in a package show at the Pleasance named *The Comedy Zone*, whose roster included fellow beginner Al Murray, who at this point was in Edinburgh with a character act in which he was a gentlemanly serial killer. In 1994, Hill's Perrier-nominated Fringe show was *Pub Internationale*, a celebration of the Great British pub and it co-starred Murray in the persona that was to make his name, Al Murray the Pub Landlord, a self-described divine idiot, with the most knuckle-headedly simple answer to every problem.

In Edinburgh during the 1990s, Murray was to develop an 'always the bridesmaid' reputation as far as the Perrier was concerned. He was nominated for *The Pub Landlord's Lock-In* (1996), *King of Beers* (1997) and *Pub Landlord's Keeper of the Pint Cosmic* (1999) and by '99 it looked like his chance had gone. In '98 he was apparently offered a spurious 'best loser ever' prize, which he declined and the following year word got out he'd been excluded from Perrier contention, apparently as he had become famous under his own steam and was already playing decent-sized gigs in London.

A furore erupted and it was pointed out that Jenny Eclair had won and Johnny Vegas had been nominated with at least comparable levels of existing fame. Murray's promoters, Avalon, put out a statement asking that he be reinstated and a hasty backtrack was performed. Under a blizzard of good reviews *And a Glass of White Wine for the Lady...* finally won Murray the award that year.

While the Perrier lists have had a massive effect on British comedy, particularly in the 1990s, it's important to make clear that a huge amount of interesting work – often of the more esoteric variety, sometimes that which is just especially rough and ready – happens outside of it every year in Edinburgh. Rob Newman, one of the highest-profile comedians of the day to be bypassed by the Perrier, used the words 'a Sunday supplement idea of what comedy is' to describe it:

> The list of people who Edinburgh's missed... reads like a roll call of
> what's happened in comedy. The Assembly Rooms bar thinks it's
> at the hub of things – it's like some bizarre Graham Greene novel.
> They think they're having an effect on things but they're not –
> they're just talking to themselves.[19]

The Award's biggest headlines in the 2000s, and the biggest dent to its credibility since its inception, would come around partly due to Newman's influence.

11

The Rise of the Stand-Up While Edinburgh Rebuilds

AROUND THE SAME time the Gilded Balloon was making its way to the Cowgate, the Comedy Boom had the same idea – to start a club on the Edinburgh Fringe for stand-up comedians alone. The idea was hatched by two promoters from London who, up until this point, had been local rivals: a 30-something stand-up, named Ivor Dembina and Addison Cresswell, son of the dean of arts at Goldsmiths College in London.

A decade younger than Dembina, Cresswell was not long graduated from a course in graphic design at his home city's Brighton Polytechnic, where he cut his teeth as entertainments officer at the student union. He had already dabbled in comedy management, beginning with the Comedy Store regular, performance poet, busker and John Peel Session veteran (with his band the Popticians), John Hegley. Cresswell was as influenced by the music business as comedy, and Dembina later remarked that he saw himself as a Brian Epstein figure to his stable of comedians' Beatles.

Cresswell had brought comedians to Edinburgh, including Tony Allen in 1982 – at the same time his brother Luke was also introducing his band Pookiesnackenburger to the Fringe – but he wanted to find his own reliable, affordable venue for them and he asked Dembina how he managed to find places to play in London. The answer was simple: Dembina just walked around and when he saw someplace he liked, he went in and asked. On the spur of the moment, the pair got on a train to Edinburgh and resolved to walk around and ask until they found a venue for the next Fringe.

The pair trudged through the snow, Dembina later recounted to writer Ben Venables of *The Skinny*. Reaching the junction of Broughton Street and Picardy Place, where the city centre begins to bleed into Leith, they found a traditional bar named the Abercraig at 2 Picardy Place, where the landlord eyed them suspiciously. When they saw the pub's snug, compact basement room, however, they knew they had to have it. One placated landlord later, they had the room which would become the Comedy Boom.

From the Comedy Boom's opening year in Edinburgh[1] it attracted a loyal bunch of regular performers, including Cresswell's old accomplice Tony Allen; prolific future radio comedian, the late Linda Smith; Sheffield poet Mark 'Miwurdz' Hurst; 'Marxist magician' Ian Saville; the groups Skint Video and Sensible Footwear; and the already-notorious Jerry (then 'Gerry') Sadowitz. One of the first acts to appear was named the Joan Collins Fan

Club, an inspired double-act featuring an actual canine named Fanny the Wonder Dog, whose schtick involved being dressed in cute outfits by her accomplice, a gay man from Teddington in bondage leathers and dazzlingly bright make-up, who took the art of sexual innuendo to new and creatively hilarious heights. He had started out in comedy not long before under the pseudonym Gillian Pieface, but now he went by his own name, Julian Clary.

Performing in the Abercraig's snug room underneath the chip shop at the top of Broughton Street, Clary stayed in a room at a vicarage for his first Fringe. His dressing room was the pub's disused kitchen, his make-up table the stove. One night he tore his rubber shorts onstage, earning a particularly big laugh. A Scot in the audience named Michael Ferri offered to mend them with a bicycle repair kit. It turned out Ferri was about to begin studying at the London School of Fashion, and he became Clary's costume designer for a number of years afterwards.

Soon after its inception, writer Tristan Davies described the Comedy Boom as:

> One of the best venues on the Fringe, best encapsulating the cellar
> bar sleaze that makes you feel as though you're living at least
> as dangerously as the performers would have you believe they
> are. Packed in shoulder to shoulder, it is almost considered good
> manners to spill your drink over the huddled figures that block your
> way to the toilets.[2]

The venue was a brief but exciting chapter in the Fringe's comedy history and it came to an end largely because all involved were getting too big for it.

Clary, with Fanny now in retirement,[3] moved on to the Assembly Rooms and eventual fame on television and as one of the 1990s' most successful British stand-up comedians. Dembina introduced some of the Pleasance's earliest stand-up shows with his late-night *Comic Abuse* strand, which featured Dave Cohen, Felix Dexter and Phil Cornwell in its first edition in '87; later guests including Jo Brand, Mark Thomas, Jim Tavare and a young Patrick Marber. In 1994, Dembina founded the Hampstead Comedy Club in North London and in recent years has continued to make Edinburgh appearances on the Free Fringe.

Dembina's modest success as a stand-up and promoter stands in contrast to that of Addison Cresswell, who was always bound for bigger and better things. Julian Clary wrote of Cresswell:

> He presented himself as a Jack the Lad, not to be messed with,
> affecting a rough south London accent. A year younger than me,

he had blonde hair and angular good looks. He swaggered around, prodded you in the chest with his pointed finger and had the habit of sometimes staring at your throat when talking to you... his bluster and machismo (was) clearly a beard for a sensitive, insecure soul who simply wanted to be loved.[4]

In his university days, Cresswell had run a bare-bones student union club in Brighton named the Basement, where early-fame bands like U2, New Order and Echo and the Bunnymen played. By the late '80s he owned a comedy promotions club named Off the Kerb, first out of his own basement flat front room and then from what Clary described as a converted old bakery in Peckham. One of his earliest clients was Clary, who he spotted at one of Dembina's gigs in a pub in King's Cross, but his roster soon filled up with many of the soon-to-be biggest artists of the day. Among them was Jo Brand, Jack Dee and Lee Evans, who Cresswell first saw supporting Craig Ferguson at the Assembly Rooms in Edinburgh.

He made them all famous, as he later did with Michael McIntyre, Alan Carr, Kevin Bridges, Rich Hall, Paul Merton and others. Off the Kerb had many connections across the country, in live performance and eventually television booking and production, but it was their foothold in Edinburgh as the 1990s began which altered the landscape of the Fringe even further. The company helped make it a laboratory for live comedy, both for raw beginners to try and get noticed by a manager, and for comedians who had already signed with management to show off their best, newest material and hope that modest stand-up fame might translate into television stardom, as it did for many of Cresswell's clients.

He wasn't alone. Founded in 1989 and arriving just in time for the next phase of comedy development in Edinburgh in the 1990s was Avalon Entertainment, a company co-created by Jon Thoday and Richard Allen-Turner, which recognised at the same time as Cresswell's Off the Kerb that the energy created by young comedians drawn all at once to the growing fraternity of an Edinburgh August could be harnessed as an even more effective promotional force than the buzz surrounding the Comedy Store had been a decade before.[5] Allen-Turner had been entertainments manager at East London Polytechnic when he met the irrepressible Thoday, the son of a Cambridge University evolutionary scientist, whose unlikely training for comedy promotion included an MSc in Biotechnology and Genetic Engineering from University College London.

A fan of comedy and musicals when he was younger, the supremely confident Thoday had been fascinated by the life of an impresario and had even asked Cameron Mackintosh for an apprenticeship when he was a student. He tried first of all to become a musical theatre producer, but the work he created failed. Soon after, Thoday took on his first clients – composers and performers of comedy songs including Steve Brown, who wrote for the BBC radio show *Radio Active* and later for television shows by Steve Coogan and Harry Hill and Richard Thomas, later the Oliver Award-winning co-writer of the Edinburgh-debuted *Jerry Springer: The Opera* with Stewart Lee.

When he couldn't get them regular work on television, Thoday instead booked his clients into live student union gigs, which went extraordinarily well and proved the appetite for more. Among Avalon's very first clients were the comedian David Baddiel, signed at the end of the Edinburgh Festival on 11 September 1989 and his roster ballooned from there, especially among the artists who won the Perrier Award in the years which immediately followed and were groomed for television success.

Live comedy promotion was hardly a new thing at the end of the 1980s, but what marked Thoday and Cresswell out in particular was their youth and hunger, often to an extent which thoroughly rubbed those they represented their clients to the wrong way. They were making space for a new generation of promoters – themselves – and of comedians and the Edinburgh Festival had known nothing like the level of vigorous promotion they brought upon the city. Fly-posters went up everywhere, flyers loaded the shelves of every bar and previous claims going back to the turn of the 1980s that the Edinburgh Fringe had surely already saturated the city began to look weak.

At the 1987 General Election, Addison Cresswell had organised the comedy leg of the national, Labour-supporting Red Wedge movement, featuring a bunch of big names and Edinburgh regulars including Clary, Ben Elton, Lenny Henry, Craig Charles, Robbie Coltrane, Phill Jupitus, Harry Enfield and Mark Miwurdz. The mission wasn't an electoral success, with all but one seat they targeted lost. After that, said Cresswell, he became a capitalist and got on with it.

Comedy followed suit. Not least in Edinburgh.

* * *

Into and from the leading names in comedy on the Fringe – the Assembly Rooms, the Pleasance and the Gilded Balloon – Avalon and Off the Kerb booked and hungrily sourced an ever-growing range of young talent, aware that the entire entertainment industry – especially delegates at the Television Festival, then a stone's throw from the Assembly Rooms at the George Hotel – would be in town and keen to see new talent.

Once the home of quirky variety and experimental work, the Perrier

Award was by now proven as the place to find the next biggest name in British stand-up. We've seen how its emphasis shifted at the turn of the 1990s, honouring a straight run of six increasingly big stand-up names in Jeremy Hardy, Simon Fanshawe, Sean Hughes, Frank Skinner, Steve Coogan and Lee Evans. Where Fringe exposure during the 1980s meant a gig on a BBC Radio 4 show or possibly a Channel 4 appearance on *Saturday Live*, the relentless savvy of Avalon and Off the Kerb meant these comedians – and others like them, who made it as far as the Perrier shortlist or the Best Newcomer award – led to the gap between a Fringe appearance and widespread television exposure narrowing.

The Pleasance's Christopher Richardson sums up the attitude that has prevailed for Fringe performers and promoters for 75 years, but which particularly flourished at the turn of the '90s. 'If you ask them, they say (their first Fringe) was disastrous, we shouldn't have done it, we should never do it again, and then you find they go on doing it and become famous. And quite rich, some of them. Look at Avalon, they're probably quite rich now'. He bonded with John Thoday. 'We used to have dinner from time to time when nobody would talk to us, both of us were thought to be rather difficult and therefore not quite the Edinburgh scene. He had people like Frank Skinner and I had the means to put him on'. Their friendship brought the Pleasance many of the best emerging comedians of the decade.

Another great Pleasance success was the artist originally known as Mother Theresa, aka Graham Norton, a complete unknown from Ireland and a graduate of the Central School of Speech and Drama in London, who turned up at the Pleasance courtyard in 1992 dressed in the robes of Mother Theresa of Calcutta, promoting his show about the religious figure's 'farewell tour'. His costume caught the press's attention, at least and he gained experience with *The Karen Carpenter Bar and Grill* (1993) and *Charlie's Angels Go to Hell* (1994), before a 1995 capacity upgrade to the Assembly Rooms in 1995 under his own name. Now he's the nation's leading chat show presenter and the host of the Eurovision Song Contest, making him one of the most powerful figures in British media.

After ten years of no profits, things began to pick up for the Pleasance in the 1990s. In '94, the Pleasance Theatre Trust was founded and in '95, the Off-West End Pleasance Islington theatre was established in London, for post-Fringe transfers and its own year-round programme. In 2000 Richardson was invited by Edinburgh University Students Association to take over the Potterrow Student Centre as a Fringe venue, with a bar in the centre's open, glass-ceilinged courtyard and a number of versatile spaces inside. Set in the new building on the site of the old Pollock Memorial Hall in 1973, this new venue was renamed Pleasance Dome for the month, while the old complex officially became Pleasance Courtyard. Around the same time, the organisation also gained use of the student sports hall at the Courtyard, double the capacity of the Pleasance One theatre at 750 seats. They now had more than 20 spaces between both venues, ranging from capacities of 48 to 750.

Line-ups for benefit gigs of the time gave an impression of the acts who were either breaking through or defining each Fringe. The *Night for Nicaragua* at the Playhouse in 1990 featured Steve Coogan, Sean Hughes, Jenny Eclair, Jo Brand, Mark Thomas, Stu Who?, Patrick Marber and Henry Normal. The AIDS benefit *Live and Lubricated* at the same venue in '91 had Jack Dee, Eddie Izzard, Sean Hughes, John Hegley, Dillie Keane and Bill Hicks, compered by Clive Anderson. With its position secured as the place to find the best of British comedy – all of British comedy, in fact – under several closely-located roofs and tented structures, Edinburgh was now going international. The extremely hotly tipped Hicks was at the vanguard of a new wave of American comics making their way to Edinburgh, bringing his set *Dangerous* to a tent on the Meadows co-created by the Assembly Rooms and Wildcat Theatre in 1991.

In fact, Hicks had been beaten to Edinburgh by a year, when the Irish-American sometime actor Denis Leary brought his show *No Cure for Cancer* to the Assembly Rooms in 1990. Both artists had developed remarkably similar sets which circled subjects like the first Gulf War, drug and policing policy, borderline conspiracy theorising about the nefarious activities of those at the highest levels of power and an outspoken joy in smoking cigarettes which seems anachronistic now. He told *The List*:

> If you're not smoking and you're eating supposedly correct food, you're still gonna have to deal with polluted riverways and ozone and the sky falling down on you. I'm just saying face up to it and take it into your own hands, start smoking and eating mad cow beef. Develop your own cancer rather than letting the government bring it to ya.[6]

The pair's quick-witted libertarianism caught some kind of mood of the times. Bombs started falling in the Middle East, while the entirely unexpected fall of the Berlin Wall was mere months away from Leary's debut. In retrospect, it was the Texan Hicks' blend of bear-like, friendly enthusiasm and raw, barely-suppressed fury that left him a lasting legacy, although perhaps his untimely death of pancreatic cancer aged just 32 in 1994 – despite Leary being the one to court the disease in the title of his show – has contributed to a legendary status to rival that of Lenny Bruce.

More transatlantic comedians arrived and – although the very white, male

British comedy environment had only a passing association with diversity, despite its avowedly right-on nature – a 1993 show at the Pleasance titled *Stand Up Black America* featured Renee Hicks, Suli McCullough and Ian Edwards. The same year a show named *The Adventures of Trick Whiteyman* appeared at the Assembly Rooms, the work of a 19-year-old from Washington DC named Dave Chappelle, who had once been booed off stage at the Harlem Apollo but bounced back and hit public recognition on the HBO show *Def Comedy Jam* the year before he came to the Fringe. His set included the unsurprising observation, 'where are all the black people in Edinburgh?'

At the Gilded Balloon, Karen Koren foregrounded what female comedians she could find, which included some of the biggest names of the day. The programme for 1990's Fringe highlighted Jo Brand with support from Patrick Marber alongside fellow headliners Mark Steel, Stu Who? and Mark Hurst. Elsewhere on the bill was *30 Somehow*, a group show featuring Jenny Eclair, Julie Baloo and the pseudonymous Maria Callous, aka future regular on television's *The Fast Show* and her friend Graham Norton's various broadcast endeavours, Maria McErlane.

Eclair had appeared at the Gilded Balloon as far back as 1987, at Late 'n' Live, the same year she gigged at the Traverse and Helen Lederer also did a run at the Balloon. By 1993, Koren was booking the up-and-coming Donna McPhail, while Lederer had moved on to the Assembly Rooms and Eclair – the first solo woman to win the Perrier in 1995 – was at the Pleasance. 'I'm pleased more women are performing at last,' says Koren in the present day. 'That's taken a long time, but I've always been supporting women'. In later years, Caroline Aherne also played her venue.

In 1990, the Balloon hosted the eventual Perrier-winning show *A One-Night Stand with Sean Hughes,* putting him for a brief time at the vanguard of the early '90s movement Janet Street-Porter was describing when she said 'comedy is the new rock 'n' roll'.[7] Hughes' reward was a move up to George Square Theatre and cult 1992 television success, although every British comedian of this period was thoroughly overshadowed by David Baddiel and Rob Newman's unprecedented *Live and in Pieces* tour date at the 12,000-capacity Wembley Arena in 1993, setting a genuine precedent for comedy as a business on a par with rock music.

Although the pair made their names alongside fellow Cambridge graduates and former Footlights[8] Steve Punt and Hugh Dennis as part of the radio and television sketch show *The Mary Whitehouse Experience*, which ran from 1989 until 1992, they cut their teeth at the Fringe. In 1987 Baddiel appeared as part of a double-double-act, the uncatchily titled Black and Baddiel/The Two Marks at Theatre ACT on Broughton Street, while Newman turned up as a solo impersonator in 1989 and '90.

Between the exposure of *The Mary Whitehouse Experience*, his impersonations for the *Steve Wright in the Afternoon* show on Radio 1 and his sketch-writing for *Spitting Image* and Harry Enfield, Newman was seen as almost too self-consciously aimed at youth audiences, a long distance from the novelist and intellectual renaissance man he later became. In the 2000s, he lobbied against Nestle's involvement in the Perrier Award and staged lower-key Fringe shows with activist roots like *From Caliban to Taliban* and *Apocalypso Now, or From P45 to AK47: How to Grow the Economy with the Use of War*. In the meantime, Baddiel and Frank Skinner first performed together on the same Fringe bill at George Square Theatre in 1991.

If the Fringe had become the centre of the UK comedy industry, then the Gilded Balloon was by this point its anarchic heart and *Late 'n' Live* was the aorta, a no-holds-barred bearpit and a rite of passage for every comedian with any ambition to count themselves among the Fringe's best. Beginning after midnight and with a late licence which stretched until 4am – an exciting Fringe novelty in those days – and most recently all the way until 5am, much of the audience would be dependably leathered by the time it got started. So, in fact, would many of the performers. Karen Koren laughs as she remembers, for example, outrageous Canadian comic troupe The Nasty Show being overshadowed in their hammered nudity by a female Australian circus artist who downed a pint of beer and peed in a glass on the stage while hanging from the scaffolding, to everyone in the room's nauseated astonishment.

Then there was the big-name comedian who used an empty tube of Pringles as an impromptu toilet before he went on. Despite such stories, though, Koren says these competitively outrageous nights in Wilkie House, often played out to the soundtrack of Bill Bailey's punk band Beergut 100, were an exercise in pure comedy discovery, rather than just an excuse to drink. These days, with the Gilded Balloon long-gone from the Cowgate, she says the late-night atmosphere on this bustling booze trap of a street is now 'sinister'. 'It was rough and ready, but it was harmless,' she says of *Late 'n' Live*. 'There wasn't anybody fighting each other, and to see all those guys onstage was brilliant.' Widely-famous names like Lenny Henry and Jo Brand tried their luck, the audience baying like the hordes of a Roman Coliseum, anticipating death or glory on a stage with no hiding place.

In those days, Steve Coogan shared his dressing room with the bar's spare beer barrels in '91, *Father Ted* star Ardal O'Hanlon fretted about not having done a lot of stand-up before he arrived in Edinburgh with big telly popularity in tow ('But he was fantastic and he did great,' says Koren) and Eddie Izzard spent three festivals at the Gilded Balloon, after first turning up at Greyfriars Kirk House in 1989. During the 1990s, Koren also began attending the big Australian comedy festivals and putting on a lot of the artists she saw in the UK. One of these was Adam Hills, a comic who she notes for his hard work in turning a tiny, disinterested audience into a significant following and eventually present-day stardom on Channel 4.

The other aspect of the Gilded Balloon's legend is the annual *So You Think You're Funny?* contest, which invites genuinely new stand-ups to try their luck. The format was actually devised by comic Simon Fanshawe for Glasgow's Mayfest in 1988. Koren was a judge for the first edition and afterwards she asked William Burdett-Coutts – then in charge of Mayfest, as well as the Assembly Rooms – if she could use the format at the Gilded Balloon that year. The rules have remained largely unchanged since then, with contestants permitted to have played no more than 15 gigs and none before the previous summer. If the contestant has ever performed or planned to perform an Edinburgh Fringe show, they entry information says, they're probably too experienced.

Among comedians, the Perrier (now the Edinburgh Comedy Award) is the contest for professionals and *So You Think You're Funny?* is for genuine newcomers and amateurs. As such, the range of talent it's discovered from scratch is truly incredible, from current Edinburgh and Gilded Balloon veteran Fred MacAulay at its Glasgow edition, to the debut winner Bruce Morton. Phil Kay, Rhona Cameron and Tommy Tiernan were among the early winners and future national treasure Peter Kay won it in 1997, going on to pick up a Perrier nomination the year after.

With a fiercely difficult and competitive selection process involving national heats, the contest – which was sponsored by Channel 4 from 1993 until 2004 – has had whole shortlists full of future stars, sometimes with surprising results. In 2002, the largely unknown Matthew Osborn beat Mark Watson, Nina Conti, Greg Davies, Rhod Gilbert, Rufus Hound and Greg McHugh. In 2005, the reasonably successful Tom Allen won out over future superstars Sarah Millican and Kevin Bridges. Both Lee Mack and Jason Byrne have spoken of the contest as the most thrilling and important thing they did in their careers.

'Culturally we were like the Left Bank,' says Koren of the Gilded Balloon's unique place in the comedy ecology of the Edinburgh Fringe and the national industry, during the 1990s and 2000s especially. Expansion was inevitable. The closure of 369 Gallery during the recession of the early 1990s saw it converted into the year-round bar and restaurant the Gilded Saloon. The original Gilded Balloon Studio space expanded into the buildings around it.

I moved across to the nightclub in Blair Street, and there was a homeless shelter across the road that we did four or five venues in. We started with the original Studio theatre and ended up with 14 venues in the late '90s. It just grew so quickly – from the late '80s and early '90s onwards, kids wanted to be a stand-up comedian rather than a pop star.

Others took notice of the Gilded Balloon's sterling reputation, namely William Burdett-Coutts and Christopher Richardson. On the last day of 1992's festival, they approached Koren and asked if she'd like to collaborate on their Fringe offering the following year, sharing brochures and marketing. Complaints about the Fringe's size had been ongoing since 1959, but this time the planned actions of the Big Three were viewed as threatening to overpower the democratic, free market nature of the Fringe, for better or worse.

Wider changes were happening in society throughout the 1990s. Tony Blair's New Labour government was on its way and with it Scottish devolution, a new Parliament in Edinburgh and eventually an arts strategy for the country. The Edinburgh Fringe had become an island of the British comedy industry in August, but the Edinburgh Festival's future has never been divisible from the city and the society around it.

* * *

The end of Frank Dunlop's reign at the International Festival brought the beginnings of real, long-needed change to the cultural landscape of Edinburgh after many decades. In the wake of the Glasgow Garden Festival of 1988, the hugely successful and well-publicised regeneration project that Michael Dale had left the Fringe for, Glasgow had woken up to the idea of cultural capital as a selling point ahead of many other cities in the UK. It had attracted 4.3 million visitors across five months – a number close to the entire population of Scotland – and was by far the most popular of the Garden Festivals.

Since 1983, the Mayfest festival had also been a fixture of Glasgow's spring arts calendar, having evolved out of trade union events going right back to the Clyde Fair International that spawned The Great Northern Welly Boot Show in '72. Mayfest was on its way to becoming the second-largest arts festival in the UK, until it closed after its funding was revoked in 1997. I found Glasgow a very different city to Edinburgh,' says Burdett-Coutts, who ran Mayfest between 1988 and 1990.

I loved the fact the council were so supportive there, whereas in Edinburgh I've always felt there was a kind of semi-reluctance. We happened despite the council in Edinburgh, really. I'd been given support to get the Assembly Rooms, but you never really got the sense that the councillors were behind you. Whereas in Glasgow, I'd be in there with the leader of the council, they wanted to make things happen. I think there was a great sense of pride in Glasgow, about the city and what it was doing, and an impetus to support community work around the city.

In 1990, Glasgow was awarded the title of European City of Culture, a move which had an extraordinary regenerative and PR effect on the city and its cultural scene. Edinburgh watched enviously and a little fearfully from afar, wondering if the place of its Festivals – way out in front in terms of Scotland's cultural recognition – was about to be usurped. As the new decade approached, even Lothian Region Transport buses had adverts featuring Glasgow's smiley Mr Men character alongside the city's cheerful new slogan 'Glasgow Smiles Better' on their sides. Someone in Edinburgh started making car stickers which read 'Edinburgh's Slightly Superior'.

With both the Festival and the City of Culture year beginning in August that year, *The Guardian* ran a profile of the Festival that noted the city of Edinburgh's serious problems with levels of HIV infection and heroin addiction in its unseen suburban council estates, beneath the wider image of a city 'whose riches in terms of banking, insurance and financial services are believed to rank in Europe below only those of London and Zurich.' In the same article, the great and good of the Fringe lambasted their city.

'It's hopeless,' said Burdett-Coutts of any attempt to extract municipal funding, compared to the helpful local politicians he found in Glasgow. 'All talk, no action. Edinburgh's so complacent.'

'The district council are a load of wankers,' steamed in 369 Gallery's Andrew Brown. 'I hate them.'[9]

Yet the example of Glasgow seemed to be spurring Edinburgh's pursestring holders into some sort of action, especially as they'd missed the boat in either bidding for European City of Culture 1990 or exploring a joint bid alongside Glasgow, after Dunlop had suggested both options back in '86. Ahead of 1990's EIF, the Festival Council instead approved a budget for the next three years, an unprecedented step that allowed some real planning to happen. The news also came that the tired Lyceum Theatre was to have £3.5 million pound spent on a revamp of the backstage area and a new, glass-fronted foyer. Buoyed, Frank Dunlop adapted and directed his own version of *Treasure Island* at the Assembly Hall, starring Peter Duncan and David Harewood, to commemorate 100 years since Robert Louis Stevenson arrived in Samoa.

Edinburgh still didn't have a world-class opera house, though, as companies and commentators endlessly remarked. Plans to develop the

Playhouse were derailed when the operators Apollo Leisure insisted on maintaining control after a publicly-funded refurbishment, while visions of building on a site at Victoria Docks in Leith were a non-starter. But circumstances finally changed when Dunlop, quite by coincidence, found himself sitting next to the head of Mecca Bingo at an event in London. With customary boldness, he asked to know about the grand Edinburgh theatre which the company was using as a bingo hall.

The theatre in question was the Empire on Nicholson Street, which already had an illustrious International Festival history, despite its specifications being less than adequate. There had been a theatre on the site since 1830, which saw use as a music hall, cinema and circus until its third destruction by fire in 1911, when the illusionist the Great Lafayette and ten of his company perished. The grand new Edwardian auditorium as it exists today was rebuilt to some of the original 1892 plans of designer Frank Matcham, who later created London's Hippodrome, Coliseum, Palladium and Hackney Empire theatres.

During the first 15 years of the International Festival the Empire hosted the Old Vic, Royal Ballet and Royal Opera, as well as regular-season variety appearances by Laurel and Hardy, Charles Laughton, Fats Waller and Morecambe and Wise. Falling out of use as a Festival venue in the 1960s, it became more well-known for hosting late-night gigs by musicians including David Bowie, T-Rex and Emerson, Lake and Palmer in the 1970s, before bingo took over. Dunlop's prodding was successful and after a period of negotiation the council purchased the building from a willing Mecca for £2.6 million in 1991.

The International Festival's director wasn't around to see the plan come to fruition, though. Aware that some on the Festival Council wanted to get rid of him, he still believed that the regeneration of the Empire would allow EIF to move out of its unsuitable former *Edinburgh Evening News* office on Market Street and make the new theatre their permanent home. He was under the impression, in fact, that he might take over the running of the new theatre, whether that job was part of remaining the International Festival's director or not. Not only did this not happen, but the office move didn't even take place.

The wheels came off in 1991. Dunlop had already decided to leave, when a planned production of *Peter Pan* directed by Bill Bryden fell through and had to be replaced by a hastily assembled and ultimately commercially unsuccessful rework of *The Three Estates*. He had also made some choice comments about the standard of theatre on the Fringe at a mid-Festival press conference – it was a 'third-rate circus' with 'very little serious theatre' – which earned a rebuke from Lord Provost Eleanor McLaughlin.

One positive of that year came when the *Bolshoi* Opera managed to make it out of Moscow amid the failed coup to oust Mikhail Gorbachev, although they and the Leningrad Philharmonic Orchestra were understandably distracted by news from home. For Dunlop, though, bridges had been burned and even 15 years later commentators were writing things in retrospect like 'Dunlop... had not been a total disaster, but the festival's music programme had begun to resemble a supermarket shelf'.[10] The flaws of his programmes, though, stood in contrast to their many great and widely popular success stories.

Dunlop returned to the directing life and at the time of writing still lives in New York at the age of 95. The applications to replace him included Richard Demarco and the Scottish Chamber Orchestra's general manager Ian Ritchie, while William Burdett-Coutts had been touted by others for the job, at least before some of his sharper comments about the district council. The eventual appointee was a surprise to many – 48-year-old Brian McMaster, previously director of the Welsh National Opera for 15 years. It wasn't that his expertise was in question, especially as he was the opera specialist Dunlop wasn't, but he was a quiet and reserved figure after the particularly forthright Dunlop and Drummond.

After the failed regeneration of Edinburgh in the 1960s, which tore down buildings and left brown patches of mud in their place, the first improvement to be made was filling in the Hole in the Ground at long last in 1992, not with an opera house after all, but with one very significant adjustment to the city's theatrical spaces. With the Little Lyceum studio now being torn down, Saltire Court was the centrepiece of a reinvention of the whole quadrant, a space that includes the Usher Hall and the Royal Lyceum Theatre, its foyer opened up into a bright glass structure.

Saltire Court itself is a pleasant, if nondescript, sandstone-clad building designed in a civic Edwardian style for bland visual sympathy with the classical Georgian buildings around it and the Exchange financial district on the other side of Lothian Road. A series of prestige office lets, no Festival-goer has ever stepped inside its main space. Within the drum-like rotunda on its north side, however, an institution was rehomed and revived. Moving from its well-worn, leaking space on West Bow after two decades of bubbling speculation, the new Traverse Theatre opened on Cambridge Street at the beginning of July 1993 and initially there was a great deal of wariness about the project.

Could a theatre with such a rich grounding in the countercultural and the anti-establishment have any kind of a credible life by choosing to transfer to what was essentially the basement of a financial institution, even if the past quarter of a century had involved a slow crawl towards the mainstream world of Arts Council subsidy? By this point, the Traverse still sought the shock of the new, but the balance had tipped decisively towards newness over shock. The new space was touted prior to opening as the first purpose-built theatre in the country dedicated to new writing since Shakespeare's Globe.

After a month to bed in, the new Traverse's first Fringe presented Simon Donald's *The Life of Stuff* in the compact 100-seat studio – which mimicked the previous Traverse's dimensions – and Communicado theatre company's *Cyrano de Bergerac*. Held in the versatile 250-seat main auditorium, the latter was adapted by Edwin Morgan and directed by Gerry Mulgrew and it proved a classic of Scots theatrical translation. The new theatre's modern, subterranean bar and café was also a popular hit, as one of the Fringe's busiest late-night meeting spots for industry and audiences alike.

The new Traverse isn't a place for artistic extremism, but it remains a beloved and unique Edinburgh theatre whose high-quality Fringe programme is one of the major single press announcements of the early-year Festival build-up. The final fate of the Hole in the Ground was only the first resolved Edinburgh embarrassment of the decade and the next one shared its history. Following the floundering of the imagined opera house project in 1975 and the controversial decision by Conservative Lord Provost Kenneth Borthwick to use his casting vote in a split council decision to sell the site for development, Circuit tents came and went in the mud while the saga dragged to a conclusion.

Various organisations came together to fund the £11 million refurbishment of the old Empire Theatre to architects Law & Dunbar-Naismith's plans, and in June 1994 the new 1600-capacity venue opened with a striking new glass frontage, a remodelled interior and a remit to accommodate Scottish Opera, Scottish Ballet and the Edinburgh International Festival in particular, alongside all manner of private hires besides. The new space was most appropriately christened the Festival Theatre and the centrepiece production of its first International Festival was the Australian Opera's production of *A Midsummer Night's Dream*, directed by Baz Luhrmann and the team behind his hit 1992 film *Strictly Ballroom*. The programme at the new theatre that year also included Beethoven's *Fidelio* by Scottish Opera, the UK premiere of Peter Handke's 1992 play *The Hour We Knew Nothing of Each Other* and works by the Mark Morris Dance Group from America.

At the other end of Chambers Street, the Festival Theatre's arrival was followed by another in 1998, when the site of the former Society Buildings on Chambers Street was filled with the new Museum of Scotland building. Linked to the old Royal Museum of Scotland, this building houses the collection of the former National Museum of Antiquities of Scotland, which previously shared a space with the Scottish National Portrait Gallery on Queen Street. The whole organisation was collectively, conveniently renamed the National Museum of Scotland in 2006.

As for the old Traverse, it's now become flats like so much else in the city centre, but not before Karen Koren was invited to run it for a few years during the 1990s as the Stepping Stones Theatre. It was a venue that took her into theatre – highlights of its life included Borderline Theatre's Fringe production of emerging writer AL Kennedy's *The Audition* in 1993 – even as the other two-thirds of the Big Three increased their comedy output.

'It was lovely,' says Koren of the old Traverse space.

> It had two venues and a bar, and the main house was at least 150. The Traverse's studio now is set up like the main house at West Bow, and then there was another smaller studio, which was great. Pleasance and Assembly's base was always theatre, and they put comedy on to support their theatre. With me theatre came later, but I want to do popular theatre – I want bums on seats, I'm not into unique, experimental things. I want a laugh.

Even as the new Traverse came to life, one Edinburgh venue that was very much concerned with the unique and experimental came to an end in 1992. It was the final year of the Richard Demarco Gallery, still a place for the truly pioneering and international spirit in which the Edinburgh Festival as a whole had been founded, with its closing Festival of Polish Art featuring dance from *Polska Teatr Tanka Balet* and *Teatr Grupa Chwilowa's* Fringe First-winning spectacle *A Stop in the Desert*, by theatrical maestro Krzysztof Borowiec. Located at a former Presbyterian church at 17–21 Blackfriars Street since 1985, the gallery finally fell victim to the cut in Arts Council funding which Demarco had weathered since 1980, although now it was apparently a quarter of a million pounds in debt and the venue was about to be taken over by the Italian Cultural Institute.

Demarco's sheer will and resourcefulness in the face of apparent financial ruin served him well, however, and he returned to programming exhibitions and performances in various found venues until the end of the decade, as he had between the closure of his Melville Crescent gallery in 1974 and the opening of Blackfriars Street in 1985. In the 2000s, he found another fixed venue at the Roxy Art House, which he co-produced with Rocket Venues' founder Xela Batchelder until 2008. During this time he was instrumental in the Edinburgh Art Festival's creation.

Demarco's tastes are for the Avant Garde and for work created with a highbrow, thought-provoking, internationalist sensitivity, regardless of whether it might be considered shocking or not. His programming often attracted flak from self-appointed censors, although as the Fringe developed and a great array of international artists arrived in the 1990s, some of their antics took the heat off him. Although these weren't the kinds of works of art with which he would want to be associated, they somehow became more representative of what the Fringe was about in the 1990s in the eyes of many.

Brought to the world's attention at the second Lollapalooza festival of grunge and alternative rock in Chicago in 1992, the Jim Rose Circus arrived in Scotland in the early months of the following year, on the first of many world tours to perform before outrage-hungry international audiences. In August 1993, they returned to Edinburgh for the Fringe, appearing at a purpose-built venue on Calton Hill named the Acropolis, in the shadow of William Henry Playfair's ill-fated and incomplete 19th century National Monument of Scotland. The show featured acts like The Tube, who regurgitated his own stomach fluids for himself and others to drink, and the notorious Amazing Mister Lifto, whose nipple and genital piercings were surprisingly load-bearing.

'I think for Calton Hill to be sullied by something like this is awful,' noted Conservative councillor and moral guardian Moira Knox, a local politician so dependably dismayed by the Fringe's moral licentiousness that a nude lesbian trapeze act later used her words on their advertising when she declared them a 'dirty-minded disgrace'. 'Worse things happen on Calton Hill', noted her Labour opposite number Steve Cardownie, aware of the hill's reputation as a well-used spot for gay men to have recreational outdoor sex.

Rose was a big draw until his show of 1999, but when he returned to Edinburgh in 2008 there was much noise that the times had left his Circus behind, following the rise of television stunt shows like *Jackass* and *Dirty Sanchez* and equally exhibitionist Fringe shows like *Puppetry of the Penis*, the Australian duo whose horrifying/entertaining show of genital manipulation made its first appearance outside its home country at the Pleasance in 2000. In 1994, Japanese sensations the Tokyo Shock Boys appeared at the Assembly Rooms, making nerve-fraying features of performers lighting fireworks in their own backside and spraying liquid out of their eyeballs.

Elsewhere, other big-tent shows with their own unique selling points grew up, albeit without the deliberate shock value. Phillip and Carol Gandey were already bringing the *Chinese State Circus* to the city in Festival time when in 1998 they booked a group of performers they'd witnessed in Thailand to run as a smaller sideshow alongside it. *The Ladyboys of Bangkok* – Thai 'kathoey', or a third gender of transgender women and perfectly female-passing gay men – seemed an unlikely choice for a hit in those days, but the Ladyboys' popular blend of risqué comedy and pop music performance became an extraordinary success not just in Edinburgh, but across the world.

* * *

In 1996 the International, Fringe and Film Festivals all made it to their 50th editions. The International Festival celebrated with a revival-of-sorts of that hit from the festival's second year, *A Satire of the Three Estates*, now updated for the 1990s and an approaching new political era by John McGrath and the radical theatre company Wildcat, in what ended up being among their final productions. Staged at the Edinburgh International Conference Centre and renamed *A Satire of the Four Estates* to include the power of the contemporary media, it was poorly reviewed and served to illustrate how times and Edinburgh had moved on since both Tyrone Guthrie and John McGrath's heyday.

The anniversary year was a milestone, a demonstration of the already-proven staying power of the Festivals, and the years preceding it saw a steadying of the International Festival ship and an increase in funding and sponsorship levels. Yet while the Edinburgh Festival had been in existence for an entire adult lifetime now, more or less, 1996 was significant for the renaissance in Edinburgh's cultural life happening around it. This had been bubbling under for most of the decade, through a group of young working-class writers from Leith, the housing schemes of North Edinburgh and elsewhere, who published through an anti-mainstream DIY magazine named *Rebel Inc* between 1992 and 1994.

Founded by Kevin Williamson, who moved from Thurso in Caithness to Edinburgh as an 18-year-old in 1979, the magazine took the temperature of working-class, post-Thatcher literary Scotland by publishing the work of writers including Alan Warner, Laura Hird, Toni Davidson, Gordon Legge, Paul Reekie and John King. Most famously, *Rebel Inc* also published the work of Edinburgh writer Irvine Welsh – memorably including the unedited transcript of a conversation between Welsh and Williamson while both were on ecstasy – in the days around the publication of Welsh's acclaimed debut novel *Trainspotting* in 1993.

Revelling in the post-acid house culture of the city, where clubs like Pure at the Venue on Calton Road surfed the wave of new trends in music and drugs, *Rebel Inc* also sought to marry the experiences of clubbing and literature through events like 1993's pre-Christmas *Invisible Insurrection* at the city's La Belle Angele nightclub, hidden up the dank lane alongside the Gilded Balloon. Welsh told *The List* magazine he actively rejected literature which was discussed 'in Waterstone's with glasses of wine'.

In 1996, Danny Boyle's film adaptation of *Trainspotting* was released and it quickly blew up into one of the great cinematic reflections of British youth culture, a 1990s rival to *A Clockwork Orange* or *Quadrophenia*. Given that the main thread of the story was the repetitive ennui of addiction amid Edinburgh's days as 'heroin capital of Europe' in the 1980s, the vibrant, sexy edge lent by breakthrough Scottish actors like Ewan McGregor, Jonny Lee

Miller and Kelly Macdonald felt somehow unsuited. Still, the attention of the nation – and even further afield – was on Edinburgh.

In the year of the film's release, Welsh had already left the city's scene behind for Amsterdam, but his work was all over the Fringe of '96. Created with Boilerhouse Theatre, a company founded from the ashes of Jimmy Boyle's Gateway Exchange art space in the city after it folded in 1988,[11] in his pre-fame days, *Headstate* was a semi-improvised piece taken from the same milieu of drugs and club culture as informed his novels. That it was soundtracked by Graham Cunnington of industrial provocateurs Test Department and staged at Café Graffiti added to its desired club ambience; that its star was Edinburgh actor Tam Dean Burn linked it to the year's big theatrical hit at the Assembly Rooms, Harry Gibson's film-predating stage adaptation of *Trainspotting*.

Burn had previously played the lead role of Mark Renton in the staged *Trainspotting*, as had the film's eventual co-star Ewan Bremner, although the part was taken at the Fringe of 1996 by a 26-year-old former Scottish Youth Theatre actor and law school drop-out from Paisley in Renfrewshire named Gerard Butler. Acting in only his second professional role,[12] Butler later went on to at least as much fame in cinema as any of the stars of *Trainspotting*.

For once, what happened during the festival wasn't viewed as being the most exciting thing happening in Edinburgh that year. In 1996, Williamson also went into partnership on the *Rebel Inc* imprint with publishers Canongate, reissuing books by a selection of counterculture authors including one-time *enfant terrible* of the 1962 Writers Conference Alexander Trocchi. Irvine Welsh, meanwhile, did indeed read from *Trainspotting* in Waterstone's on Princes Street that August.

SPOTLIGHT

The Bloody Chamber (1997) Gargantua (1998)

ONE FESTIVAL EVENING in August 1994, as dusk was settling over the moss-darkened gravestones and broken mausoleums of Greyfriars Kirkyard, an audience was promenading through an outdoor performance of the historian Owen Dudley Edwards' play *Hare and Burke*. In the scene an actor was jumping between the gravestones in character as Mary Paterson, one of the infamous Edinburgh bodysnatchers' victims, vowing revenge upon her killers from beyond the grave. In the moment that followed, the show's young director Ben Harrison had an epiphany.

'She pointed at William Burke and accused him with the line "may your body be corrupted with lust!"',' remembers Harrison.

> On the word 'lust', Edinburgh Castle turned red behind her. We all
> gasped – the audience thought we'd intended it, it was just so perfect
> for that moment. But of course, it was just the technicians from the
> Tattoo testing the lights.

This cemented in Harrison's mind how he wanted to make theatre in future. 'Going out into the world, away from the embrace of a studio or proscenium arch theatre... when it's happening in real life, you get it all for free'.

For all the visible beauty of Edinburgh, its spires and battlements and narrow alleys and leafy parks, part of its unseen character is that it's a multi-storey city, an appropriately fantastical development for a place that has fired so many great imaginations. Just as North, South and George IV Bridges pass over Market Street and the darkened Cowgate below them, so do the grandly towering libraries, courts, Georgian apartment blocks and seats of local government, which line the higher roads sit upon unseen, crypt-like cellars and antechambers whose purpose is often simply to hold the buildings up.

'Edinburgh's a really geographically interesting city, because all the places that feel underground aren't,' says Judith Doherty, who is co-artistic director of the Grid Iron theatre company with Harrison. 'They're man-made structures that are supporting buildings, because it's such a hilly bloody place'. The pair met as students at Edinburgh University in the early 1990s, where both were involved with the student-run Bedlam Theatre. Harrison had set up his own Norwich-based theatre company as an 18-year-old in 1988, so by 1994 he was certainly experienced enough to take on Edwards' play, which was part-staged at the Bedlam.

At this point, while in her third year, Doherty was the venue's general manager, responsible for programming the Bedlam's Fringe and working out the logistics of a show like *Hare and Burke* with its creative team. She and Harrison fought like cat and dog on the production, says Doherty, who's from Magilligan on the Northern Irish coast. Then 'one morning I woke up, probably intensely hungover, and thought, "oh god – I think I need to set up a theatre company to work with Ben"'. It may have seemed a rash decision at the time, but she knew *Hare and Burke* had been a success in difficult circumstances, an early example of the 'site-specific' work with which Grid Iron would make their name.

Harrison graduated and went off to study directing at the Central School of Music and Drama in London. He had longed to be an actor – his parents were in healthcare, but his grandparents were old friends with actors like George Cole and Alasdair Sim, who they introduced him to as a child – until the great Scottish theatre director and educator Maggie Kinloch pointed out that wasn't where his talents lay. Meanwhile, Doherty took work as deputy manager of the Fringe box office under then-director Hilary Strong, who poached her from the Bedlam. There, she asked advice from as many Fringe companies as she could. 'One was called Fecund Theatre, they were really quite big around '95, '96,' says Doherty.

> They did a lot of hardcore, thumping music shows – I had never
> seen anything like it in my life, as a wee girl from Northern Ireland,
> all these semi-naked people sweating buckets on a stage. Oh my
> god! But these were real, normal people that I got to speak to, that
> had to work their fingers to the bone to be able to make a career out
> of this. They were really influential.

Grid Iron's life began in modest circumstances, with a play about the ruling classes' responsibilities to society named *Clearance*, by Anita Sullivan, which appeared on the Traverse Theatre's stage in May 1996. It was directed by Doherty's old Bedlam colleague Catriona Murray and then – following his return from London that summer – restaged by Harrison for a short tour to the Scottish Borders and Glasgow's Arches in late autumn. For the follow-up, Doherty and Harrison were on the look-out for something a lot less traditional.

Harrison had befriended a fellow student named Keith Lodwick[1] while studying at Central and the pair bonded over their love of the mature fairy stories of Angela Carter. In particular, they liked the sexually disturbing title tale of Carter's 1979 collection *The Bloody Chamber*, based on the 17th century French story *Bluebeard*, in which a teenage girl is married to a wealthy aristocrat whom she discovers has been murdering his past wives. Harrison's suggestion was that he would direct a Fringe adaptation from a script by Lodwick and his and Doherty's thoughts turned to Edinburgh's gothic undercity as a stage for the kind of extra-theatrical work they knew they wanted to produce.

At first, they considered the vaults under the buildings on South Bridge, actually the concealed arches of the viaduct which originally spanned the Cowgate gorge, later boxed in under street level by the tenements built on either side of the bridge. These vaults had been rediscovered in recent years by former Scottish rugby international and local businessman Norrie Rowan. In 1989, he'd allowed Romanian international rugby player Cristian Raducanu to sneak out through one of them during a Saturday night after-match party at Rowan's Hunter Square pub the Tron, evading his Securitate handlers so he could flag down a passing policeman and defect to the West in the weeks before the fall of Nicolae Ceauşescu's dictatorship. Yet Grid Iron had their eye on a space with an even more dramatic history.

Mary King's Close wasn't exactly unknown in 1997, but it remained a mystery to most of the city's inhabitants. Originally it was just another of the 'closes' – narrow, canyon-like alleys consisting of high tenements on either side and nook-like shops along their length – which spidered down from the raised Royal Mile onto the banks of the old Nor Loch, now the valley in which Waverley Station sits. In the mid-18th century it found itself in the way of the building of the Royal Exchange, now known as the City Chambers, and despite bearing the name of wealthy local landlord Alexander King's daughter, the street was partially demolished and built over. The Royal Exchange was designed by architect John Adam, whose body is interred in his family's mausoleum at Greyfriars Kirkyard, yards from the site of Ben Harrison's theatrical epiphany with the Castle's lights.

For decades, the rumours of a supposedly haunted ghost street hidden under the cobbled setts of the Royal Mile persisted, lent a particularly eerie context by tales of it being walled up with its residents still inside during an outbreak of the Plague; in fact, the last major outbreak in the British Isles had been a century before the Royal Exchange was constructed. By the time Grid Iron turned their attention to it, Mary King's Close had been in operation as an occasional tourist attraction for two years, with Mercat Tours – one of the operators whose walking tours drum up business next to placards on the Royal Mile, offering a blend of the historic and the potentially supernatural – running sporadic trips down into the depths. 'Judith found out from Mercat that a guy from the Council had the key, and if you could find him and he'd answer his phone, he'd take you down there,' recalls Harrison.

'I wish I could remember his name, he was fabulous,' says Doherty.

An elderly gentleman, a war veteran, and he had a wooden leg. I met him at the City Chambers and he clipped down the stairs in front of me with his wooden leg, down into Mary King's Close from a door in the square, with a big bunch of keys. When I saw it, I was totally enamoured.

She's learned since that it's important not to approach a potential venue for site-specific work with many expectations or demands, but Mary King's Close was everything Grid Iron wanted and needed it to be.

'It wasn't anywhere near as horrific as we'd expected, not full of beasts and rats and dead pigeons, and it wasn't so far gone that it was going to cost money we didn't have to make it habitable,' says Doherty.

It had some electric light, not in every room, but it was just full of atmosphere. It's stayed a founding premise of our work that you shouldn't have to do too much to the space – let it be itself, because otherwise, what's the point of being in there?

The audience were gathered after dusk on Parliament Square, across the Royal Mile in the shadow of St Giles' Cathedral and led by torchlight down one of the still-existing closes alongside the City Chambers onto Cockburn Street, at the lower end of Mary King's Close. Once inside only four rooms were used in the production, but the sets were quickly redressed as the audience moved out of each, giving the impression of a much more sprawling space as they repeated their route.

'By the time we'd done that, everyone was in the Hollywood movie with the Hollywood movie set budget', says Doherty.

My brother-in-law and another very talented metalworker built a bed from iron, and we had mirrors and gargoyles. We used our little resources very well, with light and candles to heighten the atmosphere. Whether you believe the stories or not, Mary King's Close is a freaky place to be, and we had some spooky experiences in there. I was all prepared to make them up for a press release, but I didn't have to. Things moved inexplicably. When you're doing site theatre work you try and do as little as possible to the space, and Edinburgh's just a gift for that.

The Bloody Chamber was performed between Thursday 7 and Saturday 30 August 1997, in a venue described simply in the Fringe programme as the Haunted Vaults and the reviews were extremely positive. *The Herald* awarded it a Herald Angel Award to go with its Total Theatre Award nominations for Best Design and Best Newcomer. *The Guardian* and *The Scotsman*'s words also glowed.

Grid Iron had arrived, as had Mary King's Close. Mention of Mercat's tours began appearing more frequently in the media, until in 2003 it opened fully under another operator as The Real Mary King's Close, offering tours of the underground street and exhibitions of related local history – it's now one of the most widely-recognised tourist attractions in Edinburgh. As for *The Bloody Chamber*, it returned for more winter performances in December 1997 and transferred the following year to the London Dungeon and to Lagan Weir in Belfast, although Harrison says these venues didn't bear the same sense of gothic mystery as the Edinburgh original. In the meantime, Grid Iron had to do something spectacular to follow up their first hit.

* * *

Around this time, Harrison had been reading the 16th century French satirist François Rabelais' sequence of early European novels, *Gargantua and Pantagruel*. 'It's about a giant who can eat as much as he likes and not get any fatter, and drink as much as he wants and not have a hangover,' he recounts.

> There's a fantastic scene early on where the narrators go into his mouth, and because he's so large, the molars are like mountains and there's a guy at the back planting cabbages. What's joyous about that book is the guilt-free aspect to it. At the time, I felt the Calvinist inheritance was still very much alive in Edinburgh. It was dour, the weather was terrible, you couldn't get a proper cup of coffee. There was a local councillor called Moira Knox – which is a fantastic name, I wouldn't be surprised if she was descended from John – who made it her business to close down Fringe shows. A bit like Mary Whitehouse, protesting about anything that might have had any sex or anything naughty in it. So *Gargantua* was arguing against that.

In fact, Grid Iron had experienced a run-in of their own with the redoubtable moral campaigner Knox when they staged *The Bloody Chamber*. 'There is a striking resemblance between the act of love and the ministrations of a torturer,' ran the quote from the text on the promotional posters and the implied sadomasochistic subtext had caught Knox's attention. In the event, Doherty had to appeal to Hilary Strong, her old boss at the Fringe, to smooth things over with council officers and convince them she was responsible enough to be permitted to stage such a show under the City Chambers.

In 1998 then, Doherty and Harrison had their intended text to adapt in *Gargantua and Pantagruel*, they had the desire to find another unexplored, quasi-subterranean bolthole to stage the play in and they had the advantage of now being a known quantity with both audiences and the council's estates department. They approached the latter and asked what they might be able to provide.

'It still surprises me,' says Doherty.

> This was the late '90s, the Troubles were still ongoing in Northern Ireland, and a Northern Irish girl was pitching up at places asking for keys to get in. The amount of trust that people seemed to put in me, giving me keys to the City Chambers, was astounding. I think that's because Edinburgh as a cultural entity was just a bit more accepting – it didn't seem that mad that you would want to do a show. I started off walking around the city, looking at doors and

thinking, I wonder where that goes? Finally I spoke to somebody at
the National Library of Scotland, because I'd heard they had seven
whole floors in the stacks underneath – and they said yes, they're
filled with the most precious books, so off you pop. But they told
us to get in touch with the Central Library across the road, because
they knew there was definitely derelict space underneath there, as it
was holding up George IV Bridge.

Again, another man of a certain age with a set of keys accompanied a
group that included Doherty, Harrison and their lighting designer George
Tarbuck[2] into the depths. He took them as far as natural light could take
them and decided they couldn't go any further, because what lay ahead was
unknown. Doherty, ever the persuasive producer, convinced him to let the
group have his torch so they could carry on.

'Oh my god, we went from one space to the other and they just got bigger,'
recounts Doherty.

We ended up in what we called the cathedral space, which was vast,
right up underneath the Bridge. We could have cried. On the wall
there was a sort of moss, it looked like seaweed growing up the wall,
and every so often a bit would plop off. Pigeons would get in and
breed, and the wee birds would never get out, so there were these
white, pink-eyed albino pigeons.

Like the vaults under South Bridge, the spaces they had found were
essentially the enclosed viaducts underneath the street of George IV Bridge,
lent an increasingly strange aspect because these Stygian depths were reached
through disused offices straight out of Terry Gilliam's film *Brazil*. 'In the first
room there was an abandoned calendar, thick with dust, and a phone off the
hook,' says Harrison.

The calendar was from 1983, so we began to build the show from
that discovery, really listening to the space and seeing what the
building was telling us. The characters of the show were so locked
into the world of work, they didn't realise the bank had shut for
good. It was like a clown show, they do a nine to five Monday to
Friday, and then on Friday at five o'clock they go nuts, into this
carnal weekend of pleasure. They take the audience down through
the body of the giant – through the mouth and the lungs, into the
belly, and eventually out the other end into the Cowgate. It had
all these different levels, it was crazily ambitious and we were still

living like students. It was a student show, in a way. We all worked for absolutely nothing, got paid about 25 quid each, and gave two or three months of our lives to it, but it had the effect of really launching the company and that style of work.

Gargantua was another critical hit for Grid Iron, winner of a *Scotsman* Fringe First award for the writing by Harrison and the company and a Stage Award for Acting Excellence in the Best Ensemble category. Yet the show's influence on the Edinburgh Festival stretched far beyond its run. For Gargantua's residency, Grid Iron had listed its venue name as 'the Underbelly'. Soon after the production finished, an old university and Bedlam contemporary of theirs' named Charlie Wood asked if they would mind if his former school theatre company Double Edge Drama took on the space and the name to put on a few Fringe shows.

In 2000, Wood – the nephew of the Traverse Theatre's then-artistic director Philip Howard – arranged for Double Edge, now run by an Edinburgh University student named Ed Bartlam, to put on four plays they were producing at the Underbelly. In 2001, Bartlam and Wood formalised the Underbelly as a business and a receiving Fringe venue in its own right and by 2003 they had opened enough of the sprawling complex to host 50 shows, up from the previous year's 18. By 2019, they had long been arguably the key commercial player on the Fringe, with multiple venues hosting theatre and comedy shows numbering in the hundreds.

In 2000, Grid Iron completed the early trilogy of shows at the Edinburgh Fringe that made their reputation as one of the most forward-thinking and exciting theatre companies in the UK, when playwright Douglas Maxwell's *Decky Does a Bronco* was staged at Scotland Yard playground in George V Park, a leafy nook between the New Town and Canonmills. A hugely acclaimed study of childhood machismo between young boys and the loss of innocence that growing older brings, it broke new theatrical ground for the company, but didn't bend Edinburgh's landscape and the arc of its use in quite the same way as their first two Fringe productions had managed.

Since then, Grid Iron has made regular Edinburgh Festival returns in new and inventive ways. *Variety*, an examination of the old Scottish music hall tradition, was staged at the King's Theatre in 2002 with the Edinburgh International Festival, but was pilloried for a perceived lack of quality amid the supposed prestige arts of EIF. Grid Iron returned to the same festival in 2013, however, with the science fiction piece *Leaving Planet Earth*, seen at the Edinburgh International Climbing Centre in a former quarry to the west of Edinburgh.

They've also staged Fringe shows in a New Town townhouse at 32

Abercromby Place (*Those Eyes, That Mouth*, 2003), the former Debenhams department store on Princes Street (*The Devil's Larder*, 2005),[3] Doherty's former local pub the Barony Bar (the Charles Bukowski adaptation *Barflies*, 2009 and 2012), the University of Edinburgh Medical School's anatomy department (*What Remains*, 2011), the Edinburgh International Book Festival on Charlotte Square (*Letters Home*, 2014) and at the more traditional Assembly Rooms and Summerhall.

Most recently, their planned woodland adaptation of Erlend Loe's novel about misguided environmental survivalism *Doppler* was the subject of a protracted and unsuccessful effort to stage it in 2020, at the height of COVID-19 pandemic restrictions. It was eventually seen on an ingeniously-devised woodland clearing stage in the grounds of Newhailes Estate, near Musselburgh, during 2021's partially-revived Fringe. Although Grid Iron can't lay claim to the global reputation enjoyed by many key producers who have visited Edinburgh over the years, their presence has enriched the Fringe like few other companies over the decades and with these two mould-breaking early shows they changed the landscape of the Festival and the city itself in ways few other companies can match.

12

New Blood for the New Millennium

TWO YEARS AFTER 50th anniversary in 1996, the International Festival and the Fringe were at odds. Brian McMaster's relations with the Fringe had been good – especially in relation to Frank Dunlop's open dismissal of its content shortly before he left – but debate was simmering about the effect of the Festival in general. Was the International Festival too highbrow? The comedy element of the Fringe too populist? Did the Fringe lean too far towards corporate monopoly or sheer anarchy?

Amid this atmosphere, the Fringe's director Hilary Strong moved its start date forward a week. The Fringe of 1998 now ran for three weeks from 10 August, while the International Festival ran for three weeks from 16 August. Within the fragile ecology of Edinburgh's Festival environment, it triggered a firestorm.

Appointed in 1993 to replace the outgoing Mhairi Mackenzie-Robinson, Strong arrived from the Natural Theatre Company in Bath, whose eye-catching walkabout theatre characters included the alien tourists Coneheads from Outer Space. As a member of the National Campaign for the Arts, she was well-used to working with fringe theatre companies; in fact, she directed an amateur production of Dennis Potter's *Blue Remembered Hills* in Edinburgh in 1990. Strong's time in charge was seen as a capable one and the reasons expressed for moving the Fringe were plausible. The entire Festival had originally run for three weeks across the end of August and the beginning of September, although when Frank Dunlop moved the International Festival back by a week as in 1984, the Fringe had followed suit.

Dunlop reasoned that audiences tended to drop off in the third week and fitting in around the European opera festivals was no longer the issue it had been in '47. The Fringe's move in '98 was for similar reasons. Its last week, following the English bank holiday weekend in late August, was seen as lacking summer buzz, so better to partly sync up with Edinburgh school holidays and allow local families to enjoy the start of the Fringe instead. Besides, the few days of unofficial advance previews in 'Week Zero' – as defined by Alistair Moffat back in 1979 – were as well to be officially part of the Fringe.

In defence of the move, polling by the Fringe Society in 1996 reported 73 percent of responding Fringe companies were in favour. Despite the logic of it, though, the others festivals weren't pleased at the knock-on effect on their own ticket sales of not having a 'critical mass' of concurrent events, potentially generating both audience confusion and a decrease in synchronised London press coverage. McMaster was so displeased, he even suggested the Fringe could have August while his own festival might move entirely into September.

His annoyance was partly practical – the Fringe absorbed any performers who wanted to come, but the International Festival had long fought to persuade orchestras and performing companies to spend weeks away from their families *en masse* during August's traditional holiday month across continental Europe. Meanwhile David Bates, manager of the Spiegeltent on Waverley Shopping Centre, declared many Fringe operators might stick to the old dates anyway. 'The Fringe will happen, despite the Fringe Society,' he said.

Yet, although the Book Festival and the Assembly Rooms both reported impacted sales after the fact, both the Film Festival and the Pleasance reported either no change or an improvement on the year before. After the furore died down, the Fringe and the other festivals settled into an out-of-sync rhythm that appeared to affect no party substantially and certainly didn't prevent the strength-to-strength growth of the Fringe into the 21st century. In 1999, in fact, some venues attempted a four-week Fringe.

Figures released after the 1998 festival showed visitor numbers to the city had been down by eight percent, but Fringe ticket numbers sold had increased by five percent. In 2015 both major festivals were finally aligned once more, when incoming International Festival director Fergus Linehan belatedly followed Hilary Strong's lead and began his first festival a week earlier, to capitalise on the 'electricity' of everything happening all at once.

When Strong resigned from the Fringe Society at the beginning of 1999, she said it was nothing to do with the previous year's controversy. She'd made comments in the press regarding the council's funding for the Fringe – £19,000, compared to over £1 million for the International Festival – which had drawn rebuke from councillors, but as she told *The Independent*, recent political events had caused her to wonder whether the top job at the Fringe should be held by a Scot. After directing an amateur production of John Steinbeck's *The Grapes of Wrath* at the Pleasance in March, Strong's next job was executive director of Greenwich Theatre. Her successor at the Fringe was 35-year-old Paul Gudgin, who had increased attendances at Edinburgh's Queen's Hall since taking over in 1995, after spells at the Bury St Edmunds and Aldeburgh Festivals.

This moment was a changing one in Scottish politics and culture, and the two soon became interlinked. The first of a new group of venue owners to make an impact on the Fringe had his roots in politics. In fact, to look at the breadth of his career over the last 40 years, the business of stand-up comedy appears almost a two-decade diversion from Tommy Sheppard's career as a political organiser and politician. Born in Coleraine in Northern Ireland, he moved to Aberdeen in 1977 to study medicine, but by the time he graduated five years later he'd switched to sociology and politics.

'The first Edinburgh Festival Fringe I attended was in 1979, when I was an extra in an ill-fated production by the Aberdeen University Dramatic Society,' says Sheppard now. 'I can't even remember what it was, but it was in a church hall near the top of Leith Walk'. The year he graduated he became Vice-President of the National Union of Students (NUS) and moved to London. When he returned to Edinburgh in 1993, it was to work as assistant General Secretary of the Labour Party under then-leader John Smith, after serving several years as deputy leader of Hackney Council. In London, Sheppard first experienced stand-up comedy in the midst of the Alternative boom, seeing Alexei Sayle and Ben Elton give way to newcomers including Jo Brand and Mark Thomas. He was impressed by the work of Don Ward, who founded and ran the Comedy Store.

'It was comedy with a point, comedy with a message, rather than making crass jokes about bugger all,' says Sheppard.

> Politics was my first love, but here they were combining social and political satire with performance. It also took place in little rooms above pubs, and I loved the idea of somebody performing a script in the ambience of a pub, where you could drink and chat in the interval, and in those days smoke. It was a much more accessible format than going to the theatre.

Every summer he came to Edinburgh to stay with friends and take in the Fringe, but he only got a good view of what happened in the city outside August when he moved there permanently. 'The Edinburgh Festival Fringe was probably the biggest collection of stand-up comedy anywhere in the world and yet, come the fireworks, everything just disappeared. All that was left a week later was the tatty posters falling off the walls. There was nothing, literally nothing'. He and his partner Jane Mackay were perfectly placed to do something about it.

Jane – from the Scottish Highlands, a former reporter for *The Lincolnshire Echo* and an Islington Labour councillor when Sheppard was in Hackney – had become a comedian herself and was getting to know the meagre local community of Edinburgh comics who hadn't decamped to London looking for fame and fortune. In his role as councillor, meanwhile Sheppard had been active in the campaign to reopen Hackney Empire, which became a key London comedy venue.

In 1995, with the Fringe approaching and Sheppard and Mackay actively looking to start a club, Mackay's daughter Eva told them about the basement room at WJ Christie & Sons, a pub on West Port which she went to with her Edinburgh College of Art classmates. The room was small, but it was what they needed. The manager, a man named Don Tait, liked what they had in mind. So last-minute they didn't even make it into the Fringe programme, the Comic Den at Christie's ran for 12 nights, every Thursday to Sunday during that year's Fringe, with a bunch of local comics including Gordon Brunton, Viv Gee, Bathgate's only existentialist forklift driver Bill Dewar, and Mackay herself as compere.

'It was fun,' says Sheppard, 'and then we thought, "well, what do we do now?"' They decided to keep going. With the backing of the comedians they knew and Christie's itself, the couple set up a voluntary organisation and a regular Thursday night called the Stand Comedy Club. 'I remember it well,' says Sheppard of the first night.

Seven people paid for a ticket – six of them students at £3 and one of them full price at £4. The total door take was £22 door income, which we split three ways between the tech, the acts and running costs.

In the days before email accounts, they took the names and addresses of all seven people in the audience and posted them details of what was coming next. A month later, that mailing list had 100 names on it, not least because Bruce Morton had agreed to play a gig on 19 October – Sheppard left a note for him backstage at the Traverse after one of Morton's gigs and was astonished when he replied. The inaugural winner of the Gilded Balloon's *So You Think You're Funny?* award in 1988, Morton wasn't the kind of star that some subsequent winners became, but he was by some way Scotland's biggest stand-up at this point. 'As soon as he said 'yes' we promoted it, we put up posters, and that one sold out,' says Sheppard.

In fact, we turned people away. The fire capacity limit was 50, but that was really ramming people in, there were only about 20 chairs. We did it for Bruce Morton and we knew from that point we could make it work.

There were a number of factors to the Stand's success in Edinburgh, says Sheppard. One, it was all about the comedians playing, whereas other failed ventures had mainly been showcases for their performer-promoters. He and Mackay also had a knack for momentum-building promotion and marketing. They needed a weekend venue, so in early 1996 the Stand started a Saturday night club at the Moscow Bar, a 'style bar' – 'one of those soulless concrete bars built in the bottom of a development block', as Sheppard has it – on South St Andrew Street, just off St Andrew Square. The capacity was 100 at a push and they could charge a fiver because it was the weekend.

Comedians from further afield booked gigs. First, Brendan Riley, Hovis Presley and the unknown Johnny Vegas from the north of England, then a blend of more established comics and newcomers from Scotland and further afield; Norman Lovett, Jo Caulfield, Susan Morrison and the club's new compere and shock tactician, a Glaswegian studying to be a teacher in Edinburgh named Frankie Boyle. The Stand ran nightly for three weeks at both its venues during the 1996 Fringe, Dylan Moran made a guest appearance, Boyle won Avalon and *The Daily Telegraph*'s Open Mic Award and by the end the club was firmly established in the city and the Festival. The Moscow Bar closed down, so Saturday night moved to the basement of the Tron on Hunter Square. A Sunday night for beginners named *Pint-Sized Comedy* was added.

The Stand's Fringe '97 programme at the Tron and Christie's was even bigger, although on the last night a tipping point was hit. 'A new manager took over Christie's and he was always on the case about what we were doing,' says Sheppard.

> He would close the bar during performances, there was constant tension. Anyway, it breaks out into a stand-up shouting match, with him trying to come in the back door into the venue and me standing blocking him because there's a show on, and eventually both of us tumbling through the curtain into the audience. The next morning we took our kit away, and I realise that if there's to be any future in this we have to secure our own premises, because we can't be left at the whim of that sort of thing happening again.

This was the year of Labour's General Election victory and the point at which Sheppard left his job with the party. He gently describes it by saying 'the Labour Party left me,' although another rumour was that he was personally 'invited' to leave by Tony Blair. Sheppard was never a New Labour man and the feeling was clearly mutual. 'I'd been having this weird, dream-like idea,' he says. 'Could I make running the Stand work as a full-time job? Could I actually do this commercially?' Again, the only way it could work was with their own venue, where they controlled the bar and its income; as Sheppard calls it, 'the arts council subsidy for stand-up comedy'.

An unlikely candidate appeared on York Place, in old premises belonging to the Scottish Equitable insurance company, which had been unused and on the market for several years. Up a few steps off the street was the company's bespoke printing shop, while downstairs was the old document storage archive, which had potential as a single-room space if a few rooms could be knocked through. 'It took a massive leap of imagination, but I put my redundancy money into it and we persuaded a bank to give us a loan after three turned us down,' says Sheppard.

They moved in during the first week of 1998 and after a ten-week build which went right up to the wire – the sign-off on their licence came through at ten to seven on the opening evening – the Stand Comedy Club as it exists to this day was established on Friday 20 March 1998, with a two-night stand by Fred MacAulay. 'We went upstairs to look outside and there was a queue around the block, it was such an amazing sense of relief'.

At that year's Fringe, the Stand was notable as much for the position it took as for the comedy in its basement room and the tiny backroom space which later became the dressing room. Describing himself and Mackay as 'old lefties', Sheppard explains the principles of the Stand from the outset:

> We wanted value for money, no rip-offs, we were trying to keep
> ticket prices at a fair level. We were also trying to promote local
> talent – to make a contribution to Scottish culture and try and
> provide a platform in Scotland so people weren't forced to go away,
> because there was a scene that was sustainable all year round.

The Stand programmed Scottish comedians for runs – including Paul Sneddon's alcoholic ex-football manager turned pundit Bob Doolally, a popular hit for the summer of World Cup '98, Scotland's last international tournament for more than two decades – and a *Best of Scottish Comedy* bill. With discussion brewing among comedians that the Perrier wasn't the certain path to fame it had been in the past or rather that winning wasn't any more useful than just being shortlisted or gathering good word of mouth, the Stand also ran a Fringe showcase of new acts from *Pint-Sized Comedy*. Reflecting the belief that awards weren't needed, it was called *No Contest*. For a time, the Stand also refused to give free tickets to Perrier Award judges.

'We were staunchly grassroots, with an anti-corporate, anti-commercial attitude,' says Sheppard.

> We were increasingly alarmed at the commercialisation of the Fringe
> by big business, in particular the cartel that emerged – a deliberate
> attempt, I think, to create a monopoly and to capture the lion's
> share of the market. We thought this was extremely antipathetic
> to the roots of the Fringe, so there were some sporty conversations
> between us in those days. But I always felt we had a lot of tacit

support from the Fringe office and the Fringe board for what we were doing. By the time ten years had passed, I guess we cooled our heels a bit and I got elected onto the Fringe board – we became a wee bit more participative, but still quite wary of the big commercial beasts dominating the situation.

It took some years before the Stand began to make money and even more before it paid off its loan, but the reputation of Edinburgh's only year-round comedy club was assured from the start. A roster of home-grown comedians built up around it, many of whom went on to fame elsewhere, including Boyle, Greg McHugh and Kevin Bridges. During each Fringe the club expanded into Stand 2, a drawing room space upstairs, and later it also moved into the Lothian and Borders Police Association Club, a basement on the opposite side of York Place, which temporarily became Stand 3 and Stand 4 for the Fringe. A second branch of the Stand opened in Glasgow in 2000, followed by a third in Newcastle-upon-Tyne in 2011.

Having staged Fringe shows of her own including 1999's *Housewife and Marxist*, Jane Mackay became a professional comedian in 2001, at the age of 44. She left the Stand around the time she and Sheppard split in 2005 and at the age of 50 in 2007 retired from comedy altogether, although her daughter Eva remains a director.

When Sheppard stepped back from the Edinburgh comedy institution he helped build, it was because he'd won the seat of Edinburgh East for the Scottish National Party in the 2015 General Election. He remains the area's member of parliament to this day, part of a career that currently serves as a bookend to the founding of a club created around his and Mackay's own socialist values.

* * *

Charlie Wood was 17 when he first came to the Edinburgh Festival in 1991; like so many before him, with some student drama bearing modest expectations and even more modest results. He and a group of friends from Eton College set up with a couple of plays named *The Zoo Story* and *Geometry* in the Calton Centre on Montgomery Street. They gathered an audience of around half a dozen people per show, if they were lucky.

'It was just brilliant,' says Wood. 'We came back every year.' The student group was called Double Edge Drama and it still existed by the time of the last full festival in 2019, although Wood's long since left it behind. In 1997 he passed it on to a fellow student, Ed Bartlam, six years his junior, who was already part of the company.

'It's fair to say we both fell in love with doing shows at the Edinburgh Festival as teenagers,' says Bartlam.

> I was in a production of *The Merchant of Venice* at the Pleasance playing a drag queen Portia, and Charlie was a good director. That was the impetus for me to then decide to go to Edinburgh University after school. My introduction to Edinburgh was very much via the Fringe, which I think is probably the case for lots of people.

Bartlam began studying in Edinburgh soon after Wood left and now he was based in the city he wanted to try something more ambitious. Double Edge's plays that year were *Bent*, Martin Sherman's 1979 work about the persecution of gay people in Nazi Germany and Peter Weiss's *Marat/ Sade* (1963), featuring the Marquis de Sade directing a play about the assassination of political radical Jean-Paul Marat to be performed by the inmates of Charenton Asylum. These were dark subject matters and Bartlam wanted a special, atmospheric venue to suit.

Separately, he approached the Fringe's director Paul Gudgin and Wood for suggestions and both put him onto Judith Doherty. Wood had studied at Edinburgh at the same time as Doherty and Ben Harrison and all three were involved with student productions at the Bedlam Theatre. Now Doherty and Harrison had founded Grid Iron and had a lot of success with site-specific work on the Fringe, including 1998's *Gargantua* in the vaults underneath Central Library. Wood and Gudgin thought it would be perfect for Double Edge's needs and Doherty was happy to help Bartlam make the arrangements.

'It was a complete and utter shambles, in that we didn't have any idea what we were doing,' says Bartlam of Double Edge's 2000 Fringe season at the Underbelly.

> Our license came through three or four days late. We built a bar out of bookshelves that we found in there, the library was using it as a storeroom. In a brilliantly Fringy way it was very ramshackle, just beg, borrow and steal as much as we could to put the shows on – but the shows were really great, done in a site-specific way. That was the kind of beginning, that was the first year – three shows, only the top floor, using what we now call the Belly Laugh, the White Belly and the Iron Belly.

The next year, in 2001, Bartlam was still at university and Wood was training to be a lawyer, but in their spare time they pooled their efforts to do essentially what had happened the year before, with a little extra added. They invited other companies to sublet space in the cavernous stack of stone chambers between Victoria Street and the Cowgate – originally christened by Judith Doherty, who 'graciously handed [the name] on', says Wood.

That year Wood and Bartlam presented 23 shows across three stages, most notably a Double Edge production of *Cabaret* directed by Eton School Master and playwright Angus Graham-Campbell. The show starred 19-year-old Eddie Redmayne, returning to his old Eton theatre group shortly after starting a History of Art degree and a year before making his professional stage debut in *Twelfth Night* for Shakespeare's Globe. Twenty years later, Wood and Bartlam's first West End production was the 2021 revival of *Cabaret* starring Redmayne and Jessie Buckley, a collaboration instigated by the pair's work with him on that Double Edge production. It gathered seven Olivier awards in 2022, the most ever for a revival.

'There was no grand plan,' says Bartlam.

People often think, because we do more and more stuff, there must have been a grand plan. We had this little venue, we did some good shows, in 2001 we did a few more shows, and the great thing about those vaults was that we kept exploring them and opening up different rooms.

By 2001 they'd already uncovered the largest arch under George IV Bridge, which they named Big Belly and staged *Cabaret* in. The years 2001 to 2005 were very much still in keeping with that Fringe spirit, a part-time concern for the pair while Wood continued his legal career.

During this time, Underbelly's reputation built as more big names got involved. The late-night comedy package *The Late Show* built a following and there was good theatre too, including theimaginarybody's acclaimed play *100* in 2002, in which a group of characters choose one memory from their life to spend eternity in. Jerry Sadowitz played a typically confrontational late-night set and Stewart Lee returned to stand-up there in 2004, following the success of *Jerry Springer: The Opera*.

The same year Will Adamsdale's show *Jackson's Way*, played in character as US motivational speaker Chris Jackson, won the Perrier. It was a big influence on the resurgent Lee, who saw it six times and later wrote that watching Adamsdale perform 'the most improbable and engaging of conceits in the face of mass irritation and total audience boredom proved to me that one man on a stage in a room could be anything at all, go anywhere, say anything, suggest anything, do anything. This was what I needed to see'.[1]

'We were both still doing it in our spare time,' says Wood.

When I was a lawyer I had two computers on the desk in my office – one was my Underbelly computer and the other was my work

computer. The only thing we did was the Fringe, and we only did
the Underbelly on the Cowgate. It had an innocence and a naivety to
it that was fantastic, and you could only find that at the Fringe. Ed
and I really did work hard, around the year and in August.

He remembers hosting the British Council Showcase breakfast one morning,
welcoming dignitaries to the venue at 8.30am, having only just cleared out the
late night/early morning crowd three hours earlier. 'We just didn't get any sleep'.
When Underbelly began they were quirky innovators, with the combination
of a striking venue which lent itself to unusual, site-specific work and a knack
for programming interesting, attention-grabbing shows. 'People wanted to
be part of this young, upstart, experimental, interesting venue,' says Bartlam.
But they also had a sense of how they might gain a foothold on the Fringe
and attract the best talent, offering ticket splits to companies that they knew
were more favourable than those of their closest competitors.

'That disrupted things, and it made our friends [at the other big venues]
not very happy for a bit,' says Wood.

It's weird that we then became part of it, really. Why did we do it?
Because we adored the Festival, we loved being there, and if you're
going to hang around, you need to create your own shelf. That's
what we tried to do.

The past two decades have seen Wood and Bartlam gain an unwanted
reputation as the face of capitalism on the Fringe, which is largely founded on
extraordinary success paired with a willingness to grow as much as possible.
Yet there's no doubt that the roots of the company they founded were
steeped in a love of Fringe theatre and a desire to do something speculative
and unusual, entirely in keeping with the spirit of the Fringe.

In 2005, the pair heard a rumour that the University of Edinburgh might
be interested in renting out Bristo Square, the large concourse in front of the
McEwan Hall more usually occupied year-round by the city's skateboarding
community. With maximum capacity of 150 per show at the Underbelly,
they were immediately interested and imagined some kind of large tent
branded with Underbelly's purple livery. It was a night out in Soho with the
faux-French comedy duo *Priorité à Gauche* – Arnold Widdowson and Justin
McCarron – which sealed the final fate of the city's most eye-catching new
venue.

'One of them said, if you're going to build a tent, surely you've got to
make it purple, put some udders, some legs and a head on it, and it can be
your brand?' recalls Bartlam.

So we went ahead and built this tent, the Udderbelly, and launched
it in Edinburgh in 2006. The company we got to build it got loads
of stuff wrong, it was very close to the wire. Everyone thought we
were mad, but the cow made people smile. It was the first time we'd
ever run an outdoor site, and that changed the view of Underbelly as
being this underground vaults kind of venue.

The first years of the 405-capacity Udderbelly saw comedians like Stewart
Lee, Reginald D Hunter and Demetri Martin booked for the huge structure,
alongside dance troupe ZooNation's Stephen Sondheim-influenced hip-hop
musical *Into the Hoods*. In the following years it also allowed the Underbelly
organisation to expand outside of Edinburgh, taking the tent to the Brighton
Fringe in 2007 and London's South Bank in '09. By this point Underbelly were
no longer the upstart newcomers, although the 'upstart' part of the tag has taken
longer to shake off, such is their clear ambition. Unquestionably, by the time the
decade ended, they were one-quarter of the newly-minted Big Four of the Fringe.

'It wasn't about trying to directly disrupt Karen [Koren] or William
[Burdett-Coutts] or Christopher [Richardson] at all, it was just that we
wanted to do our thing,' says Bartlam.

I guess we were and still are ambitious, as people probably know,
and over the next few years, when we began to get more known and
a bit bigger, that fuelled more ambition. 'Okay, what else can we
do with this?' It was other people that started saying, 'they're the
challenger to the establishment.' That wasn't coming from us.

* * *

It was soon after 8pm on Saturday 7 December 2002 that the first hint of smoke
was detected on Hastie's Close. Back then, the narrow lane sloping down from
Guthrie Street to the Cowgate ran in between the Wilkie House nightclub and
the towering former department store that held the Gilded Balloon and the
nightclub La Belle Angele underneath. It was in the latter building that the fire
that scarred the landscape of both the Fringe and the city itself broke out.

That night, the streetfront Gilded Saloon bar, the space formerly known
as the 369 Gallery, was due to host Extra Width, a regular DJ night by Stuart
Braithwaite of the band Mogwai alongside local indie club Evol. Fortunately
the club hadn't begun when the fire broke out and the entire building had
been evacuated by the time the blaze really got going. Nobody was hurt, but
that weird and destructive night left its mark upon Edinburgh's psyche.

Crowds amassed along the cordon at the top of Blair Street, watching as firefighters struggled to contain the flames of the inferno leaping from the windows, the faces of all these drunken pre-Christmas revellers sweating in the fierce heat. Across the city centre, in the tenements of Marchmont, smoke and embers could be seen floating past windows until the small hours, with 'last days of Rome' student parties waylaid every so often as windows were opened to check whether the blaze was still going.

By the following morning, 80 firefighters had brought the fire under control, but it continued to smoulder for two days. The cause was believed to be an electrical fire and while the firefighters' efforts had saved the buildings in the immediate vicinity – the tenements of Blair Street and George IV Bridge, Wilkie House, Adam House on Chambers Street – everything in the block was lost, from the Cowgate up to North Bridge on the level above and into the upper stories. La Belle Angele was gone, as was a new jazz bar and the arcade machines of Leisureland on North Bridge, the Gilded Saloon, the Gilded Balloon and also the Gilded Balloon offices, along with 17 years of memorabilia and business records collected by Karen Koren.[2]

'It was really hard,' says Koren, who had been visiting her new-born granddaughter in hospital earlier that day.

> When bad things happen in your life you go into, not a survival mode, but a space of nothingness where you just cut off and you're a zombie for a wee while. Then you sit up and think, 'right, what are we going to do?'

The Cowgate fire had been headline news across the UK and reported around the world. People who knew and loved the Gilded Balloon moved in with offers of support; there were comedy fundraisers in London and William Burdett-Coutts' Assembly gave the organisation use of their office in Edinburgh. The Gilded Balloon recovered and evolved, although in many ways it was already halfway out of the now-destroyed building by the time of the fire. The Edinburgh University Settlement had sold Wilkie House to a private nightclub operator, meaning the Gilded Balloon could no longer use the space, while the Edinburgh University Students Association was looking to maximise the possible return from their student union spaces during Festival time.

EUSA's Potterrow centre had already been leased out to the Pleasance as Pleasance Dome from 2000, while the Fringe Club vacated the Edinburgh University union at Teviot Row House the following year. It was known to not be a warm environment for performers, with drunken hecklers turning up to make sport and a lot of vaguely-interested tourists coming along to watch the carnage. Performers were staying away. EUSA wanted to bring audiences in all day during August and Koren and the Gilded Balloon had already staged some events there during 2002's Fringe, four months before the fire. The year after the fire the Gilded Balloon was entirely re-established at Teviot, where it remains to this day.

'I tried for Potterrow as well, but Pleasance got that,' says Koren.

> I managed to get Teviot, and without that we couldn't have moved out of the Cowgate – I mean, we were forced to move out of the Cowgate, but we couldn't have gone on at all. Then Teviot turned out to be nine venues in one building, plus all the bars in the student union.

The new venue meant she could expand from strength to strength. Recently the Gilded Balloon name has grown further during the Fringe, briefly taking on the Rose Theatre at the West End of Rose Street and currently also occupying Adam House, rebranding this tall, cylinder-shaped stack of venues running off a multi-level central foyer as the Gilded Balloon Patter Hoose.

The takeover of Adam House followed the retreat of C Venues, a venue chain that began in 1992 in Princes Street's Overseas League House, formerly used by the Jazz Festival. Programming a busy repertoire of shows by student groups and small companies and perhaps most notable for its geographic diversity, C moved to Adam House at the turn of the 2000s and remained there for nearly two decades, also setting up branches at St Columba's by the Castle (C Too) and the Roman Eagle Lodge (C Aquila), both on Johnston Terrace, the Celtic Lodge at Brodie's Close (C Cubed), India Buildings on Victoria Street (C Nova), Hill Street Lodge (C Primo), Edinburgh College of Art (C ECA), the former Odeon Cinema on Clerk Street (C Electric), St Peter's Church on Lutton Place (C South), C at Makar's Court and more. While the site of the Cowgate fire was a gap site, C also filled it with the outdoor C Soco courtyard.

The Cowgate fire was just one of the changes or setbacks experienced by Fringe institutions in the 2000s. In 2005, after 20 years in charge, Christopher Richardson handed over the reins of the Pleasance to his former general manager Anthony Alderson. Much like his predecessor, Alderson traced his Fringe roots back to the seminal year of 1979. Born in Hexham in Northumberland, that was the year his mother started taking him to the Fringe following the Aldersons' move to Edinburgh, when his father took over the family business, catering company Scobie Mcintosh. Eight years later, 16-year-old schoolboy Alderson followed his elder brother into a summer job working at the Pleasance.

By the time Alderson left the Pleasance in 1999, he was general manager. He'd seen great comedians like Jo Brand, Jenny Eclair and his personal favourites the Doug Anthony Allstars, helped Graham Norton lug stacks of chairs into his venue and was now going off to try working with the producer Glynis Henderson, including on tours by *Stomp* and the comedian Ennio Marchetto. 'I got to a point where I really missed the Fringe, though,' says Alderson.

> I got in touch with Christopher and asked if he'd be interested in having me back, and he said, 'well, it so happens I was thinking of stepping down, so would you come and meet the board?' It was the year the Pleasance Grand became available, and he said to me, 'look, you've got to take it on – this is your first decision, do we open the Pleasance Grand?' It seemed such a no-brainer, because financially it would change the whole operation. So we went for it, but we only had a couple of months to programme it, so it was a seat-of-the-pants ride. That was 2004, when we sort-of transitioned, then Christopher stepped down in 2005. We had a moment in Brookes Club (at Pleasance Dome) where he handed me his hat.

The year 2005 also saw the end of Perrier's involvement with the main comedy award on the Fringe, 24 years after the UK franchise of the company had instigated their creation. In 1992 Perrier had been bought over by the Swiss food and drink multinational Nestlé, although this information hadn't percolated down to the comedians involved in the award until 2001. Since 1977, beginning in the United States, activists had protested Nestlé for its promotion of infant formulas and breast milk substitutes in developing nations. As *Scotland On Sunday* reported in 2001:

> [Nestlé] has been criticised for giving free powdered baby milk to mothers in developing countries in violation of World Health Organisation (WHO) regulations. It has been accused of encouraging mothers to give up breast feeding in favour of nutritionally inferior powdered milk.[3]

The same article quoted comedian Rob Newman, who had long since left his blockbuster comedy career alongside David Baddiel behind, to get into novel-writing and supporting various anti-capitalist activism projects.[4] Urging Fringe comedians to boycott the Perrier due to the involvement of Nestlé, he said 'I regard this as a larger struggle against corporate power'.[5]

Newman was often cited as the originator of the campaign against Perrier sponsorship, but it actually began with Suzy Merrall of Edinburgh arts organisation Out of the Blue, which began life in 1994 as a shopfront gallery on Blackfriars Street and in '96 moved into the offices of an empty former bus garage on New Street, behind Waverley Station. Here OOTB founded the Bongo Club, a countercultural late-night club space whose regular hip-hop nights were attended by the teenage future members of Edinburgh's Mercury Prize-winning Young Fathers.

The arts wing of the organisation was involved in an exchange programme with the South African Mamelodi Theatre Organisation and it was on a visit to the township that Merrall became aware of the Nestlé boycott. [6] Returning to the UK she contacted Patti Rundall, the policy director of Baby Milk Action, the UK wing of international campaign group IBFAN (International Baby Food Action Network). A plan was conceived to run an ongoing alternative protest event to the Perrier at the Bongo Club, impudently named the Tap Water Awards. Less than two years after the publication of Naomi Klein's *No Logo* and the street battles that surrounded the 1999 World Trade Organisation Conference in Seattle, the Perrier campaign captured the anti-capitalist spirit of the times.

Baby Milk Action's supporters included the actors Julie Walters, Richard E Grant and Emma Thompson. As one of the Perrier's first group of winners, Thompson was only too happy to speak up in support of the boycott, as were the comedians Victoria Wood, Mark Thomas, Stewart Lee and another past winner, Steve Coogan; he compared it to the campaign for Barclays bank to stop doing business with South Africa during the apartheid years of the 1980s. [7] With protests held outside the Perrier Award every year to the point the location was no longer announced, Nica Burns fought a rearguard PR action. It became a badge of honour for comedians to knock the Perrier and its sponsors finally withdrew following the event of 2005, when a protest message was displayed inside the awards venue.

Burns is philosophical now. 'Twenty-five years is a long time to do sponsorship, it was pretty amazing and it all just fitted together, but that was the right time to end it,' she says.

> We had discussions [with Perrier] well ahead of time to enable me to go and find another sponsor, because they were a very hard act to follow, but by now the awards were costing a lot of money to do properly. So they very amicably moved on to new things, and I took ownership of the awards.

Under different names dependant on sponsor, the Edinburgh Comedy Awards have continued ever since, although arguably their influence has waned since the Perrier controversy. Partly this is just a matter of timing; the British comedy industry is a different proposition to what it was even back in the early 2000s and while the Edinburgh Fringe is still one of its major proving grounds for stand-up talent, it's no longer the only one. Since the 1980s, the touring stand-up comedy circuit around the country has been built up and the internet and television talent development schemes have become direct routes into the media for comedians and comedy writers.

Yet the winners of the if.comedy awards, the Foster's Edinburgh Comedy Awards, the lastminute.com Edinburgh Comedy Awards and now Dave's Edinburgh Comedy Awards have, since the departure of Perrier, included a slew of star names including David O'Doherty, Tim Key, Russell Kane and Richard Gadd. In the first post-Perrier year, the Australian comedian Brendon Burns' *So I Suppose This is Offensive Now* generated much comment for its innovative surprise – a particularly offensive show which at once questioned the responses of the audience to the worst of the jokes, by way of a mid-show intervention from an outraged plant in the crowd which reviewers went out of their way not to spoil.

Over the years, the overwhelming white maleness of the British comedy industry, and by extension the Comedy Award shortlists, has not unfairly drawn comment. In recent years, this has begun to change. In 2005 only the second Perrier won by a solo female performer went to Laura Solon, who later moved into screenwriting in Hollywood, and in 2013 Bridget Christie's winner *A Bic For Her* seemed to signpost a change in the tone of the comedy industry. The show's starting point was the perceived ridiculousness of a pen designed especially for women to hold and it went on to tear into everyday sexism, taking aim at lads' mags and sexist sports commentators.[8]

Christie is hardly the only female Fringe comic who challenged the business's male hegemony, but her show captured attention and awards and outsold the previous record-holder Trevor Noah when it transferred to London's Soho Theatre. Since 2013, Hannah Gadsby and Rose Matafeo have won the main Comedy Award and since 2006 the Newcomer Award has gone to Josie Long, Sarah Millican, Roisin Conaty, Sofie Hagen, Natalie Palamides and Catherine Cohen. It's hardly full equality and diversity in other areas is only just beginning to catch up, but it's a start.

'The hardest thing was getting women to take the mantle and get on with it,' says Karen Koren, looking back across a comedy promotion career of nearly four decades.

> In the '90s they were a bit rough and ready, being a bit like a boy, and now they've found their own feet, they've developed. But it's hard for a woman to stand up and be criticised by men, which is what happens. 'Oh, she's a bit fat' or 'she's too sexy to be funny' or whatever. I applaud every woman that gets onstage and is funny.

Nica Burns was also involved in one of the most uniquely Fringe-suited Edinburgh stage trends of the 2000s, the one for pieces of classic theatre performed by high-profile comedians. This began in 2003 with *12 Angry Men* at the Assembly Rooms, an adaptation not of the Henry Fonda-starring 1957 Sydney Lumet film, but of the 1954 Reginald Rose play that inspired it.[9] The idea emerged during the Fringe of 2001, following an initial suggestion by the Assembly Rooms' associate director Mary Shields, between comedian Owen O'Neill – who had already had some Fringe theatre success with Sean Hughes during the 1990s – and actor/director/producer Guy Masterson, a singular force of Fringe nature in his own right.

Born Guy Mastroianni in North London in 1961, Masterson studied to be a biochemist at Cardiff University, then emigrated to Los Angeles in the 1980s, attending UCLA as an acting student and slipping into the familiar Californian acting student life of table-waiting around occasional stage jobs.[10] Returning to England to study at LAMBA, his first produced play was a 1991 touring revival of *The Boy's Own Story*, the 1979 play about a troubled professional footballer by County Durham playwright Peter Flannery, most well-known for his play and television series *Our Friends in the North*.

Masterton's long association with the Fringe began with his next production in 1994, an acclaimed solo performance of Dylan Thomas's *Under Milk Wood* at the Assembly Rooms, following its debut at the Traverse earlier that year. Inspired by the performance that Richard Burton first made famous on BBC Radio in 1954, it helped that Burton is Masterson's great-uncle; his death in 1984 first inspired Masterson to move into acting. In the decades since, he's performed *Under Milk Wood* internationally more than 2,000 times, while the other play he directed about his famous relative at the Assembly Rooms in '94 – playwright Mark Jenkins' one-man piece *Playing Burton*, starring Josh Richard – has been seen around 500 times.

From that point, Masterson's reputation and enduring presence on the Fringe was sealed. Under his banners Guy Masterson Productions and later Theatre Tours International, he brought an adaptation of Orwell's *Animal Farm* in '95, which later had two West End runs; actor Pip Utton's acclaimed study of Hitler, *Adolf*, which first appeared in '98 and saw many Fringe revivals in Edinburgh; Masterson's return to Thomas with *Fern Hill and Other Dylan Thomas* in 2001; a British dialect version of David Mamet's *Oleanna* in 2002; and seven Fringe First-winning plays,[11] amid a slew of Stage Awards and other Fringe accolades.

By 2003 he was a known and highly successful quantity in Edinburgh and *12 Angry Men* was a bold experiment which Masterson had absolute faith in. As he wrote in *The List*:

Comedians, to my mind, have few of the hang-ups that obscure confidence. To survive in their business, which is far more ruthless than theatre, they have utterly to trust themselves and their material and be big enough to admit they're wrong when it doesn't work – all qualities most actors struggle for.[12]

He said around 50 comedians expressed an interest in the play's 12 roles, although scheduling commitments helped whittle the number down. The final cast was Bill Bailey (arguably first among equals, given his cult fame through television's *Black Books*), O'Neill, Stephen Frost, Jeff Green, Steve Furst, Phil Nichol, Andy Smart, Dave Johns, Ian Coppinger, Gavin Robertson, David Calvitto and Russell Hunter. Those who expressed an interest before they were forced to pull out included Rich Hall, Omid Djallili, Boothby Graffoe, Nicholas Parsons, Greg Proops and Ed Byrne.

Masterson's instincts were correct and his version of this gripping courtroom drama was well-reviewed and commercially very successful, despite the size of the cast. Plans were made for a follow-up in 2004 and the play chosen was Dale Wasserman's 1973 stage adaptation of Ken Kesey's 1972 classic counter-cultural novel *One Flew Over the Cuckoo's Nest*. The idea came at the 2003 Fringe party following the closure of *12 Angry Men*, when an unnamed cast member remarked they were 'all fuckin' mad anyway!'

The role of McMurphy had been played in earlier productions by Kirk Douglas and, in the multi-Academy Award-winning 1975 film version, Jack Nicholson. A star would be ideal to lead off the show and one was found in Hollywood actor Christian Slater, who'd moved from teen heartthrob status in films like *Pump Up the Volume* (1990) to a promising emergence as an edgy indie star in movies like the Quentin Tarantino-written *True Romance* (1993). Once touted as the new Jack Nicholson – which made him perfect for the role of McMurphy – Slater's career had by 2003 stumbled due to substance abuse issues and jail terms.

Much excitement built around the show, which would once more be held at the Assembly Rooms. Once again, comedians comprised the bulk of the ensemble cast, some of them returning from *12 Angry Men* and others new for this production. They included O'Neill, Johns and Nichol once more, alongside Stephen K Amos, Lucy Porter and actor Felix Dexter. The other key stars were Frances Barber as the quietly authoritarian Nurse Ratched and Mackenzie Crook, then just becoming a bona fide star through his role in Ricky Gervais's television sitcom *The Office*. Although Crook counted as one of the experienced actors on the cast, he'd started out as a stand-up comedian before moving into screen work.

Director Masterson's idea was for an improvisational element to the work the comedians were doing in the background, that their characters' unpredictability as asylum inmates would be baked-in by the nature of their particular skills. Rehearsals in London – the show was transferring to the Gielgud Theatre in the West End immediately after Edinburgh – were fraught and chaotic, according to more than one report, but everything appeared to still be on track and the intensity of it all could even deliver something exceptional. Slater was going to the ballet in London and having dinners with Barber and mutual friends Derek Jacobi and Alan Rickman. But then Masterson quit.

'Due to an untimely amalgamation of unprecedented stresses, personal and professional, I am physically and emotionally unable to continue in my role of director on this show', he said in a statement. His replacements as director were Terry Johnson and Tamara Harvey, the former the playwright and dramatist most well-known for his 1982 Royal Court play *Insignificance*,[13] who somehow corralled the show. In interviews, Barber was talking up the sexuality of the original novel and of Slater's performance. Then he went and caught chickenpox, apparently from co-star Felix Dexter.

'It was an extremely fraught ride,' says Nica Burns, one of the co-producers of the play, who had first made the suggestion to hire a Hollywood star.

It was completely sold out, and then about ten days before we were due to come up to Edinburgh, Christian got chickenpox. It was serious, he was really sick – I had to ring Bill Burdett-Coutts and say, we're not going to make the first performances. Then there was one of the most incredible moments… I remember going to the doctor with Christian, who felt good, and he was told he wasn't infectious any more, but the doctor was signing him off for another week.

Burns says the pair got in a taxi after that and she couldn't hide the sense of panic building inside her.

'It's really bad, isn't it?' asked Slater.

'Yeah'.

'Okay, I feel good, I know all my lines. I'll do it tomorrow'.

Slater hadn't seen the finished set, or even been with his fellow actors for the previous ten days. Meanwhile, the entire production was in Edinburgh and the Festival was well underway around it.

'It was one of the most exciting mornings in a theatre ever,' says Burns of the opening performance.

Everyone knew he'd got off his sick bed and that he hadn't been in rehearsal, but he'd bloody learned his lines. It was one of these really special moments – it was the bravest piece of acting, absolutely extraordinary what Christian Slater did, and he was brilliant. He had entered into the whole Fringe spirit of what we were doing, and we cared about the audiences, about not disappointing people. They're part of the story too, you know?

Despite it all, *One Flew Over the Cuckoo's Nest* eventually opened midway through its planned run at the Fringe – with a brief, belated preview period and reviews following later in the month – and was a critical and word-of-mouth hit, finally living up to its billing as the biggest show in town that year. By his 35th birthday on 18 August, Slater was well enough to celebrate with the cast at short-lived Picardy Place members' club the Hallion, while at the end of every performance he took to slinging his sweat-soaked T-shirt into the audience. Many in the crowd, aware of the infectiousness of chickenpox, left it where it fell.

The transfer to the Gielgud was also a hit and Slater returned to the role of McMurphy in the West End in 2006, this time at the Garrick Theatre alongside Alex Kingston. In 2007 the same production toured the UK, now with Shane Ritchie and Sophie Ward in the lead roles. Guy Masterson, meanwhile, was fully recovered by the following year and he returned to the format with a version of Neil Simon's *The Odd Couple*, now with comedians Bill Bailey and Alan Davies taking on the respective roles made famous by Walter Matthau and Jack Lemmon. Another huge hit, it was performed at the Assembly Hall on the Mound, which William Burdett-Coutts has continued to use ever since.

'When the Scottish Parliament left the Assembly Hall [in September 2004, a matter of days after *One Flew Over the Cuckoo's Nest* closed at the Assembly Rooms], there was a discussion about what should happen with the building,' says Burdett-Coutts.

We were approached about whether we'd be interested, and I thought it would be a natural adjunct to what we do. I love the venue, the size and feel of the room, and the wood panelling creates a great resonance in the room. The horseshoe seating area bends around the stage and it's not a big room, so you can play to 800 people in a very intimate space. Atmosphere's a hard thing to determine in theatres, some have it, some don't, and that room is really special. It's maybe the best theatre in the city.

Despite its history as an International Festival venue, 2005's *The Odd Couple* was the first Fringe show ever performed in the Assembly Hall. The name itself meant it sat perfectly in Burdett-Coutts' portfolio alongside the Assembly Rooms. Comedians including Sarah Millican, Eddie Izzard and Julian Clary have since played there and in 2009, three years after author Muriel Spark's death, director – and future director of the National Theatre of Scotland – Laurie Sansom brought a stage production of her definitive Edinburgh novel *The Prime of Miss Jean Brodie* to the Assembly Hall's stage, at the same time as all-female Scots theatre company Stellar Quines put on Spark's *A Girl of Slender Means* at the Assembly Rooms, by this point rebranded Assembly @ George Street.[14]

In 2006, Peter Quilter's play *End of the Rainbow* also appeared at the Assembly Hall, its European premiere after dates in Australia. This play – an evolution of Quilter's earlier play *Last Song of the Nightingale*, which appeared on the Fringe at Jongleurs comedy club in the newly-built Omni Centre entertainment complex on Picardy Place in 2003 – starred Caroline O'Connor as Judy Garland in the final years of her life and went on to gather seven Olivier and Tony Award nominations for its West End and Broadway runs and an Academy Award for Renée Zellweger, star of the 2019 film adaptation *Judy*.

Although Masterson's high-profile trio of plays between '03 and '05 were the real blockbusters of the Fringe's theatre-by-comedians trend, they weren't the only ones plying this trade during the 2000s. in 2003, the same year 12 *Angry Men* debuted, Jo Brand was playing the Assembly Rooms in *Mental*, a dark comedy about her and co-writer and fellow former mental health nurse-turned-actor Helen Griffin's experiences in their old job, while Ed Byrne starred in *Kings of the Road* at the Pleasance Dome, about Belfast bus drivers during the Troubles. The Scottish-born Canadian comedian Phil Nichol, meanwhile, co-founded the Comedians Theatre Company with director Maggie Inchley in 2006.

Corky and the Juice Pigs, Nichol's Ontario-founded comedy trio alongside Greg Neale and Sean Cullen, had been nominated for a Perrier in 1993 and the by-now Fringe veteran was Perrier-nominated for his solo show *Things I Like I Lick* in 2002, the same year he appeared in the Boy George musical *Taboo* in the West End (Nichol later won the rebranded if.comedy award for *The Naked Racist* in 2006). In 2005, although not part of *The Odd Couple*'s slimmer cast, he brought a production of Edward Albee's *The Zoo Story* to the Gilded Balloon.

The following year the Comedians Theatre Company was fully up and running, with Sam Shepard's *True West* at the Assembly Rooms, directed by Inchley and starring *Cuckoo's Nest* alumni Nichol and Dave Johns alongside Tom Stade and Janice Connolly. For some years, the company became a Fringe fixture, bringing repertory productions to the Assembly Rooms, the

Pleasance and the Stand, including Kenneth Ross's *Breaker Morant*, with Adam Hills, Rhys Darby and Brendon Burns; Tracey Letts's *Killer Joe*, with Tony Law and Lizzie Roper; Gregory Burke's *Gagarin Way*, with Will Andrews and Bruce Morton; and RB Sheridan's *School for Scandal*, with Lionel Blair, Stephen K Amos, Bridget Christie and Marcus Brigstocke.

Later, Nichol took to appearing in acclaimed new plays by comedian and playwright Dave Florez, directed by Hannah Eidenow, including *The Intervention, Somewhere Beneath It All a Small Fire Burns Still* and *Angel in the Abattoir*. Where during the 1990s, the discussion about stand-up comedy's encroachment upon the long-standing theatrical aspect of the Fringe had been live and raw, the list of shows that grew out of those that followed *12 Angry Men* represented an evolution for the Festival, a cross-pollination of ideas and skills to which the hothouse creative environment of Edinburgh in August is perfectly suited.

* * *

In 2006, the year after Malcolm Hardee's accidental death by drowning while trying to get back to his houseboat in London, the Comedians Theatre Company brought his old Circuit nemesis Eric Bogosian back to Edinburgh – or rather, Nichol and Inchley brought Bogosian's 1987 off-Broadway play *Talk Radio* to the Underbelly on Bristo Square, the year before it finally made its Broadway premiere in a separate production starring Liev Schreiber and Sebastian Stan.

The Edinburgh *Talk Radio* was a worthy successor to the spirit of Masterson's plays, given *The Odd Couple* was the last of these large-scale productions. While Masterson ended the concept on a high, in fact, he simply divided his production energies in Edinburgh between a greater number of smaller shows. Whether performing them himself, directing other actors or acting as producer, his name is a Fringe ever-present.

In 2006 Masterson directed Rich Hall's debut play *Levelland*; in 2009 he directed Bob Golding in *Morecambe*, Tim Whitnall's one-man bioplay of the comedian Eric Morecambe, which won an Olivier Award the following year. In 2019 he directed *The Shark is Broken* at Assembly George Square – written by and starring Ian Shaw, son of the late actor and *Jaws* star Robert Shaw, it told the behind-the-scenes story of Spielberg's film and also won an Olivier in 2022, following its West End transfer.

The director of the Comedians Theatre Company's 2006 *Talk Radio*, meanwhile, was the other key figure in the Fringe's blurring of lines between comedy and theatre during the 2000s. Stewart Lee had been coming to the Fringe since 1987, first as a student comedian, often performing with fellow

Oxford students including his friend Richard Herring and then, from 1990, on the professional roster of Jon Thoday's Avalon:

> The bright new dawn of 90s comedy was rising, and we drove around Edinburgh under cover of darkness in a panel van, flyposting illegally with pots of paint and brushes, like the A-Team with jokes. The romance of it! [A]ll of us pasting over Jeremy Hardy's face again and again, like pathetic and ungrateful schoolboys vandalising a photo of the headmaster. Nobody on the Fringe had ever seen anything like it. Advertising![15]

Over the next decade, Lee's career developed independent of the Edinburgh Fringe, although he still came with a newly-written stand-up show every year until 2000. He worked on BBC Radio 4's *On the Hour*, original home of Steve Coogan's Alan Partridge, for which character he and Herring wrote and his Fringe show *King Dong vs Moby Dick* was instrumental in the formation of The Mighty Boosh; he directed their Perrier-nominated 1999 show *Arctic Boosh*. But mostly he was known for his silly, pop culture-drenched and often bitingly funny double act with Richard Herring on the BBC Radio One shows *Fist of Fun* and *Lee and Herring* and the Sunday Afternoon BBC Two TV programme *This Morning with Richard Not Judy*, which ended after a year in 1999.

With the new millennium came disenchantment and temporary retirement from stand-up comedy. Lee had always wanted to be a writer, but during the 1990s his career rode the wave of the 'comedy is the new rock 'n' roll' trend built by the likes of Sean Hughes, Rob Newman and David Baddiel. Yet, the student audience that enjoyed his and Herring's work grew up, as Lee also wanted to. He was unsatisfied with the limitations of the form, searching for something more complex to say while his audiences just wanted a bit of risqué humour. His 2000 show at the Pleasance, *Badly Mapped World*, was the final straw; it made him little money and picked up mediocre reviews.

After an encounter with a racist fan at a gig in Liverpool, Lee decided to give up stand-up. In 2001, he took his first year off Edinburgh in a decade and a half and worked instead with his old friend, composer and musical comedian Richard Thomas, at Battersea Arts Centre (BAC) in London. The pair were working together on Lee and Simon Munnery's very short-lived BBC Two series *Attention Scum* in the same year, an offshoot of their mid-90s Fringe show at the Pleasance *Cluub Zarathustra*, which featured Thomas, Kevin Eldon, Johnny Vegas, Sally Phillips and Munnery's Alan Parker – Urban Warrior and The League Against Tedium characters.

In 2001 Thomas, who performed his own show *Tourette's Diva* at the

Fringe in 2000, was working on a solo piano project named *How to Write an Opera About Jerry Springer*, which he was performing to small preview audiences in a semi-written state at BAC. The real Springer was very much a person of his era, a former lawyer, campaign advisor to Robert Kennedy, Mayor of Cincinnati and serious news anchor, whose self-titled television show had since 1991 become a byword for bear-baiting sensationalism, by having ordinary members of the public argue out their differences on camera.

By the turn of the 2000s, Springer's show was cult viewing internationally and already a familiar subject of topical comedy for Fringe comedians. Thomas discovered it late at night, when coming in after shows and turning on the television. '[A]ll these fat people [were] shouting at one another and you couldn't understand what they were saying, and I thought, 'that's an opera''.[16]

Under the artistic directorship of Tom Morris, brother of *On the Hour* and *The Day Today* co-creator Chris Morris,[17] BAC had introduced a series of scratch nights, where artists were allowed full use of rehearsal spaces to try out new ideas on condition they present in-progress versions to the public. Once Thomas asked Lee to write a story around his Jerry Springer songs and direct the resulting show, the rehearsal rooms in Battersea became a haven for them, especially while Lee was in the midst of a creative crisis. If it hadn't been for this theatre, said Lee, 'I doubt I would ever have written or performed anything new ever again'.[18]

As the show developed into *Jerry Springer: The Opera*, it ran for a week at BAC in late 2001 and then another three weeks in early 2002. Its official premiere and baptism of fire came at the Fringe of 2002, however, playing three weeks at the Assembly Rooms' 600-capacity Music Hall and selling out each one. This was where it was heard in full for the first time, with 21 professional opera singers and a five-piece band alongside the cast, singing operatic works with unexpected titles like 'Chick with a Dick', 'Montel Cums Dirty' and 'Poledancer'.

Meeting Lee and Thomas around one of the show's previews, before full reviews were permitted, the *Edinburgh Evening News*'s Rory Ford urged his readers, 'you should definitely book now... The West End and probably Broadway beckons. Seriously'.[19] In fact, Lee and Thomas were guaranteed to make nothing from the Edinburgh run, such was the cost of producing the show, but with Lee's agent Avalon and other financial backers involved, its continuation was more or less a foregone conclusion.

It was the perfect Fringe show – funny, topical, profane, both a talking point for audiences and thoroughly critically-acclaimed, even in the quality press. In Edinburgh it was also given the most priceless boost of all when Jerry Springer himself, in the city to give an address at the Television Festival, went to see it. Jokingly referring to his fictional murder in the show and journey into hell, to mediate between Satan and Jesus, he told *The Observer*:

Not many people get to see their future... I hope the show comes to America. I only wish I'd thought of it first. I don't object to anything in it. The whole show is tongue-in-cheek, so what is the problem?[20]

Springer stood up in the Assembly Rooms and took applause during the interval, although he later said he felt uncomfortable watching a representation of himself onstage. The Edinburgh run of *Jerry Springer: The Opera* gave way to an even larger production at the National Theatre in London in 2003 and then at the West End's Cambridge Theatre for more than a year, although the planned Broadway run never materialised. This had much to do with the high-profile campaign by Christian groups against first the televised BBC Two broadcast in early 2005 and then the 2006 UK tour.

One such group unsuccessfully attempted to take the BBC's then-director general Mark Thompson to court for blasphemy and the show became the most complained-about BBC broadcast ever, attracting 63,000 orchestrated complaints.[21] Claims were also made that the play contained several thousand profanities. According to Lee the real number is 174, which a BBC investigation said contained 96 uses of 'fuck' and nine of 'cunt'; detractors had apparently counted every instance of every member of the chorus singing the same word at the same time. Still, that's many, many times more than the usual BBC broadcast.

Jerry Springer: The Opera didn't make it to Broadway, but two dates at Carnegie Hall in January 2008 with Harvey Keitel in the title role were some kind of consolation. In 2018, it finally appeared Off-Broadway, to little consternation – by this point Springer's show was a spent cultural reference point and a few months later production of it ended. The opera was a brief but incredibly bright success and arguably a great PR boost to Springer himself, although within the context of the Edinburgh Festival Fringe, its lasting legacy was the reinvention of Stewart Lee's comedy career.

In 2002, while *Jerry Springer* was playing in the city, Lee also performed his personal, moderately well-received piece about the poet Edward Lear, *Pea Green Boat*, at the Traverse. By 2004, he was beginning to feel his way back into stand-up. Armed with a decidedly tentative title for the show – *Stand-Up Comedian* – which partially disguised the fact he hadn't written it in time for the Fringe programme deadline, Lee returned to Edinburgh in 2004.

In a mutually beneficial agreement, which gave them a big name on the bill and him a deal that meant he wouldn't lose any money, Lee took his show to the then-young Underbelly's White Belly cave. It was a winding, seemingly freeform conversation with himself, which captured the cynical flavour of the period immediately post-9/11, while making skilful and more mature use of Lee's hangdog blend of sarcasm and geekish enthusiasm. It was the kind of stand-up show a one-time wannabe novelist – who now actually was a published novelist – might write. Referring to the four Oliver Awards *Jerry Springer: The Opera* won from seven nominations in 2004, Lee wrote with customary sarcasm:

> Now that I had been ladled with theatrical accolades, previously puzzled critics had to assume that my apparent inability to write and perform stand-up properly was in fact the result of positive artistic choices, rather than an indication of a basic lack of ability, and they adjusted their star ratings accordingly.[22]

He was on a roll, his voice and audience rediscovered after a period in his career that skirted close to the marshy edge of the wilderness. Lee returned to the Underbelly in 2005 with *90s Comedian*, which railed against the religious censorship of *Jerry Springer: The Opera* while discussing his own recent health troubles. It was widely acclaimed, with *The Scotsman* comparing Lee's onstage growth to Banner become the Incredible Hulk. Some complement, for Marvel Comics fan Lee.

Jerry Springer: The Opera was Richard Thomas's big hit, although he later worked on *Anna Nicole* (2011), the opera about the life of American model Anna Nicole Smith at the Royal Opera House in London, and the stage musical version of the film *Made in Dagenham* (2014). He'd first come to Edinburgh at the same time as Lee, as one half of comedy musical duo Miles and Milner – who were successful for a time in the late '80s and early '90s – and 30 years later was still involved in Edinburgh shows.

In 2017, he played piano for *Jonny Woo's All-Star Brexit Cabaret* at Assembly George Square Gardens, with Jayde Adams as Boris Johnson and Le Gateau Chocolat in the role of Nigel Farage. The same year, he also did some songwriting alongside Scottish duo Noisemaker (Scott Gilmour and Claire Mackenzie) for the National Theatre of Scotland's disability comedy *My Left/Right Foot* at Assembly Roxy.

Lee, meanwhile, held an event named *Silver Stewbilee* at the Festival Theatre on Wednesday 18 September 2010, which marked his 25th anniversary (more or less) of coming to the Fringe and also launched his book of selected show transcriptions and writing around them, *How I Escaped My Certain Fate*. Performed to an audience of 2,000, the bill included Simon Munnery, Paul Putner, Kevin Eldon, Lee's wife and fast-rising fellow stand-up Bridget Christie, as well as Glasgow rock group Franz Ferdinand, who played their own songs 'Do You Want To' and 'Take Me Out' alongside a cover of the band Mission of Burma's 'That's How I Escaped My Certain Fate' with obscurist music fan Lee on vocals.

The night also featured 1984 Perrier Award nominees Frank Chickens, a Japanese musical troupe much-loved by Lee's hero, the DJ John Peel, who in the 1980s had toured with The Smiths and Billy Bragg. The Chickens had been the subject of a public falling-out between Lee and the Edinburgh Comedy Award the previous month. Setting up a telephone poll where the public could vote for their favourite among 173 past nominees and Fringe comedy performers, the Comedy Award and Nica Burns had been rebuked in a letter from Lee that he released publicly, including to the comedy website *Chortle*. It read:

> Don't invoke people like Simon Cowell and Andrew Lloyd Webber in an Edinburgh fringe award. What is wrong with you? It's totally inappropriate. This is the place we go to escape them![23]

It went on to collectively refer to the originators of 'this farcical, selfish idea' as 'Corporate Whores. Morons. Illiterates.'[23] With an online campaign similar to the one that saw Rage Against the Machine's anti-corporate anthem 'Killing in the Name' crowned the UK's 2009 Christmas number one ahead of the latest X-Factor winner, Frank Chickens eventually topped the poll with 30,000 votes, ahead of Tim Minchin, Russell Howard and Michael McIntyre.

It was the opening salvo in a war of words that came to a head two years later, when Lee wrote an excoriating opinion piece for *The Guardian*. He took aim at the Edinburgh Comedy Festival and the major venues, railing against many of the perceived problems of the Fringe for performers. The 2010s would prove the most successful decade yet for the Fringe and the wider Edinburgh Festival in terms of audience numbers and critical acclaim, but Lee's words struck a chord with many performers and members of the public who were growing dissatisfied with the increasingly corporate nature of the Festival.

SPOTLIGHT

Black Watch (2006) The James Plays (2014)

THE NATIONAL THEATRE of Scotland officially opened in 2006, yet to fully understand its influence upon the Edinburgh Festival – including one of the biggest hit shows British theatre has seen in recent times – we have to look at the two decades during which a surging drama scene in Scotland flowed through and around the floodgates of the Festival towards its creation. The forces that shaped the NTS' birth stretch right back to the beginning of the Edinburgh Festival and beyond, covering a century during which demands for Scotland to have its own theatre grew and faded and returned again.

While these demands intensified in the post-war years, they largely went into remission until after the failed Scottish devolution referendum of 1979, when the nation's theatre entered its most vibrant period yet. It's ironic, perhaps, that the discussions around a Scottish National Theatre pioneered by Glasgow's Scottish National Players in the 1920s and carried on after the war by notable Festival figures like James Bridie, Robert McLellan, Duncan Macrae and the Glasgow Unity Theatre group didn't just die out because these people did; they were also left in the past because the need for life support to keep Scotland's fragile playwriting and performing ecology alive in the middle of the 20th century became less necessary as the theatre scene in the country became fitter and stronger.

The big Scottish theatres went through golden eras.[1] Between 1972 and '75 the great theatre director Bill Bryden – who also worked at the Royal Court and National Theatre in London and was Head of Television Drama at BBC Scotland for nine years from 1984 – was a resident director at the Lyceum. From 1969 until 2003, the Oxford Theatre Group alumnus and former Watford Palace Theatre director Giles Havergal was AD at the Citizens Theatre alongside designer/director Philip Prowse and the prolific playwright, translator and director Robert David MacDonald. Their repertoire at the International Festival over three decades featured regular Citizens actors Ian McDiarmid, Gary Oldman, David Hayman and Ida Schuster.

In 1980 Dundonian actor Ewan Hooper, who had helped found London's Greenwich Theatre in 1969, established the Scottish Theatre Company to tour new and classic Scottish work alongside some international repertory performances. It was soon taken over by the Royal Lyceum Company's founder Tom Fleming who, prior to the company's folding in 1987, directed both of its appearances at the International Festival with *A Satire of the Three Estates* at the Assembly Hall in 1984 and '85, adding Sydney Goodsir Smith's *The Wallace* in the second year. In 1982, 7:84's Glasgow-based Clydebuilt season revived the work of playwrights like Joe Corrie and Ena Lamont Stewart to great acclaim and the decade brought new voices to Scottish theatre, including Gerry Mulgrew's Communicado company.

During the Fringe of 1985, the Traverse Theatre's programme was a watershed moment in the development of a new generation of Scottish playwrights. It was also the final act of outgoing artistic director Peter Lichtenfels, who was born in Germany in 1949 and educated in Canada and who had weathered heavy financial storms in his half-decade at the Traverse. His tenure included a psychological horror, in April 1983, about a woman having a breakdown in the Grampian hills named *Fugue*. Its writer was Rona Munro, a 23-year-old recent Edinburgh University history graduate from Aberdeen.

The same month *Fugue* was performed, Lichtenfels hired another 23-year-old as a trainee director. Jenny Killick was a University of London graduate from England who had been recommended to him after a brief spell working at Riverside Studios. Her skills and enthusiasm were such that over the next two years she worked her way up to the position of associate director; in effect a kind of unofficial joint artistic director. As a young theatre administrator just starting out, she had an affinity for new playwrights, particularly ones local to the Traverse.

In March '84, Killick directed a Royal Scottish Academy of Music and Drama production of Tom McGrath's *The Innocent*, an autobiographical piece about the writer's days of jazz, drugs and underground poetry in London in the 1960s, first seen at the Royal Shakespeare Company's Warehouse Theatre in London in 1979. Killick and the students' version was performed again without the Traverse banner at the Assembly Rooms during the Fringe of '84. In April of that year, she also co-directed, with Lichtenfels, a trio of short works by new Scottish playwrights Chris Hannan, Simon Donald and Stuart Paterson under the banner title *1984: Points of Departure*.

This event was the spark that led to the seminal Traverse Fringe of '85 and to emphasise that a new generation of Scots writers was in the midst of emerging around this period, the theatre hosted a script-in-hand reading of a brand new work named *Confessions* on 10 November 1984. The aspiring playwright, two years graduated from the University of Edinburgh, was the future crime writer Ian Rankin, three years before his book *Knots and Crosses* launched the landmark series of novels starring his definitive Edinburgh detective John Rebus.

The first of the Traverse Class of '85 to arrive that year was Peter Arnott, a lawyer's son from Glasgow who had become involved in theatre while he was studying English Literature at Cambridge University. Killick knew him from Cambridge – she had directed him in Brecht there – and he'd just turned 23 when his debut play *White Rose* appeared at the Traverse in May '85. About a female Soviet fighter pilot during the Second World War, its three-handed cast was outstandingly good in retrospect, placing 30-year-old Ken Stott alongside Arnott's fellow Cambridge alumni Kate Duchene and the 24-year-old unknown Tilda Swinton.[2] The following year Arnott was back at the Fringe, this time at the Crown Theatre on Hill Place, with a cabaret run by Glasgow's left-wing troupe *Redheads*, performing sketches aimed at Tories, the Royal Family, crooked landlords and the DHSS (Department for Health and Social Security) alongside actor Libby McArthur and a 26-year-old community drama worker and occasional writing partner of Arnott's, Peter Mullan.

The next of the new breed was Chris Hannan, who'd already picked up a couple of Traverse credits, including *Purity*, his short play about Beethoven's early life as part of *1984: Points of Departure* and a loose adaptation of Maxim Gorky's *The Life of a Useless Man* as *Klimkov: The Life of a Tsarist Agent* later that year, both directed by Killick. Hannan, like Arnott, had been raised in Glasgow and then gone south to study English Literature at an elite university, in his case Oxford, where he earned a double first. The son of a shipyard worker and a primary school teacher, he returned home soon after graduation and went to work in a night shelter for homeless people. His first play was *Screw the Bobbin*, a piece of agit-prop about a factory closure, co-written with John McGrath and staged by 7:84 at Edinburgh's Wester Hailes Community Education Centre in the autumn of 1982, when Hannan was 24.

Where *White Rose* was a powerful calling card for a new playwriting talent, it's been overshadowed by many of Arnott's other works over four prolific decades since; among them *The Boxer Benny Lynch*, the first play he wrote, which toured Glasgow community centres later in 1985 to great enthusiasm. Yet *Elizabeth Gordon Quinn*, Hannan's contribution to the Traverse season of 1985, proved to be an immediate and enduring classic of contemporary Scottish theatre and his most celebrated play of a busy career. His Quinn is a woman living amid the Glasgow rent strike of 1915 who maintains a sense of individualism and aspiration amid the grinding poverty around her, as represented by the upright piano she keeps in her flat. But does this individualism, wonders Hannan's play, mentally free her from the harsh reality of destitute times, or does it act to break up the bonds of society and the unity of collective action?

The parallels with life in Thatcher's Britain weren't hard to see. The play's stars were Eileen Nicholas as Elizabeth and Ralph Riach as her downtrodden husband William. Hannan has noted in commentary on his website that Nicholas was the daughter of working-class Glasgow communists and that 'when she was confronted with the part of Elizabeth Gordon Quinn she was able to make a very strong connection with a woman who had an alternative belief-system to those around her.'

These plays, both directed by Stephen Unwin, were soon revived for the classic Traverse Fringe of that year, alongside the debut of the biggest hit of them all.

Jo Clifford wasn't entirely a novice by this point. In fact, she was already in her mid-'30s – a later starter than the rest of the Traverse newcomer crowd, having tried to work towards becoming a novelist for 15 years.[3] Born in Stoke-On-Trent, Clifford studied at the University of St Andrews at the turn of the 1970s and returned to complete her thesis there some years later, in the meantime working all manner of jobs: a bus conductor, a yoga teacher, a student nurse. The thesis's subject was Pedro Calderón de Barca's

17th century Spanish play *The Doctor of Honour* (*El Médico de su honra*), a tragedy about a nobleman who plots brutal revenge on his wife for an imagined affair, which Clifford translated herself as part of her studies.

Clifford's partner, the journalist, academic and feminist campaigner Sue Innes, showed the script to a producer colleague at the BBC named Robert Livingston in 1982. He praised Clifford's ability to write dialogue and Livingston and Clifford decided to take another Calderón translation to the Edinburgh Fringe that year with their own Merlindene theatre company. This time the play was the 1629 comedy *The House with Two Doors* (*Casa con dos puertas*), which was staged in the hall of St Thomas of Aquin's High School near Tollcross. Clifford later wrote:

> It was a terrible venue... and we did really badly... On our best night, we had an audience of 23. But they laughed. And hearing their laughter made me understand I was a playwright.[4]

Her *The Doctor of Honour* was performed in St Andrews in 1983, the same year Clifford had new plays read on BBC Radio Scotland and BBC Radio 3. In 1984 she was asked by artistic director Ian Brown to adapt and condense *Romeo and Juliet* for performance in schools by the Citizens Theatre's outreach arm TAG (Theatre About Glasgow). Her first original play for the stage, however, was *Losing Venice*, the third of the trio of breakthrough plays at the Traverse during the Fringe of '85. It was the only one of the three making its full premiere.

Clifford wrote reviews for *The Scotsman* and made Spain of the 17th century a speciality of her writing. *Losing Venice* was set there once more, like the plays of Calderón, in a fading empire where delusional ideas of superiority and male bravado prop up the nation's power structures, until the poet Quevedo suggests a doomed adventure to 'retake' the city of Venice for Spain. In the years after the Falklands War of 1982 between the UK and Argentina, the play struck chords.

Again, Sue Innes was partly responsible for this play happening. She'd met Jenny Killick on a train from London in 1983, when Killick was on her way to Edinburgh to begin the trainee director job, and suggested she might like to meet Clifford and have a chat; Clifford had been pitching to the Traverse for a while with no success. They met in the gloomy downstairs theatre at the old Traverse off the Grassmarket and *Losing Venice* was the second idea Clifford pitched. She recalled it had a troubled, complex birth right up to its opening, with the pressure on to deliver during the Fringe. Later, she wrote:

> When the reviews came out, we found we had somehow created

a huge hit... It was everything I had wanted it to be – funny, fast-moving, lovely to look at, lovely to see, thought-provoking, entertaining, moving.[5]

Losing Venice transferred to London, Australia, Sweden, Hong Kong and the United States and Clifford became a mainstay at the Traverse and the Edinburgh Festival with plays and translations for many years to come. *Playing with Fire* (1987), *Inés de Castro* (1989) and *Light in the Village* (1991) all played at the Traverse during the Fringe. For the Edinburgh International Festival she wrote Caldéron's *Schism in England* (1989), directed by John Burgess at the St Bride's Centre on behalf of the National Theatre in London; the short opera *Anna* (1993) with composer Craig Armstrong at the Traverse; the acclaimed operatic adaptation of *Inés de Castro* (1996) with composer James MacMillan at the Festival Theatre;[6] Caldéron's *Life is a Dream* (1998) at the Lyceum; and Fernando de Rojas' *Celestina* (2004) at the King's Theatre.[7]

Peter Lichtenfels left the artistic director post at the Traverse after 1985's Fringe, taking the same job at the Haymarket Theatre in Leicester until 1991 and then splitting his time between directing and academia during spells in England and California. Jenny Killick was his replacement and she became both the Traverse's first female artistic director and the youngest AD in the UK when she took over. She stayed until 1988, going on to work as a director for stage and television, and was replaced in turn by Ian Brown, the director of Glasgow's TAG, who had commissioned *Romeo and Juliet* from Clifford some years before.

During her tenure Killick ended the Traverse's status as a members' club. During her Fringes in charge she welcomed back South African playwright Percy Mtwa and his Earth Players company with the first international tour in 1986 of *Bopha!* ('Arrested!') about an activist son and his policeman father, which was filmed for a Sidney Poitier-narrated documentary that year and adapted as Morgan Freeman's film directorial debut in 1993.

In 1987, the big Traverse hit of the Festival was the English-language premier of former Berliner Ensemble actor Manfred Karge's play *Man to Man*, in which a German woman living in Nazi Germany must take on her dead husband's identity to survive. It starred emerging star Tilda Swinton in the same year she made her film debut in Derek Jarman's *Caravaggio*, then transferred to the Royal Court in London the following year and was made into a 1992 television film, also starring Swinton and directed by John Maybury.[8]

Killick commissioned more work by Arnott, Clifford and Hannan, as well as established Scottish writers Tom McGrath and James Kelman and newcomers including Iain Heggie, John Binnie, Anne Marie Di Mambro and Annie Griffin. Scottish theatre had done well in the 1980s, especially at the Traverse, and was to boom yet further in the 1990s, although its wider story during this time – bound up as much in the theatres of Glasgow and the catalytic effect of that city's European City of Culture year in 1990 – has been told elsewhere. Yet that Traverse Fringe of 1985 was arguably the domino which set the birth of the National Theatre of Scotland 21 years later in motion. As Peter Arnott told writer Mark Fisher in 2010:

> All three plays were resisting the sense of limited possibility [in Scottish theatre]... In 1985 it felt that, even if [Scots] were impotent politically, in the cultural sphere we could say, 'More is possible'... now, with the National Theatre of Scotland, there's an assumption of grown-upness about Scottish theatre that wasn't there in 1985. That season at the Traverse was the best of the way Scottish theatre has developed since.[9]

* * *

At the heart of this development, like a wheel whose spokes touched most of the major arts work in the country, was the Scottish Arts Council, the body that had paid the Traverse to produce Clifford, Hannan and Arnott's plays in 1985. This had its deepest roots in the wartime Council for the Encouragement of Music and the Arts (CEMA), which was founded in 1940 to stimulate cultural activity at a time when the nation had war on its mind. In 1946 CEMA evolved into the Arts Council of Great Britain, the organisation whose then-chair John Maynard Keynes had turned down Rudolf Bing and Glyndebourne's John Christie for early funding towards the Edinburgh International Festival in '47.

The Scottish Art Council was formally established as its own committee within the Arts Council of Great Britain in 1967, with responsibility for funding arts and cultural projects in Scotland, and in 1994 it became its own entirely independent organisation,[10] with the added responsibility of distributing allocated National Lottery funds.[11] Through the domestic political events of these decades and the ebb and flow of Scottish nationalist desires following Winnie Ewing's Hamilton by-election win of '67, the rise of the North Sea Oil industry and the failed devolution referendum of '79, further demands for a Scottish National Theatre were not much more than a murmur in the background.

Quite simply, a lot of people didn't see the need. In 2003, after wheels had finally started turning in that direction, *The List* magazine's theatre editor Steve Cramer bluntly made the case against. While paying due regard towards the work of James Bridie, Joe Corrie and Ena Lamont Stewart, he maintained that:

> ...the Norwegians built their national around Ibsen, and Ibsen these folks aren't. I won't have the English laugh at us while we stage [Bridie's] *The Anatomist* against their *King Lear*. Scotland's greatest writers for the theatre – John McGrath, Lochhead, [David] Greig and so forth – are products of the last quarter century or so. They don't need a museum built to them, just enough money in Scottish theatre to allow existing companies to revive them.[12]

The knock-on implication was that when Scotland looked to the golden age, the high watermark of theatre in the country, it didn't need to look back nearly 400 years to the time of Shakespeare, unlike England. Scotland was living its golden age in the present, so why not bolster that in any way possible?

Everything changed in 1997, with the landslide UK general election victory of the Tony Blair-led Labour party on 1 May and then the honouring on 11 September of the winning party's manifesto commitment to hold a Scottish devolution referendum.[13] The result was nearly 75 per cent in favour of the creation of a Scottish Parliament and following the passing of the Scotland Act 1998 at Westminster, this Parliament came into being on 12 May 1999. Known first as the Scottish Executive and since 2007 as the Scottish Parliament, it sat for its first five years at the Assembly Hall on the Mound, where *The Three Estates* in 1948 linked Scotland with its theatrical history of 150 years prior to the 1707 Act of Union between Scotland and England.

One early task of the new Scottish Executive was to consult and report on a National Cultural Strategy for Scotland, which it did throughout 2000. Its Education, Culture and Sport Committee made the point early on that Scotland had a national opera company, a national ballet company and national orchestras, so the absence of a national theatre company was both a glaring omission and a missed opportunity to create inward investment in Scottish theatre, boosting a homegrown theatrical voice and industry. In July that year, the industry body the Federation of Scottish Theatre (FST) made a proposal that perhaps a National Theatre of Scotland might function like the Edinburgh International Festival – as a commissioning body that employed various theatre groups and professionals to build its programme, rather than as one building-based hub.

When the National Cultural Strategy arrived at the end of the summer, it was described by one writer as 'a confused, sometimes contradictory hotchpotch of political and economic justifications for nebulous and untameable creative forces, but at least it is an earnest attempt to take the whole business seriously.'[14] In the face of an often jargonistic attempt to hammer the raw flexibility of the creative industries into the over-planned certainties of management-speak which has often characterised these relationships in Scotland since, there came a broad agreement to publicly fund something like the FST's model. The process took more than half a decade to come together, with a final funding commitment given by the Scottish Executive on 11 September 2003 and the appointment of an artistic director in July 2004.

For some in Scottish theatre, the person chosen for the role came as a surprise. There was a longlist of 30 applicants and a shortlist of six. Rumoured contenders from those who supposed they knew who might be on them included Kenny Ireland, former *Great Northern Welly Boot Show* stalwart turned artistic director of the Royal Lyceum until 2003, and Ian McDiarmid, the Carnoustie-born Royal Scottish Academy of Music and Drama graduate and prolific Royal Shakespeare Company actor who made a popular name for himself as Emperor Palpatine in the 1983 *Star Wars* sequel *Return of the Jedi*. Between 1990 and 2001 he was also co-director of the Almeida Theatre in London.

The applicant chosen however, was 37-year-old Vicky Featherstone, whose career by this point was young but prolific. Born in Surrey and trained as an actor at Manchester University before moving into directing, she spent most of the 1990s working in various roles at theatres including the Royal Court and Bush Theatre in London, West Yorkshire Playhouse and Bolton's Octagon Theatre. For ITV, she co-created the prime-time nursing drama *Where the Heart Is* with Ashley Pharoah in 1997, then later that year took over the artistic directorship of the Paines Plough theatre company. It was this job she left for the National Theatre of Scotland in 2004.

There were mutterings from some quarters about Featherstone's appointment – generally some shade of speculation as to why the appointment couldn't have been either a Scot or someone already deeply embedded in Scotland's theatre industry. This ignored the facts that Featherstone had spent most of the first seven years of her life in Clackmannanshire and that her work with Paines Plough had borne serious fruit at the Edinburgh Fringe during her tenure. The company already had Edinburgh history, with some of founders David Pownall and John Adams' earliest success after the company's birth in 1974 coming at the Fringe. Under subsequent directors it had acquired a reasonable reputation as a home for new writing, but Featherstone took the company to new levels of popular and commercial success.

Paines Plough's arrival in Edinburgh – its *real* arrival, with Featherstone in charge and an explosive near-decade of exciting new plays to reveal – came during the Fringe of 1998, once again with a classic Traverse Fringe programme. For a time, Paines Plough and artistic director Philip Howard's Traverse became synonymous with everything that was thrilling and truly challenging in Edinburgh Fringe theatre, in a way the Trav had only achieved at certain golden points in its history. A Yorkshireman who studied at Cambridge and St Andrews, Howard took over from Ian Brown when the latter's tenure as artistic director ended in 1996 after nine years.

By far the biggest upheaval of Brown's time in charge had been the opening of the modern new Traverse space at Saltire Court in 1992 and he overcame concerns that the new venue would prove soulless compared to the dingy but atmospheric old space. Fringe hits after the reopening included 1994's *Moscow Stations*, in which Brown directed Tom Courteney in Stephen Mulrine's adaptation of Venedikt Yerofeyev's novel, which told of the life of an alcoholic Brezhnev-era Russian dissident making his way around Moscow by metro. It successfully transferred to the Garrick Theatre in London that autumn.

There were also regular Fringe returns to the Traverse for Gerry Mulgrew's Communicado during the 1990s, with distinctive adaptations including JM Synge's *The Playboy of the Western World* (1994), Athol Fugard's *A Place with the Pigs* (1995) and Pavel Kohout's *Fire in the Basement* (1998), which was Mulgrew's swansong with the company. Simon Donald's dark gangster comedy *The Life of Stuff* emerged in '92 and Brown's own farewell to the Traverse came in 1996 when he directed *Shining Souls*, Chris Hannan's return to the Scottish stage with an eccentric comedy about a superstitious woman's marriage. Brown's tenure as artistic director also saw the emergence of young Edinburgh playwright Anthony Neilson and the Traverse's first work with the bold and unique Grassmarket Projects.

Neilson's debut play arrived in early summer 1990 at the Traverse, when he was 23, a short piece mocking the bureaucracy of state benefits in film noir style named *Welfare My Lovely*. In 1991 he wrote and directed *Normal: The Düsseldorf Ripper*, a disturbing tale of the 1920s German serial killer Peter Kürten, which made the playwright's name – and his growing reputation for unsettling work – when it transferred to the Finborough Theatre in London that October. In 1993, his third play *Penetrator* was part of the Traverse's Fringe programme, another grim but darkly amusing tale, this time of two porn-obsessed flatmates and their conspiracy theorist Gulf War veteran friend. For the rest of the decade Neilson built a formidable reputation with work exclusively for the London stage, before his later return to Scotland and the Edinburgh Festival.

Grassmarket Projects, meanwhile, were founded in 1989 by director

Jeremy Weller, who was influenced by Tadeusz Kantor, especially after meeting him in Poland in 1987. The company took its title from the subject of its first production *Glad*, which was staged during the Fringe of 1990 at the Grassmarket Mission for homeless people in the heart of Edinburgh. Its performers were selected from the users of the Mission itself and the words they spoke were their own, as told to Weller and developed into a play. The effect was strikingly authentic and the play received much thoughtful coverage, later transferring to London, Dublin, Berlin and Paris. It was the first of a trilogy, the next two parts of which were *Bad* at Ainsley Park Leisure Centre in 1991, featuring young offenders on special release from Polmont detention centre, and *Mad* at Leith Theatre in 1992, featuring a group of women who had experienced mental health problems.

In '92 the company also presented *The Big Tease* at Calton Studios, directed by Jean Findlay and featuring a group of nude dancers from the bars of Edinburgh. Later they were brought into the fold of the Traverse Theatre by Ian Brown, first with *20/52* in 1995, which saw campaigner Stephanie Lightfoot-Bennet tell of her struggle to get answers about her brother Leon Patterson's death in police custody in Manchester. Then in 1998 *Soldiers* had combat veterans, war reporters and Bosnian and Croatian generals and soldiers discuss war and killing. The piece was acclaimed, but it was cancelled midway through when one of the anonymous Bosnian participants' names was revealed and others involved decided to pull out.

A debate about the purpose of theatre ensued and old paper discussions about whether Weller's work was exploitative or not were reignited. He had already affirmed his desire to share a sense of human experience onstage and his disgust that war was ever used as entertainment: 'I must entertain to inform, but underneath all that I want to engage the audience in a debate about the moral issue'.[15] Inspired by the tradition of Dickens and Orwell in using art to comment on social injustice, Grassmarket Projects' work was widely acclaimed, gathering numerous Fringe First awards, and Weller has worked internationally on community projects in the decades since. In 2016 and '17 *Doubting Thomas* and *Doglife* appeared at Summerhall during the Fringe, in which reformed criminal Thomas McCrudden told his story, and 2018's *Where It Hurts* looked at the inner workings of the NHS.

Ian Brown's replacement Philip Howard had trained as a theatre director at the Royal Court under former Traverse artistic director Max Stafford-Clark at the end of the 1980s and from 1993 he was associate director at the Traverse, which positioned him perfectly to take over when Brown left. His debut Fringe in 1997 was eye-catching, not least because Vicky Featherstone was directing the play – Scottish writer Mike Cullen's *Anna Weiss*, a disturbing piece about False Memory Syndrome, which later transferred to the West End. That year also saw the UK premier of the previous year's Irish hit *Disco Pigs*, which was Enda Walsh's debut play and Cillian Murphy's first acting role, as well as a revival of David Harrower's *Knives in Hens*.

First seen in June 1995 at the Traverse, Harrower's play was a deceptively simple piece set in 16th century East Lothian, which introduces a travelling man with the ability to read into the simple life of a farming couple. Directed by Howard and starring Pauline Knowles and Lewis Howden, it was a study of the power of knowledge and language against those who have neither and it transferred to the Bush Theatre in London that autumn. Harrower's second play *Kill the Old Torture Their Young* premiered amid the fateful Fringe of 1998, a panoramic view of multiple characters living in an unnamed city whose attention-grabbing title reflected the 'in-yer-face' theatre trend of the time.

In August 2005, Harrower's play *Blackbird* premiered at the King's Theatre, telling the difficult story of a reunion between a young woman and an older man whose relationship began when the younger woman was under the age of consent – in which case, the play's dilemma offers us, surely she was a victim of abuse and never really in an autonomous relationship? Directed by Peter Stein and starring Roger Allam and Jodhi May, *Blackbird* transferred to the Albery Theatre in London's West End and then off-Broadway and eventually to Broadway, picking up Olivier and Tony Awards along the way. It's now one of the most acclaimed and successful self-originated plays in the Edinburgh International Festival's history.

One of the supposed key practitioners of in-yer-face was Anthony Neilson, who was absent from Scotland during most of the 1990s. He returned to the Traverse and the Fringe in 2002 with *Stitched*, a challenging piece about a couple's disintegrating relationship, then the Theatre Workshop in 2003 with a stage production of his radio play *Twisted*, about the murderer of a young woman attempting to convince a prison psychologist why he should be freed. His later plays *The Wonderful World of Dissocia* (2004) and *Realism* (2006) were both co-productions by the National Theatre of Scotland and Edinburgh International Festival, each visionary and acclaimed works which managed to meld gritty drama and magic realism to powerful effect.

Neilson reportedly first coined the phrase 'in-yer-face theatre'.[16] The genre was described and archived by writer Aleks Sierz in his 2001 book *In-Yer-Face Theatre: British Drama Today*. Sierz retrospectively pulled together some exemplar works from the past few years of British theatre to define a particular trend that was broadly characterised by sex, swearing and the emphatic destruction of social taboos. 'The kind of theatre which inspires us to use superlatives, whether in praise or condemnation', summed up the writer.

In the years following Danny Boyle's 1996 youth culture-defining film version of Irvine Welsh's *Trainspotting* – as well as the music of Oasis and Blur, the devotion of 'lad's mags' and 'girl power' to decadence, dark humour and consequence-free good times – the conditions for in-yer-face theatre had become prevalent in wider media. It was no surprise, for example, that Enda Walsh's *Disco Pigs* was described as an Irish *Trainspotting*, or that Harry Gibson's stage version of the book appeared amid Sierz's summary of in-yer-face plays.

Another was Mark Ravenhill's *Shopping and Fucking*, a frank exploration of the lives of hard-partying young gay men in London, which followed its hit debut at the Royal Court in 1996 with a Fringe run at the Assembly Rooms the following year; the title became *Shopping and F***ing* on the flyers. Ravenhill and Featherstone first met at the National Student Drama Festival in the 1980s and at Paines Plough she made him literary director in 1998, working alongside another playwright as part of the steering team. Sarah Kane was writer-in-residence, an alumni of Bristol University's extremely successful drama course of the early 1990s, who had seen Jeremy Weller's *Mad* at the Fringe in 1992, the year she graduated, describing it as thepiece of theatre which changed her life.

Kane, in turn, changed British theatre in the 1990s. Her 1995 play *Blasted* also debuted at the Royal Court and instantly attracted attention for what was a multi-faceted, morally complex and formally deeply experimental examination of sex, war and human nature – yet as it featured oral sex, male rape and the cannibalism of a dead baby, puritanical tabloid knives were thoroughly sharpened on words like 'disgusting' and 'filth'. In 1996, her Seneca adaptation *Phaedra's Love* was produced and early in 1998 *Cleansed* appeared at the Royal Court, an exploration of love through the metaphor of loss of identity.

On 13 August that year her fourth play *Crave* premiered as part of the Traverse's Fringe programme, and it's now viewed as arguably one of the most significant Fringe premieres of the decade. Despite an absence of the physical violence seen in her other work, *Crave*'s frank emotional intensity was compounded by its formal style – four characters identified only by a letter of the alphabet speak, with no stage directions to illuminate the context of what they're doing or where they are.

Six months later, in February of 1999, Kane died by suicide in a London hospital at the age of 28, leaving behind a small but incredibly powerful legacy of plays. Like Ravenhill's *Shopping and Fucking*, her posthumous *4:48 Psychosis* demonstrated its popularity among younger audiences by the number of times it appeared in Fringe programmes of years to come, performed by student drama companies. Alongside Anthony Neilson and her friend, workmate at Paines Plough and accomplice in this shocking new era of playwriting Mark Ravenhill, Kane was one of the most significant figures of in-yer-face theatre.

It was a style born out of the trends of the era and the shift away from the agit-prop 1970s and '80s, towards a more interiorised view of the world through the lens of identity. These writers' work reveals so much more about their times than just people's sexual habits and substance intake. In-yer-face was born in London, particularly on the stages of the Royal Court under artistic director Stephen Daldry and the Bush Theatre while Dominic Dromgoole was in charge. Yet it also found life on the stages of the Edinburgh Fringe, because no trend in theatre escapes Edinburgh's orbit. The Traverse – particularly the Neilson plays it staged – was an important proving ground.

Vicky Featherstone's Paines Plough returned with more Fringe hits, including Scottish playwright and former teacher Linda McLean's first full-length play *Riddance* in 1999, about domestic violence and murder in a Glasgow tenement, and Abi Morgan's *Splendour* in 2000, which tells of the wife of a dictator who's about to be overthrown and the women who surround her. The following year Morgan returned with the premiere of *Tiny Dynamite*, a co-production between Paines Plough and Frantic Assembly.

Founded by a group of Swansea University students in 1994 with an acclaimed version of John Osborne's *Look Back in Anger*, Frantic Assembly came to wider attention with a trilogy of Fringe plays – *Klub*, *Flesh* and *Zero*. They graduated from the Calton Centre to the Pleasance over the three years between 1995 and '97, their novel and attention-grabbing style fusing dance, physical theatre and drama. Making a company style out of loud club music and themes aimed at the under-30s, they returned with Royal Court playwright Michael Wynne's *Sell Out* at the Assembly Rooms in 1999, then artistic directors Scott Graham and Steven Hoggett directed *Tiny Dynamite* with Featherstone.

With new Scottish groups like Grid Iron and Benchtours producing during and outwith the Fringe, another young group had their roots in the same University of Bristol drama department as Ravenhill and Kane. For one student production of Howard Barker's *Victory*, Kane and the future actor Simon Pegg performed alongside a fellow student from Blackburn named Graham Eatough and another from Edinburgh, David Greig. The latter pair began working together while still students, first with their sort-of sequel to Shakespeare's *The Tempest*, *A Savage Reminiscence*, in 1991.

Knowing the city as he did, Greig was well-placed to help his fellow students put on work during the Fringe, but his ambitions were still greater than most. That summer at the Roman Eagle Lodge on Johnstone Terrace he and fellow student Andy Thompson inaugurated a completely new venue named Theatre Zoo, which ran for three years. Its opening highlights included a double bill of *A Savage Reminiscence*; Sarah Kane's devastating account of a rape, *A Comic Monologue*; and a late-night cabaret by a group named *David Icke and the Orphans of Jesus*, featuring Arbroath-born compere and later television presenter Dominik Diamond alongside Pegg and David

Walliams. Another soon-to-be-famous Bristol student, Walliams co-created the sketch show *Little Britain* and became a well-known children's author.

Writer and dramaturg Greig, director Eatough and composer Nick Powell returned in even more emphatic form to Theatre Zoo in '92, by this time collectively known as Suspect Culture. They produced a new play named *... and the opera house remained unbuilt*, which concerned theatre workers after the Second World War, although the title bore an echo of the failed Edinburgh municipal project whose saga was coming to an end that summer. Outside of Suspect Culture's banner, Greig's play *Stalinland* also appeared, which took as its subject a small Eastern European town after the fall of Communism, winning him a Fringe First award and signalling the arrival of a major new Scottish writing talent.

In 1993, both Greig and Eatough moved to Glasgow, where Suspect Culture was formalised as a company and Greig's playwriting career took off. In late 1994, his major theatre debut *Europe* – set in a derelict European borderlands railway station – gained wider critical acclaim, and in early '95 Suspect Culture's *One Way Street* presented a man named Flannery's life story as a walking tour of Berlin. Together and apart, the pair's plays concerned themselves with modernism, place and the experience of living in Europe and in Scotland in the years immediately after the Cold War.

In 1997, Brian McMaster commissioned Suspect Culture to write a piece about lifelong friendship for the Edinburgh International Festival named *Timeless*, staging it at the Gateway Theatre and in '99 Greig joined Paines Plough's roster of playwrights with *The Cosmonaut's Last Message to the Woman He Once Loved in the Former Soviet Union*. The company and its creators were definitive of Scottish theatre throughout the 1990s and the early 2000s, in the era immediately prior to the birth of the National Theatre of Scotland. As Joyce McMillan wrote:

> The central idea of the piece told the story of a young man pursuing his lost love through the streets of East Berlin; but it illustrated the story with haunting still images of the backstreets, council flats and canals of Edinburgh, as if to assert that for all the historic drama of Berlin as a setting, the romance of love and loss could strike just as powerfully in Tollcross or Slateford... *One Way Street* was the first Scottish-made piece of theatre I had seen which simply and completely incorporated the new, post-Cold War map of Europe into its sense of identity, and moved on, without pause or argument.[17]

In light of all of this, both the arrival of the National Theatre of Scotland and Vicky Featherstone's appointment as its head seem like *fait accompli* for the beginning of the 21st century. Half a century before, the Edinburgh Festival had struggled to find a definitive play to showcase the best of Scottish theatre and had to go looking half a millennium earlier to make their choice. Now Scotland's stages were overflowing with material which spoke vividly of the country's times and its people and through her loyal return to the Traverse with new work every Fringe, Vicky Featherstone was already arguably the theatre administrator who tied much of the best of what was happening on Scottish stages to conversations happening in theatres outside Scotland.

Yet still, there were murmurs that Featherstone had never produced anything on the kind of scale that might be expected of a national theatre company – complaints that seem laughable now, in light of what she and the creators she surrounded herself with achieved during the National Theatre of Scotland's very first Fringe.

* * *

The story of the National Theatre of Scotland's first and greatest success begins with the departure of the Traverse Theatre's literary director in 2001. The son of a nurse and an engineer who was born in 1971 and raised in Huddersfield, John Tiffany moved to Glasgow to study biology at Glasgow University, although after a time he switched to classics and drama. A few years after graduation he took the Traverse job in 1997, which meant his term was concurrent with Vicky Featherstone's first four years at Paines Plough. They became friends and then colleagues, when Tiffany became associate director at the company on leaving the Traverse.

He also directed at the Traverse during his time there, and his final show before leaving was a piece by a new writer he'd plucked from the submissions pile. Gregory Burke was born in 1968 and raised around the working-class south of Fife, in the naval shipyard town of Rosyth and in historic Dunfermline, the hub of a series of disintegrating mining villages in the area. One of these, Lumphinnans, inspired the name of his debut play *Gagarin Way*, the name of an actual street in the village. In a region where the UK's only Communist MP was elected in the 1930s and a legacy of socialism exists even as the unionised industries that supported it have crumbled, it makes sense that a Russian cosmonaut might have been a folk hero.

Gagarin Way is a heist thriller in which two mismatched employees of a soon-to-close Fife electronics factory decide to kidnap their visiting Japanese boss, when they're stumbled upon by a luckless security guard.

Except the visiting 'dignitary' is a Scottish middle-manager, and the Scots-accented but Tarantinoesque single location claustrophobia of the piece hothouses a grim black humour. In Burke's play, the legacy of working-class Scottish culture of the 20th century breaks down before a renewed onslaught of capitalism.

Starring Maurice Roeves as manager Frank and presented by the Traverse during the Fringe of 2001, the play was a huge critical hit. It transferred to the National Theatre's Studio Theatre, winning a Critics Circle Award, and then to the Arts Theatre in the West End, no doubt buoyed by the fact Burke – who didn't graduate from the University of Stirling and worked doing dishes and other odd jobs through his 20s – had envisaged it as a film. He didn't go to the theatre, so had written the piece primarily as a fast-paced action thriller. The trappings of political commentary on globalisation's pitfalls gave it theatrical bite.

The Straits, Burke's second play, arrived at the Traverse during the Fringe of 2003 and told of four teenagers growing up in Gibraltar in 1982, where Burke himself lived for six formative years when his family followed his father's job in the RAF to the British Overseas Territory at the southern tip of Spain. It was received warmly, although with nothing like the acclaim that greeted *Gagarin Way*. Yet this play was directed by Tiffany and produced by Featherstone's Paines Plough.

Although the National Theatre of Scotland didn't begin to stage work until February 2006's deeply ambitious *Home* project – a series of near-simultaneous performances in non-traditional theatre spaces in cities and towns across Scotland – it began life, to all intents, with Featherstone's first day at work in November 2004, supported by just a single assistant in an office space on the Glasgow council estate of Easterhouse. From there, she built the company from scratch. As she wrote the month before starting work:

> The model is entirely radical and non-institutional. No shady
> corridors of power for the National Theatre of Scotland or
> backstage passes only for those in the know. No building to swallow
> up our money in heating bills and toilet rolls. No mausoleum for the
> elite like many other National Theatres around the world. It is an
> outstanding message to the country and beyond that theatre is vital
> to our wellbeing and we are going to be allowed to prove it. [18]

A month after she started work, Featherstone noticed the news story that six Scottish army regiments were to be combined into one as the Royal Regiment of Scotland. She asked Burke – whose upbringing was in the area that mostly recruited into the Black Watch (Royal Highland Regiment) – to keep an eye on the story and see if there might be a play in it. Aware that the Black Watch is a working-class institution in Fife, he imagined a story that examined the history and future of this historic regiment and the role identity plays in being part of the armed forces, through the lens of its 2003 deployment as part of Operation Telic during the Second Iraq War. At the regiment's base near Fallujah, nicknamed 'Camp Dogwood', insurgent attacks were a constant threat.

In 2005, Featherstone hired John Tiffany once more, as Associate Director for New Work at the NTS. Soon after his arrival he went to Edinburgh's King's Theatre to see a retrospective of the work of JM Synge. Thinking about the tradition of Irish playwriting, which Synge represented, he began to consider the Scottish tradition, which the Black Watch play could sit within: John McGrath's *The Cheviot, the Stag and the Black, Black Oil*; Liz Lochhead's *Mary Queen of Scots Got Her Head Chopped Off*; and Edwin Morgan's version of *Cyrano de Bergerac*, the latter pair Fringe hits for Communicado.

At the same time, with the play now fully commissioned, Burke and researcher Sophie Johnston were speaking to soldiers who had just returned from Iraq over several meetings in a pub in Fife, to get their real-life perspective.

These veterans' collected verbatim words were incorporated into a text with fictional scenes devised by Burke. Steven Hoggett of Frantic Assembly – a childhood friend of Tiffany's from Huddersfield, although they hadn't worked together until *The Straits* at the Traverse in 2003 – was brought in as movement director. Tiffany envisaged a raw, claustrophobic version of the Royal Military Tattoo on the Castle Esplanade, with audiences seated in a semi-circle all around. An appropriate building was found; the former premises of the University of Edinburgh Officers Training Corps at Forrest Hill, in the same complex where Richard Demarco had staged the work of Tadeusz Kantor 30 years before.

Black Watch opened on 1 August 2006 and was the runaway hit of the Fringe, with actors including Brian Ferguson, Paul Higgins and Ryan Fletcher delivering the raw Fife dialogue which Burke had taken from the mouths of those who had experienced what the play was about. Tiffany and Hoggett proved to be a dream team, building a physicality into the piece which saw its ultimate expression in a brutal but balletic representation of what actually happens when an Improvised Explosive Device goes off and bodies are caught in the blast. Glowing reviews were issued, as was a Fringe First. Yet, beyond the technical excellence of the play, it seemed to have captured exactly the right mood sought by an audience still desperately trying to make sense of the far-off conflicts in Iraq and Afghanistan.

The play transferred to London, touring across the UK and internationally, only building acclaim as it went. The second printing of the playscript in 2010 lists 22 awards won by *Black Watch* – among them four Olivier Awards, one each for Burke, Tiffany, Hoggett and sound designer Gareth Fry – and Tiffany's introduction speaks of taking the play to 'a disused hydro-electric laboratory in Pitlochry, a warehouse underneath Brooklyn Bridge in New York, a converted train factory in Sydney and an ice rink in Toronto.'[19] After two decades of the 21st century, it's been named among the century's ten best plays by *The Guardian* and the 50 best plays ever by *Time Out* and The Independent. In Scotland especially, it became that rarest of things – a stage play that was every bit as much a popular cultural touchstone as the year's biggest movie or must-see television series.

Gregory Burke later got into films, while Tiffany and Hoggett continued to work together for the National Theatre of Scotland until 2013, with Tiffany later earning huge acclaim for the Enda Walsh-scripted 2012 Broadway musical *Once* and 2016's enormously successful *Harry Potter and the Cursed Child*, written with JK Rowling and Jack Thorne. For Vicky Featherstone's National Theatre of Scotland, meanwhile, *Black Watch* was simply proof of success from the very first hurdle. Although no solid, quotable data exists, it's very likely to be the most financially successful play ever produced in Scotland by a Scottish company. For its very first home, the Edinburgh Festival Fringe, it was yet another global hit which found its feet on an Edinburgh stage.

* * *

It's about renegotiating the union in creative, modern terms in the world we live in… We don't need a state built for empire anymore. It's absurd. We don't need to reform the House of Lords; we need to start again.[20]

David Greig was speaking at the very beginning of 2014, five years after Suspect Culture went into hibernation following the end of its public funding, the new national funding body Creative Scotland having replaced the Scottish Arts Council in 2010. He was speaking in advance of the Scottish Independence referendum of that year, which was called by Prime Minister David Cameron to take place on 18 September.

The subject dominated political and cultural conversation in Scottish, UK-wide and eventually international circles as the day approached. Greig was a supporter of independence, seemingly far more interested in the issues surrounding possible political transformation from scratch than any mere question of preference or identity. He was vocal and eloquent on the subject, but far from the only person in that position in the Scottish arts.

In June of 2014, Greig created *The Great Yes, No, Don't Know Five Minute Theatre Show* for the National Theatre of Scotland, a series of five-minute theatrical responses to the question of Scottish Independence, held in

24-hour sessions at seven locations around the country over two days. The first of these was on Monday 23 June, ten days after the death of Greig's union-supporting co-coordinator David MacLennan, by this point founder and artistic director of the A Play, a Pie and a Pint lunchtime theatre series at Glasgow's Oran Mor. Among MacLennan's other co-founders of the 7:84 company nearly half a century before, John McGrath had died aged 66 in 2002. MacLennan's sister Elizabeth passed away almost exactly a year after her brother, aged 77.

During the Edinburgh Festival of 2014, the subject was one of the most dominant. Meanwhile, Philip Howard had left the Traverse in 2007, his prior notable commissions including Mark Ravenhill's scathing 2005 monologue *Product*, about the world of entertainment's co-opting of tragedy, and the same writer's series of short, daily fast-response plays *Ravenhill for Breakfast* in 2007, directed by Jemima Levick, which mutated the following year in London into his collected work *Shoot/Get Treasure/Repeat*. They were, says Ravenhill, an attempt to create a theatrical epic for the age of the soundbite.

Another major arrival of Howard's late tenure was New York's astonishing TEAM, founded by six graduates of New York University in December 2004. They were an underground hit during the following year's Fringe with two sleeper productions at C Venue on Chambers Street, *A Thousand Natural Shocks* and *Give Up! Start Over! (In the Darkest of Times I Look to Richard Nixon for Hope)*. An extraordinary feast of fragmentary drama, music, dance, physical theatre and channel-hopping cultural, political and philosophical references, from Nixon, Robert Kennedy and Shakespeare to *The Wizard of Oz*, *Gone with the Wind* and the paranoia of the nuclear age, they held a cracked mirror up to the self-image of America.

Once the TEAM's secret was out, the Traverse brought them over for *Particularly in the Heartland* in 2006, *Architecting* in 2009 and *Mission Drift* in 2011. *Architecting* was a co-production with the National Theatre of Scotland, following John Tiffany and NTS associate Davey Anderson's befriending of the company in 2006. TEAM's multigenerational gig theatre piece *Primer for a Failed Superpower* was given a reading at the 2012 Festival after *Mission Drift* won the Edinburgh International Festival Fringe Prize. *Anything That Gives Off Light* (formerly *The Scottish Enlightenment Project*) appeared at the Edinburgh International Conference Centre in 2016, their final appearance to date, a full-scale collaboration between the company, the National Theatre of Scotland and Edinburgh International Festival.

Howard was also responsible for bringing Daniel Kitson to the Traverse, following the eccentric stand-up's transition from a Perrier nomination for his show *Love, Innocence and the Word Cock* in 2001 and the winner of the award for *Something* in 2002, to quirky, semi-theatrical storyteller with *A Made Up Story* at temporary Festival Square venue The Pod in '03. Audience reaction and critical acclaim was so positive that Kitson set out on a long-term Fringe residency of shows in a similar vein at the Traverse and latterly Summerhall: *Stories for the Wobbly Hearted* (2005), *C-90* (2006), *66a Church Road: A Lament, Made of Memories and Kept in Suitcases, by Daniel Kitson* (2008), *The Interminable Suicide of Gregory Church* (2009), *It's Always Right Now Until It's Later* (2010), *A Variety of Things in a Room* (2014), *Polyphony* (2015), *Mouse: The Persistence of an Unlikely Thought* (2016), and *Shenanigan* (2019).

Howard was replaced in 2008 by Dominic Hill, former joint artistic director at Dundee Rep, whose four Fringes at the Traverse brought more voices to the theatre. These included the Mancunian playwright Simon Stephens, whose debut play *Bring Me Sunshine*, about a dying composer's life in a flat in Edinburgh's Tollcross, premiered at the Assembly Rooms during 1997's Fringe, while Stephens lived in the city. His play *Pornography*, about disconnected London lives leading up to the 7/7 terrorist bombings in the summer of 2005, was first seen at the Traverse in 2007, and in 2009 the Bush Theatre's production of his play *Sea Wall* with Andrew Scott came to the same theatre.[21]

Dominic Hill left the Traverse for the Citizens Theatre in 2011 and was in turn replaced by Orla O'Loughlin, former artistic director of the Pentabus company and associate with the Royal Court, who became only the second woman to take charge of the Traverse. One of her first acts was to inaugurate the *Traverse 50*, a hunt for 50 new playwrights to celebrate the theatre's 50th anniversary in 2013 and one of them, a Northern Irishman named John McCann, wrote *Spoiling* for 2014's Fringe, an amusingly cynical look at the days following an imagined 'Yes' vote for independence and what Scotland's relationship with the rest of the UK might look like.

O'Loughlin also brought *Theatre Uncut* to the Traverse, a radical collective founded by Hannah Price in 2011, which sought to make plays by leading playwrights in opposition to the austerity-driven policies of the then-current Conservative-Liberal Democrat coalition government, available for performance. David Greig and Mark Ravenhill both assisted in an advisory capacity and at 2014's Fringe *Theatre Uncut* performed bar readings of short plays on the subject of independence. These included works by new Scottish playwrights Kieran Hurley and Rob Drummond, both alumni of the Arches theatre in Glasgow, whose respective breakthrough plays – the 1990s free party rave flashback *Beats* and the enthralling study of stage magic *Bullet Catch* – were hits of O'Loughlin's first Fringe in 2012.

Greig's Fringe response to the upcoming referendum, meanwhile, came through the unlikely channel of the Stand Comedy Club, which had set up a tented venue on St Andrew Square that year. The club's owner Tommy Sheppard was and is a vocal supporter of Independence, and Greig's contribution was the daily chat show *All Back to Bowie's*, named after David Bowie's plea at that year's Brit Awards to 'stay with us, Scotland', as delivered by his proxy Kate Moss. A partisan but welcoming affair with an interest in ideas over dogma, the show welcomed the SNP's then-deputy First Minister of the Scottish Parliament Nicola Sturgeon – whose party had been the largest at Holyrood since 2007 – and the actor Brian Cox.

The National Theatre of Scotland and the Edinburgh International Festival, chose a joint response which dug into the subject of the time while retaining a certain sense of diplomacy – not least in the way the National Theatre in London became the third co-producer. Vicky Featherstone had left the NTS in 2013 to become artistic director of the Royal Court and her role had been taken by Laurie Sansom, former director of the Royal and Derngate Theatre in Northampton.

For 2014's Festival, Sansom directed *The James Plays*, three full-length plays – *James I: The Key Will Keep the Lock*, *James II: Day of the Innocents* and *James III: The True Mirror* – which told of the significant early events of Scottish history and its relationship with England through the first three Scottish kings named James, who lived and ruled throughout the 15th century.

There had already been major National Theatre of Scotland collaborations with the Edinburgh International Festival, including John Tiffany and David Greig's Alan Cumming-starring adaptation of Euripides' *The Bacchae* at the King's Theatre in 2007; Featherstone and David Harrower's exploration of the youth care experience *365: One Night to Learn a Lifetime* at the Playhouse in 2008; and an exploration of the story behind the 18th century's final witch to be burned in Scotland in *The Last Witch* at the Traverse in 2009.

Yet *The James Plays* were of a whole new order of ambition, a trio of Shakespearean epics which could be fitted together into one day-long narrative, if the customer chose their bookings correctly. They were written by Rona Munro, one of Scotland's most experienced playwrights, whose career was in the middle of a renaissance following *The Last Witch*. After emerging at the time of Peter Lichtenfels and Jenny Killick's joint reign at the Traverse, she had written prolifically for Scottish and English stages, including for her and actor Fiona Knowles' one-woman monologue company The MsFits; *Bold Girls*, her 1990 breakthrough play about women during the Northern Irish Troubles for 7:84; and the acclaimed *Iron*, a Traverse Fringe play in 2002, in which a daughter visits her mother – her father's murderer – in prison.

Munro's career had demonstrated her to be a powerful teller of feminist stories.[22] Like Tiffany, she was influenced by John McGrath's *The Cheviot, the Stag and the Black, Black Oil*, in her case a formative television screening in her youth, and by a visit to the Royal Shakespeare Company to see a series of Shakespeare's historical works. She went in with a degree of scepticism, and came out marvelling at both the quality of the plays and what they told England about itself:

> I realised that so much of what we understand about English history came from those plays. Even if people haven't seen them they know the stories, and we didn't have an equivalent in Scotland. So I thought, wouldn't be a fun idea to try and do that.[23]

It was Vicky Featherstone who helped inaugurate *The James Plays* when she called Munro in and asked her to name her dream project, but Laurie Sansom happily continued to support her ambition. At the point development began, in fact, none of the team had any knowledge the referendum would be taking place in 2014. Munro has said she liked the fact the plays occurred around the referendum, but weren't written with it in mind. This gave them a frisson at the time, but she hopes it means they aren't rooted in the moment.

For the International Festival's then-director Jonathan Mills, the connection to current events was more tangible. 'I was under a little bit of pressure from certain commentators saying, why will you not dedicate this Festival in 2014 to the cause of Scottish Independence?' he says. 'I said I was not going to give the festival over to one part of a political debate or not... would you be happy if I dedicated it to not leaving the union? I felt it was important that artists' voices were able to be heard, and that the interpretation was available and open to anyone who saw the show. *The James Plays*, I think, provide us with very powerful instances of how one might interpret historical events in multiple ways'.

Featuring a strong roster of talent including Blythe Duff, Jamie Sives and the Danish star of BBC Four detective series *The Killing* Sofie Gråbøl as Margaret, Queen of Denmark, *The James Plays* felt like the kind of experience that could only be fully appreciated in the open space of the Edinburgh Festival. They were seen by 30,000 people in Edinburgh and when they transferred to the National Theatre that autumn they won an Evening Standard Award and the Writers' Guild of Great Britain Award for Best Play. A fourth instalment, *James IV: Queen of the Fight*, is to be premiered in late 2022, produced by the National Theatre of Scotland with Raw Material and Capital Theatres, once again directed by Sansom. Munro wrote of the original trilogy:

We cannot know the character and thoughts of these dead kings and queens and long-gone Scots. We can speculate a whole series of possibilities from the few hard facts that we rely on, the slim historical evidence of their actions. However, I feel robustly certain that whatever their thoughts and feelings might have been, human nature is exactly the same now as it was then. Only culture and circumstances have changed.[24]

Even in the previous 67 years, since the beginning of the Edinburgh Festival, culture and circumstances had changed. The Independence referendum of 2014, the third vote on Scotland's future in 35 years, was lost by campaigners for a 'Yes' vote by a margin of 55 percent to 45 percent. Yet in nearly the same period, as we've seen, the landscape and unique identity of Scotland's theatrical landscape had boomed beyond recognition. While the political step might have been one too far for the moment, plays like *Black Watch* and *The James Plays* have been significant staging points in the exponential growth of the country's cultural confidence.

13

Edinburgh Art Festival and the Arrival of Summerhall

RICHARD DEMARCO ALWAYS put his sense of relentless, open-minded inter-nationalism in bringing artists from across Europe and the world to Edinburgh down to the experience of growing up as an Italian-Scot; especially doing so during the Second World War when both countries were at war and anti-Italian discrimination was rife in Britain. Beyond his attending every single Festival and his involvement with many of its institutions' foundation, it's this spirit of post-war reconciliation through creativity and the arts that means he exemplifies the spirit of the Edinburgh Festival more than anyone.

As he told *Scotland On Sunday* writer Dani Garavelli in 2003, when he was a youthful 73-year-old:

> In one way I was trying to make sense of the horror of the war that had caused me to be regarded as a piece of mud and that had deeply affected Scotland's psyche... What I really wanted was to prove that through the international arena of the Edinburgh Festival I could help to rebuild Europe – so instead of looking to the [United] States I looked to Poland and Romania.[1]

In the same interview, he expressed two wishes for the future: that a home could be found for his monumental archive of material related to his three decades promoting art from across the world, and that the city would finally formalise its relationship with art in August by inaugurating an official Edinburgh Art Festival. One of these dreams, at least, was imminent.

While Demarco's aspirations echoed those of the International Festival's founding, his tastes have been for that which is marginal, undiscovered and surprising, or which simply show the viewer the world from a different cultural perspective. The Traverse Gallery and then the Demarco Gallery operated in an unbroken hereditary line, albeit across ten venues as rental agreements and funding arrangements shifted around him like sand,[2] since 1964. In 1992, when Demarco finally had to vacate the premises on Blackfriars Street, he appeared all out of Plan Bs.

Yet, in many ways, he had too many plans. The year Blackfriars went, he founded the non-building-based Demarco European Art Foundation, then in '93 took on the post of Professor of European Cultural Studies at Kingston University in London, which he held until 2000. Later in '93, he also opened another building in Edinburgh, installing the Foundation at the disused former St Mary's Roman Catholic School on Albany Place in the New Town. In 2000, a celebratory exhibition named 70/2000 was held at the City Art Centre in honour of his 70th birthday and he began assisting with the Fringe programming of the new Rocket Demarco venue at the Roxy Art House, the mid-19th century former Lady Glenorchy Free Church at 2 Roxburgh Place. This had been under the Edinburgh University Students Association's ownership since the 1970s and previously used during the Fringe as the Roxburgh Hall and the Pleasance Over-the-Road.

Demarco's championing of the young Joseph Beuys, Tadeusz Kantor, Marina Abramović, Clive James and many others has already been accounted for. In March 1976, 22-year-old unknown Ruby Wax staged a version of Jean Genet's *The Maids* at the Demarco Gallery at Monteith House, just off the High Street.[3] At the time she was a student at the Royal Scottish Academy of Music and Drama in Glasgow, having arrived from Illinois after a year studying psychology at the University of California in Berkeley. During the Fringe of 1977, Irish brothers Peter and Jim Sheridan, the latter the future director of films including *My Left Foot* and *In the Name of the Father*, brought their first artistic venture the Project Theatre Company to the same venue with a production of WB Yeats's *On Baile's Strand*, the play which opened the Abbey Theatre in their home city of Dublin in 1904.

In 1979, Demarco created *Edinburgh Arts 1979: A Quest Through Europe, or the Long Way Round to the Edinburgh Festival*, a 68-day circumnavigation of the British Isles by the sailing ship Marques, with 106 artists, poets, teachers and assorted creatives on board. In 1984, the 20th anniversary of his involvement with art in Edinburgh, the International Festival staged a Demarco-curated programme of work at Edinburgh College of Art, which included *Demarcation '84;* the group show of Australian and New Zealand art, *ANZART; Bougé: New French Photography;* and the *Art and the Human Environment* conference, whose many contributors included Patrick Heron, Paul Neagu, David Nash, Alastair MacLennan, Jimmy Boyle, David Harding, Sorley MacLean, Norman MacCaig, Iain Crichton Smith and Owen Dudley Edwards.

In 1988 and '89 came one of Demarco's boldest experiments yet: the production of a version of *Macbeth* by the Roman theatre company *La Zattera di Babele* on the island of Inchcolm in the middle of the Firth of Forth. The 1988 edition was named *Towards Macbeth*, an exploratory project which began at the Demarco Gallery and saw audiences bussed to North Queensferry then sail to the island. The full production in '89, however, had to be significantly changed when *La Zattera di Babele's* artistic director Carlo Quartucci was unable to travel due to illness, leaving the Scottish actors involved in the project – Juliet Cadzow and eventual director

John Bett – to gather a new company for an all-Scottish performance with a few days' notice. For most of the 1,400 audience members across seven days of performances, the spectacle of Inchcolm island was enough.

At the old St Mary's School in 1994, the year before the artist won the Turner Prize, Damien Hirst created an installation to accompany Danny Moynihan's opera *Agongo*, which consisted of discarded medical and pharmaceutical ephemera and 25 humanely caged live rats. Their presence meant the building's electrician refused to enter the room to maintain the neon sign that displayed the opera's title.

Ever a good publicist, Demarco hinted in 2000 that he'd like to restage the Inchcolm *Macbeth* that year, this time with his friend Sean Connery and Connery's son Jason in leading roles. Bizarrely, in 1996 he even programmed the avant garde *Oskaras Kursonovas* Company of Lithuania as a Fringe show taking place at Dundee Rep Theatre (Venue 191), 60 miles from the Royal Mile, which caused the Fringe Society to tighten up their rules on where exactly an Edinburgh Fringe can be – in Edinburgh, essentially. Known as a wayward conversationalist whose digressions take the form of full conversations in their own right, interested in others but utterly consumed by his life's work of finding, championing and archiving global art through the lens of its appearance in Edinburgh, the eternally smart-suited, cravat-wearing Demarco is a force of nature.

Visiting his European Art Foundation as it prepared to open for the Fringe of '94, writer Mark Fisher summed up the experience of meeting him:

> Demarco may be a charmer, you might even call him charismatic, and deep down he's a tough cookie who knows how to get just what he wants, but what is really persuasive about him is that his heart is in exactly the right place. He has a mission and he believes in it implicitly. The chaos, the craziness, the way that at any one time there are either too many phones ringing or too many people to answer them, all this might be frustrating, but it is perfectly in keeping with a philosophy that puts art first, admin second. In these times of arts council bureaucracy, when arts organisations are expected to behave like ruthless free-market sharks, this is a deeply unfashionable philosophy. But there is a refreshing air of shoestring passion at Demarco – what people like to refer to as that original Fringe feeling – and you can see why it is infectious. Demarco and his band of happy helpers are doing it because they want to.[4]

Within the same article, Demarco gave possibly the most concise mission statement to his life's work he's every likely to deliver:

You don't stop making art if you're a real artist. You don't stop
'til you die. You don't retire. This is a princely, aristocratic work
that demands that you do it 'til the end of your days. You have to
make use of limited time so you can hand on the truth to future
generations.[5]

* * *

'Scotland could rival London or New York,' declared Demarco in 2003.
'It would be fabulous. We need to bring the spirit of Venice to Edinburgh.
What's the point of spending £300,000 sending Scottish art to Venice if
you can't do this sort of thing at home?'[6] Once again he was outlining a
grand plan, this time to use the international popularity of the Edinburgh
Festival as a launchpad for an artistic festival in the city to rival the great
Venice Biennale, which has filled the unexplored buildings and alleys of the
romantic Italian city with international art since 1895.

Never averse to a publicly-expressed flight of fantasy here or there –
although with a greater hit rate than most mortals when it comes to making
them happen – Demarco was expressing an idea which had a lot of support
among Edinburgh's artistic community. The city's art gallery scene, in fact,
had never been in better shape by this point. Glasgow of the 20th century
was responsible for waves of contemporary art and had enjoyed boom times
throughout the 1990s with a new cohort of young and exciting Glasgow
School of Art graduates who worked in non-traditional media like film,
photography and environmental installation. Emerging in parallel with the
YBA (Young British Artists) movement, their number included the 1996
Turner Prize winner Douglas Gordon, '97 nominee Christine Borland and
others including Jim Lambie and Martin Boyce.

Yet, Edinburgh had for a long time been the hub of classical art in Scotland
and by the end of the 20th century the National Galleries of Scotland were
already well-established across the city. William Henry Playfair's neoclassical
National Gallery of Scotland was built in the furrow within the slope up to
the Mound in 1859 and the National Galleries organisation grew to include
the Scottish National Portrait Gallery in Robert Rowand Anderson's striking
red gothic building on Queen Street in 1889.[7] When the Royal Scottish
Academy, the artist-led national academy of art, opened their own building
alongside Playfair's similarly grand, classically-columned design on the
junction of Princes Street and the Mound in 1911, it assumed a dual purpose
as further exhibition space for the National Galleries.

With a greater public recognition of contemporary art after the Second
World War – and Edinburgh's own link to this world to boast about, the

Leith-born Italian-Scot pioneer of Pop Art Eduardo Paolozzi – the Scottish National Gallery of Modern Art was founded in the compact 18th century stately home Inverleith House, now the hub of the city's Royal Botanic Garden. The SNGMA moved in 1984 to the far larger John Watson's Institution to the west of the city centre and by 1999 it was twinned with the equally grand Dean Gallery on the other side of Belford Road.

Named after the nearby Dean Village in the Water of Leith valley, the Dean Gallery was formerly the Thomas Hamilton-designed Dean Orphanage of 1834, a building whose stunning baroque grandeur was funded by private donations when the orphan hospital's original building in the valley between Calton Hill and the High Street was demolished to make way for Waverley Station. The new gallery houses the archival collection gifted to the National Galleries by Paolozzi five years before, much of which can be seen in the recreated Paolozzi Studio, a jumbled assortment of papers, reference books, work tools and half-constructed maquettes of his larger sculptures, which still give an insight into his busy working mind many years after his death in 2005 at the age of 81.

Since the opening of the new Scottish National Gallery of Modern Art in 1984, the director of the organisation had been Sir Timothy Clifford, 38 at the time of his arrival from Manchester City Art Gallery. A natural, gifted gallerist, Clifford and the individual directors of each of the galleries under his watch had made the National Galleries of Scotland a hugely successful collective attraction. Following the renovation of the Royal Scottish Academy building in 2003, the National Galleries' Festival-timed reopening exhibition *Monet: The Seine and the Sea*, which borrowed 90 paintings from around the world, broke the National Galleries' box office record with 173,000 visitors in its first two months. The gallery needed to be opened in the evening to keep up with demand.

Yet, Clifford's success on his own terms had a mixed effect on the wider artistic exhibition scene in Edinburgh. It meant other galleries were submerged, particularly during Festival time, under the sheer weight of the National Galleries' reputation. It also meant Clifford didn't need to stake his success on getting into the International Festival's official programme in order to attract the required number of visitors through the door. Commentators hinted at a schism between him and EIF's director Brian McMaster; certainly, McMaster was averse to the arbitrary list of other organisations' exhibitions that Dunlop had placed in the back of the programme. In fact, he wasn't keen on putting anything in which he hadn't programmed himself. By 1994 only the National Galleries' programme was listed and soon even that was gone.

Philip Long, senior curator of the National Galleries of Scotland in the early 2000s and an expert in 20th century Scottish art, observes:

As far as I can recollect, the tenet of the disagreement was that the National Galleries, as expressed by Tim Clifford, believed the visual arts should be a central part of the Edinburgh Festival, but there was a view from Brian McMaster that the Festival should be something which concentrates on the performing arts, with other organisations very welcome to put on great things round around it. I think the argument basically revolved around funding. If EIF started to effectively sponsor exhibitions as part of its programme, then it would also need to contribute to their funding. I think that was the reality at the heart of the debate.

While contemporary art had been exceptionally well-represented at the Festival, albeit just below the radar, ever since Richard Demarco first hung a work in the Traverse bar in the 1960s, the International Festival's on-off relationship with visual art was a less reliable affair. At the beginning, there were displays of Scottish arts and crafts in the shop windows of Princes Street, as well as a 1949 show of the Scottish Colourists Peploe, Cadell and Hunter, before EIF's second director Ian Hunter arranged excellent large exhibitions at the National Gallery of Scotland and the Royal Scottish Academy with the assistance of the Arts Council of Great Britain. From 1950, visiting audiences enjoyed seeing the work of Rembrandt, Spanish painters from El Greco to Goya, Degas, Renoir, Cézanne, Gauguin, Braque, Monet, the Blue Rider Group featuring Wassily Kandinsky and Paul Klee and many more.

The blockbuster Jacob Epstein retrospective of 1961 at Waverley Market was an early high point for EIF in terms of not just relying on acknowledged masters, but leading the conversation and discovering contemporary work to champion. Over the following two decades the official exhibitions increased in number, but they became more niche, exploring newer artists, illustrative displays about Festival works – for example Tyrone Guthrie at the Assembly Hall in 1973, in commemoration of his death – and national group shows. Demarco's *Strategy: Get Arts* was in the official programme in 1970 and in '76, the year after her death and the same year her St Ives studio was opened to the public as a museum, the sculptures of Barbara Hepworth were shown at the Royal Botanic Garden, where the pieces *Ascending Form (Gloria)* and *Rock Form (Porthcurno)* can still be seen.

In 1979, incoming EIF director John Drummond attempted to restore a sense of the blockbuster to the Festival with his centenary show of the French Impressionist Edgar Degas, but while the breadth of exhibitions grew during the '80s, nothing quite as bold was attempted. Instead, a diverse range of smaller exhibitions happened at Demarco's venues, the Fruitmarket Gallery, the buzzing new 369 Gallery, the City Art Centre and the Talbot

Rice Gallery. The City Art Centre, home to the city of Edinburgh's collection of Scottish art, opened in 1980 in a nine-story former extension to *The Scotsman*'s offices and sometime fruit and vegetable warehouse on Market Street, after a decade at the disused Royal High School. The Talbot Rice Gallery, meanwhile, is the University of Edinburgh's in-house gallery at the Old College, containing both an arched, two-level natural history museum from the 19th century and a contemporary 'white cube' space. It was named in honour of the art historian and former Vice Principal of the University David Talbot Rice, who died in 1972.

By the early 2000s, a diverse gallery culture existed in Edinburgh which encompassed the monolithic National Galleries, the larger, publicly and institutionally-funded spaces such as City Art Centre and Talbot Rice and a growing range of independent spaces which filled the space left by Demarco and 369. The most deep-rooted of these began life as the 57 Gallery, founded in 1957 with a pioneering artist-led constitution and based on Rose Street until 1974, when it took over the floor above the Fruitmarket on Market Street as the New 57 Gallery. The two spaces made an interesting counterpoint, with the 57 entirely self-sufficient and Fruitmarket publicly backed by the Scottish Arts Council, but when both galleries made moves to merge in 1984, many members of the 57 were unhappy with the development.

The same year these artists broke away and formed the breakaway Artists' Collective Gallery in a shopfront on Cockburn Street, which by 2000 continued to exist as the Collective Gallery, showing a diverse range of exhibitions by recent graduates. The list of early-career Scottish and Scottish-based artists to have displayed at the Collective in its first two decades includes subsequent Turner Prize nominees and winners Callum Innes, Christine Borland, Simon Starling and Richard Wright and the installation artist, Wellcome Prize-winning memoirist and singer with Scottish post-punk group Dog Faced Hermans, Marion Coutts.

During 1976's Festival, the Fruitmarket Gallery held an exhibition entitled *Recent American Stills Photography*, featuring a selection of work by definitive US photographers including Henry Wessel Jr, Harry Callahan, Garry Winogrand, Robert Adams, Lewis Baltz and Tod Papageorge. Its curator was also an American, Richard Hough, who taught photography in his home country before moving to Edinburgh at the age of 27 in 1972. He was one of a group named the Scottish Photographic Society, the organisers of the exhibition, which the following year founded the Stills Centre for Photography in Edinburgh, only the third dedicated photographic gallery in the UK. Starting out at the corner of the Royal Mile's High Street and Blackfriars Street, the Stills Gallery has been based at the foot of Cockburn Street since 1994.

Founded in 1978, the year after the Stills, the Travelling Gallery was originally a one-person art gallery on a bus operation founded by the Scottish Arts Council. Travelling to rural locations across Scotland, the bus – which has been upgraded several times since – now falls within the remit of the Edinburgh Galleries and Museums organisation and is based in the city during the Festival. Its commissioned artists include Dalziel + Scullion at the beginning of their career in 1992 and Rachel Maclean in 2014.

As the millennium came and went, more new galleries emerged, buoyed by the success of contemporary art. In 1998, sometime art critic Richard Ingleby opened his eponymous Ingleby Gallery on Carlton Terrace, a grand curve of townhouses with views towards Arthur's Seat and Easter Road. A commercial venture, it still benefited from a carefully selected curation policy, with Callum Innes, for example, featuring in the opening exhibition and getting his own show a year later. In 2001, the former art editor of *The List* magazine Susanna Beaumont set up doggerfisher, her own gallery and commercial agency for contemporary art, in a converted tyre repair garage just off Gayfield Square.

The name of her gallery referenced the shipping forecast terms for stretches of water between Scotland and mainland Europe and Beaumont was making a clear attempt to surf the post-devolution current of Scottish internationalism:

> I feel very strongly about Scotland and being in Edinburgh, but there is a tendency of being caught up in heritage. Edinburgh is knowingly a good-looking city, but I feel it's very important in the 21st century that it is seen as a very contemporary city. Obviously it cherishes its history and its beauty, but it should also look forward. A space like doggerfisher is about looking forward and being optimistic and not being caught up in tartan and shortbread.[8]

At the start of 2003, the directorship of the Fruitmarket Gallery was taken over from Graeme Murray by Fiona Bradley, an Oxford graduate who had previously been curator at the Hayward Gallery in London and before that had worked at Tate Liverpool. Since it opened for the Festival of 1974 with Richard Demarco's *11Da: Eleven Dutch Artists*, the Fruitmarket had built a strong reputation for its often exemplary contemporary art programme, programming shows by Scots like Paolozzi and Mark Boyle alongside David Hockney, Henri Cartier-Bresson, Willem de Kooning and Frank Auerbach in the 1970s.

Some eclectic 1980s and early '90s choices followed under directors Mark Francis and Fiona McLeod, including the famous Festival double bill of Jean-Michel Basquiat and John Cage in 1984, a comprehensive look at Max Ernst's metalwork during the Festival of '90 and Andy Goldsworthy in August '92.

Graeme Murray was a sculpture graduate of Edinburgh College of Art who ran a gallery and art book publishing company since the early 1980s, occasionally curating shows at the Fruitmarket himself. He became director in 1992 and immediately oversaw the redevelopment of the building, reopening for the Festival of 1993.

Whether intentionally or not, Murray's programmes bore echoes of Demarco's legacy, not least because he ran Festival retrospective shows of artists Demarco had championed in Gerhard Richter (1995) and Marina Abramović (1997). He promoted a strong international element to the gallery, with group shows of work by artists from Germany, Australia, Mali, Korea, Israel, America and Japan. Yoko Ono was among the major artists to receive a solo show, as well as Bill Viola, Jeff Koons and Dalziel + Scullion, while the *Visions for the Future* series gave space to new Scotland-linked artists including Martin Boyce, Ross Sinclair and Rosalind Nashashibi.

Philip Long was raised in Edinburgh and he remembers a vivid and interesting contemporary art scene in the '80s and '90s, particularly propelled by work he saw at the Fruitmarket and Travelling Gallery. Yet, when Graeme Murray handed over to Fiona Bradley in '03 to return to his career in wood-carving, she didn't see any kind of reputation as an artistic centre preceding the city.

'I have to say it didn't figure on my radar at all as somewhere for visual art,' says Bradley.

> I mean, obviously as somewhere for performance... I'd seen some of the best theatre I've ever seen at the Edinburgh Festival when I was a student. But no, it didn't figure in my sense of where to go and look at contemporary art. When I got here, though, it was very clear everybody involved in visual art in the city put their best foot forward in August. You were aware there was a huge increase in footfall and in attention on the city in August, so it made sense to put on a good show.

This was in contrast to the gallery calendar in the rest of the country, where programming relaxed for the summer and then took off again for the autumn season in September. From the beginning, Bradley was aware the national press would be in town for that summer's big Monet show at the freshly reopened RSA and part of her job was to entice them into the Fruitmarket for a quick visit before they got back on the train to London. Others, for their own reasons, were beginning to think about this dynamic and about how the energies of a bunch of disparate galleries putting on interesting shows under their own initiative for passing Festival audiences could be combined into something bigger.

There had already been attempts at coordination. Angela Wrapson, an old friend of former Traverse artistic director Chris Parr from London, had moved to Edinburgh to train as a teacher in 1973. She joined the board of Parr's Traverse in '79 and stayed through the changes of the 1980, helping to arrange the move to the theatre's new premises at Saltire Court. She arranged Scotland's first pavilion at the Venice Biennale in 1990, showing the large-scale sculpture of David Mach, and founded the printed Edinburgh Gallery Guide, which was the most joined-up initiative the galleries of Edinburgh had collectively undertaken by the 1990s. Wrapson was good friends with Richard Demarco and his influence inspired the attempt to go even further at the beginning of the 2000s.

No-one seems entirely sure who instigated the conversations that led to the foundation of the Edinburgh Art Festival, but Philip Long was there from near the beginning. He remembers a meeting of a small group of people at the purpose-built new offices of *The Scotsman* newspaper in 2003, down in the shadow of Salisbury Crags on the edge of Holyrood Park. The newspaper's new owners, the Barclay Brothers, had sold the classic building on North Bridge for development as a hotel in 2001, in favour of a site near the in-construction new Scottish Parliament. The reason for this meeting venue was Iain Gale, art editor of *The Scotsman*'s sister newspaper *Scotland On Sunday*, who in late July 2002 had written a prescient opinion piece about the city's lack of a dedicated visual art festival:

> Week after week, as I write my column, it becomes increasingly clear Scotland is continuing to experience an unprecedented renaissance in the visual arts. To ignore such an evident flowering of talent and achievement is not only crass stupidity but a wasted opportunity.[9]

Gale also made the compelling point that Sir John Falconer's original 1947 mission statement for the International Festival was that it would present 'all that is best in drama, music and the visual arts'.

The hope that EIF would relent and put some visual art in its programme once more, he implied, was an incomplete and compromised ambition. The will wasn't there, while the Fringe's involvement stretched to a few token exhibitions in the annual catalogue, curated mainly on the basis of which galleries had decided to pay for a place.

He counted 56 shows, most of which covered crafts like clockmaking and jewellery, with maybe 15 of the roughly 25 high-quality exhibitions happening in the city during August represented in the Fringe programme. Instead of these half-hearted efforts, said Gale, the city should aspire to create its own distinct festival of art, which could invite galleries from across Scotland and even the world to curate their own spaces.

His ideas might have been over-optimistic, but Gale was an indefatigable and outspoken campaigner for the creation of an Edinburgh Art Festival, with the support of his paper's editor John McLellan. Another with grand ideas about what could be possible was Richard Demarco, who still backed a kind of Venice Biennale of the north. He was also at the Holyrood meeting.

'There was a view that, while the visual arts organisations in the city put on their own exhibitions at the time of the Festival, they could do more to coordinate their efforts, so it could be something which could be understood more collectively,' recalls Philip Long of these discussions. Gale returned to the subjects throughout his columns on 2003's Festival, canvassing the opinions of gallery directors. While Timothy Clifford appeared to believe McMaster's inclusion of the National Galleries within the International Festival's programme was imminent once more, Richard Ingleby suggested that trying to tie the entire art activity of Edinburgh together in a theme was too ambitious. Instead, as Susanna Beaumont agreed, devising some kind of umbrella, perhaps a joint publication, would bring together everything that was happening. 'This wasn't all well-received,' says Long.

> There was a view from some quarters that the larger organisations shouldn't necessarily get into bed with the smaller ones, because it would be of inconsistent quality and scale and so on. To my mind that was a rather insensitive view which didn't respect the collegiate strength of the visual arts organisations in Edinburgh. The discussion was about instituting a body which would lead an arts festival and represent the whole range of visual arts in it. Not long after that an organisation was convened, and some funding was found.

It was Long who brought Bradley on board very soon after she arrived in the city, with Demarco's bold ideas still leading the way at this point. She joined a steering group which included Long, Demarco, Gale, the Scottish National Gallery of Modern Art's director Richard Calvocoressi and Wendy Law of the Scottish Arts Council. In November the latter organisation provided £10,000 towards the project, which allowed an administrator to be appointed – freelance arts producer Katie Nicoll, who created a feasibility study ahead of a projected opening in 2004.

'Ricky Demarco at that point was interested in something patterned on Venice, where international partners could be sought to sponsor or put forward their own manifestations in Edinburgh in August,' says Bradley.

> It was an interesting model, but all of us working in institutions in the city thought it would be hard to pull off from a standing start.

Instead we could start by thinking about what was happening in
Edinburgh in August, when all the galleries try hard anyway, and
whether those galleries could band together for a more positive
outcome for visual art in Edinburgh in August.

Although Nicoll was working independently, she did so out of the
Fruitmarket, her period as administrator lasting into 2005. In the end, the
Edinburgh Art Festival was born with a certain amount of fanfare, but there
wasn't a hard launch. The first official year of it was 2004, although this took
the form of the most modest manifestation possible – a specially-created print
supplement rounding up what was going on, proudly presented by Iain Gale
and *Scotland On Sunday*, in which Long wrote about the history of art at the
Edinburgh Festival and Nicoll described the potential of this new strand.

'Iain Gale was a massive supporter of Edinburgh Art Festival, and was
instrumental in supporting it,' says Nicoll.

The supplement was a brilliant way in which we could develop
media attention, and there was real support for the Art Festival.
It was all based on people's interest to apply for it, we wanted to
discount people paying a contribution. We didn't want to just cover
the people who could pay, and the people who couldn't wouldn't
get a look in. We very much started with an even playing field for
people to apply.

The debut Art Festival of 2004 showcased very little that wouldn't
already have happened in Edinburgh that August, but seeing the totality of
that work grouped in one place shows why it was worth shouting about
collectively. The major draw of the year was another blockbuster for the
National Galleries, *The Age of Titian: Venetian Renaissance Art from
Scottish Collections*, a historical retrospective. Its opening celebrated the
culmination of the £30m, five-years-in-the-making Playfair Project and the
opening of the Weston Link – an underground linking concourse created
from the cellars beneath the RSA and the National Gallery of Scotland on
the Mound, which created a Louvre-like underground complex with a glass-
fronted entranceway out onto East Princes Street Gardens.

Elsewhere, the Californian contemporary painter Fred Tomaselli's work
was shown at the Fruitmarket and Edinburgh College of Art hosted the BBC
Concert Orchestra-featuring 'Strings' by video artist Sam Taylor-Wood.[10] The
photography of Cecil Beaton was seen at the City Art Centre and the Scottish
painter Alison Watt's work was displayed at the Ingleby Gallery and offsite
in the Memorial Chapel of Old St Paul's Church on Jeffrey Street. Glasgow

School of Art graduate Lucy Skaer – later Scotland's representative at the 57th Venice Biennale in 2007 and a Turner Prize nominee in '09 – was shown at doggerfisher. Large-scale retrospectives of Jasper Johns and Eduardo Paolozzi appeared at the Scottish National Gallery of Modern Art and the Dean Gallery. In the commercial storefront galleries of Dundas Street, there were paintings by John Bellany, Elizabeth Blackadder and the Glasgow Boys.

Away from the high-end and commercial sides of the city's gallery landscape, a group of young and creatively ambitious current and former Edinburgh College of Art students were building an impressive underground art scene. The year 2004 also saw the debut of the Edinburgh Annuale, a thoroughly DIY series of events held in ad-hoc spaces around the city. The hub of these was the Embassy Gallery, a disused storefront on the backstreet East Crosscauseway near the Pleasance, a year-round venture instigated by art students Kim Coleman, Craig Coulthard, Tommy Grace, Jenny Hogarth, Dave Maclean, Kate Owens and Catherine Stafford in the same year.[11] Annuale events also took place at the artist-led spaces Aurora on Great Junction Street in Leith and Total Kunst on Bristo Place and at the pop-up galleries Magnifitat and Wuthering Heights in tenement flats in Bruntsfield.

The Edinburgh Art Festival was a diverse roster of concurrent exhibitions of which any major European city would be proud and while it was no different to what was already happening in Edinburgh during August, the fact all involved had found a means of shouting about it together multiplied the power of what was happening. By 2005, the steering group stepped back while the Edinburgh Art Festival professionalised further. Lisa Kapur replaced Nicoll as administrator, while the former director of the Scottish Arts Council and the Arnolfini Gallery in Bristol Tessa Jackson took over as chair. That year the Art Festival printed its own map and its unique developing identity was emphasised by a special opening event on 29 July, the American-based Chinese artist and Fruitmarket exhibitor Cai Guo-Qiang's *Black Rainbow: Explosion Project for Edinburgh*, a fusillade of black clouds exploding in the clear summer sky over the Castle for 30 seconds.

The timing of the event for 7pm was to prove sadly prophetic. 'The original idea was that we would just do it and nobody would know what had hit Edinburgh,' says Fiona Bradley, who commissioned the work.

Obviously the Council knew we were doing it, but the public would be oblivious. Then the 7/7 bombing [of London in July 2005] happened and we realised we couldn't do that, because it would be so frightening. It was incredibly loud and ominous, a comment on the way people feel unsafe in cities, and the way things happen unexpectedly and people's reaction to them. [After 7/7] it became a work absolutely everybody had to know was coming, so there was a fantastic effort to get every radio station, every news programme, every newspaper to talk about it, and the police held the traffic for 30 seconds for us. It stayed in my mind for that – most of Edinburgh held its breath, everything stopped while the rainbow exploded over the castle, and then everyone went about their business again.

The Art Festival evolved quickly. In 2006, its high-quality printed guide appeared and in 2007 it appointed its first official director Joanne Brown, an Edinburgh College of Art Graduate who'd previously worked with the Scottish Arts Council and at the Fringe Society. In her first year she inaugurated Art Late, a closing event for which galleries across the city stayed open late with drink, music and DJs. This popular series has since evolved into programmed short tours of galleries and unusual music venues.

The guide to the Edinburgh Art Festival's first edition in 2004 listed 38 shows across 23 venues and by Brown's final year in 2010 that had grown to 65 shows in 50 venues, not including an extensive programme of talks and artist-led walks and tours around the city. By this point, exhibitions had been seen in venues like Eskmills in Musselburgh, East Lothian, and on the beachfront promenade at Portobello. Ten miles to the west of Edinburgh, closer to the East Lothian town of Livingston than the city itself, one of the most distinctive success stories in the city's recent contemporary art history opened in 2009 and went straight into the programme.

Bonnington House, near the village of Wilkieston, dates back to 1622 and was owned by the city's Lord Provost Hugh Cunningham at the turn of the 18th century. In the mid-19th century it was remodelled in Jacobean style and by 1999 the house and its 100 acres of fields and wood were purchased by Nicky and Robert Wilson, who moved up from London to take it on. Dublin-raised Robert was chairman of Nelson and Son, the largest manufacturer of homeopathic medicines in the UK and Nicky was a former advertising professional from Edinburgh who had studied at Camberwell and Chelsea Colleges of Art under tutors including Phyllida Barlow and Cornelia Parker.

Looking for an artistic project to develop the grounds of the house, Nicky contacted the American land artist and Postmodernist architectural theorist Charles Jencks, who for many years had lived with his wife Maggie Keswick Jencks at their house in Dumfriesshire, Portrack House. He began his first major land project in the grounds of their home in 1988, at Maggie's urging. *The Garden of Cosmic Speculation* was completed 15 years later, eight years after his wife's death from cancer in 1995.

The following year at Edinburgh's Western General Hospital, the first of the pioneering, architect-designed cancer care Maggie's Centres was opened in Maggie's memory by a charity co-founded by Jencks. Since then, 17 more centres have been built or put into construction, designed by architects including Frank Gehry, Rem Koolhaas and, in 2006 at Kirkcaldy's Victoria Hospital, Zaha Hadid's first UK building.

By the time of *The Garden of Cosmic Speculation*'s completion, Jencks had already made a name for himself as a designer of large-scale postmodern landscapes with a grounding in scientific theories. Completed in 2002 at the Scottish National Gallery of Modern Art on Belford Road, his *Landform* – a series of shaped pools set around curving, sculpted, perfectly manicured grass hills – has since become a major piece of Edinburgh's contemporary art landscape. *Cells of Life*, which took four years to complete, was a similar project for the entrance driveway of Bonnington House. It was the first artwork created for what became Jupiter Artland, which also contains significant site-specific works by Andy Goldsworthy, Antony Gormley, Anish Kapoor and Cornelia Parker. Robert Wilson said at the time:

> This isn't a sculpture park. We think of it as something different. That's why we used the word 'artland', because we want to focus equally on the land element. The intention is that the art will increase the landscape it's in and the landscape will enhance the art.[12]

The early years of the Edinburgh Art Festival featured major studies of work by artists including Tracey Emin, Pablo Picasso and Andy Warhol and in 2010 it created its first commissions in unexplored spaces around the city: the Edinburgh College of Art-educated, Turner Prize winner Richard Wright's *Stairwell Project* at the Dean Gallery; Embassy Gallery co-founders' Kim Coleman and Jenny Hogarth's digital camera obscura *Staged* in the Playfair-designed City Observatory on Calton Hill; and Martin Creed's permanent *Scotsman Steps* on the previously run-down Waverley Steps, a small but landmark change to the landscape of the city.

In 2011, Joanne Brown left the Art Festival and was replaced by Sorcha Carey, formerly of the British Council and the Liverpool Biennial, whose first year saw a new structural glass pavilion built by artist Karen Forbes on St Andrew Square. During the Art Festival's early years, Timothy Clifford also left the National Galleries of Scotland on his 60th birthday in January 2006, after 21 years in service which transformed the organisation into one with an international reputation. This was founded in large part on his knack for smart acquisitions of artists like Botticelli, Raphael and El Greco on a budget, his attractive wall hanging tastes and an ability to programme – or delegate to his gallery directors – shows that were the correct blend of commercial, educational and sensational.

His final Festival programme was a vintage one, with Paul Gauguin, Francis Bacon and Henri Cartier-Bresson shown at his galleries in 2005. Clifford, who was knighted in 2002, said at the time:

> Most directors get forgotten about quite quickly. I'm not sad about it. It's quite right and proper. After all, there's nothing special about Tim Clifford, what's special is the collection.[13]

His replacement and the current incumbent at NGS is John Leighton, a Belfast-born graduate of both the University of Edinburgh and Edinburgh College of Art, who was previously director of the Van Gogh Museum in Amsterdam and curator of 19th century paintings at London's National Gallery. His opening Festival programme in 2006 featured Robert Mapplethorpe, Ron Mueck, a study of Van Gogh's relationship with Britain and the work of the Scottish photojournalist Harry Benson.

Also in 2006, Brian McMaster left the International Festival and was replaced by Australian composer and festival director Jonathan Mills, whose attitude towards visual art was much more relaxed. In 2007 he instigated the *Jardins Publics* project, curated by former Dundee Contemporary Arts deputy director Katrina Brown and produced by Katie Nicoll. Inspired by New Town planner Patrick Geddes and artist Ian Hamilton Finlay's use of gardens, the project placed art in the context of certain pre-existing Edinburgh surroundings.

Richard Wright engraved a window in the early 19th century stone St George's Well on the banks of the Water of Leith in Stockbridge, a short distance from the Romanesque holy site St Bernard's Well. The latter was designed in 1789 by Alexander Nasmyth, the Scottish landscape painter and friend of Robert Burns, and is referenced as a site of great Edinburgh beauty in Mary Shelley's *Frankenstein*.

Wright also created a special ceiling and wall illustration within a private flat at 28 London Street, while Taiwanese painter Michael Lin built a colourful bench seating arrangement around the base of a tree in East Princes Street Gardens. Slovakian former architect Apolonija Sustersic and her collaborator Mieke Schalk worked with residents to create a garden feature at Chessel's Court, between the Royal Mile and Holyrood Road, which would inspire communal discussion in the same manner an 18th century coffee shop might have. Bringing social and private housing in the area together, the residents bought it for one pound and kept it as a permanent feature.

'One of the amazing things when we did the *Jardins Publics* was the access into some of the brilliant spaces nobody was really using,' says Nicoll.

Below St George's Well on the Water of Leith is St Bernard's Well, and we opened that up to let people see the mosaics under the statue. That in itself, just taking people into spaces to see things they pass every single day and never get an opportunity to see, that's what we were trying to do. That's the joy of Edinburgh, as long as the development of it doesn't continue at pace. It's these hidden, delightful spaces that really talk about the heritage of the city, and then when you see it through a contemporary lens that's really interesting. That's what visual arts can do.

After many years of trying, it was the first and last involvement in visual art on the part of Edinburgh International Festival since then. With the overdue emergence of the Edinburgh Art Festival, its patronage in the field was simply no longer required.

* * *

One name that hasn't figured substantially throughout the history of Edinburgh Art Festival has been that of Richard Demarco. His European Art Foundation was listed in that first *Scotland On Sunday* programme of 2004, presenting sculptures at the Roxy Art House and a display of *Canalscapes of Scotland* at Edinburgh Quay near Fountainbridge, where the Union Canal begins in the city, running to Falkirk and all the way on to Glasgow via the Forth and Clyde Canal.

He also programmed retrospective displays of Joseph Beuys' work for the Theatre Workshop in Stockbridge and the Terence Conran-designed Ocean Terminal shopping centre by Leith Docks, then just three years old. Demarco also contributed an essay to the Art Festival programme that paid tribute to the link between Beuys and art in Edinburgh during the Festival, with which he set out his understanding that Beuys' assertion 'Kunst = Kapital' translated to mean art is 'health', not 'wealth'. Its healing power is directly linked, said Demarco, to the founding ideals of the Edinburgh Festival.

By this point, however, his direct influence upon the currents of the Edinburgh Festival was waning. Demarco was 74 when the first Edinburgh Art Festival brochure was issued and despite gathering more honours to add to a lengthy list in the years immediately after – he was made a CBE in 2006 and given the European Citizen's Medal in 2013 – the Roxy Art House stopped hosting Rocket Demarco after 2008, when rent on the place was put up. Meanwhile, St Mary's School in Stockbridge had been closed in 1998 and Demarco had to move his archive, the record of his life's work, into first the old Royal High School building on Calton Hill and then in 2005 out to

Skateraw Farm near Dunbar in East Lothian, where the helpful benevolence of the Watson family was offset by the sheer distance of the collection and any associated exhibitions from Edinburgh.

In 2011, salvation for Demarco's archive – and the arrival of a landmark venue in the development of the Fringe to match the Traverse of the 1960s or the Assembly Rooms of the 1980s – came through an old connection with Joseph Beuys. Back in 1971, when Beuys had set up the Free International University for Creativity and Interdimensional Research (FUI) in Düsseldorf, one of his accomplices had been a painter named Robert McDowell. Born in 1952, McDowell studied art in Belfast, where he was involved in the foundation of the Troubled Image group, a bunch of young artists who created work which responded to the conflict of the Troubles era in Northern Ireland.

After studying at the Slade School of Art, McDowell worked for a decade with Beuys, but later retrained at the University of Cambridge and moved into the field of macroeconomics. He became a highly-regarded advisor to banks, central banks, regulators, insurers and more, specialising in banking risks and regulations, but for all this time he maintained a friendship and a creative involvement with Demarco which dated back to their Beuys connection. In 2010 a major new site in Edinburgh became available, the old Royal Dick veterinary school at the eastern edge of the Meadows and McDowell saw an opportunity to alter the artistic landscape of the city year-round, not just during the Festival.

The Royal Dick dated back to its construction as a bespoke veterinary school in 1916, although the name went back much further, to the founding in 1823 of the first veterinary school in Scotland by the Edinburgh veterinarian William Dick. Officially named the Highland Society's Veterinary School, but unofficially known as the Dick School after its founder, it moved into a bespoke space next to his house on Clyde Street in 1833,[14] then to its Southside site as the Royal (Dick) Veterinary College in 1916, the 50th anniversary of its founder's death.

The school officially became part of the University of Edinburgh in 1951, changing its name to the Royal (Dick) School of Veterinary Studies and in 2010 it moved to another new, purpose-built Edinburgh University site at the Easter Bush Veterinary Campus, seven miles to the south of Edinburgh across the Pentland Hills. What it left behind is a stunning, atmospheric building, a functional but maze-like academic structure with bright, high-ceilinged rooms that look out across the Meadows, open halls primed for concert performances and dank, curving wooden-bench lecture theatres whose dimness and echoing acoustics make them perfect sites for challenging underground performance.

McDowell saw the potential of all this, but at the same time he was holding talks about the future of the Roxy Art House as well. In 2009 it had been purchased by Edinburgh University Settlement (EUS), a philanthropic organisation founded in 1905 by the University of Edinburgh's history professor Sir Richard Lodge. A charitable body that wasn't actually officially connected to the University, EUS was part of the popular Settlement Movement of the turn of the 20th century, in which middle-class lodging houses or student accommodation halls were placed within deprived areas, so privileged students and settlement workers could work on beneficial projects for the local community.

The first Edinburgh University Settlement building of 1905 was at High School Yards, the complex between Infirmary Street and the part of the Pleasance lined by the remains of the 16th century Flodden Wall. One hundred years later, the Settlement was jointly funded by the University and the City of Edinburgh Council and it was involved in lifelong learning classes in disadvantaged communities and activities like art therapy around the city. EUS acquired the Roxy with the intention it would become a local art centre to help raise funds for and promote its mission and a new general manager named Rupert Thomson was appointed.

Thomson grew up in Manchester and moved to Edinburgh as a teenager, where his art historian parents knew many people within the classical and contemporary art communities. He went to university in Bristol and York and when he returned he began to get involved in the local music and art scenes at places like the Embassy Gallery and the Left Bank, a hole-in-the-wall loft venue down a backstreet flight of stairs between Guthrie Street and the Cowgate, also based in premises owned by the Settlement. He was editor of Edinburgh arts magazine *The Skinny* for a few years, then took over at the Roxy in 2010, running it for that year's Fringe.

Here, Thomson programmed alongside Fringe venue Zoo, which was founded in 2001 by lighting designer James Mackenzie and a group of fellow Fringe casual workers at the former Charteris Memorial Church on the Pleasance, more recently known as the Kirk O' Field, where they were initially allowed access to only one hall as the church still wanted to run Sunday coffee mornings in the other. Although Zoo Venues was only in the Roxy for a year, as well as other temporary venues such as the upstairs space in Cowgate bar the Three Sisters, it's built a strong reputation as a Fringe chain with a particular strength for dance. It programmes work at the original Zoo on the Pleasance, Zoo Southside (the former Nicolson Street Church of 1820, since 1986 converted into Southside Community Centre) and Zoo Playground, an Edinburgh University-owned space at High School Yards.

Shortly after the Fringe of 2010, Edinburgh University Settlement fell into bankruptcy in very public fashion after 105 years in existence, threatening the future viability of a number of established Fringe venues. Among them were the Left Bank, later renamed the GRV and the Mash House; the bohemian, artist-led social centre known as the Forest Café, based at the Seventh Day Adventists Church at 3 Bristo Place since 2003, after opening in 2000 in a small West Port shopfront just off the Grassmarket; Wilkie House, another former church on the Cowgate, now a nightclub which formed part of the same space as the GRV; and the Roxy itself, which in October 2010 had just hosted the first edition of the DIY pop-up Hidden Door festival.

There was concern at the time that the Settlement's collapse might see the city's Fringe and year-round cultural scene damaged, but all of these spaces were bought out and subsequently used for the same purpose they had been previously – all except the Forest Café, whose efforts to occupy the building until purchase money could be raised were in vain, forcing a move to a shopfront at 141 Lauriston Place on the corner of Tollcross. The Roxy and the Bristo Place space have both since become Fringe venues under the banner of William Burdett-Coutts' Assembly, as Assembly Roxy and Assembly Checkpoint respectively. For a year after its closure the former Forest Café had been a rough, Berlin squat-style Fringe venue named Checkpoint Charlie and this was the kind of afterlife that Thomson had sought for the Roxy.

'When the Roxy closed due to the collapse of the Settlement, the team and I wanted to see if we could get it back up and running,' says Thomson.

> We thought there was a viable business model to run the building and pay off the mortgage, especially with the guaranteed rent of the Edinburgh Fringe. Richard Demarco, whom I'd met at the Roxy, introduced me to Robert McDowell, who came and had a look and was somewhat interested. But his much bigger project to buy the Dick Vet was already gaining momentum.

The plan for the Roxy was forgotten – in February 2011, Thomson began planning with McDowell to open the Dick Vet for the Fringe of 2011, initially on a rental agreement with the University of Edinburgh to test its effectiveness. The street on which the Dick School was based is named simply Summerhall and so was the new venue, at Thomson's suggestion.

'Robert had worked with Demarco for years, meeting Beuys through him, and had been an artist himself,' says Thomson.

> I always associated his vision with his connection to Demarco's festival endeavours, a very European aesthetic. I remember Robert in the early days saying he wanted it to feel like an Italian hill village, where everyone knew each other. We both wanted it to be internationalist, artistically ambitious, but free and fun – festive, in other words. It felt

special that someone took on such a big space with those ambitions, as he had. I was involved from the early stages of planning what the venue would be like from its identity to the styling, where we retained many of the original names of spaces and colour-schemes of the old vet school.

The main bar and gig venue was named the Dissection Room, with its jars of medical samples rather edgily retained in place, while there's another performance space named the Anatomy Lecture Theatre. 'As Artistic Director I worked on the programme identity and partnerships that formed a crucial part of that, and the range and balance of art forms we would present.'

In that first year alone, there were collaborations with Battersea Arts Centre and the British Council Showcase, as well as a Scottish Independent Record Fair. Summerhall's first extraordinary centrepiece and talking point was a show that seemed designed for this haunting new venue, *Hotel Medea*, by Brazilian theatre maker and Rose Bruford College graduate Jorge Lopez Ramos's Zecoro Ura company. Audiences experienced a spectacular, six-hour overnight promenade performance of the myth of Medea, told through dance, DJ sets, multimedia tricks and a food fight.

Although *Hotel Medea* hogged the attention, Summerhall still received plenty of acclaim as a very unusual venue with an interesting programme and also as a great place to socialise, a more important selling point than ever during a 21st century Festival. In November 2011, the McDowell family pushed the purchase of the building through and Summerhall's reputation during the Edinburgh Festival has grown exponentially since then.

Thomson's Festival programmes threw up a mini-Fringe's worth of highlights. These included the Herald Angel-winning literature programme *These Silences* in 2011; the Polish company Song of the Goat's song-based reinterpretation of Shakespeare *Song of Lear* and Cristian Ceresoli's challenging monologue for one nude woman *The Shit/La Merda* in 2012; the controversial *Süsse Duft* exhibition by German artist Gregor Schneider (the visual art strand was curated by Paul Robertson) and Phia Ménard of the French Company Non Nova's 'plastic bag ballet' *L'Après Midi d'un Foehn* in 2013; and Song of the Goat's return with the offsite, Scots Gaelic song-inspired *Return to the Voice* at St Giles' Cathedral in 2014.

Also in 2014, Paines Plough brought its portable in-the-round theatre Roundabout to Edinburgh for the first time at Summerhall, showing plays including Duncan Macmillan's *Lungs* and *Every Brilliant Thing*, Mark Ravenhill's thriller *Show 6* and the family show *Our Teacher's a Troll* by Dennis Kelly, writer of the West End's *Matilda: The Musical*. Roundabout has since brought work by performers, playwrights and companies including Daniel Kitson, Nish Kumar, Jonny and the Baptists, Chris Thorpe, Theatre

Clwyd, Theatre Uncut, Soho Theatre and Barrel Organ to the Fringe. In 2017 it presented the Royal Court's *Manwatching*, with a different male stand-up comedian reading a sight-unseen monologue about women's sexual fantasies every night. Outside of Festival time moves were made to set Summerhall up as a year-round presence and Thomson's wife Anu was instrumental in securing Edinburgh Children's Festival and Edinburgh International Science Festival as off-season tenants.

Thomson left Summerhall in 2015, through a combination of a financial dispute with McDowell and the offer of a job programming performance and dance at the Southbank Centre in London. 'Edinburgh audiences have been warm to art and Festival culture for decades, and are a bit special in that respect, but I take heart from the response we got,' he says now. 'People like to feel part of something special when it feels social and fun, even if they know they won't like everything in the mix'. His replacement as Programme Manager is Verity Leigh, also from Manchester, who brought a show to Summerhall in 2011, was asked to produce *Return to the Voice* in 2014 and then to help produce the following year's Fringe programme.

'Summerhall is a range of different spaces, which means we can present visual art, live music, theatre and dance, and also fit in a pub, a cafe and an eclectic community of artists, arts organisations and small businesses,' says Leigh.

> Lots of the venue spaces are dramatic and memorable before you even put a show in them, and where an artist is able to take advantage of the aesthetic and atmosphere of a space it can really add to the power of their performance. I'm looking for contemporary work which feels right in our spaces, and to balance international work with work made in Scotland, work from different perspectives and experiences, different genres, and a mix of established and new theatre makers. I don't see commerciality and experimentalism as opposites – there's no point having an amazing experimental performance if no-one comes to see it, but we won't pick a show just because we think it will sell tickets.

Memorable Fringe highlights of her time have been *Us/Them* in 2016, a 10am show for young audiences about a school siege in Chechnya which emerged as a sell-out hit and toured the world and producer Darkfield's shows for 20 people in a pitch-black shipping container parked in front of the venue (*Séance* in 2017, *Flight* in 2018, and *Coma* in 2019). Sh!t Theatre have been a recurring success, making, says Leigh, 'work which is carefully researched and structured with a real political message, but with a really enjoyable layer of daftness which I think audiences enjoy'.

From 34 shows in 2011's Fringe, Summerhall has grown to 90 shows, six exhibitions and another 30 shows in satellite spaces by 2019, including Army at the Fringe, an artistic collaboration with the British Army, which has grown into its own venue at Hepburn House Reseverve Centre on East Claremont Street. Summerhall has welcomed Russian artist/activists Pussy Riot and drag performer Le Gateau Chocolat's piece about acceptance and diversity for young audiences *Duckie*, both in 2018, long-serving experimental Fringe returnees The People Show and Jo Clifford's *The Gospel According to Jesus, Queen of Heaven*, which reimagines Jesus as a trans saviour. In 2012, the programme also included the memorably staged memoir piece *White Rabbit Red Rabbit* by Iranian playwright Nassim Soleimanpour.

The producers of *White Rabbit Red Rabbit* were Aurora Nova, previously more well-known for the Fringe venue of the same name at St Stephen's Church in the New Town, which they opened in 2001 through the joint endeavours of Brighton venue Komedia and German producer and dancer Wolfgang Hoffmann. Born in 1967 in East Germany and based in Potsdam when the Berlin Wall fell, Hoffman sold chunks of it to pay for dance classes, starting his fabrik Potsdam company in 1990. His first visit to the Festival was in 1999 with his hit show *Hopeless Games*, co-produced by St Petersburg's DO-Theatre and somewhat inevitably presented by the Demarco European Art Foundation and in the early 2000s his Aurora Nova shows gathered up Fringe awards. Says Verity Leigh:

> I think Summerhall arrived at the right time to benefit from the audiences that had been developed for experimental European work by Aurora Nova at St Stephens', and the way the British Council Showcase helped to influence established theatre-makers in the UK to take the Fringe more seriously, after several years when it was seen as just for students and comedians.

In 2012, Summerhall's programme once again featured a Demarco-produced production of *Macbeth* on Inchcolm Island in the Forth and both his European Art Foundation and his Demarco Archive Trust – caretaker to 4,500 artworks, over a million photographs and an extensive book and film library – are now permanently housed and displayed as much as is practical at Summerhall.

The Edinburgh Art Festival, Summerhall and the legacy of the Aurora Nova venue are all disparate strands of the Edinburgh Festival, but through each of them can be traced the guiding influence of Richard Demarco and the unbroken 60-year thread of his commitment to internationalism and experimentation in Edinburgh. At Summerhall, especially, the outsider Fringe spirit of the early Traverse and the Richard Demarco Gallery lives on.

SPOTLIGHT

The Scotsman Steps (Work No 1059, 2011)

FEW PLACES IN Edinburgh give more of a sense of the city being a multi-storey one than the spot outside the southern entrance of Waverley Station onto Market Street. Passengers are drawn up to ground level by escalators and stairs and as they step out onto the street and glance across the road, past the jostling taxis and beeping cars trying to pick up and drop their passengers off, they see an Edwardian building which currently houses a bustling bar and nightclub. They look up and up and up and see the building rise for ten grand Edwardian stories 190 feet above them.

This is the Scotsman Hotel, one of the city's landmark buildings since its three-year construction was completed in 1902 as the headquarters of *The Scotsman* newspaper. Look to their left and the visitor will see North Bridge arcing above, carrying road and foot traffic from Leith Street and the east end of Princes Street at the Balmoral Hotel towards the south. The main entrance to *The Scotsman* is somewhere up there, just off North Bridge. The nightclub used to be the gloomy printworks of the newspaper, floors slick with ink, its loading bays ready to open as the summer dawns of the 20th century cracked over the city. For decades, the morning papers were transferred under the road to the station, to be sent around the country by rail freight.

The fate of *The Scotsman* newspaper, still in widespread daily circulation but diminished from the point when it was one of the pre-eminent symbols of Edinburgh and Scotland's intellectual life, speaks more of the trajectory of print media in the age of the internet. Founded in 1817 by a group including Fife-born lawyer and journalist William Ritchie and his brother John, the newspaper was based first on the High Street and then Cockburn Street and was in the hands of the Ritchie's' grand-nephew John Ritchie Findlay when *The Scotsman* building on North Bridge was commissioned as part of an Old Town regeneration in 1897, although Findlay died in 1898 and didn't see it built.

In 2001 the paper moved to the new, purpose-made Barclay House, alongside the Scottish Parliament in Holyrood and in the shadow of Salisbury Crags, but in 2014 it left these premises and downsized to offices at Orchard Brae House on the far northern fringe of the city centre. Exemplifying the shift in media power of the new century, the world-leading Scottish videogames company Rockstar North, publisher of the *Grand Theft Auto* games, took over the sprawling Barclay House, while on North Bridge the old building was renovated into the Scotsman Hotel in 2001. Alongside it, the little-used route between Market Street and North Bridge remained untouched.

The Scotsman Steps are a strikingly-devised but often-hidden nook of the city centre, an internal staircase which rises five stories from Market Street to the side entrance of the building at the lip of North Bridge. Designed by architects James Dunn and James Finlay, much like the rest of the Scotsman building and part of both the Old Town Conservation Area and the Edinburgh UNESCO World Heritage site encompassing the Old and New Towns, as established in 1996, the steps comprise a grand turret – either above or below street level, depending on your vantage point – an octagonal spiral flight of stone stairs, decorative iron grilles in place of windows and white, glazed-tile internal walls. There are 104 steps within; 88 stairs and 16 landings. In the 1960s, this space was used to host exhibitions of hung art during the Festival.

Despite the renovation of the building when it became a hotel, the Scotsman Steps suffered from years of neglect. The dirty old tiles lining the walls enhanced the sense of the space being a public urinal and it was frequently used as such by late-night weekend drunks rushing for last trains to Glasgow or the Lothians; either that, or a living space for rough-sleepers and a heroin shooting gallery. As far as short cuts go, most citizens preferred to get to Waverley by walking across North Bridge or skipping down the steep stairs of Fleshmarket Close, which runs from Cockburn Street past the old *Scotsman* printers' drinking nook, the Halfway House. Once the area around Waverley had been dotted with similar watering holes – like The Scotsman's Lounge on Cockburn Street,[1] or city postal workers' favourite smoky upstairs lounge, The Penny Black on West Register Street – which all opened at five or six o'clock in the morning to serve an eclectic mix of shift workers, alcoholics and clubbers on an all-nighter, who each knew the precise order in which venues should be hit to effect 24-hour drinking.

Set up in the wake of Edinburgh's UNESCO listing, the Edinburgh World Heritage organisation began talks with the City of Edinburgh Council about the possible restoration of the steps and someone within EWH had the idea to involve the Fruitmarket Gallery in the planning of this.

'The Scotsman Steps are a massively important thoroughfare, but at the time we started working on them they were a source of huge embarrassment,' says the Fruitmarket's Fiona Bradley. 'They were scary and dirty and dangerous'.

She realised the Edinburgh Art Festival could be the perfect vehicle to enable their regeneration, as it allowed application to the Scottish Government Expo Fund and therefore financial assistance with artworks created in the public realm. With funding in place, she approached the artist Martin Creed, raised in Glasgow and the East Dunbartonshire town of Lenzie, who'd created a predictable 'but is it art?' public furore in 2001 when he won the Turner Prize for exhibitions that included his *Work No.227: The lights going on and off*; literally, a room in which the lights were set to switch on and off at five-second intervals.

'I wanted an artist who had a smart response to public space,' says Bradley, mentioning Creed's 2008 piece *Work No.850: Runner*, for which runners ran through Tate Britain in London at regular intervals and his 2005 'singing elevator', *Work No.409: Piece for choir and elevator*, later permanently installed in a lift at London's Southbank Centre. 'An extraordinarily beautiful work,' she says, 'where people sing up the scale as you go up the lift and down the scale as you come down.' A lift and a staircase, she reasoned, worked on fundamentally similar principles and the first idea the musician Creed came up with was for a musical staircase.

'I thought of having a musical scale, so as you walked up the steps you would hear a note of the scale,' says Creed.

> But it proved to be so complex and difficult, because the Scotsman Steps was basically famous as a toilet. The musical scale thing would be half in the open air, not totally covered, made of equipment that's going to break and have to be fixed, and then people are going to be pissing all over it.

The idea, though, got him thinking about other materials. 'I thought, what's beautiful, but you can piss on it?' One answer was hard-wearing, easily-washable marble.

With the work commissioned and funded, Creed and Bradley travelled to the marble yards of Carrara in Italy, where marble is internationally brokered and chose as many different types and colours as they could. Working with architectural studio Haworth Tompkins and local architect Chris Bowes, Creed created an artwork that encompasses a different kind of marble from a different country on each step, from Pakistani Black Forest Gold to Brazilian Azul Macaubas. Its official title in his personal artistic catalogue is *Work No.1059: The Scotsman Steps*.

> Lots of people come to Edinburgh from all over the world for the Festival, and what I like about marble is, it's from all different stones in all different parts of the world. That's what I feel about that work – it's got the whole world in it.

Creed likes bridges and staircases; they have form as well as function and they help to gather his thoughts, to hone his abstract ideas. 'A staircase has to be a certain shape, because people can only raise their legs a certain amount, then you have a certain number of steps, and it has to spiral round within that small space. [The Steps] reminds me of Venice, those spaces there which are part of a building, but also a street.

Creed's *Scotsman Steps* relates a subtle sense of internationalism, a useful part of the city landscape whose qualities someone traversing them might not notice until they're halfway up or down – and even though they might not know the background, the aesthetic beauty of them is enough to take notice. Bradley says they reflect the reinterpretation of Edinburgh's history through contemporary culture, especially during Festival time, when the city becomes a theatre. 'It literally puts art underneath people's feet and just slightly alters how they feel about their environment,' she says. 'It's the most loved work of art I've been involved in, a local landmark. The only negative comments we get about it are that we should remove the chewing gum – which we do, annually'.

Creed's association with the Edinburgh Festival has been wide-ranging, including his own performance shows *Work No.1020: Ballet* at the Traverse Theatre in 2010, *Words and Music* at the Edinburgh International Festival in 2017 and *Everything is Going to Be Alright* at the scaled-down, mid-pandemic Fringe of 2021, at Summerhall's outdoor courtyard stage. The latter shares its title with *Work No.975: Everything is Going to Be Alright*, the work installed in giant neon letters above the Scottish National Gallery of Modern Art's neo-classical entranceway in 2008. Although other identical works bearing the all-capitals words 'Everything is Going to Be Alright' have been displayed in London, New York, Italy and New Zealand since 1999, the Edinburgh edition has become a permanent fixture, both an Instagram landmark and a comfort to visitors in troubled times. 'It reminds me of the *Scotsman Steps*,' says Creed.

I'd been asked to do this thing in public (the first one in 1999), thinking, 'shit, people are going to see this who aren't art gallery goers'. Up until then I'd never done anything on the street, only exhibitions in art galleries, but I liked that thought. I realised I didn't just want to make stuff for experts, for a rarefied clique. When someone gives you a hug and says, don't worry, everything is going to be alright, it can be very comforting. These words aren't empty, cliches are cliches for a reason. People find them useful, and I like that people like that work.

He likes that people like *Scotsman Steps* too, now the huge responsibility of making his mark on the landscape of Edinburgh has passed and they've been accepted as part of the city's fabric.

14

The 21st Century Festival: Bigger… and Better?

'IT WAS THE best job I'll ever have,' says Paul Gudgin of his time in charge of the Festival Fringe Society, which lasted between 2000 and 2007 and coincided with the most exponential period of growth in the Fringe's long history.

> During those eight years, most of the specs doubled in scale. Ticket sales were about 800,000 [in 2000], then they went to about 1.6 million by the time I finished. I'm not claiming credit.

Where Gudgin had close involvement, though, was in the international reach of the Fringe. American student groups and Australian comedians had been coming to Edinburgh for decades, but other cities had tried to set up their own version of the Fringe around the world. Most famously, the Adelaide Festival of Arts started in 1960 and was joined by the first Adelaide Fringe in the same year, in the same manner as the Edinburgh Fringe had happened. Brighton Fringe grew out of Brighton Festival the same way, when both events started in 1967.

Since then, following Edinburgh's example, Fringe Festivals have boomed around the world. From a handful in 1980, the International Fringe Festival Association's figures say that 10 more were opened in the 1980s, 40 in the 2000s and more than 150 since 2010, with around 300 now in existence around the world; it's also estimated that one in three such festivals have since closed.[1]

In 2007 the Association, also known as World Fringe, was created to link a slew of increasingly varied events, some of them not even connected to a larger event, creating a somewhat aspirationally business-like definition of a 21st century Fringe Festival as

> a grassroots Festival with the freedom to celebrate and exchange…
> by administrating a programme of events and creating a platform
> and marketplace for new and established art forms.[2]

In Edinburgh these international connections already existed, with Brighton and Adelaide Fringes and Melbourne Comedy Festival, for example, already sharing work with the city. A new international player arrived in Edinburgh in 1999, when the South Korean physical comedy *Cookin'* had its European premiere at the Assembly Rooms, two years after it was first seen in Seoul. Despite the fact fire restrictions meant no food could be cooked live onstage, as it was in the original, this chaotic, wordless physical piece about a catastrophic kitchen (known as *Nanta* in Korea) was a big hit. It still plays in Korea today, after an international tour which included hit off-Broadway dates.

'When I was there, South Korea became obsessed with the Fringe,' says Gudgin. After *Cookin'* was seen in 1999 and 2000, producer Angela Kwon returned to Edinburgh, in partnership with the Assembly Rooms, to show *Jump* in '05 and '06 and *Korean Drum: Journey of a Soul* in 2011, as choreographed by Kook Soo-Ho. In 2015, an annual Korean Season of work was established around Assembly's venues.

During and after Gudgin's tenure, representatives of the international Fringe boom in Prague, Stockholm, Canada, Sydney and beyond looked to Edinburgh as their template. He and his staff helped a lot of these Fringe Festivals with advice to get off the ground, as many as five or 10 new ones every year, as well as talking to overseas performers, event organisers and scouts looking for acts. The Fringe's Promoter Liaison Office was set up to help facilitate this.[3] 'It became an exciting part of what we were doing,' he says.

I think the city also began to take the Fringe and their relationship with it more seriously. Then travel and tourism became much more of a thing and Edinburgh became a natural focus of the international cultural media's attention. It was stars aligning, really.

A world-changing development of the 2000s impacted the Fringe even further. 'The growth of the website edfringe.com is the big story around the Fringe at the start of the century,' says Gudgin. He marvels at the now-outdated memory of 20th century Fringe ticket sales being racked up through long queues of patient in-person customers snaking off the Royal Mile down past the Wireworks Playground, now filled in by a children's nursery and confidently, compellingly states that real-time online booking is the single greatest factor driving the Fringe's booming sales during his tenure and beyond.

'From a practical point of view, we wouldn't have been able to sell 1.6 million tickets the way we did formerly, we just wouldn't have had the capacity,' says Gudgin.

We weren't the only festival doing a website, but I believe we were the first event of our kind to have real-time booking online. We put a lot of money, time and effort into edfringe.com, and that really helped tell the story of the Fringe to the rest of the world. We felt we were racing to keep up with the site and the rate at which it was growing, we couldn't develop it fast enough. This undoubtedly led to that growth in international attention.

The first online Fringe booking, he recalls, came in 2000, a day of great excitement in the Fringe office.

It was very experimental – we wondered, is this thing going to work, is it going to be safe? On the very first day the office manager came running through to say we'd received our first online booking. Little did we know...

As the Fringe began to bulge, new names continued to emerge. From Wellington, New Zealand, came musical comedy duo *The Flight of the Conchords*, Jemaine Clement and Bret McKenzie, who started out in a mid-'90s comedy troupe formed by fellow Victoria University of Wellington drama students named *So You're a Man*, also featuring friend and future film director Taika Waititi. The pair struck out on their own in 1998 and were a familiar name on the New Zealand comedy circuit when they arrived in Edinburgh in 2002.

They played a late-night show at the Caves under South Bridge, just off the Cowgate, under the Gilded Balloon's banner and word got around, particularly among the Fringe's comedians. The booking came about through Karen Koren's employment of a New Zealander named Rosie Carnahan to run Gilded Balloon's bars, who suggested the Conchords as they were friends and collaborators with her boyfriend – later husband – Rhys Darby. 'All the comics started going down to the Caves to see them,' said Koren. 'I also booked them lots on *Late 'n' Live* which helped their profile, and I helped get their UK agent.'4 The Conchords returned to the same venue in 2003, with a new show named *High On Folk* which spoofed Lou Reed, Eminem and New Zealand's now-ubiquitous *Lord of the Rings* association – McKenzie played a minor role as a hobbit in one of the films – with songs including the folk rap 'The HipHopapotamus Versus the Rhymenoceros' and the ballad 'I'm Not Crying (It's Just Been Raining on My Face)'. They were nominated for the Perrier Award, returning in 2004 with *Lonely Knights*, by which point they were already developing a show for BBC Radio 2. Broadcast in September 2005, it featured Fringe regulars Daniel Kitson, Nina Conti, Dan Antopolski and Rhys Darby himself. International fame, an HBO television series and Grammy and Emmy Award nominations followed soon after.

In 2001, Scots-born comedian and cartoonist Kev F Sutherland brought his *Sitcom Trials* show to the Gilded Balloon, after premiering it in Bristol in 1999, in which the first part of new sitcom ideas were acted out and placed head-to-head in an audience vote, with only the winning ending shown. The show has returned sporadically ever since, often under the guise of the Gilded Balloon's *So You Think You're Funny?* contest, and also appeared as an ITV television show in 2003. Sutherland's subsequent show *The Scottish Falsetto Sock Puppet Theatre* describes its suitably Fringe-friendly concept within the title.

The most notable success of Sutherland's productions, however, came in the very first Edinburgh *Sitcom Trials* in 2001, when one of the entries at the vaulted Peppermint Lounge nightclub below South Bridge[5] was *You Say Potato*, starring double act the Orange Girls, aka Miranda Hart and Charity Trimm. Hart had first appeared at the Fringe in 1994, in another double act named Hurrell and Hart, a run which she later said kept her career going; she'd vowed to carry on if she got one audience of at least 20 people (some shows were cancelled as they had no audience, but one had 21) and a good review (a lukewarm three star write-up in *The Scotsman* was good enough).

Hart's *Sitcom Trials* show wasn't very well reviewed – 'the show had very little to do with 'com', but to sit through it was something of a trial', said *The Scotsman*'s Kate Copstick,[6] while *Chortle* said it was 'as unpredictable as an episode of Scooby Doo'.[7] Yet in the archive footage now available online, the style of Hart's extremely popular and award-winning 2009 BBC sitcom *Miranda* is clear in the script and performances.[8]

At the Assembly Rooms in 2005, 25-year-old future international star and creator of the hit musicals *Hamilton* and *In the Heights* Lin-Manuel Miranda made his first international appearance, performing in his co-created six-piece hip hop improvisation show *Freestyle Love Supreme*. The group busked on the Royal Mile and were described by *The Telegraph* as 'a bunch of fresh-faced, quick-witted New York kids who improvise rap tunes to audience suggestions'.

The same year, Australian musical comedian Tim Minchin made his first appearance in the UK with a Fringe run of his show *Darkside* at the Gilded Balloon, after Karen Koren saw him perform it at the Melbourne International Comedy Festival. He gave his first impressions of Edinburgh on his then-new blog: the Gilded Balloon had a 'ceiling like a chapel, balconies on three sides. Amazing'. Everywhere he looked he saw 'my silly head on bright pink posters'.[9]

The Telegraph called Minchin 'the find of the Fest'. *Time Out* advised readers to '[t]ake out a second mortgage, sell the car, and put the money on the safest bet you'll ever make in this uncertain world: that Tim Minchin will be the next big thing in musical comedy'. *Scotland On Sunday*'s Jonathan

Trew compared him to 'the bastard son of The Cure's Robert Smith and Riff Raff from *The Rocky Horror Picture Show*, [with] the kind of slightly psychotic stage presence that frightens animals'.

That year Minchin won the Perrier Best Newcomer award, returning to Edinburgh with his shows *So Rock* in 2006 and *Ready for This?* in 2008. It was after seeing the latter that director Matthew Warchus approached Minchin about writing music and lyrics for the Royal Shakespeare Company's Roald Dahl adaptation *Matilda the Musical*. Minchin agreed, the show debuted in 2010 and it won a record seven Olivier Awards, plus four Olivier Awards, following its incredibly successful West End and Broadway runs.

Among these huge visiting success stories, the artistic landscape of Edinburgh continued to adapt and alter. As a company, Dance Base had existed since 1994 for the promotion of dance in the city, but in June 2001 it became Scotland's National Centre for Dance, with the opening of a purpose-built new headquarters on the Grassmarket. A glass-ceilinged series of studio spaces with panoramic views up towards the Castle, Malcolm Fraser Architects' design won the RIAS (Royal Incorporation of Architects in Scotland) Award and was a finalist in the Royal Institute of British Architects' (RIBA) Stirling Prize in 2002.

Born in Edinburgh in 1959 and educated at George Watson's College and the University of Edinburgh, Malcolm Fraser's architectural stamp – light, welcoming, accessible builds, often transforming old and outdated spaces without ruining their character – informed a range of Edinburgh's most successful new buildings at the turn of the 21st century, among them a number of art spaces used during the Festival. The Scottish Poetry Library, founded by poet and later president of Scottish PEN Tessa Ransford in 1984, moved into a new space on Crichton's Close just off the Royal Mile in 1999 and received a RIBA Award and a nomination for Channel 4 Building of the Year in 2000.

In 2006, Fraser Architects designed the Scottish Storytelling Centre on the Royal Mile, taking the place of the Church of Scotland's old Netherbow Theatre, yet creating a new and vibrant Fringe and year-round space which incorporates the historic John Knox House. Run by TRACS (Traditional Arts & Culture Scotland), the Centre has become home to a significant festival on Edinburgh's calendar, albeit one which runs outside the Edinburgh Festival season in October. Established in 1989, when just 700 people attended, the Scottish International Storytelling Festival had grown to welcome 27,000 visitors in Edinburgh and across Scotland by 2017, the largest festival of its kind in the world, blending traditional music, dance and storytelling.

In 2009, Fraser Architects also converted the old Infirmary Street Baths – the first public baths in Edinburgh, built in 1885 – into Dovecot Studios, creating a new home for the former Edinburgh Tapestry Company, which was established in 1912 by the 4th Marquess of Bute in Corstorphine, now a suburb of Edinburgh but then an outlying village. In the 20th century the old studio was home to the great Scottish weaver, Pop Artist and former artistic director of the company, Archie Brennan, while among its annual Fringe exhibitions have been the Herald Angel-winning 2012 performance piece *A Tapestry of Many Threads*, co-written by the author Alexander McCall Smith.

Since then, Malcolm Fraser has been involved with the multiple award-winning new Collective Gallery at the former observatory on Calton Hill, as well as much-admired new housing developments at West Pilton Crescent and Leith Fort Colonies.[10] These major projects have sprung up amid a formal post-devolution recognition of Edinburgh's historic structure, which was brought to international awareness when the city's Old and New Towns were awarded UNESCO World Heritage Status.

In 1999, the Edinburgh World Heritage body was formed as a result of this designation,[11] under the direct sponsorship of the new Scottish Government and the City of Edinburgh Council, with a remit based around conservation, monitoring, promotion of and special projects involving the World Heritage site. In 2004, the city received its second major piece of international cultural recognition when it became the first UNESCO City of Literature, followed by the creation of the City of Literature Trust, an organisation designed to promote the city's literary history and current life.

As part of this, a new civic post of Edinburgh Makar was created in 2002, essentially a poet laureate and literary ambassador for the city. The first Makar was poet and former BBC Scotland head of radio drama Stewart Conn; the current appointee is poet and playwright Hannah Lavery, whose play *Lament for Sheku Bayoh*, about the real-life death of a man in police custody in 2015, was seen at the Lyceum as part of Edinburgh International Festival in 2021.[12] The City of Literature status rewards a centuries-long literary tradition in Edinburgh, from the opening of the world's first circulating library in the city in 1725 to, of course, the worldwide renown of the Edinburgh International Book Festival.

* * *

The destruction of the original Gilded Balloon and the Perrier Award's bad press over sponsorship weren't the only setbacks experienced by the Festival during the 2000s. Historically, the year 2008 will be known for the international banking crash, which hit a number of major Edinburgh-based banks through the recession which followed. Although many of their operations were by this point located in London, historic Edinburgh financial institutions like the Royal Bank of Scotland, the Bank of Scotland and TSB were greatly affected to one degree or another and many of their flagship Edinburgh city centre premises were sold off in following years.

For the Edinburgh Festival, meanwhile, 2008 was an ignominious year for its own reasons. The bankruptcy of the Lehman Brothers bank, the event that brought the crash home to the world, happened on 15 September 2008, two weeks after the end of the Festival. For the Fringe, however, the big crash of '08 happened on 9 June that year, when the new electronic ticketing system brought in to handle centralised sales began to experience problems and crashed completely the following day.

A replacement system was up and running by 17 June and web, counter and telephone sales continued for a time, until the system was taken offline twice more towards the end of July and sales were suspended again. Some half-full shows were appearing on the system as full, others with no seats left were still being sold into. A perfect storm of bad publicity followed, where reports of the problems in the press caused concern among some customers who hadn't received their postal tickets. A murmur of rolling discontent dogged the build-up to the Fringe, building here and there into alarmed – and alarmist – speculation that the whole thing might not be able to happen.

With the benefit of 14 years' hindsight, the Fringe ticketing crisis was a blip along the road in the Festival's long history, but at the time an air of existential threat seemed to hang over the event, possibly feeding on the sense of financial crisis building in the world. It didn't help that the Big Four of Assembly, Pleasance, Gilded Balloon and the now very firmly ascendant Underbelly had launched their own subsidiary Edinburgh Comedy Festival as a Fringe offshoot, with its own exclusive programme. The launch event had been the day before the Fringe's, to add to the sense of perceived gazumping.

When the original ticketing system, supplied by Glasgow-based Pivotal, went down, the Fringe was compelled to turn to IT firm Red61, a company whose services it had decided against prior to appointing Pivotal and whose freshly-installed system for the Big Four was working perfectly well. The understandable glitches of a major IT project's first phase adopted some of the drama of the perceived ongoing internal battle for the Fringe's soul and purse strings. At the time and after the fact, the box office affair had consequences. On 26 August it was announced the Fringe's takings were down nearly 10 percent for the year – the International Festival's were up by seven percent – with more than 1.5 million tickets sold, compared to 1.7 million the year before. Concluding his first year in charge of the Fringe following Gudgin's departure, director Jon Morgan declared himself pleased with these results.

It was always going to be a difficult year. Morgan said the Fringe Society had been worried about the clearly gathering financial clouds in the world and the effect of the 2008 Beijing Olympics on sales. August in Edinburgh, meanwhile, had been one of the wettest Festivals on record. Two days later, Morgan announced his own departure at the end of his only Fringe in charge, stating his desire to get back to producing work.

Morgan had arrived at the Fringe with a strong pedigree, following senior positions at the youth theatres Contact in Manchester and TAG in Glasgow, as well as advising the Scottish Arts Council, working for the British Council and being involved in the process that established the National Theatre of Scotland. Although his motives for leaving at the time fitted well with his past experience, there remained a perception he was carrying the can for the box office affair. The bitter taste left by the events of 2008 has long since gone, however, and Morgan has gone on to work in leadership positions with the Federation of Scottish Theatre and currently the Theatres Trust.

At the Fringe Society AGM in August 2009, the past year's accounts revealed the Society had made a loss of nearly £900,000, partly accounted for by the £142,000 spent on Red61 – over and above the £394,000 cost of the original system – as well as £100,000 on new staff to help and £130,000 less ticket commission than budgeted for. A £125,000 loan from Edinburgh Council and money from both the Scottish Government and the Scottish Arts Council had helped stabilise matters.

'There's no question we came very close to the edge of the abyss,' said the Stand's Tommy Sheppard, also a Fringe Society board member by this point. 'There were times around the turn of the year [2009] when we were looking at the cash flow on a week-by-week basis to make sure we had enough money to pay people'.[13]The Fringe's new chief executive Kath Mainland, meanwhile, said the whole scenario had 'highlighted what a fragile and vulnerable enterprise the arts can be'.[14]

Originally from Orkney, Mainland studied English literature at the University of Glasgow and a postgraduate in accounting at Strathclyde University and freely described herself to *The Herald* as a 'control freak' who 'love[s] spreadsheets'. She first took a summer job at the Fringe in 1991, then worked as a freelance events and festivals producer – including for William Burdett-Coutts' Assembly – until 2005, when she became administrative director of the Edinburgh International Book Festival under director Catherine Lockerbie. The latter had been in post since replacing Faith Liddell in 2001.

Remaining with the Fringe until 2015, when she left to take up the role of executive director at the Melbourne Festival in Australia, Mainland was a major figure in the development of the 21st century Fringe. 'I doubt whether the Edinburgh Fringe has ever found itself in the hands of a leader who understood it more thoroughly, or nurtured it more carefully and effectively through what could have been difficult times, than Kath Mainland', wrote

Scotsman theatre critic and columnist Joyce McMillan upon Mainland's departure in '15.[15]

Employed under the new designation of Chief Executive, with a strategic remit which more closely matched her organisational skills, Mainland effected a spectacular recovery from the events of 2008. In 2009, the number of Fringe tickets sold leapfrogged those of both 2008's troubled Fringe and 2007's previous benchmark of 1.7 million, with 1.8 million purchased. By her departure in 2015 that had leapt considerably again to 2.3 million. She was awarded a CBE for Services to Culture in Scotland in 2014.

During Mainland's time in charge avenues for new talent thrived, among them Escalator East to Edinburgh, established in 2003 by Colchester Arts Centre as a funding and development vehicle for artists from the east of England to create Fringe work with the support of the Arts Council. Between 1997 and 2019, the British Council's Edinburgh Showcase was a key development source for some urgent new voices from the UK, with boundary-pushing monologue performers Tim Crouch and Chris Thorpe, disability arts creator Jess Thom of Touretteshero and Javad Alipoor, who makes thrilling multi-media works about online culture and radicalisation, all praising its positive effect upon their ability to present work.

Made in Scotland, meanwhile, was founded for Mainland's first Fringe in '09, and continues to be a showcase of some of the finest Fringe-ready Scottish work across genres, a collaborative effort between the Festival Fringe Society, the Federation of Scottish Theatre, the Scottish Music Centre and Creative Scotland, with support from the Scottish Government's Festivals Expo Fund. More new national voices arrived from elsewhere, including the From Start to Finnish delegation from 2011.

Between 2010 and 2013, Mainland also chaired the board of one of the most significant organisations in the Fringe's recent history. Established in 2007, Festivals Edinburgh is an umbrella group founded by the 12 individual Edinburgh festivals, including those that happen outside of August. Its founding director was Faith Liddell, Catherine Lockerbie's predecessor as head of Edinburgh International Book Festival and her initial remit was for a two-day, part-time job; in 2022 the job – since 2015 held by Liddell's successor, Julia Amour – is one of six within the organisation.

The impetus for Festivals Edinburgh's creation came from a general institutional sense in the new millennium that the Festival wasn't a prestigious irritation to be borne by the city, but instead a key part of its contemporary identity and a powerful and unique tool for promoting investment and tourism. Three key documents led to its formation, the first of which was the City of Edinburgh Council's Festival Strategy of 2001. Next, co-commissioned by the City of Edinburgh Council, Scottish Enterprise

Edinburgh and Lothian, EventScotland and VisitScotland, economic development consultants SQW carried out an Economic Impact Study of the (then) 17 year-round festivals from August 2004 to July 2005.

The final piece of the puzzle that led to Festivals Edinburgh's founding was delivered on 4 May 2006 and became a major talking point in the life of the Festival up to this point. Carried out by AEA Consulting, the report named 'Thundering Hooves: Maintaining the Global Competitive Edge of Edinburgh's Festivals,' says Paul Gudgin, came about as a result of his conversation with *The Times* journalist Mike Wade. During it, Gudgin noted the amount of money being spent by Liverpool on their successful European Capital of Culture bid of 2008 and on the creation of Manchester International Festival, which soft-launched with a series of events in 2005 ahead of the full first edition in '07.

'I said, I've been to a few places recently, overseas and in the UK, and they're spending big sums of money because they want to be Edinburgh,' says Gudgin.

> He thought this was interesting, so he went to Frank McAveety, who was then culture minister [in the Scottish Government], and asked him what he thought about this. Frank McAveety got involved, put together meetings to talk to the festivals about this, and then between Edinburgh City Council and the Scottish Government, they commissioned the report.[16] I think it was Catherine Lockerbie at the Book Festival who came up with the name Thundering Hooves, which referred to the sound of all these other festivals coming up behind us.

Thundering Hooves noted that the 2004 study had found the year-round festivals brought £184 million of revenue to the Scottish economy, £135 million going to Edinburgh and the Lothians, and £75 million of it directly attributable to the Fringe. Two and a half million visitors to the city had generated this money in '04, an exact doubling of the number of visitors in 1997. 'Any fall from [the festivals'] pre-eminent position would have immediate economic repercussions for Edinburgh, the Lothians and the whole of Scotland', said the report.[17]

The 11 festivals discussed in Thundering Hooves are the same ones as comprise Festivals Edinburgh now, with one exception. These are Edinburgh International Festival, the Edinburgh Festival Fringe, Edinburgh International Film Festival, Edinburgh International Book Festival, Edinburgh Art Festival, the Royal Edinburgh Military Tattoo and the immediately pre-Festival Edinburgh Jazz and Blues Festival. These have been joined by Edinburgh

Science Festival, held in April and Edinburgh International Children's Festival, held in May.

Opening in 1989 with a 'Discovery Dome' in the Royal Botanic Garden, school engagement events and a science book fair at Heriot-Watt University, the Science Festival was inaugurated by Valentina Tereshkova, the first woman in space and has since established the Edinburgh Medal, a prestigious award given to a major figure in science who then delivers a lecture at the festival. Said the *New Scientist*'s reporters – actually their correspondent and his 12-year-old son – of the first edition 'now that the idea is a proven success, we can hope that the Edinburgh Science Festival will go from strength to strength'.[18]

Separate from earlier efforts by Frank Dunlop to start a children's event at the International Festival, the Children's Festival was inspired by founder Duncan Low's visit to the Vancouver International Children's Festival, whose bill of 'extraordinary theatre, music, dance, mime, art, designed specifically for children, young people and teenagers, and delivered by professional performing artists'[19] he sought to recreate. It had its first edition in 1990 at a tented village on Inverleith Park, with an audience of more than 20,000 watching 75 performances of 12 shows from countries including Zimbabwe, Canada and the Netherlands.

In modern Festivals Edinburgh times, the Scottish International Storytelling Festival has taken the place of Edinburgh Mela, a multi-cultural event founded by organisers from Edinburgh's Bangladeshi, Indian and Pakistani communities, with involvement of Chinese, African and other groups. The Mela was first held at Meadowbank Stadium in 1995, before moving to Pilrig Park in 2000 and Leith Links in 2010. Despite attempts to give it a curated artistic element through the employment of artistic directors Stephen Stenning and later Chris Purnell, it's returned to being more of a community meeting event in recent years.

The 11th year-round Edinburgh festival is by some way the most significant after those happening in August and a major tourist attraction in its own right. Of the money brought into the economy by the festivals, Thundering Hooves stated in 2006 that Edinburgh's Hogmanay was responsible for £44.4 million to the Scottish economy, of which £39.5 million – nearly 30 percent of the total from all 12 festivals – stays in Edinburgh and the Lothians. A four-day event built around the Scottish New Year celebration ('Hogmanay' is the Scots name for New Year's Eve, although the origin of the term is uncertain), its public celebration was a tradition in Edinburgh, as in other Scottish towns and cities.

Build around the Scottish ritual of 'first-footing', or visiting a friend or relative's house as soon as possible to toast the New Year, the inevitable parties gave way to informal street celebrations around 'the Bells' (the chimes of midnight), with the Royal Mile at the Tron Kirk becoming a particular focus of these in Edinburgh. In 1993 the City of Edinburgh Council decided to formalise an increasingly busy event by instituting Edinburgh's Hogmanay, approaching city-based event organisers Unique Events to take it on.

Formed to create the Big Day festival as part of Glasgow's European City of Culture celebrations in 1990, Unique's founding director was Pete Irvine, who with his business partner and Regular Music co-founder Barry Wright had put on the Edinburgh Rock Festival of 1979. That event wasn't successful enough to continue, but it was an early chapter in popular music's troubled history with the Edinburgh Festival. In 1997, Alex Poots and the creator of London's Meltdown festival David Sefton were invited to devise a new music festival for August in Edinburgh and for three years the Flux Festival was a critical success at the Queen's Hall, the old Jaffacake nightclub on King's Stables Road and finally Princes Street Gardens. It welcomed artists including The Kinks' Ray Davies, PJ Harvey, Nick Cave, Spiritualized and The Jesus and Mary Chain for shows which were perfectly in tune with the Festival's character, before collapsing in acrimony between the promoters and the council.

Around the same time, the short-lived Planet Pop promoted local and indie gigs in Edinburgh in August, while since 2000, Scotland's largest promoters DF Concerts have made various attempts to bring larger shows. Between 2000 and 2012 they ran T on the Fringe – rebranded as The Edge from 2008 – and booked artists including Massive Attack, Jurassic 5, Kelis and a pair of headline Princes Street Garden shows by Franz Ferdinand in 2005, with the then-emerging Arcade Fire in support. Between 2005 and 2007, T on the Fringe used Meadowbank Stadium for 25,000-capacity outdoor gigs by artists including Radiohead and Pixies, while in recent years the promoter has started a new series of August concerts in Princes Street Gardens named Summer Sessions.

Edinburgh's Hogmanay was an initially ticketless event, until overcrowding occurred on Princes Street in 1996 when over 300,000 people attended and ticketed numbers were capped at 100,000 from the following year. Featuring a Scottish-focused bill of bands during the 1990s, including Runrig, Texas, Bay City Rollers and Edwyn Collins, since the millennium the event has booked a major star to play around the Bells, among them Moby, Blondie, Pet Shop Boys and Mark Ronson. More representatives of a resurgent Scottish music industry have also featured, like KT Tunstall, Primal Scream, Simple Minds and Franz Ferdinand. Although Unique lost the contract for Hogmanay to Underbelly in 2017, it's since been restored to them for 2022.

Thundering Hooves stated that, for Edinburgh's festivals 'there are grounds for confidence in the short term.... [however] [t]he non-profit cultural sector throughout western democracies is undergoing profound changes and the festivals, by virtue of their reliance on, and relationship to, the 'global' cultural economy are sensitive to those changes'. It offered a raft of recommendations.[20] Although the festivals had been working together since Fringe director Michael Dale was approached by the Tattoo's business manager Brian Leishman in the 1980s and the Capital Group was formed – in fact, Festivals Edinburgh was tentatively formed as the Association of Edinburgh Festivals in 2004 – these fully coalesced into Festivals Edinburgh.

The years since have seen Edinburgh maintain its leading international position, although the Festival's continued growth in size and its increasing collective instinct for financial maximisation hasn't been welcomed by all, as other elements of what happens in Edinburgh in August have come under scrutiny. Yet on its own terms, Festivals Edinburgh has been a great success.

Describing the Edinburgh Festival as 'a never-ending experiment' in 2015, while she still headed up Festivals Edinburgh, Faith Liddell summed up the city's enduring appeal:

The idea of a festival as a vehicle for city marketing and branding has become very fashionable over the last 15 years, but what happens in Edinburgh couldn't happen anywhere else in the world. You cannot buy what happens here off the peg.[21]

* * *

Even as the Edinburgh Festival as a commercial entity began to realise new possibilities, clever promoters sought to turn their own relative lack of commercial potential to their advantage. One of the underground visionaries of the modern Fringe is Peter Buckley Hill, a writer of comedy folk songs in the mould of Connolly and Carrott, who was already in his 40s when he first attended the Fringe – and lost £4,000 – in 1994. Realising later that the Fringe was, as he put it, 'people spending their savings to finance their dreams', he returned in '96 with a show named *Peter Buckley Hill and Some Comedians* at the Footlights and Firkin pub on Bread Street. He decided to make it free entry, putting a hat at the door for donations instead.

The lack of admission fee caught attention and Hill played to some full houses – admittedly partly made up of the pub's regulars – and more or less broke even for the month. The show continued annually and by 1999 it had moved to the Three-Quarter sports café on the Grassmarket, with Hill doing a solo show at the Stand's old haunt WJ Christie's. Early-career acts he booked that year, he has recounted, included Jimmy Carr, Adam Hills, Lucy Porter and Robin Ince.

The model Hill established of persuading bars to forego venue hire fees in expectation of increased bar take, while performers collect donations at the end, has gone on to be a great success, spreading to other venues under his 'PBH's Free Fringe' banner. By 2015, Hill's last year in charge before handing the brand over, some 529 shows played a combined total of 9,260 performances. Other promoters like Laughing Horse and Just the Tonic have been inspired to adopt a similar strategy, not always with amicable results between those involved.

Under the name Heroes of Fringe, Bob Slayer has also booked pub comedy shows on the Fringe since 2011, including Kunt and the Gang, who in 2011 caused controversy – and won a Malcolm Hardee award – for promoting their show with adhesive stickers shaped like school graffiti penises, to be stuck to other comedians' posters in amusing positions. This episode was dubbed 'Cockgate'. Later, Slayer organised *Iraq Out & Loud* in 2016, in which 1500 comedians and members of the public continuously read all 2.6 million words of the Chilcot Report into the Iraq War over 13 days, 24 hours a day.

Hill's creation of the Free Fringe was partially inspired in '96, he says, by a barrier he saw between the residents of Edinburgh and the performers of the Fringe when he was booked for a Festival-time gig in Craigmillar and he wondered why no-one in the area made the short journey to see him in the centre of town. This view only intensified with the loss of the five pounds entry Fringe Club and the Fringe Sunday and Festival Cavalcade events during the following decade. As Hill wrote in his memoir *Freeing the Free Fringe*, a comprehensive and entertaining account of Fringe promotion in Edinburgh:

> The parade and Fringe Sunday were ways of giving back to the
> people of Edinburgh... All of this is gone now. The Fringe [Society]
> doesn't see its role as providing things like that. And arguably that
> has built up a larger barrier between the Fringe and the people of the
> city that hosts it.[22]

These weren't the only popular aspects of the Festival to depart from August in the 2000s. Since Lynda Myles's tenure in the 1970s, the Edinburgh International Film Festival had continued under the stewardship of her old accomplice Jim Hickey and then a succession of directors until the 2000s. Although its programming was highly regarded and it brought a number of UK and European premieres to Edinburgh, it had become difficult for the Film Festival to lead the way amid a booming range of similar events around the world, as it managed with the early Documentary movement and then

Myles and David Will's astute awareness of emerging '60s and '70s cinema.

Instead, the Film Festival's stock in trade was its strong programming under first Hickey's successor David Robinson, then Penny Thomson, Mark Cousins, Lizzie Francke and Shane Danielson. Now an author, broadcaster and filmmaker himself, Cousins in particular brought a blend of good connections, cinematic knowledge and programming ingenuity and made the Film Festival an exciting venue for international filmmakers and new British talent alike to be seen. In the public eye, however, it was all about the big-name red carpet appearances in the city, including Clint Eastwood (*White Hunter, Black Heart*, 1990), Ewan McGregor (*Velvet Goldmine*, 1998), Pierce Brosnan and Rene Russo (*The Thomas Crown Affair*, 1999), Kate Winslet (*Enigma*, 2001) and Sigourney Weaver and Alan Rickman (*Snow Cake*, 2006).

By the mid-2000s a perfect storm had been building for the Film Festival, including the booming growth of the Fringe and the Book Festival in particular, which placed pressure upon not just accommodation for delegates in the city, but on finding an appropriate space for the Delegate's Centre, the film industry meeting hub. There had also been a report which suggested moving to a 'shoulder month' of July or August, as the Jazz & Blues Festival had done, might be appropriate, while research said the Filmhouse's usual year-round customers tended to see fewer films in August, as they were taking in other festival events from an ever-growing selection.

With financial clouds gathering across the world ahead of the crash of 2008, that year's Film Festival was moved to June, a decision that took some by surprise and was disliked by many traditionalists. Although the move had been under consideration since before her tenure and was a board-level decision, film journalist Hannah McGill was artistic director at this point and had to front it to the press. In explaining it, she astutely described the much-changed landscape since 1947 and the competing pressures that have left the festival somewhat seeking an identity:

> International film festivals were a new concept; Cannes and Venice were in their infancy too. But things have shifted considerably since then. Film festivals have flourished, as both industry and public events; and cinema has more than established itself as a legitimate art form and academic field of study as well as a commercial entertainment medium... rather than endlessly debate our place in August and the relative positioning of other events, we've opted to do something.[23]

There was change at the International Festival too, when Brian McMaster left in 2006 after 15 years, making him EIF's longest-serving director to date, to be replaced by Australian composer and former director of Melbourne

International Arts Festival Jonathan Mills. Born in Hitchin, Hertfordshire, and originally intent on being a lawyer, McMaster's move into arts administration was partly inspired by a visit to the Edinburgh Festival at the age of 19 in 1963. His tenure brought a number of great artists to Edinburgh regularly, including the German theatre director Peter Stein – whose numerous hits at McMaster's EIF included David Harrower's *Blackbird* in 2004 – the choreographer Mark Morris and the conductor András Schiff.

Yet perhaps McMaster's greatest achievement was finally closing EIF's London office and moving the festival into its own permanent home base in Edinburgh, the Hub at the top of the Royal Mile. Opened in 1845 as Victoria Hall, the General Assembly of the Church of Scotland, this grand, gothic building had lain all-but unused since its closure in 1979, until it's reopening in '99 by Queen Elizabeth. McMaster seemed incredulous that some doubted the wisdom of closing the London office:

Someone said you will win Edinburgh but you will lose the world.
There was the feeling that it made it parochial to run it from
Edinburgh... now that idea seems totally absurd.[24]

Until 2014, the International Festival was steered by Mills as a thematic celebration of internationalism and since his departure he's continued to run the Edinburgh International Culture Summit, an international meeting of culture ministers, artists, thinkers and arts leaders from across the world, devised as a collaboration between Edinburgh International Festival, the British Council, the Scottish Parliament and the Scottish and UK governments. In conversation, Mills puts into focus what the International Festival was once about and reinvigorates it for the present:

My argument when I came to the festival in 2006, was to ask
the question that inevitably needs to be asked by every director
– what does it mean to be international today? Edinburgh is a
very international city, in terms of its influence with the Scottish
Enlightenment, its scholarship, its innovation, its philosophical
considerations, so it was an appropriate place to embark in 1947 on
a forging of ties, on not taking for granted that your perspective of
the world was the only one that mattered, because we had just had
that world shaken. It may not have existed if we hadn't been careful,
and there was a certain logic to say, maybe if we knew a little bit
more about each other, we wouldn't be so quick to kill each other.
I'm convinced that we need to continue to try to strive towards that
notion of civility and civilisation, and the hope that Edinburgh gives

us all is this notion, this simple idea that we should use the mutual trusted space of culture to learn more about other perspectives, other creeds, other societies, other human beings.

Mills began with a programme devoted to Europe, celebrating the 400th anniversary of Monteverdi's opera *L'Orfeo* and presenting Richard Strauss's *Capriccio, Op 85*, composed in the midst of the Second World War. 'In the bittersweet concluding moments of that opera Strauss leaves open the big question,' says Mills. 'What matters more – meaning, or feeling? A word, or an emotion? Something we analyse, or something we intuit?' In 2008, his programme went to the borders of Europe, in 2009 it looked to Edinburgh's Enlightenment relationship with the world. In 2010 it explored the 'New World' of Australia and the Americas and in 2011 it went to Asia, to the Far East; or as he puts it, upending traditional perspectives, bringing its artists to the Far West.

'What was the heartbeat of why I did what I did?' Mills asks.

There is, I believe, an absolute necessity to honour the origins of the festival, to imagine a compelling narrative that is worthy of those origins, and think about a context which resonates in a continuum with those original ideas.

* * *

Jerry Springer: The Opera and Guy Masterson's shows were only two of the huge successes enjoyed by William Burdett-Coutts' Assembly Rooms during the 2000s, which evolved through the decade away from just a single venue into a network of spaces across the city. In 2001 he and his good friend from the earliest days of stand-up at the Assembly Rooms, Off the Kerb co-founder Addison Cresswell, had also launched the Brighton Comedy Festival in Cresswell's home city. Cresswell sadly died of a heart attack at the age of 53 in December 2013.

Under the umbrella name Assembly, Burdett-Coutts's company began programming shows in the network of modern university lecture theatres on George Square in 2010, including the George Square Theatre (now the Gordon Aikman Theatre) and an assortment of six 'studio' venues. Assembly George Square Gardens was also set up around the same time and its Spiegeltent performance space was soon joined by Underbelly's 'purple cow' udderBelly venue in the west side of the gardens, consolidating the area's position as the outdoor focal point of the Fringe.

Neither company was responsible for first developing the Gardens during the Fringe, however. Following his first performance there with a band called Madam and Her Orkestra during the Jazz Festival in 1989, Canberra-raised musician, composer and show producer David Bates had taken on the running of the Famous Spiegeltent as 'Spiegelmaestro' in 1996, on behalf of its owners Scottish and Newcastle brewers, who had recently bought it from Jelle van der Zee for promotional events in the UK. Together with his business partner, former Book Festival director Shona Munro, Bates took the Famous Spiegeltent first to the top of the Waverley Shopping Centre, then to East Princes Street Gardens next to the Walter Scott Monument and in 2000 to George Square Gardens.

The following year, Bates bought the Spiegeltent from Scottish and Newcastle and toured it to Australia, New Zealand, Canada and the United States. Yet, the move to George Square was a true Fringe phenomenon; with a large outdoor bar built around the Speigeltent, a late-night drinks licence and food stalls throughout, the 'Spiegel Garden' became the key party hub in the city, a successor to the Fringe Club, where the last of the mild summer weather and the late, bright Scottish nights could be enjoyed. When Bates moved out and Assembly and then Underbelly moved in to George Square, this sense only intensified.

During his tenure in George Square, Bates didn't just innovate with the placement of the Spiegeltent and the environment around it. In 2004 he also created a late-night show which it's was as era-defining for the Fringe as Late 'n' Live had been nearly two decades before. *La Clique* was a fun, risqué cabaret and variety show which used the early 20th century European aesthetic of the Spiegeltent to its advantage in creating an environment that evoked Weimar Berlin, from Brecht and Weill to *Cabaret*'s Kit Kat Klub. Over its subsequent years at the Fringe and touring with the Spiegeltent across the world (although the show was building-based at the Hippodrome in London when it won an Olivier Award in 2009), *La Clique* rode and in many ways helped create the wave of edgy cabaret and burlesque-style entertainment that proliferated at the time.

Stars *La Clique* helped on their way to fame include the Irish singer and contemporary song interpreter Camille O'Sullivan (whose performance in the first *La Clique* inspired Edinburgh-based actor Ewan Bremner to recommend her for a role in Stephen Frears' 2005 film *Mrs Henderson Presents*), Australian singer Meow Meow, German MC and cabaret artist Bernie Dieter, punk cabaret group the Tiger Lillies and Nigerian-English alternative drag star Le Gateau Chocolat, all later Fringe stars in their own right with headline shows of their own. O'Sullivan's version of the song 'Look Mummy, No Hands' by Fascinating Aida's Dillie Keane was in turn covered by Amanda Palmer, who first came to the Fringe with Dresden Dolls in 2005 and immersed herself in the scene around *La Clique* and its performers.

Assembly's move to George Square was the tipping point of the Fringe's centre of gravity towards the Southside of the city, and Underbelly later setting up a Circus Hub tent on the nearby Meadows. Assembly's move, however, came with the company's eviction from the venue that had literally made its name. After talk of the Council's redevelopment of the publicly-owned Assembly Rooms had rumbled for half a decade, Assembly left the building after 30 years when it was closed after 2010's Festival. It reopened in 2012 with the ground floor rooms converted into restaurant and retail units, including a branch of celebrity chef Jamie Oliver's restaurant.

The closure came after a 'Save the Assembly Rooms' campaign founded by Burdett-Coutts, which attracted the backing of comedian Jo Brand and actors Brian Cox and Simon Callow. The argument wasn't that the upgrade of the building was unneeded, but that the change of its use to retail might fundamentally disrupt and even end its use as a Fringe venue. This point seemed to be a nadir in Burdett-Coutts's relationship with the city's council and the Festival in general. The redevelopment went ahead as planned, but he had also recently been in the press – along with many other business owners in the city – decrying the effect of the notorious first phase of the new Edinburgh tram works on traffic and footfall.

Set at a cost of £521 million when work began in 2008, the trams were subject to widely-reported time and cost overruns. When they finally opened on a shortened route between Edinburgh Airport and York Place in 2014, they had cost the taxpayer £776 million. The completion of the line to Newhaven commenced in 2019 and is scheduled to open in 2023, while the debacle of the first phase earned its own Fringe show, director Joe Douglas's verbatim piece *Bloody Trams* at the Traverse in 2014.

When the Assembly Rooms reopened with the upper spaces still intact in 2012, Assembly was no longer the tenant for August. Instead, Salt 'n' Sauce – the production company run by the Stand's Tommy Sheppard – took over the lease. 'We thought, this is an opportunity for us to put our money where our mouths are and see if we can actually run something in the Assembly Rooms according to our principles,' said Sheppard. 'To my surprise we won the contract to programme it, which ran for three years and was extended by a year'.

Among the highlights of Sheppard's tenure in charge of the Assembly Rooms was a 2013 adaptation of the film version of Stephen King's story *The Shawshank Redemption*, adapted by Owen O'Neill and Dave Johns, in a callback to the venue's great comedians-in-drama hits of the 2000s. Some big-name comedians also transferred from the Stand, with one of the venue's main loyalists Stewart Lee declaring himself happy to not be near the 'increasingly grotesque Philip K Dick-style wasteland of alcohol-banner festooned architecture' at Bristo Square.[25] 'It was a rollercoaster,' says Sheppard of the show.

> We ended up breaking even, but artistically and organisationally it was a fantastic thing to do, well-received by audiences and more or less by critics. The other thing was, because the council had done away with most of the bars and insisted on running the bar that was left themselves, we had to build an area outside on George Street. We closed off the block and put in the Spiegeltent. David Bates was looking for a new collaboration, and we were soul fellows really, so we put together a partnership and brought in some nice local sponsors.

For three years in the mid-2000s, the Stand also ran a Spiegeltent-focused venue on St Andrew Square in the heart of the city. 'I still think to this day it's the best outdoor venue the Fringe has ever had,' says Sheppard.

> It was family-friendly, open and accessible, there was a light touch on security, you could walk through the park. We did a programme of open-air free performance all through the day, there was no edge to it, but it was a real quality bill. We spent a fortune on making sure we got it right, that it looked and felt sympathetic to the setting. It was a commercial proposition, but it didn't look that way, there was hardly any branding and the sponsors and food operators we had were all local.

In a climate where the Big Four had courted controversy in 2008 and '09 by producing their own distinct Edinburgh Comedy Festival brochure alongside the Fringe's more comprehensive programme, the Stand were determined to do things differently. They capped their prices at £15 per ticket and didn't raise them at the weekend, as they realised that was when locals tended to attend. The company paid the real living wage to all employees and offered attractive deals to comedians, with an agreed budget deducted from takings first – it was covered by the venue if not enough tickets were sold – and then an 80–20 percentage split in the comedian's favour after that.

'People can overstate the importance of comedy to the Festival,' says Sheppard.

> In terms of tickets sold it's still, I think, number three as a genre, but the reason it looks so important is because large entertainment organisations have used the Edinburgh Fringe as a trade fair. I don't

say they shouldn't to some extent, but that's been their primary
purpose. They do it as a loss-leader to try [and] get people thinking,
have you heard about this guy X? Maybe he's the next big thing,
maybe we're missing out. It works, but I think the comedy business
has spent so much money on it, that it looks at times that comedy is
pretty much all there is. That's all something of a mirage.

Due to objections from businesses on St Andrew Square, the Stand
wasn't permitted to operate there in 2017. Nor was it permitted to set up the
Spiegeltent outside the Assembly Rooms on George Street, denying it the bar
revenue it needed to keep doing the venue. It's since taken over the Freemason's
Hall on George Street and run it as the New Town Theatre, although by this
point Sheppard is back in politics and no longer calling the shots.

'I don't have any day-to-day operational involvement at all, and I don't
take a salary,' he says. 'I get a dividend off my shares if we make a profit, but
it's been a few years since that happened, so it's back to being a hobby for me.'

Assembly, meanwhile, returned to the Assembly Rooms following
the Stand's departure in 2017, by which point the company was firmly
established in not just the Assembly Hall and its George Square site, but also
its new Checkpoint and Roxy venues. The Fringe's centralisation on and near
George Square comes as a result of the University of Edinburgh's increasing
involvement as a landlord for venues, reaping the financial benefits of a
summer of activity on their premises and, as one of the Big Four promoters
had it explained to them by a representative of the University, a powerful
promotional tool for attracting international students to the city.

'Initially the University offered us George Square Theatre and what we
now operate as Studio One and Two, and that didn't really work financially,'
says Burdett-Coutts.

But when we had the garden it made sense, so we took on that site.
In the early days when we just ran the Assembly Rooms, we put
on about 50 or 60 shows and played to about 100,000 people. By
2019, after we'd taken back the Assembly Rooms, we had about
575,000 as an audience, and 230 or so shows. It's grown from a
small thing into rather a massive operation.

The Fringe's growth this century hasn't been solely down to the Big Four
venues, or other major operators like the Stand and Summerhall. Across the city
in August other venues, many of them multi-site, have emerged, including C
Venues, Zoo, theSpace, Sweet Venues, Greenside and Monkey Barrel Comedy.
Some have particular specialisms, but most simply colonise church halls, bars,

hotel meeting rooms, university spaces or sites awaiting development and hire out space to whichever smaller companies or performers need it.

Debates about the purpose and desirability of the Fringe has been going on ever since those eight companies first showed up uninvited in Edinburgh in 1947, but some of the points against it – 'it', of course, being a range of individual businesses, promoters and civic policies which are relevant to its existence – have become more structured in recent years.

Working conditions have become one bone of contention. An article published by Edinburgh Poverty Commission in 2019 stated that a

> survey by the Fringe Society last year found that 54 per cent of Fringe Workers paid by the hour received less than the then national minimum wage of £7.50 per hour or were paid youth rates... that 34 per cent of those contracted to work were on zero-hour contracts despite the fact that nearly 48 per cent of them worked more than 49 hours a week [and that] 31 per cent of respondents were working more than 10 hours per day.[26]

Earlier that year, it was reported C Venues would be denied the use of the University of Edinburgh's Adam House building, its main home for nearly 20 years, after the Free Fringe campaign accused it of not paying the Living Wage to its Festival staff and using some volunteer labour.[27] Meanwhile, there has also been increasing concern that rising accommodation costs will force out those performers and tourists who don't have cash reserves to be able to afford steadily increasing prices, not to mention the effect this has on the year-round rental market in the city.

A 2015 survey by online hotel search site Trivago found Edinburgh to be the most expensive city in Europe in August – dearer even than London, Venice and Geneva – with the average price of a night's stay sitting at £207, up from £149 the month before.[28] The arrival of Airbnb also disrupted the market, with a report in 2015 finding Edinburgh was the ninth most expensive city in the world in which to use the service.[29] Both the Scottish Government and the City of Edinburgh Council have taken steps towards regulating the short-term letting market, although in the late 2010s the city was cited alongside places like Venice and Barcelona as one of the major European sites of problems associated with the recent phenomenon of 'overtourism'.

In recent years, Edinburgh heritage body the Cockburn Association has become increasingly involved in discussions about what it refers to as the 'Festivalisation' of the city; how the line between civic and commercial use of public spaces is blurred, alongside their belief that insufficient planning scrutiny is given to temporary events. One fear is that, as happened to

Liverpool in 2021 and in light of several new urban developments in the city, Edinburgh may be stripped of its UNESCO World Heritage status.

In 2018, 25-year-old PhD psychology student Jess Brough instituted the first Fringe of Colour as a reaction to what she called the 'overwhelming whiteness' of the Festival, turning a spreadsheet she had kept of all shows with at least 50 percent people of colour in the cast into a full public programme, as well as arranging a ticket discount scheme with the major venues. 'I want to create the sense that there's a community that's willing to support you,' she said at the time. 'The desire to have people in your audience that look like you or are representative of what you're doing is something that most feel really strongly about.'[30]

Comedian Sophie Duker, whose show that year, *Venus*, was about the representation of black women, echoed Brough's thoughts:

> Edinburgh is amazing, but it's such a specific audience. Knowing there will be young people of colour at some of the shows is such a gift. The presence of just one person of colour, particularly when you're talking about race, completely changes the dynamics of the room.[31]

Fringe of Colour was a success in 2018 and '19.[32] But by March 2020, an international crisis meant efforts to improve the Festival suddenly seemed entirely redundant.

SPOTLIGHT

Fleabag (2013) The Play That Goes Wrong (2013) Six (2017–18)

IN RECENT TIMES, wider discussion of the Edinburgh Festival has been less likely to look back on *Beyond the Fringe* or Tom Stoppard as examples of success in the city and more towards just how small a venue someone might have experienced, for example, The League of Gentlemen or Stewart Lee when they were starting out. Partly, this is because comedy's such a big draw, but other scale factors come into play. The Fringe is just so big these days that finding a truly undiscovered talent is a real needle in a haystack job. The three key ways of standing out are to have a truly astonishingly good show; to have an astonishingly good PR machine behind your show; or to have enough financial backing that solid preparation, promotion and venue choice can be maximised.

Many shows and performers make an early stop in the city on their way to success, but it's still possible – more than ever, perhaps – to arrive in the city with the right show at the right time and parley hard work, enthusiasm and creativity into truly international success. We'll look at three major examples here, beginning with the show that's often referred to as the greatest Fringe success story of the modern era. Televised as two BBC series between 2016 and 2019, *Fleabag* made its writer and lead performer Phoebe Waller-Bridge an international star, but the one-woman theatre show on which it was based premiered and broke through at the Fringe in 2013.

Just turned 28 when *Fleabag* arrived in Edinburgh, Waller-Bridge is a self-described 'posh' Londoner who performed for her family since the age of five. Raised in Ealing, she was independently schooled and studied at the Royal Academy of Dramatic Art. After graduation she became an underemployed actor and met Vicky Jones, a University of Birmingham politics graduate from Sheffield who'd moved into theatre. Their close friendship was cemented when Jones was let go as director of a play they were working on and Waller-Bridge quit in solidarity.

In 2007 the pair founded the DryWrite short theatre night at the George Tavern in Stepney, East London, which hosted early work by playwrights including Jack Thorne, Lucy Kirkwood, Ella Hickson and James Graham, some of whom had history with the Edinburgh Fringe. Both Kirkwood and Hickson, from London and Guildford respectively, had been students of the University of Edinburgh who were involved with student and Fringe drama at the Bedlam Theatre. In 2005, English student Kirkwood produced her first play, *Grady Hot Potato*, at the Bedlam and in 2006 her second work *Geronimo* appeared as a Fringe experiment named *The Umbilical Project*, where Kirkwood directed one version of the play and fellow student Matt Addicott directed another, with no contact or comparison between the pair.

Hickson, meanwhile, broke through as a playwright at the age of 23 at the Bedlam, when her 2008 debut play *Eight* – a series of eight individual monologues – won a Fringe First and the Carol Tambor Best of Edinburgh Award and the following year transferred to London and New York. From these Edinburgh beginnings, Kirkwood and Hickson have become two of the leading British playwrights of their time, for plays including Hickson's *Precious Little Talent* and *Boys* and Kirkwood's *Chimerica* and *The Children*.

Meanwhile, between temping jobs, Jones and Waller-Bridge were setting their writers bold challenges, like making the audience fall in love with a character during a play or writing a piece that had to elicit an audience heckle. Waller-Bridge's acting career grew steadily alongside DryWrite's reputation as a social as much as creative space. She appeared in Steve Thompson's *Roaring Trade* at Soho Theatre in 2009, directed by Roxana Silbert for Paines Plough,[1] the classic *Rope* at the Almeida Theatre in '09 and Nina Raine's *Tribes* at the Royal Court in '10, both directed by Roger

Michell and at the Noel Coward Theatre in a version of Coward's *Hay Fever* alongside Olivia Colman in 2012.

In 2012, DryWrite made the step up to becoming theatre producers in their own right, putting on Jack Thorne's bathroom-set two-hander about a failing relationship, *Mydidae,* at Soho Theatre, directed by Jones and co-starring Waller-Bridge. It opened in December, a month after Waller-Bridge had taken her tentative first steps as a writer. She'd been invited by her friend, the comedian Deborah Frances-White, to come up with a short comic monologue for a themed night entitled *Chancing Your Arm* at Frances-White's London Storytelling Festival.[2]

Frances-White later wrote that she felt Waller-Bridge had the 'electric energy of someone from the Bloomsbury Set, whom people would tell implausible stories about a hundred years after they'd first set London alight'.[3] The monologue, perhaps for convenience's sake, was also named *Chancing Your Arm.* Wary of performing her own work before an audience and taking to the stage alongside stand-up comedians, Waller-Bridge had set herself a simple challenge ahead of the gig in the basement of Leicester Square Theatre; writing something which Vicky Jones would find funny.

'[I]f I make her laugh then this whole ordeal is worth it,' she decided.[4] What emerged was essentially ten minutes of the *Fleabag* show, a frank and explicit discussion about sex in line with the kind of conversation Waller-Bridge had in private with her friends, with a poignant, bittersweet twist at the end. The reaction on the night was extremely positive and someone suggested she could work it up into a play for the Edinburgh Fringe.

Waller-Bridge and Jones agreed this sounded like a great idea, albeit with no idea what this meant, having never performed at the Fringe before. They turned to their friend Francesca Moody, an actor from London who studied at Exeter University and had become a producer accidentally. When a friend wanted to apply for funding to the IdeasTap scheme but was older than the cut-off age of 25, Moody, who was younger, agreed to produce and apply on their behalf. She was only 25 when she eventually produced *Fleabag*, but an Edinburgh veteran, having worked front of house roles at the Fringe since she was 17 and produced smaller-scale shows since she was 22. Now she set about making *Fleabag's* Edinburgh run happen.

The nine-month gestation period between the London Storytelling Festival and the Edinburgh Fringe of 2013 was essentially filled with Waller-Bridge writing the play in rehearsals in a disused office block on Whitechapel High Street and director Jones acting as dramaturg while she tried to force perfection from every line. Lots of very good material was thrown out because it didn't fit, while stage manager Charlotte McBrearty and composer and sound designer Isobel Waller-Bridge – Phoebe's sister – tried to keep up with ever-changing technical and audio cues. They were so determined to get it right that Waller-Bridge and Jones turned down other work and slowly ran out of money. They'd buy a Starbucks iced coffee to share, because they couldn't afford one each.

Every director they spoke to told them it was crucial there had to be action onstage, but Jones kept Waller-Bridge sitting on a high stool throughout, so convinced was she of the intensity of her friend's words and performance. There were two preview dates in mid-July at the Soho Theatre, where DryWrite had been associates since *Mydidae* and the original ending was scrapped after these. On the train from King's Cross to Waverley in late July, Waller-Bridge was still rewriting and McBrearty was still erasing all the cues from her script and starting again.

The show was booked into the Big Belly at the Underbelly, in the arches below George IV Bridge and their three-hour tech rehearsal was in the middle of the night. The show was on at 9.30pm, in the 'twilight zone' more suited to stand-up, but Fleabag was the perfect theatrical alternative. During the first performance Waller-Bridge blanked and left out a chunk of the text. She reasoned she'd get it right next time, then backstage afterwards was told the reviewers from *The Guardian* and *The Telegraph* had been in.

They team continued to work hard on the play from there, though. They'd do the show, go out and get drunk (only in the second and third week) and then rehearse and rewrite in their rented two-bedroom flat based on the feedback of the previous evening. 'Fleabag is a daring debut that makes up its own rules', said *The Scotsman*'s writer Matt Trueman in his five-star review. 'I've never seen a play quite like it'. The paper gave *Fleabag* and Waller-Bridge a Fringe First and before the Fringe was over she'd also won the Stage Award for Acting Excellence. Towards the end of the run, Steve Coogan was in the audience. Waller-Bridge said years later:

> God, the whole thing was so thrilling. Taking *Fleabag* to Edinburgh with our tiny team felt like true freedom. I always come back to that. It was the first time we did something completely on our own... and *that* happened.[5]

The play and its creator's histories from there are well-documented. It ran at Soho Theatre's studio the month after the Fringe, then in the theatre's main house and for a few Korean dates in 2014, later touring the UK and Australia with Maddie Rice in the lead role between 2015 and 2018.[6] Waller-Bridge won the London Critics' Circle Theatre Award for Most Promising Playwright in 2014, a BAFTA Award for the television series in 2017, then in America won three Primetime Emmy and two Golden Globe awards for its second season in 2019. She specifically thanked the Edinburgh Festival

Fringe during one of her Emmy acceptance speeches.

In the same year, Waller-Bridge also returned to the role onstage for a two-month run in the Off-Broadway SoHo Playhouse and a month at Wyndham's Theatre in the West End, after which she retired *Fleabag*. After creating the 2018 spy thriller *Killing Eve* for the BBC and co-writing the 2021 James Bond film *No Time to Die* at its star Daniel Craig's request, she continues to use her fame to support the Fringe, taking the role of honorary president and sponsoring an exclusive fundraising range from Edinburgh Gin during the COVID-hit year of 2021.

On stage and on screen, *Fleabag*'s story was one of the defining fictional works of its decade. As Deborah Frances-White put it, it arrived:

> [J]ust as the fourth ripple of feminism became a wave. Laura Bates created *Everyday Sexism*. Chimamanda [Ngozi Adichie]'s TED Talk, 'We Should All Be Feminists', went viral. Lucy-Anne Holmes started *No More Page 3*. Bridget Christie won the Edinburgh Comedy Award for *A Bic for Her*. It was a time throbbing with possibility for women who wanted more and better.[7]

Fleabag was the dark, conflicted, self-examining underbelly of this movement.

In Edinburgh, its legacy is best exemplified by the continuing career of Francesca Moody, one of the brightest and most exciting young theatre producers in the UK. She produced Brad Birch's play *Gardening for the Unfulfilled and Alienated*, which also won a Fringe First for its Pleasance run in 2013 and her later Edinburgh hits include Clara Brennan's *Spine* in 2014, Penelope Skinner's *Angry Alan* and Kieran Hurley and Gary McNair's *Square Go*, both in 2018 and Richard Gadd's *Baby Reindeer* and Remy Beasley's *Do Our Best* in 2019. Most have won Fringe Firsts, while *Baby Reindeer* won an Olivier Award and a New York transfer.[8] As Moody said in 2019:

> It's amazing to know that something that started off as a tiny little show you made with your friends is suddenly in the West End. The idea that an Edinburgh show could have that kind of success is more possible now *Fleabag* has made that journey.[9]

* * *

For a number of years around the turn of the 2010s, the Scat Pack were one of the burgeoning success stories of a Fringe that was increasingly rediscovering improvisational comedy. They weren't the only improv troupe who drew audiences; Brighton quartet The Noise Next Door and American improvised musical group Baby Wants Candy! both played to full houses at the Pleasance Courtyard and Assembly venues, while Paul Merton's Impro Chums has been a staple at the Pleasance since the 1990s. A touring quasi-version of the Comedy Store Players, which was formed in London after the Fringe of '85, the group features Merton, his wife Suki Webster, fellow comedians Mike McShane, Richard Vranch and Lee Simpson and musician Kirsty Newton.[10]

In January 2004, the Oxford Imps improv group were formed at the Wheatsheaf pub in Oxford by a student named Hannah Madsen, who was inspired by the improv scene she'd witnessed in Edinburgh the summer before. The group made their Fringe debut that summer and years later members of the troupe were among the six performers who founded the *Austentatious* improv show, which had some of its first performances at Laughing Horse at the Counting House during 2012's Fringe. Improvising a spoof Jane Austen novel from scratch during the show, this group has returned to Edinburgh annually since, winning a Chortle award and transferring to the West End's Piccadilly Theatre in 2017.

The Oxford Imps, meanwhile, have proven to be almost as reliable a talent-finder as the Cambridge Footlights before them. Also returning to the Fringe every year, their number has included *Austentatious* founders Rachel Parris and Joseph Morpurgo,[11] both celebrated young comedians in their own right – Morpurgo was nominated for the Edinburgh Comedy Award in 2015 – and comics Ivo Graham and Sophie Duker. Graham was the youngest-ever winner of the Gilded Balloon's *So You Think You're Funny?* prize when he took it home at the age of 18 in 2009 and an Edinburgh Comedy Award nominee in 2019. Duker co-founded the comedy showcase *Manic Pixie Dreams Girls* with Erin Simmons, which ran at free venues the Mash House in 2016 and the Counting House in 2017. She was nominated for the Comedy Award's Best Newcomer in 2019 for her show *Venus*.

One of the biggest hitters in terms of improvised Fringe shows, meanwhile, has been Adam Meggido, Dylan Emery and Keith Strachan's *Showstopper! The Improvised Musical*. Built for a large cast around audience suggestions, the show ran with increasing success for 12-years between 2008 and 2019, winning an Olivier Award for its West End appearance in 2015. Amid this landscape, the Scat Pack's Edinburgh years were hardly head and shoulders above those of their contemporaries, but hard work and dedication brought them to new heights.[12]

A group of foundation year students who joined the London Academy of Music and Dramatic Art (LAMDA) in 2007, the Scat Pack came to Edinburgh at the end of their first year with an improv show called *Let's See What*

Happens. Founder members Henry Lewis and Henry Shields were involved at this point, while their coursemate Jonathan Sayer joined soon after. Their 2008 show at C Venues was named *Lights! Camera! Improvise!* and it was the one the company kept performing as they came back to Edinburgh on an annual basis until 2015.

The format was simple and well-used, with the audience calling out suggestions of imaginary films for host 'Oscar' to pick from his infinite movie collection. This led to such never-to-be-repeated spectacles as a tale of gangsters on a Somerset cider farm named *Keep Your Hands Off My Apples*, a gladiator disaster film called *Maced in the Back* and a fantasy film set in a convent named *Dirty Habits*. Throughout, Oscar held the 'remote control' and could pause, rewind or speed up the action as he chose. For the eight-strong ensemble in lurid yellow and black outfits, it was the kind of steep learning curve they couldn't have found elsewhere.

'The Fringe was this incredible opportunity to not just be able to do a show for a day or two, but to do it for a full month and immerse yourself in a creative idea,' says Sayer.

> You have to work really hard to get audiences, and even if you do there are still tremendous pitfalls. But the audience is there, and they want to see new ideas. We had the best time in that first year, all living in one flat in cots and sleeping bags – it was just a big old adventure. We travelled on the bus from London, we flyered our show all day on the Royal Mile from 10am, giving out as many pieces of paper as we could – anything we could to get the show noticed and fill our 60 seats a day.

Every year they brought the show back and every year the intensity of Edinburgh brought them on in bounds as performers, in an environment where they ate, slept and breathed nothing but their performance for three weeks. There was an attempt to create an adult improv games strand called *Late Night Impro Fight*, but the group came to realise that structured, long-form improvisation around a theme was what they were really good at. The eight-strong core group of performers – artistic directors Lewis, Shields and Sayer, alongside Hearn, Nancy Zamit, Charlie Russell, Rob Falconer and Greg Tannahill – were all just hitting their 20s at the time and they decided that while the intensity of Edinburgh made them good, trying to recreate the same scenario for the other 49 weeks of the year could make them exceptional.

Lewis, Shields and Sayer moved in together in London and began writing intensively, while the group performed more and more. They wrote *The Murder Before Christmas*, a play within a play in which the *Mousetrap*-style

Edwardian murder-mystery at the show's heart is comprehensively ruined by the hilarious ineptitude of the amateur student society producing it. It opened in 2012, upstairs at the 50-seater Old Red Lion pub, to an audience of 12.

In Edinburgh, *Lights! Camera! Improvise!* shifted to ever-larger rooms at C Venues and then eventually graduated to Underbelly. At some point along the way the group finally ditched 'the Scat Pack' and became the far more family-friendly Mischief Theatre. *The Murder Before Christmas* moved to the 90-capacity Trafalgar Studios in 2013 and changed its name to *The Play That Goes Wrong*. West End producer Kenny Wax saw it and asked if the group would be interested in developing the hour-long show up to a full two-act production.

The subsequent global success of Mischief Theatre's *The Play That Goes Wrong* was instigated by those London runs, but it was the group's many years in Edinburgh that made them good enough in the first place. They were on the theatre world's radar after Trafalgar Studios, but the show's final run before it became a true phenomenon happened in Edinburgh in 2013, over three successful weeks at the Pleasance Courtyard. In January 2014 the full two-act production opened at the 12,000-seat Marlowe Theatre in Canterbury, visiting 17 cities before opening at the Duchess Theatre in the West End in September, where it remains in 2022.

Mischief still found time to bring *Lights! Camera! Improvise!* to Edinburgh for a Fringe run in 2014, with their West End opening imminent and the follow-up *Peter Pan Goes Wrong* already touring following a December 2013 debut at the Pleasance Theatre in London. It was their last major involvement with Edinburgh bar a quick, schedule-beating three-night return for *Lights! Camera! Improvise!* at the end of 2015's Fringe, which is no surprise given what happened next.

The Play That Goes Wrong won the Olivier Award for Best New Comedy in 2015, then Tony and Drama Desk Awards in scenery design for its JJ Abrams-produced Broadway transfer in 2017, which lasted for two years and 745 performances before moving Off-Broadway. In eight years since the full production of *The Play That Goes Wrong* arrived, Lewis, Sayer and Shields' spin-off plays *Peter Pan Goes Wrong*, *The Comedy About a Bank Robbery*, *Mischief Movie Night*,[13] *Groan Ups* and the Penn & Teller co-written *Magic Goes Wrong* have all debuted, played the West End, toured and gathered three more Olivier nominations between them. Mischief shows and their adaptations have played in 35 countries around the world and *The Goes Wrong Show* has run for two seasons on BBC One.

'There's absolutely no doubt in my mind that if the Fringe didn't exist, a lot of the stuff we've done wouldn't have happened,' says Sayer of the painstaking perfection that goes into onstage anarchy.

It taught us how to manage all the different kinds of crowds. What
do you do when it's going really well? What do you do when it's
going less well? The rhythm of our shows and of each other's
delivery and performance were moulded and shaped by those
Edinburgh audiences. It's an amazing playground where you can do
the thing you love for a month's time. As a company we've learned
to speak a very similar language, and that came from Edinburgh.

* * *

While Mischief is one model of contemporary success on the Edinburgh
Fringe – to grind ever closer to perfection in relative obscurity for several
years – the one enjoyed by Toby Marlow and Lucy Moss was immediately
stratospheric. They arrived at Edinburgh together in 2017, when Marlow
was 22 and Moss 23, both in their final year at the University of Cambridge.
Moss's ambition was to be a dancer, but following a year studying dance
she decided she'd rather have a behind-the-scenes role, so she switched
to a history degree at Cambridge and directed shows by groups including
Footlights in her spare time.

Marlow, meanwhile, played music and worked as a child actor in British
television shows like *Agatha Christie's Marple* and *Silent Witness* and was a
committed member of Cambridge University Musical Theatre Society while
studying for a degree in English.[14] He acted in and wrote music for student
shows, Moss choreographed or directed some of them and in their final year
the Society decided to try and take a brand new work to Edinburgh, rather
than obtain a copyrighted musical. Marlow volunteered to write it and he
and Moss began putting ideas together around some subjects they'd been
discussing. It was the first time they'd written anything together.[15]

Marlow knew some of the features he wanted the musical to have. It
needed pop music and an interesting format. It had to be an hour long to fit
the typical Fringe format and the subject needed to be something recognisably
famous. 'With an original show, you have to find a way to get people to come
and see it,' says Moss. 'The Fringe is so saturated with shows that if there
isn't a hook, no one's going to come'.

Something was in the air that year; two months after their show appeared
at the Fringe, the #MeToo movement took off in earnest. These thoughts
were already on Moss's mind, though. 'I had an understanding of revisionist
history and feminist history, and Toby and I'd had lots of conversations
about representation for women in theatre in 2017, and the way in which
women's voices have been marginalised and written out of history. It was a
big topic of conversation amongst all of us'.

The four criteria Marlow envisaged defined the show. The pair alighted on the wives of Henry VIII as 'the most famous, out-of-copyright group of women' they could think of. Pop music was the interesting form, and Marlow arrived at the concept of presenting the characters as a girl group telling their stories. 'We'd only ever planned to do it at the Edinburgh Fringe that one year, and we thought nothing else would happen [says Moss] It literally didn't cross our minds that anything else would happen.

Moss watched documentaries by the historian Lucy Worsley and the pair pooled their appreciation for the music and image of Beyonce; just the kind of odd juxtaposition on which a Fringe show out to grab attention thrives. Their subject was the six wives – Catherine of Aragon, Anne Boleyn, Jane Seymour, Anne of Cleves, Katherine Howard and Catherine Parr – whose individual lives and stories are often viewed historically as being secondary to the story of Henry, who divorced them or had then beheaded.

The society took the pair's musical – named simply *Six* (stylised as *SIX*, with the bold tagline 'Divorced, Beheaded, Live!') – to Sweet Venues' space at the Apex Grassmarket Hotel, about as raw an environment as a show might get on the mainstream Fringe. The 'theatre' was a hotel meeting room converted into a 100-seat performance space, while the show was done entirely on a budget. 'Dresses from Asos,' says Moss. Marlow's sister Annabel was one of the performers, as Katherine Howard. But it drew attention.

'The first show, there was maybe 45 people there,' says Moss.

> We thought this must be everyone we'd ever met and no-one else was going to come. But from that point onwards, it was pretty much sold out until the end of the run. I think word of mouth was what did it. People say, 'you've got to see this show' then as soon as it's sold out once and people can't get a ticket, they'll definitely get one for another day.

Beyond the demand caused by scarcity, she also knows they just had a really good show, despite its economic limitations.

> Lots of the writing was first draft stuff – much of it's remarkably similar to how it is now, but some of the songs were a bit rough and the structuring and pacing was raw. But I think the performances in particular were just amazing, with such charisma. As a show becomes more professional and gets better in lots of ways, it also loses a little something.

Edinburgh was the spur that set everything in motion for *Six*'s subsequent achievements. Producers took a look during its run and Andy and Wendy

Barnes, founders of the not-for-profit musical theatre development company Perfect Pitch, offered to work with them. Two months later the show ran for a week at the ADC Theatre in Cambridge and Kenny Wax – also Mischief Theatre's producer – decided to take a look based on the Edinburgh buzz. He immediately asked to get involved, offering Marlow and Moss a development run on the free Mondays at the Arts Theatre in London when that winter's seasonal production of *Mischief Movie Night* wasn't playing. George Stiles, composer of musicals including Cameron Mackintosh's *Mary Poppins* and *Betty Blue Eyes* and also an old friend of Marlow's father Andrew, came on board as third producer.

Of all the internationally acclaimed stage shows that have found life through the Edinburgh Festival, it's difficult to overstate just how unprecedented the success of *Six* has been. In 2018, just a year after first appearing in the most low-budget Fringe circumstances, it returned to the 'purple cow' at Underbelly George Square for an acclaimed Fringe run of the professional production which had played only a handful of dates in Norwich and Cambridge the month before. By the summer of 2019 it had toured the UK, returned to the Arts Theatre in January of that year for a West End run which continues to this day, been nominated for five Olivier Awards and started a North American tour at the Chicago Shakespeare Theatre which was seen as a try-out for Broadway.

Incredibly, the birth of *Six* in Edinburgh happened while Marlow and Moss were also creating another hit in the city. *Hot Gay Time Machine* played at the Underbelly Med Quad in 2017, directed by Moss, with Marlow and Zak Ghazi-Torbati's double act offering a loud and upbeat celebration of the events in a gay man's life through song and comedy, channelling Beyonce once more alongside the spirit of Diana Ross's 'I'm Coming Out'. It played the following year at the Brighton Fringe and London's Trafalgar Studios.

'I love the Edinburgh Fringe, it's my favourite thing in the world,' says Moss, enthusiastically.

> It's my favourite month of the year, just the amount of incredible theatre you see, the hanging out, the people you chat to. It was so inspiring, it's been so informative for all of our work, because you can see so much different stuff. I love it. I'm obsessed.

Like so many shows before it, *Six* was born – midwifed, perhaps – in Edinburgh and then it grew beyond it. In recent times, though, both *Six* and the Fringe have shared a place in the imagination as emblematic of the struggles of the performance industry to overcome the effects of the COVID-19 pandemic. While the Fringe's cancellation in 2019 was unprecedented, *Six*'s inevitable Broadway debut was one of the major casualties of March 2020's mass cancellation. The day Broadway theatres closed on 12 March 2020, in fact, was also the day *Six* was to premiere after a month of previews.

Like the Fringe, *Six* persisted during this tough time. The show has returned to touring before an ever more loyal audience in the UK, North America, Australia and New Zealand and it finally had its Broadway premier proper at the Brooks Atkinson Theatre on 3 October 2021. As co-director with Jamie Armitage, who directed the very first Fringe version back in 2017, Moss became the youngest woman to direct a musical on Broadway to date.

15

Edinburgh Without a Festival

ON WEDNESDAY 1 April 2020, the Edinburgh Festival was cancelled entirely – for the first time in its history. The joint decision surprised no-one living under nationwide lockdown since 23 March to help combat the rapid spread of the COVID-19 pandemic, but the temporary departure of this monumental tradition in the year it was to reach its 74th consecutive edition brought home the urgency of the moment. In the midst of the emergency, how easy was it to tell how soon things would return to normal, if ever?

Speculation about the cancellation was rife beforehand and in the end the International Festival, the Fringe, the Book and Art Festivals and the Royal Military Tattoo issued a joint statement soaked in regretful inevitability.

The immediate concerns were financial, not just for individual Festival performers and companies, who were largely able to access emergency business grants or government furlough and income support schemes, but for the venues and arts organisations which aren't publicly funded.

Practically, this meant most of the major venues and returning companies on the Fringe, as well as the Fringe Society itself. As a small charity with minimal public funding, the annual cycle of collecting participation fees is what keeps the Society financially afloat – yet the Fringe's director Shona McCarthy saw an urgent and unavoidable need to refund all participation fees, tickets and Fringe memberships paid or purchased for 2020. As she wrote in a personal statement on the Fringe website:

> Art has always helped shape and reshape how we think of ourselves, and will help now to pull through the threads that unite us as human beings in a globally shared experience. From its earliest beginnings in 1947, the Fringe has provided a totally uncensored platform for artists from all backgrounds, cultures and perspectives to tell their story and shape their own worlds. As we try to adapt in the face of an all-encompassing global emergency, this spirit of shared storytelling and open dialogue feels more important than ever.[1]

The entire in-person Festival of 2020 was no more, despite early hopes that restrictions might ease enough for outdoor or limited-audience shows to be staged, but its presence was still felt. As with so many live arts during the pandemic, a pivot to virtual online work was made. The Fringe Society's own website became a repository for more than 300 recordings of new shows, while its FringeMakers scheme was a bespoke crowdfunder for participating shows, initially to help companies make back any outlay they'd already made for 2020 and plan a future visit instead.

Some venues sat the year out entirely, while others creating an online replacement, among them theSpace UK and Laughing Horse. Zoo Venues' ZOO TV was a winner, not just for the adoption of the name of Irish rock group U2's highly successful early '90s concert tour. Described by Zoo's founder James Mackenzie as 'an iPlayer or Netflix for theatre,' it featured Ontroerend Goed's work *Loopstation*, a show by sound artist Graeme Leak named *Ewetube: An Infinite Eco-Opera*, live-streamed from his Stirlingshire farm and Scottish Dance Theatre and Scottish Ensemble's digital lockdown work *These Bones, This Flesh, This Skin*. Staying in tune with cutting-edge social issues, Matsena Performance Theatre's *Are You Numb Yet?* was a show about a young black British man dealing with the repercussions of Black Lives Matter amid the pandemic.

One venue that flung itself into the opportunities of a makeshift online Fringe was the Gilded Balloon, which put recorded highlights of Late 'n' Live, *So You Think You're Funny?* and other classic theatre and comedy online, while comedian Fred MacAulay held a Zoom version of his Fringe chat show with guests including Rory Bremner and Jo Brand. The most poignant element of Karen and Katie Koren's programming, however, was a production team-up with Padlox Escape Rooms on an app-based interactive game named *Fringe Search Party*, in which well-known Fringe comedians like Brand and Bill Bailey encouraged participants on a pre-recorded scavenger hunt around the city.

For residents who happened to be in tourist-free Edinburgh during August 2020, *Search Party* was an oddly unforgettable experience, a walk from the breezily empty Bristo Square – silence broken only by the occasional clatter of returning skateboarders' wheels on concrete – through the wynds and closes of the Old Town to the closed Fringe office on the Royal Mile. The presence of one lone, unplanned busker playing a guitar when the final waypoint was reached on an early August afternoon was an especially affecting sight and sound, given the near-total absence of any live music for the past five months.

When the pandemic hit, the Traverse Theatre was under the joint artistic directorship of Gareth Nicholls and Debbie Hannan, both graduates of the Royal Conservatoire and only just appointed in late 2019, following Orla O'Loughlin's departure to become Vice-Principal and Director of Drama at Guildhall School in London in 2018.[2] Nicholls' previously directed plays included Scottish playwright and performer Gary McNair's Traverse Fringe shows *Donald Robertson is Not a Stand-Up Comedian* (2014) and the Fringe

First-winning *A Gambler's Guide to Dying* (2015) and an outstanding 2016 adaptation of *Trainspotting* at Glasgow's Citizens.

Hannan directed the Traverse's hit adaptation of Jenni Fagan's young offender's institution-set novel *The Panopticon* in October 2019, while Nicholls' multiple award-winning production of David Ireland's play *Ulster American* was a big success during 2018's Fringe. A post-#MeToo dark comedy in which a hell-raising American director and a self-consciously politically correct English theatre producer discuss staging the work of – and eventually subverting the voice of – a female, Protestant, Northern Irish playwright in a London hotel room, the play asked tough questions about identity and easy ideological positioning, ending with a character being stabbed in the eyeball.

These two outstanding young talents' joint Fringe in charge of the Traverse was the most unusual in its history, with a new online 'venue' named Traverse 3 (the venue's theatres are Traverse 1 and Traverse 2) established to show newly commissioned online work, including Matilda Ibini's Hannan-directed Glaswegian Afrofuturist fantasy *Shielders* and *Declan*, a single-character adaptation of Kieran Hurley's *Mouthpiece* by Lorn Macdonald from the point of view the character he played in it. The Traverse also co-hosted a new streaming service named *Shedinburgh*, co-programmed by *Fleabag* producer Francesca Moody and Nicholls' old Fringe show collaborator Gary McNair.

A Royal Conservatoire of Scotland graduate from Glasgow, who came through the same experimental proving ground at Glasgow's Arches as Nicholls, Hurley, Rob Drummond and others, McNair had made a habit of quirky, high-concept Fringe shows, often self-performed. *Born to Run* (2012) was performed on the Traverse's stage by actor Shauna MacDonald while running on a treadmill for 55 minutes, while in 2017 the venue hosted both his solo show *Letters to Morrissey*, in which he reassessed his youthful fascination with the controversial Smiths singer and outsider idol and *Locker Room Talk*. Inspired by Donald Trump's unguarded comments about women, this play used verbatim text of interviews with men of all backgrounds about their attitudes to women and was read by female actors.

In 2018 at Summerhall, McNair's *After the Cuts* imagined a dystopian post-NHS future Britain in which patients are operated on by their loved ones and McNair and Hurley's co-written *Square Go* was an energetic two-hander about the rituals of developing masculinity as teenage boys prepared for a playground fight. In the week the Fringe was cancelled in 2020, McNair had been on a lot of calls with colleagues from his Glasgow garden office and he made the same joke to all of them; if the Fringe was cancelled, he'd be broadcasting his own 'Shedinburgh Fringe Festival' from exactly where he was sitting. When the inevitable happened, it was Moody who called him back and asked about his idea.

In the end, they created the most live festival possible under the circumstances, building garden shed studios on the stages of the Traverse and London's Soho Theatre and staging one-person shows which were only available to view during their live broadcast period. These included comedy from Sara Pascoe, Rosie Jones and Deborah Frances-White, a performance of Tim Crouch's play *My Arm* and a reading of the Traverse and National Theatre of Scotland's 2017 Fringe hit *Adam*, in which actor Adam Kashmiry performs his life story as a trans person from Egypt now settled in Scotland.

'[The Fringe is] enshrined in my year, and not having it really has discombobulated me,' Moody said when I interviewed her about Shedinburgh for *The Scotsman* at the time, giving voice to every theatre maker, comedian, producer and technician for whom August in Edinburgh is integral to their year. 'My identity is so wrapped up in my work as a producer that I had a moment of thinking, "who am I and where do I fit into all of this?"'

The National Theatre of Scotland's own project during 2020's non-Fringe was a collaboration with Edinburgh International Festival, a film named *Ghost Light* by director Hope Dickson Leach, alongside the NTS' artistic director Jackie Wylie and dramaturg and former Traverse artistic director Philip Howard. Filmed within the empty theatres of the city, it had actors including James McArdle, Siobhan Redmond, Thierry Mabonga and Anna Russell-Martin performing excerpts of past and currently planned NTS shows by writers including JM Barrie, David Greig, Rona Munro and Jackie Kay.

It was part of an Edinburgh International Festival series named *My Light Shines On*, named after the uplifting, Biblical lyric from Glasgow-founded rock group Primal Scream's 1992 single 'Movin' On Up'. Just as the title of *Ghost Light* referred to the theatrical tradition of leaving a dim light on in an unused theatre – a tradition symbolically used in darkened theatres across the world during the COVID-19 pandemic – EIF arranged illuminations beamed into the night sky from the major Festival venues, each designed to be viewed from a distance rather than have people congregate around them.

EIF also co-produced the return of two previous Edinburgh Art Festival works whose design made them perfect as a socially-distanced experience: Peter Liversidge's 2013 display 'Flags for Edinburgh', with simple white flags bearing the friendly word 'HELLO' flown from buildings across the city and Janet Cardiff and George Bures Miller's Fruitmarket-produced solo twilight walk for phone app 'Night Walk for Edinburgh.

Soundscapes of chamber music were broadcast in Princes Street Gardens and haunting live performances before non-existent audiences at Leith

Theatre were shown online, by Edinburgh musician Stina Tweeddale of Honeyblood and folk artists Breabach and Aidan O'Rourke. There was a new online performance of Gian Carlo Menotti's comic opera *The Telephone*, last heard at Edinburgh International Festival in 1984, this time performed by Scottish Opera's orchestra, with soloists Soraya Mafi and Jonathan McGovern appearing onstage and in the streets around the King's Theatre. A new online programme of Mahler's work by the Royal Scottish National Orchestra with Scottish mezzo soprano Karen Cargill also appeared.

As a publicly-funded body, says Fergus Linehan, the International Festival felt a great organisational responsibility to help, but also restricted in the manner it could distribute funds. 'Nobody knew what was going to happen,' he says of the days immediately after the pandemic-enforced shutdown and cancellation.

> We didn't know if the government [funding] was still going to be there, we didn't know if the donors were still going to be there. It was a real shock to the system until it established itself, and there were a lot of technical questions – when you're a charity that's registered to do certain things with money, it's not yours to do with as you please. You can't just become a grant-giving body.

In the end, he and his staff were surprised by how quickly they were told their funding was safe and how some donors even increased their donations. With these funds and the commitments EIF had already made, they tried to make things happen, whether they were in-person events in '20 or optimistically delayed live productions in '21.

> It was logistically and ethically really hard to work through where money should and could go. It was all done at high-speed, with very little knowledge as to what was coming next.

What online activity there was paled beside a normal Edinburgh Festival, but at least it reflected something of the energetic will to create and perform which powers Edinburgh in August. It was surprisingly successful, too. By 1 September, Edinburgh International Festival's 26 online shows had been watched a total of 1.013 million times internationally, while the 390 short videos released under the Fringe's Pick 'n' Mix banner were viewed 282,000 times. By this point the FringeMakers scheme had also raised £250,000 in crowdfunded donations.[3]

The Book Festival and its director Nick Barley were quick to adapt. 'Looking at the plans we had for August 2020 before the pandemic struck, the lost festival is a wonderful thing in my mind,' he says. He put almost his entire team on furlough, began to make plans for an online festival instead, and made arrangements to use the Assembly Rooms to build studios.

'I was adamant I didn't want to have a festival which took place just on Zoom,' says Barley.

> I wanted us to build TV studios where as many writers as possible could be brought to present in front of multiple cameras, and that's what we managed to do. It was a much smaller festival than the one we envisaged originally, only about 160 writers rather than 950, and it was free, but it gave us the opportunity to build an online platform and see whether we could make that work. After about three weeks on furlough I brought everybody back, because I thought if this is going to change how festivals are done, and if we learn how to do it now, then we'll be ahead of the game. Fortunately, that proved to be the case.

Alongside guests including Hilary Mantel, Arundhati Roy, Ian Rankin and Ali Smith, the biggest Book Festival event of 2020 was Scottish First Minister Nicola Sturgeon's interview with 2019 Booker Prize winner Bernadine Evaristo, attracting 5,000 live viewers on first broadcast and more than double that number again on catch-up. By 1 September 210,000 viewers had seen the Book Festival's broadcasts, a number which escalated even further through the catch-up facility and they were seen in every country around the world bar five, among them North Korea, Nicaragua and the Central African Republic.

The following year the Book Festival used the same online broadcast system as part of a hybrid live offering, but unlike the completely free model of 2020, in 2021 there was a pay-what-you-want element. 'We've now got a monetisable model for the online side of what we do, which I think gives us a stable, sustainable financial future for our online activity,' says Barley. 'Meanwhile we could also develop the traditionally live, in-real-life side of the festival.'

Discussions around the Edinburgh Festival at this time mirrored those happening in wider culture while live performance was restricted. The purpose of art was discussed, along with the value of it in terms of what creators are paid and the means of facilitating that payment – must every artist also be a hustling businessperson, or do they provide a public service that should draw some form of state funding? In Edinburgh the discussion became even more acute, about the viability of the whole Fringe ecosystem and – as was being asked across society – how the Festival could 'build back better' in years to come.

Speaking in spring 2020, while that year's Festival was still in tentative planning and the possibility of live events was unknown, the Pleasance's Anthony Alderson imagined a smaller Festival which 'could look like the festival of the early 1990s'. In the event his venue only hosted some online shows in 2020, but alongside many of its fellow venues, the organisation tentatively moved back towards live performance the following year. Yet as Alderson explained at the time, this period has been one of real existential threat for the Fringe and many of its component parts:

> There's a myth that the big festival venues are wealthy organisations, but we just aren't, the margins are minute. Our reserve will keep us going until November or December, but we'll need to find support to continue. The potential financial burden on us is going to be somewhere between 1.8 and two million pounds, which doesn't include the four million pounds that would have gone from our box office to the artists... to put the festival back on its feet you're looking at maybe 20 or 30 million, but it's estimated that it brings about 160 to 180 million a year into the city, so to do that would strike me as a very wise thing to do. Yet the Fringe will survive, without a question. It's a concept, a collection of ideas – even if it had to start from scratch, it will always exist.[4]

* * *

The Edinburgh Festival reaches its 75th anniversary in August 2022 and – with the official cancellation in 2020 meaning both the anniversary and the 75th edition fall in the same year – the individual festivals and the city itself have awaited it with a blend of excitement and trepidation. After a two-year period of halting lockdowns and reopening, as vaccines were rolled out and COVID-19 variants came and went, restrictions in Scotland and the UK were finally eased in early 2022. A Festival that looks something like the last full edition in 2019 appears to be possible once again.

There was a live, in-person Edinburgh Festival in 2021, however, just much more scaled-down than the city's used to. Taking a cue from the Book Festival the year before, when Barley and his team moved quickly, Linehan and the International Festival attempted to design a festival which would be, in his words, 'very hard to cancel'. On three spacious pieces of ground around the city, large, bespoke tents with open, airy sides and two-metre socially-distanced seating between groups was instituted.

Holding the concerts which would otherwise happen indoors at the

Queen's Hall, the Usher Hall or Leith Theatre, each covered structure bore a different type of programming. Largely relying on UK-based artists due to pandemic travel restrictions, with individual conductors and dance artists brought in from abroad, the large tent on the lawn of Edinburgh Academy Junior School in suburban Trinity bore a classical and opera programme including Richard Strauss's *Ariadne Auf Naxos* conducted by Sir Andrew Davis for the Royal Scottish National Orchestra, Errollyn Wallen's *Dido's Ghost* conducted by John Butt for Dunedin Consort and Verdi's *Falstaff* by Stuart Stratford for Scottish Opera.

At Edinburgh Park, on a bare patch of ground between the tram line to the airport and the business park at South Gyle to the west of the city, composer Anna Meredith, Afrobeat group Kokoroko, Scottish rock group The Snuts and singer-songwriters including Damon Albarn, Kathryn Joseph, Nadine Shah and Erland Cooper all played at night, a stack of packing containers muffling the noise of the nearby City Bypass. On the Old College Quad on South Bridge, a smaller tent featured a programme of poets including Hollie McNish, Saul Williams and Vanessa Kisuule and folk music including *A Great Disordered Heart* by Lau's Aidan O'Rourke and former Film Festival director Mark Cousins, a music and film project which considered the Irish immigrant-built area where O'Rourke lives around the Cowgate and the Old Town, in the context of the past year's pandemic induced stillness. As O'Rourke described it:

A film about Edinburgh. About multiple Edinburghs, really.
It's about centuries of layers. The Old Town has two main rhythms.
One is the rhythm of the community. People who live here, go to
school here, tend our communal gardens. The other is a rhythm
of Airbnb-ers, bus tours and cashmere scarf shoppers. This year, the
balance shifted.[5]

Elsewhere, Enda Walsh's darkly absurdist new play *Medicine* appeared with Domhnall Gleeson in the main role in a drastically socially-distanced Traverse, playwright Sara Shaarawi's *Niqabi Ninja* revisited Egypt's Arab Spring-era Tahrir Square as a graphic novel app tour of Edinburgh by twilight and Alan Cumming returned to Scotland and the International Festival with *Alan Cumming is Not Acting His Age*, two evenings of story and song at the Old College. EIF's programme in 2021 bore about 30 percent of the festival's usual capacity, but it sold very well.

The Fringe also improvised to make work happen. The Traverse, Gilded Balloon, Zoo and Dancebase collaborated on MultiStory, an outdoor venue and bar on top of NCP's Castle Terrace Car Park, with Castle Rock as the backdrop to a stage just across the road from the former site of the Hole in the Ground. The Gilded Balloon was another venue that reopened its usual space, putting on a reduced number of socially-distanced shows including former Bodger Jack Docherty's *Nothing But*, in which he reminisced of his early Fringe days in the 1980s.

Under the umbrella of the Traverse, Julia Taudevin and Kieran Hurley's company Disaster Plan presented the migration-themed music and dance piece *Move* on the wide expanse of Silverknowes Beach and Fringe regulars Grid Iron – after trying unsuccessfully to mount the outdoor production in 2020 – finally got to put *Doppler*, their adaptation of Erland Loe's novel about a misguided rejection of contemporary society, on in woodland at Newhailes House near Musselburgh in East Lothian.

Now the emergency appears to have passed, the time is right for a reassessment of the Edinburgh Festival and a reaffirmation of the founding values which drove it into being in 1947. Taking over in 2016, when Kath Mainland moved to Australia to become director of the Melbourne Festival, the Fringe's current Chief Executive Shona McCarthy. She came to Edinburgh after a career running small film festivals and then the British Council in Northern Ireland and successfully leading Derry-Londonderry's bid for UK Capital of Culture in 2013.

'I wouldn't have moved from Northern Ireland for anything else but the Edinburgh Fringe,' she says.

> I'd always loved it from afar, and I had a real romantic idea about it – that it's an uncensored, open-access platform for anyone who wants to express a creative idea, that there's no single curator, that it's made up of so many curatorial voices, and it isn't a closed shop.

It was this sense of cultural democracy, McCarthy says, that appealed to her own politics and desire for universal access to the arts. 'One of the first things that really surprised me (after starting the job) was just how much the narrative of the Fringe had become about scale and numbers,' she says.

> I always found that slightly vacuous, and it surprised me. From an outsider's perspective, you look at the Fringe with rose-coloured glasses. It's the thing every other city wants to have. When I came, the narrative had seeped in and was firmly fixed. 'What are the numbers this year? How many shows? What percentage is that up on last year?.' To me, that was the least interesting thing about it. I've set out to try and shift that narrative, to remind people of the values-driven core principles of the Fringe.

McCarthy wanted to know the truth about perceptions of the Edinburgh Festival Fringe, especially the anecdotal idea that it's imposed from outside upon the people of Edinburgh. The ticketing data was analysed and it showed that wasn't the case. A majority of Fringe ticket purchases come from Scotland; roughly one-third of total sales from Edinburgh, in fact and a further 22 percent from elsewhere in Scotland. Another approximate third of sales are made to people in the rest of the UK, with just seven percent to customers based overseas.

The figures demonstrate the Fringe is primarily a Scottish and particularly an Edinburgh festival, based on attendees, although mapping the tickets sales from the city by district painted a different picture.[6] It showed the fewest tickets were sold in the areas with the highest levels of social deprivation, a situation that inspired McCarthy to try and do something about it. In 2017, with the support of Edinburgh financial firm Baillie Gifford, she instituted a scheme named Fringe Days Out, which provides ticket vouchers – £60 for a family and £12 for an individual – and support with travel and other costs to local charities, schools and community groups, so members can experience the Fringe show of their choice. Since 2017, nearly 10,000 local people have experienced Fringe Days Out.

Relationships with participating Fringe Days Out groups are ongoing, 'a forever commitment' as McCarthy puts it. She's pleased to recount how even people otherwise critical of the Fringe have heard of and complimented the scheme as an exemplar of strong community engagement. 'I was really chuffed about that,' she says. 'Fringe Days Out is relatively unsung still, because most of our marketing and promotion is telling people about the Fringe and trying to get people to come and see shows'. Days Out is just one part of the Society's *Fringe Blueprint*, created to mark the Festival's 70th anniversary in 2017, outlining commitments to be acted on ahead of the 75th.[7] It was broadly an honest and engaged document which tried to grapple with the Fringe's own massive footprint and its great potential for change. Although the COVID-19 pandemic has disrupted the very ground upon which the Festival stands, the *Blueprint* still remains a key tenet for the Fringe.

For some, the rate of change hasn't come quick enough. Local arts producer Morvern Cunningham who, for many years, ran the grassroots and locally-involved arts festival LeithLate outside of Festival time, wrote and published three extensive, COVID-era essays on how the city's cultural landscape can be reconstructed during and after the pandemic, which are essential reading for anyone who might wish to understand the criticisms levelled against the Festival.[8] A common and not unreasonable defence of the modern Festival is that many people have criticisms of it, but very few have suggestions as to its improvement. Cunningham, at least, had both.

Invoking Hamish Henderson's reasons for helping start the People's Festival nearly 70 years before, she did the precise opposite of some of the rote, half-understood online arguments levelled against the Festival, instead offering thoughtful, constructive commentary on who a city should work for, the role of capital in the arts and an attempted reimagining of the Festival beyond the perceived commercial imperatives of the Thundering Hooves reports. As she wrote in the early days of the pandemic:

> It could be argued that the stark cultural wasteland that Edinburgh
> residents will be presiding over this summer was in the works
> before Covid struck. During those halcyon days where we could
> all be in a room together and share the same oxygen, the city was
> already far down a road that firmly equated culture with commerce,
> that fully understood the economic reasoning behind supporting
> creative activity within its city centre, but didn't focus on arguably
> its most important contribution to the human condition – that of
> increased health and wellbeing. As a consequence, Edinburgh had,
> imperceptibly, become fundamentally ill at its core, and dangerously
> close to alienating from art and culture those it was meant to
> specifically cater to – its people.[9]

In August 2020, supported by the Festival Fringe Society and the University of Edinburgh, the Future Fringe campaign was established by the Staging Change and Greenhouse Theatre groups and Cunningham and others became involved in its core steering group.[10] Delivering a report in February 2022, its headline findings included the assertion that the Fringe's growth mindset isn't helpful, that 'bigger is not always better' and that the Fringe Society's neutrality contributes to a situation where it's often unclear who takes overall responsibility for the Fringe. Most controversially, it suggested the open access model of the Fringe is troublesome, 'creating a "pay to perform" landscape that is financially and emotionally taxing'.[11]

The recommendation didn't appear to be that the Fringe should ditch its open-access element, however, instead suggesting a 'common set of standards' be implemented across the Fringe. The report also made the point that the pandemic cancellation's presented an opportunity for any flaws within the Fringe to be addressed, although it's worth bearing in mind these words in the *Fringe Blueprint*:

> We believe that everyone should have the opportunity to express
> themselves through creativity and experience the thrill of live

performance. No matter who you are or where you come from, everyone is welcome on the Fringe. No individual or committee determines who can or cannot appear. You, the audience, curate your own festival.[12]

To say the Fringe is difficult to manage due to its largely unrestricted nature might be fair, but so is the defence that the democratic imperative that first brought it to life remains fundamentally unchanged. To tinker with this and add restrictions on who's allowed to play – beyond basic rules in terms of safety, working conditions, accessibility and so on – is to essentially end the Festival Fringe and start something new, a curated, gate-kept festival much like hundreds of others around the world.

'The business model of the Fringe was creaking at the seams before COVID,' says McCarthy, a keen reformer, but with an ability to discern baby from bathwater and a desire to not thrown both out at once.

Everybody knew that. Costs were going up every year; rental of buildings, paying the supply chain to create pop-up structures, paying rent to the university or council for space. Everything goes up by inflationary rates, but accommodation in Edinburgh goes up way beyond inflation. Yet there's an expectation everybody can be part of the Fringe, so ticket prices don't go up and registration fees have stayed the same for 15 years. This has been a real moment to ask, is that sustainable going forward?

The Fringe of 2021, she says, gave a vision of what a reset might look like.

We had about 15 per cent of the scale of 2019, so venues got to experiment with putting on a scaled-back, slowed down-offering, and the result was that the shows practically all sold out. It was a great experience for artists and for audiences, so there's an opportunity for a renaissance of the fringe in 2022 that takes in some of that learning.

McCarthy wants to make sure everybody's paid the living wage, that the need for printed materials is minimised, that marketing strategies that don't involve 'endless flyering' are looked at and that street events can happen without large infrastructure around them. The Fringe is working with groups like Future Fringe and market research group ScotInform to seek improvement, but so many of the organisations involved with the Fringe, including the Society itself, have relied on bank loans and COVID-era Scottish

Government grants and loans to get through this period. Simple survival is still a priority.

'I haven't come across anyone who doesn't want to find a way to make [a set of shared values] work,' she says.

> The big challenge is, how do you make it work economically? What really made the Fringe in 2021 was, it was the first time there had ever been an acknowledgement it needed some investment from the public sector, and just a little bit was enough to ease the pressure'. Yet compared to the International Festival or the Book Festival, where one organisation oversees everything, the sheer complexity of the Fringe is difficult to explain to those not immersed in it. It's a live conversation and a good one, because I think it's the first time the officials are getting a level of detailed understanding that the Fringe has a very different model to any other festival in the world.

Despite all the talk about how the Edinburgh Fringe and Festival might reasonably be improved, apocryphal reports of a dislike for it among the people of Edinburgh appears to be greatly exaggerated. Polling carried out by ScotInform on behalf of the Fringe Society in the aftermath of 2021's Festival showed that among Edinburgh residents, 80 percent of respondents felt the Fringe makes Edinburgh a more attractive place to visit, 84 percent said they would recommend it, 86 per cent said they were likely to attend at least one event in 2022 and nearly two-thirds said they valued the Fringe more in the aftermath of the pandemic.[13] Reports of the death of public appreciation for the Fringe have been greatly exaggerated.

The pandemic is bringing necessary changes to many parts of the Festival. One which will be welcome to many is the Edinburgh International Film Festival's move back to August, at first in an online format in 2020 and then with distanced cinema and outdoor screenings in 2021. The latter strands included the returning Film Fest in the City on St Andrew Square and Film Fest on the Forth, a two-day outdoor session at Port Edgar Marina under the Forth bridges.

During the decade EIFF spent in June it was run by critic and programmer Chris Fujiwara for two years until 2014, then by critic and former Director of Cinema at the ICA in London, Mark Adams, until 2019. Due to the pandemic no overall artistic director was in charge in '20 and '21, with a team including Director of Programming Rod White and Nick Varley, the founder of Glasgow-based distributor Park Circus, among those selecting the films.

In June 2021, Kristy Matheson was appointed the new artistic director of the Edinburgh International Film Festival to take up her post after that year's festival. An Australian, Matheson came to Edinburgh from the role of Director of Film at the Australian Centre for the Moving Image (ACMI) in Melbourne. Her precise job description is Creative Director of the Centre for the Moving Image (CMI), an umbrella organisation established in 2010 which encompasses Edinburgh International Film Festival, the Filmhouse cinema and the Belmont Filmhouse cinema in Aberdeen.

'Screen culture is the most democratic of all of the arts, because it's so ubiquitous in our lives,' says Matheson.

> A trip to the cinema isn't cheap, but compared to other art forms it's something most people can engage and feel comfortable with. I love the idea that in the latter half of the 20th century humans got used to the idea we go to the movies, and we might get scared, we might cry, we might be thrilled. It's very ordinary, but it can be extraordinary. It feels very of our time.

She's travelled halfway around the world to take on this particular film festival. Why Edinburgh? Matheson says much of what attracted her was the wider 'cultural gathering' in Edinburgh itself, rather than a film festival which takes place in isolation. There's an enormous potential for us to put film back into the broader cultural conversation,' she says.

> It's often seen as a separate art, but film draws in all the other art forms – visual art, theatre, dance, music, comedy – and Edinburgh is a perfect place for us to sit in that space.

Matheson wants her version of the Edinburgh International Film Festival to collaborate with the other festivals. She wants her delegates and audience members to have an experience where they might come to the city for a film, but take in a Fringe performance on the way home, or go to a bar and get talking to, for example, a dance performer from another part of the world. She wants people who live in Edinburgh to feel proud of it and excited by the prospect of it happening. Despite the logistical challenges posed by EIFF's return to August in 2022, she feels that's the only way her ambitions can be achieved.

'If you think about a city like Austin, with South by Southwest, that's a few weeks of music and tech and film and ideas colliding,' she says, trying to think of the very few other cities which have something like what Edinburgh has.

> Then there's the Venice Biennale. There are other examples of these carnivals of culture, but they're rare. Not every city approaches

their cultural offering this way, and the potential in Edinburgh for unexpected collisions with something you didn't go looking for is what's exciting. In the arts world we're always trying to put a value on art, so we can get funding. It can be seen as a frivolous pursuit when you have important things you need to fund, like schools, roads and hospitals, but it's much more than that, and you can't easily put an economic value on it. What's the role of culture? How does it build better societies? For a city to say for a whole month, 'come and indulge in this cultural experience, come and have some fun, then go off into the world again', it's a bold proposition for that city to hang its hat on culture in such a big way.

She thinks of Australia's love of sport, of all the money that's poured into it by the government and the acceptance that sport is part of the country's social fabric and the joy that the experience of following or participating in it gives so many. You support your team and the Edinburgh Festival is the World Cup of the arts.

You might walk out of a show and think, that was a waste of my time, that was boring, that was amazing... who knows? It doesn't matter how you walk out, but you will be changed.

As Matheson arrived at the festival, Sorcha Carey – director of the Edinburgh Art Festival since 2011 – moved on to take up directorship of the Collective Gallery, which moved from its long-time shopfront space on Cockburn Street to Calton Hill in 2018. The new gallery is the centrepiece of a major redevelopment of the formerly closed-off City Observatory complex, with the compact, Greek-columned Playfair Building in its centre. Named after the great 19th century Edinburgh architect William Henry Playfair, the Observatory and City Dome complex also contains a memorial to Playfair's uncle, the mathematician and philosopher John Playfair.

The new Collective shows art in the former observatory dome and a new undercroft space named the Hillside, with a museum to the observatory in the main building and a restaurant named the Lookout with possibly the finest dining view in the city. The gallery's gift shop merchandise bears the title 'Edinburgh's Disgrace', a reference to William Henry Playfair and Charles Robert Cockerell's nearby National Monument of Scotland, an intended copy of the Parthenon in Athens which was planned as a monument to Scots who died fighting in the Napoleonic Wars.

Partly constructed then abandoned in 1829, the skeletal columns of Edinburgh's Disgrace are a unique kind of Edinburgh landmark, a monument to incompletion and thwarted ambition, rather than so many of the city's other perfect and well-preserved buildings from the same era. On the last day of April every year it serves as a backdrop for one of Edinburgh's most unique and underground festival experiences, the Beltane Fire Festival. Revived in 1988 after more than a century of dormancy, due to historic disapproval from the Kirk (the Church of Scotland), Beltane reactivates the Pagan ritual of thanks and welcome for the incoming summer, as the characters of the May Queen and the Green Man are reunited in a ceremony of fertility for the Earth.

The instigator of Beltane was Angus Farquhar, percussionist with London industrial music group Test Dept, who were known for their enthusiastic support of political causes like the striking miners of the 1980s and for guerrilla gigs in industrial spaces like the bus depot on Edinburgh's Annandale Street in 1984. 'The rituals of the druids were held on a hillside, because you could not contain the beauty of creation in a church,' he explained.[14] Calton Hill was chosen for the festival because Arthur's Seat felt inappropriate, as it's Crown property, while bonfire material was supplied by the Dalmeny Estate, contacted by Farquhar when he remembered 'childhood fireworks nights staged on the Forth shore by Lord Rosebery – a slightly eccentric pyromaniac. He acquiesce[d] immediately, offering five tons of firewood, a truck and a driver'.[15]

In creating what's still a landmark Edinburgh event of fire, drums and red-painted revelry, Farquhar was joined by co-organisers Kevin Anderson and Gus Ferguson, with the enthusiastic and educated support of 68-year-old Hamish Henderson, by this point on the cusp of retirement from the School of Scottish Studies at the University of Edinburgh. Since the People's Festivals of the 1950s Henderson had held a prominent place in Scotland's intellectual life and he continued to do so until his death in Edinburgh in March 2002, at the age of 82. The Beltane Fire Festival continues to the present, involving an annual audience of 15,000 and 300 performers.

Angus Farquhar played a further part in Edinburgh's festivals, after founding in Glasgow in the early 1990s the public art organisation NVA, an abbreviation of 'nationale vita activa,' a Greek term referring to the democratic health of participation in society. Its pioneering projects in Scotland and elsewhere reflect Farquhar's interests in landscape and public ritual, including 2012's *Speed of Light*, a co-production between Edinburgh International Festival and the London Cultural Olympiad, which saw 'ghost pelotons' of illuminated cyclists flood in streams of light across Arthur's Seat through the late-August evenings. NVA's most successful project, it was later staged in Japan and Germany and at the Grand Depart of the Tour De France in Yorkshire in 2014.[16]

A Dubliner who once acted in a Pleasance Fringe play in the early '90s, then after a period with the Liverpool Biennial moved to Edinburgh to work as senior adviser at the British Council Scotland in 2008, Sorcha Carey was hired by Edinburgh Art Festival in 2011. Her remit was to bring the festival's programme out of galleries and into public spaces and sites across the city, turning the city into a venue in much the same manner Beltane or the Venice Biennale do, in their own ways.

Carey oversaw a commissioning programme which, she says, 'brought the festival and contemporary art into direct conversation with the city, its histories and architectures'. She's particularly proud of those commissions that opened up sites in the city, including Christine Borland's 2013 work 'Daughters of Decayed Tradesmen' at the derelict watchtower in New Calton Burial ground on the south-east slope of Calton Hill, a series of suspended Jacquard weaving loom punchcards. Nearby, the Burns Monument contained Jonathan Owen's repurposed marble statue in 2016 and Emeka Ogboh's political piece 'Song of the Union' – a choir from all 21 EU member state nations singing Burns' 'Auld Lang Syne' – in 2021.

Carey also oversaw works sited in the Old Royal High School on Calton Hill and in Trinity Apse, nestled just off the Royal Mile on Chambers Close. A grand, cathedral-like church, the Apse is one of the oldest buildings in Edinburgh. It was built as Trinity College Kirk in Waverley Valley, between Calton Hill and the Old Town, at the command of Queen Mary of Gueldres on the death of her husband, King James II of Scotland and moved stone by stone to its current site in the 1840s, to make way for the train lines into the new Waverley Station.

Martin Creed's landmark *Scotsman Steps* were constructed under the wing of Edinburgh Art Festival and the Fruitmarket and in 2016 Graham Fagen's permanent neon murals 'A Drama in Time' were placed under Calton Bridge, near the site of the original Trinity Kirk. The same year Ciara Phillips' brightly decorated 'Dazzle Ship' redesign of the MV *Fingal* was berthed at Leith Docks to commemorate both the Battle of Jutland and the 14–18 NOW events around the First World War's centenary and Bobby Niven's permanent 'Palm House' (2017) was built at Johnstone Terrace Wildlife Garden just off the Grassmarket, the Scottish Wildlife Trust's smallest nature reserve.

The Art Festival also co-commissioned Isaac Julien's ten-screen 2021 film portrait 'Lessons of the Hour' with the National Galleries of Scotland, about the 19th century African-American philosopher and anti-slavery campaigner Frederick Douglass, who was based in Edinburgh for a number of years during the 1840s. Added to these, Carey's Edinburgh Art Festival also established the Platform commissioning strand for early-career Scottish artists, instituted a paid programme assistant internship and a community learning and engagement programme and grew its Art Late strand, whose early years, says Carey, were characterised by shopping trolleys of beer being shuttled between venues.

All this, against the backdrop of a city where siting public artworks is almost as difficult as finding affordable studio space for young artists.

At Liverpool Biennial I used to do a 'what might have been' tour, discussing commissions we hadn't been able to realise,' says Carey.

I could certainly lead a very lengthy tour in Edinburgh. The challenges of being a comparatively young festival with significantly smaller budgets than other August festivals are frustrating, and finding ways to establish a presence amid the noise, especially with diminutive marketing budgets, is incredibly challenging. There are enormous opportunities, though, in terms of reaching audiences and connecting across art forms. Edinburgh Art Festival was founded to ensure there was a dedicated platform for the visual arts as part of Edinburgh's festivals, and we've definitely achieved that. It's become an incredibly important space to champion the ambitious visual arts programming in Edinburgh all year round, and our programme is 100% authentically made by and in the city – a real expression of the ambition, expertise and creativity of Edinburgh's visual art sector.

Carey's replacement for the 2022 festival is Kim McAleese, arriving from the Grand Union gallery and studio complex in Birmingham.

For Edinburgh International Book Festival, under the leadership of Nick Barley, the pandemic has had the most immediately transformative effect of all. During the 1990s Barley was the publisher of art magazines including *Blueprint* and the *Tate Magazine* and was involved in the launch of international art journal *Frieze*. In 2003 he moved to Edinburgh when his wife Fiona Bradley took the job as director of the Fruitmarket Gallery, working as editor of Edinburgh-based arts magazine *The List* and then director of Glasgow centre for architecture The Lighthouse.

'It was pretty widely acknowledged I was a leftfield appointment, because I hadn't come from the traditional literary world,' says Barley of becoming Book Festival director in October 2009, replacing Catherine Lockerbie, whom he'd previously chaired events for. His pitch was to 'internationalise and broaden the Book Festival, so that as well as remaining a literary festival it was going to be increasingly about political and cultural issues outside the world of literature directly.'

He wanted to involve historians, sports people, musicians, cultural figures and politicians, talking about

the issues which make the world go round. No festival can survive by just running on a formula. However much it might appear to be stable and running on rails, behind the scenes it has to reinvent itself every year. I inherited a great reputation, a fantastic location and great people, but I knew we couldn't stand still, that we were in this period of extraordinary growth for book festivals around the world. Edinburgh had to carry on innovating or we would have been overtaken, whether that was by Hay, Cheltenham or Bradford, or Jaipur, Toronto or Buenos Aires. We needed to stay ahead, and I think the perception in the publishing world has been that we've done that.

Barley describes a vastly changed landscape from the time when Cheltenham and Edinburgh were the only major book festivals in the UK, to the current point where book festivals are an international industry. From a culture of volunteer enthusiasts or librarians running a series of events where a journalist might chat with an author onstage, now a small army of professional box office, front of house, bookselling and artist liaison staff oversee events where film, music and performance feed into the discussion of literature.

In the past decade, Edinburgh has pioneered many of these elements. A major theatrical co-production was Grid Iron's *Letters Home*, which appeared in both the Book Festival and the Fringe's programmes. Also part of the Glasgow 2014 Cultural Programme surrounding that year's Commonwealth Games, it saw work from an international programme of writers – Nigeria's Chimamanda Ngozi Adiche, the Glasgow-based Jamaican poet Kei Miller, Pakistani-British author Kamila Shamsie and Australian novelist Christos Tsiolkas – adapted into short plays at Charlotte Square Gardens.

In 2017, a continuing annual strand was developed in collaboration with the Royal Lyceum Theatre and its artistic director, the playwright David Greig, where several plays have been given similar treatment every year, followed by a discussion between author and adapting team. Books featured include Amy Liptrot's *The Outrun*, adapted by playwright Stef Smith and director Eve Nicol, James Kelman's *Dirt Road* by Greig and Wils Wilson, Ali Smith's *How to Be Both* by Julia Taudevin and Claire Duffy and David Keenan's *This is Memorial Device* by Graham Eatough, ex of Suspect Culture, with music by Stephen McRobbie of Glasgow indie group the Pastels. Greig's 2019 adaptation of Charlotte Higgins' *Under Another Sky* has become a full theatrical production at Pitlochry Festival Theatre in 2022.

Kristy Matheson's ideas around the Edinburgh Festival being unique in that it allows this cross-pollination between genres have rarely been put into action more comprehensively than by Nick Barley's Edinburgh International Book Festival. In 2010, his very first year, he brought in a free mini-festival within EIBF named Unbound, for which tickets couldn't be bought and audiences had to queue hopefully. These brought the buzz of a hot-ticket gig to Charlotte Square Gardens and the atmosphere of one too. Famous nights at Unbound include performances by singer-songwriters King Creosote and Kristin Hersh and Irvine Welsh interviewing disco idol and super-producer Nile Rodgers, who played the hits for the under-canvas crowd.

The death in 2010 of iconoclastic Leith poet Paul Reekie at the age of 48 also saw Welsh pay tribute the following year with an Unbound night on Sunday 28 August 2011, featuring writer Gordon Legge, actor Tam Dean Burn, musician Vic Godard and an extensive cast of Hibernian supporters in the audience, stopping off on their return across Edinburgh from the city's local football derby against Hearts at Tynecastle Stadium in Gorgie. Another Welsh accomplice, the founder of the former Rebel Inc imprint Kevin Williamson, in December 2010 created a new anti-establishment Edinburgh salon dedicated to words, music, film and associated arts named Neu! Reekie! in part-tribute to Paul Reekie.[17]

Founded with Edinburgh poet Michael Pedersen, Neu! Reekie!'s year-round presence has included anarchic, authentic Edinburgh representation at EIBF's Unbound, Edinburgh International Festival excursions to Leith Theatre featuring punk poet Lydia Lunch and their namesake Neu's founder Michael Rother and other non-affiliated shows during Festival time. There are many reasons why Edinburgh International Book Festival is unique among book festivals, why it has its own unique character which is distinctly Edinburgh, but Barley points to one main reason as being the level of love and participation it's had from local authors over the years. He's talking about big names like Welsh, Ian Rankin, Val McDermid, Alexander McCall Smith and the late Iain Banks.

In 1997 a 32-year-old unknown named Joanne Rowling, as she was billed, entertained a mid-afternoon Book Festival audience of schoolchildren with her debut novel *Harry Potter and the Philosopher's Stone* less than two months after its publication. For three pounds (or a concessionary price of two pounds), children over the age of seven and their carers could hear the author, who moved to Edinburgh less than four years earlier, read from what EIBF's programme that year called her 'terrifyingly imaginative debut novel... a tale of wizardry and witchcraft and... the most amazing secret of all time, the fabled philosopher's stone!'

In 2014, by this point the most famous author in the world, JK Rowling introduced the Pakistani women's rights activist and soon to be Nobel Peace Prize laureate Malala Yousafzai onstage at the Book Festival. It's one of Barley's highlights of his tenure, alongside Scottish First Minister Nicola Sturgeon's interview with Indian writer Arundhati Roy – Roy's first appearance in Edinburgh – in 2019 and the reclusive Japanese author Haruki

Murakami's visit in 2014, his first to the UK since 2003. Barley enticed him to the festival with a promise to help the author visit George Orwell's famous cottage on the Isle of Jura.

It's near-impossible to condense the diversity of household names and literary superstars brought to Edinburgh by the Book Festival in recent years. As an example, in 2019 alone it hosted more than 900 events and attracted over 250,000 individual visits, with a turnover of £4.2 million. The festival's theme was 'We Need New Stories', with authors attending from more than 60 countries including Annie Ernaux, Jokha Alharthi, Thomas Keneally, Bernadine Evaristo, Salman Rushdie, Colson Whitehead, Prue Leith, Lemn Sissay, Benjamin Zephaniah and Linton Kwesi Johnson. The programme included the former British Prime Minister Gordon Brown, the former Irish President Mary Robinson and the former leader of the Scottish Conservatives Ruth Davidson.

This sense of plurality is important to the Book Festival, says Barley. In 2014, the year of the Scottish Independence Referendum, the theme was simply 'Let's Talk'. 'It wasn't simply a question of standing on a platform and trying to persuade other people about your point of view, but also listening to each other,' he says.

> Since then, with the Brexit referendum and the political and cultural world becoming more bitterly divided, the more I think it's important the festival remains a forum where many different views can be heard. That's uncomfortable at times, and not everybody I invite is somebody with whom I might agree, but it's important we provide a properly moderated and framed discussion in which people can say what they think and disagree, and hopefully understand why they disagree by better understanding the perspective of people whose views seem odious or offensive. We play an increasingly delicate role in opposition to things like Twitter, which are obviously very bitterly divided places. We need to not close our ears, because it's important to know [what's happening].

An interest in literature is a baseline for being invited, which explains Sturgeon's returning presence, but Barley tries as far as possible to invite guests from across the political spectrum. Often they turn him down, but each person has their own reasons for doing so and he won't say who has or hasn't declined.

The changes wrought by the pandemic brought to a head issues developing around the Book Festival for some time – namely, the soil structure in the ground at Charlotte Square Gardens, with concerns that the continued construction of a small tented village for a month of every year was causing damage to tree roots. The site itself is owned by the buildings around the Square, a disparate collection of businesses, landlords and some residential owners and although Barley is on record as appreciating their collective help and goodwill over the years, he says the process of negotiating a way forward was prohibitively complex, simply down to the number of parties involved.

In 2021, with the experience of the previous year's virtual festival at the Assembly Rooms behind it, Edinburgh International Book Festival moved out of Charlotte Square Gardens for the first time in its history, to Edinburgh College of Art on Lauriston Place. This venue contains indoor rooms and halls that are easily converted into theatres for in-person talks and hybrid broadcast, while its courtyard gives the same outdoor socialising environment as Charlotte Square.

'It was an enormous wrench to leave Charlotte Square, but it had become clear that the damage we were doing to the gardens was becoming too great,' says Barley.

> The move to a new site was always going to be hard, and it will take us a while to bed down, but it offers so many opportunities to change up the festival and give it a new lease of life, bringing in a whole new generation for whom that part of town will be the home of the Book Festival. On balance, I think it's a great thing to have done.

Edinburgh International Book Festival isn't done moving yet. Following 2023's edition at the College of Art, it will take up permanent residence at the University of Edinburgh's new Futures Institute, a research and education institution which is describes by its website as 'a curious, open-minded thought laboratory' whose aim is to 'pursue knowledge and understanding that supports the navigation of complex futures'. Upon completion in 2024, the Institute will be based at the other end of Lauriston Place to the College of Art, in the last remaining structure which formed the old Royal Infirmary of Edinburgh complex, designed in 1879 by architect David Bryce and incorporating elements of the former George Watson's Hospital by William Adam.

Lothian Health Trust sold the old Infirmary site in 2001, before moving to a brand new hospital at Little France in the far southeast of the city in 2003; the Little France site sits on the outskirts, where the city meets the countryside, but the old Infirmary site had been the southern edge of Edinburgh when it was built in 1879. Some of the old buildings were demolished at the beginning of the 21st century to make way for the Quartermile development, a glassy swathe of apartment and tech company offices fringing the Meadows, but the Futures Institute – and the Book Festival – will sit within a landmark

Edinburgh building with nearly 150 years of history.

When the building site surrounding it is cleared away and the Institute opens, George Square will be barely a minute or two's walk across Middle Meadow Walk, the leafy pedestrian corridor to the city's south. The Book Festival, until now one of the Festival's last remaining outposts in the central New Town along with the Assembly Rooms and the Stand, will become part of the ever-expanding mass of August activity centring on the Southside around George and Bristo Squares.

* * *

The third and final change of leadership at one of Edinburgh's festivals in 2022 is an historic moment for the one which started it all. Despite the great talents and efforts of the ten directors who have gone before, the announcement on 1 March 2022 that Nicola Benedetti is to become Edinburgh International Festival's director in October '22 means it will have both its first female and first Scottish director.[18] Born in Irvine in Ayrshire, the Scots-Italian will be 36 when her first Festival arrives in 2023, which will also make her the youngest holder of the post in more than 60 years.[19]

Benedetti has no previous public reputation as a theatre administrator, but in 2019 she established the Benedetti Foundation, which is dedicated to all-ages music education and which has been hugely successful, especially during the lockdown period. She also brings something much more to the International Festival, something it hasn't had from other directors. A violin prodigy who won the BBC Young Musician of the Year title in 2004, Benedetti is one of the most successful and acclaimed classical musicians in the world and one of Scotland's leading musical exports. She's an MBE, a CBE and the winner of the Queen's Medal for Music, two Classical Brit Awards and a Grammy Award.

It's easy to see why both her connections and her passion were attractive to the International Festival, her proper debut with which came at the Usher Hall in 2012, performing with the London Symphony Orchestra conducted by Valery Gergiev.[20] Returning regularly throughout the 2010s, she played a week-long EIF residency during the reduced Festival of 2021, including performances of Stravinsky's *The Soldier's Tale* and her own *The Story of the Violin* show.

In 2022 she's scheduled to play alongside the Scottish Chamber Orchestra under Maxim Emalyanychev at the Usher Hall, her final EIF concert as just a simple participant. Infamously hard-working and busy, Benedetti has given no more than a brief welcome statement so far. Her last comment on EIF came in a *Scotsman* interview to promote her residency in 2021:

What the Edinburgh International Festival is demonstrating at the moment is a trend towards the increased juxtaposition of localised artists and the truly international. The EIF are having such a celebration of what's local this year, what's here in Scotland. I think it's something that will become more of a pattern for festivals all over the world.[21]

When she takes charge, it will bring the curtain down on Fergus Linehan's tenure. Appointed in 2013 ahead of his first festival in 2015, Linehan is from Dublin, part of an esteemed creative family. His late father, also Fergus, was the arts editor of the *Irish Times* and his mother Rosaleen is a well-known Irish actor and comedian; together, the pair had a popular comedy show on RTÉ Radio. Fergus Jr was involved in the founding of the college theatre company Pigsback in 1988, when he was just 19 and it later became the respected Irish touring company Fishamble, bringing new shows by celebrated writer-actors including Pat Kinevane and Eva O'Connor to the Fringe.

By this point Linehan had moved on, although in 2001 he produced Enda Walsh's *Bedbound* in his new role as director of the Dublin Theatre Festival, which transferred to the Traverse during that year's Fringe. He went around the world to run the Sydney Festival and then the music programme at the Sydney Opera House, returning to London for consultancy work – including for his EIF predecessor Jonathan Mills – before his own desire to tinker with the International Festival became too much and he applied for the job. Edinburgh already held a special place in Linehan's heart; he met his wife here in 2009, while his parents had regularly visited for years, including his mother's own one-woman appearance at EIF in 1989, as Kathleen Behan in *Mother of All the Behans* at the Assembly Rooms.

Compared to the deeply-embedded classical enthusiasms of Jonathan Mills, the 45-year-old Linehan presented as a laid-back, five-a-side playing director with a taste in contemporary music which fed into his Festival. As an introductory *Herald* profile had it he was a truly modern Festival director who listened to composers like Arvo Part and Steve Reich.

'The barbarians are not at the gate,' is how Linehan puts it. 'We're not talking about replacement.' In other words what we used to think of as high and low art now sit perfectly well together in most people's minds. The EIF, he thinks, should reflect that.[22]

Linehan remembers sitting around as a young stagehand in the theatres of Dublin, reading *A Portrait of the Artist as a Young Man* while the show was up, feeling he had to understand the classic works before he pushed beyond them. One of his brothers, the concert pianist Conor, introduced him in their youth to the songwriting of Cole Porter and Stephen Sondheim, while his other brother Hugh, now a journalist, taught him about post-punk bands like The The and Pixies. Much later, he discovered people like the dubstep artist Burial for himself.

'I grew up with this incredible respect for artists and their needs,' he says, with a nod to his parents.

> It doesn't matter who, it could be [the conductor] András Schiff, or [the opera singer] Joyce DiDonato, or someone like [indie-rock musician] Sufjan Stevens, but when they're really on fire, there's something about the alchemy and the courage of it. What it takes to get them to that point, what they need around them, and then their relationship with the audience, these are things I was always fascinated by. Just trying to understand someone like Aretha Franklin, for example. That might sound old-fashioned now, because the whole artist-as-hero thing is going out of the window, but the capacity to hold a crowd, is phenomenal and so rare. It requires so much support and air around it for it to be able to happen.

Linehan's debut programme in 2015 – following his moving EIF forward by a week to finally sync up with the Fringe once more – was an outstanding fusion of the contemporary and the classic, with an awareness of the Edinburgh Festival's rich history seemingly built-in. The centrepiece show was the return of director Ivo Van Hove with a version of Sophocles' *Antigone* at the King's Theatre which featured the film star Juliette Binoche in the lead role, while Komische Oper of Berlin and recent Underbelly Fringe darlings 1927 adapted Mozart's *The Magic Flute* at the Festival Theatre. Linehan's old Dublin colleague Enda Walsh also returned to Edinburgh alongside composer Donnacha Dennehy, with the chamber opera *The Last Hotel*.

There were also returns for Robert LePage at the Edinburgh International Conference Centre, with his piece about memory, technology and theatre *887*; Simon McBurney and Complicité with the world premiere of his acclaimed piece *The Encounter*; and the reunion of the old Suspect Culture team of David Greig and Graham Eatough, with an ambitious and visually stunning adaptation of Alasdair Gray's novel *Lanark* at the Lyceum, in celebration of both Gray's 80th year and the 70th anniversary of Glasgow's co-producing Citizens Theatre on its current site.

Linehan's indie hero Sufjan Stevens was also on the bill, a sell-out at the 2,000-capacity Playhouse, as part of a new programme of mature and critically-acclaimed popular music at EIF. FFS – the combined supergroup featuring Sparks and Glasgow's Franz Ferdinand – played the Festival

Theatre and a new series at EIF's home base entitled the Hub Sessions featured live performances from Anna Calvi with the Heritage Orchestra, electronic composer Daniel Lopatin aka Oneohtrix Point Never, Fife's King Creosote and Edinburgh regular Chilly Gonzales.

A new EIF tradition was also implemented, the opening event. 59 Productions' *Harmonium Project* took John Adams' minimalist 1981 composition 'Harmonium' as the starting point for a large-scale animated light show upon the face of the Usher Hall, which temporarily closed off Lothian Road in the late evening of Friday 7 August and finally made a use of the Festival Square plaza on Lothian Road which is appropriate to the name. Set out in 1984, in front of the just-built Sheraton Hotel and an intended centrepiece of the developing West End financial district, the Square stands on the site of the old Princes Street rail station's goods yard, long since wiped from the map when the station was closed in 1965.

The Harmonium Project featured music by the Royal Scottish National Orchestra and, in their 50th year, the Edinburgh Festival Chorus.

59 Productions created three more opening events for the International Festival at the same location, *Deep Time* (2016), *Bloom* (2017) and *Five Telegrams* (2018), the latter produced in commemoration of the centenary of the World War One armistice, with music from the North Queensferry-raised electronic musician and classical composer Anna Meredith. Intended as imagination-grabbing introductory events which were free to all, the opening concert moved to Heart of Midlothian FC's newly-redeveloped Tynecastle Stadium in 2019, with a free concert by the LA Philharmonic. A planned socially-distanced event at the Royal Botanic Gardens during the reduced Festival of 2019 had to be cancelled, but for 2022 an opening show named *Macro* will take place at Murrayfield Stadium and the Philadelphia Orchestra will play a free closing concert at the Playhouse.

Foregoing the thematic structure of Jonathan Mills' events, Linehan's International Festival programmes have mixed and matched an array of cross-genre work from around the world, highlights of which include a European revival of American Repertory Company's adaptation of Tennessee Williams' *The Glass Menagerie*, which reunited the *Black Watch* team of John Tiffany and Steven Hoggett, Cheek By Jowl and Moscow's Pushkin Theatre collaborating on Shakespeare's *Measure for Measure*, the TEAM and National Theatre of Scotland's *Anything That Gives Off Light* and Barry Humphries and Meow Meow's *Weimar Cabaret*, all in 2016.

In the same year, Matthias Pintscher conducted the BBC Scottish Symphony Orchestra in a tribute to the great late-20th century experimental composer Pierre Boulez, who died that January at the age of 90. Boulez's long association with the International Festival began in 1948, when the

23-year-old brought an operatic production of *Hamlet* to the city, and it flourished throughout Lord Harewood's tenure, around the time of Boulez's famous 1967 declaration that his plan to freshen up opera was to 'blow the opera houses up'.[23] By 2000, when he conducted yet again in Edinburgh with his *Music Boulez* night at the Usher Hall, he had been inducted, no matter how unwillingly, into the classical establishment.

Viewing Boulez's long life and death from a distance, in the context of the Edinburgh Festival, begins to demonstrate to us how 75 years of the Edinburgh Festival equals roughly one human lifetime, how most of the people alive at its birth are now no longer with us and how the values, virtues and questions about humanity that they sought to promote through art are passed on and adapted to new media and concepts.

In 2017, playwright Zinnie Harris and director Murat Daltaban created an adaptation of Eugene Ionesco's play *Rhinoceros* for the International Festival, an enduring, absurdist allegory for the rise of fascism which was first published by Edinburgh Writers Conference founder John Calder and used as an excuse for Jim Haynes' rhinoceros head on the door of the Paperback Bookshop. The same year, Anoushka Shankar carried on her late father and International Festival stalwart Ravi Shankar's legacy at the Usher Hall and the Incredible String Band's Mike Heron and Danny Thompson celebrated their own legacy in Edinburgh at the Playhouse. In 2018, a low-key workshop presentation of and discussion around *A Satire of the Three Estates* at the Festival Theatre's studio space celebrated 70 years since the play's return to a Scottish stage in 1948.

In the late 1980s, Leith Theatre – formerly known as Leith Town Hall – ended its first life as a booming if off-the-beaten-track International Festival venue, when the city council took it out of regular use. By the early years of the 2010s this proud old theatre was entirely dark, its bathrooms stripped out and paint flaking on the walls where water had crept in. The main floor of the theatre – opened in 1932 reputedly as a gift to Leith from Edinburgh, following the former's integration into the city in 1920 – was used for storing traffic cones by the council's work department.

Following work to restore the venue, first by the indefatigable Leith Theatre Trust and then the springtime Hidden Door festival, whose strategy is to clean up disused Edinburgh spaces and convert them into ad hoc temporary arts venues, Linehan's 2018 EIF programme included the *Light on the Shore* strand of contemporary concerts at the Theatre, bringing it back into International Festival life with music from Mogwai, Anna Meredith, King Creosote and local arts insurgents Neu! Reekie! After two years dark during the pandemic, the theatre will return once more in 2022 with artists including Ezra Furman, Jeff Mills and Kae Tempest.

Linehan's International Festival has welcomed back many artists whose names have been linked with the Edinburgh Festival over years, including Alan Cumming, Stephen Fry, Martin Creed, Nicola Benedetti, Sir James MacMillan, Meow Meow, Jackie Kay and 1927. In 2017 it commemorated the reopening after renovation of St Cecelia's Hall on the Cowgate, the oldest concert hall in Scotland, which first opened in 1763 and in 2019 Ian McKellen celebrated both his 80th birthday and the 50th anniversary of his first Festival appearance at the Assembly Hall with a one-man show at the same venue as part of his *Ian McKellen On Stage* tour. Contemporary singers from Scotland and around the world have expanded EIF's integral musical remit, including St Vincent, John Grant, Youssou N'Dour, Amadou and Mariam, Jarvis Cocker, Teenage Fanclub, Young Fathers and Karine Polwart.

'Leith has been amazing, but I'm loathe to take the credit for any of it,' says Linehan.

> The whole thing was driven by a bunch of really committed people there, then we came in to work with them and do work on the building. Festivals are very good at stealing other people's thunder. Edinburgh covers all the bases, but it still struggles to cover certain music areas. Out on the street you see people going to cabarets and comedies and you think, I bet they like Franz Ferdinand. In a landscape where people enjoy artistically ambitious things, a Monteverdi piece or an arthouse film, in the natural scheme of things they'd be going to a St Vincent or a Youssou N'Dour show. These things exist within people's own cultural canon, but they didn't exist in August, so [programming popular music] was some low-hanging fruit. The International Festival had been cannily moving at its own pace. I thought maybe I could take it and retain the core audience around classical music and theatre, and hopefully win their trust so I could move the organisation and the programme towards what people are culturally interested in today, to push it around the edges in terms of what it could be, without bumping into the other festivals too much.

The International Festival, he says, has the advantage over the Fringe in programming contemporary music, because it accommodates shows which need a whole day's technical get-in, while Fringe venues are built for 45-minute changeovers. This has been part of Linehan's Edinburgh experience since he first brought work to the city, when he had

> a show in the Traverse and around the corner Peter Stein has a show in the King's, and Claudio Abbado was conducting next door in

the Usher Hall. That felt like a reason to bring my little show to Edinburgh.[24]

With an initial contract for five years and a three-year extension agreed in 2019, Linehan decided now was the time to hand over control of the Edinburgh International Festival because

eight is on the cusp of too many. It's definitely as many as one should do, unless you've woken up with a revelation. It's such a big job, and in a city the size of Edinburgh where the Festival plays such a key role, you need new perspectives. Right now in particular, there's a real need to articulate a five-to-ten-year vision, so it's no time to tread water. It feels like it's time to turn the page and have a new chapter.

POSTSCRIPT

The Future

AS THESE WORDS are being typed, new Edinburgh Festival shows are steadily being announced for 2022's edition, creating a programme that looks something like the Festival most recently experienced in its last year of full health in 2019. Many veterans will make a welcome return, among them Liz Lochhead, whose *Medea* plays at the Hub under the wing of the Edinburgh International Festival, directed by Michael Boyd and starring Adura Onashile. At the Book Festival, the 50th anniversary of the publication of *Memo for Spring*, Lochhead's debut book, will also be celebrated.

After a period away from the Fringe and conquering the international theatre, Mischief Theatre make a triumphant return to the Pleasance venues with a trio of shows, the long-running *Mischief Music Night*, the brand new *Mind Mangler: Member of the Tragic Circle* and Charlie Russell's *Aims to Please*. At the King's Theatre, Alan Cumming returns with *Burn*, a fresh look at the life and poetry of Robert Burns, co-produced by Edinburgh International Festival, the National Theatre of Scotland and the Joyce Theatre in New York.

Burn is a collaboration of many eras of Fringe talents, involving comic actor of the '80s Cumming, '90s and '00s choreographer, director and Black Watch visionary Stephen Hoggett and 2010s composer Anna Meredith. Its pedigree reminds of the hit play *Leopoldstadt*, which opened at Wyndham's Theatre in London's West End weeks before the pandemic began in early 2020. Directed by 1980s Oxford student performer and stand-up comic Patrick Marber, written by Tom Stoppard, whose career emerged on the Fringe in the 1960s and set in the early 20th century Viennese Jewish district where the International Festival's founder Rudolf Bing was raised, it was a play made in Edinburgh, by one degree of removal each.

Already, the Festival of 2022 is confronting the political issues of the day. On Saturday 6 August, a free concert will be held at the Usher Hall by the Ukrainian Freedom Orchestra, a collaboration between Edinburgh International Festival and the Scottish Government. Canadian-Ukrainian conductor Keri-Lynn Wilson will lead an orchestra of Ukrainian musicians drawn from recent refugees, players with European orchestras and musicians from within Ukraine, including men of military service age who have been given leave by the Ukrainian Ministry of Culture to participate.

Seventy-five years after the International Festival was instigated by the end of war in Europe, the invasion of Ukraine is hanging heavy over the world. On the 1 March 2022 it was announced that the Russian conductor Valery Gergiev, one of the most significant figures of the contemporary International Festival, had been requested to resign his post as honorary patron with immediate effect. In the preceding days he had also been dropped by the Munich Philharmonic Orchestra, New York's Carnegie Hall and the Verbier Festival in Switzerland.

Only the International Festival's third honorary patron after Yehudi Menuhin and the late Australian conductor Charles Mackerras, since his appointment in 2011 Gergiev's performances in Edinburgh included Prokofiev's *Third Piano Concerto* with the Royal Scottish National Orchestra in 2013, Wagner's *Das Rheingold* with his own Mariinsky Opera in 2016 and a return with the RSNO in 2021. Yet he was known to be a close friend of the Russian President Vladimir Putin and his refusal to publicly condemn what was happening in Ukraine caused a domino flow of festivals and concert halls to take action.

Yet as the International Festival's statement made clear, there was a reason for this which was very specific to the city of Edinburgh. 'The board of trustees of the Edinburgh International Festival has asked for, and accepted the resignation of, Valery Gergiev as honorary president of the festival,' it said. 'Edinburgh is twinned with the city of Kyiv and this action is being taken in sympathy with, and support of, its citizens.'[1]

Since Glasgow Unity first chose *The Lower Depths* as an expression of working-class oppression in 1947 and Theatre Workshop soon joined in with Ewan MacColl's early tale of Nuclear Age anxiety *Uranium 235*, the Fringe has been deeply engaged with the political condition of the world and its expansion over the decades has only brought more voices and a wider sense of perspective to the table. It's an arts festival, so these perspectives tend to swing to the left, but full immersion in the Festival and Fringe goes beyond tribalism.

Their shared first year in '47 was forged in love of the supposedly elite arts and their use as a driver for the city's economic prosperity and in the competing energy of socialist theatre groups who sought to make art available to the working classes, particularly on the Festival's doorstep in Scotland. Over time, these very different interests have found space to co-exist and feed off one another within the same small city and in some ways have taken on the other's characteristics. This book, equally, has attempted not to pick sides, not to prioritise one motive for the act of artistic creation over another, in the spirit that all can have a voice in Edinburgh – although sometimes an artist's political motivation has been integral and required further explanation.

On the Fringe in 2022, Karen Koren will continue the Fringe's exploration into often-neglected Leith with the *Fringe Social*, a series of events at the popular Pitt food market. The International Festival's programme at nearby Leith Theatre, meanwhile, will close with Hebridean band Niteworks' show *Comann*, a celebration of the country's emerging Gaelic popular music scene. Both are attempts at the greater involvement of Scottish and particularly Edinburgh culture at a revived Festival which is aiming to pick up much of the momentum it held in 2019 – yet how this might play out after the pandemic remains uncertain.

'No-one knows what tourism is going to look like in 2022,' says Fergus Linehan.

> Edinburgh will be back very strongly in August, but will people be back with bells on, or will they be back cautiously? There are many unknowns, but I've really felt over the last 18 months that this is where the full 74-year history kicks in – this is where people go, 'we need this to continue.' Generally the sentiment in government has been that this is important, but how the arts emerge from this, and how quickly they emerge is going to be interesting to see.

Consolidating what it learned in 2020 and 2021, the Book Festival will continue to pursue a hybrid model. 'There are two directions festivals can take,' says director Nick Barley.

> There'll be those that feel that, for whatever reason, they have to be live and in person, and they'll keep cameras away. The Book Festival will continue to pursue a hybrid model, and will really make the most of that mixture of local quality and international reach. It's one of the strengths of Edinburgh as a festival city, that it can accommodate so many different kinds of festival. I do a lot of traveling to a lot of festivals, and there is no city in the world with quite the same ingredients – topography, demographic and geography – to make a festival city as successful as Edinburgh. But I'm not saying we can be complacent, and I'm not saying it will always be that way, we have to keep fighting for it. Yet the conditions are here for Edinburgh to maintain its position as a really important and leading festival city for a long time to come.

These senses of localism and internationalism are equally important to Barley. Since 2015, the Book Festival's Citizen project has taken readings and events to community spaces, social enterprises, prisons and elsewhere around Scotland. 'I don't use the word 'outreach', because it implies some central organisation reaching out to people on the periphery,' he says.

> People who live in Pilton (for example) are not on the periphery, they're in the centre of Pilton, and the festivals are not doing enough to engage people in parts of the city. We've looked at the reasons why people have felt alienated – it might be to do with economic deprivation, or it might be migrant communities who've not necessarily had as much exposure to Scottish culture. We do a lot of work, and it's a long-term program which I believe is crucially important. We've got to make sure that Edinburgh engages with its citizens, there's got to be some kind of dividend. We've got to find a way that the benefits of this incredible festival the city's able to put on are felt by as many people as possible.

At the beginning of June 2022, at a launch event in Edinburgh attended by the Fringe's President Phoebe Waller-Bridge, the Fringe Society launched a 'Vision and Values' document which seeks to produce a new, post-COVID contract between the Fringe and all involved with it. An update of the previous *Fringe Blueprint*, it set out six Fringe Development Goal targets and a number of commitments to be carried out before the end of the year.[2]

'There's nothing else like the Fringe,' said Shona McCarthy earlier in the year, while this document was still in preparation.

> For all of the things people would love to see fixed or changed or adjusted about it – and hopefully we can address a lot of that in this renaissance moment – even its biggest critics in the arts would still say, 'but I love it and it's magical'. But more than those kinds of platitudes, it's still a place where anyone can come and put on a show, and only how and where you put on that show is what varies. There's still every possible type of model, and every year I see glorious new emerging works put together by people on a wing and a prayer. I would never want to take that way, because it gives everybody a chance.

In 2019, she says, the number of media representatives and arts industry scouts attending the Fringe from around the world numbered in the thousands. Beyond the famous names introduced in this book, the number of careers, new pieces of work and even personal relationships and marriages attributable to the Festival must be beyond calculation. Before he passes on the mantle inherited from Rudolf Bing's earliest inspiration and efforts, Edinburgh

International Festival's director Fergus Linehan shares his thoughts on the responsibility he's carried. 'All a festival is, is context,' he says.

> It's a juxtaposition of things alongside the expectations of the audience. When Richard Wagner set up the Bayreuth Festival, he spoke of certain types of art where, if you completely give yourself over to it, it can have an incredible effect upon you. It's an experiential thing which draws a line from a 16-year-old kid doing stand-up for the first time, all the way through to the Komische Oper onstage at the Festival Theatre. Salzburg has an opera festival and Avignon has a theatre festival, but this is the only place where it all exists, and that has an effect on you (as a performer or an audience member), where you come out of it feeling more is possible in your life and in the world. It has to sustain that.

During our interview just prior to the 2021 Festival, before Nicola Benedetti had been appointed as his successor, Linehan went on to expand on the philosophy of the Edinburgh Festival – particularly the Edinburgh International Festival – in the present moment. His words bear repeating at length:

> There's questions of what internationalism means into the future. The Festival came about predominantly out of an idea of internationalism which was western capitalism. To a degree some of that has held, but I think the world is looking for a new definition of internationalism – not a neoliberal thing. For those of us who were around during the Cold War, we had this idea of internationalism as being one of the great healing factors in our lives, whereas now there's suspicion around it. The global cosmopolitan individual was the icon for a while, zipping from city to city, and there has been a certain amount of change in relation to that idea. That's partly driven by sustainability and environmentalism, but I think globalism also got caught up with the Davos view of the world, where globalism is actually to do with global economy; a lot of things inferred [by the word] certainly wouldn't have been inferred in 1947. There's a real role for internationalism at the moment, but also a focus on not just the local, but the hyperlocal, [and] there might need to be more conversation around creating a vision of what is possible internationally. Whoever's going to come in [after me] will have to figure that out, because I think generationally, finding the idea of internationalism as exciting as the Boomer generation did is going to be a job.

In 2019, 3,841 Fringe shows were staged in Edinburgh. By June 2022, 3,131 had been booked in for the coming August. The Edinburgh Festival in all its forms will continue, a force of nature driven by the deep love of all who regularly experience it, but like every natural organism, shaped by the changes around it.

Amid the sunlit sandstone temples of the Old and New Town, the same rain-washed setts trodden by Scott, Stevenson, MacDiarmid, Muir and Spark will be walked by thousands of curious visitors from around the world. For three weeks in summer, this Scottish village of more than half a million people will continue to pursue a very 21st century form of Enlightenment.

Timeline

1934   Austrian opera administrator Rudolf Bing comes to the United Kingdom to take the job of General Manager at Glyndebourne Opera Festival in East Sussex.

1940   Touring with a Glyndebourne production of *The Beggar's Opera*, Bing visits Edinburgh at the beginning of the year and likens it to the city of Salzburg.

1944   Bing develops his idea for a healing post-war international festival of the arts. During a London meeting late in the year with the British Council's Henry Harvey Wood, Edinburgh is suggested as a venue.

1945   In February Bing and Wood meet Edinburgh's Lord Provost John Falconer, who likes the idea of a festival for Edinburgh. The Second World War ends on 2 September.

1946   In September the Edinburgh International Festival of Music and Drama is approved by Edinburgh's city corporation and will be going ahead in 1947. In November the Edinburgh Festival Society is founded as a steering committee of interested parties.

1947   The first Edinburgh International Festival of Music and Drama begins; the Assembly Rooms on George Street is its social Festival Club. Eight unofficial, 'uninvited' companies also bring work to the city, the precursor of the later Festival Fringe; one of its venues is the Pleasance Theatre. The first Edinburgh International Festival of Documentary Films is also held, later becoming the Edinburgh International Film Festival.

1948   For the first time in approximately 400 years, Sir David Lyndsay's *A Satire of the Three Estates* (in the original Scots, *Ane Pleasant Satyre of the Thrie Estaites*) is staged, here in an International Festival production at the Church of Scotland's Assembly Hall on the Mound. It's a watershed moment in Scottish theatre.

1950   The first official Edinburgh Military Tattoo happens on the Castle Esplanade, following on from military performance events of increasing size held during the Festival since 1947.

1951   The inaugural Edinburgh People's Festival takes place at Oddfellows Hall, with the involvement of Hamish Henderson, Theatre Workshop, the musicologist Alan Lomax and figures from the Labour movement. The festival's final edition is in 1953, with some further small events in 1954, yet its impact on the wider Festival and the Scottish folk scene is significant.

1953   Queen Elizabeth II's coronation takes place at Westminster Abbey.

1958   The Edinburgh Festival Fringe Society is founded, after a meeting of 25 'unofficial' groups at Cranston Street Hall.

1959   The first official Edinburgh Festival Fringe takes places under the Society's guidance (although the Fringe as an unnamed concept is recognised as beginning in 1947).

1961   Eager to catch up with the Fringe's trend for late-night revues, International Festival director Robert Ponsonby and his assistant Johnny Bassett recruit four Oxford and Cambridge graduates – Alan Bennett, Peter Cook, Jonathan Miller and Dudley Moore – for their own show at the Lyceum. *Beyond the Fringe* launches the satire boom of the 1960s.

1962   The Edinburgh International Writers' Conference takes place at McEwan Hall, welcoming writers including Norman Mailer, Henry Miller, Mary McCarthy, William Burroughs, Hugh MacDiarmid, Muriel Spark and Alexander Trocchi for a week of fierce, headline-grabbing debate.

1963   The Traverse Theatre opens in a compact loft space on the Lawnmarket in January. In August the Edinburgh International Writers' Conference takes place, again at McEwan Hall. It becomes infamous for a very 1960s artistic Happening in which a nude female model appeared, scandalising the Festival.

1968   Film Festival director Murray Grigor takes on two young Edinburgh University graduates, Lynda Myles and David Will, as programmers. The pair reinvigorate the festival with their taste for radical cinema and the new generation of American 'Movie Brat' auteurs. Myles becomes director of the Film Festival from 1973 until 1980.

1969   The Traverse Theatre moves to its second home on the Grassmarket.

1970   Among the many hundreds of artists and shows he's brought to Edinburgh, local art impresario Richard Demarco's *Strategy Get Arts* exhibition of German contemporary artists at Edinburgh College of Art is his masterpiece. It introduces Joseph Beuys to an international audience. Later, Demarco welcomes Tadeusz Kantor's Cricot 2 company to the Festival in 1972 and in 1973 he presents Marina Abramović's first international performance as part of *Eight Yugoslav Artists*.

1971   Future film star Robin Williams, then a 20-year-old, appears in a student production of *The Taming of the Shrew* at Viewforth Church.

1972   Starring Billy Connolly, *The Great Northern Welly Boot Show* at Waverley Market is instrumental in launching a new generation of Scottish theatre makers. Also key is the 7:84 company, presenting their own show nearby at the same time.

1978   Mike Hart hosts a three-day jazz event in Abbeyhill, the informal beginning of the Edinburgh Jazz and Blues Festival.

1979   The Edinburgh Jazz Festival begins properly during the Festival. A group including performer Rowan Atkinson and writer Richard Curtis convert a building off the Royal Mile into the Wireworks Theatre, a one-year venture which inspires many of the major venue owners who are about to emerge. In politics the Scottish devolution referendum fails to win a majority, although this and the election of Margaret Thatcher's Conservative government give new energy and material to theatre makers and comedians with a political edge.

1981   William Burdett-Coutts takes over the Assembly Rooms as a Fringe venue, following its closure as the International Festival's Festival Club in 1979 after 32 years. The first Perrier Award for comedy is given to the Cambridge Footlights – featuring Stephen Fry, Hugh Laurie, Emma Thompson and Tony Slattery – for their show *The Cellar Tapes*. Although the award won't become synonymous with strand-up for another decade, its arrival, the Assembly Rooms' opening and the emergence of Alternative Comedy are the spurs that develop stand-up comedy as a major part of the Fringe. Outgoing Fringe director Alistair Moffat institutes the first Fringe Sunday on the Royal Mile, a one-day event which continued in Holyrood Park and then the Meadows until 2009 and which catalysed the daily street theatre performances which have now become the norm on the Royal Mile.

1982   The derelict space alongside the Royal Lyceum Theatre known as the Hole in the Ground becomes a tented venue called the Circuit. It ends in 1983, although the space is used again later in the decade for the Elephant Tent.

1983   The first Edinburgh Book Festival takes place in Charlotte Square Gardens.

1985   Karen Koren runs her first comedy club at McNally's, a townhouse in the West End. After many years in use by Fringe companies, the Pleasance as we know it now opens under the management of Christopher Richardson. Book Festival director Jenny Brown brings a Spiegeltent to Charlotte Square Gardens, the first sighting of a performance structure that has become synonymous with the Edinburgh Festival.

1986   The Gilded Balloon opens on the Cowgate as a single 150-seat theatre under Koren's management. The infamous after-midnight Late 'n' Live revue comes with it from McNally's.

1988   The Gilded Balloon's *So You Think You're Funny?* contest for new comedians begins in Edinburgh, later discovering winners including Dylan Moran and Peter Kay, and finalists Sarah Millican, John Bishop and Alan Carr. The idea was originally conceived and executed by Simon Fanshawe and William Burdett-Coutts at Glasgow's Mayfest festival in May '88 and adapted by Karen Koren with permission.

1989   The major comedy promoter Avalon Entertainment is founded. Off the Kerb has already been backing artists like Julian Clary at the Comedy Boom stand-up club on Picardy Place, which closes this year. Both agencies have a transformative effect on the UK comedy industry and the Edinburgh Fringe.

1990   Sean Hughes wins the Perrier Award, taking stand-up's presence at the career-making Fringe to new and still-ongoing heights.

1992   The current Traverse Theatre opens on Cambridge Street.

1994   The Empire Theatre on Nicholson Street, until recently a bingo hall, at last becomes the fully-renovated Festival Theatre.

1995   Tommy Sheppard and Jane Mackay put some local comedians on over 12 nights of the Fringe in the tiny basement of WJ Christie & Sons' pub on West Port. The following month they start a weekly comedy night there named the Stand Comedy Club.

1996   Edinburgh Jazz Festival rebrands as the Edinburgh Jazz & Blues Festival.

1997   Following the General Election win for Labour in May, a Scottish devolution referendum is called for September. The vote is 74 percent in favour of a Scottish Parliament.

1998   The Stand Comedy Club opens in its permanent home at York Place. The Fringe Society controversially moves its start and finish dates forward, making it a week out of sync with the International Festival. This arrangement continues for two decades.

1999   The Scottish Parliament is founded. Until the move to a purpose-built building in Holyrood, it sits at the Church of Scotland's Assembly Hall on the Mound, a sometime Edinburgh International Festival venue.

2001   Ed Bartlam and Charlie Wood open their Underbelly venue in the atmospheric vaults below Central Library. One of their first shows is a school production of Cabaret starring 19-year-old later stage and film actor Eddie Redmayne. Their organisation has grown, sometimes controversially, into new venues including the tented Udderbelly 'purple cow' on Bristo Square and more recently George Square Gardens.

2004   The first Edinburgh Art Festival takes place. At first a printed guide encompassing the many already-exhibiting galleries in the city, it has since become a commissioning entity in its own right.

2006   After many years of debate and speculation, the National Theatre of Scotland is founded. The same year its most famous and successful play to date, *Black Watch*, opens at the Fringe.

2007   Festivals Edinburgh is founded as the combined representative body of all 12 of Edinburgh's year-round festivals. It signals a new era in the professionalisation of the Edinburgh Festival and its relationship with the city as a source of tourism and investment.

2011   Entrepreneur Robert McDowell opens the Summerhall arts complex in the former Royal Dick Vet School on the Southside, with the assistance of producer Rupert Thomson. It's since become one of the Fringe's key and most widely-acclaimed venues.

2013   Phoebe Waller-Bridge's Underbelly solo show *Fleabag* makes her name and later becomes an acclaimed television series, an emblem of contemporary Fringe success. Waller-Bridge later becomes President of the Fringe Society.

2020   The COVID-19 pandemic leads to the entire cancellation of the Edinburgh Festival, although a lot of work transfers online. Fears are expressed about the future of the Festival, particularly by various Fringe operators, amid the crisis.

2021   A reduced, socially-distanced Edinburgh Festival takes place. After 38 years, Edinburgh International Book Festival moves out of Charlotte Square Gardens and into the courtyard of Edinburgh College of Art.

2022   For its 75th anniversary, something much like the last full Fringe of 2019 is planned. After pandemic-hit editions in the previous two years, Edinburgh International Film Festival officially moves back to its August slot. Edinburgh International Book Festival announces its intention to move again in 2023, to a permanent home at the new Edinburgh Futures Institute in the Quartermile development.

Who's in Charge of the Edinburgh Festival?
A complete chronological list of directors of the major festivals

Edinburgh International Festival

1947–1949: Rudolf Bing
1950–1955: Ian Hunter
1956–1960: Robert Ponsonby
1961–1965: George Lascelles, 7th Earl of Harewood
1966–1978: Peter Diamand
1979–1983: John Drummond
1984–1991: Frank Dunlop
1992–2006: Brian McMaster
2006–2014: Jonathan Mills
2014–2022: Fergus Linehan
From October 2022: Nicola Benedetti

Edinburgh Festival Fringe

Prior to 1971, the Fringe had no formal lead and prior to 1959 the Festival Fringe Society didn't exist, although events that can be described as 'fringe' happened from 1947. Known variously as Fringe Administrator, Director and currently Chief Executive, the role has no commissioning element–each individual Fringe show is its own entity, although some are commissioned or programmed by organisations or Fringe venues. The role of Fringe head is essentially about communication, coordination and wider strategy.

1971–1976: John Milligan
1976–1981: Alistair Moffat
1981–1986: Michael Dale
1986–1993: Mhairi Mackenzie-Robinson
1993–1999: Hilary Strong
2000–2007: Paul Gudgin
2007–2008: Jon Morgan
2008–2016: Kath Mainland
2016–present: Shona McCarthy

Edinburgh International Film Festival

Between 1947 and 1953 the Film Festival was run by the members of the Edinburgh Film Guild, chaired by Norman Wilson, with an advisory committee consisting of Basil Wright, Charles Oakley, Paul Rotha and Forsyth Hardy.

1954–1956: Forsyth Hardy
1957: Callum Mill
1958: Theo Lang
1959: Donald M. Elliott
1960: RB MacLuskie
1961–1964: Michael Elder
1965–1966: David Bruce
1967–1972: Murray Grigor
1973–1980: Lynda Myles
1981–1988: Jim Hickey
1989–1991: David Robinson
1992–1994: Penny Thomson
1995–1996: Mark Cousins
1997–2001: Lizzie Francke
2002–2006: Shane Danielsen
2007–2010: Hannah McGill
2011: James Mullighan (producer only, films were 'guest-curated')
2012–2014: Chris Fujiwara
2015–2019: Mark Adams
2022–present: Kristy Matheson

Edinburgh Jazz & Blues Festival

1978–1996: Mike Hart
1997–2007: Mike Hart, Jim Thompson and Assembly Direct (Roger Spence and Fiona Alexander)
2008–2020: Roger Spence and Fiona Alexander
2021–present: Fiona Alexander

Edinburgh International Book Festival

1983–1993: Jenny Brown
1993–1996: Shona Munro
1996–1997: Jan Fairley
1998–2001: Faith Liddell
2001–2009: Catherine Lockerbie
2009–present: Nick Barley

Edinburgh Art Festival

2004–2006: Katie Nicoll (co-ordinator)
2006–2006: Lisa Kapur (co-ordinator)
2007–2011: Joanne Brown
2011–2022: Sorcha Carey
2022–present: Kim McAleese

APPENDIX 2

Festival Winners

From its foundation in 1981 until 2005, the star-making main comedy award in Edinburgh was sponsored by the mineral water company Perrier and was widely known as the Perrier Comedy Award, or just 'the Perrier'. Since 2006, there have been various successive sponsors – to date, banking company Intelligent Finance, Absolute Radio, Foster's Lager, lastminute. com and the comedy-focused television channel Dave. Since Perrier's departure the award has widely been known as simply the Edinburgh Comedy Award, sometimes shortened to the 'Eddie'.

In 1992, a Best Newcomer Award was added for an act performing their first show; these acts are also eligible for the main award, but can't be on both shortlists in the same year. In 2006 an additional Panel Prize was added, with looser eligibility rules for anyone (or no-one, as in 2017) who has contributed to the Fringe, particularly in comedy.

All winners in bold. There was no Comedy Award shortlist until 1984 and no Best Newcomer Award shortlist until 1998. Due to the COVID-19 pandemic, no awards were issued in 2020 or 2021.

Edinburgh Comedy Award

1981 **Cambridge Footlights** (Penny Dwyer, Stephen Fry, Hugh Laurie, Paul Shearer, Tony Slattery, Emma Thompson)

1982 **Writer's Inc** (Gary Adams, Steve Brown, Vicki Pile, Trevor McCallum, Heather Murray, Jamie Rix, Nick Wilton)

1983 **Los Trios Ringbarkus** (Neill Gladwin, Steve Kearney)

1984 **The Brass Band**; The Bodgers; Fascinating Aida; Frank Chickens; Hank Wangford Band; Paul B. Davies and Dave Cohens

1985 **Theatre de Complicité**; The Bodgers; John Dowie; Merry Mac Fun Show; Sue Ingleton

1986 **Ben Keaton**; Jenny Lecoat; Merry Mac Fun Show; Paul B. Davies; Roy Hutchins

1987 **Brown Blues** (Arnold Brown, Barb Jungr, Michael Parker); Jeremy Hardy; John Sparkes; Nick Revell; Simon Fanshawe

1988 **Jeremy Hardy**; Doug Anthony Allstars; Robert Llewellyn; Roy Hutchins; The Wow Show

1989 **Simon Fanshawe**; Al and George; John Hegley; Live Bed Show; Will Durst; The World of Les and Robert

1990 **Sean Hughes**; Dillie Keane; Jimmy Tingle; Pete McCarthy

1991 **Frank Skinner**; Avner the Eccentric; Eddie Izzard; Jack Dee; Lily Savage

1992 **Steve Coogan** (with John Thomson); Bruce Morton; Jo Brand; John Shuttleworth; Mark Thomas;

1993 **Lee Evans**; Corky and the Juice Pigs; Donna McPhail; Greg Proops, Johnny Meres; Parrot; Phil Kay

1994 Alan Davies; Harry Hill (with Al Murray); Jeff Green; **Lano and Woodley**; Owen O'Neill; Robert Schimmel

1995 **Jenny Eclair**; Boothby Graffoe; Scott Capurro; Simon Bligh; the Umbilical Brothers

1996 **Dylan Moran**; Al Murray; Alexander Armstrong and Ben Miller; Bill Bailey; Dominic Holland; Rich Hall

1997 **The League of Gentleman**; Al Murray; Graham Norton; Johnny Vegas; Milton Jones

1998 **Tommy Tiernan**; Al Murray; Ed Byrne; Peter Kay; Seán Cullen

1999 **Al Murray**; The Arctic Boosh (aka The Mighty Boosh – Noel Fielding, Julian Barratt, Rich Fulcher); Ross Noble; Simon Munnery; Terry Alderton

2000 **Rich Hall**; Dave Gorman; Garth Marenghi's Fright Knight (Matthew Holness; Richard Ayoade, Alice Lowe); Lee Mack (with Catherine Tate and Dan Antopolski); Sean Lock

2001 **Garth Marenghi's Netherhead** (Matthew Holness; Richard Ayoade, Alice Lowe); Adam Hills; Dan Antopolski; Daniel Kitson; Jason Byrne

2002 **Daniel Kitson**; Adam Hills, Jimmy Carr; Noel Fielding; Omid Djalili; Phil Nichol

2003 **Demetri Martin**; Adam Hills; Flight of the Conchords; Howard Read and Little Howard; Reginald D. Hunter

2004 **Will Adamsdale**; Chris Addison; Ethan Sandler and Adrian Wenner; Reginald D. Hunter; Sarah Kendall

2005 **Laura Solon**; Chris Addison; Dutch Elm Conservatoire; Jason Manford; Jeremy Lion (aka Justin Edwards, with George Cockerill)

2006 **Phil Nichol**; David O'Doherty; Paul Sinha; Russell Howard; We Are Klang

2007 **Brendon Burns**; Andrew Lawrence; Andrew Maxwell; Pappy's Fun Club; Tom Binns

2008 **David O'Doherty**; Kristen Schaal and Kurt Braunohler; Rhod Gilbert; Russell Kane

2009 **Tim Key**; Idiots of Ants; John Bishop; Jon Richardson; Russell Kane; Tom Wrigglesworth

2010 **Russell Kane**; Bo Burnham; Greg Davies; Josie Long; Sarah Millican

2011 **Adam Riches**; Andrew Maxwell; Chris Ramsey; Josie Long; Nick Helm; Sam Simmons

2012 **Doctor Brown**; Claudia O'Doherty; James Acaster; Josie Long; Pappy's; Tony Law

2013 **Bridget Christie**; Carl Donnelly; James Acaster; Max & Ivan (Max Olesker and Ivan Gonzalez); Mike Wozniak; Nick Helm; Seann Walsh

2014 **John Kearns**; Alex Horne; James Acaster; Liam Williams; Romesh Ranganathan; Sam Simmons; Sara Pascoe

2015 **Sam Simmons**; James Acaster; Joseph Morpurgo; Kieran Hodgson; Nish Kumar; Sarah Kendall; Seymour Mace; Trygve Wakenshaw

2016 **Richard Gadd**; Al Porter; James Acaster; Kieran Hodgson; Nish Kumar; Randy Feltface; Tom Ballard; Zoe Coombs Marr

2017 **Hannah Gadsby; John Robins** (joint winners awarded); Ahir Shah; Elf Lyons; Jordan Brookes; Mae Martin; Mat Ewins; Sophie Willan; Spencer Jones

2018 **Rose Matafeo**; Ahir Shah; Alex Edelman; Felicity Ward; Glenn Moore; Kieran Hodgson; Larry Dean

2019 **Jordan Brookes**; Darren Harriott; the Delightful Sausage; Demi Lardner; Goodbear; Ivo Graham; Jessica Fostekew; London Hughes; Spencer Jones

2020 No award.

2021 No award.

Edinburgh Comedy Award: Best Newcomer

1992 Harry Hill

1993 Dominic Holland

1994 Scott Capurro

1995 Tim Vine

1996 Milton Jones

1997 Arj Barker

1998 **The Mighty Boosh** (Noel Fielding, Julian Barratt, Rich Fulcher);Chris Addison; Jason Byrne; Jon Reed; Paul Foot

1999 **Ben 'n' Arn's Big Top** (Ben Willbond, Arnold Widdowson, Bernard Hughes); The Arthur Dung Show (James Lamb and Jim North); Infinite Number of Monkeys (Tim FitzHigham, James Cary); Wil Anderson

2000 **Noble and Silver**; Andrew Clover; Dan Antopolski; David O'Doherty

2001 **Garth Cruickshank and Eddie McCabe**; Andy Zaltzman; Cambridge Footlights (with Edward Jaspers, Tim Key, Day Macaskill, James Morris, Mark Watson, Sophie Winkleman): Danny Bhoy

2002 **The Consultants**; Hal Cruttenden; Natalie Haynes; Reginald D Hunter

2003 **Gary LeStrange**; Alex Horne; Michael McIntyre; Miles Jupp

2004 **Wil Hodgson**; Alun Cochrane; Joanna Neary; Sabotage (Shenoah Allen and Mark Shavez)

2005 **Tim Minchin**; Charlie Pickering; Mark Watson; Rhod Gilbert; Toulson and Harvey

2006 **Josie Long**; Fat Tongue (Sophie Black, Seb Cardinal, Dustin Demri Burns); God's Pottery; Russell Kane

2007 **Tom Basden**; Jon Richardson; Micky Flanagan; Zoe Lyons

2008 **Sarah Millican**; Mike Wozniak; Pippa Evans

2009 **Jonny Sweet**; Carl Donnelly; Jack Whitehall; Kevin Bridges; Pete Johansson

2010 **Roisin Conaty**; Asher Treleaven; the Boy with Tape on His Face; Gareth Richards; Imran Yusuf; Late Night Gimp Fight!

2011 **Humphrey Ker**; Cariad Lloyd; the Chris and Paul Show; Hannibal Buress; Holly Walsh; Josh Widdicombe; Thom Tuck; Totally Tom

2012 **Daniel Simonsen**; David Trent; Discover Ben Target; Joe Lycett; Sam Fletcher

2013 **John Kearns**; Aisling Bea; Liam Williams; Matt Okine; Romesh Ranganathan

2014 **Alex Edelman**; Dane Baptiste; Gein's Family Giftshop; Lazy Susan; Lucy Beaumont; Steen Raskopoulos

2015 **Sofie Hagen**; Adam Hess; Daphne; Larry Dean; John Henry Falle; Tom Ballard; Tom Parry

2016 **Scott Gibson**; Bilal Zafar; Brendan Reece; Jayde Adams; Michelle Wolf; Nath Valvo

2017 **Natalie Palamides**; Chris Washington; Darren Harriott; Ed Night; Kwame Asante; Lauren Pattison; Lucy Pearman; Rob Kemp

2018 **Ciarán Dowd**; Maisie Adam; Olga Koch; Sara Barron; Sarah Keyworth; Sindhu Vee

2019 **Catherine Cohen**; Crybabies; Helen Bauer; Huge Davies; Janine Harouni; Michael Odewale; Nigel Ng; Sophie Duker

2020 No award

2021 No award

Edinburgh Comedy Award: Panel Prize

2006   **Mark Watson**
2007   **Arthur Smith**
2008   Every performer on the Fringe
2009   **Peter Buckley-Hill**, founder of PBH's Free Fringe
2010   **Bo Burnham**
2011   **Max & Ivan** (Max Olesker and Ivan Gonzalez)
2012   **The Boy with Tape On His Face**
2013   **Adrienne Truscott**
2014   **Funz and Gamez** (Phil Ellis)
2015   **Karen Koren**
2016   **Iraq Out & Loud: Reading the Chilcot Report in Full**
2017   No award
2018   **Home Safe Collective** (Angela Barnes, Pauline Eyre, Sameena Zehra)
2019   **Fringe of Colour**
2020   No award
2021   No award

So You Think You're Funny? Winners

Originally created for Glasgow's Mayfest festival in May 1988 by comedian Simon Fanshawe and artistic director William Burdett-Coutts, founding director of the Fringe's Assembly venue, the competition format was transferred with permission to the Gilded Balloon for 1988's Fringe by original judge Karen Koren. The contest is for genuinely new comedians (among the list of entry conditions, they must have no agent, have played no more than 15 gigs and not started before June in the year prior to their entry). Under these conditions, the number of subsequently A-list comedians who have won or been among the finalists is truly astonishing.

Only winners and (since 2000) runners-up and third-placed entrants are listed, in order and with the winner in bold. Other finalists to have not been among the top three over the years include Dan Antopolski, John Bishop, Kevin Bridges, Jason Byrne, Greg Davies, Rhod Gilbert, Russell Howard, Reginald D Hunter, Josie Long, Zoe Lyons, Jason Manford, Greg McHugh, Lucy Porter, Romesh Ranganathan, Ahir Shah, Daniel Sloss, Jack Whitehall, Josh Widdicombe and the future screenwriter and creator of *Being Human* and *No Angels* Toby Whithouse. No awards were issued in 2020 or 2021 due to the COVID-19 pandemic.

1988   **Bruce Morton**
1989   **Phil Kay**
1990   **Trio Brothers Troup** (Rab Christie, Greg Hemphill, Neil Warhurst)
1991   **Alan Francis**
1992   **Rhona Cameron**
1993   **Dylan Moran**
1994   **Martin Trenaman**
1995   **Lee Mack**
1996   **Tommy Tiernan**

1997 Peter Kay
1998 Rob Rouse
1999 David O'Doherty
2000 Drew Rokos, Des Clarke
2001 Miles Jupp, Stefano Paolini, Alan Carr, Michael Downey (joint third place)
2002 Matthew Osborn, Mark Watson, Nina Conti
2003 Tom Wrigglesworth, Andrew Lawrence, Stuart Hudson
2004 Nick Sun, Russell Kane, Chris McCausland
2005 Tom Allen, Sarah Millican, Joe Wilkinson
2006 Wes Packer, Hannah Gadsby, Ginger & Black
2007 Richard Sandling, Ben Davis, Joanne Lau
2008 Daniel Simonsen, Seann Walsh, Sara Pascoe
2009 Ivo Graham, Kevin Shevlin, Naz Osmanoglu
2010 James Allenby-Kirk, Liam Williams, Rob Beckett
2011 Tommy Rowson, Dayne Rathbone, Lucy Beaumont, Fern Brady (joint third place)
2012 Aisling Bea, Jonathon Pelham, Murdo Haggs, Wayne Mazadza (joint third place)
2013 Edward Hodges, Demi Lardner, Laura Mclenaghan (joint winner)
2014 Aidan Strangeman, Elliot Steel, Joe Hart
2015 Luca Cupani,, Yuriko Kotani, Ed Night (as Ed Day)
2016 Heidi Regan, Ruth Hunter, Danielle Walker
2017 Maisie Adam, Sarah Mann, Morgan Rees
2018 Danny Garnell, Liam Farrelly, Bec Melrose, Joe Hobbs (joint third place)
2019 Finlay Christie, Shane Daniel Byrne, Charlie George
2020 No award
2021 No award

Fringe First Winners

Concerned by the poor box office performance of new plays on the Fringe in 1972, the Fringe Society sought ways of promoting new work. Administrator John Milligan collaborated on the idea of a new writing award with *The Scotsman's* publicist Ian Thomson and arts editor Allen Wright, the latter creating the definition of a Fringe First award. The award is open to any new play or other rehearsed piece of theatre that is having its premiere on the Fringe (not the International Festival), with a provision for up to six preview performances elsewhere being permitted. A member of *The Scotsman* festival review team can nominate a play for its outstanding quality, which will then be seen by other reviewers and generally earn an award if there's broad consensus that it's merited.

The first Fringe First awards were announced in the pages of *The Scotsman* in 1973 and have continued to appear every year since, the cancellation of 2020 and limited programme of 2021 notwithstanding. There is no set number of awards, but usually around five or six are given out at a weekly ceremony hosted by a star guest, totalling 15 to 20 awards per year. For an example of winning odds, 511 out of 1,542 Fringe shows were eligible in 2003, the 30th anniversary year and 15 awards were given. Although other high-profile and well-regarded theatre awards have been distributed in Edinburgh, including the **Herald Angels**, the **Stage Awards**, the **Total Theatre Awards** and the **Amnesty Freedom of Expression Award**, the Fringe Firsts are the longest-running and the most comprehensive guide to grassroots new writing trends on the Fringe.

The list below contains internationally-famed plays by playwrights at various stages of their careers; well-decorated regular returnees for whom the Fringe is an annual event and who have hit upon the perfect formula for an hour of thought-provoking Edinburgh entertainment; international and experimental works which might not have found a stage anywhere else; and 'one-hit wonders' by writers and companies who have hardly been heard of since, but who perfectly captured the imagination of the city for three weeks.

Between 2001 and 2003, a **Best of the Fringe Firsts** award was given to the play chosen as the finest of that year's selection, which was replaced in 2004 by the **Carol Tambor Best of Edinburgh Award**. Announced at the final Fringe First ceremony of the year, it's open not just to every Fringe First winner, but to every production awarded a four- or five-star review in *The Scotsman* that hasn't previously been produced in New York City. As such, some of the awarded productions may not also appear on the Fringe First list due to not meeting the eligibility criteria. The prize is an all-expenses-paid four-week run in an Off-Broadway theatre.

All plays are listed by name of play and playwright or devising company only, in something close to the order they were given. No central databank of Fringe Firsts exists prior to this one – all information has been drawn and matched from various online and offline sources, including archival copies of *The Scotsman*, so errors may have slipped in.

Allen Wright first reviewed at the Festival in 1957 and was the first arts editor of the Scotsman from 1964 until his retirement following a stroke in 1993. He died in November 1997 at the age of 65 and the 25th anniversary of the Fringe Firsts in 1998 was celebrated with the foundation of the Festival Fringe Society's **Allen Wright Award**, which honours the best Fringe arts journalist under the age of 27 who submits their work with a cash prize. It continues to this day and now awards prizes in two categories, Features and Reviews.

1973

Man of Sorrows by Enzo Toppano, Peggy Mortimer, Lorrae Desmond; Union Jack and Bonzo by Stanley Eveling; Pool Lunch Hour Theatre Club (jointly awarded to all theatre productions at the venue: Dreyfus on Devil's Island by Michael Almax, Bondi's Dream by John Hall, The Sash by Hector MacMillan and The Erik Satie Show by John Cumming and Roger Savage); Thunder by Richard Crane; Three Dances to Japanese Music by Jack Carter; Pilobolus Dance Theatre; Sarah Bernhardt by Stephanie Rich; Lovelies and Dowdies by Tadeusz Kantor; The Ecstasy of Rita Joe by George Ryga.

1974

The Quest by Richard Crane; Knox by W. Gordon Smith; Shylock by Roger Haynes and Paul Bentley; The Creation of the World and Other Business by Arthur Miller; Stallerhof by Franz Xaver Kroetz; The Archangel Michael by Georgi Markov; Hugh Miller by Colin MacLean and Reginald Barrett-Ayres; The Golden City by Hugo Clifford and Strathclyde Theatre Company; Schippel by C.P. Taylor; After Brecht by George Froscher and Freies Theater Munchen; Jazzart by Matt Mattox; Drumbuie/Faustus by John Abulafia; Edgar Allan's Late Night Horror by Robert Nye.

1975

Clownmaker by Richard Crane; Moon by Annie Stainer; Morecambe by Franz Xaver Kroetz; The Mutants by Yves Marc and Claire Heggen.

1976

Un Jour La Terre by Jean-Pierre Amiel; An Exotic in Edinburgh by John Irvine; The Contrast by Royall Tyler; The Wasting of Dunbar by Leonard Maguire; The Farndale Avenue Housing Estate Townswomens' Guild Dramatic Society's Production of Macbeth by David McGillivray and Walter Zerlin; Music to Murder By David Pownall; Woody Shavings and Sir Herbert MacRae by West Midlands Umbrella Group; Light Shining in Buckinghamshire by Caryl Churchill; Tapestries: A Travesty by Playback Theatre; Mockhero's Heron by Stuart Delves; The Dead Class by Tadeusz Kantor; Tea with Dick and Jerry by Bill Schoppert; The Third Arabian Night by Shared Experience; The Ballad of Solomon Pavey by Jeremy James Taylor and David Drew-Smythe.

1977

Writer's Cramp by John Byrne; Navigator in the Seventh Circle by Leonard Maguire; The Ancient Mariner by Annie Stainer and Emil Wolk; Richard III Part II by David Pownall; Recollections Between the Wars by Harry Stamper; Player King by Patrick Williams; Satan's Ball by Richard Crane; When Hair Was Long and Time Was Short by Billy Connolly; Bed of Roses by Mike Bradwell; A Respectable Family by Maxim Gorky; Walter by CP Taylor; Whistling at Milestones by Alex Glasgow; Private Dick by Richard Maher.

1978

The Robber Bridegroom and Miss Hamford Beauty Pageant and Battle of the Bands, both by Rio Hondo College; Henrysoun and the Plowdame by Leonard Maguire; Lunatic and Lover by Michael Meyer; Follies by Stephen Sondheim, staged by the University of Southern California; Traverse Theatre and Old Chaplaincy Centre 'for an outstanding programme of new work'; All Ayre and Fire by the Royal Lyceum Theatre Company; Privitus, Privitorum, Privet Hedge by Angie Farrow and Mobile 4 by Stephen Jeffreys, both National Student Theatre Company; Don Juan by ATC Paris, from the poem by Lord Byron; Lenny Bruce by Paul Bennett; Jellies, Jam and Jubilation by Ray Johnson; Black to Black by Greg Light.

1979

Pulse by Alem Mazgebe; Buried Child by Sam Shepard, staged by the University of

Southern California; **Seven Faces of Sinbad** by Triad Stage Alliance; **Creeps** by David Freeman; **Krassivy: The John Maclean Show** by Freddy Anderson; **The World of My America** by Paulene Myers; **An Evening with Rowan Atkinson** by Rowan Atkinson; **The Game** by Paul Pender; **Technicolour Dreams** by Chris Rohmann; **Heroes** by Doug Lucie; **The Widows of Clyth** by Donald Campbell; **Great Expectations** by Edward Argent and the Royal Scottish Academy of Music and Drama, from the novel by Charles Dickens; **Salford Road** by Stefan Rudnicki and Skyboat Road Company, based on poems by Gareth Owen; **Colour Radio** by Nigel Force; **Fun in Futility** by Bob Berky; **Heartache and Sorrow Theatre Company**; **Talk About It** by John Bett.

1980

Ya'acobi and Liedental by Hanoch Levin; **Lyrics of the Hearthside** by Joseph Mydell; **Guys Like Me and Bogie** by California State University; **The Roman Invasion of Ramsbottom** by Jeremy James Taylor and David Nield; **Vanity** by Richard Crane; **The Ice Chimney** by Barry Collins; **The Trial** by Andrew Visnevski, from the novel by Franz Kafka; **Chekhov on the Lawn** by Elihu Winer; **Captain Stirrick** by Jeremy James Taylor and David Scott, based on the ballads of Richard Brett; **Cambridge Mummers** 'for an outstanding programme of new work' (including work by Stephen Fry); **Running Around the Stage Like a Lunatic** by Walter Zerlin Jr; **NewsRevue 1980** by the Strode-Jackson company; **Play It Again, Tam** by Morag Fullerton; **Gru-Gru** by Henry Gruvman; **Somewhere Resting** by Wigan Young People's Theatre; **Summer Days** by Jack Carter (billed as the 100th Fringe First); **I Die For None of Them** by J.E. Cox; **The Rise and Fall of the Entire Human Race** by Steve Hanson; **Island Protected by a Bridge of Glass** and **The Pursuit of Pleasure**, both Garry Hynes for Druid Theatre Company.

1981

Bozzy by David McKail (as Frederic Mohr); **Heaven and Hell** by Dusty Hughes; **Herman** by Stewart Conn; **Slaying of the Dragon King** by John Strehlow; **Hot Burlesque** by David McNiven; **Twilight Zone** by Trevor Laird; **Of Arrows and Roses** by Touchstone Mime Theatre; **Night of the Jockstrap** by Richard and Laura Beaumont; **Treatment** by Jonathan Moore; **Superman on Ice** by Oxford Theatre Group; **Follies Berserk** by Three Women Mime Company (Peta Lily, Claudia Prietzel and Tessa Schneideman); **Maurice the Minotaur** by Gavin Pagan, Ian Johnston and Gerard Lohan of Edinburgh Youth Theatre; **The Decameron** by Justin Greene and Steve Cook; **Cramp** by John Godber; **In the Eye of the Sun** by John Clegg; William Burdett-Coutts and Roger Spence for the first year of **Assembly Rooms**; special award to **Alistair Moffat** 'for extending the frontiers of the Fringe'.

1982

Charan the Thief by Naya Theatre Company; **Raspberry** by Tony Marchant; **Bracknell Waste Products Company**; **Cults Academy Operatic Society**; **The Circuit** venue. (Note: there don't appear to have been many awards and/or details of them recorded in 1982. In particular, the Bracknell and Cults companies or what they presented are unknown.)

1983

Quilters by Molly Newman and Barbara Damashek, **The Fifty Minute Hour** by Jack Klaff, **Bread 'n' Butter and Guns** by Mike Elliston, **Third Class Carriage** by John Kendrick, **What a Way to Go** by W. Gordon Smith; **Circe** by Cambridge Mummers, based on the novel Ulysses by James Joyce; **Nastassia Filippovna** by Andrzej Wajda and Teatr Stary, based on the novel *The Idiot* by Fyodor Dostoyevsky; **Spoon River Anthology** by Edgar Lee Masters; **Vanity Fair** by Declan Donnellan and Nick Ormerod, adapted from the novel by William Makepeace Thackeray; **Pula and Imbaba** by Soyikwa African Theatre; **Die Hose** by Carl Sternheim, produced by the National Student Theatre Company; **Coda** by Jim Addison and David Ward; **Spike in the First World**

War by Jim Sheridan, based on the novel *Good Soldier Svejk* by Jaroslav Havek; **Odour of Chrysanthemums** and **The Metamorphosis** by Nick Ward, respectively adapted from the short story by David Herbert Lawrence and the novel by Franz Kafka.

1984

Up 'n' Under and **Bouncers** by John Godber; **Gertrude Stein and a Companion** by Win Wells; **The Odyssey** by Aberystwyth University Anaber Theatre Company; **Carmen: The Play** by Stephen Jeffreys, adapted from the opera by Georges Bizet; **Two-Way Mirror** by Arthur Miller, staged by Salford University Theatre Company; **To Marie With Love** by Pauline Devaney; **Precarious Living** by Amy Hardie; **Sikes and Nancy** by Cambridge Actors; **Talk of the Devil** by Tom Wright; **Charlie and Marie** by Peter Jukes; **In Nomine Patris** by Paul MacGee; **Amelia Lives** by Laura Shames; **Stonewater Rapture** by Doug Wright; **Styx** by Jim Addison and David Ward; **This Side of Paradise** by Cambridge Fringe Theatre, from the novel by F Scott Fitzgerald; a special award to the **Traverse Theatre** 'for its outstanding programme'.

1985

A Prayer for Wings by Sean Mathias; **Howard's Revenge** by Donald Campbell; **The Hunchback of Notre Dame** by Andrew Dallmeyer, based on the novel by Victor Hugo; **Losing Venice** by Jo Clifford; **Mr Carnegie's Lantern Lecture** by W. Gordon Smith; **Jack Spratt VC** by Jeremy James Taylor, David Scott and Peter Allwood; **Fire in the Lake** by Karim Alrawi; **The Puddok an' the Princess** by David Purves; **Auto-Da-Fe** by Theatr Osmego Dnia; **Beatrix and Sigmund** by Keith Sturgess; **A Day Down a Goldmine** by Bill Paterson and George Wylie; **Cupboard Man** by Ian McEwan; **Tryst** by Jim Addison and David Ward; **Present Continuous** by Sonja Lyndon; a special award to **Teatr Nowy** 'for its important contribution to the Edinburgh Festival Fringe'.

1986

Bopha! by Percy Mtwa; **The Great Hunger** by Tom MacIntyre; **Request Programme** by Franz Kroetz; **Comedy Without Title** by Federico Garcia Lorca, adapted by Yorick Theatre Company; **Between the Devil and the Deep Blue Sea** by Peter Granger-Taylor; **Whalers** by Michael Elder; **Quemadmodum, At Last** by East Lothian Youth Theatre; **Bodycount** by Les Smith; **Soldier, Soldier** by Richard Crane, adapted from the book by Tony Parker; **Playing for Time** by Arthur Miller, staged by Studio Theatre Productions; **SUNA: Zoo of the Desert** by Banyu-Inryoku Company; **The Dining Room** by A.R. Gurney; **Kathie and the Hippopotamus** by Mario Vargas Llosa; **Fanny Kemble at Home** by Laurier Lister; **Grave Plots** by David Kane; **Hooligans** by Jon Gaunt; **Fallen** by Polly Teale.

1987

Tattoo Theatre by Mladen Materic; **Hauptmann** by John Logan; **La Lavoir** by Dominique Durvin and Helene Prevost; **Have You Seen Zandile?** by Geina Mhlope, Thembi Mtshali and Maralin Vanrenen; **Chakravyuha** by Ratan Thiyam; **Mary Queen of Scots Got Her Head Chopped Off** by Liz Lochhead; **The Grapes of Wrath** by Peter Whitebrook and Duncan Low, from the novel by John Steinbeck; **Pushkin** by Richard Crane; **Nightmare Abbey** by Eleanor Zeal, adapted from the novella by Thomas Love Peacock; **Hours by the Window** by Margaret Douglas; **France to Fortheringhay** by Douglas Currie; **In the Image of the Beast** by Jonathan Holloway; **No Further Cause For Concern** by Rib Davis; **Trailing Clouds of Glory** by Jenny Fraser; **Company** by Katherine Worth, adapted from the novella by Samuel Beckett; **Tom McGrath**, a special award 'for enterprise in promoting new writing' with *Words Beyond Words*.

1988

Bag Lady by Frank McGuinness; **Hugh Miller** by Stewart Conn; **A Man with Connections** by Stephen Mulrine, translated from the novel by Alexander Gelmam; **Dom Juan** by

Mikhail Tumanishvili, adapted from Moliere; **Red Magic** by Richard Crane; **Salt of the Earth** by John Godber; **Blood Wedding** by Federico Garcia Lorca, translated by David Johnston; **The Tainted Honey of Homicidal Bees** by Eleanor Zeal; **Undertow** by Shimon Wincelberg; **P'tit Albert** by Jean-Marie Frin; **Woman of Hiroshima** by Chieko Kurihara; **Le Misanthrope** by Neil Bartlett, adapted from the play by Moliere; **Wendy Darling** by Peta Lily, adapted from Peter Pan by JM Barrie; **The Turn of the Screw** by Jon Pope, adapted from the novella by Henry James; **Gulliver's Travels** by Alan Leigh and Lords of Misrule, adapted from the book by Jonathan Swift. A special award was given to Teatro Arte Livre of Brazil for its show **Sideways Glance.**

1989

Heart and Bone by Stephen Greenhorn; **Frida and Diego** by Greg Cullen; **Hanging the President** by Michel Celeste; **The Lady and the Clarinet** by Michael Cristofer; **Poor Lisa** by Mark Rozovsky and Nikitsky Gate Theatre, from the book by Nikolay Karamzin; **Terminal** by James Mavor; **Red King Rising** by Grant Morrison; **Ecocide** by Sandy Walsh; **Mother of All the Behans** by Peter Sheridan, from the book by Brian Behan; **The Man Who Had Three Arms** by Edward Albee; **The Ugly Noo Noo** by Andrew Buckland; **Falling for a Dolphin** by Heathcote Williams; **Lucky People** by Bim Mason; **Rolling Stone** by Richard Crane; **Consider the Lilies** by Harriet Smyth, from the novel by Iain Crichton Smith; **E5, 6B** by CragRats Theatre in Education Company; **When Five Years Pass** by Federico Garcia Lorca, translated by Gwynne Edwards; **Beyond the Rainbow** by John Binnie; **How to Kill** by Angus Reid; **Water of Life** by Chris Balance.

1990

The Boys Next Door by Tom Griffin; **Waiting for Sir Larry** by Greg Crutwell; **Tverboul** by Alexei Paperny; **The Wake** by Paul O'Hanrahan, based on *Finnegan's Wake* by James Joyce; **Curl Up and Dye** by Susan Pam-Grant with Michael's Company and Market Theatre; **Dads in Bondage** by Robert More with music by Tom Doyle; **Gary** by Roy Winston; **Glad** by Jeremy Weller; **Lament for Arthur Cleary** by Dermot Bolger; **Maria Malibran: Bright Star in a Dark Sky** by Sally Bradshaw and Ian Jessup; **Theatre for Africa** of South Africa and **Meridian Theatre** of Zimbabwe for a joint programme of five plays at Springwell House in Gorgie; **Can't Stand Up for Falling Down** by Richard Cameron; **Hour of the Lynx** by Per Olav Enquist, translated by Kim Damback; **Olsnienie** by Janusz Wisniewski and Teatr Nowy, based on *The Story of a Horse* by Tolstoy; **Here to Be There** by Aleksandr Vvedensky and Daniil Kharms, performed by the Lithuania Conservatoire. A special award was made to **Michael Westcott** 'on his retiral as vice-chairman of the Fringe Society. He has held the post for 16 years and been a staunch supporter of the Fringe First award scheme'. *An award was also made in the first week to* The Guise *by David Mowat, although it was later publicly withdrawn due to the show having more than six previews in Britain prior to the Fringe.*

1991

Booth by David Beeler; **Plaisir d'Amour**; **Are There Tigers in the Congo?** by Bengt Ahlfors and Johan Bargum; **The Canterbury Tales** by Nottinghamshire Education, from the stories by Geoffrey Chaucer; **Carlucco and the Queen of Hearts** by George Rosie; **Bad** by Jeremy Weller; **Stabat Mater** by Laboratorio Teatro Settimo; **Shelter** by Tmu-Na Theatre; **The Magic Toyshop** by Mick Yates, adapted from Angela Carter; **Boardroom Shuffle** by Greg Ward; **Autogeddon** by Heathcote Williams; **Kvetch** by Steven Berkoff; **Theatre for Africa** 'for their programme of new work at the Netherbow'; **A Stop in the Desert** by Krzysztof Borowiec, **Aesop** by Charles Causley and Stephen McNeff.

1992

Mad by Jeremy Weller; **Cyrano de Bergerac** by Edwin Morgan, adapted from the play by Edmond Rostand; **Studs** by Paul Mercier; **Eclipsed** by Patricia Burke Brogan; **Sex III**

by Emily Woof, **Exile** by David Ian Neville; **Stalinland** by David Greig; **Grimm: The Telling of the Tales** by Toby Gough; **The Dig** by Carran Waterfield; **The House of Doors** by Attraction Theatre Company; **Richard Demarco Gallery's Polish programme,** especially *From Heaven Through the World of Hell* by Provisorium and *The Loneliness of Faun* by Polska Teatr Balet; **No Mean Fighter** by Willy Maley, Barlinnie Special Unit and the Royal Scottish Academy of Music and Drama; **A Wilderness of Monkeys** and **Every Inch a King,** both by John Cargill Thompson; **Believer** by Angus Reid; **Tearsheets: Letters I Didn't Send Home** by Joan Hotchkis.

1993

The Tender Mercies by Sladjana Vujovic; **Our Brutus** by David Beeler; **Accustomed to Her Face** by John Binnie; **Tonight I'm Entertaining Richard Gere** by Cecilia Delatori; **Port and Lemon** by John Cargill Thompson; **Storybook** by Richard Davidson; **The Truman Capote Talk Show** by Bob Kingdom; **Bloodstream** by Andrew Buckland; **Dead Fish** by Gordon Steel; **One Moment** by Jeremy Weller; **The Admiral Jones** by Frederic Mohr; **Roll-a-Pea** by Tadeusz Slobodzianek; **The Woman on a Tree on a Hill** by Ovidia Yu; **The Audition** by AL Kennedy; **Klytemnestra's Bairns** by Bill Dunlop, based on *The Oresteia* by Aeschylus; **The Legend of St Julian** by Michael Nardone.

1994

When the Cradle Falls by Lucy Thompson and Paul James; **Nancy Sleekit** by Donald Campbell, adapted from the poems of James Smith; **Killer Joe** by Tracey Letts; **Spell in the Well** by Joseph Hart; **Linnaeus: Prince of Flowers** by Toby Gough; **Off Out** by Gill Adams; **Merlin** by Piotr Tomaschuk and Teatr Wierszalin; **Mirjam** by Mariela Stefanski; **An English Education** and **Guerrilla** by John Cargill Thompson; **Jack** by Aspect Touring Company; **The Pierglass** by Tim Norton; **Pendragon** by Peter Allwood, Frank Whately, Joanna Horton and Jeremy James Taylor; **Mary Stuart** by Denise Stoklos; **Noc/Night** by Zygmunt Duczynski.

1995

The Holy Ground by Dermot Bolger; **Hey Joe** by Leicester Youth Dance and Sue Rosenbloom; **Don't Start Me** by Ford Kiernan and John Paul Leach; **Ningali** by Ningali Josie Lawford, Robyn Archer and Angela Chaplin; **Soup** by Michael Mears; **20/52** by Jeremy Weller; **Peasouper** by Tim Hibberd; **Romeo et Juliette** by Nada Theatre, after William Shakespeare; **Feedback** by Andrew Buckland; **Road Movie** by Godfrey Hamilton and Mark Pinkosh; **Carmen Funebre** by Teatr Biuro Podrozy; **Jekyll** by John More and Alex Went; **Saucy Jack and the Space Vixens** by Charlotte Man; **Glasgow Hard Tickets** by Kathleen Ruddy; **Some People** by Danny Hoch. An honorary award was also made to **Emilio Coia** for 40 years of Festival illustrations in *The Scotsman.*

1996

Martin and John by Sean O'Neil, adapted from the novel by Dale Peck; **Parallel Lines** by Theatre Cryptic, based on the novel *Ulysses* by James Joyce; **The Fever** by Wallace Shawn; **Dubliners** by Edinburgh University Theatre Company, adapted from the novel by James Joyce; **The Woman Who Thought She Was a Dog** by Nick Joseph; **Trance** by David Hauptschein; **Plant Hunter** by Toby Gough; **Catalpa** by Donal O'Kelly; **The Last Supper of Dr Faustus** by Anita Sullivan, based on the play by Christopher Marlowe; **Where Ravens Rule: A Theatrical Response to the War in Bosnia** by Joan Evans and Lafayette Workshop; **Here Lies Henry** by Daniel McIvor and Daniel Brooks; **Behind the Aquarium at the Last Pizza Show** by Jonathan Hall; **See Base of Can** by Andy MacLean; **Guardians of Eden** by Nicholas Ellenbogen; **My Life with Kenneth Williams** by David Benson; **Sabina** by Chris Dolan; **The Land of Ham** by Josh Norman; **Viper's Opium** by Godfrey Hamilton. A special award was made to **Ian Brown**, artistic director of the Traverse Theatre between 1988 and 1996.

1997

Anna Weiss by Mike Cullen; **Dr Felix** by Piotr Tomaszuk, translated by Barry Keane; **Life's a Gatecrash** by Terry Hughes; **Elephant Wake** by Joey Tremblay and Jonathan Christenson; **Hellcab** by Will Kern; **Fool House** by Joff Chafer and Toby Wilsher; **Jump to Cow Heaven** by Gill Adams; **Talking to the Wall** by Mannix Flynn; **The Story of the Fallen Hero** by Guandaline Sagliocco; **Russian Anguish** by Yuri Pogrebnichko and Krasnaya Presnya; **Dusty Fruit** by Tom Hibberd; **Blue Heart** by Caryl Churchill; **Diriamba!** by Robert Rae and Nixtayoleros; **After Penny** by Richard Bickley.

1998

Gargantua by Grid Iron Theatre Company; **The Last Obit** by Peter Tinniswood; **OJ/Othello** by Maarten van Hinte; **Moscow** by Nick Salamone and Maury R. MacIntyre; **The Water Carriers** by Theatre Talipot; **Hatches, Matches and Dispatches** by Alan Cochrane; **Kill the Old, Torture Their Young** by David Harrower; **A Little Requiem for Kantor** by Zofia Kalinska; **Soldiers** by Jeremy Weller; **Perfect Days** by Liz Lochhead; **Romantic Friction** by Michelle Read; **Once** by Anton Adassinski and Derevo; **Amsterdam Parade** by Terts Brinkhoff and De Parade; **Death in New Orleans** by John Murrell; **Skin Tight** by Gary Henderson.

1999

Nixon's Nixon by Russell Lees, **Fantasia** by Victor Kramer; **Anonymous Society** by Andrew Wale and Perrin Allen, based on the music of Jacques Brel; **Car** by Chris O'Connell; **The House of Pootsie Plunkett** by Joey Tremblay and Jonathan Christenson; **Hopeless Games** by DO-Theatre and fabrik Potsdam; **Lyrebird: Tales of Helpmann** by Tyler Coppin; **Krishnan's Diary** by Jacob Rajan; **Riddance** by Linda MacLean; **Dream State** by Theatre Works, based on the original Polygon anthology; **Messengers** by Robin Wilson; **Wreck the Airline Barrier** by Adriano Shaplin; **The Man Who Committed Thought** by Patrice Naiambana with Ian Leonard; **William Shakespeare's Othello: A Play in Black and White** by Royston Abel; **Dehydrated and Travellin' Light** by Sean Hughes and Owen O'Neill; **Danny's Wake** by Jim Sweeney; **Sweet As You Are** by Jonathan Hall.

2000

The King of Scotland by Iain Heggie; **Further Than the Furthest Thing** by Zinnie Harris; **Soho** by Rebecca Lenkiewicz; **Achilles** by Elizabeth Cook; **The Gimmick** by Dael Orlandersmith; **Splendour** by Abi Morgan; **The Bogus Woman** by Kate Adshead; **Woman in Waiting** by Thembi Mtshali; **Messiah** by Steven Berkoff; **Too Much Light Makes the Baby Go Blind** by Neo-Futurist Theatre Company, from a format by Greg Allen; **Decky Does a Bronco** by Douglas Maxwell; **Chagal Chagal** by Vladimir Drazdow; **White Men with Weapons** by Greig Coetzee; **Vomit and Roses / Wolverine Dreams** by Brian Parks; **Static** by Chris Thorpe; **No 2** by Toa Fraser; **Bertrand's Toys** by blackSKYwhite Theatre Company.

2001

Wiping My Mother's Arse by Iain Heggie; **Ferdydurke** by Allen Kuharski, based on the novel by Witold Gombrowicz; **Gagarin Way** by Gregory Burke; **Like Thunder** by Niels Fredrik Dahl, translated by Steven T. Murray; **Runt** by Michael Philip Edwards; **Bedbound** by Enda Walsh; **Neutrino** by Unlimited Theatre with Chris Goode; **Man in the Flying Lawnchair** by 78th Street Theatre; **Raw** by Chris O'Connell; **Jesus Hopped the A Train** by Stephen Adly Guirgis; **Moving Objects** by David Mark Thomson; **School for Fools** by Andrey Moguchy, from the novel by Alexandr Sokolov; **Do Teatr** by Evgeny Kozlov and Alexandr Bondarev; **Cracked** by Skye Loneragan; **Mental** by Lynn Ferguson and Stephen Powell; **Midden** by Morna Regan. Best of the Fringe Firsts: *Gagarin Way*.

2002

Outlying Islands by David Greig; The Laramie Project by Moises Kaufman; Silent Engine by Julian Garner; The Drowned World by Gary Owen; La Divina Commedia by Derevo; Horse Country by CJ Hopkins; 100 by Neil Monaghan; Mousson (Monsoon) by Au Cul du Loup; The Al-Hamlet Summit by Sulayman Al-Bassam, after William Shakespeare; Kiss of Life by Chris Goode; Victory at the Dirt Palace by Adriano Shaplin; Hyperlynx by John McGrath; Cincinnati by Don Nigro; Fallen by Jess Curtis; Double Trouble by Yvette Boszik; Who's Harry? by Henry Fleet; Black to My Roots by Kathya Alexander. Best of the Fringe Firsts: *Horse Country*.

2003

Pandora 88 by fabrik Potsdam; Boy Steals Train by 78th Street Theatre; Pugilist Specialist by Adriano Shaplin; The People Next Door by Henry Adam; Those Eyes, That Mouth by Ben Harrison and Grid Iron Theatre Company; Love, Sex and Cider by Paul Charlton; Thebans by Liz Lochhead; White Cabin by Akhe Theatre; Ladies and Gents by Paul Walker; A Very Naughty Boy by Adrian Poynton; NE 2nd Avenue by Teo Castellanos; The Pickle King by Jacob Rajan and Justin Lewis; Baby Jane: People Show 113 by The People Show; The Birds of Sarajevo by Harris Burina; The Echo Chamber by Oliver Birch. Best of the Fringe Firsts: *Pugilist Specialist*.

2004

Fatboy by John Clancy; Dias de la Noches by Teatr Novogo Fronta; Bombshells by Joanna Murray-Smith; Bang, You're Dead by William Mastrosimone; How to Act Around Cops by Logan Brown and Matthew Benjamin; Take Me Away by Gerard Murphy; The Pull of Negative Gravity by Jonathan Lichtenstein; Chronicles: A Lamentation by Teatr Piesn Kozla; Gone by Glyn Cannon, adapted from Sophocles' *Antigone*; The Ignatius Trail by Oliver Birch; Manchester Girl by Sue Turner-Cray; Thom Pain (Based on Nothing) by Will Eno; Rosebud: The Lives of Orson Welles by Mark Jenkins; Peacefire by Macdara Vallely; Rumble by Renegade Theatre; The Jammer by Rolin Jones; Works of Temporary Solace by Highway Diner; Raw Beef by Al Seed. Carol Tambor Best of Edinburgh Award: *Sisters, Such Devoted Sisters* by Russell Barr and *Rosebud: The Lives of Orson Welles* by Mark Jenkins.

2005

Switch Triptych by Adriano Shaplin; East Coast Chicken Supper by Martin J. Taylor; Children of the Sea by Toby Gough; The Devil's Larder by Ben Harrison, adapted from the novel by Jim Crace; Give Up! Start Over! (In the Darkest of Times I Look to Richard Nixon for Hope) by The TEAM; Stories for the Wobbly Hearted by Daniel Kitson; The Exonerated by Erik Jensen and Jessica Blank; Guardians by Peter Morris; Breakfast at Audrey's by John Binnie; Basic Training by Kahlil Ashanti; Broken Road by Ryan Craig; Screwmachine/Eyecandy by CJ Hopkins; Trad by Mark Doherty; Chamber Made by David Bolger and Katie Read; The Girls of the 3.5 Floppies by Luis Enrique Gutirrez Ortiz Monasterio. Carol Tambor Best of Edinburgh Award: *Absence and Presence* by Andrew Dawson.

2006

The Adventures of Tom Thumb by Finn Caldwell, Eliza Wills-Crisp and Elena Riu (Blue Scream Theatre); Food by Joel Horwood and Christopher Heimann; (I Am) Nobody's Lunch by Steve Cosson; The Receipt by Will Adamsdale and Chris Branch; Black Watch by Gregory Burke; Particularly in the Heartland by the TEAM; Sclavi: The Song of an Emigrant by Farm in the Cave; Tom Crean: Antarctic Explorer by Aidan Dooley; Finer Noble Gases by Adam Rapp; Clean Alternatives by Brian Dykstra; What I Heard About Iraq by Simon Levy, from an article by Elliot Weinberger; C-90 by Daniel Kitson; The Pool by James Brough and Helen Elizabeth; Knots by Coisceam Dance; Goodness by Michael Redhill; **Johnny Boskak is Feeling Funny** by Greig Koetzee; **Meeting Joe Strummer** by Paul Hodson. Carol Tambor Best of Edinburgh Award: *Goodness* by Michael Redhill.

2007

Damascus by David Greig; **Truth in Translation** by Michael Lessac; **The Walworth Farce** by Enda Walsh; **England** by Tim Crouch; **Scarborough** by Fiona Evans; **The Container** by Clare Bayley; **Between the Devil and the Deep Blue Sea** by Suzanne Andrade; **Ravenhill for Breakfast** by Mark Ravenhill; **Hangman** by DO-Theatre; **Popsicle Departure 1989** by Madi Distefano; **The Smile Off Your Face** by Ontroerend Goed; **Emergence-See!** by Daniel Beaty; **Wish I Had a Sylvia Plath** by Edward Anthony; **Hugh Hughes in... Story of a Rabbit** by Shôn Dale-Jones; **Subway** by Vanishing Point; **Mile End** by Analogue. Carol Tambor Best of Edinburgh Award: *Between the Devil and the Deep Blue Sea* by Suzanne Andrade and 1927.

2008

The New Electric Ballroom by Enda Walsh; **Deep Cut** by Philip Ralph; **Architecting** by the TEAM; **Stefan Golaszewski Speaks About a Girl He Once Loved** by Stefan Golaszewski; **The Tailor of Inverness** by Matthew Zajac; **66a Church Road** by Daniel Kitson; **Terminus** by Mark O'Rowe; **The Caravan** by Look Left Look Right; **Itsoseng** by Omphile Molusi; **Paperweight** by Tom Frankland and Sebastien Lawson; **Motherland** by Steve Gilroy; **Eight** by Ella Hickson; **In a Thousand Pieces** by Jemma McDonnell, Elle Moreton, Kylie Walsh; **Crocosmia** by Little Bulb Theatre; **In Conflict** by Douglas C. Wager, based on the book by Yvonne Latty; **Once and For All We're Gonna Tell You Who We Are So Shut Up and Listen** by Ontroerend Goed; **Slick** by Jamie Harrison and Candice Edmunds (Vox Motus); **The Idiot Colony** by Lisle Turner and RedCape Theatre. Carol Tambor Best of Edinburgh Award: *Eight* by Ella Hickson.

2009

Orphans by Dennis Kelly; **East 10th Street: Self Portrait with Empty House** by Edgar Oliver; **Internal** by Ontroerend Goed; **Crush** by Paul Charlton; **The Event** by John Clancy; **The Unravelling** by Fin Kennedy; **Found** by Curious Seed; **The Rap Guide to Evolution** by Baba Brinkman; **The World is Too Much: Theatre for Breakfast** by Simon Stephens, David Greig, Enda Walsh, Rona Munro, Chris Hannan and Zinnie Harris; **The Interminable Suicide of Gregory Church** by Daniel Kitson; **The Hotel** by Mark Watson; **Morecambe** by Tim Whitnall; **Barflies** by Charles Bukowski, adapted by Ben Harrison; **A Life in Three Acts** by Mark Ravenhill and Bette Bourne; **The 14th Tale** by Inua Ellams; **White Tea** by David Leddy; **Party** by Tom Basden. Carol Tambor Best of Edinburgh Award: *Little Gem* by Elaine Murphy.

2010

Beautiful Burnout by Bryony Lavery; **Speechless** by Linda Brogan and Polly Teale; **Bare** by Renny Krupinski; **White** by Andy Manley and Ian Cameron; **Real Babies Don't Cry** by Stewart Permutt; **My Romantic History** by DC Jackson; **Lockerbie: Unfinished Business** by David Benson; **It's Always Right Now, Until It's Later** by Daniel Kitson; **Penelope** by Enda Walsh; **Roadkill** by Stef Smith; **Bound** by Jess Briton; **Running On Air** by Laura Mugridge; **Do We Look Like Refugees?** by Alecky Blythe; **Primadoona** by Doon Mackichan; **Flesh and Blood and Fish and Fowl** by Geoff Sobelle and Charlotte Ford; **Lidless** by Frances Ya-Chu Cowhig; **Bunny** by Jack Thorne; **Another Someone** by Abbi Greenland, Helen Goalen, Becky Wilkie and Marc Graham (RashDash). Carol Tambor Best of Edinburgh Award: *Ovid's Metamorphoses* by Pants on Fire.

2011

Silent by Pat Kinevane; **Somewhere Beneath It All, A Small Fire Still Burns** by Dave Florez; **2401 Objects** by Hannah Barker, Lewis Hetherington, Liam Jarvis and

Analogue; **The Table** by Blind Summit Theatre; **Mission Drift** by The TEAM; **The Wheel** by Zinnie Harris; **Futureproof** by Lynda Radley; **Allotment** by Jules Horne; **An Instinct for Kindness** by Chris Larner; **The Oh F**k Moment** by Chris Thorpe and Hannah Jane Walker; **Release** by Icon Theatre; **Scary Gorgeous** by Abbi Greenland and Helen Goalen (RashDash); **Tuesday at Tescos** by Simon Callow; **Ten Plagues** by Mark Ravenhill and Conor Mitchell; **Your Last Breath** by Curious Directive; **Leo** by Circle of Eleven; **Mad About the Boy** by Gbolahan Obisesan; **Minute After Midday** by Ross Dungan; **A Reply to Kathy Acker: Minsk 2011** by Belarus Free Theatre, adapted by Vladmir Shcherban; **You Once Said Yes** by Morgan Lloyd Malcolm and Katie Lyons. Carol Tambor Best of Edinburgh Award: *Leo* by Circle of Eleven.

2012

Bravo Figaro! by Mark Thomas; **Juana in a Million** by Vicky Araico Casas; **Continuous Growth** by Catherine Grosvenor; **All That is Wrong** by Ontroerend Goed; **Why Do You Stand There in the Rain?** by Peter Arnott; **Educating Ronnie** by Joe Douglas; **Mies Julie** by Yaël Farber, adapted from August Strindberg; **Dirty Great Love Story** by Katie Bonna and Richard Marsh; **The List** by Jennifer Tremblay; **As of 1.52 GMT on Friday April 27 2012, This Show Has No Title** by Daniel Kitson; **Theatre Uncut** by Neil Labute, Lena Kitsopoulou, Anders Lustgarten, Kieran Hurley, Marco Canale, Hayley Squires, David Greig, Clara Brennan, Mohammad Al Attar, Andri Snaer Magnason, Stef Smith; **Monkey Bars** by Chris Goode; **The Shit/La Merda** by Cristian Ceresoli; **Flaneurs** by Jenna Watt; **Songs of Lear** by Song of the Goat; **The Wheelchair On My Face** by Sonya Kelly; **Thread** by Jules Horne; **Rainbow** by Emily Jenkins. Carol Tambor Best of Edinburgh Award: *Mies Julie* by Yaël Farber and *Midsummer* by David Greig.

2013

The Events by David Greig; **Ciara** by David Harrower; **Grounded** by George Brant; **Quietly** by Owen McCafferty; **Feral** by Tortoise in a Nutshell; **Nirbhaya** by Yaël Farber; **Kiss Me, Honey, Honey!** by Philip Meeks; **Brace – Fionnuala** by Donal O'Kelly; **Fleabag** by Phoebe Waller-Bridge; **Dark Vanilla Jungle** by Philip Ridley; **Theatre Uncut** by Neil Labute, the TEAM, Davey Anderson, Clara Brennan, Tanika Gupta, Theatre Ad Infinitum, AJ Taudevin, Rob Drummond, Tim Price, Mark Thomas, Kieran Hurley, Lewis Hetherington; **These Halcyon Days** by Deirdre Kinahan; **Dumbstruck** by Fine Chisel Theatre Company; **Water Stain** by Armazem Theatre Company; **For Their Own Good** by Arzhang Pezhman; **Gardening for the Unfulfilled and Alienated** by Brad Birch; **Credible Likeable Superstar Rolemodel** by Bryony Kimmings; **Choose Your Own Documentary** by Nathan Penlington; **Mercy Killers** by Michael Milligan; **Freeze!** by Nick Steur. Carol Tambor Best of Edinburgh Award: *The Events* by David Greig.

2014

Cuckooed by Mark Thomas; **Confirmation** by Chris Thorpe; **Men in the Cities** by Chris Goode; **Chef** by Sabrina Mahfouz; **The Collector** by Henry Naylor; **Spoiling** by John McCann; **The Carousel** by Jennifer Tremblay; **The Day Sam Died** by Armazem Theatre Company; **The Initiate** by Alexandra Wood; **Lippy** by Bush Moukarzel with Mark O'Halloran; **The Object Lesson** by Geoff Sobelle; **Pioneer** by Curious Directive; **Sanitise** by Melanie Jordan and Caitlin Skinner; **Handmade in China: Moons, Migrations and Messages** by Dumpling Dreams Theatre and Migration Project; **Letters Home** by Chimamanda Ngozi Adiche, Kei Miller, Christos Tsiolkos and Kamila Shamsie; **No Guts, No Heart, No Glory** by Common Wealth; **Pondling** by Genevieve Hulme-Beaman; **Spine** by Clara Brennan; **Travesti** by Rebecca Hill. Carol Tambor Best of Edinburgh Award: *Object Lesson* by Geoff Sobelle.

2015

The Christians by Lucas Hnath; **A Gambler's Guide to Dying** by Gary McNair; **Going**

Viral by Daniel Bye; **The History of the World Through Banalities** by Johan De Smet; **The Deliverance** by Jennifer Tremblay; **Swallow** by Stef Smith; **Underneath** by Pat Kinevane; **Citizen Puppet** by Mark Down; **The Great Downhill Journey of Little Tommy** by Jonas Vermeulen and Boris Vanseveren; **Labels** by Joe Sellman-Leava; **Light Boxes** by Grid Iron Theatre Company, from the novel by Shane Jones; **Raz** by Jim Cartwright; **Tar Baby** by Desiree Burch; **Trans Scripts** by Paul Lucas; **A Girl is a Half-Formed Thing** by Annie Ryan, from the novel by Eimear McBride; **Our Ladies of Perpetual Succour** by Lee Hall, from the novel *The Sopranos* by Alan Warner; **Penny Arcade: Longing Lasts Longer** by Penny Arcade; **A Reason to Talk** by Sachli Gholamalizad; **What I Learned From Johnny Bevan** by Luke Wright. Carol Tambor Best of Edinburgh Award: *Key Change* by Katrina McHugh.

2016

Counting Sheep: A Guerrilla Folk Opera by Mark and Marichka Marczyk; **The Interference** by Lynda Radley; **Expensive Shit** by Adura Onashile; **Angels** by Henry Naylor; **World Without Us** by Ontroerend Goed; **Heads Up** by Kieran Hurley; **Two Man Show** by Abbi Greenland and Helen Goalen (RashDash); **Us/Them** by Carly Wijs; **Tank** by Breach Theatre; **Fabric** by Abi Zakarian; **The Red Shed** by Mark Thomas; **Daffodils** by Rochelle Bright; **One Hundred Homes** by Yinka Kuitenbrouwer; **Letters to Windsor House** by Sh!t Theatre; **Joan** by Lucy Jane Parkinson; **Growth** by Luke Norris; **The Duke** by Shon Dale Jones; **Scorch** by Stacey Gregg. Carol Tambor Best of Edinburgh Award: *Life According to Saki* by Katherine Rundell.

2017

Nassim by Nassim Soleimanpour; **Flesh and Bone** by Elliot Warren; **Letters to Morrissey** by Gary McNair; **Enterprise** by Brian Parks; **The Believers are but Brothers** by Javaad Alipoor; **Adam** by Frances Poet; **Woke** by Apphia Campbell; **The Shape of the Pain** by Rachel Bagshaw and Chris Thorpe; **A Super Happy Story (About Being Sad)** by Jon Brittain; **How to Act** by Graham Eatough; **Borders** by Henry Naylor; **£ ¥ €$ (Lies)** by Ontroerend Goed; **Education Education Education** by the Wardrobe Ensemble; **Fag/Stag** by Chris Isaacs and Jeffrey Jay Hunt; **Foreign Radical** by Theatre Conspiracy; **(More) Moira Monologues** by Alan Bissett; **Old Stock: A Refugee Love Story** by Hannah Moscovitch; **Stand By** by Adam McNamara. Carol Tambor Best of Edinburgh Award: *The Flying Lovers of Vitebsk* by Kneehigh and *Borders* by Henry Naylor.

2018

Angry Alan by Penelope Skinner; **The Basement Tapes** by Stella Reid, Jane Yonge, Thomas Lambert and Oliver Morse; **Class** by Iseult Golden and David Horan; **First Snow / Premiere Neige** by Davey Anderson, Philippe Ducros and Linda McLean; **Status** by Chris Thorpe; **Ulster American** by David Ireland; **What Girls Are Made Of** by Cora Bissett; **Dressed** by Josie Dale-Jones, Lydia Higginson, Nobahar Mahdavi and Olivia Norris; **DUPed** by John McCann; **Check Up: Our NHS at 70** by Mark Thomas; **My Left/Right Foot: The Musical** by Robert Softley Gale; **On the Exhale** by Martin Zimmerman; **Square Go** by Kieran Hurley and Gary McNair; **Underground Railroad Game** by Jennifer Kidwell and Scott R. Sheppard; **Archive of Educated Hearts** by Casey Jay Andrews; **It's True It's True It's True** by Breach Theatre; **Power Play: Funeral Flowers** by Emma Dennis-Edwards; **Trojan Horse** by Helen Monks and Matt Woodhead; **Unsung** by Valentijn Dhaenens Skagen; **Valerie** by Robin Kelly, Cherie Moore and Tom Broome. Carol Tambor Best of Edinburgh Award: *Ulster American* by David Ireland.

2019

Arthur by Daniel Bye; **Enough** by Stef Smith; **How Not to Drown** by Nicola McCartney and Dritan Kastrati; **Mustard** by Eva O'Connor; **Raven** by Still Hungry Collective;

Rich Kids: A History of Shopping Malls in Tehran by Javaad Alipoor; **Are We Not Drawn Onward to New Era** by Ontroerend Goed; **Bobby & Amy** by Emily Jenkins; **Everything I See I Swallow** by Mary Taylor and Tamsin Shasha; **Lipsync** by Kirsty Young with Jenna Watt; **The Patient Gloria** by Gina Moxley; **Sh!t Theatre Drink Rum with Expats** by Sh!t Theatre; **Subject Matter** by Nadia Cavelle; **The Afflicted** by Jake Jeppson and Groupwork; **Baby Reindeer** by Richard Gadd; **The Desk** by Reetta Honkakoski Company; **Dispatches on the Red Dress** by Rowan Rheingans; **E8** by Marika Mckennell. Carol Tambor Best of Edinburgh Award: *Mouthpiece* by Kieran Hurley.

2020

No awards.

2021

No awards.

Bibliography

Bannister, Winifred, *James Bridie and his Theatre*, Rockliff, 1955

Bartie, Angela, *The Edinburgh Festivals: Culture and Society in Post-war Britain*, Edinburgh University Press, 2014

Bassett, Kate, *In Two Minds: A Biography of Jonathan Miller*, Oberon, 2014 (first published 2012)

Bean, JP, *Singing from the Floor: A History of British Folk Clubs*, Faber & Faber, 2014

Bell, Eleanor and Gunn, Linda (eds.), *The Scottish Sixties: Reading, Rebellion, Revolution?*, Rodopi, 2013

Bennett, Alan, Cook, Peter, Miller, Jonathan and Moore, Dudley, *The Complete Beyond the Fringe*, Methuen, 2003 (previously published 1963, 1987)

Bennett, Alan, *Writing Home*, Faber and Faber, 2006 (first published 1994)

Bennett, Alan, *Untold Stories*, Faber and Faber, 2006 (first published 2005)

Bergan, Ronald, *Beyond the Fringe... and Beyond: A Critical Biography of Alan Bennett, Peter Cook, Jonathan Miller and Dudley Moore*, Virgin, 1989

Billington, Michael, *Stoppard the Playwright*, Methuen, 1987

Bing, Rudolf, *5000 Nights at the Opera*, Hamish Hamilton, 1972

Bing, Rudolf, *A Knight at the Opera*, G.P. Putnam's Sons, 1981

Birrell, Ross and Finlay, Alec (eds.), *Justified Sinners: An Archaeology of Scottish Counter-Culture 1960–2000*, Pocketbooks, 2002

Bort, Eberhard (ed.), *Borne on the Carrying Stream: The Legacy of Hamish Henderson*, Grace Note Publications, 2010

Bort, Eberhard (ed.), *'Tis Sixty Years Since: The 1951 Edinburgh People's Festival Ceilidh and the Scottish Folk Revival*, Grace Note Publications, 2011

Bort, Eberhard (ed.), *At Hame wi' Freedom: Essays on Hamish Henderson and the Scottish Folk Revival*, Grace Note Publications, 2012

Bort, Eberhard (ed.), *Anent Hamish Henderson: Essays, Poems, Interviews*, Grace Note Publications, 2015

Boyle, Frankie, *My Shit Life So Far*, Harper Collins, 2010

Brown, Ian, *Journey's Beginning: The Gateway Theatre Building and Company 1884-1965*, Intellect, 2004

Bruce, George, *Festival in the North*, Robert Hale, 1975

Burke, Gregory, *The National Theatre of Scotland's Black Watch*, Faber and Faber, 2007

Calder, Jenni, *Essence of Edinburgh: An Eccentric Odyssey*, Luath Press, 2018

Calder, John, *Pursuit: The Memoirs*, Alma Books, 2016 (first published 2001)

Callow, Simon, *My Life in Pieces: An Alternative Autobiography*, Nick Hern Books, 2010

Campbell, Donald, *Playing for Scotland: A History of the Scottish Stage 1715-1965*, Mercat Press, 1996

Campbell, Donald, *Edinburgh: A Cultural and Literary History*, Signal Books, 2003

Carpenter, Humphrey, *OUDS: A Centenary History of the Oxford University Dramatic Society 1885-1985*, Oxford University Press, 1985

Carpenter, Humphrey, *A Great Silly Grin: The British Satire Boom of the 1960s*, Da Capo Press, 2003 (first published as *That Was the Satire That Was*, 2000)

Chambers, Colin, *The Story of Unity Theatre*, Lawrence and Wishart, 1989

Clary, Julian, *A Young Man's Passage*, Ebury Press, 2006 (first published 2005)

Clary, Julian, *The Lick of Love: How Dogs Changed My Life*, Quercus, 2021

Cleese, John, *So, Anyway...*, Random House, 2014

Connolly, Billy with Gittins, Ian, *Made in Scotland: My Grand Adventures in a Wee*

Country, BBC Books, 2018

Connor, John, *Comics: A Decade of Comedy at the Assembly Rooms*, Papermac, 1990

Coogan, Steve, *Easily Distracted: My Autobiography*, Arrow, 2015

Cook, Peter and Cook, William (ed.), *Tragically I Was an Only Twin: The Comedy of Peter Cook*, Arrow, 2003

Cook, William, *Ha Bloody Ha: Comedians Talking*, 4th Estate, 1994

Crawford, Iain, *Banquo on Thursdays: The Inside Story of 50 Years of the Edinburgh Festival*, Goblinshead, 1997

Daiches, David (ed.), *Edinburgh: A Traveller's Reader*, Robinson, 2004 (first published 1986)

Dale, Michael, *Sore Throats and Overdrafts: An Illustrated Story of the Edinburgh Festival Fringe*, President Publications, 1988

Demarco, Richard, *A Life in Pictures*, Northern Books, 1995

Demarco, Richard and others, *The Demarco Collection and Archive: An Introduction*, The Demarco Archive Trust Limited and Lodz-Edinburgh Foundation, 2009

Demarco, Richard, *The Road to Meikle Seggie*, Luath Press, 2015 (first published 1978)

Demarco, Richard, *A Unique Partnership: Richard DeMarco, Joseph Beuys*, Luath Press, 2016

DiCenzo, Maria, *The Politics of Alternative Theatre in Britain 1968-1990: The Case of 7:84 (Scotland)*, Cambridge University Press, 1996

Dick, Eddie (ed.), *From Limelight to Satellite: A Scottish Film Book*, Scottish Film Council and British Film Institute, 1990

Dickson, Barbara and Eunson, John KV, *A Shirt Box Full of Songs: The Autobiography*, Hachette Scotland, 2009

D'Monte, Rebecca and Saunders, Graham, *Cool Britannia? British Political Theatre in the 1990s*, Palgrave Macmillan, 2008

Double, Oliver, *Alternative Comedy: 1979 and the Reinvention of British Stand-Up*, Methuen Drama, 2021 (first published 2020)

Drummond, John, *Tainted by Experience: A Life in the Arts*, Faber and Faber, 2000

Eatough, Graham and Rebellato, Dan (eds.), *The Suspect Culture Book*, Oberon, 2013

Edinburgh Festival Fringe Society, *The Fringe Blueprint*, Edinburgh Festival Fringe Society, 2018

Edinburgh Gateway Company, *The Twelve Seasons of the Edinburgh Gateway Company 1953-1965*, St Giles' Press, 1965

Elliott, Patrick, Hare, Bill and Wilson, Andrew, *Boyle Family*, National Galleries of Scotland, 2003

Ferguson, Craig, *American on Purpose: The Improbable Adventures of an Unlikely Patriot*, It Books, 2010 (first published 2009)

Fifield, Christopher (ed.), *Letters and Diaries of Kathleen Ferrier*, Boydell Press, 2003

Findlay, Bill (ed.), *A History of Scottish Theatre*, Polygon, 1998

Findlay, Bill (ed.), *Scottish People's Theatre: Plays by Glasgow Unity Writers*, The Association for Scottish Literature Studies, 2008

Fisher, Mark, *The Edinburgh Fringe Survival Guide: How to Make Your Show a Success*, Methuen Drama, 2012

Forsyth, James, *Tyrone Guthrie: A Biography*, Hamish Hamilton, 1976

Fowler, Jim, *Unleashing Britain: Theatre Gets Real 1955-64*, V&A Publications, 2005

Franklin, Bob (ed.), *Television Policy: The MacTaggart Lectures*, Edinburgh University Press, 2005

Fry, Stephen, *The Fry Chronicles*, Penguin, 2011 (first published 2010)

Games, Alexander, *Backing Into the Limelight: The Biography of Alan Bennett*, Review, 2002 (first published 2001)

Gillon, Jack, McLean, David and Parkinson, Fraser, *Edinburgh in the 1950s: Ten Years That*

Changed a City, Amberley, 2014

Grierson, John and Hardy, Forsyth (ed.), *Grierson on Documentary*, Faber and Faber, 1979 (previously published in 1946, 1966)

Griffin, Roger, *David Bowie: The Golden Years*, Omnibus Press, 2016

Guthrie, Tyrone, *A Life in the Theatre*, Columbus Books, 1960

Hall, Julian, *The Rough Guide to British Cult Comedy*, Rough Guides, 2006

Hardy, Forsyth, *John Grierson: A Documentary Biography*, Faber and Faber, 1979

Hardy, Forsyth, *Scotland in Film*, Edinburgh University Press, 1990

Hardy, Forsyth, *Slightly Mad and Full of Dangers: The Story of the Edinburgh Film Festival*, Ramsay Head Press, 1992

Harewood, Lord, *The Tongs and the Bones: The Memoirs*, Weidenfeld and Nicolson, 1981

Harper, Colin, *Dazzling Stranger: Bert Jansch and the British Folk and Blues Revival*, Bloomsbury, 2006 (first published 2000)

Harris, Paul, *Edinburgh Since 1900: Ninety Years of Photographs*, Lomond Books, 1994 (previously published 1987, 1988)

Haynes, Jim, *Thanks for Coming!*, Faber & Faber, 1984

Henderson, Hamish and Finlay, Alec (ed.), *The Armstrong Nose: Selected Letters of Hamish Henderson*, Polygon, 1996

Heron, Mike and Greig, Andrew, *You Know What You Could Be: Tuning Into the 1960s*, Riverrun, 2017

Hewison, Robert, *Footlights!: A Hundred Years of Cambridge Comedy*, Methuen, 1983

Hill, Harry, *Fight!*, Hodder Studio, 2021

Hill, Peter Buckley, *Freeing the Free Fringe: The Quest to Make Performers Better Off By Charging the Public Nothing*, Desert Hearts, 2018

Howard, Philip (ed.), *Scottish Shorts*, Nick Hern Books, 2010

Hutchison, David, *The Modern Scottish Theatre*, Molendinar Press, 1977

Itzkoff, Dave, *Robin: The Definitive Biography of Robin Williams*, Pan Macmillan, 2018

Jack, Robbie with Edwards, Owen Dudley, *The Edinburgh Festival: A Pictorial Celebration*, Canongate, 1990

Johnston, John, *The Lord Chamberlain's Blue Pencil*, Hodder & Stoughton, 1990

Kelly, Katherine E. (ed.), *The Cambridge Companion to Tom Stoppard*, Cambridge University Press, 2001

Lee, Hermione, *Tom Stoppard: A Life*, Faber, 2020

Lee, Stewart, *How I Escaped My Certain Fate: The Life and Deaths of a Stand-Up Comedian*, Faber and Faber, 2010

Lee, Stewart, *The 'If You Prefer a Milder Comedian, Please Ask For One' EP*, Faber and Faber, 2012

Lennie, Valerie, *Edinburgh People's Theatre 70th Year 1943-2013*, self-published at ept.org.uk, 2013

Leonard, Maurice, *Kathleen: The Life of Kathleen Ferrier 1912-1953*, The History Press, 2008 (first published 1988)

Linklater, Eric, *Edinburgh*, Newnes, 1960

Littlewood, Joan, *Joan's Book: The Autobiography of Joan Littlewood*, Bloomsbury Methuen Drama, 2019 (first published 1994)

Lloyd, Matthew, *How the Movie Brats Took Over Edinburgh: The Impact of Cinephilia on the Edinburgh International Film Festival 1968-1980*, St Andrews Film Studies, 2011

Lochhead, Liz, *Five Plays*, Nick Hern Books, 2012

Lyndsay, Sir David and Kemp, Robert, with Fleming, Tom, *Ane Satyre of the Thrie Estaites*, Polygon, 1985

MacColl, Ewan, *Journeyman: An Autobiography*, Manchester University Press, 2009 (first published 1990)

MacDonald, Ian, *The New Shostakovich*, Pimlico, 2006 (first published 1990)

Maclennan, Dolina with Gilchrist, Jim and Eydmann, Stuart, *Dolina: An Island Girl's Journey*, Islands Book Trust, 2014

MacLennan, Elizabeth, *The Moon Belongs to Everyone: Making Theatre with 7:84*, Methuen, 1990

Margolis, Jonathan, *The Big Yin: The Life and Times of Billy Connolly*, Chapmans, 1994

Marshall, James Scott, *The Life and Times of Leith*, John Donald, 1992 (previously published 1985, 1986, 1988)

Martine, Roddy, *Edinburgh Military Tattoo*, Robert Hale, 2001

Mavor, Ronald, *Dr Mavor and Mr Bridie: Memories of James Bridie*, Canongate and the National Library of Scotland, 1988

McBride, Joseph, *What Ever Happened to Orson Welles? A Portrait of an Independent Career*, University Press of Kentucky, 1977

McGrath, John, *A Good Night Out – Popular Theatre: Audience, Class and Form*, Nick Hern Books, 1996 (first published 1981)

McGrath, John, Six-Pack: *Plays for Scotland*, Polygon, 1996

McGrath, John, *Plays for England*, University of Exeter Press, 2005

McGrath, John, with MacDonald, Graeme, *The Cheviot, the Stag and the Black, Black Oil*, Bloomsbury Methuen Drama, 2015 (previously published 1974, 1981, 1993)

McMillan, Joyce, *The Traverse Theatre Story 1963-1988*, Methuen, 1988

McMillan, Joyce with Howard, Philip (ed.), *Theatre in Scotland: A Field of Dreams*, Nick Hern Books, 2016

Melly, George, *Owning Up: The Trilogy*, Penguin, 2006 (first published 1965)

Miles, Barry, *William Burroughs: A Life*, Weidenfeld & Nicolson, 2014

Miller, Eileen, *The Edinburgh International Festival 1947-1996*, Scolar Press, 1996

Moffat, Alistair, *The Edinburgh Fringe*, Johnston & Bacon, 1978

Morgan, Ted, *Literary Outlaw: The Life and Times of William S. Burroughs*, Norton, 2012

Morris, David and Mackay, John, *Festival City*, CJ Cousland & Sons, 1949

Muir, Edwin, *Scottish Journey*, Mainstream, 1996 (previously published 1935, 1979)

Munro, Rona, *The James Plays*, Nick Hern Books, 2014

Nadel, Ira, *Double Act: A Life of Tom Stoppard*, Methuen, 2002

Neat, Timothy, *Hamish Henderson, A Biography: Volume I – The Making of the Poet*, Polygon, 2007

Neat, Timothy, *Hamish Henderson, A Biography: Volume II – Poetry Becomes People*, Polygon, 2009

O'Connor, Garry, *Ian McKellen: The Biography*, Weidenfeld & Nicolson, 2019

O'Leary, Chris, *Rebel Rebel: All the Songs of David Bowie from '64 to '76*, Zero Books, 2015

Ostende, Florence (ed.), *Michael Clark: Cosmic Dancer*, Prestel, 2020

Paskin, Barbara, *Dear Dudley: A Celebration of the Much-Loved Comedy Legend*, John Blake, 2018

Ponsonby, Robert, *Musical Heroes: A Personal View of Music and the Musical World Over Sixty Years*, Giles de la Mare, 2009

Ponsonby, Robert, *In and Out of Tune: Personal and Public Memoirs 1926-2015*, Diadem, 2016

Pye, Michael and Myles, Lynda, *The Movie Brats: How the Film Generation Took Over Hollywood*, Faber and Faber, 1979

Rees, Jasper, *Let's Do It: The Authorised Biography of Victoria Wood*, Trapeze, 2021 (first published 2020)

Roberts, JF, *The True History of the Black Adder*, Preface, 2012

Roberts, Jem, *Soupy Twists! The Full Official Story of the Sophisticated Silliness of Fry and*

Laurie, Unbound, 2018

Rosebery, The Countess of, *The Ambitious Girl*, Thomas Nelson and Sons Ltd, 1943

Royle, Trevor, *Precipitous City*, Mainstream, 1980

Ryding, Erik and Pechefsky, Rebecca, *Bruno Walter: A World Elsewhere*, Yale University Press, 2001

Sayle, Alexei, *Thatcher Stole My Trousers*, Bloomsbury, 2016

Scotsman, The, *Festival City: A Pictorial History of the Edinburgh Festivals*, Breedon, 2009

Scott, Andrew Murray, *Alexander Trocchi: The Making of the Monster (Second Edition)*, Kennedy & Boyd, 2012 (first published 1991)

Scott PH and Davis, AC (eds.), *The Age of MacDiarmid: Essays on Hugh MacDiarmid and His Influence on Contemporary Scotland*, Mainstream, 1980

Shellard, Dominic, *Kenneth Tynan: A Life*, Yale University Press, 2003

Shuttleworth, Ian, *Ken & Em: The Biography of Kenneth Branagh and Emma Thompson*, Headline, 1995 (first published 1994)

Sierz, Aleks, *In-Yer-Face Theatre: British Drama Today*, Faber and Faber, 2001

Skinner, Frank, *Frank Skinner*, Arrow, 2002

Snowman, Daniel, *The Hitler Emigres: The Cultural Impact on Britain of Refugees from Nazism*, Pimlico, 2003 (first published 2002)

Stephenson, Pamela, *Billy*, Harper Collins, 2002 (first published 2001)

Stevenson, Randall and Wallace, Gavin (eds.), *Scottish Theatre Since the Seventies*, Edinburgh University Press, 1996

Stoppard, Tom and Delaney, Paul (ed.), *Tom Stoppard in Conversation*, University of Michigan Press, 1994

Szwed, John, *The Man Who Recorded the World: A Biography of Alan Lomax*, Arrow, 2011

TEAM, The, *Five Plays by the TEAM*, Oberon, 2015

Test Dept, *Total State Machine*, PC Press, 2015

Thompson, Harry, *Peter Cook: A Biography*, Sceptre, 1997

Waller-Bridge, Phoebe, *Fleabag: The Special Edition*, Nick Hern Books, 2019

Ward, Robin, *Exploring Edinburgh: Six Tours of the City and its Architecture*, Luath Press, 2021

Weikop, Christian, *Strategy Get Arts: 35 Artists Who Broke the Rules*, Studies in Photography, 2021

Wilmut, Roger, *From Fringe to Flying Circus: Celebrating a Unique Generation of Comedy 1960-1980*, Methuen, 1982 (first published 1980)

Wilmut, Roger and Rosengard, Peter, *Didn't You Kill My Mother-in-Law? The Story of Alternative Comedy in Britain from The Comedy Store to Saturday Live*, Methuen, 1989

Wishart, Ruth, *Edinburgh international Festival: Celebration! 50 Years in Photographs*, Edinburgh Festival Society, 1996

Endnotes

Introduction: The Past

1. The seven hills are Castle Rock, Arthur's Seat, Calton Hill, Corstorphine Hill, Craiglockhart Hill, Braid Hill and Blackford Hill. The presence of seven hills within the city is just one reason why Edinburgh is frequently compared to Athens.

2. The five older universities are Oxford and Cambridge in England, and St Andrews, Glasgow and Aberdeen in Scotland. There are numerous older universities which were established in non-English-speaking Europe.

3. The 'Corri' of the name was Domenico Corri, an Italian immigrant to Edinburgh in 1771, who also organised concerts at St Cecilia's. His hall was later rebuilt as the Theatre Royal, which burnt down in 1946 and was not rebuilt due to a shortage of materials. A bar bearing the Theatre Royal's name still stands next to the current Playhouse nearby on Picardy Place.

4. The Theatre Royal on Shakespeare Square was the original building by that name, bearing a statue of Shakespeare above its entrance. It stood there from 1769 until 1859, when it was demolished and reopened as the new theatre on the site of the former Corri's Concert Hall. With it went Shakespeare Square itself, and it was replaced by the great Victorian Post Office building which stands there today, albeit now entirely restructured internally as an office complex named Waverley Gate.

5. It now encompasses 'Poets, Playwrights, Editors, Essayists, Novelists'.

6. Muir, Edwin, *Scottish Journey*, p.5.

7. Even in the early years of the 2000s, incredibly, it was still possible for a woman to enter certain traditional city centre Edinburgh pubs and be gruffly asked to leave. Fortunately the practice seems to have died out completely now.

8. Now James Gillespie's High School, in a new building on the same site.

9. Muir, Edwin, *Scottish Journey*, p.38.

Spotlight: Bruno Walter and the Vienna Philharmonic Orchestra (1947)

1. Now the *Deutsche Oper Berlin*.

2. 'Festival Notes: Arrival of Vienna Orchestra', *The Scotsman*, 5 September 1947.

3. 'Close of the Festival: Lord Provost's Tribute to 'Most Cosmopolitan Club", *The Scotsman*, 15 September 1947.

4. Quoted in Miller, Eileen, *The Edinburgh International Festival 1947–1996*.

1. The Birth of the Edinburgh International Festival

1. Bing, Rudolf, *5000 Nights at the Opera*, p13.

2. Wood, H Harvey, 'Aims of the Enterprise: Attractions of Highest Standard', *The Scotsman*, 7 August 1947.

3. Lord Provost is a Scotland-specific role which involves chairing the city council and taking on Mayoral-style ceremonial duties.

4. Rosebery, The Countess of, *The Ambitious Girl*, p125.

5. Although Falconer wasn't knighted by King George VI until 1946, and his first

encounter with Bing happened in early 1945.

6. Unless they're actually from England, of course.

7. 'Sunlit pageantry of the opening day', *The Scotsman*, 25 August 1947.

Spotlight: A Satire of the Three Estates (1948–1996)

1. Bannister, Winifred, *James Bridie and his Theatre*, p39.

2. ibid p237.

3. Later revisited at his Tyrone Guthrie Theater in Minneapolis, opened in 1963.

4. John Home's *Douglas*, also considered by Bridie for the 1948 Festival, was itself finally directed in Edinburgh by the Citizens' John Casson in 1950.

5. Campbell, Donald, *Playing for Scotland: A History of the Scottish Stage 1715-1965*.

2. 'On the fringe of the Festival...'

1. 'Letters to the editor', *The Herald*, 30 January 1947.

2. 'Letters to the editor', *The Herald*, 1 February 1947.

3. 'Letters to the editor', *The Herald*, 4 February 1947.

4. 'Letters to the editor', *The Herald*, 24 February 1947.

5. 'Letters to the editor', *The Herald*, 22 February 1947.

6. Findlay, Bill (ed.), *Scottish People's Theatre: Plays by Glasgow Unity Writers*.

7. Now a chain restaurant on the newly-rechristened Nelson Mandela Place.

8. Who was, if anything, more versatile than his father – a doctor turned playwright and Scotsman theatre critic who became director of the Scottish Arts Council, deputy chair of the Edinburgh Festival Committee from 1975 to 1981 and a painter in later life.

9. Bannister, Winifred, *James Bridie and his Theatre*.

10. Apparently due to Sir Ernest Pooley replacing John Maynard Keynes; Bridie disagreed with Pooley's position on Lord Chamberlain censorship.

11. 'Play cancelled: result of Arts Council decision', *The Scotsman*, 12 August 1947.

12. 'Semi-Official: Ill-province of the smaller stages', *The Scotsman*, 14 August 1947.

13. Lennie, Valerie, *Edinburgh People's Theatre 70th Year 1943-2013*.

14. Both company and theatre later appeared in Michael Powell and Emeric Pressburger's classic 1948 film *The Red Shoes*.

15. 'Scottish drama: beginning of a native theatre', *The Scotsman*, 13 September 1947.

16. Bannister, Winifred, *James Bridie and his Theatre*.

17. 'Semi-Official: Ill-province of the smaller stages', *The Scotsman*, 14 August 1947.

Spotlight: The Edinburgh People's Festival and Ceilidh (1951–53)

1. Szwed, John, *The Man Who Recorded the World: A Biography of Alan Lomax*.

2. Neat, Timothy, *Hamish Henderson, A Biography: Volume I – The Making of the Poet*.

3. ibid.

4. Bort, Eberhard (ed.), *'Tis Sixty Years Since: The 1951 Edinburgh People's Festival Ceilidh and the Scottish Folk Revival*.

5. ibid.

6. Szwed, John, *The Man Who Recorded the World: A Biography of Alan Lomax*.

7. Gramsci died of chronic, prison-induced ill-health in 1937, at the age of just 46.

8. It was suggested his name change was a practical necessity following his probable desertion from the Navy during the war.

9. Littlewood, Joan, *Joan's Book: The Autobiography of Joan Littlewood*.

10. ibid.

11. Bort, Eberhard (ed.), *'Tis Sixty Years Since: The 1951 Edinburgh People's Festival Ceilidh and the Scottish Folk Revival*.

12. Now, with a certain amount of irony, an Irish theme pub.

13. No-one knows who 'Sandy' was.

3. The Film Festival, the Military Tattoo and the 1950s

1. Hardy, *Slightly Mad and Full of Dangers*, p.1.

2. The Princes Cinema was opened in 1912 and survived under various names until its closure as the Jacey Cinema in 1973. In a 21st century context, it's the nondescript shop unit to the left of the former site of the HMV record store on Princes Street.

3. *The Scotsman*, 'Edinburgh Guild's Purpose', 4 February 1931. Mackenzie's novel *Whisky Galore* was published in 1947, and its 1949 film adaptation as *Whisky Galore!* by Alexander Mackendrick is recognised as one of the enduring classics of Scottish-made film.

4. *Cinema Quarterly* ceased publication in 1935, returning briefly in the late '30s as *World Film News and Television Progress*, and then as *SEE: World Film News* until it finally folded in 1938.

5. Hardy, *Slightly Mad and Full of Dangers*, p.16.

6. 'Documentary's Gratitude to Scotland', *The Herald*, 1 September 1947.

7. Known as *Paisan* for its later English-language release.

8. Hardy, *Slightly Mad and Full of Dangers*, p.18.

9. Although a critical and commercial success at the time, *Louisiana Story* later attracted criticism for being semi-fictionalised, and funded as a promotional tool by a big oil company.

10. Although the scheduled premiere of Vittorio de Sica's future classic *Bicycle Thieves* was cancelled when the film found UK distribution and the distributors pulled it from the festival.

11. In 1950 with *Francis, God's Jester*, more commonly known in English as *The Flowers of St Francis*.

12. Which still exists as the Bath Festival.

13. This is likely to be an exaggeration, given the Gardens' size.

14. *The Herald*, 25 Aug 1949.

15. Tickets could also be bought at the Rae, Mackintosh & Co. music shop on George Street.

16. Fielding was a year into her performing career at this point; by the end of the decade her West End roles in Wilson's adaptation of Ronald Firbank's novel *Valmouth* and the Kenneth Williams revue *Pieces of Eight*, co-scripted by a pre-*Beyond the Fringe* Peter Cook, set her up as one of Britain's most prolific screen comedy actors of the 1960s.

17. Now the building-based Pitlochry Festival Theatre.

18. Except in 1959, when many Gateway regulars were needed in Tyrone Guthrie's final presentation of *A Satire of the Three Estates*.

19. *The Herald*, 11 Sept 1958.

20. Although no alcohol was available, due to the YMCA's religious origins.

21. It's often claimed this was the first production of *Under Milk Wood*, but there are technicalities involved. It was part of tour of the first full stage production, although it had opened in Newcastle a week earlier, and there had been a number of radio broadcasts – including Richard Burton's famous one of January 1954 – and informal stage readings going back to 1953.

22. 'Opera Singer and Her Temperament', *The Herald*, 24 August 1957.

23. ibid.

24. 'Taking Good Music to the People', *The Herald*, 10 August 1958.

25. Crawford, Iain, *Banquo on Thursdays: The Inside Story of 50 Years of the Edinburgh Festival.*

Spotlight: Beyond the Fringe (1960)

1. Tynan, Kenneth, 'English satire advances into the Sixties', *The Observer*, 14 May 1961.

2. Even though director Stanley Daniels insisted he wasn't to do it when Bennett appeared in *Better Never*, Oxford Theatre Group's 1959 Edinburgh revue.

3. Introduction to *The Complete Beyond the Fringe*.

4. Miller had already departed, to be briefly replaced by the American-based former Royal Shakespeare Company actor Paxton Whitehead. The West End run limped on until 1966, some way past its sell-by date, with an all-new cast.

5. Quoted in Cook, Peter and Cook, William, *Tragically I Was an Only Twin: The Comedy of Peter Cook.*

4. The Conferences and the Birth of the 1960s

1. Longtime site of the Urban Angel café in recent years.

2. He also co-directed the 1951 version.

3. Now part of the Murrayfield Hospital complex on the south side of Corstorphine Hill.

4. McMillan, Joyce, *The Traverse Theatre Story 1963-1988.*

5. Calder, John, *Pursuit*, p.185.

6. And also the inspiration for one of Haynes' tall stories about the Paperback Bookshop's rhino.

7. It lost out to Billy Wilder's *The Apartment.*

8. At birth, he became sixth in order of succession to the British throne.

9. Calder, John, *Pursuit*, p.199.

10. Although the Conference was their first meeting.

11. Calder, John, *Pursuit* p.205.

12. Quoted in Birrell, Ross and Finlay, Alec (eds.), *Justified Sinners: An Archaeology of Scottish Counter-Culture 1960-2000.*

13. McMillan, Joyce, *The Traverse Theatre Story 1963-1988.*

14. Calder, John, *Pursuit*, p.252.

15. Calder, John, *Pursuit*, p.259.

16. Brecht's widow had sent a telegram suggesting a follow-up Drama Conference be staged in Berlin in '64.

17. Although Jim Haynes held a tiny replacement at the Traverse.

18. Cornwell, Tim, 'Lady MacChatterley's £4 furore in the raw', *The Scotsman*, 5 August 2012.

Spotlight: Rosencrantz & Guildenstern Are Dead (1966)

1. Bradshaw, Jon, 'Tom Stoppard, Nonstop: Word Games with a Hit Playwright', *New York*, 10 January 1977.

2. Snell's subsequent career in factual television included a gig as one of the founding director-producers of long-running British arts programme *The South Bank Show* – including a special on Tom Stoppard in its debut 1978 series.

3. Watts, Janet, 'Stoppard's half-century', *The Observer*, 28 June 1987.

4. Bryden, Ronald, 'Wyndy Excitements', *The Observer*, 28 August 1966.

5. The Howff, The Traverse and the Demarco Gallery

1. Also named the Howff.

2. McMillan, Joyce, *The Traverse Theatre Story 1963-1988*.

3. Used solely for their collaborative work by mutual agreement at the time, although Hills was later given full retrospective credit. The pair later produced work as Boyle Family with their adult children.

4. McMillan, Joyce, *The Traverse Theatre Story 1963-1988*.

5. Greer's own career had begun with the 1965 Cambridge Footlights revue *My Girl Herbert*, which played at the Edinburgh Festival Fringe while she was still a student.

Spotlight: Strategy: Get Arts (1970)

1. Duncan Macmillan, in *The Demarco Collection and Archive: An Introduction*, The Demarco Archive Trust Limited and Lodz-Edinburgh Foundation, 2009.

2. *Demarco, A Unique Partnership*, p.37.

3. The stories and affiliations of Beuys' earlier life have long been a matter of uncertainty to those who have followed and written about him. Joining the Hitler Youth came three years before this became compulsory for all young Germans, although there would still have been a level of expectation and peer pressure involved when he did so. The perception of him in later life was as an artistic left-liberal. For many decades Beuys promoted the story that he'd been saved from his plane wreck by nomadic Tatars who had swaddled him in regenerative animal fat, healing his wounds, although this story was subsequently disproven, throwing suspicion on other stories of his wartime experience. On the English language publication of his multi-volume Beuys biography in 2021, Swiss writer Hans Peter Riegel expressed the belief that mental illness may have played a part in his life and work; he was known to suffer from depression. (https://www.swissinfo.ch/eng/culture/joseph-beuys--great-art-built-on-even-greater-lies/46606814) These contradictions and uncertainties, if nothing else, contribute to the view of Beuys as a very 20th century enigma.

4. The former folk musician and broadcaster who had previously organised Fringe and International Festival folk concerts, now switched to a career as a wildlife artist.

5. The college building had closed in 1972 and merged with Daniel Stewart's College in the latter's grand old 1855 hospital for needy children on Queensferry Road. Today it's known as Stewart's Melville College.

6. Searle, Adrian, 'Wreckers of civilization: Hull embraces its frenzied sexual past', *The Guardian*, 5 February 2017, accessed at https://www.theguardian.com/artanddesign/2017/feb/05/hull-city-of-culture-best-visual-art-coum.

7. Pollock, David, 'Interview: Richard Demarco on Joseph Beuys', *The List*, 17 August 2016, https://edinburghfestival.list.co.uk/article/83586-interview-richard-demarco-on-joseph-beuys/

6. Changing Landscapes in the 1970s

1. An alternative site alongside the Usher Hall was also proposed.

2. John Lennon suggested he pawn his gold chain of office instead.

3. Conflicting accounts say it was either called the New Edinburgh or the West End.

4. Harewood, *The Tongs and the Bones*, p.201.

5. Harewood, *The Tongs and the Bones*, p.203.

6. This was also performed in Edinburgh in 1962.

7. Shostakovich was generally believed to have been less than willing, but felt he had no choice for reasons of personal and professional liberty.

8. Ex-Africa, a 'Black odyssey in jazz, rhyme and calypso', was on the late-night bill in 1963, and the National Company of Guinea presented Les Ballets Africains in 1964.

9. Who studied at Edinburgh University's School of Music under Donald Tovey.

10. As herself, in the Audrey Hepburn-starring *Paris When It Sizzles* in 1964. She did make one final appearance years later, in David Hemmings' Berlin-set 1978 film *Just a Gigolo*, starring David Bowie.

11. Harper, *Dazzling Stranger*, p101.

12. Haymarket Ice Rink sat just to the north-west of Haymarket rail station. It was closed and demolished in the late 1970s, and the current Murrayfield Ice Rink a short distance away was opened.

13. Campbell's sons Ali, Robin and Duncan later founded the group UB40.

14. Now Liverpool Hope University.

15. https://projects.handsupfortrad.scot/hall-of-fame/dr-john-barrow/

16. The first student rector was Jonathan Wills, elected the previous year on a promised one-year term in order to give the student body a voice within the University establishment.

17. Featuring actor Miriam Margolyes, at 26 making one of her first post-Cambridge Footlights appearances in Edinburgh.

18. McMillan, *The Traverse Theatre Story*, p62-63.

19. The Georgian Group still exists, greatly expanded, as the Architectural Heritage Society of Scotland.

20. David Hume Tower was renamed 40 George Square in 2020, in response to Black Lives Matter-era protests concerning Hume's statements on race. George Square Theatre was renamed the Gordon Aikman Lecture Theatre in 2018, in honour of the Edinburgh graduate, activist and motor neurone disease fundraiser, who died of the disease the year before, aged 31.

Spotlight: The Great Northern Welly Boot Show (1972)

1. Whose 1972 hit 'Stuck in the Middle with You' gained new infamy when it was used on the soundtrack of Quentin Tarantino's *Reservoir Dogs* 20 years later.

2. Who then and for many years went by the name Ian Ireland.

7. The Film Festival Meets the Movie Brats

1. Although Bergman never attended the Film Festival.

2. Pierre Boulez conducted the BBC Symphony Orchestra performing *The Rite of Spring* in Edinburgh at the Usher Hall on 2 September 1967.

3. The Ivor Novello Awards, named after the prolific writer of songs including 'Keep the Home Fires Burning', which were established in 1955 and generally known for rewarding proficient but conventional music.

4. Through the Committee, Hardy had commissioned Grierson to produce Hilary Harris's 1961 short *Seaward the Great Ships*, about the Clyde shipbuilding industry, which was the first Scottish film to win an Academy Award. The Committee also commissioned early work from the film director Bill Forsyth and the writers William McIlvanney and Alasdair Gray.

5. Hardy, *Slightly Mad and Full of Dangers*, p.92.

6. Ranvaud, Don, 'An Interview with Sam Fuller', *Framework*, No.19, 1982.

7. And in the 1970s a rock music venue, with bands going on after bingo calling finished at 11pm.

8. Now Mill Hill School.

9. Which merged with Cranley School in 1979 and was subsumed into St Margaret's School for girls in 1998. This school closed in 2010.

10. O'Connor, Garry, *Ian McKellen: The Biography*, p. 72.

11. Haymarket Ice Rink closed in 1978, and the present-day Murrayfield Ice Rink opened soon after.

12. The former were public, the latter was for a BBC broadcast.

13. 'It was a very small operation, and I think often we were told on no account could we publish, and somehow miraculously a book would appear,' says Myles of the Film Festival retrospective publications. 'The books were very cheaply done, and the Douglas Sirk book is famous because the glue was cheap and every copy explodes as soon as you try to open it.'

14. Mulvey, Laura, 'Visual Pleasure in Narrative Cinema', *Screen* No.16, Autumn 1975.

15. EIFF programme 1975, quoted by Stanfield.

16. McGrath, quoted in Franklin (ed.), *Television Policy: The MacTaggart Lectures*, p.41-42.

17. Later managing director of Scottish Television and a Labour peer under Tony Blair in the House of Lords.

18. Franklin (ed), *Television Policy: The MacTaggart Lectures*, p.10.

19. A close friend of Bill Forsyth's, who went on to direct the Scottish films *Living Apart Together* and *Heavenly Pursuits* in the 1980s.

20. Bryce's later landmark buildings included Fettes College and Edinburgh Royal Infirmary by the Meadows.

21. Hardy, *Slightly Mad and Full of Dangers*, p.143-144.

Spotlight: Cambridge Footlights – The Cellar Tapes (1981)

1. Kendall later earned a place in British television history when she spoke the first words in the long-running soap *Emmerdale* in 1972.

2. Despite being involved in shows, Eleanor Bron, Margolyes and Kendall weren't officially admitted to the Footlights club.

3. It became the Royal National Theatre while he was there.

4. McGrath left Hat Trick in 1992, although it continues to produce series with comedians and broadcasters who started on the Fringe, including *Whose Line is it Anyway?*, *Have I Got News For You*, *Paul Merton: The Series* and *The Armstrong & Miller Show*.

5. Fry, *The Fry Chronicles*, p.98.

6. Shuttleworth, *Ken & Em*, p.67.

7. Fry, *The Fry Chronicles*, p.155.

8. Including an opening party for the film *Chariots of Fire*, in which Fry had been an extra, that took place precisely as John Hinckley Jr attempted to assassinate US President Ronald Reagan on March 30 1981. Much of the audience left to make phone calls.

9. Other members considered were the actors Chris Langham and Alfred Molina, and Scottish poet and playwright Liz Lochhead, who according to Fry 'was clearly not impressed with what she found and declined to take part.' In the end, the Glaswegian actor Siobhan Redmond joined the cast.

10. Fry, *The Fry Chronicles*, p.199.

11. Complicité also co-produced *I'll Take You to Mrs Cole!* and *The Last of the Pelican Daughters* in Edinburgh, both of which premiered at the Pleasance in 2019.

8. The Fringe Gets Serious

1. The SNP's Motherwell by-election victory in 1945 was short-lived, being overturned in the General Election three months later.

2. It didn't, despite the pre-fame presence of both Terence Stamp and Michael Caine in the cast. The latter was poached to appear in the film *Zulu*, co-written by *Highland Clearances* author John Prebble.

3. McGrath, *Six-Pack*, preface.

4. McGrath, *A Good Night Out*, p12.

5. McGrath, *A Good Night Out*, p4.

6. McGrath, *Cheviot* script, p.xi.

7. This was Arnold's first job in professional theatre, having come from a purely community theatre background himself. In 1986, he ran Edinburgh International Festival's ill-fated Dome tent on Pilrig Park. In 1991 he founded Glasgow's famed multi-arts venue and club, the Arches. He's currently the artistic director of the Tron Theatre in Glasgow.

8. Although Edinburgh by-laws again using animals in circuses meant many of their other tricks were mercifully off-limits.

9. Arrabal was also one of the playwrights whose work was staged by the Traverse on its opening night.

10. Alistair Moffat says this latter venue was nicknamed 'Fort Knox'.

11. The *Guardian*, 18 August 1972, p.10.

12. Co-founded by David Hare in 1968 at Jim Haynes' Drury Lane Arts Lab, although Hare had left by '71.

13. 'Reading, (w)riting and (a)rithmetic'.

14. Crummy's younger son is artist Andrew Crummy, whose tapestry projects include the national-renowned *Great Tapestry of Scotland* (2013), based on an idea by the Edinburgh author Alexander McCall Smith.

15. Although billed headliners the Clash didn't appear.

16. https://www.davidharding.net/?page_id=33

17. Moffat was elected rector himself at the same university in 2011.

18. https://www.warp-experience.com/Plays/warp-edinburgh-1979.html

19. Irvine, Lorna, 'Ken Campbell, theatrical trickster, memorialized in Fringe show 'Ken'', *The List*, https://edinburghfestival.list.co.uk/article/103088-ken-campbell-theatrical-trickster-memorialised-in-fringe-show-ken/

20. This is in contrast to local music in Edinburgh. In the late '70s and early '80s, bands like Josef K, the Scars, Fire Engines and the Rezillos (the latter with later Human League member Jo Callis among their number) created an energetic scene.

21. In an interview for Dale's 1988 book *Sore Throats and Overdrafts*.

22. Helen Atkinson-Wood had been the only other performer in the Fringe version of '77, although an unnamed friend of Atkinson's from Dundee University Theatre Group hadn't made it through the early edits.

23. Founded in 1628 by the royal goldsmith and philanthropist George Heriot to provide free education to the 'faitherless bairns' (fatherless children) of the city, the Foundation also built the large school on Lauriston Place which bears Heriot's name.

24. There was debate among *The Scotsman*'s team as to whether it was eligible.

25. The New Revue co-starred Atkinson's old Oxford accomplice Angus Deayton as straight man, who made his own mark in television presenting and acting with *Have I Got News For You* and *One Foot in the Grave*.

Spotlight: Mary Queen of Scots Got Her Head Chopped Off (1987)

1. Moving to Scotland as part of the scheme was the Canadian writer and husband of Margaret Atwood, Graeme Gibson.

2. *Alfresco* was known as *There's Nothing to Worry About!* when it was first broadcast in 1982.

9. 'Supervenues' and the Arrival of the Big Three

1. Dale, *Sore Throats and Overdrafts*, p24.

2. The Mackenzie Building in which the Wireworks was housed was bought by the Faculty of Advocates in 1984 and became their training and education centre.

3. Sayle, *Thatcher Stole My Trousers*, p.207.

4. Future Hollywood stars Grant and Myers also befriended one another at McNally's, and Grant's later partner Elizabeth Hurley played her defining screen role alongside Myers in the first *Austin Powers* film.

5. The characters were the pantomime dames in an eclectic Christmas production of *Sleeping Beauty* at Glasgow's Tron Theatre, as written by Craig Ferguson and Peter Capaldi.

Spotlight: I Am Curious, Orange (1988)

1. Maconie, Stuart, 'The History Man Whose Head Expanded', *NME*, 17 September 1988, accessed at https://thefall.org/gigography/88sep17.html.

2. The fee was £65,000, now spare change to one of the world's richest clubs.

3. Perry, Kevin E.G., 'We Only Have This Excerpt', *The Quietus* (online), 24 January 2018.

4. 'Mark E Smith on Edinburgh', *Granada Tonight*, broadcast on 21 November 1994,

accessed at https://www.youtube.com/watch?v=KRZFhrV6iFQ.

5.Cooper, Neil, 'Obituary – Mark E Smith, riotous lead singer of The Fall', *The Herald*, 25 January 2018.

6. 'Mark E Smith on all things Scottish', *The Herald*, 20 November 2012.

7. As he stated in Perry, Kevin EG, 'We Only Have This Excerpt', *The Quietus* (online), 24 January 2018.

10. The Birth of the Jazz and Book Festivals

1. The other was St George's Hall in Liverpool.

2. In more recent times, C Venues used the building as a Fringe venue.

3. Melly, *Owning Up*.

4. The precursor of the annual Sacramento Music Festival, which ended in 2017.

5. Spence also staged jazz concerts at the Assembly Rooms soon after William Burdett-Coutts' takeover.

6. Established in the 19th century, James Thin booksellers' was a leading business in the city until its sale in 2002.

7. The lead role was taken successively by John Wood, John Neville, Robert Stephens and Leonard Nimoy.

8. *The New York Times*, August 14 1983.

9. Drummond, *Tainted by Experience*, p.233.

10. Heath was founding President in 1976 of the orchestra, now the European Union Youth Orchestra.

11. Morrison's fee, reported to be somewhere between £30,000 and £50,000, was apparently the highest ever paid for a rock performance in Scotland.

12. Drummond, *Tainted by Experience*, p.300.

13. *The Guardian*, 11 September 1983, p.34.

14. *The Guardian*, 21 August 1983, p.2.

15. Drummond spent a third of his working year living out of a hotel in Edinburgh, third at EIF's London office and a third visiting artists internationally. In his memoir he wrote of being stopped by a woman conducting a survey in Heathrow Airport, who wanted to know how many times he had travelled through the airport in the last year. After a bit of consideration, his answer was 146.

16. Dale also managed the Cambridge Arts Theatre before arriving at the Fringe.

17. The Glasgow Garden Festival site at Pacific Quay is now home to the Glasgow Science Centre and a media park containing the offices of BBC Scotland and Alistair Moffat's old employer STV (Scottish Television). The Garden Festivals, held every two years from 1984 until 1992, were in Liverpool, Stoke-on-Trent, Glasgow, Gateshead and Ebbw Vale.

18. *The Herald*, 24 August 1984, p.4.

19. *The Herald*, 20 August 1984, p.4.

20. At a time when cultural and economic sanctions against the apartheid-era South Africa were a hot subject, the works performed were Barney Simon's 'living newspaper' *Born in the RSA* in '86, by his dissident Market Theatre company, and David Kramer and Taliep Petersen's fiercely anti-apartheid *District Six: The Musical*, about the forced removal of black communities from the titular area in Cape Town.

21. Parsons was also scheduled to perform four appearances of the show in 2019, but had to pull out for health reasons and was replaced by Fred MacAulay. Parsons died at the age of 96 in 2020.

Spotlight: A One Night Stand with Sean Hughes (1990) Frank Skinner (1991)
Steve Coogan in Character with John Thomson (1992)

1. A 16th century masonic lodge at Brodie's Close.

2. Ian Albery was the person who suggested to Dillie Keane that her show needed a director.

3. Since 2002, this formerly open space has housed the Cowgate Under-5s nursery.

4. http://www.theweb-uk.com/archive-john-helmer.html.

5. A prolific left-wing activist, Hardy was perhaps best known as the host of BBC Radio 4's *Jeremy Hardy Speaks to the Nation* for two decades until 2014. He died on 1 February 2019. Fanshawe broke boundaries as a queer voice in UK comedy, and was one of the 14 founders in 1989 of the Stonewall LGBT rights charity, a response to the infamous Section 28 of the UK's Local Government Act 1988, which related to 'promotion of homosexuality'.

6. *The List*, 31 August 1990.

7. Dessau, Bruce, 'Sean Hughes obituary', *The Guardian*, 16 October 2017.

8. In recent years Izzard has expressed a preference for female pronouns: 'If they call me 'she' and 'her', that's great - or 'he' and 'him', I don't mind. I prefer to be called Eddie, that covers everything. I'm gender fluid.'

9. O'Grady, Paul. *Open the Cage, Murphy!*, p.156.

10. O'Grady, Paul. *Open the Cage, Murphy!*, p.171.

11. Coogan, Steve, *Easily Distracted*.

12. Skinner, Frank, *Frank Skinner*.

13. Marber was born in September 1964, Coogan in October 1965.

14. Lee and Herring were both writers for *On the Hour*, but disputes about attribution of character creation meant they didn't return for *The Day Today*.

15. Coogan, *Easily Distracted*, p.337.

16. Alan Partridge appeared in his own film in 2013, and Coogan made a jump to dramatic acting in films including Michael Winterbottom's *24 Hour Party People* (2002) and Stephen Frears' *Philomena* (also 2013).

17. Different sources say that Moran was either the second youngest solo Perrier winner when he triumphed, or that he replaced Hughes as the youngest. The answer is marginal, as both were 24 when they won and both had their birthdays in early November. Taking for granted that the award was given out at the same point in the Fringes of 1990 and 1996 – it's usually the last Saturday – that would mean Hughes was two months and nine days away from his 25th birthday and Moran was two months and four days away, so Hughes remained the youngest winner.

18. Hill, Harry, *Fight!*.

19. Cook, *Ha Bloody Ha*, p.245.

11. The Rise of the Stand-Up while Edinburgh Rebuilds

1. There are conflicting reports as to when the club ran. Ivor Dembina says it opened in 1987, although Julian Clary has written that he performed there in 1985. Contemporary listings suggest it was in business from 1987 until 1989; possibly Clary was mistaken.

2. *The List*, 21 August 1987, p.10.

3. She sadly died in 1999.

4. Clary, *A Young Man's Passage*, p.199-200.

5. There was – and is – a third major force in the promotion of UK comics, Phil McIntyre Entertainment. McIntyre started out with Billy Connolly in 1974 and was mainly known as a rock promoter until the late 1980s, with occasional forays into big comedy names like Lenny Henry and Rowan Atkinson on the way. Numerous other promoters of all sizes have become involved since then.

6. *The List*, 10 August 1990, p.9.

7. This phrase is widely attributed to Street-Porter, although even she's unsure whether she first said it. Another version of the its origin has it that original Comedy Store Player Dave Cohen said it off-the-cuff at a gig in Islington, and was quoted in London listings magazine *City Limits* a couple of weeks before Street-Porter said it.

8. Except Newman, a graduate but not a Footlight.

9. All quotes in this exchange from *The Guardian*, 5 August 1990, p.51.

10. *Financial Times*, 3 April 2006.

11. Boilerhouse's four co-founders had produced the Gateway Exchange's last play, a piece named *Requiem for a Woman's Soul* starring the future comedian Rhona Cameron.

12. The first was in Stephen Berkoff's *Coriolanus* in London, acting opposite Berkoff himself. Tam Dean Burn also appeared in this production.

Spotlight: The Bloody Chamber (1997) Gargantua (1998)

1. Lodwick was later the curator of the theatre department at the V&A Museum in London.

2. Tarbuck had formerly played piano with Essex art-punks Crass.

3. The Debenhams department store closed in 2020 and is currently being converted into a hotel.

12. New Blood for the New Millennium

1. Lee, *How I Escaped My Certain Fate*, p.39.

2. Early in their life Underbelly had also been given office space by Koren, which was also destroyed in the fire.

3. Davidson, Gail and Rimmer, Louise, 'Link with Nestlé provokes comedian to call for boycott over baby milk', *Scotland On Sunday*, 22 July 2001.

4. Newman's very informative and funny later comedy-lectures included *From Caliban to Taliban: 500 Years of Humanist Intervention* (2002) and *Apocalypso Now, or From P45 To AK47: How To Grow The Economy With The Use Of War* (2005), the latter debuting at the Bongo Club during the Fringe.

5. *The List*, 2 August 2001, p.4.

6. *Tap Into the Talent: Nestlé and the Birth of the Tap Water Awards* (2001), a film by Baby Milk Action, viewed at https://www.babymilkaction.org/archives/6940 and https://www.youtube.com/watch?v=M4RVLGUMT5A).

7. ibid.

8. Christie's first Edinburgh show was 2006's modest character comedy piece *The Cheese Roll* at the Holyrood Tavern, and *A Bic For Her* came in the midst of more than a decade of Fringe shows which took her from the Underbelly to the Gilded Balloon and her eventual spiritual home, the Stand. *Because You Demanded It* (2016) was a rapidly-written response to the same year's Brexit referendum, which *The Guardian*'s comedy critic Brian Logan labelled the 'only... comedy show (which) has risen to the challenge

(Brexit's) posed' as he named it the best of the year.

9. Which appeared first on television, and was adapted for the stage at the Selwyn Theatre on Broadway the following year.

10. He also had a bit part in English director Colin Chilvers' 'Smooth Criminal' segment of Michael Jackson's *Moonwalker* film in 1988.

11. Fringe First winners produced by Masterson in his early Fringe career were Gary Henderson's *Skin Tight* (1998), Jacob Rajan's *Krishnan's Diary* (1999), Brian Parks' *Americana Absurdum*, Toa Fraser's *No.2* (both 2000), Nick Salamone's *Moscow* (2001), CJ Hopkins' *Horse Country* and Don Nigro's *Cincinnati* (both 2002).

12. Masterson, Guy, 'Court in the act', *The List*, 31 July 2003.

13. Johnson's debut play, *Days Here So Dark*, was produced by Paines Plough at the 1981 Edinburgh Fringe.

14. The internet-inspired 'at' symbol became an affectation in multi-location venue names during the 2000s, and sadly still hasn't quite been shaken off.

15. Lee, *How I Escaped My Certain Fate*, p.16.

16. Quoted by Lee in *How I Escaped My Certain Fate*, p.27.

17. Tom Morris was also a sometime Fringe performer, the co-writer and director with Nick Vivian of *Tom Tom* at the Heriot Watt Theatre on Grindlay Street, presented by their Stage of Fools company in 1987.

18. Lee, *How I Escaped My Certain Fate*, p.27.

19. Ford, Rory, 'Springer time for opera and Edinburgh', *Edinburgh Evening News*, 8 August 2002. Accessed at www.stewartlee.co.uk/jsto/springer-time-for-opera-and-edinburgh.

20. Thorpe, Vanessa, 'Springer watches us watching him', *The Observer*, 25 August 2002.

21. The show's record was finally overtaken in April 2021, when blanket, simultaneous coverage of the death of Prince Philip across all channels attracted in excess of 110,000 complaints.

22. Lee, *How I Escaped My Certain Fate*, p.38.

23. 'Nica Burns said she was 'absolutely stunned' by the use of the word 'whore' – and Lee later issued a clarification saying: 'I wasn't using the word in a sexual or sexist sense, but in the commonly understood metaphorical sense of "corporate whore"'. Source: 'Ye Gods: Stewart Lee attacks 'inane' comedy poll', *Chortle*, 20 July 2010, https://www.chortle.co.uk/news/2010/07/20/11398/ye_gods!

Spotlight: Black Watch (2006) The James Plays (2014)

1. Perth Repertory Company was the trailblazer building-based company in Scotland. It was founded at Perth Theatre in 1937 and, although it no longer exists, Perth is still a producing theatre. Dundee Repertory Theatre was founded as a semi-professional company in 1939, which moved into its current theatre in 1982 and launched its permanent acting Ensemble in 1999. The tented Pitlochry Festival Theatre – inspired by and named in tribute to the Edinburgh Festival – opened in 1951, with the current building opened in 1981.

2. Duchene had been a Cambridge Footlight in '83, the year after *Cellar Tapes*, when Tony Slattery was president and members included Neil Mullarkey and Morwenna Banks.

3. Her early theatre work was produced under the credited name of John Clifford.

4. Quote from Jo Clifford on her website www.teatrodomundo.com.

5. Quote from Jo Clifford on her website www.teatrodomundo.com.

6. *The Observer*'s reviewer Paul Griffiths called the Inés de Castro opera 'an appalling display of artistic and moral ignorance', and suggested that Scottish Opera would be wise to 'avert any further damage by dropping the other performances it has planned.' (*The Observer*, 1 September 1996, p.72) Clifford jokes that 'it's a review I am very proud of.' (www.teatrodomundo.com).

7. Her play *The Girl Who Fell to Earth or Shoot the Archduke!*, about the murder of Archduke Franz Ferdinand, was intended for production by EIF in 1988, but as both Clifford and director Giles Havergal disliked the only available venue, the Church Hill Theatre, it was pulled and eventually seen on tour in 1991.

8. Maybury was a defining British visual stylist of the era, having directed the pop videos for Pet Shop Boys' 'West End Girls' and Sinead O'Connor's 'Nothing Compares 2 U'.

9. Fisher, Mark, 'How a bumper programme at the Traverse Theatre in 1985 changed Scottish culture', *The List*, 23 November 2010, www.list.co.uk/article/29446-how-a-bumper-programme-at-the-traverse-theatre-in-1985-changed-scottish-culture.

10. The Arts Council of Wales followed the same chronology.

11. Established in 1994 under John Major's Conservative administration, the National Lottery is a countrywide gambling franchise which allocates 25% of income to its 'good causes' fund, 20% of which goes to the arts in the UK. Although the Lottery has been criticised as a stealth tax and for its association with gambling, the good causes fund had raised and distributed £32 billion by 2014.

12. *The List*, 27 March 2003, p.21.

13. This manifesto commitment was inspired by the signing of the symbolic 'Claim of Right for Scotland' in March 1989 at the Assembly Hall on the Mound in Edinburgh, with which many dozens of civic dignitaries declared their support for Scotland's sovereignty – among them Blair's Chancellor of the Exchequer Gordon Brown and the later Chancellor during Brown's term as Prime Minister, Alistair Darling. From this point on the Scottish Constitutional Convention, which promoted devolved power within the UK for a Scottish Assembly or Parliament, became a Labour party position.

14. Fisher, Mark, 'Art of the Matter', *The List*, 7 September 2000, p.20.

15. Burnet, Andrew, *The List*, 'Fighting Spirit', 23 July 1998.

16. In a 1995 interview with *Financial Times* and former *List* writer Sarah Hemming, according to Aleks Sierz.

17. *The Suspect Culture Book*, p.43-44.

18. Featherstone, Vicky, 'Staging a Revolution', *The List*, 7 October 2004, p.10.

19. Burke, Gregory, *Black Watch* script, p.xi.

20. Carrell, Severin, 'Scottish independence yes vote would drive change in England, says writer', *The Guardian*, 3 January 2014.

21. Stephens' most successful play of a prolific career has been the 2012 adaptation of Mark Haddon's novel *The Curious Incident of the Dog in the Night-Time*, with movement direction by the Frantic Assembly team of Scott Graham and Black Watch's Steven Hoggett.

22. Munro is also a screenwriter, who wrote Ken Loach's 1994 film *Ladybird, Ladybird*. She has a unique distinction in British television as the only person to have written stories for both the old and new series of *Doctor Who*, in 1989 and 2017.

23. 'The SRB Interview: Rona Munro', *The Scottish Review of Books*, 11 November 2014, https://www.scottishreviewofbooks.org/2014/11/the-srb-interview-rona-munro/

24. Munro, Rona, *The James Plays*, p.vii–viii.

13. Edinburgh Art Festival and the Arrival of Summerhall

1. Garavelli, Dani, 'Richard Demarco: Still Fighting Art's Corner', *Scotland On Sunday*, 26 October 2003.

2. The Demarco Gallery's addresses included 18a Great King Street, Monteith House at 61 High Street, Gladstone's Court at 179 Canongate, 32 High Street and 10 Jeffrey Street.

3. More recently a restaurant named Monteith's.

4. Fisher, Mark, 'Rebel with a cause', *The List*, 19 August 1994, p.10.

5. ibid. p.11.

6. Gale, Iain, 'Is Wee Ricky the answer for Big Tam?', *Scotland On Sunday*, 24 August 2003.

7. The Scottish National Portrait Gallery has a minor yet specific historical distinction in that, although the National Portrait Gallery in London was founded earlier, the fact its own building didn't open until 1896 means the Scottish National Portrait Gallery is the first building specifically build to house a Portrait Gallery anywhere in the world. The Scottish Society of Antiquaries also made the building its home, until it merged with the Royal Museum of Scotland on Chambers Street in 1985 and moved its collection there a decade later.

8. Monaghan, Helen, 'Nautical but nice', *The List*, 10 May 2001, p.28.

9. Gale, Iain, 'The Edinburgh Festival may be a great arts festival. But where is the art?', *Scotland On Sunday*, 28 July 2002.

10. Later the director of the 2015 erotic thriller *50 Shades of Gray* under her married name Sam Taylor-Johnston.

11. Grace and Maclean later founded the successful art-pop band Django Django in London. Maclean is the younger brother of fellow Edinburgh College of Art graduate John Maclean, who was a member of Edinburgh group The Beta Band and later a filmmaker with the Michael Fassbender-starring *Slow West* (2015).

12. Pollock, David, 'Outdoor pursuits', *The List*, 23 July 2009, p.87.

13. Allan, Vicky, 'The End of the Affair', *Sunday Herald*, 22 January 2006.

14. Clyde Street no longer exists. The modern pedestrian shopping lane Multrees Walk occupies roughly the same site.

Spotlight: The Scotsman Steps (Work No. 1059, 2011)

1. Which still exists, but very much tidied up.

14. The 21st Century Festival: Bigger... and Better?

1. Figures from http://www.worldfringe.com/history-of-fringe/.

2. Definition from http://www.worldfringe.com/what-is-a-fringe/.

3. The Promoter Liaison Office is now named the Arts Industry Office.

4. Venables, Ben, 'When Flight of the Conchords played a plague pit', *The Skinny*, 8 June 2018, accessed at https://www.theskinny.co.uk/comedy/opinion/when-flight-of-the-conchords-played-a-plague-pit.

5. Now Cabaret Voltaire on Blair Street.

6. Copstick, Kate, 'Review: The Sitcom Trials', *The Scotsman*, 7 August 2001.

7. Bennett, Steve, 'The Sitcom Trials', *Chortle*, August 2001, accessed at https://www.chortle.co.uk/review/2001/01/01/33886/the-sitcom-trials.

8. *The Sitcom Trials: You Say Potato*, accessed at https://www.youtube.com/watch?v=UDvm4hN-qds.

9. 'Arrival in Edinburgh', Tim Minchin's blog entry on 30 July 2005, accessed at https://www.timminchin.com/2005/07/30/arrival-in-edinburgh/.

10. Malcolm Fraser Architects closed in 2015. A new partnership with Robin Livingstone as Fraser Livingstone Architects opened in 2019, with Fraser taking various contract jobs in between.

11. Edinburgh World Heritage is an amalgam of two former existing bodies; Edinburgh New Town Conservation Committee, established in 1971, and Edinburgh Old Town Renewal Trust, founded in 1985.

12. The full list of Edinburgh Makars and their year of appointment is Stewart Conn (2002), Valerie Gillies (2005), Ron Butlin (two terms from 2008), Christine De Luca (2014), Alan Spence (2017) and Hannah Lavery (2021). The holder of the role is jointly chosen by the Scottish Poetry Library, Scottish Pen, the Saltire Society, the City of Edinburgh Council and the UNESCO City of Literature Trust.

13. Boztas, Senay, 'Edinburgh Fringe left £900,000 out of pocket by collapse of new box office', *The Guardian*, 23 August 2009.

14. ibid.

15. McMillan, Joyce, 'Kath Mainland leaves the Fringe', *The Scotsman*, 10 November 2015, accessed at https://joycemcmillan.wordpress.com/category/other-theatre-writing/page/2/.

16. The report's other commissioners were the Scottish Arts Council, Festivals Edinburgh (newly-renamed from the Association of Edinburgh Festivals), EventScotland and Scottish Enterprise Edinburgh and Lothian.

17. *Thundering Hooves*, p.4, accessed at https://www.edinburghfestivalcity.com/assets/000/000/355/Thundering_Hooves_Report_-_04.05.06_original.pdf?1411049125.

18. Gribbin, John and Gribbin, Ben, 'Forum – All the Fun of the Fair: the first Edinburgh Science Festival', *New Scientist*, 6 May 1989, accessed at https://www.newscientist.com/article/mg12216636-400-forum-all-the-fun-of-the-fair-the-first-edinburgh-science-festival/.

19. YouTube interview with Duncan Low by Edinburgh International Children's Festival, accessed at https://imaginate.org.uk/timeline/1990/.

20. These recommendations were grouped under the headings long-term planning and strategy, investing in quality over quantity, talented and experienced direction, focused and innovative programming, excellent facilities, strategic promotion, strategic intelligence, political will matched by strong leadership and political independence, and coordinated processes of monitoring and evaluation.

21. 'The Edinburgh Festivals: an endless experiment', TedxUniversity of Edinburgh talk, posted 20 April 2015, accessed at https://www.youtube.com/watch?v=2WNo4LITSfQ.

22. Hill, Peter Buckley, *Freeing the Free Fringe*, p.48.

23. McGill, Hannah, 'Why we're moving the Edinburgh film festival to June', *The Guardian*, 7 August 2007, accessed at https://www.theguardian.com/film/filmblog/2007/aug/07/whyweremovingtheedinburghfilmfestivaltojune.

24. Scott, Kirsty, 'The quiet showman', *The Guardian*, 5 August 2006.

25. Brocklehurst, Steve, 'Assembly battle splits Edinburgh Fringe', *BBC News*, 3 August 2012, https://www.bbc.co.uk/news/uk-scotland-19096877.

26. Alexander, Mary, 'Fringe Benefits for Who?', *Edinburgh Poverty Commission*, 13 November 2019, accessed at https://edinburghpovertycommission.org.uk/2019/11/13/fringe-benefits-for-who/.

27. As reported in Ferguson, Brian, 'Major Edinburgh Fringe show producer booted

out of venue in wake of staffing row', *The Scotsman*, 10 February 2019, the University's statement read: 'This change follows our yearly review of tenants, venues and operating models, with 2018's review looking in particular at terms and conditions around staff employment. We are aware that Fringe venues employ a variety of employment practices. As part of our yearly review of tenants, venues and operating models we consider amongst other things the employment practices of our tenants. After the last Fringe, and in light of our yearly review, it was decided not to renew the relationship with one client. We are comfortable that our continuing Fringe tenants satisfy our aspirations with regards to terms and conditions around volunteers and employment.'

28. Witts, Sophie, 'Edinburgh festivals drive hotel prices up 39 per cent', 6 Aug 2015, accessed at https://www.bighospitality.co.uk/Article/2015/08/07/Edinburgh-festivals-drive-hotel-prices-up-39-per-cent.

29. Bradley, Jane, 'Edinburgh among most expensive cities on Airbnb', *Edinburgh Evening News*, 4 October 2015, accessed at https://www.edinburghnews.scotsman.com/news/edinburgh-among-most-expensive-cities-airbnb-882024.

30. Wolfe-Robinson, Maya, 'Grassroots project addresses Edinburgh Fringe's 'overwhelming whiteness'', *The Guardian*, 29 July 2016, accessed at https://www.theguardian.com/stage/2019/jul/29/grassroots-project-addresses-edinburgh-fringes-overwhelming-whiteness.

31. ibid.

32. Fringe of Colour migrated to an online film festival during the COVID years of 2020 and '21, and is on hiatus for '22.

Spotlight: Fleabag (2013) The Play That Goes Wrong (2013) Six (2017–18)

1. Her co-star was *Fleabag*'s future 'hot priest' Andrew Scott.

2. The Australian Frances-White is also a prolific Edinburgh Fringe performer, including her debut show *How to Get Almost Anyone to Want to Sleep with You* in 2007, *Cult Following* in 2012, which was about growing up as a Jehovah's Witness, and *Half a Can of Worms* in 2013, about tracking down her birth family. With Sofie Hagen, she also co-founded the hit podcast *The Guilty Feminist* in 2015.

3. Waller-Bridge, *Fleabag* script, p.7.

4. http://www.theatrevoice.com/audio/phoebe-waller-bridge-discusses-her-award-winning-fleabag/

5. Waller-Bridge, Fleabag script, p.26.

6. This production also played a week at the Udderbelly 'cow tent' on Bristo Square during the 2017 Fringe.

7. Waller-Bridge, *Fleabag*, p.9.

8. Albeit the latter was postponed during COVID-19.

9. Wyver, Kate, 'Frankly, it's ridiculous! Fleabag super-producer Francesca Moody', *The Guardian*, 10 July 2019, https://www.theguardian.com/stage/2019/jul/10/fleabag-super-producer-francesca-moody-phoebe-waller-bridge-edinburgh-fringe

10. The Comedy Store Players also came to Edinburgh, at the George Square Theatre and Assembly Rooms in the '80s and '90s. Other early Fringe improv sets included Stephen Frost's shows *Impro All Stars* and *Celebrity Pub Quiz* at La Belle Angele, which involved Merton, Colin Mochrie and Steve Steen. In 2014 Webster wrote a Fringe play for the Pleasance named *My Obsession*, in which she played a fan who met her idol, a comedian played by Merton.

11. The comedian Cariad Lloyd, an Edinburgh Comedy Award Best Newcomer nominee

in 2011 for her show *Lady Cariad's Characters*, was an Austentatious founder, but not an Oxford Imp.

12. 'I will absolve myself of all responsibility because I didn't want to be called that, but it was done by some of the guys,' pointed out Pack member Dave Hearn, concerning the name Scat Pack. 'Scat is from improvisational jazz. But it's also faecal pornography.' Quote from 'The Spotlight Podcast: Making and Performing Comedic Work with Dave Hearn from Mischief Theatre', https://www.spotlight.com/news-and-advice/interviews-podcasts/the-spotlight-podcast-making-and-performing-comedic-work-with-dave-hearn-from-mischief-theatre/

13. The retitled *Lights! Camera! Improvise!*

14. The Society's acronym is CUMTS, which amuses Moss.

15. It was also Marlow's first Fringe show, although Moss had directed a family show named *Bobalong* in 2015 at Assembly George Square, by former Footlights Joshan Chana and Tom Fraser, and Cambridge University Amateur Dramatic Club's version of Kae Tempest's *Wasted* at the Greenside venue on Infirmary Street in 2016.

15. Edinburgh Without the Festival

1. '2020 Fringe announcement from Shona McCarthy, Chief Executive', *edfringe.com*, 1 April 2020, accessed at https://www.edfringe.com/covid-19.

2. Hannan left the Traverse in March 2021, and Nicholls is now sole AD.

3. Figures from Carrell, Severin, 'Edinburgh international festival to hold more online events after 1m views', *The Guardian*, 1 September 2020; 'Fringe 2020 draws to a close with almost 300 shows online and £250,000 raised for artists and venues', edfringe.com, 1 September 2020, https://www.edfringe.com/learn/news-and-events/fringe-2020-draws-to-a-close-with-almost-300-shows-online-and-ps250-000-raised-for-artists-and-venues.

4. Pollock, David, 'The Fringe will survive – even if it has to start from scratch', *The Stage*, 27 April 2020, https://www.thestage.co.uk/features/the-fringe-will-survive--even-if-it-has-to-start-from-scratch. Text from original interview.

5. Edinburgh International Festival 2021 Brochure.

6. Attendance, venue, geographical, Scottish Index of Multiple Deprivation and cycle route data was compiled by the Edinburgh Culture and Communities Mapping Project and published at https://www.edinburghculturalmap.org/research/festivals-communities-map/.

7. The full list of *Fringe Blueprint* commitments are: 'remove barriers to entry to ensure that everyone is welcome at the Fringe and anyone can take part; develop the Fringe's international reputation as the place to discover talent; tackle the rising cost of attendance at the Fringe to ensure the festival is affordable for all; secure a new home for the Fringe to provide year-round assistance to participants and support a vibrant Fringe community; foster a lifelong passion for the arts amongst Scotland's young people and champion creative learning in our schools and colleges; support and develop the world's greatest street festival at the heart of the Fringe; reduce the festival's carbon footprint and champion initiatives that limit our impact on the environment; tell the remarkable story of the Fringe and build awareness of, and support for, our charitable mission all over the world.'

8. Cunningham's essays were published online at: 'Building Edinburgh better in a post-pandemic world', *The Skinny*, 29 July 2020, https://www.theskinny.co.uk/art/features/building-edinburgh-back-better-in-a-post-pandemic-world; 'Edinburgh reimagined: the future will be localised', *sceptical.scot*, 13th March 2021, https://sceptical.scot/2021/03/

edinburgh-reimagined-the-future-will-be-localised/; 'Time to rebuild: Edinburgh Reimagined Part 2', *sceptical.scot*, 7 April 2021, https://sceptical.scot/2021/04/time-to-rebuild-edinburgh-reimagined-part-2/.

9. Cunningham, 'Building Edinburgh better in a post-pandemic world', July 2020.

10. The groups and individuals involved were zero-waste theatre company Greenhouse Theatre, which first appeared at the Fringe in 2019; Staging Change, which supports theatre makers responding to the Climate Crisis; Fringe of Colour, the initiative to support black people and artists of colour at festivals in Scotland and beyond; the Working Class Artist Group collective; the inclusive Scottish theatre company for disabled and non-disabled actors Birds of Paradise, under artistic director Robert Softley Gale; queer theatre group Activism for Change; Something to Aim For, a group which provides advocacy and capacity-building for marginal artists, with a particular focus on health and wellbeing; Power Play, which aims to provide platforms for women's stories; and Morvern Cunningham.

11. Future Fringe Steering Group Report, 2022, accessed at https://www.thegreenhousetheatre.com/wp-content/uploads/2022/02/Future-Fringe-Steering-Group-Final-Report.pdf.

12. Edinburgh Festival Fringe Society, *The Fringe Blueprint*, Edinburgh Festival Fringe Society, 2018.

13. Ferguson, Brian, 'New poll suggests three quarters of residents believe the Fringe makes Edinburgh a better place to live', *The Scotsman*, 31 January 2022.

14. Mab, 'Beltane Fire', *The List*, 7 April 1989.

15. Farquhar, Angus, 'For luck and reconnection', extract from *Test Dept: Total State Machine*, accessed at https://beltane.org/2015/06/29/angus-farquhar-for-luck-and-reconnection/.

16. Under the NVA banner, Farquhar also directed Dael Orlandersmith's monologue *The Gimmick* at the Traverse during the Fringe of 2000.

17. Also in part-tribute to German kosmische rock group Neu! and Edinburgh's old-fashioned nickname 'Auld Reekie'.

18. Benedetti will be, more precisely, the first Scottish-born director of the Edinburgh International Festival. Ian Hunter and John Drummond both had Scottish fathers, and Hunter was part-raised in the country when he went to school at Fettes College in Edinburgh. Robert Ponsonby described Hunter as 'at heart a canny Scot.'

19. Ian Hunter was 31 at the time of his first International Festival in 1950. Robert Ponsonby was 29 for his in 1956, and still only 33 when he left in 1960.

20. She did play one previous EIF concert with the Scottish Chamber Orchestra at the Ross Bandstand on Princes Street Gardens, which *The Scotsman*'s Ken Walton later recalled was interrupted by the Tattoo flypast and the jingle of a nearby ice cream van.

21. Walton, Ken, 'Nicola Benedetti: "The EIF are having such a celebration of what's local this year"', *The Scotsman*, 2 August 2021.

22. Didcock, Barry, 'Edinburgh's new broom: meet EIF director Fergus Linehan', *The Herald*, 2 August 2015.

23. Quoted in Kohda, Claire, 'Boulez in his own words', *The Guardian*, 26 March 2015.

24. Abbado conducted his Mahler Jugendorchester orchestra at the Usher Hall in 2002, Stein directed Chekov's *The Seagull* at the King's Theatre in 2003. Both collaborated on Wagner's *Parsifal* at the Festival Theatre in '02.

Postscript: The Future

1. 'Statement on Valery Gergiev', Edinburgh International Festival, 28 February 2022, accessed at www.eif.co.uk

2. The six published Fringe Development Targets are:

'1. Thriving artists – Be the best place in the world for emerging artists to perform and the best platform for talent to emerge. 2. Fair work – Eradicate any remaining unfair or exploitative work conditions at The Fringe. 3. Climate action – Become a carbon net zero event by 2030. 4. Equitable Fringe – Who you are and where you are from is not a barrier to attending or performing at the Edinburgh Fringe. 5. Good citizenship – The Fringe, a force for good in and for the city of Edinburgh. 6. Digital evolution – Enhance the live Fringe experience by ensuring a world-class digital experience.' The headline commitments for 2022 are: 'source new income streams, sponsorship and investment to support Fringe artists and particularly those who face the greatest barriers; introduction of a three-stage system of monitoring and penalty to address inappropriate or poor working conditions and practices: Warning / Notice / Suspension; an annual free-to-access family event for Edinburgh residents; support, and champion, as a priority, under-represented artists and arts professionals, the exclusive use of e-tickets in 2022 and a reduction of the programme print run by 50%; support digital literacy and inclusion for all artists and audiences, ensuring there are no barriers for engaging fully with the Fringe.'

All text from 'Edinburgh Fringe signals time for change on 7th anniversary', *edfringe.com*, 9 June 2022, accessed at https://www.edfringe.com/learn/news-and-events/edinburgh-fringe-signals-time-for-change-on-75th-anniversary.

Acknowledgements

DURING THE 75 years of the Edinburgh Festival's existence – the combined existence of every festival which forms a part of it, that is, and the many parts of the wider cultural and civic life which feed into it – a huge cast has been involved. Hundreds of people have directly steered the course of the festivals. Thousands of people have contributed significantly, perhaps by creating or producing famous shows, managing venues or committing themselves to reviewing and recording events with diligence and professionalism. Quite probably, the number of people who have been involved at the lowest levels – producing low-key but hopeful DIY shows which are long forgotten, but which brought small audiences pleasure at the time, or served at a bar or rigged a set or cleaned a hotel room – must stretch into the millions.

To each of these people, thanks are due for helping make the Edinburgh Festival one of the greatest forums for art and shared human perspective in the world. Thanks are also due to those who constructively criticise the Festival in good faith, with a mission to improve and not wreck. For every single person who has been involved in every way over the years, there will be a unique and quite possibly differing perspective on every single part of the Festival they've been involved in, no matter how small. Many of their own memories, reliable or otherwise, might contradict or elaborate upon any part of the story told in this book. It will be surprising if they don't, in fact.

In attempting to compile this biography as faithfully and accurately as possible, I'm indebted first of all to the writers of each of the books mentioned in the bibliography. Some were key texts, some provided a page or two of reference, others were simply scene-setters. All have reminded me of the importance of attempting to record social, cultural and personal history as accurately as possible for those who come after, which is what I've tried to do here.

In particular, the memoirs of those who have led festivals in Edinburgh have been extremely useful; Rudolf Bing, Michael Dale, John Drummond, Forsyth Hardy, the 7th Earl of Harewood George Lascelles, Alistair Moffat and Robert Ponsonby. Special thanks also to Richard Demarco and the late Jim Haynes for writing so vividly and comprehensively of their lives and times. Joyce McMillan's history of the Traverse theatre is an excellent if sadly out-of-print read.

From around midway through the story on, readers may notice a slight shift in tone, with longer quotes from those involved. By and large, where quotes are unattributed, these come from direct interviews with many Festival leaders, producers and artists who are still around, and who were able to give me the benefit of their first-hand knowledge. Whether they sat for a full interview or checked odd details by email, my thanks go to Fiona Alexander, Anthony Alderson, Ginnie Atkinson, Nick Barley, Ed Bartlam, Fiona Bradley, Jenny Brown, Joanne Brown, William Burdett-Coutts, Nica Burns, David Cairns, Sorcha Carey, Martin Creed, Michael Dale, Judith Doherty, Paul Gudgin, Ben Harrison, Lisa Kapur, Karen Koren, Verity Leigh, Fergus Linehan, Liz Lochhead, Philip Long, Kristy Matheson, Shona McCarthy, Jonathan Mills, Lucy Moss, Lynda Myles, Katie Nicoll, Mark Ravenhill, Christopher Richardson, Jonathan Sayer, Tommy Sheppard, Rupert Thomson and Charlie Wood. Their words may have been edited for reasons of clarity and space, but their intent remains intact.

Many thanks also to those PRs and other individuals who arranged interviews, and who are generally extremely helpful and hard-working, especially during the Festival. For this book, these have included Susie Gray, Michelle Mangan, Hugo Mintz, Morag Neil, Magda Paduch and Frances Sutton.

Thanks also to the many journalists who have covered the Edinburgh Festival over the decades, some of whom are colleagues, some of whose entertaining words have simply popped up regularly throughout the research process for the book, and others who are lost in the abyss known as the days before bylines. Among the above, in no particular category or order other than alphabetical, and with apologies to anyone I've missed, are Michael Billington, Mary Brennan, William Cook, Neil Cooper, Kate Copstick, Steve Cramer, Bruce Dessau, Thom Dibdin, Mark Fisher, Lyn Gardner, Lorna Irvine, Alice Jones, Brian Logan, Allan Radcliffe, Jay Richardson, Robert Dawson Scott, Ian Shuttleworth, Natasha Tripney, Ben Venables, Gareth K Vile, Allen Wright, and many, many others. Thanks to Joyce McMillan for all of the above, and for her dedicated service to writing about theatre over several decades; her collected output is the last word on the history of Scottish theatre during this period. Thanks also to Andrew Eaton-Lewis, who first invited me onto *The Scotsman*'s reviewing team, and to all of the other editors who have commissioned me during August, including Roger Cox.

When so much reporting and commentary on culture and society, the stuff of which future history is made, is now stored online and subject to server crashes or website licence expiries, the research process has been a stark reminder about preserving the past. The National Library of Scotland, Edinburgh's Central Library and McDonald Road Library off Leith Walk were all used during the process, as were the archives – largely those available online – of *The Scotsman*, *The Herald*, *The Guardian* and *The Times* newspapers, and *The List* magazine.

Many thanks to Gavin MacDougall at Luath for taking an interest in the project, and to all the staff there who have helped see it through, including Eilidh MacLennan, Caitlin Mellon, Jennie Renton and Madeleine Mankey.

Personal love and thanks to Caroline (who is very patient), Henry, Malcolm and my parents.

Luath Press Limited

committed to publishing well written books worth reading

LUATH PRESS takes its name from Robert Burns, whose little collie Luath (*Gael.*, swift or nimble) tripped up Jean Armour at a wedding and gave him the chance to speak to the woman who was to be his wife and the abiding love of his life. Burns called one of the 'Twa Dogs' Luath after Cuchullin's hunting dog in Ossian's *Fingal*. Luath Press was established in 1981 in the heart of Burns country, and is now based a few steps up the road from Burns' first lodgings on Edinburgh's Royal Mile. Luath offers you distinctive writing with a hint of unexpected pleasures.

Most bookshops in the UK, the US, Canada, Australia, New Zealand and parts of Europe, either carry our books in stock or can order them for you. To order direct from us, please send a £sterling cheque, postal order, international money order or your credit card details (number, address of cardholder and expiry date) to us at the address below. Please add post and packing as follows: UK – £1.00 per delivery address; overseas surface mail – £2.50 per delivery address; overseas airmail – £3.50 for the first book to each delivery address, plus £1.00 for each additional book by airmail to the same address. If your order is a gift, we will happily enclose your card or message at no extra charge.

Luath Press Limited
543/2 Castlehill
The Royal Mile
Edinburgh EH1 2ND
Scotland
Telephone: 0131 225 4326 (24 hours)
Fax: 0131 225 4324
email: sales@luath.co.uk
Website: www.luath.co.uk